Rick Steves

EUROPE
THROUGH THE
BACK DOOR

CONTENTS

EUROPE
THROUGH THE
BACK DOOR

Preface

This guidebook, based on lessons learned from more than 30 years of exploring Europe, is your handbook for traveling smart. With the tips and advice I've assembled here, you can plan, create, and enjoy a trip that will live up to your dreams.

My first five trips to Europe were purely for kicks. I made my share of blunders—I missed train connections, wasted money on dreary hotels and bad restaurants, and showed up at sights after they had closed. But each new trip became smoother than the last. It was clear: I was learning from my mistakes.

While traveling, I saw others making the same costly and time-consuming errors that I'd once made. It occurred to me that by sharing the lessons I'd learned, I could help people enjoy better, easier trips. And I'd have a good excuse to go back to Europe every summer to update my material.

Throughout the late 1970s I taught my "European Travel Cheap" class in Seattle during the school year, and traveled to Europe every summer. I developed a good sense of the fears and apprehensions that troubled people before their trips, and I gathered lots of great "Back Door" discoveries and experiences throughout Europe.

So, in 1980, with all that material, writing the first edition of *Europe Through the Back Door* was easy. I rented an IBM Selectric typewriter, sweet-talked my girlfriend into typing the manuscript, and cajoled my roommate into sketching the illustrations. I gingerly delivered that precious first pile of pages to a printer, and, on my 25th birthday, picked up 2,500 copies.

I sold all those first editions of *Europe Through the Back Door* through my travel classes. With the second edition, in 1981, I got a bit more professional, taking out my personal poems and lists of the most dangerous airlines. I found a distributor who got the book into stores throughout the Pacific

Northwest. The third edition, although it was typeset, still looked so simple and amateurish that reviewers repeatedly mistook it for a "prepublication" edition.

All this time I was supporting myself as a piano teacher. But my recital hall was gradually becoming a travel lecture classroom, and I needed to choose what I would teach: Europe or music. I chose Europe, let my piano students go, and began building my travel business. At the same time, an actual publisher agreed to bring out the fourth edition of *Europe Through the Back Door*. Happily, I could now focus on researching and writing rather than publishing.

Since then I've kept to the same teaching mission— although now this mission is amplified by 100 workmates at my company in Edmonds, Washington, and by technology I never could have dreamed of back when I started. Working together, we've developed a wide-ranging program of travel material—guidebooks, guided bus tours, a public television series, a weekly public-radio program, information-packed apps, personally designed gear, a generous website, and more. Everything we do is designed to inform and inspire American tourists to turn their travel dreams into smooth and affordable reality—and this book is the foundation of our work.

My favorite part of this job remains my on-the-ground research. I typically spend four months every year in Europe: April and May in the Mediterranean, July and August north of the Alps. I use some of that time to film my TV series, but for the majority of it, I'm alone, eyes and ears open: exploring new places, revisiting old favorites, tracking down leads, collecting experiences, and updating my guidebooks. When I

get home, I can't wait to splice the lessons I've learned from my most recent travels into the book you're about to read.

Home took on a new meaning as the Covid-19 pandemic swept the globe in 2020. Travel dreams were put on hold as scientists raced to find treatments and vaccines, and countries embarked on mass inoculation campaigns. This new edition is being released as Europe figures out how to welcome travelers back in a post-pandemic world. I get excited thinking about all that pent-up travel energy, ready to fuel your trips and mine. And I can't wait to hit the road again—once it's safe to do so.

Between now and then, some details in this book will likely change, but the underlying fundamentals are as true as ever: You can be your own top-notch tour guide—simply equip yourself with the best information. Expect to travel smart...and you will.

Happy travels!

Rich Steves

Introduction

Why do I find Europe so endlessly fun and entertaining? Because I know where to look. And I know how to experience more by spending less.

Europe is my beat. For more than three decades, it's been my second home. Sure, I love the biggies...from the Eiffel Tower to "Mad" King Ludwig's castles to Michelangelo's David. But even more than the must-see sights, I value the Back Door experiences that Europe has to offer: meeting pilgrims at Santiago, sampling stinky cheese in a Czech town, pondering an ancient stone circle in Dartmoor, and cheering for a youth soccer team with new friends in Greece. Looking back on my European travels, having spent much of my adult life living out of a carry-on-sized bag, I'm thankful that, for me, Europe never gets old. When I first started traveling, I wanted to "feel the fjords and caress the castles"...and I still do. My curiosity will always take me back to that wonderful continent.

But many American travelers miss the real Europe because they enter through its grand front door. This Europe greets you with cash registers cocked, $10 cups of coffee, high-rise hotels, and service with a purchased smile. Instead, you can give your trip an extra, more real dimension by coming with me through the back door, where a warm, relaxed, personable Europe welcomes us as friends. Rather than simply being a part of the economy, we become part of the party.

Sure, Europe is expensive. Prices are high for locals—and even steeper for travelers. But the Back Door style of travel is better because of—not despite—your budget. Spending money has little to do with enjoying your trip. In fact, as we can learn from Europeans, even those who don't have much money can manage plenty of la dolce vita.

When I reread my trip journals, I'm reminded that the less I spend, the richer the experience I have. Often the best travel memories have cost little or nothing. If you see dancers in Barcelona celebrating their Catalan heritage in the *sardana* circle dance, join in. In Rome, climb up the Scala Santa Holy Stairs on your knees to learn what it feels like to be a pilgrim. Watch tourists run for their lives from the bulls in Pamplona. At a French produce market, gather a gourmet picnic to enjoy in the garden of a Loire château... or perched in a Provençal hill town amid fields of lavender. Even in London (Europe's most expensive city), you can have a world-class experience by soaking up its many free museums: Visiting the Tate Gallery, British Museum, and National Gallery won't cost you a pence.

Participate in sports and games, and everyone wins. Join the Scotsman who runs your B&B in a game of lawn bowling, the Frenchman who runs your *chambre d'hôte* in a game of *pétanque,* or the Greek who runs your *dhomatia* for backgammon. Even if you don't know the rules, you'll end up with a memory that's easy to pack and costs nothing.

ABOUT THIS BOOK

The first half of this book covers the practical skills of Back Door European travel: how to plan a smart itinerary, pack light, take public transportation, find good-value accommodations, eat cheaply but well, stay healthy, use technology wisely, avoid theft and scams, save money and time—and best of all, connect with locals. Even more important than saving you money, my travel tips (which apply whether you're traveling on your own or with a tour group) will steer you toward matchless experiences that become indelible memories. These are the kind of souvenirs you'll enjoy for a lifetime.

The second half of the book gives you a vivid sampling of the experiences that await you across Europe. With limited vacation time, it's important to understand what each place has to offer. These country introductions will help you sort through the many options so you can come up with a terrific trip, immersing yourself in the Europe of *your* dreams.

STOKE YOUR TRAVEL DREAMS

Kicking off your European adventure can be a matter of simple logistics (you've got 10 days off in April) or the fulfillment of a lifetime dream (you've always wanted to see where your French grandmother was born). Whether your trip is fueled by practicality or inspiration, the planning part can be instrumental in its success and an enjoyable part of the experience itself. Start by finding out all you can about the destinations you'd like to visit. Many resources are standing by to help inform and inspire your planning. For in-depth itinerary-planning advice, see "Designing an Itinerary" on page 41.

Find inspiration from other travelers. Firsthand, fresh information can be good stuff—whether you're at home or in Europe. Travelers love to share the tips and lessons they've learned. Take advantage of every opportunity to confer with fellow travelers who've been to where you want to go. Solicit tips and ideas from your Facebook friends, ogle images of places you may want to visit, read travel blogs, and talk to travelers in online forums.

Keep in mind, however, that these assessments of a place's touristic merit are a product of that person's personality and experiences there. Maybe it was raining, or the crowds were out of control that particular weekend, or that person got sick in "that lousy, overrated city." Every year, I find travelers hell-bent on following bad advice from friends at home. Treat opinions as opinions (except, of course, those found in this book).

Look through travel books and magazines. Spend some time in the travel section of a bookstore, thumbing through guidebooks. (Make it a date with your travel partner.) Page through coffee-table books with eye-candy pictures of the places you're thinking of visiting. Your hometown library has a lifetime of valuable reading on European culture. Navigate toward nonfiction: Dewey gave Europe the numbers 914 and 940. (For reading recommendations by country, check the "Explore Europe" pages at RickSteves.com.)

Pick up a few travel magazines loaded with beautiful photographs of enticing destinations. For glitz, try *Travel & Leisure* or *Condé Nast Traveler;* for a more scholarly approach turn to *Smithsonian* or *National Geographic.*

Feast on videos. My public television series, *Rick Steves' Europe,* captures the best of Europe in 100 episodes (www.ricksteves.com/tv), getting you up-close with awe-inspiring

Free Travel Resources from Rick Steves

This book is just the tip of a flying wedge of information I've produced and designed to make your trip smooth, efficient, and affordable. By tapping into the resources listed below, you'll have access to the collective travel experience of my 100-person staff and legions of smart travelers.

My goal is to inspire, inform, and equip Americans to have European trips that are fun, affordable, and culturally broadening.

RickSteves.com

My mobile-friendly website is the place to explore Europe. You'll find thousands of fun articles, videos, photos, and radio interviews organized by country, a wealth of money-saving tips for planning your dream trip, monthly travel news dispatches, a video library of my travel talks, my travel blog, and my latest guidebook updates.

Our Travel Forum is an immense yet well-groomed collection of message boards, where our travel-savvy community answers questions and shares their personal travel experiences. Learn, ask questions, and share your own opinions as you browse topics on each country, other travelers' tips, and reviews of restaurants and hotels. You can even ask one of our well-traveled staff to chime in with an answer.

You'll also find information on our small-group European bus tours, rail passes for independent travelers, and a wide array of guidebooks, luggage, and accessories for sale.

Rick Steves' Europe on Public Television

My television series, airing on more than 300 public television stations across the United States, covers my favorite continent in 100 half-hour episodes, and we're working on new shows every year. Each half-hour show takes you to Europe's most interesting places, from great cities to off-the-beaten-path discoveries. Several shows devoted to travel skills help illustrate this book. All of my TV shows are available free on demand at RickSteves.com/tv, where you'll also find scripts and a behind-the-scenes look at filming Rick Steves' Europe.

art, centuries-old churches, colorful markets, romantically cobbled streets, pristine lakes, and peaceful vineyards. All of my shows are available to stream at no cost.

Watching movies, television series, and documentaries set in Europe can also stoke your wanderlust. The Tuscan picnic scene in A Room with a View will have you packing your bags for Italy. Downton Abbey makes English manors and manners enthralling. The Sound of Music sends fans

Producer Simon Griffith, cameraman Karel Bauer, and writer/host Rick Steves—working together to bring the best of Europe home to you on public television.

Our free audio tours cover the top sights in London, Paris, Rome, Florence, Venice, Vienna, Athens, and other locales.

Travel with Rick Steves on Public Radio

My one-hour weekly radio show airs on 400 public radio stations across the US. I talk with experts and everyday travelers about the places, people, and ideas we encounter as we explore our world. You can also listen to it as a podcast on all major platforms. Excerpts from the weekly broadcast are featured in my free Rick Steves Audio Europe app. A list of local broadcast times, and on-demand archives of the show, are at RickSteves.com/radio.

Rick Steves Audio Europe

My free app includes dozens of self-guided audio tours of Europe's top neighborhoods, museums, and sights, and hundreds of my radio interviews, all organized into handy geographic playlists. Find it in your app store and you'll have me as your tour guide anytime. For more information, see RickSteves.com/audioeurope.

Rick Steves Classroom Europe

My free online video clip library is a powerful tool for teachers but is also useful for travelers. This video database is packed with more than 400 short clips excerpted from Rick Steves' Europe TV episodes. Teachers can search it, select any number of short clips, and build playlists to enhance their lesson plans. Travelers can use it to sort through options for your trip and better understand what you'll see in Europe. Check it out at Classroom.RickSteves.com (just enter a topic to find everything I've filmed on a subject).

singing into the streets of Salzburg, and *Midnight in Paris* will inspire you to stay out after dark in the City of Light.

Documentaries can be equally compelling: *The Rape of Europa,* telling the fascinating story of the rescue of Europe's great art from Nazi plunderers, adds an extra dimension to your museum going. *The Singing Revolution* gives you stirring background on how the people of Estonia literally—and courageously—sang their way to freedom. (For more TV and film suggestions by country, check the "Explore Europe" pages at RickSteves.com.)

Take classes. Understanding a subject makes it interesting. To avoid getting "cathedraled" or "museumed" out, take an art history class, especially if you're going to Italy or Greece. A European history class will bring "dull" museums to life, while a conversational language class can be fun and practical. My travel talks, available on my website, range from lectures on countries and travel skills to lessons in art history (www.ricksteves.com/travel-talks).

Study this book. I've been teaching Americans how to travel smart in Europe on a budget for more than three decades, and the tips in this book are tried and tested on the ground every year. The feedback from my readers makes it clear: Enjoying Europe through the back door can be done—by you.

MAKING THE MOST OF YOUR TRIP

On the road, I get out of my comfort zone and meet people I'd never encounter at home. In Europe, I'm immersed in a place where people do things—and see things—differently. That's what distinguishes cultures, and it's what makes travel interesting. By being open to differences and staying flexible, I have a better time in Europe—and so will you. Be mentally braced for some surprises, good and bad. Much of the success of your trip will depend on the attitude you pack.

Don't be a creative worrier. Some travelers actively cultivate pretrip anxiety, coming up with all kinds of reasons to be stressed. Every year there are small problems turning into large problems, and old problems becoming new again... and yet the world keeps turning. Don't sweat stuff that hasn't yet happened (and is very unlikely to happen) to you. And don't underestimate yourself. Think you're too old to travel? I've learned that age only matters if you're a cheese: If you want to travel with a youthful spirit, you certainly can.

Expect problems and tackle them creatively. Travel is exciting and rewarding because it requires you to ad-lib, to be imaginative and spontaneous while conquering surprise challenges. Make an art out of taking the unexpected in stride. Relax—you're on the other side of the world playing games in a continental backyard. Be a good sport, enjoy the uncertainty, and frolic in the pits. For many situations, the best defense is a good offense—arm yourself with good information and a knack for improvisation.

When I see a bunch of cute guys on a bench, I ask 'em to scoot over... and 30 years later, I'm still one of the gang.

No trip is without its disappointments: If your must-see cathedral isn't covered with scaffolding, or your must-visit museum isn't closed for restoration, then your favorite artist's masterpiece will be out on loan—probably to the US.

Many of my readers' richest travel experiences have been the result of seemingly terrible mishaps: the lost passport in Slovenia, the doctor visit in Ireland, the blowout in Portugal, or the moped accident on Corfu.

Most of the time, the worst result is a missed museum or two, and maybe a blown budget for the week. But you may well make some friends and stack up some fond memories. This is the essence of travel that you'll enjoy long after your journal is shelved and your photos are archived in your mind.

KISS: **"Keep it simple, stupid!"** Don't complicate your trip. Simplify! Travelers can get stressed and clutter their minds over the silliest things, which, in their niggling ways, can suffocate a happy holiday: standing in a long line at the post office on a sunny day in the Alps, worrying about the correct answers to meaningless bureaucratic forms, having a picnic in pants that make you worry about grass stains.

If people stare... sing cowboy songs.

Concerns like these are outlawed in my travels.

People can complicate their trips with clunky camera gear, special tickets for free entry to all the sights they won't see in England, inflatable hangers, immersion heaters, and instant coffee. They ask for a toilet in 17 words and use a calculator to convert currencies to the third digit. Travel more like Gandhi—with simple clothes, open eyes, and an uncluttered mind.

Head off screwups before they happen. You make a rental-car

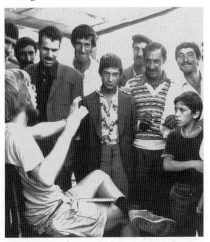

reservation six weeks early, have everything in careful order, show up to pick up your car...and it's not there. The rental agency's fault? Sure. But if you'd called a day ahead to confirm, you'd have avoided an annoying hiccup in your travel plans. Double-checking things along the way minimizes the chances of having your trip marred by other people's mistakes.

Don't be penny wise, pound foolish. Smart travelers will spend a little extra to polish off the rough edges of a trip. Take a taxi instead of a bus when catching an early morning flight at the airport. Enjoy a touristy town without the crowds by spending the night there. If you're traveling solo and feeling lonely, just hire a guide and you've got a buddy to hang out with who really knows the local culture.

Be militantly humble—Attila had a lousy trip. All summer long I'm pushing for a bargain, often for groups. It's the hottest, toughest time of year. Tourists and locals clash—often due to misunderstandings compounded by linguistic and cultural differences. Many tourists leave needlessly soured.

Don't let an unpleasant interaction ruin your travel day. When I catch a Spanish merchant shortchanging me, I correct the bill, smile, and say *"Adiós."* When a French hotel owner blows up at me for no legitimate reason, I wait, smile, and try again. Usually the irate ranter comes to his senses, and we work things out.

"Turn the other cheek" applies perfectly to those riding Europe's magic carousel. If you slap back, the ride is over. The militantly humble and hopelessly optimistic can happily spin forever.

Ask questions. If you are too proud to ask questions, your dignity will stay nicely intact...until you hop the wrong train, order the dish you didn't want, or lead your travel partner in circles. Many tourists are too timid to ask questions, even to prevent mistakes that can cost precious time and money. Locals are a wealth of information: Use them. Most people are happy to help a traveler. Hurdle the language barrier. Use a paper and pencil, charades, or whatever it takes to be understood. Don't be afraid to butcher the language.

Ask questions—or be lost. If you are lost, get help. Perceive friendliness and you'll find it.

Make yourself an extrovert, even if you're not. The meek may inherit the earth, but they make lousy travelers. Be a catalyst for adventure and excitement. Meet people. Don't wait for cultural experiences—reach out and make them happen. The American casual-and-friendly social style

Extroverts Have More Fun

I'm not naturally a wild-and-crazy kind of guy. But when I'm shy and quiet, things don't happen, and that's a bad rut to travel in. So when I'm on the road I make myself an extrovert...and everything changes. Let me describe the same evening twice—first with the mild-and-lazy me, then with the wild-and-crazy me.

> *The traffic held me up, so by the time I got to that great museum I'd always wanted to see, it was 12 minutes before closing. No one was allowed to enter. Disappointed, I walked to a restaurant and couldn't make heads or tails out of the menu. I recognized "steak-frites" and settled for a meat patty and French fries. On the way home I looked into a pub but it seemed dark, so I walked on. A couple waved at me from their balcony, but I didn't know what to say, so I ignored them. I returned to my room and did some laundry.*

That's not a night to be proud of. An extrovert's journal would read like this:

> *I got to the museum only 12 minutes before closing. The guard said no one could enter, but I pleaded with him, saying I'd traveled all the way to see this place. I assured him that I'd be out by closing time, and he gave me a glorious 12 minutes in a hall slathered with Renaissance frescoes. At a restaurant that the guard recommended, I couldn't make heads or tails out of the menu. Inviting myself into the kitchen, I met the cooks and got a firsthand look at what was cookin'. What I chose was delizioso! On the way home, I passed a pub, and, while it seemed uninviting, I stepped in anyway, and was greeted by a guy who spoke broken English. He proudly befriended me, and we shared stories about our kids (he had pictures...and so did I)—while treating me to his favorite brew. As I headed home, a couple waved at me from their balcony, and I waved back, saying "Buon giorno!" I knew it didn't mean "Good evening," but they understood. They invited me up to their apartment. We joked around—not understanding a lot of what we were saying to each other—and had fun. What a lucky break to be welcomed into a local home! And to think that I could've been back in my room doing laundry!*

Pledge every morning to do something entirely different that day. Meet people and create adventure—or bring home a boring journal.

is charming to Europeans who are raised to respect social formalities. While our slap-on-the-back friendliness can be overplayed and obnoxious, it can also be a great asset for the American interested in meeting Europeans. Consider that cultural trait a plus. Enjoy it. Take advantage of it.

Every town in Europe has an amazing open-air market. If you're like me, you might feel a little awkward—you don't speak the language, you're not good with the metric system, you just want to buy one apple and two carrots, the coins are new to you, and there's a long line of locals. Hold your ground. You're not a gawky tourist who is out of your league; you're one in a thousand-year-long line of hungry travelers.

You're legit. Stop looking at it as if you were on a stage, get out there, and risk making mistakes. Connect.

Accept that today's Europe is changing. Europe is a complex, mixed bag of the very old, the very new, and everything in between. Among its palaces, quaint folk dancers, and dusty museums, you'll find a living civilization grasping for its future while we romantic tourists grope for its past.

This presents us with a sometimes-painful dose of truth. Europe can be crowded, tense, seedy, polluted, industrialized, and increasingly hamburgerized. Hans Christian Andersen's statue has four-letter words scrawled across its base. Amsterdam's sex shops and McDonald's share the same streetlamp. In Paris, armies of street vendors bait tourists with knock-off purses and light-up Eiffel Towers. Drunk punks do their best to repulse you as you climb to St. Patrick's grave in Ireland, and mountains of trash make their way into the Mediterranean Sea. A 12-year-old boy in Denmark smokes a cigarette like he was born with it in his mouth. On town squares, tattooed violinists play Vivaldi while statue-mime Napoleons jerk into action at the drop of a coin.

Cherish the cultural diversity—your Dublin B&B host is as likely to be Polish as he is Irish. Europe is a society of 400 million people just like us, sorting through social challenges and dealing with them in a creative, productive, and positive way. Contemporary Europe is alive and in motion. Keep up!

Savor the differences. Europeans' eating habits can be an adjustment. They may have next to nothing for breakfast, mud for coffee, mussels in Brussels, snails in Paris, and dinner at 10 p.m. in Spain. Beer is room-temperature here and flat there, coffee isn't served with dinner, and ice cubes are only a dream.

Germans wait patiently—in the rain—for the traffic light before they cross an empty street, while Roman cars stay in their lanes like rocks in an avalanche. Trains are speedy but rail strikes are routine.

Locals are more attracted to sidewalk cafés and modern malls than medieval cathedrals. The latest government tax or protest march has everyone talking. Today's problems will fill tomorrow's museums. Feel privileged to walk the vibrant streets of Europe as a student—not as a judge. Be open-minded. Absorb, accept, and learn.

If you can think positively, travel smartly, adapt well, and connect with the culture, you'll have a truly rich European trip. So raise your travel dreams to their upright and locked positions, and let this book fly you away.

Rick Steves' Back Door Travel Philosophy

Travel is intensified living—maximum thrills per minute and one of the last great sources of legal adventure. Travel is freedom. It's recess, and we need it.

Affording travel is a matter of priorities. (Make do with the old car.) You can eat and sleep—simply, safely, and enjoyably—anywhere in Europe for $100 a day plus transportation costs. In many ways, spending more money only builds a thicker wall between you and what you traveled so far to see. Europe is a cultural carnival, and time after time, you'll find that its best acts are free and the best seats are the cheap ones.

Experiencing the real Europe requires catching it by surprise, going casual..."through the Back Door." A tight budget forces you to travel close to the ground, meeting and communicating with the people. Never sacrifice sleep, nutrition, safety, or cleanliness to save money. Simply enjoy the local-style alternatives to expensive hotels and restaurants.

Connecting with people carbonates your experience. Extroverts have more fun. If your trip is low on magic moments, kick yourself and make things happen. If you don't enjoy a place, maybe you don't know enough about it. Seek the truth. Recognize tourist traps. Give a culture the benefit of your open mind. See things as different, but not better or worse. Any culture has plenty to share. When an opportunity presents itself, make it a habit to say "yes."

Of course, travel, like the world, is a series of hills and valleys. Be fanatically positive and militantly optimistic. If something's not to your liking, change your liking.

Our Earth is home to seven billion equally precious people. It's humbling to travel and find that other people don't have the "American Dream"—they have their own dreams. Europeans like us, but with all due respect, they wouldn't trade passports.

Can travel be a political act? Yes. Travelers learn that the world is basically a good place, and that caring for our environment and finding international solutions can be a win-win rather than a win-lose. In the Industrial Age (RIP), the adage was, "What's good for GM is good for America." But now we live in a global age, and we can't make that go away by denying facts and building walls. A new maxim might be, "What's good for the world is good for America."

Thoughtful travel engages us with the world. It reminds us what is important and teaches new ways to measure quality of life. I believe that if Americans were required to travel before they could vote, the US would be safer, stronger, and happier. That's why, rather than saying, "Have a safe trip," I say, "Keep on travelin'."

Globetrotting destroys ethnocentricity, and helps us understand and appreciate other cultures. Rather than fear the diversity on this planet, celebrate it. Among your most prized souvenirs will be the strands of different cultures you choose to knit into your own character. The world is a cultural yarn shop, and Back Door travelers are weaving the ultimate tapestry. Join in!

Travel Skills

In Europe, life's very good—even if you're on a budget.

Budgeting & Planning

The best travelers aren't those with the fattest wallets, but those who take the planning process seriously. Jack might jet off to Europe as a free spirit, without much planning and no real itinerary—and return home with a backpack full of complaints about how expensive and stressful it all was. Jill does her homework and travels with a detailed day-to-day plan—and returns home with rich stories of spontaneous European adventures. It's the classic paradox of good travel: Structure rewards a traveler with freedom, and "winging it" can become a ball-and-chain of too many decisions, too little information, and precious little time to relax.

In this chapter, I'll help you create a budget for your trip, guide you through the best resources for researching and planning, give you the scoop on Europe's travel "seasons," and walk you through creating a smart itinerary.

PLANNING YOUR BUDGET

Anticipating costs, knowing your options, and living within your budget are fundamental to a good trip. You can travel comfortably in Europe for a month for about $5,500 (plus airfare). Students and rock-bottom travelers can enjoy a month in Europe for about 40 percent less—$3,300 plus airfare. See the sidebar and read the next section for details.

Budget Breakdown
Run a reality check on your dream trip. Start by getting a handle on your biggest expenses. Five components make up your trip costs: airfare, transportation within Europe, room

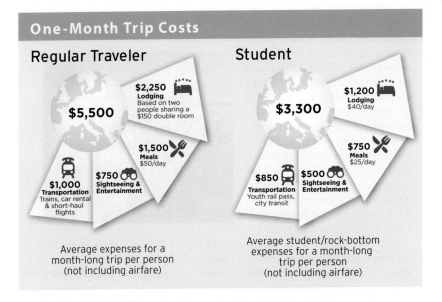

One-Month Trip Costs

Regular Traveler

$5,500

$2,250
Lodging
Based on two
people sharing a
$150 double room

$1,500
Meals
$50/day

$750
Sightseeing &
Entertainment

$1,000
Transportation
Trains, car rental
& short-haul
flights

Average expenses for a
month-long trip per person
(not including airfare)

Student

$3,300

$1,200
Lodging
$40/day

$750
Meals
$25/day

$500
Sightseeing &
Entertainment

$850
Transportation
Youth rail pass,
city transit

Average student/rock-bottom
expenses for a month-long
trip per person
(not including airfare)

and board, sightseeing and entertainment, and shopping and miscellany.

Airfare: The same round-trip flight between the US and Europe can cost anywhere from $900 to $1,500, depending on the time of year, where you are flying from, and various fees (such as airport taxes, fuel surcharges, and baggage fees). Traveling outside of peak season alone can save you several hundred dollars per ticket. The Flying chapter later in this book will help you understand all your alternatives.

Transportation Within Europe: This can be reasonable if you use Europe's excellent public transportation system (taking advantage of the best deals) or split a car rental among several people. And cheap flights—about $100 one-way between most major European cities—can save time and money on long journeys. For transit within cities, figure about $2-3 for each bus or subway ride. Your budget shouldn't dictate how freely you travel in Europe. If you want to go somewhere, make the most of whatever money-saving options you can. You came to travel. See the Trains, Buses, & Boats chapter for more details.

Lodging and Meals: The costs of sleeping and eating can make or break your budget. Luckily, you have a good degree of control over these expenses. Thrifty travelers can thrive on $125 a day for lodging and meals: $75 per person in a $150 hotel double with breakfast, $15 apiece for lunch, and $30 for dinner. That leaves you $5 for cappuccino or gelato. Remember that these costs are averages—Scandinavia,

Go with a Group or on Your Own?

Putting together a dream trip requires time and skills. As with any do-it-yourself project, at the outset it's wise to honestly assess whether you want to handle your endeavor (in this case, exploring Europe) on your own. Some people are not inclined to figure things out for a trip, and that's OK. They make their living figuring things out 50 weeks a year, and that's not their idea of a good vacation. These people should travel with a tour or a partner.

Tours and cruises are an easy way to see Europe and can make a lot of sense for people with limited time. You won't waste any mental energy determining where to sleep or how to get to the next town. With a good tour company, you'll enjoy the insights of local guides who'll bring Roman life alive in Pompeii or help you recall recent history in Berlin. And cruises offer the undeniable efficiency of sleeping while you travel to your next destination, allowing you to tour six dynamically different destinations in a single week—experiencing Europe as day trips in port rather than as a 24/7 immersion course.

Some tours and cruises can be cheaper than independent travel. Large tour companies get deals on hotels and restaurants, and using your cruise ship as a floating hotel can be less expensive than paying separately for hotels and city-to-city transportation (see the Bus Tours & Cruises chapter).

On a bus tour or cruise, you dip into Europe here and there, and tend to see a veneered version of Europe. For a more intimate challenge, an educational and experiential time, and a break from other Americans, you'll get the most satisfaction from traveling independently. Just as someone trying to learn a language will do better by actually experiencing that culture rather than sitting in a classroom for a few hours, I believe that travelers in search of engaging, enlightening experiences should eat, sleep, and live Europe.

Britain, and Italy are more expensive, while Spain, Portugal, Greece, and Eastern Europe are cheaper. Also, as a general rule, you'll pay less in the countryside and more in big cities.

If $125 per day is too steep for your budget, that's no reason to stay home—you can get by on less by picnicking more and staying in simpler accommodations. If you trade white tablecloths and black-tie waiters for a street market bench, your tomato salad will cost 20 times less. What you'd pay in a day for accommodations will cover a week if you opt for a basic double instead of a suite with fancy room service and chocolate on your pillow. For more money-saving advice, see the Sleeping and Eating chapters.

Sightseeing and Entertainment: Admissions to major attractions are roughly $8-20; smaller sights usually charge $2-5. Concerts, plays, and bus tours cost about $30. Plan for an average of about $25 per day. Don't skimp here. This category powers most of the experiences that all of the other expenses are designed to make possible. And fortunately, some of the best sights are free. See the Sightseeing chapter for strategies to make the most of your time and money.

Shopping and Miscellany: Shopping can vary in cost from nearly nothing to a small fortune. Good budget travelers find that this category has little to do with assembling a trip full of lifelong and wonderful memories. But if souvenirs are part of your travel dreams, see the Shopping chapter.

Budget Tips

I traveled every summer for years on a part-time piano teacher's income (and, boy, was she upset). My idea of "cheap" is simple, not sleazy. I'm not talking about begging and groveling around Europe. I'm talking about enjoying a one-star hotel rather than a three-star hotel ($100 saved), ordering a carafe of house wine at an atmospheric hole-in-the wall rather than a bottle of fine wine in a classy restaurant ($40 saved), and taking the shuttle bus in from the airport rather than a taxi ($50 saved). There are plenty of ways to keep your expenses in check without compromising your travel experience. In many ways, the less you spend, the more engaged you are with the culture around you, and the more you actually experience life as a temporary European.

Sleep in inexpensive hotels. I go for safe, central, friendly, local-style hotels, shunning swimming pools, people in uniforms, and transplanted American niceties. Hotels are pricey just about everywhere in Europe. But, equipped with good information, you can land some fine deals—which often come with the most memories, to boot. In Dubrovnik, for example, I pick a centrally located room in a small family-run hotel over a pricey resort hotel on a distant beach.

Find deals at local institutions. Rome has several convents that rent out rooms—the beds are twins and English is often in short supply, but the price is right. In London, you don't need to be a student to stay at colleges (such as the London School of Economics), which have openings in their dorms during student vacation periods in spring, summer, and winter.

Try inexpensive, unique alternatives to standard accommodations. On recent visits, I slept well in a former

medieval watchtower along Germany's Rhine River (Hotel Kranenturm, $90 double), a view room in a Franciscan convent in Italy's Umbria region (St. Anthony's Guest House in Assisi, $120 double), and a welcoming guesthouse in Dubrovnik's old town (Villa Ragusa, $100 double). If you're willing to rough it, you'll save even more. Consider a renovated jail in Ljubljana (Hostel Celica, $30 for a bunk in a 12-bed dorm) or a summer-only circus tent in Munich ($10 per foam mattress).

Delve into the "sharing economy." Staying in the home of a local is interesting and affordable, whether through pay-for-stay arrangements like Airbnb, home exchanges, or organizations that emphasize intercultural exchange such as Couchsurfing and Servas.

Patronize family-run restaurants with a local following. The best values are not in the places with glossy menus in six languages out front. I look for family-run restaurants away from the high-rent squares, filled with enthusiastic locals and offering a small, handwritten menu in the local language only. You'll get more for your money at mom-and-pop places; they pay less in labor (family members) and care more about their customers.

Look for daily deals. You can eat well for less nearly anywhere in Europe by taking advantage of daily specials, lunch deals, and early-bird dinners. In Britain, you'll find restaurants offering a three-course "set menu" deal before 7 p.m. In Stockholm, eat your main meal at lunch, when cafés and restaurants have daily special plates called dagens rätt.

Economize where it's expensive and splurge where it's cheap. The priciest parts of Europe (Scandinavia, Britain, and much of Italy) can be twice as expensive as Europe's cheapest corners (Spain, Portugal, Greece, and Eastern Europe). Exercise budget alternatives where they'll save you the most money. A hostel may save you $10 in Crete but $50 in Finland. In Scandinavia I picnic, walk, and sleep

Comparing *Apfels* to *Pommes*: Relative Prices in Europe's Top Cities

Budget alone should not determine where you go in Europe. People on a shoe-string budget can have a blast in Europe's most expensive countries...if they travel smart. But knowing roughly what you'll pay in various destinations can help you craft a more wallet-friendly itinerary. This chart attempts to compare apples to apples by showing rough costs in US dollars for basic tourist expenses in several of Europe's major cities (and, by way of comparison, my hometown in the USA). Prices are based on midrange hotels and restaurants, second-class trains, and first-class museums.

	Double Room	Main Dish at Dinner	One-Hour Train Ride to a Nearby Town	Museum Entry Fee
Amsterdam	$165	$22	$15	$18
Athens	$115	$15	$5	$17
Budapest, Kraków	$120	$15	$5	$8
Copenhagen, Oslo	$160	$25	$21	$15
London	$200	$25	$39	$25
Madrid, Lisbon	$130	$16	$14	$15
Munich	$125	$21	$28	$10
Paris	$190	$25	$19	$15
Prague	$170	$12	$6	$12
Rome	$210	$15	$13	$17
Vienna	$145	$21	$21	$15
Zürich	$195	$28	$25	$10
Seattle	$175	$20	$14	$20

on trains, but I live like a king in Portugal or Poland, where my splurge dollars go the farthest. Those on a tight budget manage better by traveling more quickly through the expensive countries and lingering in the cheap ones.

Eastern European hotels are nearly as pricey as in the West, but other items are a relative steal. A mug of Czech beer costs $2 (versus $6 in Britain or Ireland, or $10 in Oslo). A ticket for Mozart in a sumptuous Budapest opera house runs $20 (versus $65 in Vienna). And your own private Slovenian guide is $100 for a half-day (versus $200 in London).

Learn from the locals. When you're in Europe's priciest places, take the high cost of living gracefully in stride by following the lead of people who live there. Instead of paying dearly for dinner at a restaurant, Norwegians "eat out" in parks, barbecuing their groceries on disposable "one-time grills" ($5 in supermarkets). The last time I was in a restaurant in Oslo, 16 of 20 diners were drinking only tap water. While you'll see crowds of young people drinking beer along Copenhagen's canals, that doesn't mean alcohol consumption is higher in Denmark—it's just that many young adults can't afford to drink in the bars, so they pick up their beer at the grocery store and party al fresco. Why not drop by the local equivalent of a 7-Eleven and do the same?

Look for transportation discounts. You'll save on city transportation by purchasing transit passes for multiple rides or all-day usage. Some locales offer discounts if you travel in off-peak hours.

Swallow pride and save money. Many people cringe every time I use the word "cheap"; others appreciate the directness. Find out the complete price before ordering anything, and say "no thanks" if the price isn't right. Expect equal and fair treatment as a tourist.

Sightsee smartly. If you're an avid sightseer, look into combo-tickets or passes that cover multiple museums. If a town doesn't offer deals, prioritize the top sights you want to see, and then seek out free sights and experiences. Plenty of big-city museums have a free day or evening (but expect crowds); some sell discounted tickets if you enter late in the day (such as the Orangerie or Musée d'Orsay in Paris).

Spend money to save time. When you travel, time really is money. (Divide the complete cost of your trip by your waking hours in Europe, and you'll see what I mean. My cost: $20 per hour.) Don't waste your valuable time in lines. In Europe's most crowded cities (especially Paris, Rome, Florence, and Barcelona), advance tickets/reservations let you skirt long ticket-buying lines. If it costs $1 to use your mobile phone to confirm museum times, but it saves you trekking across town to discover the sight is closed, that's a buck very well spent.

Go communal. If you're traveling with a buddy or small group of friends, pool your money for everyday expenses. Separate checks and long lists of petty IOUs are a pain. Plus, combining costs can save you money; for instance, a group of four often travels more cheaply in a shared taxi or rental car than by subway, bus, or train. Enjoy treating each other to taxis and dinners out of your "kitty," and after the trip, divvy up the remains. Keep track of major individual expenses, but don't worry about who got an extra postcard or cappuccino. Just assume everything equals out in the long run. If one person consumed $40 or $50 more, that's a small price to pay for the convenience and economy of communal money.

Don't take budget tips too far. The true "value" of a trip isn't just a function of how cheaply you travel, but how much you enjoy it. If everyone says, "Portugal is cheap," but your travel dreams feature the Swiss Alps, then *your* best value is in Switzerland.

RESEARCHING YOUR TRIP

Europe is always changing, and it's essential to plan and travel with the most up-to-date information. Study before you go. Guidebooks, maps, and travel apps and websites are all key resources in getting started—and guiding you as you go.

While information is what keeps you afloat, too much can sink the ship. So winnow down your resources to what best suits your travel needs and interests. WWII buffs research battle sites, wine lovers brainstorm a wish list of wineries, and MacGregors locate their clan's castles in Scotland.

A word of warning as you hatch your plans: Understand what shapes the information that shapes your travel dreams. Information you seek out yourself is likely to be impartial, whereas information that comes at you is often propelled by business. Many publications and websites are supported by advertisers who have products and services to sell; their information may be useful, but it's not necessarily unbiased.

Online Resources

For travelers hitting the road post-pandemic, the internet is a critical resource for current restrictions, requirements, and health guidance; and for reconfirming details as you plan and travel.

Online resources also can help you save time and zero in on your interests. Thinking about visiting the Eiffel Tower, but worried about getting stuck in a long line? Use the official website to buy tickets in advance. Want to eat at the latest hot spot in Berlin? Get the inside scoop from a local blog, then check the open hours on the restaurant's own website. Wondering where a certain hotel is in Barcelona? Map it with Google Maps, then check "street view" to get the neighborhood vibe (though be aware that you might be looking at an early morning photo taken when the area is not as bustling as usual).

Start your web research with the professionals: Every guidebook publisher has a website, as do travel magazines and major newspapers with good travel sections. But don't overlook homegrown talent and opinions from other travelers. Here are some sources to consider:

Government Websites

Two websites to bookmark as resources for travel restrictions by destination, health requirements, and more are the Centers for Disease Control and Prevention's travel website (www.cdc.gov/travel) and the US State Department's international travel website (www.travel.state.gov). US embassy websites are also good resources for individual countries (www.usembassy.gov).

Tourist Information Office Websites

Just about every European city has a centrally located tourist information office loaded with maps and advice. This is often my first stop upon arrival in any town, but you don't need to wait until you get to Europe to access their information. Each European country has its own official tourism website—a great place to begin researching your trip. Many of these sites are packed with practical information, suggested itineraries, city guides, interactive maps, colorful photos, and free downloadable brochures describing walking tours and more.

Local Websites

I'm a big fan of local websites and blogs loaded with insider tips. Not only do they fill you in on the latest happenings and hot spots, but they help you feel like a native in no time.

Any major city has a host of online resources dedicated to arts, culture, food, and drink. Serious foodies looking for Paris restaurants and specialty shops should consult the always appetizing ParisByMouth.com. The Local, the largest English-language news network in Europe,

Resources for Trip Planning

CDC.gov/travel: US Centers for Disease Control and Prevention travel site, with recommendations by destination

Travel.State.Gov: US State Department's official travel site, with foreign entry requirements, travel warnings, and more

TripAdvisor, Booking.com: Traveler reviews, hotel prices and availability

VisitaCity.com: Itinerary planning, budgeting, and sharing

ViaMichelin.com: Maps and route planner

Bahn.com: German rail website listing schedules for trains all over Europe

Rome2Rio.com: Compiles different transportation options from one destination to another

WeatherPlanner.com: Weather prediction site that uses historical data

RickSteves.com: Destination info, trip-planning advice, festival and holiday dates, travel forum, and a trove of Rick's TV shows, radio interviews, articles, and travel-skills talks

TripIt app: All-in one travel organizer

has websites devoted to Germany (www.thelocal.de), Italy (www.thelocal.it), and several other countries.

One of my favorite resources, Matt Barrett's Athens Survival Guide (www.athensguide.com), covers emerging and off-beat neighborhoods as well as recommendations for vibrant, untouristy restaurants. The Florentine (www.theflorentine.net) takes an insider look at culture, art, and food in Florence and Tuscany. Expat websites, such as AngloInfo.com for the French Riviera, collect tips on local events, markets, and the like.

Traveler Reviews

To plan a trip, I once relied on travel agents, other travel writers, and the word-of-mouth advice of friends. Those sources are still valid—but my circle of "friends" has increased exponentially. With the advent of user-review sites and apps such as Yelp, Booking.com, and TripAdvisor, the opinions of everyday travelers are changing the way we approach trip planning.

User reviews can be helpful as you plan, allowing you to browse destinations and get a consensus of traveler opinions about everything from hotels and restaurants to sights and nightlife. But these reviews also have their drawbacks.

When I started traveling, there wasn't enough information. Now there's too much. Those enamored with crowdsourcing might plan an entire trip based solely on user reviews. But it's risky: Your reviewer may be someone who visited once and had a bad day; a company on another continent that's being paid to say good (or bad) things about European businesses; a couple who promised to write a good review of a B&B in exchange for a free breakfast; or a guy who goes to Paris to eat Tex-Mex. I've seen estimates that one-third to one-half of the travel reviews you see on the internet are fake.

Review sites can also become an echo chamber, where one or two well-located, flashy businesses camp out atop the ratings. Travelers rave about these already-popular places, creating a self-perpetuating cycle of positive reviews. Meanwhile, a better, more affordable, and more authentic alternative may sit ignored, tucked down a side street. Or a hotel can pay a website to be a "preferred property" and get its listing bumped to a high spot—even if the reviews are mediocre. And hotels or B&Bs who refuse to pay a commission won't be listed at all.

The most helpful crowd-sourced ideas for travelers

usually come from the categories for tours, sightseeing experiences, and entertainment. If I'm coming into Amsterdam and I want to know what's new, I might look at TripAdvisor: It lists every food tour, every bike tour, every zipline, and every goofy goblin tour. You can sort through those options and decide what you want to do with your time. But keep in mind that good guidebook writers have already done most of the work for you—read on!

Guidebooks and Planning Maps

I am amazed by the many otherwise smart people who base the trip of a lifetime on a borrowed copy of a ten-year-old guidebook. Guidebooks are $30 tools for $4,000 experiences. As a writer—and user—of guidebooks, I am a big believer in their worth. When I visit somewhere as a rank beginner, I equip myself with a good, up-to-date guidebook. I travel like an old pro, not because I'm a super traveler, but because I have reliable information and I use it.

Guidebooks: With a good guidebook, you can come into Paris for your first time, go anywhere in town for less than $2 on the subway, enjoy a memorable bistro lunch for $25, and pay $150 for a double room in a friendly hotel on a pedestrian-only street a few blocks from the Eiffel Tower—so French that when you step outside in the morning, you feel you must have been a poodle in a previous life.

Before buying any guidebook, check the publication date. If it's been in print for a while, find out when the new edition is due out. Many guidebooks get an update only every five or six years. Only a handful of titles (including my titles) are updated in person with regularity. When I'm choosing between guidebooks for a certain destination, the publication date (often on the copyright page) is usually the deciding factor.

Planning Maps: When you pick up your guidebook, choose a map or two for planning purposes. The *Michelin Map Europe 705* provides an excellent overall view of Europe. Many guidebook publishers (including Rough Guides, Lonely Planet, and my series) make maps or combination map-guidebooks. While online mapping tools are excellent for help in planning the finer points of your itinerary (especially if you're driving), there's nothing quite like laying out a large map on the table to get a sense of relative locations and distances, then inking in your intended route.

Ebooks: Many guidebook series, including most of my titles, are available as ebooks. While I still consider myself a paper guy, there are advantages to going digital. You

LEFT Never underestimate the value of an up-to-date guidebook.

RIGHT My planning maps highlight what you want to see...not just the biggest cities.

can carry multiple titles without adding weight to your bag (great for long, multidestination trips), and you can buy books on the go (convenient for spur-of-the-moment detours). But ebooks have limitations: Flipping from page to page is awkward and maps—often designed to run across two pages—don't always appear correctly. Until the perfect digital solution arrives, I believe a printed guidebook is the most practical format.

Rick Steves Guidebooks

The book you're holding is the foundation of a series of books—written and refined over the last three decades—that work together to help smooth your travels and broaden your cultural experiences. With the help of my research partners, I update my guidebooks lovingly and in person. In order to experience the same Europe that most of my readers do, I insist on doing my research in the peak tourist season—from April through September. And I'm stubbornly selective, writing about fewer destinations than other guidebooks. For example, Italy has dozens of hill towns, but my Italy book zooms in on the handful that are truly worth the trip. I base my depth of coverage on a place's worthiness, rather than its population or fame.

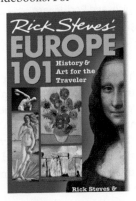

A trio of my books is best read before your trip. This book, *Europe Through the Back Door,* teaches you the nuts and bolts of how to travel affordably and efficiently, with maximum opportunities to connect to the culture. *Europe 101: History and Art for the Traveler* (co-authored with Gene Openshaw)

Rick Steves Guidebook Series

My take-along guidebooks create a blueprint for your trip, weaving my favorite sights, accommodations, and restaurants into strategies designed to make the most out of every mile, minute, and dollar. I focus on helping you explore and enjoy Europe's big cities, small towns, and regions, mixing must-see sights with intimate Back Door nooks and offbeat crannies. For a complete list of titles, see the ad pages at the end of this book.

Rick Steves City, Regional, and Country Guidebooks

These comprehensive guidebooks cut through the superlatives to give you the best possible plan for your trip, with all the info and tips you need to tour Europe's top destinations and sights.

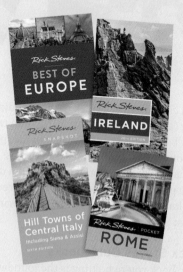

Rick Steves "Best Of" Guidebooks

This series covers Europe's best destinations in condensed form. Full-color and easy-to-scan, they focus on the top cities and sights across Europe.

Rick Steves Pocket Guidebooks

For travelers taking short, focused trips, my colorful Pocket guidebooks cover many of Europe's most popular destinations and slip right into your pocket.

Rick Steves Snapshot Guidebooks

Excerpted from my bigger country guidebooks, these slim titles zoom in on many of my favorite cities and regional destinations.

Rick Steves Cruise Guidebooks

My cruise-focused guidebooks help you choose and book a cruise, enjoy your time on board, and make the most of your time in port.

Rick Steves Phrase Books

Fun and practical, these guides will help you get along in French, Italian, German, Spanish, and Portuguese.

will help you achieve a deeper understanding of the story of Europe. (It's for smart people who slept through their art history classes before they knew they were going to Europe... and now wish they knew who the Etruscans were.) The next step, *Travel as a Political Act,* illustrates how Americans who travel with an open mind and a curious spirit can have the time of their lives and come home smarter—with a keener appreciation for the interconnected-ness of the world around them.

This trilogy forms a pyramid—similar to Abraham Maslow's "hierarchy of needs"—for the thinking traveler. You start off with the basics: Pack light, stay safe, catch the train, and eat and sleep well. When those needs are met, you can enjoy the art, history, and culture. Finally you reach the pinnacle of travel: gaining a deeper understanding of our place on this delightful planet.

Other Guidebook Series

Every guidebook series has an area of specialization: Some are great for hotels, but fall down on restaurants. Other series can't be beat for history and culture. Some guidebooks (like mine) are more opinionated and selective, choosing the most worthwhile destinations in each country and covering them in depth. Others seek to cover every possible destination you might find yourself in. When I travel to areas I don't cover in my books, I routinely use guidebooks from these publishers, and find them helpful.

A good guide-book allows you to play "tour guide" and brings Europe's museums to life.

Lonely Planet: The worldwide standard for a solid guidebook, Lonely Planet covers most countries in Europe, Asia, Africa, and the Americas. The Lonely Planet series offers comprehensive, no-nonsense facts, low- and mid-budget listings, and helpful on-the-ground travel tips.

Frommer's Guides: The granddaddy of travel publishing, Frommer's has reinvented its longstanding series to be leaner and more focused on the budget traveler. These books are especially well attuned to the needs of older travelers, but some readers may feel like they're being handled with unnecessary kid gloves.

Fodor's Travel: A stalwart of travel publishing, Fodor's has been producing good basic European guidebooks for American travelers since the 1930s. Their coverage is more encyclopedic than inspiring.

DK Eyewitness Travel: These visual guides offer appealing color photos and illustrations (like cutaway cross-sections of important castles and churches). They are great for trip planning and visual learners, but the written information is scant—I don't travel with them.

National Geographic Traveler: These guides are well

Guidebooks: Small, Handy, and Tailored to Your Trip

I often buy several guidebooks for each country I visit, rip them up, and staple the pertinent chapters together into my own personalized hybrid guidebook. On the road, I bring only the applicable pages—there's no point in carrying 100 pages of information on Madrid to dinner in Barcelona.

As I travel in Europe, I've met lots of people with clever book treatments. One couple was proud of the job they did in the name of packing light: cutting out only the pages they'd be using and putting them into a spiral binding. Another couple put their guidebook in a brown-paper-bag book cover so they wouldn't look so touristy (a smart move, I'll admit).

I love the ritual of customizing the guidebooks I'll be using: I fold the pages back until the spine breaks, neatly slice out the sections I want with a utility knife, then pull them out with the gummy edge intact. I use a monster stapler to "rebind" the sections I'm keeping, then finish it off with some clear, heavy-duty packing tape to smooth and reinforce the spine. Another option is to tear out the chapters you don't need and bring the rest in the original binding. To make things easy for travelers who like this approach, I've created a slide-on laminated cover to corral your pages (for details, see www.ricksteves.com/shop).

produced, with beautiful maps and sharp photos. They're highly selective and a bit stingy with information, but great for trip planning and dreaming.

Rough Guides: This British series is written by Europeans who understand the contemporary social scene better than most American writers. While their hotel listings can be skimpy and uninspired, the historical and sightseeing information tends to offer greater depth than others.

Michelin Green Guides: From a French publisher, these tall, green books are packed with color maps and photos, plus small but encyclopedic chapters on history, lifestyles, art, culture, and customs. Recent editions also list hotels and restaurants. The **Michelin Red Guides** are the hotel and restaurant connoisseur's bibles.

Bradt Travel Guides: This British series, specializing in off-the-beaten-track destinations throughout Europe (and the world), offers plenty of cultural insights in addition to solid nitty-gritty details.

Blue Guides: Known for a dry and scholarly approach,

these guides are ideal if you want a deep dive into history, art, architecture, and culture. With the Blue Guide to Greece, I had all the information I needed about every sight and never needed to hire a guide. Scholarly types actually find a faint but endearing personality hiding between the sheets of their Blue Guides.

DESIGNING AN ITINERARY

Filling in the blanks between your flight out and the flight home is one of the more pleasurable parts of trip planning. It's armchair travel that turns into real travel.

I never start a trip without having every day planned out. Your reaction to an itinerary may be, "Hey, won't my spontaneity and freedom suffer?" Not necessarily. Even with my well-thought-out plan, I maintain my flexibility and make changes as needed, using my itinerary to see the consequences of any on-the-fly revisions I make. With the help of an itinerary, you can lay out your goals, maximize their execution, and avoid regrettable changes.

Your itinerary depends on several factors, including weather, crowds, geography, timeline, and travel style. (Are you antsy to see as much as you can, or do you like settling into a place for a few days?) Take the following considerations into account as you build your European itinerary.

Europe by (Tourist) Season

Some people have flexible enough jobs and lifestyles to cherry-pick when to take their vacations, but many others have less choice. Fortunately, Europe welcomes visitors 365 days a year—and each season offers a different ambience and experience.

In travel-industry jargon, the year is divided into three seasons: peak season (roughly May through September), shoulder season (April and October), and off-season (November through March). Each has its pros and cons. Regardless of when you go, if your objective is to "meet the people," you'll find Europe filled with them any time of year.

Peak Season

Summer is a great time to travel—except for the crowds and high temperatures. Sunny weather, long days, and exuberant nightlife turn Europe into a powerful magnet. I haven't missed a peak season in 30 years. Families with school-age children are usually locked into peak-season travel. Here are a few tips to help you keep your cool:

Arrange your trip with crowd control in mind. Go to the busy places as early or late in peak season as you can. Consider, for instance, a six-week European trip beginning June 1, half with a rail pass to see famous sights in Italy and Austria, and half visiting relatives in Scotland. It would be wise to do the rail pass section first, enjoying fewer crowds, then spend time with the family during the last half of your vacation, when Florence and Salzburg are teeming with tourists. Salzburg on June 10 and Salzburg on July 10 are two very different experiences.

Spend the night. Popular day-trip destinations near big cities and resorts such as Toledo (near Madrid), San Marino (near huge Italian beach resorts), and San Gimignano (near Florence) take on a more peaceful and enjoyable atmosphere at night, when the legions of day-trippers retreat to the predictable plumbing of their big-city or beach-resort hotels. Small towns normally lack hotels big enough for tour groups and are often inaccessible to large buses. So, at worst, they experience midday crowds. Likewise, popular cruise-ship destinations, such as Venice and Dubrovnik, are hellishly packed during the day—but more bearable at night, when the cruise crowds sail off.

Prepare for intense heat. Europeans swear that it gets hotter every year, with more frequent and persistent heat-waves. Even restaurants in typically cooler climates (like Munich or Amsterdam) now tend to have ample al fresco seating to take advantage of the ever longer outdoor-dining season. Throughout Europe in July and August, expect high temperatures—even sweltering heat—particularly in the south.

Don't discount cities in July and August. In much of Europe, especially Italy and France, cities partially shut

In peak season, sunbathers are packed like sardines on Europe's beaches. In shoulder season, the beaches are wide open.

St. Mark's Square in July—no wonder Venice is sinking...but any time of the year, walk a few blocks away and it's just you and Venice.

down in July and August, when local urbanites take their beach breaks. You'll hear that these are terrible times to travel, but it's really no big deal. You can't get a dentist, and many launderettes may be closed, but tourists are basically unaffected by Europe's mass holidays. Just don't get caught on the wrong road on the first or fifteenth of the month (when vacations often start or finish, causing huge traffic jams), or try to compete with all of Europe for a piece of French Riviera beach in August.

Some places are best experienced in peak season. Travel in the peak season in Scandinavia, Britain, and Ireland, where you want the best weather and longest days possible, where crowds are relatively rare, and where sights are sleepy or even closed in shoulder season. Scandinavia has an extremely brief tourist season—basically from mid-June to late August; I'd avoid it outside this window.

Shoulder Season
"Shoulder season"—generally April and October—combines the advantages of both peak- and off-season travel. In shoulder season, you'll enjoy decent weather, long-enough daylight, fewer crowds, and a local tourist industry still ready to please and entertain.

Shoulder season varies by destination. Because spring and fall bring cooler temperatures in Mediterranean Europe, shoulder season in much of Italy, southern France, Spain, Croatia, and Greece can actually come with near peak-season crowds and prices.

Spring or fall? If debating the merits of traveling before or after summer, consider your destination. Both weather and crowds are about the same in spring or fall. Mediterranean Europe is generally green in spring but parched in fall. For hikers, the Alps are better in early fall,

European Weather

Make sure to consider weather conditions when you make your travel plans. Europe and North America share the same latitudes and a similar climate. This map shows Europe superimposed over North America (shaded) with latitude lines. Use the map as a general weather guide. For example, London and Vancouver, Canada, are located at a similar latitude and are both near the sea, so you can assume their climates are nearly the same. But you can't go by latitude alone. While it might seem that Rome and New York City should have similar weather, Rome is hotter because it's surrounded by the warm Mediterranean. Inland areas have colder winters, so Prague can get as chilly as Minneapolis. Elevation affects climate as well. For average temperatures, check Wunderground.com.

because many good hiking trails are still covered with snow through the late spring.

Off-Season

Every summer, Europe greets a stampede of sightseers. Before jumping into the peak-season pig pile, consider a trip during the off-season—generally November through March. In the off-season, you'll enjoy an amazing slice of Europe where the only crowds are festive locals.

Expect to pay less (most of the time). Off-season airfares are often hundreds of dollars cheaper. With fewer crowds in Europe, you may find you can sleep for less: Many fine hotels drop their prices, and budget hotels will have plenty of vacancies. And while some smaller or rural

LEFT In the north, darkness falls early in the winter. This is Oslo at 3:30 p.m.

RIGHT Italy's Cinque Terre villages are empty in the winter...and the good restaurants close for a much-needed holiday.

accommodations may be closed, those still open are usually empty and, therefore, more comfortable. The opposite is true of big-city business centers (especially Berlin, Brussels, and the Scandinavian capitals), which are busiest with corporate travelers and most expensive off-season.

Enjoy having Europe to yourself. Off-season adventurers loiter undisturbed in Leonardo da Vinci's home, ponder Rome's Forum all alone, kick up sand on lonely Adriatic beaches, and chat with laid-back guards by log fires in French châteaux. In wintertime Venice, you can be by yourself atop St. Mark's bell tower; below, on St. Mark's Square, pigeons fidget and wonder, "Where are the tourists?"

Off-season adventurers enjoy step-right-up service at shops and tourist offices, and experience a more European Europe. Although many popular tourist-oriented parks, shows, and tours are closed, off-season is in-season for high culture: In Vienna, for example, the Boys' Choir, opera, and Lipizzaner stallions are in all their crowd-pleasing glory.

Be prepared for any kind of weather. Because much of Europe is at Canadian latitudes, winter days are short. It's dark by 5 p.m. The weather can be miserable—cold, windy, and drizzly—and then turn worse.

Pack for the cold and wet—layers of clothing, rainproof parka, gloves, wool hat, long johns, waterproof shoes, and an umbrella. Dress warmly. Cold weather is colder when you're outdoors trying to enjoy yourself all day long. But just as summer can be wet and gray, winter can be crisp and blue, and even into mid-November, hillsides blaze with colorful leaves.

Beware of shorter hours. Make the most of your limited daylight hours. Some sights close entirely in the off-season, and others operate on shorter hours, with sunset often determining the closing time. Winter sightseeing is fine in big cities, which bustle year-round, but it's more frustrating in small tourist towns, which can be boringly quiet, with many sights and restaurants closed down. In December, most beach resorts shut up as tight as canned hams. While Europe's wonderful outdoor evening ambience survives all year in the south, wintertime streets are empty in the north after dark. English-language tours, common in the summer, are rarer off-season, when most visitors are natives. Tourist information offices often have shorter hours in winter.

Itinerary Considerations

When planning your trip itinerary, deal thoughtfully with issues such as weather, culture shock, health maintenance, fatigue, and festivals—and you'll travel happier.

Establish a logical flight plan. Avoid needless travel time and expense by flying into one airport and out from another. You usually pay just half the round-trip fare for each airport. Even if this type of flight plan is more expensive than the cheapest round-trip fare, it often saves you lots of time and money when surface connections are figured in. For example, you could fly into London, travel east through whatever interests you in Europe, and fly home from Athens. This eliminates the costly, time-consuming, and needless return to London.

I used to fly into Amsterdam, travel to Rome, then ride one full day by train back to Amsterdam to fly home because I thought it was "too expensive" to pay $200 extra to fly out of Rome. Now I understand the real economy—in time and money—in breaking out of the round-trip mold.

Plug various cities into flight websites and check the fares. For more on choosing flights, see page 98.

See countries in order of cultural hairiness. If you plan to see Britain, the Alps, and Italy, do it in that order so you'll grow steadily into the more intense travel. If you've never been out of the US, flying directly into Rome can be overwhelming. Even if you did survive Italy, everything after that would be anticlimactic. Start mild—that means England. Compared to any place but the United States, England is pretty dull. Don't get me wrong—it's a wonderful place to travel. But go there first, when cream teas and roundabouts will be exotic. You're more likely to enjoy Naples, Athens, or Sarajevo if you gradually work your way south and east.

Match your destination to your interests. If you're passionate about Renaissance art, Florence is a must. England's Cotswolds beckon to those who fantasize about thatched cottages, time-passed villages, and sheep lazing on green hillsides. For World War II buffs, there's no more stirring experience than a visit to Normandy. Beer connoisseurs make pilgrimages to Belgium. If you like big cities, you'll enjoy London, Paris, Rome, and Madrid. Want to get off the beaten path? Nothing rearranges your mental furniture like a trip to Bosnia's Mostar or Morocco's Tangier.

If you have European roots, a fun part of travel is to discover a kinship with people from the land of your ancestors. I can't tell you how many American Murphys, Kellys, and O'Somethings I meet in Ireland, in search of their roots and a good beer. I'm Norwegian, and anywhere in Scandinavia, I feel like I'm among cousins, but when I cross the border into Norway, it's like I'm among brothers and sisters.

Seek out less-visited alternatives. Keep in mind that accessibility and promotional budgets may determine a place's fame and popularity just as much as its worthiness as a tourist attraction. And the most touristed locales are less likely to show you today's Europe.

I enjoy visiting Europe's less glamorous second cities—the Chicagos of Europe—such as Antwerp (Belgium), Marseille (France), Liverpool (England), and Hamburg (Germany). A lot of money and effort are being put into revitalizing these once-depressed, former Industrial Age powers, giving them a certain energy that you don't find in their more well-known siblings. If you have three days to spend in Edinburgh, consider spending one of them in Scotland's second city: Glasgow (just 45 minutes away).

Some underpromoted locales can even be more pleasant than their more popular counterparts. The beaches of Greece's Peloponnesian Peninsula enjoy the same weather and water as the highly promoted isles of Santorini and Ios, but are out of the way and wonderfully deserted. In England, you can find yourself all alone at your own private little stone circle, and even though it's not as grandiose as Stonehenge, there's more magic there. If you're traveling by car, take advantage of your mobility by leaving the well-worn tourist routes. Europe away from the train tracks is less expensive and feels more peaceful and relaxed. Overlooked by the rail pass mobs, it's one step behind the modern parade.

Don't let well-advertised tourist traps trump more worthwhile sights.

Moderate the weather conditions you'll encounter. Over my many years of travels, my routine

Numbers and Stumblers

Europeans convey numerical information differently than we do, from measurements to schedules and even dates. Knowing the differences will save needless confusion when planning itineraries or making reservations.

Time and Date

The 24-hour clock (military time) is used in any official timetable. This includes bus, train, and tour schedules. Learn to use it quickly and easily. Everything is the same until 12:00. Then, the Europeans keep on going—13:00, 14:00, and so on. For any time after noon, subtract 12 and add p.m. (18:00 is 6 p.m.).

To figure out the time back home, remember that European time is generally six/nine hours ahead of the East/West Coasts of the US. (These are the major exceptions: British, Irish, and Portuguese time is five/eight hours ahead; Greece and Turkey are seven/ten hours ahead.) Europe observes Daylight Saving Time (called "Summer Time" in the UK), but on a slightly different schedule than the US: Europe "springs forward" on the last Sunday in March (three weeks after most of North America) and "falls back" the last Sunday in October (one week before North America). For a handy time converter, use the world clock app on your mobile phone.

When it comes to dates, remember—especially when making reservations—that European date order is written day/month/year. Christmas 2022, for example, is 25/12/22 instead of 12/25/22, as we would write it. Also, European wall calendars tend to start on a Monday, not Sunday.

Written Numbers

A European's handwritten numbers look different from ours. The number 1 has an

has been spring in the Mediterranean area and summer north of the Alps. Match the coolest month of your trip with the warmest area, and vice versa. For a spring and early-summer trip, enjoy comfortable temperatures throughout by starting in the southern countries and working your way north. If possible, avoid the midsummer Mediterranean heat and crowds of Italy and southern France. Spend those weeks in Scandinavia, Britain, Ireland, or the Alps (which may also increase your odds of sun in places prone to miserable weather).

Alternate intense big cities with villages and countryside. For example, break a tour of Venice, Florence, and Rome with an easygoing time in Italy's hill towns or on the Italian Riviera. Judging Italy by Rome alone is like judging America by New York City.

Join the celebration. If you like parties, hit as many festivals, national holidays, and arts seasons as you can (or, if you hate crowds, learn the dates to avoid). An effort to visit the right places at the right times will drape your trip with festive tinsel. This takes some planning. One of the

upswing (*4*). The number 4 often looks like a short lightning bolt (*4*). If you don't cross your 7 (*7*), it may be mistaken as a sloppy 1, and you could miss your train. Don't use "#" for "number"–it's not common in Europe.

On the Continent, commas are decimal points and decimals are commas, so a euro and a half is €1,50 and there are 5.280 feet in a mile. (Britain and Ireland use commas and decimal points like North America.)

Metric Conversion

Expect to confront the metric system in your European travels. Here are some easy ways to guesstimate metric conversions: Since a meter is 39 inches, just consider a meter roughly equivalent to a yard. A kilometer is a bit more than a half-mile (1 kilometer = 0.62 mile). A liter is nearly the same as a quart (1.056 quarts, to be exact)–about four to a gallon. A centimeter is about half the distance across a penny (1 inch = 2.54 centimeters), while a millimeter is about the thickness of a penny (1 inch = 25 millimeters). In markets, it's handy to know that 1 ounce = 28 grams, and 2.2 pounds = 1 kilogram.

Temperature Conversion

Europeans measure temperatures in degrees Celsius (zero degrees C = 32 degrees F). To roughly convert to Fahrenheit, it's easiest (if not perfectly accurate) to double the Celsius temperature and add 30. So if it's 27° C, double to 54 and add 30 to get 84° F (it's actually 81° F, but that's close enough for me). To convert Fahrenheit to Celsius, just subtract 30 and divide by 2. A memory aid: 28° C = 82° F–balmy summer weather.

best places to start is with my country-by-country list of major holidays and festivals at RickSteves.com/festivals. Remember that event dates can change, so be sure to verify them on each festival's website or with a local tourist information office (and book your room well in advance).

Train or plane within Europe? Do a cost and time analysis to help you decide the best mode of transportation for your trip. Not too long ago, I'd piece together a trip based on which towns could be connected by train. Today, there are fewer night trains, and it's relatively cheap and easy to combine, say, Portugal, Poland, and Palermo on a single itinerary by air (for more on cheap flights, see page 112).

A train ride itself may take longer than a flight, but for most train journeys you just hop aboard (no lengthy check-in), and most trains arrive right in the heart of town. For a flight, you'll need to add in the time it takes to get to and from the airport, as well as how early you'll need to arrive for check-in. Flying also has a bigger environmental impact.

Minimize one-night stands. Even the speediest itinerary should be a series of two-night stands. It can be worth taking a late-afternoon drive or train ride to settle into a town for two consecutive nights—and gain a full uninterrupted day for sightseeing. Staying in a home base and making day trips can be more time-efficient than changing locations and hotels (see later for more on home-basing).

Leave some slack in your itinerary. Don't schedule yourself too tightly (a common tendency). Everyday chores, small business matters, transportation problems, constipation, and planning mistakes deserve about one day of slack per week in your itinerary. For long trips, schedule a "vacation from your vacation" in the middle. Most people need several days in a place where they couldn't see a museum or take a tour even if they wanted to. A stop in the mountains or on an island, in a friendly rural town, or at the home of a relative is a great way to revitalize your tourist spirit.

Assume you will return. This "General MacArthur" approach is a key to touristic happiness. You can't cover all of Europe in one trip—don't even try. Enjoy what you're seeing. Forget what you won't get to on this trip. If you worry about things that are just out of reach, you won't appreciate what's in your hand. I've taken dozens of European trips, and I still need more time. I'm happy about what I can't get to. It's a blessing that we can never see all of Europe.

Your Best Itinerary in Eight Steps

Trying to narrow your choices among European destinations is a bit like being a kid in a candy shop. The options are endless and everything looks delicious (and consuming too much isn't good for you). Guidebooks, tour company websites, travel blogs and other sources can provide you with well-thought-out itineraries to crib from. Start by listing every place you'd like to visit, then turn that list into a smart itinerary by following these steps.

1. Decide on the places you want to see. Write out your wish list ("Places I want to see—London, Alps, Bavaria, Florence, Amsterdam, Paris, the Rhine, Rome, Venice, Greece"). Then make sure you have a reason for

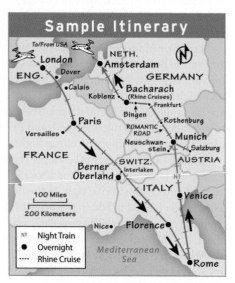

Sample Itinerary

Planning an Itinerary

SEPTEMBER

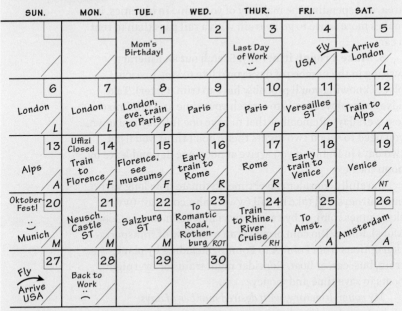

SUN.	MON.	TUE.	WED.	THUR.	FRI.	SAT.
		1 Mom's Birthday!	2	3 Last Day of Work ☺	4 USA / Fly →	5 Arrive London / L
6 London / L	7 London / L	8 London, eve. train to Paris / P	9 Paris / P	10 Paris / P	11 Versailles ST / P	12 Train to Alps / A
13 Alps / A	14 Uffizi Closed Train to Florence / F	15 Florence, see museums / F	16 Early train to Rome / R	17 Rome / R	18 Early train to Venice / V	19 Venice / NT
20 Oktober-Fest! ☺ Munich / M	21 Neusch. Castle ST / M	22 Salzburg ST / M	23 To Romantic Road, Rothen-burg / ROT	24 Train to Rhine, River Cruise / RH	25 To Amst. / A	26 Amsterdam / A
27 Fly → Arrive USA	28 Back to Work ☺	29	30			

Use abbreviations in the bottom right of each calendar day to indicate where you'll spend the night (for example, L = London).
NT = Night Train; ST = Side Trip

every stop. Don't visit Casablanca because you liked the movie. Just because George Clooney bought a villa on Lake Como doesn't mean you should go there, too.

2. Establish a route and timeline. Circle your destinations on a map, then figure out a logical geographical order and length for your trip. Pin down any places that you have to be on a certain date (and ask yourself if it's really worth stifling your flexibility). Once you've settled on an order, be satisfied with your efficient plan, and focus any more study and preparation only on places that fall along your proposed route.

3. Decide on the cities you'll fly in and out of. Flying into one city and out of another is usually more efficient than booking a round-trip flight. Think carefully about which cities make the most sense as a first stop or a finale. If you'll be renting a car, remember that a one-way drop-off fee can add to your costs, especially if you are crossing country borders.

4. Determine the mode of transportation. Base this not solely on cost, but by what's best for the trip you envision. Study the ins and outs of the many ways of getting from point A to point B—whether flying, riding the rails, driving, biking, or hiking.

For example, if you're traveling alone, traversing a huge area, and spending the majority of your time in big cities, it makes more sense to go by train with a rail pass than to rent a car.

5. Make a rough itinerary. Sketch out an itinerary, writing in the number of days you'd like to stay in each place (knowing you'll probably have to trim it later). Take advantage of weekends to stretch your time and minimize lost workdays. Remember that to have one full day in a town, you need to spend two nights there: don't think you'll get two days in Dublin if you arrive at noon one day and leave by noon the next.

Carefully consider travel time. Estimate how long various journeys will take by rail (www.bahn.com), air (www.skyscanner.com), or by car (www.viamichelin.com or Google Maps). Rome2Rio.com provides an overview of transportation options from Point A to Point B, including by plane, train, bus, car, or boat. Consider night trains or overnight boats to save time and money.

My rough itinerary, with desired number of days:

3	London
5	Paris
3	Alps
2	Florence
3	Rome (flight or train)
7	Greece (flight or train + night boat)
1	Bologna
2	Venice (night train)
3	Munich/Bavaria
3	Romantic Road/Rhine Cruise
3	Berlin
4	Amsterdam
39	TOTAL DAYS

6. Adjust to fit your timeline or budget. If your rough itinerary exceeds your available time or money, look for ways to save on travel time and/or cost. If two destinations are equally important to you but you don't have time for both, cut the place that takes the most time, hassle, or expense to reach. For example, my rough itinerary (on previous page) is too long: I have only 22 days for my trip. Based on time saved, I cut Greece, and even though I'd like to see both Amsterdam and Berlin, I drop Berlin because it takes longer to get to.

Then I minimize clutter. A so-so destination (Bologna) breaking up a relatively short train ride (Rome-Venice) is clutter.

Next, eliminate repetition. On a quick trip, focus on only one part of the Romantic Road (my favorite stop is Rothenburg). The Rhine Valley is chock-a-block with castles. Choose one (Rheinfels, above the town of St. Goar).

Finally, I trim time from each stop. Five days in Paris would be grand, but I can see the high points in four. There's a slope of diminishing return for each day that you stay in a town. Day number five in a great city is not as good as day number one in a secondary city.

It can also help to consider economizing on car rental or a rail pass. For instance, a 22-day trip can be managed with a 15-day train pass by seeing London, Paris, and Amsterdam before or after using the pass.

My final itinerary, with number of days adjusted to time limitations:

3	London
4	Paris
2	Alps
2	Florence
2	Rome
2	Venice
3	Munich/Bavaria
2	Romantic Road/Rhine Cruise
2	Amsterdam
22	TOTAL DAYS

7. Fine-tune your itinerary. Study your guidebook. Take advantage of online tools and apps that allow you to browse destinations, compare itineraries, and even get advice from friends or fellow travelers. Be sure crucial sights are open the day you'll be in town. Remember that most major tourist attractions close for one day during the week (usually Monday). It would be a shame to be in Paris only on a Monday, when the Orsay is *fermé*. Write out a day-by-day itinerary that takes into account any can't-miss sights, festivals, or markets. Note that when flying from the United States, you'll most likely arrive in Europe on the next day. When returning, you arrive home the same day (or so you hope).

Tracking Your Itinerary

Once I've fine-tuned my itinerary, I put everything into a chart like this one. This system keeps me organized, since I can collect all my reservations, train times, and other trip notes in one place. As I travel, I can see at a glance where I'll be sleeping a week from now, or what time the train leaves on Saturday. Even if you're not a detail person, it pays to be disciplined about this. And it's handy to give to family, friends, and coworkers who are curious about where you'll be.

Once you've created the chart, use it to keep track of your progress as you systematically set up your trip. Work your way through your list and request rooms, slogging away until the entire trip is confirmed. Make any advance reservations you'll need (for this itinerary, I'd reserve the Eurostar and overnight trains ahead of time, and buy advance tickets for the Eiffel Tower). Then...travel, enjoying a well-planned trip.

Date	Travel	Sleep/Notes
Fri, Sept 4	Fly to London after work (depart 6 p.m.)	Plane
Sat, Sept 5	Arrive London at 11:45 a.m., check in at hotel, take orientation bus tour	Luna Simone Hotel, London Original London Sightseeing Bus Tour is discounted with guidebook
Sun, Sept 6	Sightsee London (Tower of London, Shakespeare's Globe tour, Tate Modern)	Luna Simone Hotel, London Many sights closed today; Speaker's Corner open today only
Mon, Sept 7	See more London (Westminster Abbey, National Gallery, evening play)	Luna Simone Hotel, London Parliament open late; check for discount theater tickets at Leicester Square

8. Share your final itinerary. Whether you want to meet up with friends along the way, let family members know where you'll be, or just corral all your travel details in one place—an itinerary chart saved in a Word document or Excel chart makes it easy to share your plans. Tools such as TripIt can also help; using your confirmation emails, the app creates an itinerary—with maps, directions, and recommendations—that you can access from your phone and share.

The Home-Base Strategy

Staying longer in one spot can be a good way to make your trip itinerary smoother, simpler, and more efficient. Set yourself up in a central location and use that place as a base for day trips to nearby attractions.

The home-base approach minimizes set-up time. Changing hotels frequently can be exhausting, frustrating,

Date	Travel	Sleep/Notes
Tue, Sept 8	Wrap up London (St. Paul's/ The City, British Museum); take evening train to Paris (6 p.m.)	Grand Hôtel Lévêque, Paris Confirm Paris hotel before leaving London
Wed, Sept 9	Sightsee Paris (historic core, incl. Sainte-Chapelle; also Louvre, Eiffel Tower at night)	Grand Hôtel Lévêque, Paris Louvre open late
Thu, Sept 10	Sightsee Paris (Champs-Elysées, Rodin Museum, Orsay)	Grand Hôtel Lévêque, Paris Orsay open late
Fri, Sept 11	Side trip to Versailles	Grand Hôtel Lévêque, Paris
Sat, Sept 12	Take morning train (7 a.m.) to Interlaken, Swiss Alps; maybe hike in late afternoon	Olle and Maria's B&B, Gimmelwald
Sun, Sept 13	Sightsee Alps (breakfast at the Schilthorn, Männlichen-Kleine Scheidegg hike)	Olle and Maria's B&B, Gimmelwald If rainy, visit Bern
Mon, Sept 14	Short morning hike and/or visit Trümmelbach Falls, afternoon train to Florence (from Interlaken 1:30 p.m.)	Hotel Centrale, Florence If rainy, take morning train to Florence (from Interlaken 7:30 a.m); on arrival, do walking tour (most museums closed)

and so on...

and time-consuming. Many hotels give a better price, or at least more smiles, for longer stays. Some B&Bs don't accept those staying only one night.

You are freed from your luggage. Being able to leave your luggage in the hotel lets you travel freely and with the peace of mind that you are set for the night.

You feel "at home" in your home-base town. This comfortable feeling takes more than a day to get, and when you're changing locations every day or two, you may never enjoy this important sense of rootedness. Home-basing allows you to become attuned to the rhythm of daily life.

Day-trip to a village, enjoy the nightlife in a city. The home-base approach lets you spend the evening in a city, where there is more exciting nightlife. Most small countryside towns die after 9 p.m. If you're not dead by 9 p.m., you'll enjoy the action in a larger city.

Transportation is a snap. Europe's generally frequent and punctual train and bus systems (many of which operate out of a hub anyway) make this home-base strategy practical. With a train pass, trips are "free"; otherwise, the transportation is reasonable, sometimes with reductions offered for round-trip tickets (especially for "same-day return").

Good Home-Base Cities

Here are some of my favorite places to call home, along with the best day trips from each.

Madrid: Toledo, Segovia, El Escorial, and even Sevilla and Córdoba with the AVE bullet trains

Amsterdam: Most of the Netherlands, particularly Alkmaar, Enkhuizen's Zuiderzee Museum, Arnhem's Netherlands Open-Air Museum and Kröller-Müller Museum, Delft, The Hague, Scheveningen, and Edam

Copenhagen: Frederiksborg Castle, Roskilde, Helsingør, and Odense

Paris: Versailles, Chartres, Vaux-le-Vicomte, Fontainebleau, Chantilly, Giverny, Reims

London: Bath, Stonehenge, Cambridge, York, and many others; even Paris is less than three hours away by train

Arles: Pont du Gard, Nîmes, Avignon, and the rest of Provence

Florence: Siena, Pisa, San Gimignano, and many other hill towns

Venice: Padua, Vicenza, Verona, and Ravenna

Munich: Salzburg, "Mad" King Ludwig's castles (Neuschwanstein and Linderhof), the Wieskirche, Oberammergau, and other small Bavarian towns

Sorrento: Naples, Pompeii, Herculaneum, Mount Vesuvius, Amalfi Coast, Paestum, and Capri

High-Speed Town-Hopping

When I tell people that I saw three or four towns in one day, many think, "Insane! Nobody can really see several towns in a day!" Of course, it's folly to go too fast, but many stop-worthy towns take only an hour or two to cover. Don't let feelings of guilt tell you to slow down and stay longer if you really are finished with a town. There's so much more to enjoy in the rest of Europe. Going too slow is as bad as going too fast.

If you're efficient and use the high-speed town-hopping method, you'll amaze yourself with what you can see in a day. Let me explain with an example:

You wake up early in A-ville. Checking out of your hotel, you have one sight to see before your 10 a.m. train. (You checked the train schedule the night before.) After the sight-seeing and before getting to the station, you visit the open-air market and buy the ingredients for your brunch, and pick up a B-burg map and tourist brochure at A-ville's tourist office.

From 10 to 11 a.m. you travel by train to B-burg. During that hour you have a restful brunch, enjoy the passing scenery, and prepare for B-burg by reading your literature and deciding what you want to see. Just before your arrival, put the items you need (camera, jacket, tourist information) into your small daypack. Then, as soon as you get there, check the rest of your luggage in a locker. (Check ahead to confirm the availability of storage lockers or a baggage-check desk.)

Before leaving B-burg's station, check on the departure times of the next few trains to C-town. Now you can sight-see as much or as little as you want and still know when to comfortably catch your outbound train.

B-burg is great, so you stay a little longer than antici-pated. After a snack in the park, you catch the train at 2:30 p.m. By 3 p.m. you're in C-town, where you repeat the same procedure you followed in B-burg. C-town just isn't what it was cracked up to be, so after a walk along the waterfront and a look at the church, you catch the next train out at 5 p.m.

You arrive in D-dorf, the last town on the day's agenda, by 5:30 p.m. The TI in the station directs you to a good budget pension two blocks down the street. You're checked in and unpacked in no time, and, after a few horizontal moments, it's time to find a good restaurant and eat dinner. After a meal and an evening stroll, you're ready to call it a day. As you write in your journal, it occurs to you: This was a great sightseeing day. You spent it high-speed town-hopping.

PRIORITIZING YOUR TIME

So much to see, so little time. How to choose? It depends on your interest and your tastes. One person's Barcelona is another person's Bucharest.

Sightseeing Priorities, Country by Country

Use this chart to prioritize your sightseeing time in various countries. Add places from left to right as you build plans for the best of that country in 3, 5, 7, 10, or 14 days. So, according to this chart, the best week in Britain would be spread between London, Bath, the Cotswolds, and York; with more time, depending on your interests, you might dash up to Edinburgh or spend more time in Bath, taking day trips to Glastonbury, Wells, or Avebury. For help in linking your trip destinations in a logical route, consult the suggested itineraries in my country guidebooks.

3 Days	5 Days	7 Days	10 Days	14 Days
BRITAIN				
London	Bath, Cotswolds	York	Stratford, Edinburgh	North Wales, Wells, Glastonbury, Avebury
ICELAND				
Reykjavík, Golden Circle	South Coast	Westman Islands	West Iceland, Ring Road	Akureyri, Þorsmörk, Skaftafell
IRELAND				
Dublin	Dingle Peninsula	Galway, Aran Islands	County Clare/ Burren, Kilkenny/ Cashel	Belfast, Antrim Coast, Kinsale, Kenmare/Ring of Kerry
FRANCE				
Paris, Versailles	Normandy	Loire	Dordogne, Carcassonne	Provence, Riviera
GERMANY				
Munich, Bavarian castles	Rhine Valley, Rothenburg	More Bavaria, Salzburg (Austria)	Berlin	Baden-Baden, Black Forest, Dresden
AUSTRIA				
Vienna	Salzburg	Hallstatt	Danube Valley, Tirol, Bavaria (Germany)	Innsbruck, Hall, Bratislava (Slovakia)

The Best and Worst of Europe (with No Apologies)

Good travel writers should make hard choices and give the reader solid opinions. Just so nobody will accuse me of gutlessness, I've assembled a pile of spunky opinions. Chances are that you have too many stops on your trip wish list and not enough time. To make your planning a little easier, heed these warnings. These are just my personal feelings after

3 Days	5 Days	7 Days	10 Days	14 Days
SWITZERLAND				
Berner Oberland	Luzern and Central Switzerland	Bern, Lake Geneva area, Golden Pass scenic rail	Zermatt, Appenzell, Glacier Express train	Lugano and Pontresina area, Bernina Express and Gotthard Panorama Express trains
ITALY				
Florence, Venice	Rome	Cinque Terre	Civita di Bagnoregio, Siena	Sorrento, Naples, Pompeii, Amalfi Coast, Paestum
SCANDINAVIA				
Copenhagen, side trips	Stockholm	Oslo, Norway in a Nutshell train trip	Bergen, Helsinki	Ærø, Odense, Roskilde, Frederiksborg
SPAIN				
Madrid, Toledo	Barcelona	Sevilla, Granada	Andalucía, Morocco	Salamanca, Segovia
PORTUGAL				
Lisbon, Sintra	Algarve	Évora, Nazaré	Sights near Nazaré, Coimbra	Porto, Douro Valley
EASTERN EUROPE				
Prague	Budapest	Kraków and Auschwitz	Slovenia, Český Krumlov	Ljubljana, Lake Bled, Vienna
CROATIA & SLOVENIA				
Dubrovnik	Mostar, Split	Korčula/Hvar, Montenegro, or Sarajevo	Lake Bled, Plitvice Lakes, Julian Alps	Ljubljana, Istria
GREECE				
Athens	Hydra	Delphi	Nafplio, Epidavros, Mycenae	Olympia, Monemvasia, Kardamyli and the Mani Peninsula

more than 150 months of European travel. And if you disagree with any of them, you obviously haven't been there.

Let's start with the dullest corner of the British Isles, southern Scotland. It's so boring the Romans decided to block it off with Hadrian's Wall. However, like Venice's St. Mark's Square at midnight and Napoleon's tomb in Paris, Hadrian's Wall itself covers history buffs with goose bumps.

London, York, Bath, and Edinburgh are the most

interesting cities in Britain. Belfast, Liverpool, and Glasgow are quirky enough to be called interesting. I enjoy both Oxford and Cambridge, but seeing one university town is enough. Stratford-upon-Avon is little more than Shakespeare's house—and that's as dead as he is.

The west coast of Ireland (the Dingle Peninsula), Wales' Snowdonia National Park, and England's Windermere Lake District are the most beautiful natural regions of the British Isles. The North York Moors disappoint most creatures great and small.

Extra caution is merited in southwest England, a mine- field of tourist traps. The British are masters at milking every conceivable tourist attraction for all it's worth. Here are some booby traps: the Devil's Toenail (a rock that looks just like a...toenail), Land's End (pay, pay, pay), and cloying Clovelly (a one-street town lined with knickknack shops selling the same goodies—like "clotted cream that you can mail home"). While Tintagel's castle, famous as the legend- ary birthplace of King Arthur, offers thrilling windswept and wave-beaten ruins, the town of Tintagel does everything in its little power to exploit the profitable Arthurian legend. There's even a pub in town called the Excali Bar.

Germany's Heidelberg, Ireland's Blarney Stone (slob- bered on by countless tourists to get the "gift of gab"), Spain's Costa del Sol, and the French Riviera in July and August are among Europe's most overrated spots. The tackiest souvenirs are found next to Pisa's leaning tower and at the pilgrimage site in Lourdes.

Sognefjord is Norway's most spectacular fjord. The Geirangerfjord, while famous as a cruise-ship stop, is a dis- appointment. The most boring countryside is Sweden's (yes, I'm Norwegian), although Scandinavia's best medieval castle is in the Swedish town of Kalmar.

Norway's Stavanger, famous for nearby fjords and its

LEFT Geneva's newspaper objects to my "denigrating" its dull city on the internet.

RIGHT In Switzerland, special scenic trains give you front row seats and the Alps in your lap.

status as an oil boomtown, is a large port that's about as exciting as...well, put it this way: Emigrants left it in droves to move to the wilds of Minnesota. Time in western Norway is better spent in and around Bergen.

Geneva, one of Switzerland's largest and most sterile cities, gets the "nice place to live but I wouldn't want to visit" award. It's pleasantly situated on a lake—just like Buffalo, New York. While it's famous, name familiarity is a rotten reason to go somewhere. If you want a Swiss city, see Bern or Luzern. However, it's almost criminal to spend a sunny Swiss day in a city if you haven't yet been high in the Alps.

Bordeaux must mean "boredom" in some ancient language. If I were offered a free trip to that town, I'd stay home and clean the fridge. Connoisseurs visit for the wine, but Bordeaux wine country and Bordeaux city are as different as night and night soil. There's a wine-tourism information bureau in Bordeaux that, for a price, will bus you out of town into the more interesting wine country nearby.

Andorra, a small country in the Pyrenees between France and Spain, is as scenic as any other chunk of those mountains. People from all over Europe flock to Andorra to take advantage of its famous duty-free shopping. As far as Americans are concerned, Andorra is just a big Spanish-speaking outlet mall. There are no bargains here that you can't get at home. Enjoy the Pyrenees elsewhere, with less traffic. Among Europe's other "little countries," San Marino and Liechtenstein are also not worth the trouble.

Germany's famous Black Forest disappoints more people than it excites. If it were all Germany offered, it would be worth seeing. For Europeans, any large forest is understandably a popular attraction. But I'd say the average American visitor who's seen more than three trees in one place would prefer Germany's Romantic Road and Bavaria to the east, the Rhine and Mosel country to the north, the Swiss Alps to the

Understanding the Travel Industry

When sorting through options for your trip, you need to understand that we travelers are consumers—and the travel industry is all about selling us things.

Travel media—TV shows, magazines, newspaper articles, and websites—are careful not to offend advertisers. Just like big business lobbies our government, big travel lobbies the travel media. There's a huge appetite these days in travel journalism for lists. "The Top Ten This" and "Top Twenty That" are what the typical tourist is gobbling up. Plenty of factors that aren't in your interest shape these reports.

The industry in general is geared toward filling resorts, cruise ships, big tour buses, and fancy hotels. There's very little money to be made from independent travel. Consequently, there's little reason to sing its praises in the glossy media that shape many people's travel dreams.

As promotion is expensive, attractions and activities that are free or unprofitable are rarely marketed. It's important to be smart about which information you use to determine your itinerary. Don't be too influenced by the attractions promoted by leaflets in your hotel lobby, by advertising disguised as tourist information, or by the recommendations of your commission-hungry concierge.

And don't believe everything you read. Many sources are peppered with information that is flat-out wrong. (Incredibly enough, even this book may have an error.) Some "writers" succumb to the temptation to write travelogues based on hearsay, travel brochures, other books, public-relations junkets, and wishful thinking. A writer met at the airport by an official from the national tourist board learns tips that are handy only for others who are met at the airport by an official from the national tourist board.

Enjoy the highly publicized attractions—many of them are popular for a reason. But don't let the promotion lead you away from the wonderful world of travel experiences that are most likely to put you in touch with the people, nature, and culture of Europe. These dimensions, which no big business is pushing with slick publicity, are most likely to be the highlights of your trip.

south, and France's Alsace region to the west—all high points that cut the Black Forest down to stumps.

Kraków (Poland) and Budapest (Hungary) are, after Prague, Eastern Europe's best cities. Bucharest, Romania's capital, has little to offer. Its top-selling postcard is of the InterContinental Hotel. If you're heading from Eastern Europe to Greece, skip Thessaloniki, which deserves its place in the Bible but doesn't belong in travel guidebooks.

Europe's most scenic train ride is the Glacier Express, across southern Switzerland from Chur to Zermatt. The most scenic boat ride is from Stockholm to Helsinki—countless islands and blondes. Europe's most underrated sight is Rome's ancient seaport, Ostia Antica, and its most misunderstood wine is Portugal's *vinho verde* (green wine).

The best French château is Vaux-le-Vicomte, near Paris. The best Gothic interior is found in Paris' Sainte-Chapelle church. The top two medieval castle interiors are Germany's Burg Eltz on the Mosel River, and northern Italy's Reifenstein, near the Brenner Pass. Lisbon, Oslo, Stockholm, Brussels, and Budapest are the most underrated big cities.

To honeymoon (or convalesce), try these tiny towns: Beilstein on Germany's Mosel River; Hallstatt on Austria's Lake Hallstatt; Varenna on Italy's Lake Como; Ærøskøbing on an island in south Denmark; and Gimmelwald, high in the Swiss Alps. Have fun (or get well)!

LEFT Ancient Ostia Antica, outside Rome, is among Europe's most underrated attractions.

CENTER Vaux-le-Vicomte, near Paris, gets my vote for the most beautiful château in all of France.

RIGHT The soaring interior of Sainte-Chapelle is the best lesson in Gothic you can find.

Paper Chase

Someday, perhaps, travel will be completely paperless. But we're not there yet, so you'll need to be equipped with the necessary documents, identification, and insurance coverage. Here's how to stay ahead in the inevitable paper chase.

TRAVEL DOCUMENTS

Your trip won't get off the ground if you don't prepare your documents well before your departure date. Give yourself plenty of lead time.

Passports

The most important travel document a US or Canadian citizen needs is a passport. (The US Passport Card works only for those driving or cruising to Canada, Mexico, Bermuda, and the Caribbean.) And for most American travelers, that passport gets the most scrutiny from a customs official...as you reenter the United States.

Canadian citizens can refer to the government of Canada's travel site at Travel.gc.ca for passport information.

Getting or Renewing Your Passport: US passports, good for 10 years, cost $145 ($110 to renew). The fee for minors under 16 (including infants) is $115 for a passport good for five years—kids under 16 must apply in person with at least one parent and the other parent's notarized permission. (See page 460 for other document needs when traveling abroad with children.)

You can apply at some courthouses, libraries, and post offices, as well as municipal buildings, such as your city hall. For details and the location of the nearest passport-acceptance facility, see Travel.state.gov or call 877-487-2778. Allow ample time to receive your passport. Processing time varies; the current wait is posted on the State Department website. During busier periods, waits of six weeks or more (up to 18 weeks) are common. After you apply, you can check online for the status of your application and your passport's estimated arrival date.

If you need your passport faster than current processing times, make an appointment to go in person to the nearest US Passport Agency. You'll pay an additional $60 expediting fee (plus overnight shipping both ways), which shaves off several weeks from the turnaround—check online for estimated waits. In a last-minute emergency, call the above number and speak to a customer-service representative. If you can prove that you must travel within two weeks (by showing evidence of a purchased airline ticket or a letter from work requiring you to go overseas on short notice), you may be able to receive a passport in 24-72 hours.

Your passport is your most important travel document.

Keep an eye on your passport's expiration date. Many European countries require that your passport be valid for at least six months *after* your ticketed date of return to the United States. This means that even if your passport doesn't expire for a few months, you may be denied entry to a country. Check your destination country's requirements, and if necessary, get your passport renewed well before you go.

Some countries can have surprising entry requirements. For example, the Czech Republic and Poland technically require visitors to carry proof of medical insurance, such as a health insurance card. For requirements per country, check with the US State Department at Travel.state.gov.

Traveling with Your Passport: Guard your passport carefully. Keep it in your money belt, and if you're asked to show it, put it back in your money belt right away. For tips on keeping your money belt—and its contents—safe, see page 377.

Replacing Your Passport: If you need to replace a lost or stolen passport in Europe, it's much easier if you have a copy of it and a couple of passport photos, either brought from home or taken in Europe. For details on getting a replacement, see page 387. For tips on preparing and protecting important documents while traveling, see page 69.

European Borders (or Not)

Thanks to a series of treaties known as the Schengen Agreement, there are virtually no border checks between 26 European countries: Austria, Belgium, the Czech Republic, Denmark, Estonia, Finland, France, Germany, Greece, Hungary, Iceland, Italy, Latvia, Liechtenstein, Lithuania, Luxembourg, Malta, the Netherlands, Norway, Poland, Portugal, Slovakia, Slovenia, Spain, Sweden, and Switzerland. Countries that are not part of Schengen include Croatia, the Republic of Ireland, and the United Kingdom.

So what does Schengen mean for your travels? Schengen or no, you always need to show your passport at your first point of entry into Europe, when you exit Europe, and to reenter the US. Within the next few years, you'll also need to register with ETIAS to travel to any Schengen country (see "ETIAS Registration" in this section). When traveling between participating countries, you usually won't have to stop or show a passport: You'll blow past abandoned border posts on the superhighway or high-speed train. Non-Schengen countries still have border checks—but the border crossing is generally just a quick wave-through for US citizens.

Free movement within the Schengen area can be affected by events that cause countries to increase security; if this happens, you may encounter internal border checks in some countries (such as at an airport, train station, or highway border crossing).

Covid Entry Requirements

You'll likely need to carry proof of vaccination against the coronavirus, or a negative Covid-19 test result. Some countries may require proof of medical insurance. You may be able to gather this health information in a single certificate or digital app (a.k.a., a "vaccine passport"). You'll likely be asked to present this documentation at your departure airport, at customs in Europe, and upon return to the US. For current requirements, consult the travel pages of the Centers for Disease Control and Prevention (www.cdc.gov/travel) or the US State Department (www.travel.state.gov). For more on Covid-19 restrictions, see page 407. Travelers may also be able to obtain an EU Digital COVID Certificate to make it easier to travel between countries (for the latest, check https://ec.europa.eu/info/index_en and search for "Covid Certificate").

Visas and Travel Authorizations

A travel visa is a stamp placed in your passport by a foreign government, allowing you to enter that country. Visas are not required for Americans or Canadians traveling in Western Europe and most of the east (including the Czech Republic, Slovakia, Poland, Hungary, Slovenia, Croatia, Bosnia-Herzegovina, Montenegro, and the Baltic states). Note that travelers entering a country in the Schengen area may need to register with the European Travel Information and Authorization System (ETIAS)—see below.

Visas *are* required to visit Turkey and Russia. For travel beyond Europe, get information on visa requirements from your travel agent or the US State Department.

No Visa Required: When you enter a country without a visa you're officially on "short stay visitor"

Your passport will be stamped when you enter your first European country.

status. Within the Schengen area, that means you can stay up to 90 days within a 180-day period; most non-Schengen countries in Europe also have a 90-day limit (one big exception is the UK, which allows you to stay up to six months within a 12-month period). If your trip will extend beyond the three-month mark, you'll need to get creative with your travel plans (for example, spend the requisite amount of time outside the Schengen area before reentering) or look into a long-stay visa.

ETIAS Registration: Beginning in late 2022 or 2023, US and Canadian citizens will be required to undergo an online security screening before entering Schengen countries (see sidebar). The European Travel Information and Authorization System (ETIAS) application will cost about $8; once approved, the travel authorization will be valid for three years. A useful private website with more details is SchengenVisaInfo.com/etias/.

Turkey: Canadians and Americans must obtain a visa before entering Turkey. You can get your "e-visa" online (www.evisa.gov.tr) or by visiting a Turkish consulate or embassy. US residents pay $50; Canadians pay $60—that's US dollars, not Canadian. Cruise-line passengers don't need a visa if they visit Turkey by day but spend nights aboard their ship. But cruise passengers arriving in Turkey to start their cruise, departing from Turkey at the end of their cruise, or staying on Turkish soil for more than 72 hours must get a visa before arriving in Turkey. For more information, see the websites Washington.emb.mfa.gov.tr (Turkey's embassy in the US) or Ottava.be.mfa.gov.tr (Turkey's embassy in Canada).

Russia: Travelers to Russia also need visas. The process can be expensive, and you should begin at least 60 days before your departure. Before applying for a visa, you must first get an official document called a "letter of invitation" or a "visa support letter" (generally from a hotel or visa agency). You'll also need to fill out an electronic visa application. The Russian embassy does not accept visa applications by mail, so it's smart to use an agency that specializes in steering your application through the process. Passport Visas Express is one of many such vendors (www.passportvisasexpress.com). The costs add up; figure around $350 total per person to cover the visa, visa invitation, service fee, and secure shipping. For more details, go to RickSteves.com/russianvisa or see Washington.mid.ru (which lists Russian consulate locations in New York, Houston, and Washington, DC). If you live near one of these consulates, you can save some money (but go through a lot of steps) by applying for your visa in person at the consulate.

Trusted Traveler Programs

To expedite airport security, you may want to consider enrolling in a trusted traveler program.

More than 50 airlines at over 200 US airports participate in the TSA Precheck program, which allows you to register to skip lines and elements of TSA screening ($85, valid for 5 years, www.tsa.gov/tsa-precheck).

If you're a frequent international traveler, consider the US Customs' Global Entry Program, which includes TSA Precheck privileges at the start of your trip and lets you bypass passport control when you return ($100, valid for 5 years, www.globalentry.gov).

Any US citizen can use the free Mobile Passport app (www.mobilepassport.us), which lets you use an express lane to pass through customs at major airports. Download it before you leave, enter your personal information and flight info when you return to the US, then scan your phone at a Mobile Passport express lane.

Student Cards

Students in high school or college can save money by carrying their school ID cards when traveling. In general, people under age 26 are eligible for many discounts in Europe: Show your student ID at ticket counters, museums, and bus and train stations, and you'll be surprised at the number of discounts you'll receive. Be aware that some discounts apply only to EU residents.

Some young travelers like to carry the International Student Identity Card (ISIC), an internationally recognized student ID card that provides discounts on transportation and sightseeing throughout Europe and includes some basic trip insurance. Cards cost $25 and are good for one year from the date of issue (you must be a full-time student). They're available on the ISIC website (www.isic.org) or from your university foreign-study office.

Car Documents

If you're renting a car, be aware that an International Driving Permit is required in Austria, Bosnia-Herzegovina, Croatia, the Czech Republic, Greece, Hungary, Italy, Poland, Romania, Slovakia, Slovenia, and Spain ($20 plus tax, get it at AAA before your departure). Even if you aren't renting a car in Europe, bring along your driver's license—it can come in handy if you need to leave a piece of ID to rent a bike or audioguide and you don't want to part with your passport. For specifics, see the Driving & Navigating chapter.

Copying Key Documents

Before your trip, scan, make photocopies, and/or take photos of your documents (front and back) to pack along, upload to the cloud, or leave with someone at home in case of an emergency. It's smart to make copies of the following:

- Passport, visa, and proof of vaccination and/or negative Covid-19 test
- Rail pass
- Car-rental voucher
- Prescriptions for eyewear and medicine

Don't copy a debit or credit card—instead, keep just the number in a retrievable place. Consider bringing a couple of extra passport-type pictures, which can expedite the replacement process for a lost or stolen passport (to replace a passport, see page 387. If you're traveling with a companion, carry copies of each other's passports and other important documents. Guard your physical copies as carefully as you would the originals. I hide mine in a pouch clipped into the bottom of my luggage (don't tell anyone).

Some people scan their documents and email them to their account, or store them on a cloud service such as Dropbox for easy access from the road (see page 432 for more about online storage). If you're concerned about electronic copies of your key documents floating around in cyberspace, you could save them to a USB flash drive and tuck it into your money belt.

It's also smart to have a backup physical or digital copy of your itinerary, including hotel and car-rental confirmations and sight reservations. An itinerary-storage website, such as TripIt.com, is handy. Or go completely old-school and tuck a list of contacts, including your hotels—printed as small as you can read on a slip of paper—in your money belt.

TRAVEL INSURANCE

Travel insurance can minimize the considerable financial risks of traveling: accidents, illness, missed flights, canceled tours, lost baggage, theft, terrorism, travel-company bankruptcies, emergency evacuation, and getting your body home if you die. What are the chances you'll need it? Hard to say. How willing are you to take risks? That's up to you. Travel agents can guide you, but they are not insurance agents (and their advice can be colored by commissions). Always direct specific questions to an insurance provider (for a list, see the sidebar).

Each traveler's potential loss varies, depending on how much of your trip is prepaid, the refundability of the air ticket you purchased, your state of health, the value of your luggage, where you're traveling, the financial health of your tour company and airline, and any coverage you already have (through your medical insurance, homeowners or renters insurance, and/or credit card).

Take these considerations into account, understand your options, and make an informed decision for your trip. While not essential, travel insurance can provide peace of mind.

Insurance Basics

The insurance menu typically includes five main courses: trip cancellation and interruption, medical, evacuation, baggage, and flight insurance. These days, pandemic-related options are also available. Supplemental policies can be added to cover specific concerns, such as identity theft or political evacuation. The various types are generally sold in some combination—rather than buying only baggage, medical, or

Travel Insurance Providers

For extensive travel insurance coverage, go with a reputable company. Avoid buying insurance from a no-name company you found online. Consider the package deals sold by:

- **Betins** (Betins.com, tel. 866-552-8834)
- **Allianz** (AllianzTravelInsurance.com, tel. 866-884-3556)
- **Travelex** (TravelexInsurance.com, tel. 800-228-9792)
- **Travel Guard** (TravelGuard.com, tel. 800-826-5248)
- **Travel Insured International** (TravelInsured.com, tel. 800-243-3174)

You can compare insurance policies and costs among various providers at SquareMouth.com (tel. 800-240-0369) and at InsureMyTrip.com (tel. 800-487-4722); both also sell insurance.

cancellation insurance, you'll usually purchase a package that includes most or all of them. "Comprehensive insurance" covers all of the above (plus expenses incurred if your trip is delayed, if you miss your flight, or if your tour company changes your itinerary).

Companies such as Travelex and Travel Guard offer comprehensive packages that serve as your primary coverage; they'll take care of your expenses regardless of what other insurance you might have (for instance, if you have health insurance through your job). That means they pay first and don't ask questions about your other insurance. This can be a real plus if you want to avoid out-of-pocket expenses.

Insurance prices can vary widely. Most standard insurance covering emergency health care and cancellations runs about 5-10 percent of the total trip. A policy that covers nonemergency cancellations can cost from 20-50 percent of the trip. Age is one of the biggest factors affecting the price: Rates go up dramatically for every decade over 50, while coverage is generally inexpensive or even free for children 17 and under.

Available travel policies vary by state, and not all insurance companies are licensed in every state. If you need to make a claim and encounter problems with a company that isn't licensed in your state, you don't have a case.

Note that some travel insurance, especially trip-cancellation coverage, is reimbursement-only: You'll pay out-of-pocket for your expenses, then submit the paperwork to your insurer to recoup your money. With medical coverage, you may be able to arrange to have expensive hospital or doctor bills paid directly. Either way, if you have a problem, it's wise to contact your insurance company immediately to ask them how to proceed. Many major insurance companies are accessible by phone 24 hours a day—handy if you have problems in Europe.

Types of Coverage

For each type of insurance, I've outlined some of the key legalese. Note: These are only guidelines. Policies can differ, even within the same company. Certain companies and policies have different levels of coverage based on whether you purchase the car rental, hotel, or flight directly or through a travel agent. Ask a lot of questions, and always read the fine print to see what's covered (e.g., how they define "travel partner" or "family member"—your great-aunt might not qualify).

Trip Cancellation or Interruption Insurance

For me, this is the most usable and worthwhile kind of insurance—and it's particularly useful now, with the uncertainty inherent in post-pandemic travel. It's expensive to cancel or interrupt any prepaid travel, and for a small fraction of the trip cost, you can alleviate the risk of losing money if something unforeseen gets in the way.

Trip cancellation or interruption insurance can be used whether you're on an organized tour or cruise, or traveling independently (in which case, only the prepaid expenses—such as your flight and any nonrefundable accommodation reservations—are covered). Note the difference: Trip *cancellation* is when you don't go on your trip at all. Trip *interruption* is when you begin a journey but have to cut it short; in this case, you'll be reimbursed only for the portion of the trip that you didn't complete. If you're taking a tour, it may already come with some cancellation insurance—ask.

The rugged, healthy, unattached, and gung-ho traveler will probably forego trip cancellation or interruption coverage. I have skipped it many times, and my number has yet to come up. If it turns out that I need to cancel or interrupt, I'll just have to take my financial lumps—I played the odds and lost. But in many cases it's a good idea to get this coverage—for instance, if you're paying a lot of up-front money for an organized tour or short-term accommodation rental (which can be expensive or even nonrefundable if you cancel); if you have a loved one at home in poor health; or if a virus outbreak closes borders to travel. (For more on Covid-19, see later.)

Before purchasing trip cancellation or interruption coverage, check with your credit-card issuer; yours may offer limited coverage for flights or tours purchased with the card.

A standard trip cancellation or interruption policy covers the nonrefundable financial penalties or losses you incur when you cancel a prepaid tour or flight for an acceptable reason, such as:

- You, your travel partner, or a family member cannot travel because of sickness, death, layoff, or a list of other acceptable reasons.
- Your tour company or airline goes out of business or can't perform as promised (for example, due to inclement weather—an increasingly common occurrence due to climate change).

- A family member at home gets sick (check the fine print to see how a family member's preexisting condition may affect coverage).
- You miss a flight or need an emergency flight for a reason outside your control (such as a car accident, inclement weather, or a strike).

Trip-cancellation insurance can be worthwhile if your travel plans go haywire.

So, if you or your travel partner accidentally break a leg a few days before your trip, you can both bail out (if you both have this insurance) without losing all the money you paid for the trip. Or, if you're on a tour and have an accident on your first day, you'll be reimbursed for the portion of the tour you were unable to use.

Buy your insurance policy within a week of the date you make the first payment on your trip. Policies purchased later than a designated cutoff date—generally 7 to 21 days after that first payment—are less likely to cover tour company or air carrier bankruptcies, preexisting medical conditions (yours or those of family members at home), or terrorist incidents. Mental-health concerns are generally not covered.

Some insurers won't cover certain airlines or tour operators. Many are obvious—such as companies under bankruptcy protection—but others can be surprising (including major airlines). Make sure your carrier is covered.

Insuring against high-impact travel unknowns—terrorist attacks, natural disasters, and pandemic disease—is possible but tricky. Ask your company for details. Insurers traditionally have excluded pandemic disease from their coverage, but Covid-19 is now being recognized as an unexpected illness, eligible for trip cancellation and trip interruption coverage. Be sure to study your provider's pandemic exclusions and potential extra charges—and don't assume you'll be covered in every scenario. At the time of this printing, most Covid policies won't cover you if you cancel for fear of contracting the virus, or if you travel somewhere your government deems unsafe. But if you contract coronavirus midtrip (or right before traveling), you may be covered for certain prepaid expenses.

A terrorist attack or natural disaster in your hometown may or may not be covered. You'll likely be covered only if your departure city or a destination on your itinerary becomes the target of a terrorist incident within 30 days of your trip. Even then, if your tour operator offers a substitute itinerary, your coverage may become void. As for natural disasters, you're covered only if your destination is uninhabitable (for example, your hotel is flooded or the airport is gone).

Jittery travelers can avoid the question of what is and what isn't covered by buying a costly "Cancel For Any Reason," or CFAR, policy. These offer at least partial reimbursement (generally 50-75 percent) no matter why you cancel the trip. But the premiums are very hefty, so weigh it carefully against the cost and chance of a cancelled trip.

For my latest advice on trip cancellation and interruption insurance, see RickSteves.com/travel-tips/trip-planning/travel-insurance.

Medical Insurance

Before buying a special medical insurance policy for your trip, check with your insurer—you may already be covered by your existing health plan. While many US insurers cover you overseas, Medicare does not. Also, be aware of any policy exclusions such as preauthorization requirements.

Even if your health plan does cover you internationally, you may want to consider buying a special medical travel policy. Much of the additional coverage available is supplemental (or "secondary"), so it covers whatever expenses your health plan doesn't, such as deductibles. But you can also purchase primary coverage, which will take care of your costs up to a certain amount. In emergency situations involving costly procedures or overnight stays, the hospital will typically work directly with your travel-insurance carrier on billing (but not with your regular health insurance company; you'll likely have to pay up front to the hospital or clinic, then get reimbursed by your stateside insurer later).

For routine care, a visit to a doctor will likely be an out-of-pocket expense (bring home your documentation to be reimbursed). Whatever the circumstances, it's smart to contact your insurer from the road to let them know that you've sought medical help. Many preexisting conditions are covered by medical and trip-cancellation coverage, depending on when you buy the coverage and how recently you've been treated for the condition. If you travel frequently to Europe, multitrip annual medical policies can save you money. Check with your agent or insurer before you commit.

For travelers over age 70, buying travel medical insurance can be expensive. Compare the cost of a stand-alone travel medical plan with comprehensive insurance (described earlier), which comes with good medical and evacuation coverage. A travel-insurance company can help you sort out the options. Certain Medigap plans cover some emergency care outside the US; call the issuer of your supplemental policy for the details.

The US State Department periodically issues warnings about traveling to at-risk countries—see Travel.state.gov. If you're visiting one of these countries, your cancellation and medical insurance will likely not be honored, unless you buy supplemental coverage.

Other Insurance

Medical Evacuation (MedEvac) insurance covers the cost of getting you to a place where you can receive appropriate medical treatment in the event of an emergency. (In a worst-case scenario, this can mean a medically equipped—and incredibly expensive—private jet.) This is usually not covered by your regular medical-insurance plan back home. Most policies just get you as far as the nearest major hospital— worth buying if you're planning an adventure in a remote area. "Medical repatriation"—that is, getting you all the way home—is likely to be covered only if it's considered medically necessary. Before purchasing a policy, ask your insurer to explain exactly what's covered before *and after* you get to the hospital.

Keep in mind that medical and evacuation insurance may not cover you if you're injured while participating in an activity your insurer considers to be dangerous (such as sky-diving, mountain climbing, bungee jumping, scuba diving, or even skiing). Some companies sell supplementary adventure-sports coverage.

Baggage insurance—for luggage that is lost, delayed, or damaged—is included in most comprehensive policies, but it's rare to buy it separately, and there's a strict cap on reimbursement for such items as jewelry, eyewear, electronics, and camera equipment. If you check your baggage for a flight, it's already covered by the airline (ask your airline about its luggage liability limit; if you have particularly valuable luggage, you can buy supplemental "excess valuation" insurance directly from the airline). Homeowners or renters insurance typically covers your possessions anywhere you travel; the baggage insurance covers the deductibles and items excluded from your homeowners policy. Double-check the particulars with your agent. If your policy doesn't cover

Theft Protection

Theft is especially worrisome when you consider the dollar value of electronics (laptops, tablets, cameras, smartphones, ereaders, etc.) and other valuables we pack along.

One way to protect your investment is to purchase travel insurance from a specialized company such as Travel Guard, which offers a variety of options that include coverage for theft. Before buying a policy, ask how they determine the value of the stolen objects and about any maximum reimbursement limits for jewelry, electronics, or cameras.

Thieves rifled through this backpack before dumping it—minus any valuables—on the street in Rome.

It's also smart to check with your homeowners or renters insurance company. Under most policies, your personal property is already protected against theft anywhere in the world—but your insurance deductible still applies. If you have a $1,000 deductible and your $700 tablet is stolen, you'll have to pay to replace it. Rather than buying separate insurance, it may make more sense to add a rider to your existing policy to cover expensive items while you travel.

Before you leave, it's a good idea to take an inventory of all the high-value items you're bringing. Make a list of serial numbers, makes, and models of your electronics, and take photos that can serve as records. If anything is stolen, this information is helpful to both your insurance company and the police. If you plan to file an insurance claim, you'll need to get a police report in Europe. (If dealing with the police is intimidating, ask your hotelier for help.) For tips on avoiding theft while traveling, see the Theft & Scams chapter.

expensive rail passes, consider Rail Europe's Rail Protection Plan, which must be purchased when you buy your pass; it covers loss and theft of the pass—but doesn't cover trip interruptions.

Flight insurance ("crash coverage") is a statistical rip-off that heirs love. It's basically a life insurance policy that covers you when you're on the airplane. Since plane crashes are so rare, there's little sense in spending money on this insurance.

Collision coverage, an important type of insurance for rental cars, is covered on page 165. Collision insurance may be included in some comprehensive travel-insurance plans or available as an upgrade on others.

BEFORE YOU GO

You'll have a smoother trip if you tackle a few things ahead of time.

❏ Get a proper **guidebook** (see page 36). If traveling with one of mine, check for recent changes to your destinations at RickSteves.com/update.

❏ Make sure your **passport** is valid—and get any visas you may need for your destinations. If your passport is due to expire within six months of your ticketed date of return, you need to renew it. Allow up to six weeks to renew or get a passport (see page 64).

❏ Check **Covid-19** vaccination and testing requirements for your destination and/or airline, and gather the necessary documentation (see page 66). Research Covid testing sites at your point of departure in Europe (if required to reenter the US by air; see page 407).

❏ If visiting a Schengen country, file your security screening application with **ETIAS,** the European Travel Information and Authorization System (see page 67).

❏ Book your **international flights** (see page 98).

❏ Figure out your main form of **transportation** in Europe: Get a **rail pass** (see page 125), **rent a car** (see page 157), and/or **book flights within Europe** (see page 112). You can generally buy rail tickets as you travel (see page 120), but it can be smart to reserve seats on certain trains before you leave (see page 133).

❏ If you'll be renting a car, consider getting an **International Driving Permit,** which is required in some countries (see page 164).

❏ Make **reservations** well in advance, especially during peak season, for accommodations (see page 211), major sights (see page 323), popular restaurants, and local guides.

❏ Do your homework if you want to buy **travel insurance.** Compare the cost of the insurance to the cost of your potential loss. Check whether your existing insurance (health, homeowners, or renters) covers you and your possessions overseas (see page 70).

❏ Call your bank. Alert them that you'll be using your **debit and credit cards** in Europe. Ask about transaction fees and get the PIN for your credit card (see sidebar on page 189). In most cases you don't need to bring European currency for your trip; you can withdraw local cash at ATMs in Europe. Note your bank's emergency phone number in the US (but not its 800 number) to call if you have a problem.

❑ If you're bringing the **kids,** make sure you have the right paperwork, including passports, and, if applicable, a letter of consent to travel without both parents and documentation for adopted children (see page 460).

❑ Make backup **copies of important travel documents,** including your itinerary (see page 69).

❑ **Students** should carry a valid school-issued ID (or consider an International Student Identity Card) to take advantage of discounts throughout Europe.

❑ Prepare your **mobile phone** for international travel. Know what your phone plan covers internationally, or sign up for an international plan to reduce your costs. Plan to rely heavily on Wi-Fi (see page 292). Follow common-sense safety precautions to protect your phone and its data (see page 300).

❑ Download any **apps** you'll use on the road (maps, translators, transit schedules, and Rick Steves Audio Europe—with free audio tours of major sights, city walks, and travel interviews; see page 17). If you plan to watch TV shows or movies in your downtime, download these in advance, as licensing restrictions can block streaming services in Europe (see page 299).

❑ Enroll in the State Department's **Smart Traveler Enrollment Program** to get safety updates about your destination and to help loved ones get in touch with you in case of emergency (http://step.state.gov).

❑ Take care of any **medical needs.** Visit your doctor for a checkup, and see your dentist if you have work that needs to be done. If you use prescription drugs, stock up before your trip (see page 407), and pack a copy of the prescription, plus prescriptions for any contact lenses or glasses.

❑ Attend to **household needs.** Cancel your newspapers, hold your mail delivery, and prepay your bills.

❑ Make a **list of valuables** that you're bringing (such as electronics). Include serial numbers, makes, and models, and take photos of your items to serve as a record for the police and your insurance company should anything be stolen.

❑ Check **airline carry-on restrictions.** The Transportation Security Administration's website (www. tsa.gov) has an up-to-date list of what you can bring on the plane with you...and what you must check.

Pack Light

The importance of packing light cannot be overemphasized, but for your sake, I'll try. You'll never meet a traveler who, after five trips, brags: "Every year I pack heavier." You can't travel heavy, happy, and cheap. Pick two.

ONE BAG—THAT'S IT

My self-imposed limit is 20 pounds in a 9″ × 21″ × 14″ carry-on-size bag (it'll fit in an airplane's overhead bin, at least on your transatlantic flight; some intra-European airlines restrict carry-on luggage to even smaller specs). At my company, we take tens of thousands of people of all ages and styles on tours through Europe. We allow only one carry-on bag. For many, this is a radical concept: 9″ × 21″ × 14″? That's my toiletries kit! But they manage, and they're glad they did. After you enjoy that sweet mobility and freedom, you'll never go any other way.

No matter your age, you can travel like college kids: light, mobile, and wearing your convertible suitcase/backpack.

You'll walk with your luggage more than you think you will. Before flying to Europe, give yourself a test. Pack up completely and walk around your house or block. Or practice being a tourist in your hometown for an afternoon. Fully loaded, you should enjoy window-shopping. If you can't, stagger home and thin things out.

When you carry your own luggage, it's less likely to get lost, broken, or stolen. Quick, last-minute flight changes become simpler. A small bag sits on your lap on the bus or taxi and stashes easily overhead on an airplane. When you arrive, you can hit the ground running. It's a good feeling. When I land in London, I'm on my way downtown while everyone else stares anxiously at the luggage carousel. When I fly home, I'm the first guy the dog sniffs.

You can also save money by bringing less. While major airlines used to allow one free checked bag on overseas flights, that's changing. Read the fine print when you are choosing flights to understand add-on fees for baggage. Many airlines are linking fares to the weight of your bag—even your carry-on. (Some cheaper carriers may charge extra for overhead bin space.) If you're taking a separate flight within Europe, expect to be charged to check a bag (see "Baggage Restrictions," later). Take it as a challenge and see if you can pack according to the most restrictive baggage policy.

Pack light. You won't have a mule to haul your bags around. (If you do, you're taking advantage of your spouse.)

It can be a drag, dragging your bag through airports, and even I sometimes wonder why I followed my own advice to bring only a carry-on. But then I'm reminded of the joy of having everything with me—like the time I avoided a long layover by hopping on an earlier flight from Copenhagen to Bergen. After getting to my hotel two hours before planned, I enjoyed a jumpstart on my Norway time with a lovely evening in a salty port town, where summer's "magic hour" lasts until 11 p.m.

Packing light isn't just about saving time or money—it's about your traveling lifestyle. Too much luggage marks you as a typical tourist. It slams the Back Door shut. Serendipity suffers. Changing locations becomes a major operation. Con artists figure you're helpless. Porters are a problem only to those who need them. With only one bag, you're mobile and in control. Take this advice seriously.

Choosing a Bag

A fundamental packing decision is your luggage. When shopping for a bag, consider these factors:

External Dimensions: Is the bag small enough to work as a carry-on? (If not, are you willing to put up with the extra fees and potential delays that come with checking your bag?)

Comfort and Mobility: Consider whether you want a bag with wheels or without, and remember you'll need to maneuver it not just through airport terminals but also along uneven surfaces (cobblestones, gravel) and stairs. If picking a bag without wheels, consider how easily you can carry 20–25 pounds on your back.

Efficiency of Space: Look for the most (usable) capacity. Compartments help you stay organized; a zip-out expandable section is handy for bringing souvenirs home.

Quality: Go with a well-established and/or well-reviewed brand. As for cost, it's easy to spend a fortune on your luggage, but you don't need to. If your bag costs more than $250, you're probably paying more for a brand name than quality. Just make sure your bag is made well enough to withstand at least a few trips' worth of wear and tear; a product guarantee is a good sign. Sturdy stitching, front and/ or side pockets, padded shoulder straps (for backpacks), and a low-profile color are virtues.

Bag Breakdown

Here's my take on your main options. Note that I only consider carry-on-size luggage.

Soft Backpacks: To me, this kind of bag (see photo at the start of this chapter) makes the most sense. These bags hang on your shoulders and work fine for getting from the train station to the hotel. They're also well-suited as carry-ons, since they can squish down to fit in virtually any overhead bin. And I really appreciate the mobility and practicality of having both hands free while en route—I can eat a sandwich or buy a bus ticket and hop on board without breaking my stride. I live out of my backpack for four months each year—and I absolutely love it. The day will come when I'll be rolling my bag through Europe with the rest of the gang. But as long as I'm hardy enough to carry my gear on my back, I will.

A 9" × 21" × 14" carry-on bag (with or without wheels) is the ideal size.

Internal-Frame Backpacks: An internal-frame backpack is the most comfortable bag to wear, as the frame and hip belt keep the weight off your shoulders and balanced over your hips. However, these bags can be expensive, they're often "taller" than carry-on size, and I don't think the comfort is worth the trade-off. If you pack light, a soft backpack won't cause too much strain (and shorter carry-on-size framed backpacks force you to limit your stuff).

Rolling Bags: If carrying a pack on your back isn't for you, wheels are the way to go. A rolling bag frees your back for a smaller day bag, or you can set your smaller bag on top and roll it along. The drawbacks: Bags with wheels usually cost more, weigh more, and offer a little less capacity than backpacks of similar dimensions (since wheel wells and the retractable handle cut into the internal space). Wheeled bags are great in airports but can be cumbersome when negotiating narrow B&B staircases, crowded subways, and villages with stepped or cobbled lanes.

Unless you're traveling with your own butler, remember that you'll need to lift and lug your wheeled bag from time to time—up stairs, into and out of overhead compartments, on and off transit, over muddy footpaths, etc. Look for a rolling bag that's as roomy as possible while still being small and light enough to lift and fit in a plane's overhead bin. Plenty of wheeled bags are well-designed—most of my staffers prefer to roll with one. Just don't let wheels delude you into packing heavier.

Rolling bags come in soft- and hard-sided formats. In general, I prefer a soft-sided suitcase. Hard-sided bags tend to be expensive, and even the newest ultra-light models are still a pound or two heavier than most soft-sided bags. Their major advantage is the protection they offer any breakables you're hauling home. (I sell a hybrid hard-side/canvas bag on my website.)

Rolling Backpacks: Having both wheels and backpack straps seems like the best of both worlds—but the wheels and retractable handle eat up interior space. Many travelers tell me that, while they appreciate having flexibility, they end up using their rolling backpack almost exclusively as a wheeled bag. Personally, I'd go with one or the other.

You can see a comparison chart of my backpacks and rolling bags—and purchase them—at RickSteves.com.

Baggage Restrictions

Pack light...and pack smart. You can't bring anything potentially dangerous—such as knives, lighters, or large quantities of liquids or gels—in your carry-on bag. (This list can change—for details, see "What Can't I Carry On?" on page 106.) Don't let these restrictions deter you: I leave my Swiss Army knife at home, bring small bottles of toiletries, and carry on my bag as usual.

When you carry your bag onto the plane, all liquids, gels, creams, and aerosols must be in 3.4-ounce or smaller containers, all of which must fit into one clear, quart (or liter)-size, plastic zip-top bag. You can also find sturdier,

TSA-approved toiletry bags. Exceptions are made for certain prescription and over-the-counter medicines, as well as contact-lens solution (see www.tsa.gov for details), but European airports don't always hew to the same guidelines. If you check your bag, you can pack all the liquids you want (but I wouldn't).

Before checking, mark your bag inside and out with your name, address, and emergency phone number. If you have a lock on your bag, you may be asked to remove it to accommodate a security check, or it may be opened or even cut off so the bag can be inspected (even a TSA-approved lock may be cut by European inspectors). An alternative is to use a heavy-duty wire or nylon cable tie—but be sure you have a carry-on safe tool to cut it off (such as a nail clipper). I've never locked my bag and have never had a problem. Still, just in case, don't pack anything valuable (such as cash, a camera, or jewelry) in checked luggage.

Be aware that some airlines, particularly Europe's budget carriers, have more stringent carry-on regulations than what we're used to in the US: Confirm policies before you book. For flights within Europe—especially on cheapo airlines like Ryanair or EasyJet—it's best to pay for a carry-on or checked bag when booking the flight, as on-the-spot baggage-check fees can easily top the cost of the flight itself. Even with just a carry-on, airline personnel may ask you to check your bag at the gate if bin capacity is limited (gate-checking your bag at the airline's request is free as long as your bag complies with the airline's policies).

PACKING 101

How do you fit a whole trip's worth of luggage into a small backpack or suitcase? The answer is simple: Bring very little.

Spread out everything you think you might need on the living-room floor. Scrutinize each item. Ask yourself, "Will I really use my snorkel and fins enough to justify carrying them around all summer?" Not "Will I use them?" but "Will I use them enough to feel good about hauling them over the Swiss Alps?" Frugal as I may be, I'd buy a set in Greece and give them away before I'd carry that extra weight for weeks.

When getting way off the beaten path—like this traveler, who's staying at a tiny guesthouse in Italy's Civita di Bagnoregio—you'll be glad you're packing light.

One Carry-on Bag

Here's what I travel with for two months (photos taken naked in a Copenhagen hotel room): 9″ × 21″ × 14″ soft backpack; lightweight day bag; ripped-up sections of several of my guidebooks, notes, maps, journal, tiny pocket notepad; money belt (with debit card, credit card, driver's license, passport, rail pass, cash reserve, sheet of phone numbers and addresses); second money belt clipped inside my bag for "semiprecious" items and documents (flash drive for back-ups, house key, leftover foreign currency, advance tickets and documentation of hotel reservations, car rental, flights, etc.); toiletries bag (with squeeze bottle of shampoo, soap in a plastic container, shaver, toothbrush and paste, comb, nail clippers, squeeze

bottle of liquid soap for clothes); bag with electronic gear (travel alarm clock, phone charger, laptop power cord, plug adapters); miscellaneous bag (with family photos, business cards, back-up toiletries, first aid kit, odds and ends); light rain jacket, long khaki cotton pants (button pockets) in summer or dark jeans off-season, super-light long pants, shorts, five pairs of socks and underwear, two long-sleeved shirts, two short-sleeved shirts, two T-shirts; stuff bag with sweater and plastic laundry bag; light pair of shoes; and lightweight laptop, camera, and noise-canceling headphones.

Don't pack for the worst-case scenario. Pack for the best-case scenario and buy yourself out of any jams. Bring layers rather than a heavy coat. Think in terms of what you can do without—not what might be handy on your trip. When in doubt, leave it out. I've seen people pack a whole summer's supply of deodorant or razors, thinking they can't get them in Europe. The world is small: You can buy Dial soap, Colgate toothpaste, Nivea cream, and Gillette razors in Sicily and Slovakia. Tourist shops in major international hotels are a sure bet whenever you have difficulty finding a personal item. If you can't find one of your essentials, ask yourself how half a billion Europeans can live without it. Rather than carry a whole trip's supply of toiletries, take enough to get started and look forward to running out of toothpaste in Bulgaria. Then you have the perfect excuse to go into a Bulgarian department store, shop around, and pick up something you think might be toothpaste.

Whether I'm traveling for three weeks or three months, I pack exactly the same. To keep my clothes tightly packed and well organized, I fold and roll them before zipping them up in packing cubes. To really maximize bag space, consider airless baggies or a clothes compressor (look for heavy-duty ones made to withstand everyday use). I also like specially designed folding boards (such as Eagle Creek's Pack-It Folder) to fold and carry clothes with minimal wrinkling. Mesh bags also come in handy. I use one for underwear and socks, another for miscellaneous stuff such as a first-aid kit, earplugs, clothesline, sewing kit, and gadgets. (Note that I sell many of these organizational items, including packing cubes and compression packs, on my website.)

Pack your bag only two-thirds full to leave room for souvenirs, or bring along an empty featherweight nylon bag to use as a carry-on for your return flight, then check your main bag through (this is when expandable compartments really come in handy).

Go casual, simple, and very light. Remember, in your travels you'll meet two kinds of tourists—those who pack light and those who wish they had. Say it out loud: "PACK LIGHT PACK LIGHT PACK LIGHT."

> ## Resources for Packing Light
>
> **TSA.gov:** Official list of what you can and cannot carry on
> **Europa.eu/youreurope/citizens/travel:** EU version of TSA website
> **OneBag.com:** More tips on traveling light
> **RickSteves.com/packing:** Rick's packing list and more
> **RickSteves.com/travel-talks:** Rick's travel skills talks, including one on packing
> **Pack the Bag, Packing Pro, TripList apps:** Customizable packing lists with reminders

What to Pack

I've broken the contents of your bag into five major categories: clothing, travel documents (including money), toiletries, electronics, and miscellaneous extras. My core packing recommendations—including quantities for each item of clothing—are all included on my Packing Checklist (see page 87). At the end of this chapter, I've also included a list of optional bring-alongs. In this chapter, an asterisk (*) indicates an item you can purchase at RickSteves.com.

Clothing Basics

Experienced travelers bring only things that will be worn repeatedly, complement other items, and have multiple uses (for example, I don't swim much, so I let my shorts double as a swimsuit). Pack with color coordination in mind. Neutral colors (black, navy, khaki) dress up easily and can be extremely versatile.

To extend your wardrobe as you travel, plan to spend 10 minutes doing a little wash every few nights, or consider a visit to a local launderette, which is in itself a Back Door experience (for details on doing laundry in Europe, see page 420). Choose fabrics that resist wrinkling or look good wrinkled. If you wring with gusto, lightweight clothing should dry overnight in your hotel room. Do a test wash before your trip and pick items that hand-wash well.

In Britain, they say there's no bad weather...only inappropriate clothing.

Many travelers are concerned about appropriate dress. During tourist season, even Europe's concert halls go casual. I have never felt out of place at symphonies, operas, or plays wearing a decent pair of slacks and a good-looking sweater or collared shirt. Some cultural events require more formal attire, particularly outside of high season, but the casual tourist rarely encounters these. Women who don't pack a dress or skirt will do just fine with a pair of nice pants.

While Europeans do wear casual clothing, their definition of casual is a bit dressier than ours. Shorts are uncommon on older women and in big cities, and the cutoff temperature for "hot enough for shorts" is much higher than in the US. Especially in southern Europe, women can blend in with the locals by wearing capri pants or a skirt; men can pack a pair of as-light-as-possible pants.

Shorts, tank tops, and other skimpy summer attire can put a crimp in your sightseeing plans. Some churches, mostly in southern Europe, have modest-dress requirements: no shorts or bare shoulders. Except at the strict St. Peter's Basilica (in Rome) and St. Mark's (in Venice), the dress code is often loosely enforced. Synagogues and mosques may require women to cover their hair. If necessary, it's usually easy to improvise some modesty (buy a cheap T-shirt to cover your shoulders, or carry a scarf to cover your hair). At some heavily touristed churches with strict dress codes, people hand out sheets of tissue paper you can wrap around yourself like a shawl or skirt.

It can be worth splurging a little to get just the right clothes for your trip. For durable, lightweight travel clothes, consider ExOfficio, TravelSmith, Tilley, Eddie Bauer, and REI.

Packing Checklist

Whether you're traveling for five days or five weeks, you won't need more than this. Pack light to enjoy the sweet freedom of true mobility.

Clothing

- ❑ 5 shirts: long- & short-sleeve
- ❑ 2 pairs pants (or skirts/capris)
- ❑ 1 pair shorts
- ❑ 5 pairs underwear & socks
- ❑ 1 pair walking shoes
- ❑ Sweater or warm layer
- ❑ Rainproof jacket with hood
- ❑ Tie, scarf, belt, and/or hat
- ❑ Swimsuit
- ❑ Sleepwear/loungewear

Money

- ❑ Debit card(s)
- ❑ Credit card(s)
- ❑ Hard cash ($100-200 in US dollars)
- ❑ Money belt

Documents

- ❑ Passport
- ❑ Other required ID: Entry visa, vaccination card, etc.
- ❑ Driver's license, student ID, hostel card, etc.
- ❑ Tickets & confirmations: flights, hotels, trains, rail pass, car rental, sight entries
- ❑ Photocopies of important documents
- ❑ Insurance details
- ❑ Guidebooks & maps

Electronics

- ❑ Mobile phone
- ❑ Camera & related gear
- ❑ Tablet/ebook reader/laptop
- ❑ Headphones/earbuds
- ❑ Chargers & batteries
- ❑ Phone car charger & mount (or GPS device)
- ❑ Plug adapters

Toiletries

- ❑ Basics: soap, shampoo, toothbrush, toothpaste, floss, deodorant, sunscreen, brush/comb, etc.
- ❑ Medicines & vitamins
- ❑ First-aid kit
- ❑ Glasses/contacts/sunglasses
- ❑ Face masks & hand sanitizer
- ❑ Sewing kit
- ❑ Packet of tissues (for WC)
- ❑ Earplugs

Miscellaneous

- ❑ Daypack
- ❑ Sealable plastic baggies
- ❑ Laundry supplies: soap, laundry bag, clothesline, spot remover
- ❑ Small umbrella
- ❑ Travel alarm/watch
- ❑ Notepad & pen
- ❑ Journal

Optional Extras

- ❑ Second pair of shoes (flip-flops, sandals, tennis shoes, boots)
- ❑ Travel hairdryer
- ❑ Picnic supplies
- ❑ Disinfecting wipes
- ❑ Water bottle
- ❑ Fold-up tote bag
- ❑ Small flashlight
- ❑ Mini binoculars
- ❑ Small towel or washcloth
- ❑ Inflatable pillow/neck rest
- ❑ Tiny lock
- ❑ Address list (to mail postcards)
- ❑ Extra passport photos

But ultimately—as long as you don't wear something outrageous or offensive—just dress in a way that makes you comfortable. No matter how carefully you dress, your clothes will probably distinguish you from Europeans. And so what? To blend in and be culturally sensitive, I watch my manners, not the cut of my clothes.

Here's a rundown of what should go in your suitcase. For recommended quantities of each item, see my Packing Checklist on the previous page:

Shirts: Bring a mix of short-sleeved and long-sleeved shirts or blouses. Shirts with long sleeves that roll up easily can double as short-sleeved. Look for a wrinkle-camouflaging pattern or fabric. Synthetic-blend fabrics (such as Coolmax or microfiber) usually dry overnight. Lightweight, light-colored clothes are more comfortable in very hot weather.

Pants/Shorts/Skirts: I suggest one pair of lightweight cotton pants and another super-lightweight pair (or a skirt) for hot and muggy destinations. If you prefer jeans, choose the lightest-weight pair you have (heavy denim can be too hot for summer travel and is slow to dry). Some travelers like convertible pants/shorts with zip-off legs. While not particularly stylish, they're especially functional in southern Europe, where you can use them to cover up inside churches while still beating the heat outside. Button-down wallet pockets are safest (though still not nearly as thief-proof as a money belt). Shorts can double as a swimsuit when swimming in lakes or the sea.

Underwear and Socks: As with most clothing I recommend, lighter material dries quicker. Bamboo or cotton/nylon-blend socks dry faster than 100 percent cotton. Double-layer socks can help prevent blisters.

Shoes: Comfortable walking shoes with good traction are essential. Mephisto, Ecco, and Rieker look dressier than sneakers, but are still comfortable. Sturdy, low-profile tennis shoes with a good tread are fine, too. If you bring more than one pair, consider sandals in summer or waterproof shoes in winter or rainy weather. Flip-flops are handy if you'll be using bathrooms down the hall. Whichever shoes you bring, make sure they're well broken in before you leave home.

Sweater or Warm Layer: Warm and dark is best for layering and dressing up. Consider a cashmere sweater or a

Packing Tips for Women

Thanks to our tour guide Joan Robinson for the following tips. For tips on women's health and medication, see page 413.

Skirts: Skirts (knee-length is appropriate for churches) are as cool and breathable as shorts, but dressier, and have a key advantage over dresses: They can be worn with a money belt. A lightweight skirt made with a blended fabric packs compactly. Make sure it has a comfy waistband. Skirts can easily be mixed and matched, and can be dressed up with a pair of tights with flats or boots.

Underwear and Swimwear: Silk, microfiber, or stretch lace underwear dries faster than cotton, but breathes more than nylon. A sports bra can double as a hiking/sunning top. You don't need a bikini to sunbathe topless on European beaches—local women with one-piece bathing suits just roll down the top.

Accessories: Scarves give your limited wardrobe just the color it needs. They dress up your outfit, are lightweight and easy to pack, and if purchased in Europe, make a great souvenir. Some women bring a shawl-size scarf or pashmina to function as a sweater substitute, head wrap, skirt at a church, or even a blanket on a train. Functional, cheap, but beautiful imitation pashminas can be found all over Europe. Leave valuable or flashy jewelry at home. Bring a few pieces you can live with losing, or buy some interesting artisan jewelry in Europe.

lightweight fleece. Vests and cardigans can be mixed-and-matched to give you several different looks as well as layers.

Jacket: Bring a light and water-resistant windbreaker with a hood. A hooded jacket of Gore-Tex or other waterproof material is good if you expect rain. (For summer travel, I wing it without rain gear—but always pack for rain in Britain and Ireland.) For travel to cooler climes, come prepared to add an insulating layer, or consider a super lightweight puffer coat that can squish compactly.

Swimsuit: To use public pools, you'll need a swimsuit (men can't just wear shorts; and in France, men need to wear Speedo-type swimsuits—not swim trunks).

Sleepwear/Loungewear: Comfy streetwear—such as shorts, leggings, T-shirts, tank tops, yoga pants, and other lightweight athletic gear—can get triple use as pajamas, loungewear, and a modest cover-up to get you to the bathroom down the hall.

Accessories: For instant respectability, bring a **tie** or **scarf,** which can break the monotony and make you look snazzy. Consider a light, crushable, wide-brimmed **hat** for sunny days, especially if you're prone to sunburn. Don't forget a **belt** if you need one.

Winter Travel: Even if traveling in winter, you can pack

just about as light. Wear heavier, warmer, waterproof shoes.
I wear my heaviest pair on the plane to save room in my suitcase. Add a coat, long underwear (super-light silk or other
quick-drying fabric), scarf, gloves, hat, and an extra pair of
socks and underwear, since things dry more slowly. Layer
your clothing for warmth, and assume you'll be outside in the
cold for hours at a time.

Documents, Money, and Travel Info

Organizing your possessions, travel documents, money,
guidebooks, and maps is just as important as assembling
your wardrobe. Be sure anything you'll need at the airport
or absolutely cannot lose is either on your body or in your
carry-on—not in checked luggage.

*Money Belt:** This flat, hidden, zippered pouch—worn
around your waist and tucked under your clothes—is essential for the peace of mind it brings. You could lose everything
except your money belt, and the trip could still go on. Get
a lightweight one with a low-profile color (I like beige). A
*neck wallet** or *hidden pocket** (which attaches to your belt
and tucks into your pants) are other alternatives. For more
about money belts, see page 377.

Money: Bring a debit card, a credit card, and an emergency stash of hard US cash. For detailed recommendations,
see page 185.

Documents: Bring your **passport, driver's license,** and
any other **required or useful documents** (entry visa, vaccination record, student ID and so on). In your luggage, pack a
record of all reservations, including flights, hotels, trains,
rental cars, and tickets for sights. Bring any necessary health
or travel **insurance** contact info. Scans or photocopies of **key
documents** and a couple of **passport-type photos** can help
you get replacements more quickly if the originals are lost
or stolen (for more information on the travel documents you
need and what to copy, see page 64).

Guidebooks and Maps: Pack the travel info you'll need
on the ground, whether in paper or electronic form. I like
to rip out appropriate chapters from guidebooks and staple
them together (see page 40 for a how-to), or use a special
slide-on *page binder.**

Notepad and Pen: A small notepad in your back pocket
or daypack is a great organizer, reminder, and communication aid.

*Journal:** An empty book to be filled with the experiences of your trip will be your most treasured souvenir (for

LEFT Looking things up on your mobile phone is generally cheaper using Wi-Fi.

RIGHT Wireless hotspots allow you to get online from a park bench.

more on journaling, see page 438). Attach your itinerary. Use a hardbound type designed to last a lifetime, rather than a floppy spiral notebook. A great brand with a cult following among travel writers is Moleskine (www.moleskine.com).

Electronics

Go light with your electronic gear—you want to experience Europe, not interface with it. Consider insuring particularly high-ticket items (see page 76).

Mobile Phone: Bring your phone to snap photos, keep in touch with folks back home, and access email, travel apps, and GPS on the road. For more on using phones in Europe, see the Staying Connected chapter.

Camera: If you bring a separate camera, take along an extra memory card and battery, and don't forget the charger (and a cable if you plan to download images). For a list of camera gear, see page 430.

Tablet/Ebook Reader: Download apps, ebooks, videos, and music before you leave home (or download on the go with a Wi-Fi connection in Europe).

Laptop: If you're traveling with a laptop, consider bringing a **flash drive** for backing up files and photos (in case the internet connection is too spotty to access cloud storage—see page 432).

Headphones/Earbuds: These are a must for listening to music, tuning in to audio tours, or simply drowning out whiny kids on the plane. (I never travel without my

Adapters and Converters

Europe's electrical system is different from ours in two ways: the voltage of the current and the shape of the plug.

American appliances run on 110 volts, while European appliances are 220 volts. Most gadgets are "dual voltage," which means they work on both American and European current. If you see a range of voltages printed on the item or its plug (such as "110-220"), you're OK in Europe. Some older appliances have a voltage switch marked 110 (US) and 220 (Europe)—switch it to 220 as you pack.

Even older devices (and some handheld gaming systems) aren't equipped to deal with the voltage difference—you'll need a separate, bulky **converter.** Consider replacing your appliance instead.

A small ***adapter** allows American-style plugs (two flat prongs) to fit into British or Irish outlets (which take three rectangular prongs) or continental European outlets (which take two round prongs). Adapters are inexpensive—bring a handful. Even on a continent-only trip, I keep a British adapter on hand for London layovers. Secure your adapter to your device's plug with electrical or duct tape; otherwise it can easily get left behind in the outlet (hotels and B&Bs sometimes have a box of abandoned adapters—ask). Many sockets in Europe are recessed into the wall; your adapter should be small enough so that the prongs seat properly in the socket. (Although you can get universal adapters that work Europe-wide—or even worldwide, these tend to be large and expensive.)

In Europe, two kinds of adapters fit virtually all outlets: two little round prongs for the Continent, three big rectangular ones for Britain and Ireland.

Although sockets in Switzerland and Italy differ from others on the continent, most continental adapters work just fine. (Swiss and Italian outlets accept plugs with three slim round prongs arranged in a triangular shape; two-pronged adapters work as long as they don't have the thicker "Schuko" style prongs—and if the body of the adapter is small enough to fit in the recessed outlet.) If, for some reason, your adapter doesn't work in your hotel, just ask for assistance; hotels with unusual sockets will invariably have the right adapter to loan you.

Some budget hotel rooms have only one electrical outlet, occupied by the lamp. Hardware stores in Europe sell cheap three-way plug adapters that let you keep the lamp on while you charge your camera battery and phone.

noise-canceling Bose headphones.) Bring a Y-jack so you and a partner can listen together.

Chargers/Batteries: Bring each device's charger, or consider a charger capable of charging multiple devices at once. Portable chargers are a handy way to keep your electronics running throughout a long day of sightseeing—just remember to charge the charger at night.

Car Phone Charger and Mount (or GPS Device): If

you'll be doing a lot of driving and plan to use mapping apps on your phone, remember a car charger and car mount. Or bring your GPS device (preloaded with Europe maps). For details on both, see page 172.

*Plug Adapters: You'll need several adapters so you can plug your various devices into European outlets (see sidebar).

Toiletries and Personal Items

Even if you check your suitcase on the flight, always carry on essential toiletries, including any prescription medications (don't let the time difference trick you into forgetting a dose). Because sinks in many hotels come with meager countertop space, I prefer a *toiletries kit that can hang on a hook or a towel bar (there are also TSA-approved toiletry bags for carrying on liquids in case you don't want to use a plastic baggie). In-flight pressure changes can cause bottles to leak, making it a good idea to seal all squeeze bottles in plastic baggies, whether you carry on or check your bag.

> ## Traveler's First-Aid Kit
>
> You can buy virtually anything you need in Europe. But if you prefer a specific name-brand medication, bring it from home (see page 414 for addressing first-aid needs in Europe). It's also handy to pack:
> - hand sanitizer and disinfecting wipes
> - Band-Aids
> - antibiotic cream (in Europe, you may need a prescription to buy skin ointments with antibiotics)
> - moleskin (to prevent or cover blisters)
> - tweezers
> - over-the-counter pain reliever
> - thermometer
> - any medication you may need, including for colds, diarrhea, constipation, motion sickness, allergies, and sleep (if possible, bring nonliquids)
> - prescription medications (preferably in labeled, original containers)

Basics: Unless you plan on using the hotel bathroom "itsy-bitsies," pack your own soap and small bottle of shampoo (and conditioner if needed). Other essentials include a toothbrush, toothpaste, floss, sunscreen, deodorant, hairbrush/comb, razors, and nail clipper. Before cramming in every cleanser, lotion, and cosmetic you think you might use, ask yourself what toiletries you can live without for a short time.

Medicine and Vitamins: Keep medicine in original containers, if possible, with legible prescriptions. For a list of items to pack in a first-aid kit, see the sidebar. For advice on handling prescriptions in Europe, see pages 408 and 418

Glasses/Contacts/Sunglasses: Contact-lens solutions are widely available in Europe. Carry your lens prescription, as well as extra glasses, in a hard protective case. If it's a sunny destination or season, bring your sunglasses.

Packing Tips from Rick's Readers

Rick's readers—his Road Scholars—have a wealth of travel information to share. To read many more hot-out-of-the-rucksack tips on travel topics (and to contribute your own), visit our Travel Forum at RickSteves.com/travel-forum.

Pencil Pouch: I use a cloth pouch with a plastic window to corral my passport, itinerary, emergency contact papers, and other important information. I use one of the holes along the edge to clip it inside my bag for extra security.

Backpack Cinch: I "cinch-tied" the opening of my backpack to make it less accessible for would-be thieves (punched holes in the band at the top of the bag and ran an extendable cable lock through the holes, pulled it tight, and locked it).

Dental Floss or **Fishing Line:** Strong, versatile, waterproof, nearly weightless. Tied backpack together when it broke, doubled as a shoelace, etc.

White Noise Machine: In noisy hotel rooms, its various soothing sounds are a true godsend.

Pillowcase: To put your backpack/travel bag in while you sleep on it on an overnight train. It's another obstacle thieves must overcome.

S-Shaped Double Carabiner: I use two cheap carabiners to clip a pouch with small essentials to the top edge of my seatback pocket.

Cotton Bandanas: Use them as hand towels, washcloths, picnic blankets, emer-

Face Masks: If coronavirus restrictions are still in place, bring enough masks so that you have at least one fresh (or freshly washed) mask for each day.

Hand Sanitizer: A small container of hand sanitizer keeps hands clean when you don't have access to soap and water.

*Small Towel/Washcloth: You'll find bath towels at all fancy and moderately priced hotels, and most cheap ones. Some people bring a thin hand towel for the occasional need. Washcloths are rare in Europe, so you might want to pack a ***quick-drying microfiber cloth.** Disposable washcloths that pack dry but lather up when wet (such as Olay 4-in-1 Daily Facial Cloths) are another option; cut them in half to make them last longer.

With a hangable toiletries kit, you know the hairs on the toothbrush are yours.

*Sewing Kit: Clothes age rapidly while traveling. Add a few safety pins and extra buttons.

Packet of Tissues: Carry these in your daypack, in case you wind up at a bathroom with no toilet paper.

Personal Care Items: If you use disposable personal hygiene products, bring a supply to avoid buying full boxes in Europe.

Earplugs: If night noises bother

gency seat covers, and even towels (use two to dry your entire body). Tie a bandana on your luggage so you can quickly identify it.

Comfy Slippers: If your feet aren't happy, YOU aren't happy. Pamper them!

Inflatable Hangers: Clothes dry faster.

Wrinkle Wiz: Sprays out the wrinkles after I've unpacked my clothes—no more travel iron!

Binder Clips: I always take a few small, medium, and large binder clips to hang clothes to dry, keep window curtains together, weigh down shower curtains, and keep plastic bags shut.

Reusable Plastic Utensils: Great for take-away food, picnics, or when clean utensils aren't available.

Travel Blanket: Look for a "parachute blanket" that rolls up into its own nylon bag and has four corner pockets—it can be used for beaches, picnics, and shade in a sunny area. It also serves as an extra blanket at night and even as a pillow when rolled up.

Mailing Tube: To collect prints and posters (cut tube to fit your luggage).

Large, Strong Rubber Bands: Use them to keep shoes compactly fitted together in your luggage.

you, you'll love a good set of expandable foam plugs. They're handy for snoozing on trains and flights, too.

Miscellaneous

Consider the following:

Small Daypack: A lightweight pack is great for carrying a sweater, camera, guidebook, and picnic goodies while you leave your large bag (with most of your belongings) at the hotel. Don't use a fanny pack—they're magnets for pickpockets.

Laundry Supplies: Bring a bag for dirty laundry (such as a *mesh bag* or a plastic baggie). Travel-size packets of detergent or a squeeze bottle of concentrated, multipurpose, biodegradable *liquid soap* is handy for laundry. I find hotel shampoo works fine as laundry soap when I'm doing my wash in the sink (for tips on doing laundry in Europe, see page 420). For a spot remover, bring a few Shout wipes or a dab of Goop grease remover in a small plastic container. A small *clothesline* lets you hang laundry in your hotel room (the twisted-rubber type needs no clothespins).

Small Umbrella: Consider bringing a collapsible umbrella or plan to buy one in Europe. Umbrella vendors, like worms, appear with the rain.

Travel Alarm: Make sure you have an alarm to wake

yourself up (your phone, a travel clock, etc.). At budget hotels, wake-up calls are particularly unreliable.

Sealable Plastic Baggies: In addition to holding carry-on liquids, these are ideal for packing leftover picnic food, containing wet clothes, and bagging potential leaks before they happen. The two-gallon jumbo size can be used to pack (and compress) clothing or do laundry. Bring a variety of sizes, and extras for the flight home.

Optional Bring-Alongs

I don't advocate bringing everything listed here. Choose the items that fit with your travel style and needs.

Hairdryer: These are generally provided in $100-plus rooms or are available from your hotel's reception desk. If you can't risk a bad-hair day, buy a cheap, compact hairdryer in Europe or bring a travel-friendly one from home.

Picnic Supplies: Bring a plastic plate (handy for dinner in your hotel room or on the go), cup, spoon, fork, and maybe salt and pepper. Fozzils dishware folds completely flat (see www.fozzils.com). Buy a Swiss Army-type knife with a corkscrew and can opener in Europe (or bring one from home if you're checking your luggage on the plane).

Disinfecting Wipes: These are handy for sanitizing surfaces as you travel, such as the seatback tray table on an airplane or train.

***Water Bottle:** The plastic half-liter mineral water bottles sold throughout Europe are reusable and work great. If you bring one from home, make sure it's empty before you go through airport security.

***Fold-up Tote Bag:** A large-capacity tote bag that rolls up into a pocket-size pouch is useful for laundry, picnics, and those extra souvenirs.

***Small Flashlight:** Handy for reading under the sheets after "lights out" in the hostel, late-night trips down the hall, exploring castle dungeons, and hypnotizing street thieves. Tiny-but-powerful LED flashlights—about the size of your little finger—are extremely bright, compact, and lightweight. Your phone's flashlight function also does the trick.

***Small Binoculars:** For scenery or church interiors.

***Inflatable Pillow/Neck Rest:** These are great for snoozing in planes, trains, and automobiles. Some travelers also swear by an ***eye mask** for blocking out early-rising or late-setting sun.

Duct Tape: A small roll of duct tape can work miracles as a temporary fix—mending a punctured bag, solving an emergency shoe problem, and so on. Conserve space by spooling only as much as you might need (less than a foot) around a short pencil or dowel.

Insect Repellent: Bring some along if you're prone to bites or going somewhere especially buggy.

*****Tiny Lock:** Use it to lock your backpack zippers shut. Note that if you check your bag on a flight, the lock may be broken to allow the bag to be inspected. Improve the odds of your lock's survival by buying one approved by the Transportation Security Administration—security agents can open the lock with a special master key. Or use zip-ties or *****flight locks** to secure zippers—be sure to pack nail clippers or TSA-approved scissors so you can open them when you arrive.

Office Supplies: Bring paper, pens, and sticky notes to keep your place in your guidebook.

Address List: If you plan to mail postcards, you could print your mailing list onto a sheet of adhesive address labels before you leave. You'll know exactly to whom you've written, and the labels will be perfectly legible.

Reading Material: There's plenty of time on a trip to either be bored or enjoy a good book. Popular English-language paperbacks are often available in European airports and major train stations (usually costing more than at home). An ebook reader makes it easy to carry and buy books as you go.

Gifts: If you'll be the guest of local hosts, show your appreciation with small, unique souvenirs from your hometown.

Universal Drain Stopper: Some hotel sinks and tubs have no stoppers. This flat, flexible plastic disc—which works with any size drain—allows you to wash your clothes or take a bath.

Hostel Sheet: Sheets are usually included in the price of a hostel, but if they aren't, you can rent one for about $5 per stay. Still, you might want to bring your own sheet (silk is lighter and smaller, cotton is cheaper), which can double as a beach/picnic blanket and cover you up on overnight train rides. See page 245 for hosteling tips.

A Guilty Pleasure: It's worth sacrificing space to bring something that makes you happy. My guilty pleasure is my pair of Bose noise-canceling headphones. I love these things. When I'm on a plane or train, I can slip these on my head and relax with my music or movie without hearing the rumble and noise around me.

Flying

Before you can enjoy Europe, you have to get there.
And unless you're a romantic who's signing up
to crew on a tramp steamer, you'll be riding on
a jet plane. This chapter will help you figure out
how to get the lowest fare, both for transatlantic
and intra-European flights, and also provides tips
for flying comfortably and navigating European
airports smartly.

BOOKING YOUR FLIGHT

Your plane ticket to Europe will likely be your biggest trip
expense. It pays to be on your toes to get the best deal.

Using Flight Search Websites

If you're not using a travel agent, your first step is to
research your options. Rather than checking each airline's
website, I begin my search with a site that compiles my
choices.

Flight search websites compare fares available at multiple
airlines, online travel agencies, or both, then sort them by
price. I've tested a number of them on a variety of journeys,
both transatlantic and within Europe. Overall, **Kayak** has
the best results for both intercontinental and intra-European
flights on a combination of mainstream and budget carriers.
An alternative is Google Flights, which has an easy-to-use
system to track prices and lets you see how much you'd save
by departing a day earlier or later.

A couple of sites are better for flights *to* Europe than
flights *within* Europe, and some nice features make their
results easier to navigate. **Expedia** is easy to use and consistent at finding good fares. **CheapoAir** offers pricing tables
for mixed-airline flights to and from Europe. (For cheap

flights within Europe, I prefer **Skyscanner;** see "Flying within Europe," later.)

Flight-Search Tips

Here are some things to keep in mind when looking for flights.

Look around. No single flight search engine includes every possible airline—and some airlines deliberately limit where their airfares appear. It's always smart to check more than one website, and to look directly on airlines' websites as well.

Think flexibly about airports and dates. If you are flying into a city with several airports, select either "all airports" or simply the city name ("LON" for London) rather than a specific airport name ("LHR" for London Heathrow). If offered, select "include nearby airports"—doing so will return more flight options (for example, Pisa for Florence or Bratislava for Vienna). Choosing "flexible dates" lets you see what you might save by flying a few days before or after your ideal time frame.

Consider flying into one city and out of another. Since it rarely makes sense to spend time and money returning to your starting point, this strategy can be very efficient. For most "multi-city" flights, the fare is figured simply by taking half of the round-trip cost for each of those airports.

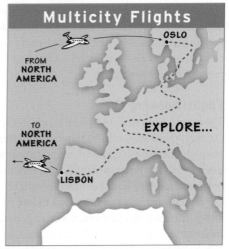

Wipe your browser's memory. If you repeatedly search for the same itinerary, it may help to regularly delete your search history and "cookies" (identifying data stored on your computer by the websites you visit). Cookies remember what you've searched in the past. If you look again and again for the same flights on the same website, the site may become aware of your search habits...and increase the prices (the industry claims this is myth). To delete your browser's search history and cookies, look in your browser's privacy settings.

One option is to use your browser's "incognito" or "private" mode when searching for fares. In the Google Chrome web browser, select the three vertical dots in the upper right corner and then select "new incognito window." When searching in this mode, Chrome will not save your cookies or browsing history. Firefox and Safari have similar features.

Buying Tickets

While it's possible to book your flights on most search sites (they certainly hope you will, to garner their commission), I typically use these sites only as a first step. Once I've zeroed in on which airline has the best deal for my trip, I check the airline's own site to compare fares. You can often avoid added costs by booking direct (the commissions are charged either as higher prices or in the form of fees for booking through a third party). And airlines may offer bonuses (such as extra frequent-flier miles) to those who book direct.

Search sites occasionally beat the fares on the airline's official site, sometimes by using "mix and match" journeys to connect the legs of a single trip on multiple airlines. (However, these trips can be difficult to rebook in case of a delay or missed leg—review the schedule carefully, watching out for very tight connections or extremely long layovers.)

For maximum peace of mind, it's usually best to book directly with the airline, which can more easily address unexpected problems or deal with rescheduled flights. If you do buy tickets through a third-party site, make sure you carry their phone number with you—you'll need to speak to a person if you have a problem.

Flight-Booking Tips

There's no such thing as a free lunch in the airline industry. (In fact, there's usually no lunch at all.) Before grabbing the cheapest ticket you can find, make sure it meets your travel needs with the best combination of schedule, economy, and convenience—without being too restrictive.

Buy your tickets at the right time (to the extent possible). Airfares flex like crazy, but in general it's wise to start looking for international flights at least four to six months before your trip, especially for travel in spring, summer, or fall. Good deals on winter travel (November through March) can usually be purchased a month or so in advance, with the exception of winter breaks and holidays, which require even earlier booking. Year-round, it's generally cheaper to book midweek.

All that said, knowing the best time to buy is still a guessing game, though you can improve your chances by taking advantage of Google's Flight Explorer (www.google.com/flights/explore), which shows the best prices to your destination in an easy-to-read graph and can be tailored to your time frame. And several search sites, including Kayak and Expedia, offer price-trend graphs.

Be ready to buy. Given how erratic airline pricing can be, you want to be ready to pounce on a good fare when you see it. As you delay, dates sell out and prices generally go up. Figure out in advance what constitutes a good fare, then grab it when you find it. A few airlines will let you pay a small fee to hold a fare for three days. US Department of Transportation regulations state that you're entitled to cancel or change a flight within 24 hours of purchase without a fee, but if you're changing flights, you may have to pay the fare difference. Read the fine print before buying to make sure you understand cancellation and change fees.

Pick a seat as early as possible. Most airlines let you choose your seat when you book, and most charge extra for roomier seats. If your first choice is not open, select another seat and try to change it later. If seat assignments aren't available at booking, ask about the earliest possible date that you can request your seat (for example, 90 or 30 days before your flight)—and put it on your calendar or set a reminder on your phone. A week before your flight,

---

Resources for Air Travel

Kayak.com: Top site (and app) for flight options to and within Europe

Google.com/flights: Another good search site with easy tracking and price alerts

Skyscanner.com: Best search engine for cheap flights within Europe

Expedia.com, CheapoAir.com: Alternative search engine for flights to Europe

Momondo.com: Alternative search engine for intra-European flights

AirfareWatchdog.com, FareCompare.com: Low-fare alerts and deals, but clunky user interface

TravelZoo.com, Priceline.com: Search engines and deals best for those with flexible itineraries

Google.com/flights/explore: Graphs the best prices to your destination

SeatGuru.com: Airplane-seat maps and advice

FlyerTalk.com: Travel forum site with tips on frequent flyer miles

TSA.gov: Latest US flight rules and regulations

RickSteves.com/hub-airports: Advice for passing through Europe's hub airports

RickSteves.com/travel-talks: Rick's travel skills talks, including one on transportation

TripIt app: Itinerary organizer with flight-change alerts

FlightAware app: Live flight tracker

LoungeBuddy app: Airport-lounge locator that lets you book immediate access

---

airlines will sometimes release extra seats or change equipment: Check to see if you can get a better seat. Try to check in online exactly 24 hours before your flight, when even more seats may be released—including bulkhead and exit-row seats. For pointers on which seats are best on specific airplanes, see SeatGuru.com.

Consider different ticket tiers. Most US airlines offer several ticket tiers based on various amenities, such as class of service (first, business, economy), type of seat (main cabin with more leg room, main cabin toward the back, etc.), baggage allowances, whether the ticket is changeable and/or refundable, whether you can preselect seats (versus waiting until check-in), and more.

The lowest fare—usually called "basic economy" or similar—looks tempting but is also the most restrictive (for instance, not allowing you to select seats or limiting the size of your carry-on). Before selecting this fare, read the rules (each airline differs) and make sure the savings are worth the sacrifices or won't cause you to spend more money in the long run (such as on checked luggage or change fees).

Larger or taller travelers, or anyone who wants a little more personal space, may find it worth the extra cost for the extra legroom afforded by "Economy Plus" seats (or whatever your airline calls their intermediate class between Economy and Business).

Understand cancellation and change policies. Many airlines eliminated aggressive change fees during the pandemic, but as travel picks back up, those fees are coming back. Even without a change fee, if you change your itinerary, you are responsible for the fare difference; so if you get a good deal on a ticket, changing a date or time may result in a higher ticket price. Note that basic economy tickets (described above) typically have change fees—and on some carriers, can't be changed at all. Unexpected circumstances can happen to anyone, so understand your ticket's change policies before you buy.

If you cancel a flight, you will likely pay a cancellation fee and receive credit toward a future flight, not a refund. One exception is if you purchase a refundable ticket (which typically costs significantly more than a nonrefundable ticket); in that case you will get a refund to your original form of payment (though there may be a processing fee). Basic economy tickets generally cannot be cancelled—meaning you'll receive neither a credit nor a refund if you can't use the ticket.

If you need to alter your return date once you're in Europe, call your airline's European office. If you absolutely must get home early, go to the airport and talk to your airline's representatives at the ticket desk: If you're standing at the airport two days before your ticket says you can go home, and seats are available, they may just let you fly.

Review your ticket information carefully when you

book. Double-check your dates, times, destinations, baggage allowance, and exact spelling of your name. Confirm that the name on your reservation exactly matches the one on your passport; this can be an expensive hassle to correct later. Decline extras that you don't want. On each page of the transaction, be sure that no boxes are checked unless you want them to be.

Money-Saving Tips

Here are some additional ideas for finding low fares.

Comparison-shop "air plus hotel" promotional deals. Some airfare aggregators and airlines offer "getaway" deals. For one low price, you get a round-trip flight to a European city as well as a few nights' lodging. Given Europe's high accommodation costs—especially in big cities—these can be a good value, though you can expect to be put up in a soulless business hotel.

Sign up for low-fare alerts. Many airfare search sites—as well as the official airline sites—will email and tweet automated updates about low fares for specific routes. Or check out the website AirfareWatchdog, a free service that does a particularly good job of finding the cheapest fares across multiple airlines (including those that don't show up on most search sites) and limits their alerts to flights that actually have seats available. A similar site called FareCompare tweets alerts specific to your home airport.

Consider budget European airlines. A few of Europe's low-cost carriers have flights between the US and Europe; these don't normally show up in the search results of most US-based airfare comparison sites. Check the list later in this chapter for carriers with hubs near your European destination, then find out if they fly to any US airports. Be forewarned that passenger reviews of these budget carriers' trans-Atlantic flights are mixed regarding their legroom, onboard services, and overall comfort—all of which are more important on a long overseas flight than a quick intra-European hop. Do your homework before committing to a lengthy flight on a budget airline.

Use any scheduling flexibility to your advantage. At certain times—for instance, when shoulder season turns into peak season (and vice versa) for your destination—shifting your flight by one day could save you hundreds of dollars. And consider that fares are generally a bit cheaper for travel Monday through Thursday than for weekends.

If your travel dates aren't set, you may be able to score a

great deal—try sites like AirfareWatchdog and TravelZoo, both of which keep track of the latest deals. Priceline offers the option to purchase a discounted ticket without knowing full details about your airline and flight times. Just keep in mind that you're just as likely to stumble upon deals on the airlines' own websites—particularly if you sign up for their email alerts.

Frequent-Flier Miles

Personally, I don't collect frequent-flier miles. (It's my own quirky hang-up, but I view frequent-flier programs as a cynical way for airlines to produce nothing while prodding their customers to jump through needless hoops and compromise flexibility.) However, for a traveler who's willing to play the game, frequent-flier miles can be a useful budget tool. Here are some strategies for getting the most travel out of your miles. For more tips, check out FlyerTalk.com.

Book as far ahead as possible. Airlines reserve only a handful of "award seats" on each flight, and they go fast. Book months in advance—or even close to a year for peak travel season.

Maximize the miles you earn. Booking direct with the airline, rather than on a third-party booking site, may earn you bonus miles. Many credit cards allow you to accrue miles with each purchase you make, flight-related or not.

Know about alliances. Most major airlines belong to one of three gigantic frequent-flier collectives: Star Alliance, SkyTeam, or OneWorld, all of which cover North American airlines as well as European carriers. Before booking, check the latest on which airlines belong to which group (these partnerships are as slippery as political alliances). If you have miles on one airline in the alliance, you can redeem them on any of the others.

Redeem miles online if possible. Check if the flight you want is available on the airline's website. If not, try speaking directly with an airline agent. While this can come with a small additional fee, it may be worth it to talk with a live person who has all your options at his or her fingertips—especially if you...

Research and know your options. If you try to redeem miles over the phone, the agent might say you're out of luck just because the most straightforward route is sold out. Before you call, make a list (in order of preference) of the connections that would work for your trip, or ask the agent to try a less convenient alternate route.

If you're a little short on miles, get creative. Look into buying miles from the airline or paying a fee to transfer them from someone else (such as a family member). Many airlines also allow you to "pay" for one leg of the ticket with miles and the other in cash.

Watch the expiration date. Miles generally expire at a certain point after you accrue them. It's a good idea to note these expiration dates in your calendar, with a reminder several months ahead. Typically, the miles must be redeemed for a ticket before the expiration date, but the flight can occur anytime—even months later. If you've got miles but aren't ready to redeem them, you can usually extend their life by keeping your airline account active (for instance, booking a cheap domestic flight or doing some online shopping through the airline's website).

Expect to pay fees. Even if your ticket is "free," you'll likely pay taxes and booking fees, which can be hundreds of dollars (British Airways is notorious for charging a hefty "fuel surcharge"). The amount depends on the airline, class of service, and destination.

Using a Travel Agent

While travel agents may seem like an antiquated notion—or perhaps only the purview of business travelers and wealthy jetsetters—even the web-savviest budget traveler shouldn't be too quick to rule out using the services of a living, breathing agent. A good travel agent will almost certainly save you time, may also save you money, and can be a vital ally should you or your trip run into problems. Like many of my readers, I value the personal touch and expertise that only an experienced agent can provide.

Most agents charge a $35-150 fee per ticket. In the long run, paying a modest fee could be a worthwhile expense—think of it as a reasonable charge for the hassle of tracking down flight options, and/or a consulting cost for your travel agent's expertise. I enjoy the convenience of explaining my travel plans to my agent, getting a briefing on my options, and choosing the best flight.

Travel agents not only save you the time of looking up your own flights, but sometimes have access to cheaper fares. A good travel agent, especially one who specializes in the region you're traveling to, offers both regular airline fares and discounted consolidator fares. (Consolidators are wholesalers who negotiate with airlines to get deeply discounted fares, then sell those tickets cheaply but with a markup;

check cancellation policies and other restrictions carefully.)

Using an agent can be beneficial if you are booking a complicated trip (whether coordinating a group and/or a complex, multileg itinerary), need to obtain visas, or if you're taking a cruise (most cruise lines prefer that you book through an agent).

An agent can also be helpful in smoothing any bumps in the road. Once, just after boarding my plane in the US and settling in for my flight to London, the flight crew announced that a fire had shut down Heathrow. Back in the terminal, you can imagine the chaotic scene as everyone from my flight scrambled to sort out their plans. But I simply called my agent and asked her to get me to my end destination, Berlin, any way but through London. With little fuss, I was rebooked on a flight early the next morning via Amsterdam, and made it to Berlin before noon.

While I often use an agent for my plane ticket, car rental, advice on visas, and possibly travel insurance, I turn to a good guidebook for everything else (such as hotel advice). Although an agent may be able to give you tips on Irish B&Bs or sporadic advice on biking in Holland, it's safe to assume you'll get more helpful information from your guidebook. For intra-Europe flights, do your own search, as a travel agent's reservations networks don't include most cheap, no-frills European airlines.

What Can't I Carry On?

The list of prohibited carry-on items can change without notice—especially just after a terrorist threat. And while most security rules are similar on either side of the Atlantic, carry-on restrictions can differ between the US and Europe, as well as between any two European countries. Don't assume you know what's allowed. Shortly before your flight, check TSA.gov/travel, as well as the websites for your airline and any airports you're flying through. (This is an especially good idea if you're flying through London, which often enforces tighter restrictions than other European hubs; see Gov.uk/hand-luggage-restrictions.)

Tempted to pick up some duty-free booze or perfume on your way back home? It's no problem if you have a nonstop flight. Passengers with a connection are permitted to carry liquids (or oil- or liquid-packed foods) in excess of 3.4 ounces if they were purchased in a duty-free shop and are packaged in a "STEB"—a secure, tamper-evident bag. Your STEB sack will be screened when you transfer to your connecting flight. But stay away from liquids in opaque, ceramic, or metallic containers, which usually cannot be successfully screened (STEB or no STEB); place these products in your checked baggage or forfeit them. For more tips, see "Hauling Home Heavenly Wines" on page 372.

If you're seeking a good travel agent, recommendations from other travelers provide excellent leads. But the right agency doesn't guarantee the right agent. You need someone whose definition of "good travel" matches yours. When you contact an agency, ask for their "independent Europe specialist."

FLYING TO EUROPE

I love a nonstop Seattle-to-Europe trip. Just about ten hours (five hours of work, one hour for dinner, then pop a quarter-tab of Ambien to get four hours of sleep, happy to wake learning I missed breakfast, eat my clean-the-cupboard peanut butter sandwich from home as we touch down)...and I'm in Europe.

Your flight and arrival are part of the adventure—here's how to make them go efficiently and enjoyably.

Preparing to Fly

Before you leave for the airport, double-check you have all the required documents for flying, and keep them in a secure but accessible place in your carry-on bag (not in a checked bag). These include your passport, boarding pass, and possibly a "vaccine passport" that shows either proof of vaccination against the coronavirus or a negative Covid-19 test (see page 66 and page 407). If using electronic documents (such as a mobile boarding pass), be sure that your phone is adequately charged before you head to the airport. (It's also important to charge your other electronic devices, as security checks may require you to turn them on.)

Most carriers allow you to check in and retrieve your boarding pass 24 hours before departure. Even if you check in beforehand, plan to arrive at the airport at least two hours in advance (some airlines—and the TSA—recommend three hours). If your flight includes a connection to a different carrier, you may not be able to check in online (even if they're partnered—for example, the first leg on United and the second leg on Lufthansa). First try checking in on the website of the company from which you bought the ticket; if that doesn't work, try the other carrier's site. Otherwise, you'll have to check in for the entire journey at the airport; in rare cases, you may have to wait until your layover to check in for your connecting flight.

Don't dawdle at the airport. Try to get through security screening as quickly as possible, in case there are long lines or hiccups. Passengers with TSA Precheck clearance can usually go to a special security line and do not have to remove their shoes, jackets (provided they're light), belts, liquids, or electronic devices (see page 68 for more on TSA Precheck and Global Entry). Seniors 75 and older and children 12 and under also can skip several screening procedures, including shoe and jacket removal.

Making the Most of Your Flight

Flying economy class doesn't have to be miserable. I've never paid for anything more than coach—and many times I've ended up on a full flight, spending ten hours in a middle seat. These aren't ideal conditions for a good night's sleep, but I make it work. Here are my tricks for a comfortable flight in cattle-car "luxury":

Dress for comfort and relaxation. I dress warm and loose, taking off my shoes and belt, and cuddling up with a sweater and scarf. Next, I slip on my noise-canceling headphones, which both mute the rumble of the engines and the mind-numbing chatter of people around me. With headphones on, I get into conversations only if I want to, which makes the flight much more restful.

Come prepared to stay busy. I board the plane with a fully charged laptop or tablet—and lots of reading or writing to do. This provides me with a mental escape and an opportunity to prepare for my upcoming travels, and it helps the time race by. Most airlines offer charging ports on long-haul flights, including in coach. Some flights also include Wi-Fi, though access isn't fast enough for streaming video (either download videos or use the in-flight entertainment).

Get some rest. For me, just a quarter-tablet of Ambien (*zolpidem*) is good for a couple of blissful hours of sleep. And a neck rest can do wonders. When I wake up, I'm thankful for the shut-eye. It enables me to function much better on my first day in Europe (for more on how to handle jet lag, see page 409). I also believe that good health on your trip starts with the flight over—see my tips on page 411.

Use your layovers well. If your flight requires a connection and layover, use the time to charge your mobile devices and handle routine tasks (e.g., if it's your first stop in Europe, get cash at an ATM if your layover shares a currency with your destination). With a very long layover, consider a brief excursion downtown—most of Europe's airports are connected to the city center by fast, frequent, and affordable public transit. For key details on Europe's hub airports (London, Amsterdam, Frankfurt, and Paris), see RickSteves.com/hub-airports.

Dealing with Delays

Even the best-planned travel arrangements can run into snags. Planes have mechanical problems, hurricanes and blizzards blow through, and flight delays cause missed connections. Planning ahead is the key to diminishing the downside of delays.

The Fear of Flying

I can understand why many people are afraid to fly. It's easy to think of the little rubber wheels splashing down on a rain-soaked runway and then hydroplaning out of control. Or the spindly landing gear crumbling. Or, if not that, then the plane tilting just a tad, catching a wing tip, and flipping over and bursting into flames.

I overcome these concerns with simple logic. The chances of being in an airplane crash are minuscule. I remind myself that worldwide, only one passenger plane is involved in a fatal accident for every 4,125,000 flights that take to the sky. That means that I could catch a flight each day for an average of 123,000 years before dying in a plane crash. There's a good reason that the pilot and crew don't seem terrified, even though they fly daily. For more than 30 years, my company has had countless tour-group members fly over to meet us—30,000 tourists a year these days—and, as far as I know, never has one of our travelers even picked up a scratch while flying.

Consider this: The odds of dying in a commercial airplane accident are 1 in 11 million. Worldwide, more than a million people die each year in road accidents—about the same as if a fully loaded 747 crashed every four hours. If you worry about safety, the real time to panic is during the drive to the airport.

I comfort my nervousness with the knowledge that flying is a matter of physics and aerodynamics. Air has mass, and the plane maneuvers itself through that mass. I can understand a boat coming into a dock—maneuvering through the water. That doesn't scare me. So I tell myself that a plane's a boat with an extra dimension to navigate, and its "water" (air) is a lot thinner. Also, the pilot, who's still "flying" the plane after it lands, is as much in control on the ground as in the air. Only when good and ready does a pilot allow gravity to take over.

Turbulence scares me, too. But a United pilot once told me that he'd have bruises from his seat belt before turbulence really bothered him. Still, every time the plane comes in for a landing, I say a prayer, close my eyes, and take my pen out of my shirt pocket so it won't impale me if something goes wrong. And every time I stick my pen back in my shirt pocket, I feel thankful.

Sign up for alerts from your airline. You can also get info about flight changes from third-party apps such as TripIt or FlightAware.

If your flight is canceled, your airline is likely to rebook you on the next flight that has available seats or offer you a refund. Consider calling the airline as you wait in line to get rebooked; you may reach someone by phone before you make it to the counter. Remember that jumping on another flight—especially if it's leaving soon—is much easier to do if you haven't checked any bags (another good reason to pack light and carry on).

It's important to know your rights as a passenger in case you get grounded by a long delay. The Department of Transportation requires that US airlines give passengers waiting inside the plane food, water, and bathroom access by the time the delay reaches two hours. After waiting for three hours on the tarmac, passengers must be allowed to leave the plane.

For longer delays, you may need to figure out where in the airport to while away several hours...or make plans to spend the night. Some airports have hotels right in the terminal (for instance, Yotel in London's Heathrow and CitizenM inside Amsterdam's Schiphol). If you need a place to sleep, ask if the airline can arrange a discount for you at a local hotel. Or consult SleepingInAirports.net, which provides tips for where to sleep at various airports, from the best benches to the closest airport hotels.

In the US, don't expect much help from your airline, such as hotel reimbursement or food vouchers, especially in the case of delays or cancellations caused by weather. Each airline's "conditions of carriage" details what passengers are entitled to receive when flights are canceled. Many major carriers have contracts that remove liability for problems related to weather.

If you are flying in the European Union, you have much stronger passenger rights; see the "EU Passenger Rights" sidebar, later in this chapter.

If you don't need a full night's sleep, consider purchasing a one-time pass for an airport lounge (about $50). You can rest, freshen up, have a drink and a snack, charge your devices, and do a little work. The LoungeBuddy app can help you locate and book access to lounges in airports across North America and Europe. Be aware that many lounges are closed after midnight or limit how long you can stay—check the hours before you buy a pass.

Navigating European Airports

Most European airports are slick, modern, and well-connected to the city center, but they still can be a jumble of tired travelers, torn-up terminals, and tardy taxis. Use these tips to navigate the airport smartly once you arrive.

Use airport services. You may be jet-lagged and just want to get to your hotel, but take advantage of airport services before you leave. Stop by the tourist information office for maps, museum passes, subway tickets, and advice (usually they're less crowded than the downtown office). I've also found that free Wi-Fi at executive lounges in airports often leaks into the main hall. Sitting nearby, I can get online for free.

Just say no to exchange booths. At airport exchange booths, you lose around 15 percent when you change dollars to euros or other currency. To get local cash, find an airport ATM.

Know where you're going. Some airlines offer apps that provide airport maps and tips for navigating them upon arrival. Google offers Street View maps of the interiors of a number of major airports. Also have on hand instructions for getting to your hotel so you'll know which train, shuttle bus, or taxi stand to look for.

Don't get lost in translation. Nearly everything is labeled in English at European airports, but you still need to pay careful attention. For example, the shuttle train between terminals at Paris' Charles de Gaulle Airport is called the CDGVAL—you have to look carefully to see that it is also marked "Airport Shuttle" in smaller letters.

If taking public transit, consider buying a transit pass at the airport. Airport buses and trains are usually part of a city's larger transport network, which means you can often include the ride on whichever transit card you'll be using while you're in town. For example, when I fly into London Heathrow, I buy the one-week public transit pass covering the Tube and city buses, and pay a small airport supplement. I get to my hotel from the airport and I get the whole week of travel covered for what I would spend if I took a taxi from the airport to my hotel.

Ensure happy returns. Before you leave the airport upon your arrival, note which terminal you'll use for your departure (assuming you're flying out from the same airport). Don't count on the taxi driver or shuttle bus driver knowing where you should be dropped off when you come back for your flight home. At some airports, terminals are very far apart, and arriving at the wrong one will mean wasted time riding around the airport on a shuttle bus.

LEFT European airports are modern, efficient, and filled with tired travelers.

RIGHT Helpful airport staff can point you in the right direction.

FLYING WITHIN EUROPE

Before buying a long-distance train or bus ticket, it's smart to first check the cost of a flight—you might be surprised. The proliferation of extremely competitive discount carriers revolutionized European-itinerary planning and turned vagabonds into jetsetters. You can hop just about anywhere on the Continent for less than $250 a flight.

Using Budget Airlines

After Europe deregulated its airways in the 1990s, a flock of budget-conscious, no-frills airlines took flight. Some established ones (such as EasyJet and Ryanair) have route maps that rival their mainstream competitors. Meanwhile, dozens of smaller, niche airlines stick to a more limited flight plan.

Budget airlines typically offer flights between major European cities for $50-250. You can also fly within Europe on major airlines affordably—and without all the aggressive restrictions. If your timing is right, you may even find some remarkable, it-must-be-a-typo deals (for example, Ryanair routinely flies from London to any one of dozens of European cities for less than $30). Even after adding taxes and a boatload of fees, these flights can still be a good value. To get the lowest fares, book long in advance. The cheapest seats sell out fast (aside from occasional surprise sales).

One-way flights on low-cost airlines are generally just as affordable as round-trips. Consider linking a couple of cheap flights, either with the same or different airlines, to reach your destination. But be careful to leave plenty of time for connections—you're on your own if a delay on one airline causes you to miss your next flight on a different airline. Pay attention to which terminal your flights use, as low-cost carriers are often in a different terminal than traditional carriers, and you'll need extra time to get between them. If you're using a budget carrier to connect to your US-bound flight, allow enough of a layover to absorb delays—maybe even an overnight.

Smart travelers use low-cost airlines to creatively connect the dots on their itinerary. If there's no direct cheap flight to Florence, maybe there's an alternative

Europe's no-frills, smaller airlines offer cut-rate fares and scaled-down services.

Budget Airlines in Europe

These are some of the budget airlines crisscrossing the European skies, along with their main hubs. To discover more, check out Skyscanner.com, or search online for "cheap flights" plus the cities you're interested in flying to/from. New airlines appear—and old ones go out of business—all the time.

Airline	Main Hubs
Aer Lingus	Dublin
AirBaltic	Riga
Blue Air	Bucharest
Condor	Frankfurt
EasyJet	London (Gatwick), Milan, Berlin, Paris (Charles de Gaulle, Orly), and more
Eurowings	Cologne, Düsseldorf, Hamburg, Vienna, Berlin
Icelandair	Reykjavík
Norwegian	Oslo, London (Gatwick), Helsinki
Pegasus Airlines	Istanbul
Ryanair	London (Stansted), Dublin, and many other European cities
SmartWings	Prague
Transavia	Amsterdam
TUIfly	Berlin, Hannover, Munich
Vueling	Barcelona, Rome
Widerøe	Oslo, Bergen
Wizz Air	Budapest

that goes to Pisa (1.5 hours away by train); remember that many flight-search websites have a "nearby airports" option that broadens your search. Even adding the cost of the train ticket from Pisa to Florence, the total could be well below the price of a long overland journey, not to mention several hours faster.

Booking Cheap Flights Within Europe

Most budget airlines focus on particular hubs. When looking for cheap flights, first check airlines that use either your starting point or your ending point as a hub. For example, for a trip from Budapest to Oslo, I'd look at Wizz Air (with a hub in Budapest) and at Norwegian (which has a hub in Oslo). Be aware that some airlines forego this "hub-and-spoke" model for a less predictable "point-to-point" schedule.

My first stop when seeking budget flights online is

Skyscanner; this straightforward website specializes in European budget airlines and gives an overview of all of my options. Skyscanner also includes major nonbudget carriers.

Several other websites, including the all-purpose **Kayak,** are worth a look. The visually engaging **Momondo** shows which days surrounding your scheduled dates have the cheapest fares; it also includes nearby airports in search results (be clear on which airport it's using).

What's the Catch?

Budget tickets are usually nonrefundable and nonchangeable. Many airlines take only online bookings, so it can be hard to reach a customer service representative if problems arise. (Read all the fine print carefully, so you know what you're getting into.) Flights are often tightly scheduled to squeeze more flying time out of each plane, which can exaggerate the effects of delays. Deadlines are strictly enforced: If they tell you to arrive at the check-in desk an hour before the flight, and you show up with 50 minutes to spare, you've just missed your plane. Also, it's not uncommon for budget carriers to unexpectedly go out of business or cancel a slow-selling route—leaving you scrambling to find an alternative.

Since budget airlines aren't making much money on your ticket, they look for other ways to pad their profits by bombarding you with ads every step of the way (as you book, via email after you've bought your ticket, on board the plane), selling you overpriced food and drinks on board (nothing's included), and gouging you with fees. The initial fare you see on the website can be misleadingly low: Once you begin the purchasing process, each step seems to come with another charge. Extra charges can include reserving a seat, choosing a seat near the front, line skipping and priority boarding privileges, and—of course—checking bags.

Even if the name of your budget airline (such as Wizz Air) doesn't exactly inspire confidence, these carriers can get you to many destinations cheaper and a whole lot faster than the train.

If you plan to check a bag, pay the fee when you purchase your ticket—on many budget airlines, the price per bag gets progressively higher the closer you get to your departure. Be aware that you may have to pay extra for a second carry-on, checking larger or heavier bags, and checking odd-sized bags such

EU Passenger Rights

You don't have to be European to benefit from the EU's consumer-protection laws, which are particularly robust when it comes to air travel. The most important one to know: If your European airline is at fault for a sudden cancellation or significant delay—say, if your plane has a mechanical problem—you're entitled to compensation for hotel and food costs you incurred while in air-travel limbo. Reimbursement depends not only on the length of your delay but on the length of your flight, with an upper limit of €600 per traveler. (Weather-related changes are exempt.)

This law applies to any last-minute change of plans, including being moved to an earlier flight. Both US- and UK-based carriers are bound by this law for any flights departing *from* the EU (the regulations also apply to non-EU members Norway, Iceland, and Switzerland).

Not surprisingly, airlines don't automatically fork over these reimbursements—but gate agents or customer-service reps must inform affected passengers about their rights. And all airlines that serve Europe must list the details on their websites (usually under "passenger rights" or "claims," albeit in fine-print legalese). For details, see Europa.eu/european-union/life/travel-tourism and choose "Passengers Rights."

If you need to seek reimbursement, the websites Refund.me and AirHelp explain what you're entitled to and how to request it. And for a 25 percent commission (plus VAT), these companies will handle the whole process for you.

as baby equipment. Don't assume your bag qualifies as carry-on in Europe; many budget airlines use smaller dimensions than other carriers. To avoid unpleasant surprises, read the baggage policy carefully before you book.

Another potential headache: Budget airlines sometimes use obscure airports. For example, one of Ryanair's London hubs is Stansted Airport, one of the farthest airports from London's city center. Some of Ryanair's flights to "Frankfurt" actually take you to Hahn, 75 miles away. You may even wind up in a different (though nearby) country: For example, a flight advertised as going to Copenhagen, Denmark, might go to Malmö, Sweden, or a flight bound for Vienna, Austria, might land in Bratislava, Slovakia. These are still safe and legal airstrips, but it can take money and time to reach your final destination by public transportation. On the other hand, the money you save often more than pays for the difference.

Finally, and perhaps most importantly, be aware that flying has a big environmental impact. While that's hard to avoid when getting *to* Europe, once you're there, trains are the more environmentally conscious way to go.

Trains, Buses & Boats

In Europe, public transportation works. Over the years, Europeans have invested hugely in their public transit, and it's generally fast and effective. Of course, digging the 35-mile-long Gotthard Tunnel in Switzerland, building a bridge between Denmark and Sweden, and adding bullet trains all cost money, and train travel is not as cheap as it once was. But savvy travelers can still get around on a tight budget.

Europe's commitment to public transportation is not just limited to populated areas—it's nearly everywhere. For example, in Scotland's Highlands—way up north—if the population is too sparse to justify a public bus service, citizens needing to get to a remote farmstead are welcome to ride with the mail delivery person for the cost of a bus ticket. In Europe, I use this rule of thumb: If there are people here and people there, there's a way to get between them by public transit. I can't think of a popular European sight that you can't reach by bus, boat, or train.

Throughout Europe, you may encounter public-health measures intended to stifle a recurrence of the coronavirus among transit riders, such as increased cleaning, mandated mask wearing, and ridership limits (to allow physical distancing). If your plans involve public transportation, check in advance for any restrictions that might affect your travel.

This chapter pays special attention to buying and using rail passes and point-to-point train tickets, figuring out train schedules, and navigating Europe's train stations. Travel by bus and ferry is covered at the end of the chapter; for information on subways, city buses, and taxis, see the Getting Around in Cities chapter. For information on taking flights within Europe, see the Flying chapter.

The Benefits of Train Travel

The European train system shrinks what is already a small continent, making the budget whirlwind or far-reaching tour a reasonable and exciting possibility for anyone. The system works great for locals and travelers alike, with well-signed stations, easily accessed schedules, and efficient connections between popular destinations. First-time train travelers get the hang of it faster than they expect. Generally, European trains go where you need them to go and are fast, frequent, and affordable. Lace this network together to create the trip of your dreams.

For many travelers, the pleasure of journeying along Europe's rails is as good as the destination. As Americans, we're accustomed to being shoehorned into cramped airline seats or enduring long road trips by car. On the train, you can walk around, relax in comparatively wide seats, and enjoy a picnic spread onboard. It's also time-efficient, especially with Europe's ever-growing network of super-fast trains. With night trains, you can eat dinner in Paris, sleep on the train, and awaken for breakfast in Venice. And (with the exception of the Eurostar, which goes under the English Channel and connects London with Paris, Brussels, and Amsterdam) you don't need to show up early. As long as you're on board when the train leaves, you're on time.

When to Choose Train Travel

So how does train travel compare to driving or flying? Though not as flexible as having a rental car, trains can be less stressful. On a train, you can forget about parking hassles, confusing road signs, speed limits, bathroom stops, and Italian drivers. You can watch the scenery instead of the road, and maybe even enjoy a glass of the local wine (for more guidance on choosing between trains and cars, see page 158).

Trains connect big cities, but also small towns—such as Manarola—in Italy's Cinque Terre.

Although flying can save both time and money when making long journeys in Europe, that's not always the case. For instance, taking the Eurostar from London to Paris can be faster than flying when you consider the train zips you directly from downtown to downtown. And if you're focusing on a single country or region and connecting nearby destinations, the train is generally more practical than a flight (and has a smaller environmental impact).

Compared to air travel, both trains and cars keep you close to the scenery, to Europe, and to Europeans. Ground transportation is also less likely to be disrupted by bad weather, mechanical problems, or scheduling delays, and it allows for more spontaneity. If a town looks too cute to miss, just jump off the train (or stop the car).

For me, trains remain the quintessentially European way to go, and the best option for romantics. Driving to the Austrian lakeside hamlet of Hallstatt is easy, but arriving by train is more memorable: Hop off at the hut-sized station across the lake, catch the waiting boat, and watch the town's shingled roofs and church spires grow bigger as the mist lifts off the water.

TRAIN TICKETS AND PASSES

A train traveler's biggest pretrip decision is whether to get a rail pass or stick with point-to-point tickets (or use a mix of both). Many travelers make a costly mistake by skipping over the details of this decision. It pays to know your options and choo-choose what's best for your trip.

Tickets or Passes?

Point-to-point tickets are just that: tickets bought individually to get you from Point A to Point B. It's simple to buy these in train stations as you travel, but they're becoming easier to purchase online (especially handy if you need to secure an advance reservation for a certain train). By contrast, a **rail pass** covers train travel in one or more countries for a certain

Train Travel Tips at RickSteves.com

While this chapter provides a good start in planning your train travel, the Trains & Rail Passes section of my website has even more details and one-stop shopping for rail passes, seat reservations, and point-to-point tickets.

At RickSteves.com/rail you'll find clear, concise advice for figuring out the smartest options for your train trip. Our goal: to create smart consumers (and sell a few rail passes) by providing all the information you need to make the best rail-pass decision for your trip. For each European country I cover, you'll get my frank opinion on which passes are a good value, handy region-specific ticket-price maps, and tips for saving money on point-to-point tickets.

number of days (either a continuous span of days or a number of days spread over a wider window of time). Until recently, rail passes were available only as paper tickets and had to be purchased prior to your trip. But now, many rail passes are available digitally, and you can generally buy them online with little notice. However, I still recommend weighing your options, making a decision, and buying your rail pass before your trip. If you prefer the paper version, allow time for home delivery.

Major Considerations

To figure out whether you want to buy a rail pass, sketch out your itinerary, then answer the following questions:

How many days do you expect to ride the train? If you'll be on the train for just one or two days, you almost certainly won't benefit from a pass. The more time you expect to spend on the train, the more likely you'll want a pass.

How many countries will you be visiting by train? The more countries you plan to visit, the more probable it is that you'll save money with a pass. If you're planning a whirlwind trip around the continent, a Eurail Global Pass is almost certainly the way to go.

Roughly how much would point-to-point tickets cost? You don't have to laboriously look up exact train fares—to get a rough idea of what you'd pay for bigger journeys, scan the "Point-to-Point Train Tickets: Cost & Time" map, later in this chapter. If you're traveling in just one or two countries, you can check the more detailed regional maps at RickSteves.com/cost-maps. Connect the dots and add up the fares to get an approximate cost for your tickets. Don't worry if some destinations aren't shown: Ticket prices are mostly based on distance, so you can estimate fares. For example, if you're going to Italy's Orvieto, about halfway between Florence and Rome, it's safe to assume the train fare to Orvieto from either Florence or Rome is roughly half the total shown for the whole Florence-Rome stretch.

Resources for Trains

Bahn.com: User-friendly, Europe-wide timetable (and source of reservation info)

RailFanEurope.net: Compendium of other national railway websites (click on "Links")

Seat61.com: Rail-travel advice, including route details, ticket-buying help, and particularly useful night-train info

DB Navigator app: Schedules for trains throughout Europe

Rail Planner app: Eurail timetables and mobile rail passes

Reading

Europe by Rail: The Definitive Guide for Independent Travellers (Nicky Gardner and Susanne Kries, 2018): Details on major train routes, from planning and ticketing advice to colorful descriptions

How does your point-to-point ticket cost compare to the price of a pass? Look up the cost of a pass that covers the region you'll be in and the number of days you'll be on the train (see "Choosing Among Passes," later). Several countries, mostly in southern and eastern Europe, have train fares so low that rail passes rarely beat out point-to-point tickets. If you're sticking to moderate distances in Italy, for example, it's unlikely a pass will save you money. If you're traveling in Germany, however, a pass is likely a smart move.

Other Factors

If your price comparison doesn't produce an obvious winner, take a closer look at factors that could tilt your decision, such as:

Sparse Rail Coverage: In some areas, such as southern Spain, coastal Croatia, much of Scotland, and all of Greece and Ireland, rail passes make little sense because trains don't reach many of the places you're planning to go. (To learn whether your destinations are served by train, see the "Looking Up Train Schedules" section, later.)

Pricey Fast-Train Supplements: Passes lose their luster when fees are tacked on. In some countries, pass holders are required to pay extra for each trip on a high-speed train. In Italy, for instance, it costs about an additional $15 per ride for mandatory fast-train reservations on most convenient connections between major cities. On the Thalys train that monopolizes direct service between Paris and Brussels (and Amsterdam), pass holders pay extra fees of up to $35 in second class and $45 in first class (explained in more detail later, under "Seat Reservations").

Advance-Purchase Discounts: If you don't mind forgoing some spontaneity, you'll probably be able to save money with advance-purchase discounts on point-to-point tickets. But what you save in dollars you will lose in flexibility, as these discounts are usually valid only for nonrefundable, nonchangeable reserved tickets.

Convenience: In countries or regions where reservations usually aren't required, a pass allows you to hop on and off trains without buying multiple tickets; if all other things are equal, a pass can make sense for ease of travel.

Point-to-Point Tickets

It's generally easy to buy point-to-point train tickets at European stations. But it can be smart to buy in advance for certain trains and destinations, especially if your dates are

First or Second Class?

First class is plusher and roomier, but second class is where you'll make friends.

Nearly every European train has both first- and second-class cars (and some newer fast trains even have one or two extra rungs of "premier" or "executive" fanciness), all going at precisely the same speed. Yet on most trains in most countries, tickets in second class cost about a third less than those in first class.

Many Americans, familiar with the huge difference between first- and coach-class seating on airplanes, are surprised by how small the difference is on European trains. Second class is plenty comfortable; it's generally a no-brainer for anyone on a budget. It can also be more fun. Many first-class travelers are businesspeople trying to work; you'll have an easier time striking up a conversation in second class. Most Europeans don't travel in first class unless someone else is paying for it.

First class is often less crowded—a significant plus on popular routes at peak times, when it can be hard to find a seat in second class. First class also has wider seats and aisles, and is more likely to have amenities such as air-conditioning and power outlets (though outlets are still fairly rare on Europe's trains, in any class). While first class is less conducive to conversation, it's more conducive to napping.

set and you don't want to risk a specific train journey selling out, or if you're hoping for an advance-purchase discount.

While rail passes offer the ultimate in spontaneity, unreserved point-to-point tickets have some flexibility, since you can make any number of stops and connections along the most direct route between the starting and ending stations printed on your ticket. A trip within a single country usually must be completed within the same calendar day; in Italy, it's within a few hours. For many international point-to-point tickets, you have four days to complete the journey.

Where to Get Train Tickets

You have three main options for buying point-to-point tickets: through a US-based retailer before leaving home (such as RickSteves.com/rail), through the website of one of Europe's national railways, and in person at Europe's train stations

Point-to-Point Train Tickets: Cost & Time

This chart shows the approximate cost of second-class train tickets. Connect the dots for your itinerary, then add up the cost to see which is better for your trip: point-to-point tickets or a rail pass.

The first number between cities is the **cost** for a one-way, second-class ticket. (For first-class fares, add 50 percent.) The second number is the trip duration in **hours**.

The fares shown here are for the fastest trains on a given route. Actual prices may vary (and may be cheaper with advance purchase). For more detailed regional maps, see www.ricksteves.com/cost-maps.

(and at some European travel agencies). For big discounts, buy tickets up to three months ahead (just note that these tickets are nonrefundable and nonchangeable).

US Retailers: You may pay a little more to purchase tickets through a US retailer than if you were to buy those same tickets in person at a European train station—but for a can't-miss train, the extra cost can be worth it for the peace of mind. Rail-pass holders who need tickets and/or seat reservations on certain trains—most notably the Eurostar, Thalys, and any TGV InOui (France's high-speed rail)—are smart to get their tickets through a US-based site, as pass-holder fares can sell out far in advance and aren't available elsewhere online.

National Railway Websites: Many European national rail companies allow customers to buy tickets online at the going European price (usually for faster classes of trains for which reservations are required, or at least recommended). If you're looking for the cheapest ticket between A and B—especially if A and B are in the same country—this is the way to go. Advance tickets can be an especially smart buy for popular high-speed trains (such as France's TGV InOui and Italy's Le Frecce), which frequently sell out.

Not all national-railway sites are created equal. While many are fairly easy to navigate (including the British, French, German, Irish, Italian, Swedish, and Swiss railway sites), some are difficult for foreigners to use (notably the Austrian, Norwegian, and Spanish railway sites; PayPal solves some credit-card difficulties).

Your "ticket" may be a barcode on your phone, an emailed confirmation code redeemable at the station (in the same country that operates the website you bought it on), or a print-at-home document. Online tickets are valid for a specific date and time and have strict refund restrictions, so read the fine print carefully.

In Europe: Once in Europe, you can purchase tickets at the station, usually without much fuss, either on your day of travel or in advance (for tips, see "Buying Tickets at the Station," later). This is the best option if you'd prefer to keep your itinerary more spontaneous. You can even get tickets for trains in another country: For example, if your trip starts in Paris, you can buy your Berlin-Prague ticket at any Parisian train station. Tickets bought at train-station windows tend to be easier to change (or refunded) than tickets bought online.

In some cities you can avoid trekking to the train station by visiting a neighborhood travel agency or branch office of the national railroad. This convenience may come with a fee, but if the agency is easier for you to get to than the train station, it can save lots of time and hassle (and travel agents may have more time and English-language skills than the people behind the train-station counter).

Train Fares and Discounts

European train fares are based primarily on distance traveled. Each country has its own "euros per kilometer" formula, though the type of train also affects the price (slower trains are usually cheaper than faster ones). For faster classes of trains, many European rail companies have moved to dynamic pricing—similar to how airfares work—in which a fare can vary depending on demand, restrictions, and how early you purchase.

The cost-estimate map earlier in this chapter gives a rough idea of regular second-class fares for any given train trip in Europe on short notice. If you're buying point-to-point tickets, be aware of the ways you can qualify for a discount (whether buying through a national-railway website or in person):

Advance purchase (a week to several months in advance) can save you money in many countries (most notably Austria, Britain, Finland, France, Germany, Italy, Spain, and Sweden), especially for faster or longer rides. On-sale dates vary by country, route, and time of year, with most starting two to four months in advance of travel, and six months ahead for Germany and the Eurostar train. In some areas (such as Switzerland and most eastern countries), advance-purchase deals either don't exist or aren't worth the hassle. In most places, tickets for slower regional or medium-speed trains cost the same whether they're bought two months or two minutes before the train leaves.

Round-trip tickets can be cheaper than two one-way tickets in some countries (Britain, Ireland, and Spain; sometimes in combination with advance purchase). In Britain, a "day return" ticket (round-trip in a single day) can be only a little bit more expensive than a single one-way ticket.

Children get ticket discounts in most of Europe (typically about 50 percent off for ages 4-11, sometimes free with an adult). Whether you're traveling with tickets or a rail pass, kids under 4 always travel free on your lap (though if there's an empty seat, feel free to use it).

"Youths" (usually ages 12–25, depending on the country) can buy discount cards in Austria, Belgium, Britain, France, Germany, and Italy.

Do You Speak Rail Pass?

When shopping for a rail pass, you'll likely come across these terms:

Global Pass: The classic "Eurail" pass, letting you travel freely throughout most of continental Europe

Eurail: Brand name under which many, but not all, European rail passes are sold (commonly used as a generic term for any European rail pass)

Continuous pass: Covers train travel for the full duration of the pass

Flexipass: Covers a certain number of train travel days within a specified window of time (for example, any 10 days within a two-month period)

Youth pass: Discounted pass for travelers ages 12-27 (ages 16-25 on BritRail and Swiss passes)

Rail-pass bonuses: Mostly boat and bus trips that are either covered or discounted with a rail pass

Activation: Step required before using your pass for the first time—have it stamped by someone behind a station counter

Reservation: Paid seat assignment (required for pass holders on many faster trains), or **overnight berth** assignment on a night train

Couchette (koo-shet): Night-train bunk bed in a compartment (with a blanket, pillow, clean linen, and up to five compartment mates)

Sleeper: Compartment with more privacy than a *couchette,* with one, two, or three beds

Point-to-point ticket: Covers travel from Point A to Point B (unlike a rail pass, which covers a certain area)

Private train: Any train that isn't run by Europe's national railways. Private operators may accept rail passes or offer a discount to pass holders, but many do not (as outlined in the fine print that comes with a pass)

Seniors can find a few ticket deals, most of which require a discount card purchased in Europe (discounts start between ages 60 and 67; see page 485).

Off-peak travel (such as midday or midweek) can be cheaper than peak-time journeys, mainly in Britain and France.

Rail Passes

For independent travelers armed with a rail pass, Europe is a playground. You can travel virtually anywhere, anytime, often without seat reservations. Just step on the right train, sit in an unreserved seat, and when the uniformed conductor comes, flash your pass. There are exceptions—Europe's high-speed trains often require reservations (as do most international trains and the few remaining overnight trains)—but even then, a rail pass is a joy.

All rail passes work in more or less the same way: Every pass covers a specific geographical area (one or more countries), has a fixed number of travel days, is either good for a continuous block of time ("continuous pass") or selected days in a window of time ("flexipass"), and comes in a choice of first or second class. Most offer discounts for seniors (60+) and youths (12-27, for most passes) and free travel for younger kids with adults (these are ages as of the day the pass is activated in Europe).

Choosing Among Passes

Carefully compare passes to find the best fit for your itinerary and style of travel. The range of options may seem intimidating, but mostly it's a matter of knowing which countries you intend to travel in and for how many days.

Where to? First find the pass that best matches the area in which you'll be traveling. If you're planning on covering a lot of ground by train, you probably want a **Global Pass,** which buys you unlimited travel on public railways in most of Europe. If you've got a whirlwind trip planned, the Global Pass is probably the best way to go, as it generally makes little sense to cobble together several single-country passes.

A few **multicountry regional passes,** available for Scandinavia and parts of eastern Europe, can be cheaper than a Global Pass if one of them happens to fit your plans.

Virtually every country has its own **single-country pass.** The relative value of a single-country pass over individual tickets really varies across Europe, so price it out before buying one. But remember to factor in convenience; rail passes can save some hassle in countries where seat reservations usually aren't required. Also consider the unique bonuses offered by certain passes, such as Switzerland's (which covers much more than just trains) and Germany's (which also covers a few international routes).

Flexipass or continuous? Decide which type of pass works best for your trip (but note that the continuous option isn't available in all destinations).

A **flexipass** lets you pay only for the days on which you actually travel. You don't have to decide beforehand which days you'll travel on, but you do have a certain window in which you must use up your train days (for most passes, that's either one or two months after you start using the pass). You can take as many trips as you like within each travel day, which runs from midnight to midnight (though most direct overnight rides can count as only one travel day).

A **continuous pass** can save you money if you plan to travel nearly daily and cover a lot of ground (whereas a flexipass is likely better if you plan to linger for a few days at most destinations). So if you have a 15-day continuous pass, you can ride the trains as many times as you like for 15 days. Only some passes offer the continuous option, including Global, BritRail, German, and Swiss passes.

Passes that span a certain number of months last through the date of the start day, minus one. So if you start a month-long pass on May 12, it'll be good through midnight of June 11 (31 days). If you set off with a one-month pass on February 15, it's good through March 14 (28 days).

For those with open-ended plans, continuous passes can provide extra flexibility. Let's say you're planning a three-week trip and choosing between two versions of a Global Pass: a three-week continuous pass and a cheaper 10-days-in-two-months flexipass. For not much more money, the continuous pass gives you the freedom to take any train without calculating whether a particular trip justifies the use of a travel day.

Getting the Most Out of a Rail Pass

Many people spend more on their rail pass than they have to. Consider the following tips before purchasing one:

Stretch a flexipass by paying out of pocket for shorter trips. If you plan to ride the train on, say, eight different days, but two of those days have very short trips, you may save money by getting a six-day pass and buying point-to-point tickets for your short-haul days. Use your flexipass only for those travel days that involve long hauls or several trips. To determine whether a trip is a good use of a travel day, divide the cost of your pass by the number of travel days (or look at what it costs to add a day onto the pass's base price). If the pass you're considering costs about $60 per travel day, it makes no sense to use one of your days for a trip that would otherwise cost $10.

One rail pass is usually better than two. To cover a multicountry trip, it's almost always cheaper to buy one Global Pass with lots of travel days than to buy several one-country passes with a few high-cost travel days per pass. If you travel over a border using separate rail passes, you'll use up a day of each pass.

Understand bonuses. Some rail passes include bonuses, such as free or discounted boat, bus, or high-mountain rides within that country (examples of bonuses include some Swiss lake boats and Italy-Greece ferry crossings). A bonus trip is no different from a train trip: To use your flexipass to cover the cost of a bonus boat or bus, you must have filled in that day's date as a travel day on your pass. Trips offered only at a discount (rather than those that are completely covered by the pass) usually don't cost you a flexipass travel day, but you must use the discount within your pass's validity period.

With careful juggling, a shorter pass can cover a longer trip. For a one-month trip, you don't necessarily need a one-month pass. You may be able to get by with a three-week continuous pass by starting and/or ending your trip in a city where you'd like to stay for several days or in a country not covered by your pass.

It can make sense to buy a longer pass for a shorter trip. One long, expensive train ride at the end of a 25-day trip can justify jumping from a three-week continuous rail pass to a one-month pass (though I'd also consider doing that long leg by plane).

Using Your Rail Pass

Rail passes are straightforward but come with a lot of fine print (worth reading). It's important to understand at least the basics before your first day of train travel.

Activate your pass before your first use. In order for your rail pass to be valid for train travel, you must activate it by providing passport information and a travel start date. (Swiss passes and a few special offers come preactivated—if

Sample Rail Pass

BritRail

BRITRAIL FLEXI PASS

CIV No. 128872030*A

	R CHI R
E	28 Feb 2019 E
I	Issuing Stamp I

Valid: 3 Days within 1 Month   Standard Class Adult

First
Day   Day Month Year

Last
Day   Day Month Year
         1   2   3
Day: I __ I __ I __ I
Mth: I __ I __ I __ I
Only valid with your passport. Please see conditions of use.

Name: **MR GENE OPENSHAW**
Country of Residence: United States
Passport #: _____
Signature: _____

MUST BE VALIDATED
BEFORE 31 Jan 2020

Validating Stamp

USD $180

Don't write anything on your rail pass before it's activated. When you're ready to use it, the ticket agent will fill in validity dates and your passport number, and stamp the activation box on the far right. Each day when you take your seat on the train, write down the date in ink (day first, then month) before the conductor comes around.

your pass has a specific travel period printed on it, skip this step.) Your pass comes with an issue date (usually the day you bought it) and in most cases must be activated within 11 months. For example, if the issue date is May 24, 2022, you must start the pass by April 23, 2023. A few passes must be activated within six months of the issue date—check the fine print before purchasing.

Activation is easy. If using a mobile pass, activate it via the Rail Planner mobile app: Add your pass to the app, connect it to your trip, then activate the pass. If you have a paper pass, you'll activate it in person with a ticket agent at a European train station. The ticket agent (not you) writes in your passport number, and the first and last dates of your travel period, and stamps the activation box on the far right. Never write anything on your rail pass before it's been activated.

Agents will assume that you intend to use the pass on the same day you present it, so if you're activating it a few days beforehand, write your desired dates (European style, e.g., 15/05/22 - 14/06/22) on a slip of paper to show the agent before handing over the pass. All train trips and nontrain bonuses (covered or discounted boats, buses, and high-mountain rides) must be started and finished within the valid life of your rail pass.

You may activate your rail pass before arriving in the (first) country it covers. Let's say you're in Copenhagen with a German rail pass, you're heading to Berlin, and you want the German portion of your route to be covered by your rail pass. At the Copenhagen train station, buy a ticket to the German border and have the agent activate your rail pass at the same time.

Don't get caught with a pass that hasn't been activated: If you forget to do it before boarding, approach the conductor right away to activate it on board (you may be charged a fee of $5-30).

Enter travel days (for flexipasses) and trip details. With a continuous rail pass, you can travel as many days as you want during the validated period, and you don't need to record anything. But if you're using a flexipass, you must enter your travel days as you go. On your paper flexipass, you'll see a string of blank boxes, one for each travel day available to you. Either just before or after boarding, fill in that day's date in ink in one of the blank boxes on your pass before the conductor reaches you. (Don't fill out any dates in advance, in case your plans change.) Before boarding a train with a mobile pass, you'll need to add the specific journey you're taking in the Rail Planner app (which has a train schedule search function). The app generates a barcode that the ticket inspector will scan (not the same as a seat reservation).

A travel day is a calendar day, running from midnight to midnight. You can take as many trips as you like within each travel day. A nice bonus is that a direct overnight train uses only one travel day (not two) on a flexipass. You'll fill in your departure date as your travel day; assuming the pass's longer validity window hasn't expired, you're covered until you get off that train the next day. Most paper passes also require you to fill in your trip destinations on the foldout sheets of your pass cover.

Show your pass if asked. After the train starts, the ticket inspector heads down the aisle, asking for tickets and passes, and checking that they are dated correctly. You may be asked to present your passport, too.

Plan ahead for groups. If you have a paper group pass (such as a "twin" pass for Germany, a "saver" pass for Britain, or kids traveling for free with an adult), all group members must be present when the rail pass is activated at the train station. This document cannot be divided into parts. On the other hand, a family traveling with individual mobile passes can load them all onto one mobile device, but cannot later transfer them to a different device.

Keep your pass safe. Your rail pass is valuable, so guard it carefully. Even if you bought a protection plan when you got your pass, a lost or stolen pass presents a logistical headache. Store paper rail passes in a money belt. If you lose a mobile phone that contains an electronic pass, you can replace it by filling out some paperwork (but you may have to pay out of pocket for tickets until the issue is resolved).

Looking Up Train Schedules

Online timetables are generally user-friendly, making it easy to find the fastest connections, and to see the frequency and length of any train trip (and whether reservations are required). Schedules can also be important for basic itinerary planning, as they tell you which train routes are even possible.

No matter where you're traveling in Europe, Germany's

Deutsche Bahn website (www.bahn.com) should be your
first stop for timetable information. (While each country's
national rail company has its own website with schedules,
the German site has schedules for virtually all of Europe.) I
use this site, along with their DB Navigator app, to plan my
connections for almost every trip in Europe. The Rail Planner
app (for mobile Eurail Passes) uses the same technology.

Finding Schedules on the Deutsche Bahn Site

The German railway's online schedule is an invaluable tool
for any European train traveler. Here's how to use it:

1. Start with a station-to-station search. Enter just the
city name, unless you know the name of the specific station
you want. Since many cities have several stations, you'll then
need to specify one from the drop-down menu. To avoid
accidentally selecting a bus stop instead of the train station,
select the option with just the city name (if available). Main
stations are often called "central," "terminus," or "Hbf" (for
Hauptbahnhof); you can also try re-entering your destination
with "main station" after the city's name. If the city's name
spelled in capital letters is among the options, select it (the
site will look up the best connections for that city, regardless
of the station).

2. Enter the date and time. Make your best guess about
when you might travel (using the 24-hour clock). Don't
worry about the exact date and time of your train trips,
as schedules for most trains don't vary much (except for
Sundays and holidays, when trains are less frequent). Though
many schedules aren't available more than three months
out, you can still get a good idea of trip length and frequency
by trying a closer date on the same day of the week you'll be
traveling.

3. Skip the extra search fields. If you're just looking
up schedules, there's no need to fill in any fields beyond the
stations, date, and time—just skip right to "Search." (If you're
then prompted to select from a drop-down list of stations,
see #1, above.)

4. Review your options. The results will show a few
possibilities for your journey; use the "Earlier" and "Later"
buttons to see more. Each result shows the start and end
points (with stations specified), departure and arrival times,
trip duration, number of changes, and train category (usually
indicated by an acronym). Results may show local names for
cities (for example, "Praha" instead of "Prague").

A circled "R" indicates that the train requires a

City Name Variations

English Name	European Name
Athens, Greece	Athina (Greek), Athenes (German)
Basel, Switzerland	Bâle (French)
Bolzano, Italy	Bozen (German)
Bratislava, Slovakia	Pressburg (German), Pozsony (Hungarian)
Basel, Switzerland	Bâle (French)
Brussels, Belgium	Bruxelles (French)
Carlsbad, Czech Republic	Karlovy Vary (Czech), Karlsbad (German)
Cologne, Germany	Köln or Koeln
Copenhagen, Denmark	København
Cracow, Poland	Kraków
Dubrovnik, Croatia	Ragusa (Italian and German)
Florence, Italy	Firenze
Gdańsk, Poland	Danzig (German)
Geneva, Switzerland	Genève (French), Genf (German)
Genoa, Italy	Genova
Gothenburg, Sweden	Göteborg
The Hague, Netherlands	Den Haag, 'S Gravenhage
Helsinki, Finland	Helsingfors (Swedish)
Liège, Belgium	Luik (Flemish/Dutch), Lüttich (German)
Lisbon, Portugal	Lisboa
London, England	Londres (French)
Lucerne, Switzerland	Luzern (German), Lucerna (Italian)
Milan, Italy	Milano (Italian), Mailand (German)
Munich, Germany	München or Muenchen (German), Monaco di Baviera (Italian)
Naples, Italy	Napoli (Italian), Neapel (German)
Nice, France	Nizza (Italian)
Nuremberg, Germany	Nürnberg or Nuernberg
Padua, Italy	Padova
Pamplona, Spain	Iruña (Euskara)
Paris, France	Parigi (Italian)
Prague, Czech Republic	Praha
Rome, Italy	Roma
San Sebastián, Spain	Donostia (Euskara)
Tralee, Ireland	Trá Lí
Venice, Italy	Venezia (Italian), Venedig (German)
Vienna, Austria	Wien (German), Bécs (Hungarian), Dunaj (Slovene), Vídeň (Czech), Viedeň (Slovak)
Warsaw, Poland	Warszawa (Polish), Warschau (German)

reservation. Note that Italy's fastest classes of trains may not display the circled "R" but do require seat reservations; these are labeled as "IC," "EC," "FR," "FA," or "FB."

5. Know where to find more details. Clicking "show details" for a journey will give you more information, including transfer points. Select "show intermediate stops" to see every stop on your route or the train number to see the entire route, including stops before and/or after your stations.

The Deutsche Bahn site generally only displays fares and sells tickets for trains that touch Germany, Austria, or Switzerland. For full-fare estimates for other countries, use the cost-estimate map earlier in this chapter. You can also check exact ticket prices on each country's own national railway site, but I wouldn't bother unless you're looking for advance-purchase discounts.

If you can't find your destination on the Deutsche Bahn site, it likely doesn't have train service. But before giving up—especially for train travel in Spain and Italy—double-check their national railway sites.

For even more tips on using the Deutsche Bahn website, head to RickSteves.com/schedules.

Seat Reservations

Some trains require all passengers to have reservations (which guarantee you a specific seat), and sometimes it's smart to reserve even when it's not compulsory. But most trains don't require reservations, and the vast majority usually have more than enough seating—so don't make the mistake of over-reserving. Many American travelers waste money and surrender their flexibility after being swayed by US-based agents who profit from exaggerating the need for reservations.

Do I Need Reservations?

Your best resource for identifying trains that truly require a reservation is the Deutsche Bahn's online schedule—it's objective, complete, and easy to use.

Though relatively few train types require reservations, those that do are among the most popular. They include a few privately run international trains, such as the Eurostar, the Brussels-based Thalys, and a handful of special just-for-tourists trains (such as several of Switzerland's specially designated scenic trains).

Aside from these, many countries have at least one category of high-speed train that always requires

Key Train Vocabulary

English	French	Italian	German	Spanish
train	*train*	*treno*	*Zug*	*tren*
ticket	*billet*	*biglietto*	*Fahrkarte*	*billete*
station	*gare*	*stazione*	*Bahnhof*	*estación*
main station	*gare centrale*	*stazione centrale*	*Hauptbahnhof*	*estación principal*
platform/track	*quai/voie*	*binario*	*Bahnsteig/Gleis*	*andén/vía*
timetable	*horaire*	*orario*	*Fahrplan*	*horario*
supplement	*supplément*	*supplemento*	*Zuschlag*	*suplemento*
delay	*retard*	*ritardare*	*Verspätung*	*retraso*
strike	*grève*	*sciopero*	*Streik*	*huelga*
reservation	*réservation*	*prenotazione*	*Reservierung*	*reserva*
car	*voiture*	*wagone*	*Wagen*	*vagón, coche*
seat	*place*	*posto*	*Platz, Sitzplatz*	*plaza, asiento*
berth/couchette	*couchette*	*cuccetta*	*Liegeplatz*	*litera*
validate	*valider*	*convalidare*	*entwerten*	*validar*
stamp	*composter*	*timbrare*	*abstempeln*	*estampar*

reservations—most notably France, Italy, Spain, and Sweden. Some countries have a few long-distance (though not necessarily high-speed) routes that must be reserved. And you'll need to book ahead (or at least pay a little extra) for a spot on nearly all overnight trains.

In many cases, required reservations aren't so much a matter of space constrictions, but a surcharge for the privilege of riding the fastest (or fanciest) train. But on certain routes where all passengers must have an assigned seat, spots can sell out quickly (see "How Far Ahead?" later).

Reservations can sometimes be a good idea on trains that don't require them. For example, it's wise to reserve at least several days ahead if you're traveling during a peak time (summer, weekends, holidays), on a route with infrequent service, if you need several seats together (families with small children), or for a train you simply cannot afford to miss.

Otherwise, I wouldn't recommend reserving a seat if you don't have to; slower regional trains don't even give you the option. Most of the time, trains have plenty of seating for everyone, and even if you wind up on a crowded train, the worst-case scenario is that you'll stand a while before a seat frees up.

Typical Train Ticket

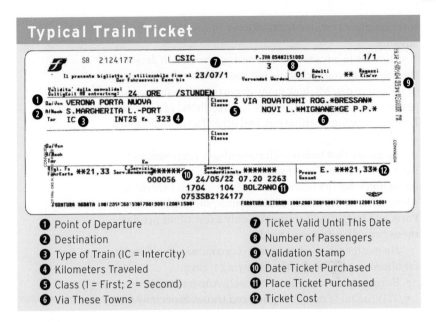

1 Point of Departure
2 Destination
3 Type of Train (IC = Intercity)
4 Kilometers Traveled
5 Class (1 = First; 2 = Second)
6 Via These Towns
7 Ticket Valid Until This Date
8 Number of Passengers
9 Validation Stamp
10 Date Ticket Purchased
11 Place Ticket Purchased
12 Ticket Cost

How to Reserve

For trains that don't need to be booked very far in advance, it's best to simply make all your reservations at one time at any staffed station in Europe.

If you need to lock in a key reservation before your trip, book it ahead of time from home through a US-based retailer (such as www.ricksteves.com/rail).

If you're using a rail pass to cover your train travel, seat reservations cost extra (except in Britain, where they're free for BritRail pass holders). The fee is typically between $5 and $35, with a few more-expensive exceptions. Some reservations are available as e-tickets (from websites or within Eurail's Rail Planner mobile app), while others are issued as paper tickets.

With point-to-point tickets, the ticket price includes the cost of any mandatory reservations (dates, times, and seat assignments are built in, just like with most airline tickets). If you opt to reserve a seat on a train that doesn't require reservations, you'll need to pay a small extra fee.

For more information on pass holder reservation fees for popular trains, check the country-specific rail pages at www.ricksteves.com/rail.

How Far Ahead?

Whether you're traveling with a rail pass or buying tickets as you go, you can purchase seat (or overnight berth) reservations anywhere from an hour to several months in advance.

How far in advance to reserve any given train depends on the rigidity of your schedule (do you have hotel reservations or a flight to catch?), how many departures in a day could get you there on time (2 or 20?), the likelihood of seats (or at least reservations) selling out, and other factors mentioned above.

Be aware that trains with compulsory reservations may have a limited number of seats available to pass holders (most notoriously France's fastest international services). Along some of the most popular routes, such as between Paris and Italy, direct trains run only a few times per day; these can sell out weeks ahead.

No matter when you're going, I recommend booking as far ahead as possible for the following trains:

- Eurostar (London-Paris/Brussels/Amsterdam)
- TGV InOui (France's high-speed trains, especially international routes)
- Thello (direct trains between Paris and Italy)
- Thalys (high-speed Brussels-based trains)
- Nightjet (international Austria-based night trains, including the popular Munich-Venice route)

TRAIN STATIONS

Great European train stations stir my wanderlust. Stepping off a train in Munich, I stand under the station's towering steel and glass rooftop and study the departure screen. Every few minutes, the letters and numbers flicker as cities and departure times work their way to the top, only to disappear one by one as another train glides away from its platform.

Surrounded by Germany on the move, I notice businessmen in tight neckties, giddy teenage girls, and a

Whether old or new, bustling European train stations are temples of travel. Just pick a platform...and explore Europe.

Karl-Marx-like bum leaning on a *Bierstube* counter. The fast and the slow, the young and the old, we're all in this together—working our way up life's departure board.

There's plenty of romance here, but the hustle and bustle at train stations can also be confusing. Here are some tips on navigating Europe's temples of transportation.

Buying Tickets at the Station

Nearly every station has at least a few old-fashioned ticket windows staffed by human beings, usually marked by long lines; avoid them by using ticket machines, which almost always offer instructions in English.

Be aware that some ticket machines won't take American credit cards (even if they claim to), or accept them only if you key in your card's PIN. If the machines won't cooperate with your card, try cash (most machines are labeled according to the kind of payment they accept), or head for the ticket window.

If you use a ticket window, find the appropriate line—larger stations may have different windows for domestic, international, sleeper cars, or immediate departures. When buying tickets, you can most clearly communicate your intentions by writing what you need and showing it to the ticket agent: destination, date, time, how many people, and first or second class.

It's often possible to buy tickets aboard the train, but expect to pay an additional fee. Be sure that you have enough cash in case the conductor can't process your credit card. If you're buying on board, find the conductor before the conductor finds you; otherwise, your fee could turn into a much heftier fine for traveling without a valid ticket. Be aware that

LEFT Savvy travelers save time by using ticket machines: Choose English, then follow the instructions.

RIGHT Bridge communication gaps by writing out your plan: departure and destination, date, time (if you want a reservation and/or a printout of your departure options), how many people, first or second class.

on most local trains (especially commuter lines), all trains in Switzerland, and many others around Europe, you can be fined for traveling without a ticket—or for not validating your local ticket on the station platform before boarding—no matter what the circumstances are. Look for warning signs on train doors and platforms.

Schedule Information

Even if you've looked up train schedules in advance, always confirm your plans at the station. Every station has some kind of schedule information available, whether it's posted in printed or electronic form, or at information counters staffed by people eager (or at least able) to help you. All European timetables use the 24-hour clock.

Learning to decipher printed schedules makes life easier on Europe's rails. Posters list all trains that arrive at and depart from a particular station each day. This information is clearly shown in two separate listings: Departures are usually in yellow, and arrivals in white. In some stations, you'll find free schedule booklets listing all their daily departures.

Familiarize yourself with the symbols in schedules that indicate exceptions: Crossed hammers, for instance, mean the train goes only on workdays (daily except Sundays and holidays); a cross signifies that it runs only on Sundays and holidays. Most other symbols are easy enough to guess—for instance, a little bed means the train has sleeping compartments, and crossed silverware indicates a dining car.

Many stations also have big boards that list the next several departures. These often befuddle travelers who don't realize that all over the world, the same five easy-to-identify columns are listed: destination, major stops along the way, type of train, track number, and departure time. I don't care

LEFT Posted train schedules show departure times, destinations, arrival times, and track numbers.

RIGHT In Munich's train station, easy-to-read electronic boards list departures and arrivals. Railroad staff is standing by to answer questions.

what language they're in; without much effort you can easily guess which column is which.

Stations may also have self-service kiosks—many of which are ticket machines—where you can look up schedule information. These computers are almost always multilingual and can be real time-savers. Use them to understand all your options. Many even print out a schedule tailored to your trip.

Of course, your best authority is the person at the train station information window. Staff in uniforms on platforms and on board the trains can also help.

Other Services

Besides offering travel-related services, most stations are great places to take care of your basic to-do list, with ATMs, grocery stores (usually with longer hours than you'll find in the town center), restaurants, bike-rental kiosks, and in many bigger stations, full-fledged shopping malls.

Baggage Check: Most major stations have storage lockers where, for about $5 a day, you can leave your bags. People traveling light can fit two bags into one locker, cutting their storage costs in half. Some security-conscious train stations have removed lockers; in this case travelers can check bags at a luggage-deposit desk—often after going through an airport-type security check. You'll pay about $10-15 per bag. Lock your bag and don't leave valuables inside—both for your own security and because some luggage desks won't accept unlocked bags. They may not take laptops, so be prepared to haul yours. Allow plenty of time to retrieve your bag before boarding your train. Bag-check desks come with lines, can close for lunch in smaller stations, and usually aren't open all night—confirm opening and closing times before storing your bag.

If the station doesn't offer a place to leave your bag, look into services offering luggage storage nearby. Companies like Stasher.com, RadicalStorage.com, NannyBag.com, and LuggageHero.com partner with hotels, hostels, and other businesses where you can stow your stuff (often bookable with your phone and about half the cost of left-luggage services inside stations). Failing that, head to a nearby tourist information office, hotel, or gift shop: Ask nicely (consider offering a small fee), and you'll likely find someone willing to keep an eye on your things for a few hours.

Wi-Fi: You'll find Wi-Fi hotspots at major train stations throughout most of Europe, sometimes for a fee. Wi-Fi is typically free in the first-class lounge. Finding Wi-Fi onboard is more serendipitous than reliable, with the exception of high-speed trains on some common business routes.

Tourist Information: Many stations have a tourist information office either in the station or very nearby. Pick up a map, find out about local transit, and double-check the hours of your

must-see sights (for more on these offices, see page 315).

Waiting Rooms: Most stations have comfortable waiting rooms, and travelers with fancy tickets often enjoy fancy business or VIP lounges. But before you spend time between trains idling in one of these rooms, take advantage of the station's services (look up schedules for the next leg of your trip, get groceries) or explore the area around the station. You may well find yourself within a short walk of something really cool. For example, if you're changing trains in Cologne, even on a tight schedule you can easily pop outside for a jaw-dropping look at its cathedral, just across the square. Waiting rooms can be decent last-ditch sleeping options (but guard your valuables).

Transit Connections: Train stations are also major transit hubs, so connections from train to bus, subway, or tram are often as simple as crossing the street. If an airport is nearby, you'll find airport-train or transit services (usually well marked) at the train station.

Buses connect from the station to nearby towns that lack train service. If you have a bus to catch, be quick, since many are intended for commuters and are scheduled to connect with the train and leave promptly.

Getting on the (Right) Train

For many Americans, Europe presents their first experience with a bustling train station, and the task of navigating the system and finding the right train can sound daunting. But anyone who's managed to find their way in a sprawling American airport will find Europe's train stations a snap. As you head for your train, ticket or pass in hand, keep these pointers in mind.

Get to the right station. Many cities have more than one train station: Paris has six, Brussels has three, and

Train stations often have good, long-hours grocery stores. This one in Vienna is open every day, from 5:30 a.m. until 11:00 p.m.

The train on track 5 will stop at Olten, Bern, Thun, and Spiez en route to Interlaken's East Station. But it's two hours late *(später)*.

even Switzerland's little Interlaken has two. Be sure you know whether your train is leaving from Interlaken East or Interlaken West, even if that means asking what might seem like a stupid question.

Find your track. A few countries publish track numbers in their train schedules, but in most places you'll need to look for platform information once you get to the station. Upcoming departures are displayed on large boards; the specific track and/or platform is usually posted about a half-hour before the train departs.

Ask for help. I always ask someone on the platform if the train is going where I think it is. Uniformed train personnel can answer any question you can communicate. Speak slowly, clearly, and with caveman simplicity. Resist the urge to ask, "Pardon me, would you be able to tell me if this train is going to Rome?" Just point to the train or track and say, "Roma?"

Be observant. If the loudspeaker comes on while you're waiting for your train at track 7, gauge by the reaction of those around you whether the announcement affects you. If everyone dashes over to track 15, assume your train is no longer leaving from track 7, and follow the pack.

Allow sufficient time to navigate the station. Stations are generally laid out logically, with numbered tracks lined up in a row. But the biggest stations are so extensive they can take time to navigate. Some large stations have entirely separate sections for local and long-distance trains. For example, Madrid's Atocha station is divided into sections for *cercanías* (local trains) and AVE (high-speed, long-distance trains). A Paris train station might have some tracks devoted to Grandes Lignes ("grand lines" to other cities), and others for Transilien (local milk-run trains). At the Frankfurt airport, regional trains depart from the *Regionalbahnhof,* while long-distance trains use the *Fernbahnhof.* Many large stations also have vast sections devoted to subway trains or regional buses.

Be on guard for pickpockets. With travelers already distracted by announcements and luggage, a busy train station is an ideal work environment for thieves. Keep your valuables zipped up in your money belt, have your bags in hand, and be very wary of "helpful" locals hanging around ticket machines. For more tips, see the Theft & Scams chapter.

Train cars are usually labeled. This nonsmoking second-class car has video surveillance and room for wheelchairs but not bikes. The eye (top left) means you'll be fined if a ticket patroller catches you without a valid ticket or pass.

Where required, validate your ticket and/or seat reservation before boarding. In France and Italy, many point-to-point tickets and seat reservations printed on special ticket paper aren't valid until you've date-stamped them by inserting them into a machine near the platform. (Tickets printed at home and electronic tickets don't need validating.) If you have multiple parts to your ticket (for example, a ticket and a reservation), each one must be validated. Watch (or ask) others, and imitate—but don't assume that you can skip this step just because others have, as locals with commuter passes don't need to date-stamp them.

If you have a paper rail pass, you need to activate it in person at a ticket window before using it for the first time. If you have a flexipass, you must fill in your travel date before boarding the first train of the day (for details, see "Using Your Rail Pass," earlier).

Expect no-hassle boarding. For the majority of Europe's trains, you stroll (or dash) right to your boarding platform, ticket or pass in hand, without any check-in formalities.

There are a few exceptions where you will encounter pre-boarding security or ticket checks (and should plan to arrive early). The Eurostar, for example, has check-in deadlines (30-45 minutes before departure) and an airline-style security procedure. In Spain your tickets will be checked and luggage scanned before you access the platform to board fast AVE trains. Big-city stations in France and Italy are beginning to

Know Where to Stand

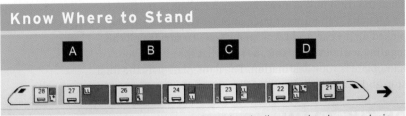

For some high-speed or long-distance trains, a handy diagram showing your train configuration can help you decide where to stand while waiting to board. (The letters indicate the platform section at which each car will arrive.) Understanding this can make the difference between snagging a great seat...or scrambling for what's left.

allow only ticketholders in the platform area. Many stations in Britain require you to slide your paper ticket or tap your barcode on a turnstile reader to enter and exit boarding areas (if you're traveling with a rail pass, just show it to the attendants at these gates), and train doors close 30 seconds before departure. If traveling in the Netherlands, you must tap OV-chipkaart and TripKey cards at the reader when entering and exiting the station. And across Europe, some night trains conductors check tickets at the doors to each car.

Scope out the train ahead of time. Display cases on platforms sometimes show the configuration of major trains. As you wait, study the display to note where the first-class, second-class, restaurant, and sleeping cars are, and which cars are going where. First-class cars are always marked with a big "1" on the outside, second-class cars with a "2." Some train schedules will say, in the fine print, "Munich-bound cars in the front, Vienna-bound cars in the rear." Knowing which cars you're eligible for can be especially handy if you'll be competing with a mob for a seat.

If your train is at the start of its run, it may already be waiting at the platform, in which case you can open the door and board early. If not, and I'm expecting a real scramble for seats, I stand on a bench at the far end of the track and study each car as the train rolls by, looking in the windows to note where the empty places are. If there are several departures within an hour and the first train looks hopeless, I'll wait for the next.

Never assume the entire train is going where you are. For long hauls, pay attention to each car's label, as trains usually add and drop cars along the journey. I'll never forget one hot afternoon in the center of Spain. My train stopped in the middle of nowhere. There was some mechanical rattling.

Then the train pulled away, leaving me alone in my car—in La Mancha. Ten minutes later, another train came along, picked up my car, and I was on my way. To survive all this juggling without any panic, be sure that the city on your car's nameplate is your destination. The nameplate lists the final stop and some (but not all) of the stops in between.

ON THE TRAIN

Once you're on board, it's time to sit back and enjoy the journey.

Find a seat. If you have a seat assignment, locate it and settle in. If you're traveling without a seat reservation, you can claim any unreserved seat. If these are in short supply, take a closer look at the reservation tags posted above the seats or on compartment doors. Each tag shows which stretch of the journey that seat is reserved for. You may well be getting off the train before the seat owner even boards. For example, if you're headed from Luzern to Lugano, and you see a seat that's only reserved from Lugano to Milan, it's all yours.

Stow your luggage. In more than 30 years of train travel, I've never checked a bag. Simply carry it on and heave it up onto the rack above the seat or wedge it into the triangular space between back-to-back seats. I've seen Turkish families moving all their worldly goods from Germany back to Turkey without checking a thing. People complain about the porters in European train stations. I think they're great—I've never used one.

Be savvy with your bags. I assume every train has a thief planning to grab a bag. Store your luggage within sight, rather than at the far end of the train car. Before leaving my luggage in a compartment, I establish a relationship with everyone there. I'm safe leaving it among mutual guards. I don't lock my bag, but to be safe, I often clip my rucksack straps to the luggage rack. When thieves make their move in the darkness of a train tunnel, and the bag doesn't give, they're not going to ask, "*Scusi*, how is your luggage attached?"

Use train time wisely. The time you spend on long train rides can be an opportunity to get organized or make plans for your next destination. Read ahead in your guidebook, write journal entries, curate your photos, double-check your connection information with the conductor, organize your daypack, or update your trip's blog. If the train has power

Strikes

Some travelers worry about getting stranded because of a strike. But in general, they're nothing to stress about.

Strikes can affect rail service anywhere in Europe (especially in France and Italy). They're usually announced long in advance in stations and online. Most last a day, or even just several hours. Anticipate strikes—ask your hotelier, talk to locals, look for signs, check online—but don't feel bullied by them. In theory, train service shuts down (with anywhere from 20 to 80 percent of trains affected), but in reality, at least some "essential service" is preserved.

If a strike occurs on your travel day, check the national railway website—special strike schedules are generally posted. Otherwise, head to the station, where the few remaining station personnel can tell you the expected schedule. You'll likely find a workable train or bus to your destination, though it may leave earlier or later than normally scheduled. If your train is cancelled, your reserved-seat ticket will likely be accepted on any similar train running that day (but you won't have a seat assignment), and should be exchangeable without penalty ahead of the departure time; otherwise, it can be refunded (have an agent mark it "unused," and check refund deadlines). A rail pass works on any train operating, but partially used rail passes can't be refunded—so make full use of any pass you have to continue your trip.

Know the local word for "strike": *sciopero* (Italian), *grève* (French), *apergia* (Greek), and so on. They're a nuisance but, in many countries, a normal part of life.

For the Back Door traveler, strikes can be a cultural experience. On one visit to Marseille, I was surrounded by thousands of strikers marching through the streets. It was a festive occasion. The museums were closed, so I explored the markets and observed strikers, including parents with children on their shoulders, learning firsthand what labor action is all about.

outlets (rare but becoming more common), charge your gadgets. Don't, however, get so immersed in chores that you forget to keep an eye out the window for beautiful scenery around the next bend.

Use WCs—they're free. To save time and money, use the toilets on the train rather than those in the station (which can cost money and are often less clean). Toilets on first-class cars are a cut above second-class toilets. I "go" first class even with a second-class ticket. Train toilets are located on the ends of cars, where it's most jiggly. A trip to the train's john always reminds me of the rodeo. Some toilets empty directly on the tracks, so never use a train's WC while stopped in a station (unless you didn't like that particular town). A train's WC cleanliness deteriorates as the journey progresses.

Follow local train etiquette. Pay attention to the noise level in your car. If everyone else is speaking in hushed tones, follow suit. Watch for signs indicating that you're sitting in a designated quiet car, where businesspeople come to work and others to nap. No matter where

I'm sitting, I make an effort not to be the loudest person in earshot (easily done on the average Italian train, but takes extra awareness in, say, Germany). Don't rest your feet on the seat across from you without taking off your shoes.

Talk to locals or other travelers. There is so much to be learned. Europeans are often less open and forward than Americans. You could sit across from a silent but fascinating and friendly European for an entire train ride, or you could break the ice by asking a question, quietly offering some candy, or showing photos of your family. This can start the conversation flowing and a friendship growing.

Pack a picnic. For the best dining value and variety, stock up at a local deli, bakery, supermarket, or wine cellar before you board; most train stations offer at least one of these. Food sold on the train costs more, with options ranging from a basic coffee and sandwich cart to a more extensive bar car or sit-down dining car (noted on most schedules when available). A few trains offer a "complimentary" meal, in first class only, usually covered by a higher seat-reservation fee.

Strategize your arrival. Use your guidebook to study up on your destination city while you're still on board—it's far more time-efficient and less overwhelming to arrive in a station already knowing how to reach the city center (or your hotel). If you're trying to make a tight connection, it's good to know from which platform your next train leaves. If you don't already have that information, flag down a conductor, who either knows the answer or can find it out for you.

As you approach your destination, have a game plan ready for when you get off the train. Know what you need to accomplish in the station before heading out—e.g., looking up the schedule (and perhaps making seat reservations) for the next leg of your train trip, picking up a map from a trackside information office, hitting an ATM, buying a transit pass, or

Europe's trains are so fast, they pull into stations with squashed birds on their windshields. You'd wait all your life to see a bird squashed onto the windshield of a train back home. I guess with Europe's impressive transportation infrastructure, "DB" stands for "dead bird."

grabbing provisions from a grocery store (especially if you're arriving late, after most city-center shops and restaurants have closed). If you'll depart from the same station later, pay attention to the layout.

Know where to get off. In Dresden, I twice got off my train too early—at two different suburban stations—before arriving at the central station. Know which station you need before you arrive, and be patient. When arriving in a city (especially on a commuter train), you may stop at several suburban stations with signs indicating your destination's name and the neighborhood (e.g., Madrid Vallecas, Roma Ostiense, or Dresden Neustadt). Don't jump out until you've reached the central station (Madrid Chamartín, Roma Termini, or Dresden Hauptbahnhof)—ask fellow passengers or check your guidebook to find out which name to look for. Learn the local word for "main station."

Be aware that some trains (especially express trains) stop only at a major city's suburban station—if you stay on board, expecting to get off in the center a few minutes later, you'll bypass your destination city altogether. For instance, several trains to "Venice" leave you at Venice's suburban station (Venezia Mestre), where you'll be stranded without a glimpse of a gondola. (You'll have to catch another train to reach the main Venezia Santa Lucia station, on the Grand Canal.) On the other hand, it can be handy to hop out at a suburban station if it's closer to your hotel than the main station. Many trains headed for Barcelona's big Sants station also stop at the Plaça de Catalunya subway station, which is near many recommended accommodations. If you do find yourself at the wrong station, don't stress: It's a safe bet that a city's stations are connected by frequent trains, and probably subway or buses as well. If all else fails, you can link by taxi.

Sleeping on Trains

The economy of night-train travel is tremendous. Sleeping while rolling down the tracks saves time and money: For every night you spend on the train, you gain a day for sight-seeing and avoid the cost of a hotel.

The first concern about night travel is usually, "Aren't you missing a lot of beautiful scenery? You just slept through half of Sweden!" The real question should be, "Did the missed scenery matter, since you gained an extra day for hiking the Alps or biking through tulips?" The answer: No. Maximize night trips.

Your overnight options may look slim, at least at first—as

daytime trains speed up and flights within Europe become cheaper, night-train service is being reduced. When you're checking schedules for night trains, pay attention to details. A connection doesn't have to be direct to be a workable overnight option—it all depends on the timing. If you need to change trains a half hour after boarding, you'll still get some sleep. But if the connection involves getting off at 2:00 a.m. and waiting until 5:30 a.m. for the next leg, that's not a night train, it's a nightmare.

Book your night-train reservation at least a few days in advance. Reservations can sell out even further ahead on popular routes, such as Nightjets trains connecting Austria and Germany to some neighboring countries; for these, it's worthwhile to buy tickets before you leave for Europe. For advice, see "Seat Reservations," earlier in this chapter.

Some train travelers are ripped off while they sleep—they're usually the ones who haven't safely stashed their money and valuables in a money belt. And while you may hear stories of entire train cars being gassed and robbed in Italy, Spain, and countries farther east, it's extremely rare and I wouldn't lose sleep over it.

Types of Compartments

Most overnight trains offer one or two different ways to sleep; the more comfortably you sleep, the more you pay. For much more on night trains in Europe, go to www.seat61. com/sleepers.htm.

Couchettes: To ensure a safer and uninterrupted night's sleep, you can reserve a sleeping berth known as a couchette (koo-shet). For a surcharge of about $35, you'll get sheets, a pillow, clean linen, and blankets on a bunk bed in a compart-ment with up to five other people—and, hopefully, a good night's sleep.

Most *couchettes* are the same in first and second class. However, some trains have more spacious four-berth *couchette* compartments (two sets of doubles rather than triple bunks for about $50 apiece). These may be considered second-class options, but occasionally require a first-class ticket or pass.

When booking your *couchette,* you can request the top, middle, or bottom berth. While the top bunk gives you more privacy and luggage space, it can be hotter and stuffier than lower bunks and a couple of inches shorter (a concern if you're six feet or taller). Compartments may be co-ed or single gender, depending on the route.

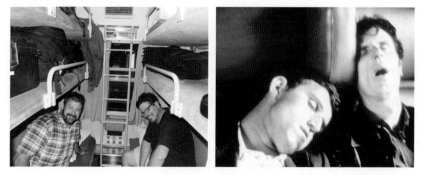

As you board, you'll give your *couchette* voucher and rail pass or ticket to the attendant. This is the person who deals with the conductors and keeps out the thieves so you can sleep uninterrupted. In case of a border check (unlikely in most of Europe these days), you'll either be woken up to show your passport, or your attendant will ask for your passport in advance and handle this task for you.

LEFT You can rent a *couchette* (bunk bed) on your overnight train. Top bunks give you a bit more room and safety—but B.Y.O.B. & B.

Private Sleepers: These sleeper compartments are more comfortable but pricier than *couchettes*. Compartments with two or three beds range from about $40 to $150 per person. Single-sleeper surcharges range from $70 to $190.

RIGHT They didn't rent a *couchette*.

Sleeping Free

Shoestring travelers just sack out for free, draping their tired bodies over as many unoccupied seats as possible. But trust me: Trying to sleep overnight without a bed can be more lumpy than dreamy. And even free seat "sleeping" isn't always an option, since not all night trains offer standard seats—and many that do require a paid seat reservation. One night of endless head-bobbing, swollen toes, glaring overhead lighting, a screaming tailbone, sitting up straight in an eternity of steel wheels crashing along rails, trying doggedly—yet hopelessly— to get comfortable, will teach you the importance of finding a spot to stretch out for the night. (If you decide you want a *couchette* after all, seek out a conductor—provided there's a *couchette* available, you can book one onboard.)

Some older trains have seats that you can pull out to make a bed—assuming your compartment isn't too full. Skilled shoestring travelers know to look for traditional train cars: the kind that have about 10 compartments, each with six or eight seats (three or four facing three or four). Some have seats that pull out and armrests that lift, turning your compartment into a bed on wheels. These cars make sleeping free quite manageable, but they're increasingly rare.

BUSES

In most countries, trains are faster, more comfortable, and have more extensive schedules than long-distance buses. But in some places—especially Greece, Turkey, and large areas of Ireland, Croatia, Portugal, the Czech Republic, Spain, and Morocco—buses are often the better (or only) option. And even countries with extensive rail networks may have certain connections where the bus is more direct and/or faster than the train; good guidebooks point these out.

Note that in British English, and therefore in much of Europe's English-language signage and websites, a long-distance bus is called a "coach," while a "bus" provides in-city transit.

Just about everywhere, bus trips are almost always less expensive than trains—often significantly so. In recent years, a flock of new European bus lines have given railways some especially tough competition—for example, a full-fare (second-class) train ticket between Munich and Nürnberg costs about $65, while a bus ticket for this route can be $25 or less (even under $10 if you're willing to buy a few days ahead and aren't picky about departure times).

I use buses mainly to pick up where Europe's great train system leaves off. Buses fan out from the smallest train stations to places trains can't get to. For towns with train stations far from the center (such as Italian hill towns), buses are often scheduled to meet each arrival and shuttle passengers to the main square (often at no extra cost—show your train ticket to the bus driver and see what happens). Many bus connections to nearby towns not served by train are timed to depart just after the train arrives. Miss that connection in a remote place and you'll wait with the ghosts in an empty station until the next train arrives.

Schedules

In most European countries, bus routes are operated by multiple private companies, each with its own timetables and fares. In addition to guidebooks and local resources, aggregator websites like Google Maps, BusBud, GetByBus, and Rome2Rio can help identify bus operators. But finding a reliable, date-specific, and unified source for schedule and price information can be very difficult. If you're lucky, the city you're traveling from will have one main bus station that offers consolidated timetables online. But it's more

likely that you'll have to check several websites, run by the various companies that serve the cities you're connecting. If you're going from a small town (with no online timetable) to a big city, try checking the "arrivals" schedules on the big city's website instead. Always confirm the schedule in person. Keep in mind that bus service can be less frequent on holidays, Saturdays, and especially Sundays.

Learn the code words for deciphering local schedules. For example, in Spain, *pista* or *autopista* means the bus takes the freeway—the fastest option. Buses that are *directa* are faster than those labeled *semidirecta* or *ruta* (roundabout journeys with several stops en route). Posted schedules list many, but not all, stops on each route. If you don't see your destination listed, ask at the ticket/information window.

If your trip involves a connection at an intermediate station, it can be difficult to get schedule details for your onward journey. Try calling the tourist information office or bus station in the transfer town (or at your final destination) for details.

LEFT Buses can help you reach places trains don't go.

RIGHT Budget lines like FlixBus connect large cities.

Bus Stations
It's common for a big city to have a number of smaller bus stations serving different regions, rather than one terminal for all bus traffic. Sometimes a bus "station" can just be an open parking lot with lots of stalls and a tiny ticket kiosk. Your hotelier or the local tourist information office can usually point you in the right direction.

Larger bus stations have an information desk (and, often, a telephone number) with timetables. In smaller stations, check the destinations and schedules posted on the window of each company's office. Bus-station employees are less likely to speak English than train-station staff. Larger bus stations have WCs (often without toilet paper) and cafés that offer quick, forgettable, overpriced food.

Tickets and Passes

For popular routes during peak season, ensure you'll get a seat by buying your tickets online (most upstart bus lines have user-friendly apps) or in person at the station (drop by a few hours in advance to buy tickets). If the station isn't central, you can ask at the tourist information office about travel agencies that sell bus tickets.

If you arrive in a city by bus and plan to leave by bus, it's smart to check schedules for your outbound trip and perhaps buy your ticket when you arrive. Keep in mind that a few railway-operated buses are covered under certain rail passes (and in Switzerland all buses are covered by the Swiss Travel Pass).

If you're planning on getting around Europe primarily by bus, consider a bus pass, such as the FlixBus €99 InterFlix Pass (covers up to five trips within three months virtually anywhere FlixBus goes in Europe). Or look into hippie-type "magic bus" companies such as Busabout, which offers hop-on, hop-off connections around Europe.

Riding the Bus

Before you get on a bus, ask the ticket seller and the conductor if you'll need to transfer. If so, pay attention (and maybe even follow the route on a map) to be sure you don't miss your change. When you transfer, look for a bus with the same name/logo as the company you bought the ticket from.

For long trips, your ticket might include an assigned seat. If your bag doesn't fit in the overhead storage space, you may be required to check it under the bus (sometimes for a small fee). Your ride likely will come with a soundtrack: recorded pop music, radio, sports games, movies, or TV shows. Earplugs and/or headphones can go a long way toward preserving your sanity. In most of Europe, smoking is not allowed on buses.

Drivers may not speak English. Buses generally lack toilets, but they stop every two hours or so for a short break. Drivers announce how long the stop will be, but if in doubt, ask the driver so you know if you have time to get out. Listen for the bus horn as a final call before departure.

Package Bus Excursions

One-day bus tours from big cities into the countryside are designed for sightseeing, but can also serve as useful transportation. For example, rather than buy a train ticket from London to Bath (about $40), consider taking a one-day

Croatia's bigger ferries offer plenty of space for foot passengers, but spots for cars can fill up.

bus tour from London (about $130) that visits Salisbury, Stonehenge, and Bath. Bring your luggage and leave the tour in Bath before it returns to London, having enjoyed a day of transportation, good sightseeing, and a live guide bubbling with information. It can be well worth the extra cost, and it's more efficient and faster than lacing together the stops on your own, using a combination of trains and public buses. If you do look into taking a bus tour as transportation, confirm the order of stops with the company (will they be stopping at your end destination last?), and check your plans with them.

FERRIES

Boats can be a romantic mode of European travel. They're particularly useful for island-hopping in Greece or Croatia, day-tripping from Spain to Morocco, gawking at Norwegian fjords, and connecting Scandinavian destinations overnight—saving both time and the expense of a pricey hotel room. (But for any ferry ride of more than a couple of hours, it's smart to compare the cost of the ferry trip with the cost of a budget-airline flight.)

Ferries rarely bunny-hop along the coastline of any one country, though Norway's Hurtigruten ferries still do. Instead, ferries primarily serve islands or connect two countries. For instance, rather than the Eurostar train, you can take a Portsmouth-Normandy ferry between England and France.

Most ferries are either big and slow, or small and fast (catamarans). The hulking, slow-moving ferries usually carry cars as well as passengers, run in almost any weather, and tend to be cheaper than catamarans. They have virtually unlimited deck space for walk-on passengers, though their space for cars is limited. On many islands, big car ferries arrive at a different point (usually farther from the main town) than smaller catamarans (which may drop you right in the town center).

Some overnight Scandinavian ferries offer the delights of a luxury cruise ship at affordable prices.

The sleek, speedy passenger-only catamarans generally cost more, but save time. However, they do have to slow down (or sometimes can't run at all) in high winds or other inclement weather. Catamarans have limited seating that can sell out. They're also the less-romantic option, as most require you to stay inside the boat while en route (for safety's sake—they're that fast). Instead of watching the coastline lazily slide by, as you do on slower boats, on fast boats you'll sit inside and peer out through saltwater-spattered windows.

Schedules

Some countries have a national ferry company (such as Croatia's Jadrolinija), but in most places, routes are operated by a variety of smaller companies. You can usually find schedules online; however, particularly in Mediterranean countries, they may not be posted more than a few days before the season starts, making it challenging to plan your midsummer trip in the springtime. It's a good idea to confirm the boat's sailing time at least one day ahead—the boat you researched two months ago might run earlier, later, or less frequently than you'd expected. Service to smaller Mediterranean islands is particularly prone to seasonal changes: Routes that run once daily in summer may drop to four days per week in shoulder season and two days per week in winter. Small, tourist-oriented boats along Italy's Cinque Terre and Amalfi Coast run roughly from Easter through October.

To search for schedules, look up the name of the company that operates a particular route. You can also check the websites AFerry.co.uk for most of Europe; CalMac.co.uk for ferries to the Scottish isles; Danae.gr, GreekFerries.gr, and Gtp.gr for Greek island services; VisitNorway.com for Norwegian fjord boats; and Jadrolinija.hr, Krilo.hr, and GV-Line.hr for Croatian boat service.

Getting Tickets

You can buy most ferry tickets online, and some offer advance-purchase discounts (such as those to or from the UK). In person, either visit a local travel agency or ticket office—or in some cases, simply show up at the ticket window an hour before departure (most tickets cost the same whether you buy them in advance or at the last minute). During peak

times in popular destinations (July-August along Croatia's Dalmatian Coast and between Greece's more famous islands), get advice from your hotelier, the tourist information office, or a local travel agency about how far ahead you should book your ticket.

If you'll be setting sail very soon after your arrival in Europe, do your research from home, and book a ticket in advance. Otherwise, the ferry could sell out and you'll be stranded on a castaway isle—or unable to reach it—for longer than you intended. This is particularly important if you're driving a car onto a ferry—in which case you may need to line up hours in advance. (If it's possible to book a space in advance, do so.)

Some international ferry routes are covered or discounted with a rail pass (such as Ancona or Bari, Italy, to Patra, Greece; and Sweden to Germany or Denmark). Swiss lake boats are integrated into that country's comprehensive public transportation system (and rail pass).

If you're taking an overnight ferry, consider your sleeping options. A basic passenger ticket is "deck class," meaning you'll simply have to camp out wherever you can find room. You can pay a little more for an assigned seat. A "berth" (bed) costs more, similar to a night train. The more private your lodgings, the more you'll pay, especially if a toilet and shower are included in the compartment. You usually can (and should) reserve overnight accommodations in advance. Some Greek island ferries, however, allow you to reserve beds only upon boarding.

On Board

While many ferry companies tell foot passengers to be at the dock 30 minutes before the boat leaves, there's usually no need to show up that far ahead, especially for short-haul daytime boats. One advantage to turning up early is the chance to grab a better seat, which does make a difference if your ferry has open seating.

On the ferry, you may be able to stow your luggage on a public rack on the boarding level; otherwise you'll haul it up several flights of stairs to the passenger decks. You can buy food and drinks on board most boats. It's not too expensive, but it's usually not top quality, either. Bring your own snacks or a picnic instead. Dining is a featured attraction on a few ferries, such as the smorgasbord service on Scandinavian overnight cruises. Ferries of all sizes typically have bathrooms on board. Some ferries offer Wi-Fi (generally for a fee) and/or charging outlets, but don't count on either.

For information about taking a cruise in Europe, see the Bus Tours & Cruises chapter.

Driving & Navigating

While many European travel dreams come with a clickety-clack "rhythm of the rails" soundtrack—and most first trips are best by train—you should consider the convenience of driving. Behind the wheel you're totally free, going where you want, when you want. Start your engine!

Driving is ideal for countryside-focused trips—and places accessible only by car typically have fewer tourists and more locals. If you glimpse a cute Italian hill town out the window, you can easily stop and linger. If you're exploring the lochs of Scotland, you're going to be glad you've got a car.

The mobility of a car lets you find cheaper accommodations in small towns and away from the train lines. You can also play it riskier, arriving in a town with no reservation—if the hotels are full, simply drive to the next town. And driving is a godsend for those who don't believe in packing light—you can even rent a trailer. As train prices go up, car rental becomes a better option for budget travelers in Europe. Three or four people sharing a rented car will usually travel for less than they would by train.

Small car, big scenery

RENTING A CAR

Renting a car in Europe isn't much more complicated than in the US, except for some byzantine insurance options. Making informed choices can help you avoid hassles and save money. Once you're free and easy behind the wheel of a European car, it's all worth it.

Car-Rental Costs

Basic rental rates vary from company to company, month to month, and country to country. The cheapest company for rental in one country might be the most expensive in the next. Comparison-shop to figure out which one is best for your trip (see "Booking a Car," later).

The basic rates you'll see quoted nearly always include unlimited mileage, value-added tax, and (legally required) third-party liability insurance. When getting estimates, be sure to include any extras (second driver, child seat, automatic transmission).

Here are some components of your car-rental rate:

Taxes: Value-added tax (VAT) generally runs 18-27 percent (varies by country). Other nonnegotiable fees, such as a "road tax" or "eco tax," also differ per country (road tax is usually no more than $6-10 per day). Taxes are typically included in any price quote, but it's smart to double-check. If it's not clear whether these taxes are included in a price, ask.

Insurance: Your biggest potential extra cost when renting a car is insurance. Your credit card may already cover the extra insurance you need—check in advance. If you buy insurance from the rental company, figure on paying roughly 30-40 percent extra, or about $15-30 a day, for a collision damage waiver supplement (described on page 165).

Theft Protection: This charge, about $15-20/day, is required in Italy; most companies include this in their advertised rates for Italy.

Extra Driver(s): Expect to pay about $15-25/day to add another driver. This is worthwhile if you plan to share the driving duties; if you let an unlisted driver take the wheel and an accident occurs, your insurance won't cover it.

Child-Safety Seats: Every country has different requirements for child-safety seats; it's good to check the rules before you travel. Expect to pay about $15/day to add a child-safety seat to your rental (this fee is usually capped at $100 per rental).

Automatics and Other Add-Ons: You'll pay extra for a car with automatic transmission (about 40 percent more than the same car with stick shift), GPS (about $20/day, though often included in more expensive models), winter tires (required in snowy conditions by some countries; often

Car or Train?

Consider these variables:
- Geographical range (trains cover broad areas more easily)
- Rail coverage (for example, Switzerland is crisscrossed by an extensive train network, whereas Ireland's trains are sparse)
- Urban vs. rural (a car is a hassle in big cities, but helpful in the countryside)
- Number of travelers (a car can be cheaper when shared by more than 2 people)
- Luggage (a car is better if you're bad at packing light)
- Kids in tow (car travel is more flexible; trains allow room to roam)

included in basic rental rates), and ski racks. Emergency roadside assistance is usually included in the cost of your rental to cover mechanical failure, but be sure to clarify this. Roadside service for a flat tire may or may not incur a charge; if you aren't comfortable changing a tire, ask about an extra protection plan.

Pickup and Drop-Off Fees: In some countries, you'll pay 10-25 percent more to pick up a car at the airport or train station than in the town center. A one-way rental (pick up in one location and drop off at another) can also incur fees. If you stay within one country, the drop fee is usually minimal (or free), but dropping a car in a different country can be costly, ranging anywhere from $250 to $1,200 extra. See "Choosing a Pickup (and Drop-Off) Place and Time," later, for tips.

From sleek German autobahns to windy, cliffside Irish lanes, driving is a fun part of European travel.

Other Fees: Make sure you understand any fees for cancelling or changing your reservation after booking. Be aware that rental companies usually charge extra if you plan to drive the car to certain points in eastern Europe (a line that generally follows old Iron Curtain borders). Wintertime driving can carry extra costs beyond the required snow tires. Some fees are easily avoided: Return your car on time to avoid late drop-off fees, fill 'er up shortly before returning to avoid refueling fees, and return your car in good shape to sidestep a cleaning fee.

Other Driving Costs

When budgeting for your trip, remember that renting a car involves some significant costs beyond what you'll pay for the car itself.

Fuel: About $100-150 a week will get you roughly 840 miles in a car that gets 40 miles to the gallon; most rental agencies offer hybrid or diesel cars with better fuel efficiency.

Tolls: You'll pay tolls figured on the distance you drive for expressways in certain places (especially Mediterranean countries). Some countries, mostly in central Europe, require drivers to buy and display a sticker ("vignette") to signify they've paid a road tax ($10-20). And in a few countries, freeways really are free (such as Germany's autobahn system).

Parking: Estimate $35 a day in big cities (more like $40-55/day in London and Paris—don't park there); otherwise it's usually free, or at least fairly cheap.

Booking a Car

For the best deal on long-term rentals, book in advance from home. If you decide to rent a car while in Europe, drop by or call a local car-rental agency or book through a travel agency. You'll need to decide from whom to rent, what kind of car to get, and where to pick it up and drop it off.

Which Rental Company?

Most of us start our search on a travel-booking site such as Kayak, Expedia, or AAA. If you have a favorite car-rental agency at home, consider using the same company in Europe.

> ## Ballpark Cost of Renting a Car
>
> This rough estimate is for a one-week rental of a compact car with unlimited mileage. Base prices for car rentals can flex dramatically with demand, length of trip, location, additional services, and fees.
>
> **Compact Rental:** $275/week (including tax)
> **CDW Insurance:** $175/week
> **Fuel:** $150/week ($7/gallon, 40 mpg, 120 miles/day)
> **Parking:** $90 ($70 for 2 days in big cities, $20 for 4 days in small towns)
> **Freeway Tolls:** $10 (about 80 miles on toll roads)
> **Ballpark Total:** $700/week

When shopping around, don't stop at comparing initial price quotes. You'll want to determine which company's offer involves the best combination of rates (including all fees and any extras you want), service, and pickup/drop-off locations (with workable office hours) for your trip.

It's generally an advantage to go with a larger company, with a wider choice of pickup and drop-off locations. Most of the big US rental agencies have offices throughout Europe, as do the two major Europe-based agencies, Europcar and Sixt. With these companies, if you get into car trouble, a replacement car is likely to be close at hand.

It's also worth considering a consolidator, such as Auto Europe (my favorite). Consolidators compare rates among various rental companies (including many of the big-name firms), find the best deal, and—because they're wholesalers—pass the savings on to you. You pay the consolidator, and they issue you a voucher to pick up your car in Europe. Auto Europe's European website (www.autoeurope.eu) may have better deals (and a wider selection) than the US version (www.autoeurope.com)—check both and compare.

With a consolidator as a middleman, it's especially important to ask ahead of time about add-on fees and restrictions; otherwise you might not learn this critical information until you pick up the car. If a dispute arises when you show up at the rental desk, call the consolidator to resolve the issue before signing anything or driving off (the consolidator should provide a toll-free number that works in your rental country). The consolidator may not be able to intervene to your satisfaction, but at least you'll have someone in your corner.

No matter which company you choose, be sure to hang onto all your paperwork (including the checklist used by the company to check the car's condition when you turn it in) for a few months after the rental period, in case a billing dispute arises.

Choosing a Car

Expect some differences between your typical American rental car and what you'll likely get in Europe, where mid-range cars have less passenger room, trunk space is smaller, and manual transmissions are the norm. Automatics are more expensive (usually about 40 percent more) and may only be available in a bigger, pricier car. (Some Americans find automatics worthwhile in Great Britain and Ireland, where it can be challenging enough just to drive on the left.) Since supplies are limited, you'll need to book an automatic farther in advance than a manual-transmission car. You'll find a better selection of automatics in big cities and at airports.

When checking out options for budget rentals, you'll see some familiar makes (Ford, VW)—though not always familiar models—as well as some less familiar ones, most commonly Opel, Fiat, Citroën, Peugeot, Renault, Škoda, and Seat. Don't waste time carefully choosing among models, since you're not guaranteed to get the exact car you signed up for, just a "similar" model.

I normally rent the smallest, least expensive model with a stick shift—not just to save money, but because larger cars are not as maneuverable on Europe's narrow, winding roads. If more than two adults are traveling, it can be worth it to move up to a larger class of car.

Choosing a Pickup (and Drop-Off) Place and Time

It's best and less stressful to begin your driving experience away from big cities, so try picking up your car away from major destinations. A pleasant scenario for a trip to England would be to start out (*sans* car) in the smaller city of Bath, rent a car when leaving Bath, explore Britain at your driving leisure, then drop off the car in York and take the train into London, where you can rely on the excellent public transportation system. That way you'd enjoy the

When Booking a Rental Car

Keep These Factors in Mind
- Coverage included in the car company's basic insurance
- Office locations and hours (consider the most efficient pickup and drop-off points)
- Age limitations (under age 25 or over age 69)
- Geographic restrictions (such as eastern European countries)

Nail Down Extra Costs
- CDW insurance (or zero-deductible "super CDW")
- Theft insurance (required in Italy)
- Additional driver(s)
- One-way rental (returning the car to a different location/country)
- Airport, train station, city center pickup—or hotel delivery
- Extras such as automatic transmission, child-safety seats, and GPS
- Mandatory road taxes or winter-tire fees
- Cancellations or changes to drop-off location or time

three major city stops on your England itinerary without having to pay for a car.

That said, beware the possible inconveniences of picking up your car in a small town—a tiny regional office almost certainly has a smaller fleet than a major airport agency. Don't plan to pick up or drop off your car in a small town on a Saturday afternoon, Sunday, or holiday, when offices are likely to be closed.

Picking up a car at an airport or city train station usually costs more than from other locations. (Airport/train-station fees apply only to your pickup, not drop off.) If you don't need a car immediately after your arrival, look into a cheaper rental with an in-town pickup price. Weigh the cost savings versus the potential inconvenience: Many in-town agencies have shorter hours (and may close at midday) or are buried in a maze of narrow streets. Before choosing a rental location, find it on a map. Some rental agencies will drop the car off at your hotel for a fee.

European cars are rented in 24-hour periods, so select your pickup and drop-off times carefully. If you pick up the car at 10 a.m. on the first day and drop it off at noon on the last day, you'll be charged a whole day's rental for just those two hours. Don't book your pickup time for earlier than you really need the car. Book a drop-off time that falls within that location's office hours (or make sure the drop-off location has an after-hours drop box).

Sometimes it can make sense to start and end your car

rental in different cities. One-way rentals are often free within the same country, but dropping off in another country will likely cost extra. Expect fees ranging from $250 to more than $1,000. One-way cross-border trips are especially expensive when renting in Italy, Spain, Scandinavia, and far eastern Europe.

Depending on which borders you will be crossing, the extra cost of a one-way rental could still be worth it. But if the last leg of your trip isn't too far from the border of the country you started in, a small tweak to your itinerary can save you plenty. Let's say you're renting a car in France for a trip that ends in Barcelona, Spain. By dropping the car off within France (as close to the border as possible) and hopping a train to Barcelona (roughly $40 per person), you could save hundreds in drop-off fees.

When booking, also ask about your options (and the costs involved) in case you change your plans en route and want to drop off your car at an office in another city or on a different date.

More Tips for Renting a Car

Get quotes for weekly rentals. Typically, the longer you rent, the less it'll cost per day. You may find that renting for a full seven days costs the same as, or even less than, five or six days.

Double-check currency conversions when comparing prices. Some foreign-based rental-company sites use fudged conversion rates that make the price in dollars look cheaper than the price that'll show up on your credit-card bill. Convert prices yourself on a conversion site such as Oanda.com.

Pay up front. If your itinerary is set, it's almost always smarter to pay for a rental car when you book, rather than at the agency counter in Europe. Not only are you likely to get a discount, but, assuming that your quote was in dollars, you'll know you're paying the exact amount you were quoted. You'll also avoid paying an international transaction fee on your credit card. If you're purchasing a collision damage waiver from the rental company, that'll likely also be cheaper when paid up front. But beware cancellation fees: Don't pay up front if your itinerary is likely to change, and be clear on the company's cancellation policy.

Read the fine print. Carefully read your entire reservation voucher before you leave home. By asking about fees in advance and double-checking the charges at pickup, you can avoid unpleasant surprises.

Reconfirm your plans. It's a good idea to confirm your reservation a day or two in advance. When filming my public-television show in Ireland, I took a minute to call Avis in England to reconfirm my car pickup the next day at the ferry dock in North Wales. The man at Avis said, "Right-tee-o, Mr. Steves, we'll have your car waiting for you, noon tomorrow, at Heathrow Airport." No, in North Wales! "Oh, sorry, Mr. Steves. It's good you called ahead."

Red Tape and Restrictions

Every country has its own take on who can rent/drive a car. Follow these tips to make sure you'll be able to take the wheel at your destination.

Passports, Driver's Licenses, and International Driving Permits: If you're American or Canadian, your passport and driver's license are all you need in most European countries. However, some countries also require an International Driving Permit (IDP). An IDP is an official translation of your US license (making it easier for a police officer to write out a ticket). Anyone can get an IDP from the American Automobile Association or Canadian Automobile Association ($20 permit fee, requires two passport pho-tos, www.aaa.com). AAA is authorized by the US State Department to issue permits; avoid scam artists peddling overpriced, fake international licenses.

You may hear contradictory information on exactly where you need an IDP. People who sell them say you should have them almost everywhere. People who rent cars say you need them almost nowhere. People who drive rental cars say the IDP is overrated, but can come in handy as a comple-ment to your passport and driver's license. It's a good idea to get one if you'll be driving in Austria, Bosnia-Herzegovina, Croatia, Czech Republic, Greece, Hungary, Italy, Poland, Romania, Slovenia, Slovakia, or Spain—countries where you're technically required to carry a permit. If all goes well, you'll likely never be asked to show it—but the permit is a must if you end up dealing with the police. That said, I've never been asked to show one.

Age Limits: Minimum and maximum age limits for rent-ing a car vary by country, type of car, and rental company. Younger renters can get stuck with extra costs, such as being required to buy extra insurance or pay a surcharge of $15-40 per day (fortunately, there are usually maximum surcharge limits). Many companies will not rent a car to someone under age 21 (with some exceptions, depending on the country and type of car), but those who are at least 25 years old should have no problem.

Drivers over age 70 may have trouble renting in the Czech Republic, Great Britain, Greece, Northern Ireland, Poland, Slovakia, Slovenia, and Turkey; drivers over 80 may have trouble in Denmark. If you're over 69, you may be required to pay extra to rent a car in the Republic

In the mountainous northwest corner of Slovenia, you're just a few miles' drive from both Austria and Italy.

of Ireland, where the official age limit is 75 (although some rental companies will rent to those ages 76-79 if they provide extensive proof of good health and safe driving). If you're considered too young or too old, leasing (explained on page 168) could be an option. Leasing has less stringent age restrictions but isn't available in all countries.

Crossing Borders: Your car comes with the paperwork you need to drive wherever you like throughout most of Europe (always check when booking). But if you're heading to a country in far eastern or southeastern Europe, especially one that has closed borders (such as Croatia, Bosnia-Herzegovina, or Montenegro), you may need to pay extra for the rental itself and/or for additional insurance. State your travel plans up front to the rental company when you book. Some companies may have limits on eastward excursions because of the higher incidence of car thefts (for example, you can only take cheaper cars, and you may have to pay extra insurance fees). When you cross these borders, you may be asked to show proof of insurance (called a "green card"). Ask your car-rental company if you need any other documentation for crossing the borders on your itinerary. It's a bad idea to take your rental car anywhere that's prohibited by your contract, as doing so voids any insurance coverage.

If you want to drive on the Continent as well as in Britain and/or Ireland, it's probably cheaper to rent separate cars, thanks to the high cost of taking cars on ferries or the Eurotunnel car train. Some companies allow you to take a rental car from Britain to the Continent or to Ireland, but be prepared to pay high surcharges and extra drop-off fees.

Insurance and the Collision Damage Waiver

When you rent a car in the US, your personal car insurance, with collision and comprehensive coverage, typically carries over to your rental. But when driving abroad, your own insurance is unlikely to cover you. Fortunately, there's usually more than one way to limit your financial risk in case of an accident.

Baseline rates for European rentals nearly always include liability coverage—for accident-related damage to anyone or anything outside the car. (The company may offer additional liability insurance, but I wouldn't buy this without some extenuating reason.)

It's (usually) up to you, however, to decide how to cover the risk of damage to or theft of the car itself. You have three main options: Buy a "collision damage waiver" (CDW; also called "loss damage waiver" or LDW by some firms) through the car-rental company (easiest but most expensive), use your credit card's coverage (cheapest), or get collision insurance as part of a larger travel-insurance policy.

If you're renting in either Ireland or Italy, you'll have little choice but to buy the company's CDW. If you need a car for at least three weeks, you're probably better off leasing (described later), which includes zero-deductible collision and theft insurance (and is tax-free to boot). Note that theft insurance covers just the loss of the car itself, not anything stolen from inside it.

Car-Rental Company CDW

The simplest solution is to buy a CDW supplement from the car-rental company. This coverage technically isn't insurance—it's a waiver: The car-rental company waives its right to collect a high deductible from you in the event the car is damaged. Note that this "waiver" doesn't actually eliminate the deductible, but just reduces it. CDW covers most of the car if you're in a collision, but usually excludes the undercarriage, roof, tires, windshield, windows, interior, and side mirrors.

CDW Fees: CDW generally costs $15-30 a day (figure roughly 30-40 percent extra). Sometimes the CDW charge itself is a little less when combined with theft/loss insurance as part of an inclusive rental rate, and it's often cheaper to pay for this kind of coverage when you book than when you pick up the car.

When purchasing CDW, the deductibles can still be substantial, with most hovering at about $1,000-1,500 (or more, depending on the car type). Most rental companies also offer a second tier of coverage, called "super CDW" or "zero-deductible coverage" to buy down the deductible to zero or near zero (if you didn't opt for this when booking from home, expect to hear a sales pitch from the counter agent). This is pricey—figure an additional $10-30 per day—but, for some travelers, the peace of mind is worth it. There's a huge comfort in knowing you can bring your car back in an unrecognizable shamble and say, "Sorry, I'm new in this country."

Inclusive CDW: CDW coverage is most often offered as extra option, making it easy to compare costs online. But some European rental agencies quote "basic" rates that include CDW/theft coverage. In this case, it's not an optional extra, so you can't decline it and take advantage of other coverage you might have (see next). If a CDW-inclusive rate seems too good to be true, it probably is: The unwaived deductible is almost certainly high (expect $2,000-3,000), so you'll have to spend extra to buy the "super CDW" anyway to get the deductible down to a reasonable level.

Credit-Card Coverage

Car-company CDW surcharges can seem like a racket when you consider that most American credit cards already include collision coverage. By paying with the right credit card, you get zero-deductible collision coverage (comparable to "super" CDW)—and likely for free. In other words, if your car is damaged or stolen, your credit card company will cover whatever costs you're liable for. The major downside: If you do end up in an accident, dealing with credit-card coverage can be more of a hassle than you'd encounter with the car-company CDW. But if a potential headache seems like a worthwhile trade-off for significant cost savings, look into this option.

Confirm your credit card's coverage. First, check that your credit card does indeed offer this coverage (Visa, MasterCard, and American Express usually do, but not Discover). Remember that restrictions apply and coverage varies between issuers: Get a complete description of the coverage offered by your credit-card company. Ask in which countries it is applicable, which parts of the car (if any) are excluded, the types of vehicles that are eligible, whether it covers theft/loss, the maximum reimbursement allowed (if it's less than the price of the car, the rental company may require you to buy their CDW), and the maximum number of rental days covered (often 30 or 31 days; if your rental period exceeds that number, your card won't cover any of the rental). Have them explain the worst-case scenario to you. It can be smart to ask for a "Letter of Coverage" and take a hard copy of it with you to the rental counter in Europe.

A credit card's collision coverage applies even if the damage happens while the car is being driven by someone else, as

Alternatives to Renting

For longer car trips, leasing a car can be more affordable than renting; for short jaunts, consider a car-share program. Neither is as widely available as rentals. For a cheap lift, consider ride sharing.

Leasing: Leasing gets around many tax and insurance costs, and is a great deal for three weeks or more. Leases are available for periods of up to five and a half months. Prices include all taxes, as well as zero-deductible theft and collision insurance valid all over Europe, including eastern countries. You won't pay extra for additional drivers or for venturing too far east, and you get a shiny new car. Leased cars can most easily be picked up and returned in France, but for an additional fee you can lease in some locations in the Netherlands, Belgium, Germany, Spain, Portugal, and Italy. Auto Europe, for example, leases no-frills Peugeot 208s for as few as 21 days for about $1,000. Renault Eurodrive and IdeaMerge (leasing Citroën cars) offer similar deals. In general, the longer you lease the car, the lower the price.

Car Sharing: Car sharing makes the most sense for day trips. Car-sharing providers place cars throughout a city, let users rent them for just a few hours or days, and charge no enrollment or annual fees. You book your car online, pick it up at a set location, and return it to the nearest location when you're done. The fee includes insurance, fuel, and GPS. There's no extra fee for drivers ages 21-24, and prices are relatively reasonable—in London a Ford Fiesta costs about $9 per hour or $68 per day. Europe's main car-sharing provider is Hertz 24/7 (www.hertz247. com), currently available in Britain, France, Germany, Italy, Spain, Portugal, Belgium, and the Netherlands. Zipcar operates primarily in Great Britain, plus Iceland and Istanbul. Car2go, which rents the smallest Smart model, operates mostly in Germany and Italy, plus Paris, Amsterdam, Madrid, and Vienna.

Ride Sharing: BlaBlaCar (www.blablacar.com), operating throughout Europe, connects passengers with drivers who are making long-distance trips. Riders pay a low fare (called a "cost contribution") that is often cheaper than public transit. The fee is paid through the website, and drivers can't profit off the service (fees cover fuel, tolls, maintenance, insurance, and other car-related costs). The website allows passengers and drivers to rate each other, and for drivers to indicate how chatty they are (from one to three "bla's").

long as the other driver and the cardholder are both listed as drivers on the rental contract.

Use the same card to book and pay. Remember to use the same card not only to reserve the car, but also to pay for it and any other related fees, whether when booking at home, or when picking up or dropping off the car in Europe. Switching cards can invalidate the coverage.

Decline the rental-company's CDW. Once you've confirmed your credit card's coverage, be sure to decline the CDW offered by your car-rental company. If you accept any coverage offered by the rental agency, you automatically forego your credit-card coverage. (In other words, if you buy CDW that comes with a $1,000 deductible, your credit card will not cover that deductible.) This may also be the case if you book and prepay for a rental that already includes CDW and/or theft coverage—don't sign any rental contract until you're sure that by doing so you're not accidentally accepting the rental company's coverage.

Be warned that, as far as some rental companies are concerned, by declining their CDW offer, you're technically liable for the full deductible (which can equal the cost of the car). Because of this, the car-rental company may put a hold on your credit card for the full value of the car. This is bad news if your credit limit is low—particularly if you plan on using that card for other purchases during your trip. (Consider bringing two credit cards: one for the rental car, the other for everything else.) If you don't have enough credit on your card to cover the car's value, the rental company may require you to purchase their CDW.

Since most credit card companies don't offer collision insurance to European cardholders, counter agents—especially those unaccustomed to American clients—may be skeptical that declining their CDW is a prudent move (another reason to have hard-copy proof of your credit-card coverage on hand). Don't be surprised if you hear a warning about how credit cards provide only "secondary" coverage—that's moot as long as you've declined the rental company's coverage. By clearly understanding the coverage from your credit-card company, you can ward off a hard sell on the rental-company CDW.

In case of an accident, collect your paperwork. If you get in an accident, the rental company will charge your credit card for the value of the damage (up to the deductible amount) or, if the vehicle is stolen, the value of the deductible associated with theft. It's then up to you to seek reimbursement for these charges from your credit-card company when you get home. You'll need to submit the police report and the car-rental company's accident report. (When deciding between rental companies, consider that American-based rental companies can be easier to work with if you have a claim to resolve.)

Collision Coverage Through Your Travel-Insurance Provider

If you're already purchasing a travel-insurance policy for your trip, adding collision coverage is an option. Travel

Guard, for example, sells affordable renter's collision insurance as an add-on to its other policies. It's valid everywhere in Europe except the Republic of Ireland, and some Italian car-rental companies refuse to honor it.

If you do go with an insurer's comprehensive travel coverage, be sure to add the insurance company's name to your rental agreement when you pick up the car. For more on travel insurance, see page 70.

Picking Up Your Car

When you arrive at the rental counter, ask for a copy of the contract in English if it's not provided as a matter of course. If you haven't already paid for the car, know what your quote is in the local currency. Be sure to decline any offer of "dynamic currency conversion" (explained on page 197).

If you can, avoid prepaying for your first tank of gas (although some offices won't let you out of this). Prepaying for fuel is always a rip-off, since agencies charge far more than the going rate. The only upside is that you can return the car with a nearly empty tank.

Be sure to check the entire vehicle for scratches or dents. Rental agencies in Europe are very strict when it comes to charging for even minor damage, so be sure to mark everything on the checklist. Some travelers photograph all dings and scratches, even the tiniest ones (be sure the date/time stamp is on). If any damage is not already noted on the rental agreement, return to the counter to make adjustments.

Before you drive off, get to know your car. Try out all the features and gadgets: Run the front and rear windshield wipers and sprayers, figure out whether the headlights come on automatically with the engine, switch the headlights to high-beam, get comfortable with the gearshift (including shifting into reverse), check if you have a locked fuel cap, and so on.

This is also a good time to quiz the rental agent on a few things, including:
- grace period for drop-off, if any
- how to use features such as the alarm system, lights, radio, GPS, etc.
- what type of fuel the car takes (diesel vs. unleaded), the local term for that fuel and how it's labeled at filling stations, and how to release the gas cap
- for diesel cars, how to add the fuel additive called AdBlue (commonly used to reduce harmful exhaust gases); if your car runs out of AdBlue, it may not start

- location of insurance "green card" and other paperwork
- whether your car has a valid toll-highway vignette (if needed) or a transponder for electronic toll collection
- info on making repairs and any included emergency roadside services
- location of spare tire and directions for using it (don't accept a car without a spare)
- location of breath-testing kit for measuring alcohol levels (required in France, included with rental or available at counter for small fee)

Before leaving, make sure the tank is full and get instructions for driving to your next stop (or at least to the expressway). Then drive around the parking lot for a few minutes to test rearview mirrors, the gearshift and clutch, backing up, and the lights and signals.

Dropping Off Your Car

Be on time to drop off your car or you could be charged an extra day's rent. Most companies allow only a 30-minute grace period, and once that's up you'll be liable for another full day's rental. If you know you'll be late, notify the rental company in advance.

Unless you've already prepaid for a tank of gas, top up your car before returning it. If you don't, you may end up paying more than double the going rate, plus an additional "refueling fee." To avoid last-minute hassles, I check online in advance for gas stations close to my drop-off point. Save your final gas receipt as proof that you filled the tank, and don't toss it until you've seen your credit-card bill.

Once you're at the rental office, inspect the car with the attendant to be sure there are no new problems. Some drivers take pictures of the returned vehicle as proof of its condition (an especially good idea at unstaffed after-hours drop-off points). Ask for a copy of the final condition report and keep it until you've seen your credit-card statement. Unexpected charges that show up on your credit-card statement are easier to dispute if you have good documentation on hand.

If you're relying on your credit card's collision coverage and you have a balance to pay at the returns desk, remember to use that same card—using a different card could invalidate your coverage.

BEHIND THE EUROPEAN WHEEL

Horror stories about European driving abound. They're fun to tell, but driving is really only a problem for those who make it one. The most dangerous creature on the road is the panicked foreign visitor. Drive defensively, observe, fit in, avoid big-city streets when you can, have a good map on hand, and wear your seat belt.

Some places are easier to handle than others. The British Isles are good for driving, with reasonable rentals, no language barrier, exciting rural areas, and fine roads—and after one near head-on collision scares the bloody heck out of you, you'll have no trouble remembering which side of the road to drive on.

Other good driving areas are Scandinavia (hug the lip of a majestic fjord as you meander from village to village); Belgium and the Netherlands (yield to bikes—you're outnumbered); Spain and Portugal (explore out-of-the-way villages and hill towns); Germany (zip along wonderfully engineered freeways much loved by wannabe race-car drivers); Switzerland and Austria (drive down sunny alpine valleys with yodeling on the radio for auto ecstasy); and Slovenia (enjoy its many diverse, picturesque sights that are hard to reach by public transit).

Once you're behind the wheel, you may curse the traffic jams, narrow roads, and macho habits, but it's all part of the experience. Driving at home is mundane; driving in Europe is memorable.

Maps and GPS

Online or on paper, a good map is a must-have on any European road trip. Don't rely blindly on your phone's mapping app or a GPS device for directions; always have at least a vague sense of your route, keep a paper map handy, and pay attention to road signs so you can consider alternatives if you feel the GPS route is Getting Pretty Screwy.

One time, driving from St. Moritz to Lugano via Italy's Lake Como, I realized that my GPS had just directed me right past the Lugano turnoff. Hitting the brakes and checking my paper map, I figured out that the GPS was aiming to send me on the freeway, then on a ferry across the lake. I stuck with the "slower" roads on the correct side of the lake—and arrived an hour earlier.

Your Mobile Device: The mapping app on your phone works fine for navigating Europe's roads. The downside is that to get real-time turn-by-turn directions and traffic updates, you'll need internet access (a concern abroad, where you are likely paying more for data; see the Staying Connected chapter).

For most travelers concerned about data roaming, the best option is an app that works offline: Google Maps, Here WeGo, and Navmii give you turn-by-turn voice directions without a data connection—and if you make a wrong turn, they recalibrate and send you on the right way. They're basically a GPS system on your phone, for free.

To use one of these apps offline, download your map before you head out (it's smart to select a large region). Then turn off your cellular connection so you're not charged for data roaming. Call up the map, enter your destination, and you're on your way. For the best performance in Google Maps, use standard view (not satellite view). Be aware that the traffic setting on Google Maps does not work offline, so check for slowdowns and detours before you hit the road, or use data roaming for a brief period to get current conditions.

GPS apps from TomTom, Garmin, CoPilot, and others work offline but can be expensive. Mobile apps like Waze require a data connection to provide live traffic and construction updates for your route.

No matter which app you use, bring a car charger for your device: Mapping apps gobbles up battery life, even offline. It's also smart to bring a car mount for your phone that works for many different vehicles.

GPS Devices: Some rental cars come equipped with a GPS device in the dash; otherwise you can generally rent one for about $20 per day. It'll give you real-time turn-by-turn directions and traffic without the data limitations of a phone app. Note that the unit may come loaded only with maps for its home country; if you need additional maps, ask when you

Resources for Driving & Navigating

ViaMichelin.com, Maps.Google.com: Reliable route planners with estimated driving times and distances

TheAA.com: Country-by-country driving tips and local road laws

RickSteves.com/travel-talks: Rick's travel skills talks, including one on transportation

Google Maps, Here WeGo, Navmii: Apps with turn-by-turn driving directions that work offline

Waze: Crowd-sourced app with navigation and traffic info, including cheapest nearby gas

Tolls.eu: Info on toll collection and fees throughout Europe.

rent. Also make sure the device is set to English before you drive off.

The other option is to bring a GPS device from home. You'll likely need to buy and download European maps before your trip (check that the maps available through the manufacturer are detailed enough for the areas you're visiting). Remember to bring your unit's car charger and a portable car mount.

Like most goats, I appreciate a good, old-fashioned map.

Paper Maps and Atlases: Even when navigating primarily with a phone app or GPS, I always have a paper map on hand. It's invaluable for getting the big picture, understanding alternate routes, and filling in when my phone runs out of juice.

The free maps you get from your car-rental company usually don't have enough detail. Better maps and atlases are sold at European gas stations, bookshops, newsstands, and tourist shops. Michelin offers good individual regional maps and road atlases for each country (with good city maps and detailed indexes). Atlases are compact, a good value, and easier for drivers to use than big foldout maps.

Sometimes the best regional road maps are available locally. For example, if you're exploring your roots in the Norwegian fjord country, Cappelen Damm 1:200,000 maps are detailed enough to help you find Grandpa Ole's farm. Other quality European brands include Hallwag, Freytag & Berndt, Marco Polo, Berndtson & Berndtson, AA (Britain's AAA-type automobile club), Road Editions (for Greece), and Kod & Kam (for Croatia and Slovenia).

Study the map legend; most maps include navigational as well as sightseeing information, such as types of roads, scenic routes and towns, ruined castles, hostels, mountain huts, viewpoints, and so on. Good maps even include such specific details as tolls and opening schedules of remote mountain roads.

Tips for the Road

The mechanics of driving in Europe aren't all that different from home, but the first day or two can be an adjustment. For a country-by-country list of driving rules and tips, see the website of the British Automobile Association (www.theaa. com/motoring-advice), and look for "Driving in Europe." You can also find road rules at Travel.State.Gov (choose

"International Travel," then select your country of interest). Below are my top tips for driving safely, and enjoyably, on European roads.

Road Rules

Drivers in Europe tend to be more aggressive than in the US, and some Europeans, particularly Italians and Greeks, seem to make up their own rules of the road. In Rome, for instance, red lights are considered discretionary. On one trip, my cabbie went through three red lights. White-knuckled, I asked, "*Scusi*, do you see the red lights?" He explained, "When I come to light, I look. If no cars come, red light *stupido*, I go through. If la polizia sees no cars—*no problema*. He agree—red light *stupido*."

Passing: When you pass other drivers, be bold but careful. On winding, narrow roads, the slower car ahead of you may use turn-signal sign language to indicate when it's OK to pass. This is used inconsistently—don't rely on it blindly. Be sure you understand the lane markings: In France a single, solid, white line in the middle of the road means no passing in either direction; in Germany it's a double white line.

After a few minutes on the autobahn, you'll learn that you don't linger in the passing lane. For passing, use the left-hand lane on the Continent and the right-hand lane in Britain and Ireland. In some countries (such as France, Germany, and the Netherlands), it's illegal to use the slower lane for passing. In Greece, slower drivers don't pull over, but drift as far right as possible to let cars pass.

Roundabouts: In roundabouts, traffic continually flows in a circle around a center island. While you'll see them sporadically throughout continental Europe (where vehicles move counterclockwise), roundabouts are everywhere in the British Isles (where traffic flows clockwise). These work wonderfully if you follow the golden rule: Traffic in a roundabout always has the right-of-way, while entering vehicles yield.

A roundabout: Take a spin... or two.

For many, roundabouts are high-pressure circles that require a snap decision about something you don't completely understand: your exit. To replace the stress with giggles, make it standard operating procedure to take a 360-degree case-out-your-options exploratory circuit. Discuss the exits with your navigator, go

How to Navigate a UK Roundabout

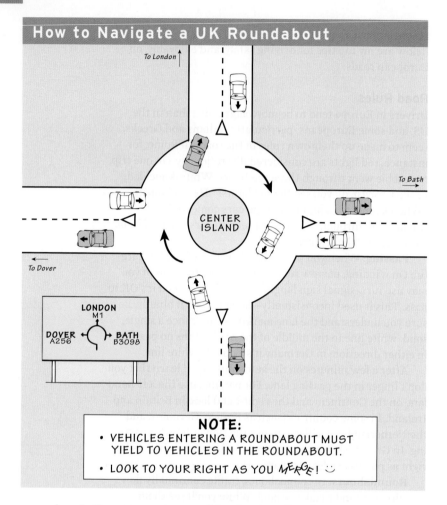

NOTE:
- VEHICLES ENTERING A ROUNDABOUT MUST YIELD TO VEHICLES IN THE ROUNDABOUT.
- LOOK TO YOUR RIGHT AS YOU MERGE! ☺

around again if necessary, then confidently wing off to the exit of your choice. (Don't worry. No other cars will know you've been in there enough times to get dizzy.) When approaching an especially complex roundabout, you'll first pass a diagram showing the layout and the various exits. And in many cases, the pavement is painted with the name of the road or town to which the lane leads.

Signs: All of Europe uses the same simple set of road symbols (see graphic on next page). It takes just a few minutes to learn them. Many superhighway rest stops have local driving almanacs (or cheap maps) that explain common signs, roadside facilities, and exits.

No Right on Red: Across Europe, it's illegal to turn right on a red light, unless a sign or signal specifically authorizes it (most common in Germany).

Speeding: In many countries, traffic is monitored by automatic cameras that check car speed, click photos, and send speeders tickets by mail. It's smart to know—and follow—the area speed limit. See page 184 for more on tickets.

Driving with Children: Most countries require safety seats for children under age three, and a few—including Ireland and Germany—require booster seats for older kids. In nearly all countries, children under 12 aren't allowed to ride in the front seat without a booster seat; a few ban kids from the front seat no matter what, and some have front-seat rules for kids up to age 18.

Drinking and Driving: The legal blood-alcohol limit is lower across the Continent and in Ireland than in the US, and punishment ranges from steep fines to imprisonment. In

STOP AND LEARN THESE ROAD SIGNS

50	▽		
Speed Limit (km/hr)	Yield	No Passing	End of No Passing Zone
⟶	△	◇	
One Way	Intersection	Main Road	Expressway
△!	⊖		◯
Danger	No Entry	Cars Prohibited	All Vehicles Prohibited
T	⦸	↓↑	⊗
No Through Road	Restrictions No Longer Apply	Yield to Oncoming Traffic	No Stopping
P	⊘	⊖	☮
Parking	No Parking	Customs or Toll Road	Peace

France, all cars must have an unused Breathalyzer on board (supplied if your rental starts in France, but ask about this if you're picking up the car elsewhere). Europe takes its DUI laws seriously, and so should you.

Planning for Traffic: Online mapping apps are a big help for drivers looking to avoid backups, and at least occasional data use can be worth it for traffic updates. Just like at home, alternate routes aren't always an option—especially on rural roads, where construction work can leave you sitting still for long stretches. In summer (prime time for roadwork) I budget at least an extra half-hour for construction delays on any long-distance drive.

Note that Europeans have the same rush hours we do, especially in the north. And Mediterranean resort areas are extremely congested on summer weekends.

Tolls and Expressways: Some drivers skip tolls by sticking to smaller, scenic, and free national highways. But the shortest distance between any two European points is the *Autobahn/strada/route/cesta*.

In some countries it's free to drive on expressways, such as nearly all highways in Great Britain and Germany's famous autobahn. But on major expressways in much of

Mediterranean Europe—including Italy, France, Spain, Portugal, Greece, and Croatia—you'll encounter toll booths; fees are based on the distance you drive. Some countries, including France, Italy, Spain, and Portugal, use electronic toll-collection systems. Rental cars are typically equipped with a transponder that automatically collects fees (which your rental company will charge back to you); if not, there is usually a toll-booth option to pay with cash or a card.

Other countries require expressway drivers to display a permit sticker (called a "vignette") in their windshields (Austria, Bulgaria, Czech Republic, Hungary, Romania, Slovakia, Switzerland, and Slovenia). You'll pay about $40 for the decal in Switzerland (good for a year); other countries offer a short-term permit (7-10 days) for $10-20. Your rental car may already have an unexpired sticker; if not, you can usually buy one at border crossings, gas stations, and post offices. If you don't have a sticker, you'll soon meet your first local...in uniform. Fines start at around $150.

Although expressway tolls can add up (for example, it's about $95 to get from Paris to Nice, and about $20 from Rome to Naples), the fuel and time saved justifies the expense. For a rundown of tolling costs throughout Europe, see Tolls.eu.

Other Rules: Nearly all countries forbid using a hand-held mobile phone while driving. Many European countries require you to have your headlights on anytime the car is running, even in broad daylight, and many require each car to carry a reflective safety vest or kit with a reflecting triangle (typically supplied by the rental company). In many cities, cars must meet a certain emission standard to enter the city limits. Your car-rental company should be aware of these rules—just ask.

Smart Navigation

Your trip will go more smoothly if you familiarize yourself with the quirks of navigating in Europe.

Metric Distances: European countries (except the UK) use kilometers instead of miles. One kilometer is six-tenths of a mile. To convert kilometers to miles, cut the kilometers in half and add 10 percent of the original number (360 km = 180 + 36 = 216 miles; 90 km/hour = 45 + 9 = 54 mph—not very fast in Europe). Some people prefer to drop the last digit and multiply by 6 (if 80 km, multiply 8 × 6 = 48 miles), though this can be challenging with large numbers (340 km × 6 = ?). Use whichever formula works for you.

When estimating how long a drive will take, figure you'll average 100 kilometers per hour on expressways (about the same as going 60 mph back home). Determining how much ground you can cover off the freeway is a crapshoot. I use a trick an Irish bus driver taught me: Figure a minute for every kilometer (covering 90 km will take you about an hour and a half). Double that for slow, curvy roads, such as in Italy's Dolomites or along its Amalfi Coast.

LEFT As you approach a tollbooth, check the signs. Here the lanes on the right take credit cards while those on the left require a special pass.

RIGHT Urban driving can involve some tight squeezes.

Navigating by Road and Town Names: Study the roads and major interchanges you'll be using before you set out. If you're headed for a small or midsize town, know which big city is nearby (and most likely to be signposted) to keep you headed in the right direction.

In some countries, road numbers can help you find your way: For example, take road A-1 to London, then B-23 to Bristol, then C-456 to Bath. Normally, the more digits the road number has, the smaller it is; so in Britain, M-1 is a freeway, A-34 is a major road, and B-4081 is a secondary road. In other countries, local signs ignore the road numbers (which can change along the way), so it's necessary to navigate by town name. Signs are often color-coded: yellow for most roads, green or blue for expressways, and brown for sightseeing attractions.

Most international European expressways are designated with an "E" (similar to the "I" designation on American freeways), but they may also be labeled on maps and signs with their national letters (for example, the main route between Paris and Lyon is known as both A-6 and E-15).

Navigating in Towns and Cities: You can drive in and out of European towns fairly smoothly by following a few basic signs. Most places have signs directing you to the "old town" or the center (such as *centrum, centro, centar, centreville, Zentrum, Stadtmitte*). Most tourist offices, normally right downtown, are clearly signposted (*i, turismo, VVV,* or various abbreviations that you'll learn in each country). The tallest spire often marks the center of the old town. Park in its shadow and look for the tourist information office. When leaving a city, look for "all directions" signs (*toutes directions, alle Richtungen*, etc.) pointing you out of town.

If visiting big cities, it's best to park your car on the outskirts and use public transportation or taxis to get to the center (see "Parking," below). Cities across Europe have taken measures to discourage urban driving. For example, to drive anywhere in downtown London or Stockholm, you'll pay a "congestion charge." You'll pay a toll to drive into Oslo and Bergen—but because of their automated systems, you may not know it until you get a bill two months later.

Car traffic is banned altogether in many Italian city centers, including Rome, Naples, Florence, Pisa, Lucca, Siena, San Gimignano, Orvieto, and Verona. Don't drive or park anywhere you see signs reading *Zona Traffico Limitato* (ZTL; often shown above a red circle). If you do, even briefly by accident, your license plate will be photographed, usually without your knowledge, and a hefty ticket—or tickets, if you did it multiple times—will be waiting for you at home (for advice on tickets, see page 184).

When you reserve your hotel room, ask your hotelier for detailed directions on how to reach the place and where to park. If possible, figure out your arrival route before you enter the city limits. While some small towns helpfully post signs directing you to individual hotels, in many cases you're on your own. If your hotel is within a restricted driving area, ask your hotelier to register your car ahead of your arrival or direct you to legal parking.

Parking

The best advice for avoiding parking hassles in Europe: Use common sense, and if you're unclear on the rules, ask locals. Park carefully—Europe's narrow streets are responsible for more than their fair share of insurance claims.

Street Parking: Learn what the pavement markings mean (different curb colors can mean free parking—or no parking), look for signs indicating where and when you can't park, and double-check with a local that your car is parked legally. Don't assume that an absence of meters means you can leave your car there: You may need to get a timed ticket from a nearby pay-and-display machine, or display a clock disc that shows when the car was parked, allowing you to use free, time-limited spots (see photo).

Lots and Garages: "Parking" is the European word for a parking lot or garage, universally marked with a blue *P* sign. In midsize towns, I generally just pull into the most central and handy lot I can find. In bigger cities, I avoid the center (often an unpleasant grid of one-way streets) and head straight to a parking lot outside the core. In an effort to make well-touristed places more pedestrian-friendly, some cities have stopped providing any parking at all in the city center. Look for huge government-sponsored park-and-rides on the outskirts of town, where local transit will zip you easily into the center. The affordable parking fee usually includes a transit ticket (or the transit is cheap and the parking itself is free).

Parking Prices: Just like at home, the bigger the city, the more you'll pay for parking. Small towns don't usually charge more than $10 per day (and are likely to have free limited-time spots), whereas in bigger cites you'll pay upwards of $35 per day. Street parking can be cheaper than parking in a lot or garage, but often comes with a time limit too short for sightseeing. In smaller towns, you may find a cheaper hourly rate by parking farther from the big-name sight. Parking machines on the street or at unstaffed garages might not accept your American credit card, and many don't give change, so keep plenty of coins and bills on hand.

Your vacation is limited, so don't spend a lot of time cruising around looking for a free spot. Get as close as you can to the city center and simply pay the fee. You'll save time and have a safer place to leave your car.

Parking Clocks

Dashboard "parking clocks" *(left)* are used in some areas instead of parking meters. Common in Germanic countries, these clocks (simple cardboard) come with rental cars or can be bought cheaply at gas stations, newsstands, or tobacco shops. Park, set the clock to indicate the time you arrived, and leave it on your dash. The street sign *(right)* tells you the hours when free parking is allowed (here parking is limited to *2 Stunden*—two hours).

Overnight Stops: If parking overnight, it's crucial to choose a safe, well-traveled, and well-lit spot for your car. Ask your hotelier about parking options (and rules governing overnight parking); the hotel may offer a permit or free spot, whether in their own lot or through an agreement with a neighbor. For advice on theft-proofing your car, see page 380.

Filling the Tank

The cost of fuel in Europe (about $7 a gallon) sounds worse than it is. Distances are short, petite cars get great mileage, and, when compared to costly train tickets (for the price of a two-hour train ride, you can fill your tank), expensive gas is less of a factor. You'll be impressed by how few miles you need to travel to enjoy Europe's diversity.

Buying Fuel: Pumping gas in Europe is easy; the English word "self-service" is universal. Paying, however, may be more complicated—observe other customers and follow suit. At some stations, you pump the gas first and then pay the cashier (your pump may be "frozen" until the previous customer pays up). At others, you pay at a central kiosk and then select your pump number. Some places offer full service. Other stations are like the ones in the US, where you pay at the pump.

Fuel prices are listed by the liter (about a quart—four to a gallon). Some payment machines (especially those in the UK, France, the Low Countries, and Scandinavia) won't accept US credit cards (be sure you know your card's PIN in case you need to enter it; for details, see the Money chapter). If your card doesn't work, pay the cashier (with cash; in some cases they might be able to process your card manually). Note that gas stations can be unattended: For instance, if you're traveling on rural highways, automated gas stations—which don't take cash—may be the only ones open on Sundays, holidays, and late at night. It's best to fill up ahead of time.

Freeway gas stations are more expensive than those in towns, but sometimes (e.g., during the lunchtime siesta) only freeway stations are open. Giant suburban supermarkets often offer the cheapest gas.

Fuel Types and Labeling: As in the US, most cars take unleaded, but diesel is widely in use. In Europe, unleaded gas is called *essence*, *petrol*, or *benzine*, while diesel is known as *gasoil*, *gasol*, *gaz-oil*, *gasolio*, *gasóleo*, *dieselolie*, *mazot*, *motorina*, *nafta*, or just plain *diesel*. In Spain, gasoline is *gasolina* and diesel is sometimes called a confusingly similar *gasóleo*.

Standard labeling is used on fuel pumps in all EU nations

European Fuel Pump Labels

Gasoline

E5 E10 E85

Diesel

B7 B10 XTL

Pumps in Europe indicate gas with circles and diesel with squares

as well as non-EU countries such as Switzerland, Turkey, Iceland, Liechtenstein, Norway, Macedonia, and Serbia. Gasoline pumps are labeled with an "E" inside a circle (E5, E10, E85, etc.; numbers indicate biofuel/ethanol levels). Diesel fuel is labeled with a "B" inside a square (B7, B10, etc., numbers indicate biodiesel content); "XTL" stands for synthetic diesel. Some older pumps may indicate regular gas as "95" and super or premium gasoline as "97" or "98."

Be sure to ask your rental company which fuel your car takes. Also, be aware that in some countries there's no size or color difference between the nozzles for diesel and gasoline, so make sure you're not putting the wrong fuel in your car.

If Something Goes Wrong

Some travelers obsess about the possibility of a car accident while driving in Europe. Most come back bragging about their road skills and missing the freedom of the autobahn. Those who do have a mishap usually tell me it was the result of a tight squeeze in a parking garage. Still, it's good to know what to do if you hit a bump in the road. Figure out where to find your rental company's emergency service number *before* you need it (it's likely on a windshield sticker, your keychain, and the rental paperwork).

Traffic Accidents: If there's major damage to your vehicle, call your rental company's 24-hour roadside assistance line. If the accident involves another car, you'll need to show your driver's license and insurance "green card" to the other driver and/or the police. Fill out the European Accident Report form that the agency includes with your rental documents. If you plan to submit an insurance claim, notify your insurer as soon as possible, and file a police report—and get copies of that report—even if no other cars are involved. Both steps must happen within your policy's time limit. If the police refuse to write up a report ("it's only a scrape"), ask your hotelier to help you type up a report, take it to the police station, and ask them to stamp it. It's a good idea to take photos of the damage to your car and the license plate of any other vehicles involved.

Flat Tires and Mechanical Problems: Rental companies typically include roadside assistance or a towing service in the event your car becomes undrivable (sometimes for a fee). Ask about this possibility when you pick up the car. If your car has a serious issue, in theory, you

Roadside assistance may be slow to arrive if you break down on a Tuscan country road, but at least the view is nice!

should be able to swap it out for a replacement car at the rental company's nearest office. In reality, it may not be so convenient, especially if you break down in the middle of nowhere. If that happens, call your 24/7 roadside assistance number right away...then expect a wait for the tow truck. (If you rented through a consolidator, they may be of some help in speeding things up, but call roadside assistance first.) The repair will be covered by the rental company as long as it's clear it was the car's fault, not yours. It's worth noting that burnt clutches account for the vast majority of breakdowns experienced (and paid for) by American drivers in Europe— go easy on the transmission.

Traffic Tickets: Just because there was no police car in sight when you ran a red light (or ignored the speed limit, drove into a restricted zone, or even tailgated too closely) doesn't mean you weren't caught—traffic cameras are everywhere. Quite likely, you won't know about the infraction until months later, when a letter arrives in your mail and/or a charge shows up on your credit card.

You likely won't get a chance to dispute a fine. Europe doesn't have traffic courts—you're simply expected to pay up. In some cases, the fine may be automatically billed to your credit card by your rental company. In other cases, the rental agency may charge you $50 just for providing your address to local authorities.

Of course, many renters just ignore any notices that show up months after their trip. It's understandable—paying the fine may not be all that straightforward, and it's not as if Interpol's on your tail. But be aware that fees go up the longer you delay, an unpaid ticket can follow you for years, and you'll likely be forced to pay it the next time you rent a car in Europe (especially if it's in the same country).

Money

Let's face it: Any international trip is going to put a strain on your wallet—but savvy spenders know how to keep expenses in check. Being aware of banking pitfalls is one of the easiest ways to keep your trip from costing more than it has to. When it comes to money, it's all about maximizing ease, minimizing fees, and keeping it safe.

At the end of this chapter, we cover another money topic on every traveler's mind: tipping.

MONEY STRATEGIES

Money-wise, Europe's never been easier. Thanks to the ubiquity of cash machines, long gone are the days of having to go to your hometown bank for travelers' checks or foreign cash, of lining up at AmEx offices overseas, or getting fleeced at exchange bureaus at every border.

Here's my basic strategy for using money wisely in Europe:

- Upon arrival, head for a cash machine (ATM) at the airport and withdraw local currency, using a debit card with low international transaction fees.
- Pay for most purchases with your choice of credit card or cash. Most people pay for bigger expenses by credit card, but cash is still the standby for small purchases and tips. Save money by minimizing your credit and debit card exchange fees.
- Keep your cards and cash safe in a money belt.
- Smile and enjoy your trip, feeling very clever for avoiding unnecessary hassle and expense.

Plastic Versus Cash

Although credit cards are widely accepted in Europe, cash is sometimes the only way to pay for cheap food, bus fare, taxis, tips, and local guides.

Even if you don't keep cash in your wallet at home, there are several reasons to carry cash in Europe. Some businesses (especially smaller ones, such as B&Bs and mom-and-pop cafés and shops) may charge you extra for using a credit card—or might not accept credit cards at all. Having cash on hand helps you out of a jam if your card randomly doesn't work.

I use my credit card to book and pay for hotel reservations, to buy advance tickets for events or sights, and to cover most other expenses. It can also be smart to use plastic near the end of your trip, to avoid another visit to the ATM. If you'll be shopping a lot, you might use your credit card more than I do—but you'll still be better off using cash for smaller purchases.

When traveling, overdependence on plastic can shape the Europe you experience. Pedro's Pension, the friendly guide at the cathedral, and most merchants in the market don't take credit cards. Going through the Back Door often means using hard local cash.

Of course, there are always exceptions. Sweden and Iceland, with their preference for electronic payments, are practically cashless societies. On the other hand, cash is still king in Germany, where many locals prefer paying for regular expenses (such as groceries) in cash, and where some shops and restaurants still do not accept credit cards (though the pandemic has driven an increase in contactless payment).

What to Bring

I pack the following and keep it all safe in my money belt.

Debit Card: Use this at cash machines (ATMs) to withdraw local cash.

Credit Card: Handy for bigger purchases (at hotels, shops, restaurants, travel agencies, car-rental agencies, and so on), payment machines, and ordering online.

Backup Card: Some travelers carry a third card (debit

Resources for Money

FTC.gov/idtheft: Advice on bank-card theft and more

Oanda.com: Currency conversion tool

NerdWallet.com: Objective advice on debit- and credit-card options for overseas trips

Bankrate.com: Compares bank-card fees

RickSteves.com/travel-talks: Rick's travel skills talks, including one on money

Welcome to €uroland

The 21 countries labeled on this map use the euro, including 19 European Union countries along with Montenegro and Kosovo (not in the EU). Eight EU countries use their own currency, including Denmark and Sweden.

Several EU members in Eastern Europe (Czech Republic, Poland, Hungary, Croatia, Romania, and Bulgaria) are committed to adopting the euro sometime in the future. For now, these countries still use their traditional currencies (see the "Non-Euro Currencies" sidebar, later).

The United Kingdom, Norway, and Switzerland also have their own currencies, but aren't EU members.

or credit; ideally from a different bank), in case one gets lost, eaten by a temperamental machine, or simply doesn't work.

While debit cards can serve as backup credit cards (provided your card has a Visa or MasterCard logo), credit cards make rotten backup debit cards because of their sky-high withdrawal fees and cash-advance interest rates. I'd only use a credit card at an ATM as a last resort. (Note that an extra

For information about using traveler's checks..see the 1995 edition of this book.

credit card can be helpful if you rent a car and use your card to cover a collision damage waiver—see page 165).

A Stash of Cash: I carry $100-200 in US dollars as a cash backup. A stash of cash comes in handy for emergencies, such as when banks go on strike or your ATM card stops working. I've been in Greece and Ireland when every bank went on strike, shutting down without warning. But hard cash is hard cash. People always know roughly what a dollar is worth. (You'll find info on exchanging money later in this chapter.)

What NOT to Bring: Resist the urge to buy foreign currency before your trip. Some tourists feel like they just have to have euros or British pounds in their pockets when they step off the airplane, but they pay the price in bad stateside exchange rates. Wait until you arrive to withdraw money. I've yet to see a European airport that didn't have plenty of ATMs.

BEFORE YOU GO

Before you travel, alert your bank as to when and where you're headed. Studious travelers will want to dig a little deeper to find out about fees and hidden charges. If fees are exorbitant, it may be worthwhile to apply for a new card.

Pretrip Checklist
Before you leave on your trip, you'll need to sort out a few details to ensure smooth use of your debit and credit cards.

Know your cards. Debit cards from any major US bank will work in any standard European bank's ATM (ideally, use a debit card with a Visa or MasterCard logo). As for credit

Ask Your Bank

It's smart to find out the answers to these questions:
- What fees do you charge for withdrawals or purchases made in Europe (percentage, flat fee, or both)?
- Are other currency conversion or foreign transaction fees added?
- If my credit/debit card is lost or stolen, what is my liability?
- What phone number should I call in an emergency?

For Debit Cards:
- What is my daily limit for ATM withdrawals in Europe? (You may need to change it.)
- Do you have partner banks in Europe with ATMs that I can use without a fee?
- What transaction fees will I be charged for making a purchase with my debit card (as opposed to a cash withdrawal)?

For Credit Cards:
- What's my PIN? (Request one if you don't have one, as it may be required for some purchases in Europe. Allow time for it to be mailed to you.)

cards, Visa and MasterCard are universal, American Express is less common, and Discover is unknown in Europe.

Check the expiration dates on your cards. If your card will expire during or soon after your trip, get a new one.

Report your travel dates. Let your bank(s) know that you'll be using your debit and credit cards in Europe. Banks will want to know the countries you're visiting and the dates you'll be gone.

Know your PIN. Make sure you know the four-digit PIN for all of your cards, both debit and credit. Request it if you don't have one, as it may be required for some purchases in Europe (see "Using Credit Cards," later). Contact your bank well before your trip to request a PIN (if your bank says the PIN is only for cash withdrawals, ask for it anyway); allow time to receive this information by mail. Memorize your PIN by number rather than by letter, since you may encounter a keypad with only digits.

Adjust your ATM withdrawal limit. Find out how much you can take out daily and ask for a higher daily withdrawal limit if you want to get more cash at once. If your bank charges a flat fee per transaction (explained later), you'll save money by withdrawing larger amounts. I prefer a higher limit that allows me to take out more cash at each ATM stop; some travelers prefer to set a lower limit as a security measure, in case their card is stolen.

Note that European ATMs will withdraw funds only from checking accounts. Make sure your checking account

balance is healthy before you go or plan to use your bank's app to move funds. (You are unlikely to be able to dip into your savings account or transfer funds between accounts from a European ATM.)

Find out about fees. American travelers often discover they paid more for their trip than they thought they had, thanks to banks charging high fees for overseas transactions. For any purchase or withdrawal made with a card, you may be charged any or all of the following fees:

1) A currency conversion fee (usually 1-3 percent of the whole amount)

2) A Visa or MasterCard international transaction fee (1 percent; a few banks absorb this fee for you)

3) For debit cards, a flat $2-5 transaction fee each time you use a foreign ATM (note that some major US banks partner with European bank chains, allowing you to use those ATMs with no fees at all—ask)

While these fees are legal, they're basically just a way for banks to wring a few more dollars out of their customers. Before you travel, ask your bank how much you'll pay in fees for debit-card cash withdrawals and credit-card charges (for a list of questions to ask your bank, see the "Ask Your Bank" sidebar; to see how fees add up, read the "Transaction Fees Add Up" sidebar).

If you're getting a bad deal, consider getting a new debit or credit card. Shop around; you can compare credit cards on Bankrate.com. Some companies offer lower international fees than others—and some don't charge any at all. Reputable no-fee cards include those from Capital One, as well as Charles Schwab debit cards. Most credit unions and some airline loyalty cards have low-to-no international transaction fees.

Avid coin collectors have the joy of filling in coin books with the eight denominations of euro coins from 19 different countries (plus the tiny nations of Vatican City, Andorra, Monaco, and San Marino). Europhiles can buy these books in Europe and chart their travels by gradually completing the collection.

IN EUROPE

Once you're on the ground, you'll navigate the world of foreign currencies, unfamiliar ATMs, exchange desks, European credit-card machines, and a cryptic thing called dynamic currency conversion.

Getting Cash

ATMs are the easiest and smartest way for travelers to get cash. You'll usually pay withdrawal fees, but you'll still get a much better rate than you would exchanging dollars for local cash at a currency exchange booth. If you do need to exchange money, you'll find advice later in this section.

Finding Cash Machines

In most places, cash machines are easy to locate—ask for a **distributeur** in France, a "cashpoint" in the UK, and a **Bankomat** just about everywhere else. Small towns may have a limited number of or even no ATMs. To avoid getting into a bind, consider stocking up on cash before heading to a small-town or rural destination.

When possible, withdraw cash from bank-run ATMs located just outside that bank. Ideally, use the machine during the bank's opening hours, so you can go inside for help if your card is munched. Bank ATMs usually do not charge usage fees and are generally more secure, as a thief is less likely to target a cash machine near surveillance cameras (see "Card Security Tips," later). Many European banks place their ATMs in a small entry lobby, which protects users from snoopers and bad weather. To get in, look for a credit-card-size slot next to the door and insert your card.

Avoid "independent" ATMs, such as Travelex, Euronet, Moneybox, Your Cash, Cardpoint, and Cashzone. These have high fees. Note that these "independent" ATMs are often found next to bank ATMs in the hope that travelers will be too confused to notice the difference. Their machines may even have signs that scream "Free Cash Withdrawals"— don't believe it.

Also beware of ATMs that offer to convert your withdrawal amount to US dollars (see "Dynamic Currency Conversion: Just Say No," later, for details).

How to use a European cash machine: Insert card, pull out cash.

Transaction Fees Add Up

If you're considering switching banks or opening a special account for your travels, it pays to shop around for the best rates, both for debit-card ATM withdrawals and credit-card transactions. See NerdWallet.com and Bankrate.com for a helpful comparison of issuers' rates. Consider these examples and you'll see how fees can add up over the length of your trip.

$300 ATM withdrawal (with debit card)

	Bank A	Bank B	Bank C
International ATM fee*	$5 (flat)	$3 (1%)	$5 (flat)
Currency conversion fee	$6 (2%)	$1 (.33%)	$0 (0%)
Visa/MC international fee	$3 (1%)	$3 (1%)	$0 (0%)
Total fees	**$14**	**$7**	**$5**

$300 credit-card purchase

	Bank A	Bank B	Bank C
Currency conversion fee	$6 (2%)	$0 (0%)	$0 (0%)
Visa/MC international fee	$3 (1%)	$3 (1%)	$0 (0%)
Total fees	**$9**	**$3**	**$0**

Note that most banks charge a 1-3 percent (but no flat per-transaction fee) for debit-card purchases, as opposed to cash withdrawals.

Withdrawing Cash

Cash machines are easy to use. They always have English-language instructions and work just like they do at home—except they spit out foreign cash instead of dollars, calculated at the day's standard bank-to-bank rate.

It's best to use a debit card that charges low fees for international ATM transactions (explained earlier). To further reduce fees, limit the number of withdrawals you make by taking out larger sums.

Remember that you're withdrawing cash in the local currency. If your daily limit is $300 in US dollars, you may be able to withdraw just €250 or so (depending on the exchange rate). Many frustrated travelers get an "insufficient funds" message and walk away from ATMs thinking their cards were rejected, when actually they had asked for more cash in euros than their daily limit allowed.

Be aware that ATMs themselves have withdrawal limits. If the ATM won't let you withdraw your daily maximum, try several smaller withdrawals to get the total amount you want. (Or, to avoid excessive per-transaction fees, try another cash machine—maximum withdrawals vary by bank and location.) Note that few ATM receipts list the exchange rate, and some machines don't dispense receipts at all.

In some countries (especially east of the eurozone), an ATM may give you high-denomination bills, which can be difficult to break. My strategy: Request an odd amount (such as 2,800 Czech *koruna* instead of 3,000), and/or head right inside a bank to exchange your withdrawal for smaller bills.

Exchanging Cash

In general, I avoid exchanging money in Europe; it's a big rip-off. On average, at a bank you lose about 8 percent when you change dollars to euros or another foreign currency. When you use an airport currency exchange booth such as Forex or Travelex, the hit can be as much as 15 percent.

But exchanging money can make sense in certain situations, including emergencies (if your card—or the only ATM in town—doesn't work), or when crossing into a country that uses a different currency. For instance, if you have a few Czech korunas in your pocket when you cross the border into Poland, an exchange booth can convert them into złotys.

If you do need to exchange money, look for places that don't charge a commission. Note the difference between the rates for buying (the bank buys foreign currency from you to exchange into local cash) and selling (the bank sells foreign currency to you). A good rule of thumb: The difference between the buy and sell rates should be less than 10 percent.

Transactions are based on the local currency. For example, if you exchange money in England on your way to France, the bank will "sell" you euros in exchange for your

---

Debit Card Help

If your debit card doesn't work...
- Try a lower amount; your request may have exceeded your withdrawal limit, or the ATM's limit.
- Try a different ATM.
- Come back later. Your card's 24-hour withdrawal maximum is based on US time, or your bank's network may be temporarily down.

If all else fails, and you can't get your debit card to work at all...
- Use the emergency dollars stashed in your money belt.
- Use your credit card to get a cash advance (you'll need your credit-card PIN for the ATM, and you'll pay a sizeable cash-advance fee).
- Have a friend or relative wire you money via Western Union (see page 388).
- Contact the nearest American embassy/consulate; they can help arrange a wire transfer.

The small gap between the buying and selling rates suggests this Polish exchange bureau is a good deal.

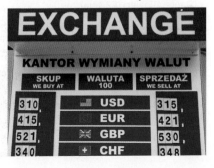

Anatomy of a Euro Coin

The first euro coins and notes were introduced in 2002 and today are used in 19 EU countries, meaning more than 340 million Europeans have the same coins jangling in their pockets. It also means that the design of these coins has to make as much sense to the crêpe vendor in Paris as it does to the fisherman in Santorini. Despite the fact that each country issues its own money, euro coins have several standard features, and using them is remarkably easy (compare that to American coins—for instance, where on a dime does it say that it's worth 10 cents?).

Size and Look: There are eight euro coins. Each has its numeric value prominently displayed on one side. Generally, the bigger the coin, the greater the value. The smallest coins (1, 2, and 5 cents) are bronze. The next coins (10, 20, and 50 cents) are gold. While the 10- and 50-cent coins are ridged (like a quarter), the 20-cent euro is distinguished by its scalloped edge. The two-toned €1 coin is mostly silver with a gold border, whereas the €2 coin—the largest of the bunch—is mostly gold with a silver border. There are no €1 or €2 bills, only coins. So that handful of change that you might toss in the tip jar at home can actually pay for your lunch in Europe.

The common, or "European," side of the euro coin shows its value and is identical throughout Europe.

Common, or "European" Side: Each coin denomination shares a universal design on one side, no matter which country it's issued in. The common side displays its value, an image of the European continent, the 12 stars of the EU flag, and the small initials "LL" for its Belgian designer, Luc Luycx.

National Side: Akin to the different US quarter designs, the reverse side of each euro coin varies from country to country. The only common requirements are the designer's initials, the year of issue, and an outer ring featuring the 12 stars of the EU. The national side can be the same for all eight denominations—Ireland's Celtic harp, a traditional symbol of that country, appears on all of its coins. Or each coin can have a unique national design. For example, each of Italy's eight coins pictures a national masterpiece, from Botticelli's *Birth of Venus* (10-cent coin) to the equestrian statue of Marcus Aurelius (50-cent coin) to Raphael's portrait of Dante Alighieri (€2 coin).

pounds. If you're returning to the US from Spain, the desk at the Madrid airport will "buy" your euros in exchange for dollars.

Note that banks in many countries will exchange money only for customers. In a pinch you can always find exchange desks at major train stations or airports—convenient but with crummy rates. You can also try a post office: In some

Non-Euro Currencies

Country	Currency	Abbreviation
Bosnia and Herzegovina	Konvertibilna Marka	KM/BAM
Bulgaria	Lev	Лв/BGN
Croatia	Kuna	kn/HRK
Czech Republic	Koruna	Kč/CZK
Denmark	Krone	Kr/DKK
Hungary	Forint	Ft/HUF
Iceland	Króna	kr/ISK
Norway	Krone	kr/NOK
Poland	Złoty	zł/PLN
Romania	Leu	lei/RON
Russia	Ruble	py6/RUB
Sweden	Krona	kr/SEK
Switzerland	Swiss Franc	SF/CHF
Turkey	Türk Lirası	₺/TL/TRY
United Kingdom	Pound Sterling	£/GBP

countries, the post office runs its own bank, and usually has the best rates.

Using Credit Cards

Despite some differences between European and US cards, there's little to worry about. US-issued Visa and MasterCard credit cards typically work fine in Europe.

While European credit cards use the chip-and-PIN standard (in which card holders enter a PIN code to complete the transaction), most US chip cards instead request a signature (though even that is being phased out in many places). In Europe, be prepared for anything: Some card readers will accept your card with no need for further authentication, others may generate a receipt for you to sign, and a few may prompt you to enter your PIN. Because of that, it's a good idea to know the code for each of your cards, including your credit card (see "Pretrip Checklist," earlier).

Just like at home, at some merchants you can "tap and pay" using your credit card's contactless option (indicated by a graphic resembling a Wi-Fi symbol). Tap-and-pay typically does not require either a PIN or signature.

Though uncommon, you may run into a situation where your US credit card doesn't work. If you do experience any issues, it likely will be at self-service machines, such as transit-ticket kiosks or parking machines. If this happens, trouble-shoot using the tips in the next section. Drivers in particular need to be aware, as unattended gas stations, parking garages, and toll roads sometimes pose payment problems. Be prepared to move on to the next gas station if necessary (don't let your tank get too low, especially if driving at night or on Sundays). When approaching a toll plaza, err on the easier (if slower) side by using the "cash" lane.

When Europeans buy something with their chip-and-PIN card, they insert the card in a machine like this one, then enter their PIN.

Payment Apps: In some places, you can pay with your mobile phone using apps such as Apple Pay, Google Pay, and PayPal (for instance, at the London Underground payment machines). Instead of inserting your credit card into a machine, you hold your phone near a contactless reader. The app then uses either fingerprint or facial recognition to verify your identity and authorize the payment. While this may sound risky, it's actually more secure than a credit card. Instead of recording your credit card number, a "token"—a one-time encrypted number—enables the purchase and expires shortly afterward.

What to Do if Your Card Won't Work

If you don't know your credit-card PIN, try the following:
- Press the "Continue" button without entering any numbers; you may be able to skip the PIN step.
- Use your debit card, as most people have that PIN memorized.
  If a payment machine won't accept your card—even with a PIN code—try to find an alternative way to pay.
- Look for a cashier who can process your card manually. This is why it's a good idea to allow a little extra time at train stations and the like, as staffed service windows almost always have longer lines than ticket machines.
- Pay in cash. Since most payment machines take coins (and possibly small bills), it's smart to keep spare change handy (especially for highway toll booths, parking garages, luggage lockers, bike-rental kiosks, etc.).
- Use a mobile phone app to make your payment.
- In a pinch, you could ask a local if you can pay them cash to run a transaction on their card.
  If your card is rejected by a cashier, you'll likely need to

contact your bank—you may have forgotten to authorize the card for use overseas.

Dynamic Currency Conversion: Just Say No

Some European merchants and hoteliers—capitalizing on the fact that some Americans are intimidated by unusual currencies—cheerfully charge you for converting your purchase price into dollars. If it's offered, refuse this "service" (called dynamic currency conversion, or DCC). You'll pay extra for the expensive convenience of seeing your charge in dollars. The price is usually based on a lousy exchange rate set by the merchant's bank—and even though you're paying in "dollars," your credit-card issuer may still levy its standard foreign-transaction fee.

DCC charges are common all over Europe; in some countries major banks require merchants to offer it. If you're handed a receipt with two totals—one in the local currency and the other in US dollars—circle the amount in the local currency before you sign.

According to Visa and MasterCard, consumers have the right to decline DCC service: If your receipt shows the total in dollars only, ask that it be rung up again in the local currency. If the merchant refuses to run the charge again, pay in cash, or mark the receipt "local currency not offered" and warn the clerk that you will be disputing the charges with your bank.

A number of ATM machines also try to trick users into DCC by using purposefully confusing or misleading wording. If an ATM offers to "lock in" or "guarantee" your conversion rate, choose "continue without conversion." Other prompts might state, "You can be charged in dollars: Press YES for dollars, NO for euros." Always choose the local currency.

Card Security Tips

While you're not at any more risk for bank fraud when on the road than at home, the hassle involved is greater. Here are some tips for protecting your debit and credit cards on the road.

At Cash Machines

Be vigilant, and look out for various ATM scams.

Safeguard your PIN code. Memorize your PIN; you'd be surprised how many people foolishly write it on their card. (If you don't trust your memory, you can keep a clue to your code in your money belt and/or your phone—just be sure that your reminder is utterly inscrutable to a thief.) "Shoulder surfing"—a thief watching you as you type your PIN into a keypad—is worth being aware of. When entering your PIN, block other people's view of the keypad by covering it with your free hand.

Inspect the ATM for card skimmers. Before inserting your card into a cash machine, inspect the front (especially if it's not inside a bank). If anything looks crooked, loose, or damaged—or if the entry to the card slot bulges out dramatically—it could be a sign of a card-skimming device (which captures your keystrokes as you enter your PIN).

Beware of stuck cards. Keep an eye out for anything in the card slot that could trap your card (or in the cash dispenser that could trap the cash). If your debit card gets stuck in an ATM, don't re-enter your PIN. Thieves have been known to insert a thin loop of tape cleverly designed to trap your card in the slot, then promptly arrive on the scene posing as a good Samaritan. They'll either tell you that you can retrieve it by retyping your PIN, or point to a sign recommending that you enter your PIN twice if there's trouble. Either way, someone is nearby watching you enter your code. Once you give up on getting your card to eject and leave the scene, the criminals collect it and use it.

If your card or cash does get stuck, try to avoid leaving the machine. If you're traveling with a partner, have one person go inside the bank while the other one stands by the machine—if your card or cash has indeed been trapped, the thieves won't wait long to retrieve it.

Don't trust "helpful" strangers. Honest strangers willing to lend a hand abound in Europe, as they do here at home—but when it comes to troubles with your bank card, politely decline any offers of help.

Also, pay attention to strangers loitering near a cash machine, especially if they're in pairs (most commonly, the first one distracts you; the second one grabs your cash). Remember that you're most vulnerable just after you have entered your PIN and the withdrawal amount. Be savvy about the many clever ruses used to distract ATM-goers. The scammer may pretend to sell you a newspaper, place a €5 bill at your feet and tell you that you dropped some money, or ask you for a charitable donation. Sometimes the scammers are children.

General Security

Here are a few other tips for protecting your cards.

Bring fewer cards and keep tabs on them. Take to

Europe only the credit and debit cards that you expect to use, plus a backup, and keep them in your money belt. Upon returning home, verify the balance and charges on your debit and credit cards. Some travelers monitor balances as they travel (see page 300 for hints on doing so safely). For tips on money belts and foiling pickpockets, see page 375.

Don't use a debit card for purchases. Because a debit card pulls funds directly out of your bank account, potential charges incurred by a thief are scary—it's *your* money that's gone, and it will stay gone until the fraudulent use is investigated by your bank. For that reason, I limit my debit card use to cash-machine withdrawals. To make purchases, I pay with a credit card or cash.

Act quickly if your card is lost or stolen. Report it immediately by calling your credit-card company (see the sidebar on page 387 for details), as your liability can be linked to timely reporting. You'll likely be on the hook for only $50, but you should still act quickly.

Cash and Currency Tips
With the following tips, you'll make the most of every cent you spend.

Don't bother with prepaid cards. It's possible to buy prepaid "cash cards" before you leave, then use them like any other credit or debit card, but they come with high fees and aren't worth considering for most trips.

Use local cash. Many Americans are thrilled to find a store advertising "We accept dollars." But the happy sales clerk doesn't tell you that your purchase is costing about 20 percent more because of the store's terrible exchange rate. Without knowing it, you're changing money—at a lousy rate—every time you buy something with dollars.

Likewise, even outside the eurozone countries, the euro is commonly accepted, but usually a bad deal. For example, in Switzerland, which officially uses Swiss francs, some ATMs give euros, prices in touristy areas are listed in both currencies, and travelers can get by with euro cash. But if you pay in euros, you'll get a rotten exchange rate. Ideally, if you're in a non-euro country for more than a few hours, head to the ATM and use local currency instead.

Use your credit card to get cash only in emergencies. If you lose your debit card, you can use your credit card at an ATM to get a cash advance—but you need to know your PIN, and you'll pay a sizeable cash-advance fee.

Don't stress over currency conversions. Local

currencies are all logical. Each system is decimalized just like ours. There are a hundred "little ones" (cents, pence, groszy, stotinki) in every "big one" (euro, pound, złoty, lev). Examine the coins in your pocket soon after you arrive, and in two minutes you'll be comfortable with the nickels, dimes, and quarters of each new currency.

It's important to know approximate exchange rates. The mathematically challenged can do real-time conversion with an app, but I've never bothered. I see no need to have it figured to the third decimal.

Very roughly determine what the unit of currency (euros, kroner, Swiss francs, or whatever) is worth in American dollars. For example, let's say the exchange rate is €1 = $1.20. If a strudel costs €5, then it costs five times $1.20, or $6. Ten euros is about $12, and €250 = $300 (figure 250 plus about 20 percent or one-fifth more).

Make a game out of quizzing yourself or your travel partner, and soon it'll be second nature. Survival on a budget is easier when you're comfortable with the local currency.

Assume you'll be shortchanged. In banks, restaurants, at ticket booths, everywhere—expect to be shortchanged if you don't do your own figuring. Some people who spend their lives sitting in booths for eight hours a day taking money from strangers have no problem stealing from clueless tourists who don't know the local currency. For 10 minutes I observed a man in the Rome subway shortchanging half of the tourists who went through his turnstile. Half of his victims caught him and got their correct change with apologies. Overall, about 25 percent didn't notice and probably went home saying, "*Mamma mia*, Italy is really expensive."

Plan your cash withdrawals wisely. Avoid having a lot of unused currency left over when you cross borders between countries that use different currencies.

Coins become worthless when you leave a country. Since big-value coins are common in Europe, exporting a pocketful of change can be an expensive mistake. Spend them (on knickknacks or snacks), change them into bills, or give them away. Otherwise, you've just bought a bunch of round, flat souvenirs. Note, however, that while euro coins each have a national side (indicating where they were minted—see "Anatomy of a Euro Coin" sidebar, earlier), they are perfectly good in any country that uses the euro currency.

Consider getting back to dollars at the end of your trip. If you have foreign cash left at the end of your trip, and some time to spare, you can change it into dollars or simply

spend it at the airport before you fly home. Although you might get a few more dollars from your hometown bank for that last smattering of foreign bills, to me it feels clean and convenient to simply fly home with nothing but dollars in my pocket.

LEFT In many countries it's common to round up your bill by leaving a few coins.

RIGHT Be smart about money and you'll get the right change back from your cabbie.

TIPPING

Here's a tip: Don't stress over tipping.

While tips are appreciated no matter where you travel, tipping in Europe isn't as automatic and generous as it is in the US, and in many countries, tips aren't expected at all. The proper amount depends not only on the country you're in, but also on your resources, tipping philosophy, and the circumstances. Since most European credit card slips don't have a line for adding a tip, plan on tipping in cash. Still, some general guidelines apply.

Restaurants: You don't need to tip if you order your food at a counter. At restaurants that have a wait staff, check the menu to see if service is included in the prices—in some countries, you don't need to tip extra; in others, it's common to round up 5-10 percent (since the service charge may go to the owner, not the wait staff). If a service charge is not included, you're generally safe in tipping about 10 percent after a good meal (for a rundown of restaurant tipping recommendations by country, see page 268).

Taxis: For a typical ride, round up your fare a bit (for instance, if your fare is €4.70, pay €5; for more advice, see page 313).

Local Guides: Guides who give talks at public sights or on bus or boat tours sometimes hold out their hands for tips after they give their spiel. If I've already paid for the tour or admission to the sight, I don't tip extra (but if you want to tip, a euro or two is enough for a job well done).

If taking a group tour—for instance, a two-hour city walking tour—a tip of €2-5 per person is appropriate, depending on the size of the group (the higher tip is for small groups). For a couple of hours with a private guide, a tip of €10-20 for the group is fine (more if the guide goes above and beyond, such as booking tickets or arranging for a driver for you).

Other Services: At hotels with porters, give a euro for each bag they carry. It's nice (but optional) to leave a small tip in your room for the housekeeping staff when you depart. In general, if someone in the service industry does a super job for you, a small tip of a euro or two is appropriate...but not required.

When in doubt, ask. The French and British generally tip hairdressers, the Dutch and Swedish usually don't. If you're not sure whether (or how much) to tip for a service, ask a local for advice; they'll fill you in on how it's done on their turf.

Sleeping

A major expense of any European vacation is the cost of accommodations. No matter where you go—whether a bustling city like Paris or a midsize destination like Siena—the neighborhood and hotel you choose help shape your experience. But you don't have to spend a fortune to find a nice, comfortable place to rest your head every night. I've found that, in many cases, the less you spend, the more you experience. The key is to seek out good information and consider your options thoroughly. When chosen properly, your lodging can connect you with Europe's culture and its people, making your overnight stays a beautiful part of the trip itself.

Europe offers a wide variety of accommodations: homey guesthouses, traditional old hotels, impersonal business-class chains, chic boutiques, and rustic farm stays—plus hostels, apartments and other short-term rentals, and a slew of other options.

Wherever possible, I opt for a family-run guesthouse—a pension or B&B that offers a good price to stay with welcoming locals in a characteristic old home. A close second is a small, friendly, independently owned hotel in a central

My favorite European hotels are well located, small, friendly, charming, and moderately priced.

Independent Traveler Seeks Good-Value Accommodations

People often ask me how I choose which accommodations to list in my guide-books. There's no secret trick to it: I collect recommendations, do online searches, and then explore the neighborhoods of my choice in person. By the end of the day, the best-value options stand out.

I seek places that are centrally located and family run. I love the thrill of being immersed in local culture, with hosts who take pride in offering a good value. In Paris, I go for the two-star hotel on a pedestrian-only street in a vibrant neighborhood: There's a market outside in the morning, it's just seven blocks from the Eiffel Tower, and $150 for my double room. Europe is filled with these types of characteristic places to sleep. Although they may be small and lack comforts like fluffy robes and room service, they offer a warmth and intimacy that you won't find in larger establishments—and they won't break the bank.

After visiting and evaluating countless accommodations across Europe, it's still striking to me how little correlation there is between what you pay and what you get. After spending a day in Amsterdam, scaling the stairs and checking out rooms at different 20 places, I found that you are just as likely to spend $150 for a double room in a big, impersonal hotel on a noisy highway as you are to spend the same or less for a double in a charming, family-run guesthouse on a bikes-only stretch of canal.

The bottom line: If you do your homework, you can sleep in an authentically local hotel at a fair price.

location. But don't rule out other types of accommodations. While B&Bs and small hotels are a specialty in some destinations, they aren't as easy to find in other places, where a business-class or chain hotel may be the best option. For families and long stays, it can make sense to rent an apartment or a house. Budget travelers should consider hostels or room rentals.

There's certain to be a perfect home-away-from-home for you. In this chapter I'll first cover the basics of finding and reserving a room. Then we'll take a spin through the various types of lodging.

Value for Your Money

Expensive hotels can rip through a tight travel budget like a grenade through a dollhouse. I've overheard people complaining about that "$300 double in Frankfurt" or the "$400-a-night room in London." True, you can spend $400 for a double, but I never have. That's three days' accommodations budget for me.

As far as I'm concerned, spending more for your room often just builds a bigger wall between you and what you traveled so far to see. Consider the typical, amenity-laden, high-rise intercontinental hotel. The experience is the same everywhere you go—designed for people who, deep-down inside, wish they weren't traveling, people spending someone else's money, people who need a strip of paper over the toilet promising them no one's sat there yet. It's uniform sterility, a lobby full of stay-press Americans, English menus, and lamps bolted to tables. It may be spacious and comfortable, but you won't know where you are.

One of my joys as a guidebook writer is connecting my readers with the small-hotel owners I've come to know over the years. Even if you're willing to spend more, you'll have a far richer trip if you stay in places with a strong sense of local character. Europe's small guesthouses and midrange hotels may not have fancy bars and turn-down service, but their staffs are more interested in seeing pictures of your children and helping you have a great time than in thinning out your wallet. And that's something you can't put a price on.

FINDING AND RESERVING ROOMS

You could spend days sorting through information on Europe's lodging options. But with the right resources and focus, finding a room that fits your budget and needs should be fairly painless.

Resources for Accommodations

TripAdvisor, Booking.com: Prices, availability, and traveler reviews

Expedia, Orbitz, Hotels.com: Good sites for hotel research

Trivago, HotelsCombined, Kayak: Search engines for comparing rates at multiple hotel sites

Priceline, GetARoom: Booking sites with deep discounts for flexible travelers

EuroCheapo: Curated online listings of budget hotels

HotelTonight: Last-minute hotel deals in about 100 European cities

Airbnb: Top site for booking private apartments and rooms

RickSteves.com/travel-talks: Rick's travel skills talks, including one on sleeping in Europe

Resources

To find a good hotel, a little research goes a long way. Most people use several resources to explore their accommodation options.

Guidebook listings for B&Bs will lead you to friendly hosts eager to invite you into their homes.

Guidebook Listings: A trusted guidebook remains the best place to start your search for a great hotel. It offers a curated list of recommendations, organized by price and neighborhood, and selected with a certain quality standard. Most important, the opinions in a guidebook come from professionals who take their jobs seriously and know what they're talking about. Guidebook writers tramp in and out of a good share of a town's rooms to get a sense of what each has to offer and how they compare. Guidebook writers have been to—and likely stayed in—many of the places they recommend; the best guidebooks offer insights and tips that you can't find anywhere else.

Find and use at least one guidebook that has a travel philosophy that matches your own. (For a rundown of various guidebook series, see page 39.) A guidebook can give you a good overview of reasonable rates and desirable neighborhoods.

User-Review and Booking Sites: TripAdvisor, Booking. com, and other aggregator websites, with loads of listings and consumer reviews, are a good resource for comparison shopping. The evaluations may not be objective, but they can still be helpful. The reviews at Booking.com are generally more reliable than TripAdvisor, since they are limited to those who have actually stayed at a property.

To winnow down the seemingly endless list of options on these sites, filter listings by price range, number of beds, location (say, in a certain neighborhood or close to the train station), must-have amenities, and so on. Plug in your travel dates to screen out any places that are already full (but be aware that even if a hotel appears booked on one of these sites, it may have a few rooms available for direct booking).

I don't use these big sites (which take big commissions) to book rooms at small family-run hotels and B&Bs. Instead, I use booking sites to narrow down my options, then contact the place where I want to stay. By booking direct, you'll establish a relationship with your host, get more complete information, and you may save money or get an upgrade. For more tips, see "Reserving Rooms," later.

Hotel and Guesthouse Websites: A hotel or guest-house's own website is an essential stop on your quest. Here you'll find additional details, photos of rooms, exact prices, special offers, and direct contact information.

Hotel Star Ratings: Europe's hotel-rating system varies quite a bit from country to country. In general, you can make these basic assumptions: In a well-chosen one-star place, budget travelers can usually sleep well and safely in simple no-frills rooms. Two-star hotels generally offer a balance of price and comfort—still basic but with good beds, an attached bathroom, and often small but appreciated elevators. Three-star hotels can be a decent value, but you'll pay for extras like a lounge and room service. Four- and five-star places bring luxury that I generally find not worth the price.

LEFT Family-run hotels offer the warmest welcome and the best value.

RIGHT 1977: It slowly dawns on Rick that cheap beds aren't always good beds.

Rates and Deals

Room prices can fluctuate significantly with demand and amenities. At guesthouses and smaller hotels, rates generally change depending upon the season. So a standard double at a Santorini guesthouse may be €150 in peak season, €130 in shoulder season, and €70 in the off-season. At popular week-end getaways, rates may be higher for Friday and Saturday night stays. Other factors that affect prices are room size and class (i.e., standard versus superior double), special features (view, balcony, bathtub, etc.), and length of stay (possibly cheaper if you stay longer). City taxes, which can vary from place to place, are generally insignificant (around €1-5 per person per night).

Room rates are especially volatile at hotels and chains that use dynamic pricing to respond to demand: If reservations are thin, rates drop, but if rooms are filling fast, prices rise. Rates can skyrocket during festivals and conventions, while business hotels can have deep discounts on weekends when demand plummets.

Using Online Services to Your Advantage

From booking services to user reviews, online businesses play a greater role in travelers' planning than ever before. Take advantage of their pluses—and be wise to their downsides.

Booking Sites

Booking websites such as Booking.com and Hotels.com offer one-stop shopping for hotels. While convenient for travelers, they're both a blessing and a curse for small, independent, family-run hotels. Without a presence on these sites, small hotels become almost invisible. But to be listed, a hotel must pay a sizable commission... and promise that its own website won't undercut the price on the booking-service site.

Here's the work-around: Use the big sites to research what's out there, then book directly with the hotel by email or phone. This allows hotel owners to avoid the commission paid to booking sites, giving them wiggle room to offer you a discount, a nicer room, or a free breakfast (if it's not already included). If you do book online, be sure to use the hotel's own website. The price will likely be the same as via a booking site, but your money goes to the hotel, not agency commissions.

As a savvy consumer, remember: When you book with an online service, you're adding a middleman who takes a cut. To support small, family-run hotels whose world is more difficult than ever, book direct.

Short-Term Rental Sites

Rental juggernaut Airbnb (along with other short-term rental sites) allows travelers to rent rooms and apartments, often providing more value, space, and amenities than a cookie-cutter hotel. Airbnb fans appreciate feeling part of a real neighborhood and getting into a daily routine as "temporary Europeans." Depending on the host, Airbnb can provide an opportunity to get to know a local person, while keeping the money spent on your accommodations in the community.

As a result, it's difficult to say which hotel will be the better value on a given day—until you do your homework. Once your dates are set, confirm the specific price at several hotels. You can do this by comparing prices online on the hotel websites, or by emailing several hotels directly and asking for their best rate. Even if you start your search at TripAdvisor or Booking.com, you'll usually get the lowest rates by contacting the hotel directly.

Additionally, many hotels offer a discount if you pay cash, pay in advance, stay longer than three nights, or mention your Rick Steves guidebook. For more ideas on how to save money on accommodations, see "Booking Tips for the Budget-Minded," later.

When establishing prices, confirm if the charge is per person or per room (if a price is too good to be true, it's probably per person).

Critics of Airbnb see it as a threat to "traditional Europe." Landlords can make more money renting to short-stay travelers, driving rents up—and local residents out. Traditional businesses are replaced by ones that cater to tourists. And the character and charm that made those neighborhoods desirable to tourists in the first place goes too. Some cities have cracked down, requiring owners to obtain a license and to occupy rental properties part of the year (and staging disruptive "inspections" that inconvenience guests).

As a lover of Europe, I share the worry of those who see residents nudged aside by tourists. But as an advocate for travelers, I appreciate the value and cultural intimacy Airbnb provides.

User Reviews

User-generated review sites and apps such as Yelp and TripAdvisor can give you a consensus of opinions about everything from hotels and restaurants to sights and nightlife. If you scan reviews of a restaurant or hotel and see several complaints about noise or a rotten location, you've gained insight that can help in your decision-making.

As a guidebook writer, my sense is that there is a big difference between the uncurated information on a review site and the vetted listings in a guidebook. A user review is based on the limited experience of one person, who stayed at just one hotel in a given city and ate at a few restaurants there. A guidebook is the work of a trained researcher who forms a well-developed basis for comparison by visiting many restaurants and hotels year after year.

Both types of information have their place, and in many ways, they're complementary. If something is well reviewed in a guidebook and it also gets good online reviews, it's likely a winner.

Comparing Your Options

The place you temporarily call home can color your travel experience. Landing in the right room in the right neighborhood merits a little research.

Consider your priorities; this is especially important if you're traveling with others. For many, price is the primary concern. For others (including me), location is the most important factor; character also counts. I'm more impressed by a convenient locale—near the sights and public transportation—and a fun-loving philosophy than flat-screen TVs and a fancy gym.

When evaluating rooms, I look for places that are clean, centrally located, relatively quiet at night, reasonably priced, friendly, small enough to have a hands-on owner and stable staff, and run with a respect for local traditions. I can tolerate dingy wallpaper, stairs, and a bathroom down the hall, but I won't compromise when it comes to safety and being able to get a decent night's sleep. Most places I recommend in my guidebooks fall short of perfection. But if I can find a place with most of these features, it's a keeper. And, if I save a few dollars on a room, that's money better spent on a good meal or a local tour.

As you select accommodations, consider these factors:

Location: I love being steps away from the action—not only to feel at home in an atmospheric neighborhood, but to avoid wasting time getting to and from major sightseeing and good restaurants. In bigger cities, being near a transit stop is almost as good as being in the middle of town.

Room Needs: If **air-conditioning** is important, make sure the hotel has it. Air-conditioning is not as ubiquitous in Europe as in the US. It's common to find hotels in northern Europe that lack air-conditioning, and even some places in southern Europe don't have it. I don't sweat this when booking rooms north of the Alps—I'm OK with the risk of suffering through an uncomfortably hot day now and then. But for a summer visit in southern Europe, air-con is a must.

Likewise, **elevators** are not a given in European accommodations. I prefer a place in the center without an elevator over one a long walk away with an elevator. But an elevator—or at least minimal stairs—can be a welcome feature for those with mobility challenges.

Some rooms come with **kitchenette** facilities, which can help save on food costs. Even with just a minifridge, you'll be able to stock snacks or breakfast items and save money on eating out.

If you're planning a relaxing vacation to a Greek island or the French Riviera, consider whether it's worth seeking out and paying for **other amenities,** such as extra space, a view, or a balcony. If you're a go-go sightseer staying for a night or two, you're unlikely to be in the room long enough to make such features worth a splurge: Any affordable, reasonably appealing room with a convenient location will do the trick. Remember, all hotels look the same when you're asleep.

Extras: When comparing prices, pay attention to whether **breakfast** is included in the rate. If it's extra, this per-person charge can add up, particularly for families. While hotels hope you'll buy their breakfast, it's optional unless otherwise noted.

Consider any other costs that aren't included in the basic room rate. For example, if you'll be traveling by car, ask about **parking.** If two nearly identical, neighboring hotels have similar room rates but one charges $20 a night to park while the other has a spot for free, you know where you're staying.

Cancellation Policy: One thing the coronavirus pandemic made clear is that it's really smart to understand cancellation policies, which may remain in place even in circumstances beyond your control. Take this into account, especially if there's anything uncertain about your itinerary or conditions at your destination. If all other things are equal, opt for the place with a willingness to be flexible and the most forgiving fine print.

Reserving Rooms

Booking a place to stay in Europe is not too different from booking a place in the US. But there are a few things to be aware of.

When to Book

I used to travel with absolutely no reservations. Europe at that time was relatively ramshackle, things were cheaper, and fewer people could afford to travel for fun, so there was less competition for budget rooms. I could make itinerary decisions on the go, show up in a new town, browse a handful of lodging choices, and take my pick of affordable, perfectly acceptable rooms.

These days Europe's best-value rooms are generally found by booking ahead. If flexibility isn't a concern, book your rooms as soon as your itinerary is set. When I want to be certain to get my first choice, I reserve weeks or even months in advance (lately I've been getting aced out by my own readers at my favorite accommodations).

It's especially important to make reservations as early as possible for stays that fall on national holidays and during big festivals (for a rundown, see RickSteves.com/festivals). I also book far in advance for stays during peak season and in big, popular cities, such as London, Paris, Barcelona, or Venice.

European innkeepers at small hotels offer friendly advice.

Book Direct

My best tip for booking rooms: Skip the middleman. While third-party sites and room-booking services may seem convenient, booking directly with a hotel or guesthouse can often save you money and puts you in contact with your host.

Booking sites and most local room-booking services extract a commission—up to a whopping 20 percent—from the hotel. Personally, I prefer that my hardworking hosts pocket all of my money. Logically, booking through a third-party service closes the door on any special deal you might negotiate if you book directly with the hotel. In addition, plenty of hotels, especially big chains, offer special rates only to guests who book direct.

Booking directly also increases the chances that the hotelier will be able to accommodate special needs or requests, such as shifting your reservation. Going through a middleman makes it more difficult for the hotel to adjust your booking.

If you find a special or promotional discount on a booking site that's lower than the hotel's price, it's worth asking the hotel to match it. If at first you don't succeed, try (politely) asking for the owner or manager. If a hotel can't match the price, go ahead and reserve through the booking site—but first be aware of any restrictions, such as a tighter cancellation policy.

Requesting a Reservation

For business-class and chain hotels, it's usually easiest to book your room through the hotel's website. For independent, family-run hotels and B&Bs, call or send a short email. Most hotels in Europe are accustomed to guests who speak only English, but it helps to keep your email short and simple. Skip the pleasantries and stick to the facts the hotelier wants to know:

- Type(s) of room(s) you want and number of guests
- Number of nights you'll stay
- Arrival and departure dates, written European style as day/month/year
- Special requests (see below)
- Applicable discounts (such as a Rick Steves reader discount, cash discount, or promotional rate)

Special Requests: When you make a reservation, let the hotel know about any special requests or preferences. These can include room features (air-conditioning, balcony, quiet, view, ground floor, fewer stairs, wheelchair accessibility, and so on), bathroom style (for a private bathroom connected to your room, use the European term "en suite"), and bed types (twin beds vs. double bed). If you wait to mention these requests until you arrive, the hotelier may not be able to accommodate you.

Sample Room Request

From: rick@ricksteves.com
Sent: Today
To: info@hotelcentral.com
Subject: Reservation request for 19-22 July

Dear Hotel Central,

I would like to stay at your hotel. Please let me know if you have a room available and the price for:
• 2 people
• Double bed and en suite bathroom in a quiet room
• Arriving 19 July, departing 22 July (3 nights)

Thank you!
Rick Steves

Nonsmoking Rooms: Nearly all of Europe's hotels are completely nonsmoking. In a few countries (such as Germany, Greece, Spain, Ireland, and Britain), some hotels still have a floor or two of designated rooms where guests are allowed to smoke, though lobbies, halls, and breakfast rooms are required to be smoke-free. It's been years since I noticed smokiness in a hotel room. But if you don't want a room that may have been occupied by a smoker, let the hotelier know when you make your reservation.

Confirming a Reservation

Once a guesthouse or hotel replies to your emailed room request citing availability and rates, you must write back to say you want the room.

Most places request a credit-card number to hold your room. If the hotel's website doesn't have a secure form where you can enter the number directly, share this info via a phone call. Smaller guesthouses that don't take credit cards will usually accept deposits via PayPal.

This is also a good time to re-read the fine print of the hotel's cancellation policy, especially if your itinerary is at all iffy.

Once you receive a final confirmation, keep the email: It can come in handy on the off chance the hotel loses track of your reservation (or the details of your room request). Some travelers like to bring along a printed copy of each confirmation.

Types of Rooms

When requesting rooms, be specific about your needs. If you're particularly tall, let them know: They'll try to avoid putting you in the attic or giving you the short bed with a footboard.

Double Rooms: These can have either a double bed or two twins. Double-bedded rooms are usually cheaper; twin-bedded rooms tend to be larger. If you request a "double," the hotelier may assume you'll only take a double bed. To keep your options open, ask for "a room for two people." If you do want a double bed, it can help to specify "one big bed for two people." Most hoteliers understand "double bed" in English, but here's some local lingo: *französische Bett* (German), *un grand lit* (French), *matrimoniale* (Italian), and *matrimonial* (Spanish).

Single Rooms: If you're traveling on your own, it's worth seeking out a true single room, as these are generally a better deal than paying the single-occupancy rate for a double room. True singles are much smaller and sometimes more basic than a hotel's doubles, and usually lack a view.

True single rooms can offer the perfect fit—and price—for a solo traveler.

Triples and Quads: A triple comes with a double or queen-size bed plus a sliver-sized single; sometimes it has three singles. Quad rooms usually have two double beds.

Family Rooms: A three- or four-bed family room is much cheaper than two smaller rooms. Generally, kids sleep for free or a small fee, and teenagers are charged as adults. If you need a small extra bed or a crib, let the hotelier know. Always be upfront about the size of your entourage: Hotels cannot legally allow more people to sleep in the room than what's shown on their official price list.

A triple room works well for small families.

Reconfirming While You Travel

Always email or call to reconfirm your room reservation a few days in advance. This gives you time to improvise in the unlikely event that something has gone wrong with your reservation. For B&Bs or small hotels, I also call on my arrival day to tell my host what time to expect me (especially important if arriving late—after 5 p.m.). If you end up running behind on your arrival day, it's helpful to follow up to assure the front-desk staff that you're coming.

Cancellations

If you must cancel your reservation, it's courteous—and smart—to do so with as much notice as possible, especially for smaller family-run places. Request confirmation of your cancellation in case you are accidentally billed.

It's good form to let your B&B host know what time you plan to arrive.

Be warned that cancellation policies can be strict—if you cancel on short notice, you could lose your deposit or be billed for one night...or even your entire stay. Many discount deals require prepayment and can be expensive to change or cancel.

Booking Tips for the Budget-Minded

If your accommodation costs are adding up, there are ways to scale back. These tricks work for me.

Don't consume above your needs. A three-star hotel is not necessarily a bad value, but if I stay in a three-star hotel, I've spent $50 extra for things I probably don't need. Amenities such as air-conditioning, elevators, room service, a 24-hour reception desk, and staff in uniforms each add about $10 to your per-night rate.

Stick with smaller places. Larger hotels are often pricier than small hotels and guesthouses, partly because of taxes (for example, in Britain, once a B&B exceeds a certain revenue level, it's required to pay an extra 20 percent tax). Hoteliers who pay high taxes pass their costs on to you.

Hotels that cater to the expense-account crowd can be especially bad values. For example, while small hotels generally offer free Wi-Fi, expensive business-class places might charge heartily for it. One exception: In many northern European capitals, you can sometimes land a deeply discounted room in an upscale business-class hotel if you're there when the corporate crowd is not (summer and weekends year-round).

Ask for the best price and cheapest room. Room prices can vary within a hotel according to facilities provided. If you're looking for the cheapest possible room, scour the hotel's website for pricing details. You may find that a room with a shower costs less than one with a bathtub, or a double bed is cheaper than twins. If you would be happy with either, let the hotelier know when you book.

Don't dismiss bathrooms down the hall. While demand has pushed many hoteliers to cram a tiny bathroom into the corner of every room, some older places—especially guesthouses—may have one or two rooms that lack an en suite bathroom. Instead, the room has a "private bathroom," which means that it's not attached, but it's for your use only. If you'd happily cross the hall for a shower or toilet to save about $20 a night, say so when you book (many hoteliers will say they're full rather than offer this type of room to Americans, because they assume we'll find it unacceptable).

Try to wrangle a discount. Prices can soften if you stay three nights or longer (fewer bedding changes), pay in cash (saves the hotelier credit-card fees), pay in full in advance (be careful, though, as these deals are almost always non-refundable), or visit in low season (when prices are discounted anyway). It doesn't hurt to ask. Outside of high season (July and August in much of Europe, though this can vary by region), try haggling: If the place is too expensive, tell them your limit; they might meet it.

Skip the hotel's breakfast. Check to see if room rates include breakfast; if so, ask what you'd save by skipping it. Especially in northern Europe, hotel breakfasts can be a great value and a fun chance to sample some regional treats (see page 255). But in countries where the hotel breakfast is skimpy—or if you're not a big breakfast person—ask for the rate without breakfast when you book. You can buy a thriftier breakfast at the supermarket or corner bakery.

If you're a small group, put more people in a room. Many doubles come with a small double bed and a tiny single, so a third person pays very little (usually about $30 extra). If there's room for a cot, they'll cram it in for you. Family suites with two private bedrooms are a fine option for two couples who don't mind sharing a bathroom, as it's much cheaper than paying for two separate doubles.

Avoid room-and-board deals. Some hotels offer room rates that include dinner in their dining room (called "half-board" or "half-pension"); a few places (often resorts) even require it, especially in peak season. While it might not be that expensive, it does limit when and where you eat. I prefer the freedom to explore and sample local restaurants or shop for picnics. On the other hand, if half-pension is required, but the charge is less per meal than you'd pay for an average restaurant meal, it can be worth considering—especially if the chef is good or if you're in a village with no convenient alternatives.

Check out discount-hunting search engines. Sites such as HotelsCombined and Trivago compile prices from travel agencies, consolidators, and hotel websites, while EuroCheapo specializes in budget hotels. If your travel dates are flexible, consider the deep discounts available on sites such as Priceline and GetARoom. It's also worth checking out the cost of "air plus hotel" packages available on Kayak, Expedia, and similar sites. Just keep in mind that what you save in dollars you'll likely lose in customer service.

Finding Rooms on the Fly

Thinking back on my vagabonding days reminds me of the fun of tossing the schedule and living in the moment. There's nothing more liberating than stepping onto a platform, realizing the train on track 6 is going to Hamburg and the train on track 7 is Copenhagen-bound...and you're free to go where the spirit moves you. Or to be tired of the rain in Munich, hop on a train, and a couple of hours later be on the other side of the Alps in hot and sunny Italy.

To leave room for this kind of spontaneity, book your lodging as you go. This works best when there's relatively little demand for rooms (in low season or in less-crowded destinations).

To ease your entry into Europe, I advise booking in advance for the first few nights, as finding a room when jet-lagged can be stressful. After that, you can book your next hotel once you know where you're going and when you'll arrive. Nail down a place in the morning so you know where you'll sleep that night; you'll spend your day sightseeing and traveling relaxed, knowing a room is waiting for you. (One tactic that can work well for longer stays: Book just the first night or two before arriving, then use some of your first day to explore lodging options for the rest of your visit.)

Ask today's hotel to call tomorrow's hotel to make a reservation for you in the native language.

Besides the usual channels for finding a room, some booking sites, such as HotelTonight, specialize in last-minute rooms. You can also ask your current hosts to recommend accommodations at your next destination. They may even be

willing to call around to see what's available. A good time to contact the next hotel is around 9 or 10 a.m., when the receptionist knows who'll be checking out and which rooms will be available.

If you show up in a new town with no reservations, your approach to room-finding will be determined by whether it's a buyer's or seller's market. These trends can be obvious (a beach resort will be crowded in summer, empty in winter). Sometimes you can arrive late, be selective, and even talk down the price. Other times you'll happily accept anything with a pillow and a blanket.

I'll never forget struggling off the plane on my arrival on a Greek island. Fifteen women were begging me to spend the night. Thrilled, I made a snap decision and followed the most attractive offer to a very nice budget accommodation.

If you do find yourself in a new place without a reservation, keep the following advice in mind.

Shop around. It's worth 20 minutes of poking your head into a few different hotels to see which of your options feels like the best value. Never judge a hotel by its exterior or lobby: Lavish interiors with shabby exteriors are a cultural trait of Europe.

View a room before accepting it. Think about heat, noise, and general comfort level. If you don't like what you see, ask about another room. Or point out any negative attributes—the price may come down. If the room's no good, just leave.

Use room-finding services as a last resort. Popular tourist cities usually have a room-finding service at the train station or tourist information office. For a small fee, they can probably get you a room in the price range and neighborhood of your choice. These services normally make no judgments about hotel quality or value, so what you get is potluck. They'll recommend places that have paid for the service but fail to mention cheaper options.

Ask hoteliers to help. Nobody knows the hotel scene better than hotel managers do. If one place doesn't have a vacant room, ask for tips on where else to look. They're usually happy to phone a friend's place for you. The priciest hotels have English-speaking staff willing to help out the polite traveler in search of a cheap room.

Follow taxi tips. One way to find a place in a tough situation is to let a cabbie take you to his favorite hotel.

If all else fails, leave the trouble zone. If you simply cannot find a vacancy, head away from the trouble zone.

An hour by car, train, or bus from the most miserable hotel situation anywhere in Europe is a town—Dullsdorf or Nothingston—with the Dullsdorf Gasthaus or the Nothingston Inn just across the street from the station or right off the main square. It's not full—never has been, never will be. There's a guy sleeping behind the reception desk. Drop in at 11 p.m., ask for a bed, and he'll say, "Head to the third floor—the keys are in the door." The rooms are dingy, and probably not a great value...but you've got a bed. It always works. Oktoberfest, Cannes Film Festival, Easter at Lourdes—your bed awaits in nearby Dullsdorf.

GUESTHOUSES AND HOTELS

"Guesthouse" is a catch-all term for the small, warm, family-run accommodations that thrive across Europe—from prim British B&Bs, to cozy German pensions, to a set of keys and a basic bed in the spare room of a Croatian grandma's house. They have different names from country to country, but all give you the privacy of a hotel and the comforts of home—at a price you can afford.

While a guesthouse is my go-to when I'm looking for a place to stay, a small hotel is a close runner-up (usually family-run but much like a guesthouse). Both are described in this section.

Guesthouses

Guesthouses offer double the cultural intimacy for less money than most hotel rooms of comparable comfort. While you may lose some of the conveniences hotels offer—such as lounges, in-room phones, daily towel changes, and credit-card payments—I happily make the trade-off. For instance, I love it when Kathleen in western Ireland runs out after me because she's noticed I've left for the day without an

LEFT Staying at a guesthouse can come with a good workout.

RIGHT Never judge a B&B by its name.

Guesthouse Etiquette

Pensions, B&Bs, and other guesthouse-style accommodations come with their own etiquette and quirks. Keep the following in mind.

Let your host know if you're coming or going at odd times. Owners' daily schedules can be built around the whim of their guests. If you're getting up early, so are they; if you check in late, they must wait up for you. Be considerate.

Be careful around the house. Treat these lovingly maintained homes as you would a friend's house. Be gentle when maneuvering your bag up narrow staircases with fragile walls and banisters. Use the suitcase rack rather than setting your bag on the bedspread. A charming, inexpensive room only stays that way through the care of its owner, who counts on having thoughtful guests like you. (It's one of the reasons so many guesthouses offer discounts for my readers—you're well known as some of the best guests in the biz.)

Be eco-conscious. Green travel is thoughtful travel. You'll endear yourself to your hosts if you turn off lights and air-conditioning when you leave and avoid excessively long showers.

Keep the noise down. Guesthouses tend to come with thin walls and creaky floorboards that can make for a noisy night. If you're a light sleeper, bring earplugs. And please be quiet in the halls and in your rooms at night (talk softly and keep the TV volume low)...those of us getting up early will thank you for it.

Join in—if you want. The "part of the family" element of a guesthouse stay is usually your choice. Chatty friendliness is not forced on guests. Depending on my mood and workload, I often keep to myself during my stays—hosts are hardly offended. But when I have the time and opportunity, I join the children in the barn for the sheep-shearing fun or grandma at the TV for tea and cookies.

umbrella, hands me hers...and reminds me to be back by 8 o'clock that night, when her brother's playing folk music in the pub around the corner. It's a bit like having your own temporary mother while you travel.

You'll find guesthouses in every European country, though they're more popular in certain regions. In general, you're more likely to find guesthouses in the countryside and smaller towns. They're an especially smart choice in regions where budget hotels are hard to come by. In Scandinavia, for example, guesthouse rooms are often good quality and surprisingly cheap compared to nearby hotels. And in Croatia—where mass tourism and overpriced resort hotels reign—rooms in private homes provide a safe, comfortable place for value-minded independent travelers.

Guesthouses don't work for every type of traveler. For instance, some places don't allow kids or require them to be over a certain age (often around 8-12). If mobility is a challenge, you're probably better off at a hotel with an elevator, as guesthouses commonly have rooms tucked away in attics or perched at the top of several flights of stairs (inquire about a ground-floor room before ruling a place out). En suite bathrooms aren't a given, nor are the usual hotel trappings (such as air-conditioning, TV, or a staff that's reliably fluent in English). Many guesthouse owners are also pet owners. If you're allergic, ask about resident pets when you reserve. Absentee management—where the proprietors live off-site (or even in another town)—is becoming more common.

It's not uncommon for guesthouses to require a two-night stay, especially in popular vacation areas and in private homes. Some guesthouses give a discount for longer stays, while others levy a surcharge for single-night stays. In popular weekend-getaway spots, you may have a hard time finding a guesthouse willing to take you for Saturday night only.

Finding and booking a guesthouse is no different than reserving a hotel. Even most smaller places are listed on hotel-booking sites—but a direct booking is especially appreciated at mom-and-pop places and will likely net you a better price.

B&Bs

Bed-and-breakfasts are my favorite way to sleep cheap—or at least reasonably affordably—in Britain and Ireland. (True B&Bs are somewhat rare on the Continent, though there are some in the Low Countries, Scandinavia, and elsewhere.) Across the British Isles, small towns and villages are littered with charming, older B&Bs with three to eight lovingly tended guest rooms. Don't confuse these with their frilly, fancy cousins in America. In a European B&B, rather than seven pillows and a basket of jams, you get a warm welcome and a good price.

B&Bs are typically run by a charming couple or family who call their guesthouse home. Hosts tend to be gregarious and genuinely invested in your visit (it's hard work—those who don't love meeting their guests don't tend to stick with it).

Some places have a common room that you're free to use for reading or hanging out. Free Wi-Fi and a well-stocked tea table are standard in your room. Your hosts may offer to make you a simple dinner for a good price,

B&B travelers scramble at the breakfast table.

LEFT A special bonus when enjoying Britain's great B&Bs: You get your own temporary mother.

RIGHT In most British towns, B&Bs line up along the same street—find one, and you've found a dozen.

and if you have time to chat, you might get in on an evening social hour.

Of course, breakfast comes with the bed (something to remember when comparing prices against hotels)—and in the British Isles, this is no ordinary breakfast (for details, see page 635). Because your host is often also the cook, breakfast hours are usually relatively short: It's bad form to show up at the very end of the breakfast period and expect the whole shebang.

While you are finishing your tea, your host may present you with her guest book, inviting you to make an entry and pointing out others from your home state who have stayed in her house. When you bid your hosts farewell in the morning and thank them for the good sleep and full stomach, it can be difficult to get away: Determined to fill you with as much information as food, your hosts want you to have the best day of sightseeing possible.

Pensions

Continental Europe's equivalent to the B&B is the pension. Typically located in charming older buildings, with 10 or fewer rooms, most pensions are relatively inexpensive, cozy, and friendly. Most hosts—though generally not as chatty as B&B owners in Ireland and Britain—speak at least some basic English. Rooms are reasonably simple, but usually well cared for.

In many countries the name for this kind of guesthouse is a variant of the French word *pension*. They may also go by local names, such as *Gasthaus* and *Gasthof* in German; *albergo* and *locanda* in Italian; or *fonda*, *casas de huespedes*, and *hostal* in Spanish (not to be confused with "hostel"—two very different things).

Breakfast isn't always included (even at places that

Family-run pensions provide a welcoming place to call home.

have appended "B&B" to their name in hopes of attracting English-speaking guests). When it is offered, a pension's breakfast rarely approaches the magnificence of the full British or Irish version. Quality and quantity depend mostly on what's considered standard in each country. For instance, a cheap place in Austria will likely serve up a heartier spread than a fancier pension in Sicily (for more on what to expect for breakfast in various countries, see page 255).

The lines separating a charming small hotel from a larger pension are pretty blurry—but on the whole hotels are more formal, more regulated, and more expensive. Legally, Italy's *albergo*, *locanda*, and *pensione* all technically belong to a nationwide hotel-rating system—but places boasting these traditional names tend to be synonymous with family-run enterprises offering simple, budget beds.

Rooms in Private Homes

The cheapest guesthouse is a (mostly) private residence that runs a business regularly rent-ing out a room or two to travelers. For about $20-40 per person you get your own room, a bathroom down the hall, and an even more intimate peek into small-town Europe (like other guesthouses, these kinds of rooms are most common outside big cities).

Staying in one of these places is not too different from being in a small pension. You'll likely have your own entrance, with a clear separation between your space and the owner's residence. One-night stays are discouraged in the smallest operations (in

Rooms in private homes, like this cozy *soba* in Croatia, offer affordable accommodation.

Croatia, for example, most charge extra for guests staying less than three nights).

Rooms like this are often listed on Airbnb and similar sites, and at the tourist information office. If you're scouting for a place, keep your eye out for posted signs with the local word for "rooms": *Zimmer* in Germany and Austria, but also commonly used across eastern Europe, *chambres (d'hôte)* in France (often abbreviated "CH"), *(affitta) camere* in Italy, *sobe* in Croatia and Slovenia, *pokoje* in Poland, *dhomatia* in Greece, *(hus) rum* in Sweden, *rom* in Norway, *værelser* in Denmark, and *quartos* in Portugal. In Spain, look for *camas* (beds), *habitación*, or *casa particular*.

In more remote but touristy locales, hardworking entrepreneurial hosts await the arrival of trains and buses at any hour, eager to whisk backpackers away to see their rooms. Along the Croatian coast, *soba* skimmers meet every arriving ferry. If you don't see any promising prospects on arrival, ask around town. Italy's small-town bars are plugged into the *affittacamere* grapevine. In Greek villages with no hotels, ask for *dhomatia* at the town *taverna*.

Expect some personal attention from your host (but no more than you'd like), simple, stripped-down rooms, and little or nothing in the way of public spaces. Your bathroom may be across the hall, but at most you'll share it with just one other set of guests. You probably won't have a TV or air-conditioning, and breakfast may or may not be included. In

Resources for Rural Guesthouses

AgriturismoItaly.it: Farm stays in Italy

Gite.com, Gites-de-France.com: Countryside rental homes in France

EcoTurismoRural.com, MiCasaRural.co.uk: Rural rentals in Spain and Portugal

FarmStay.co.uk, NationalTrust. org.uk/holidays, OriginalCottages. co.uk: Countryside rental homes in Britain

Stay on a working farm *(agriturismo)* for an authentic slice of rural Italy.

southwestern Europe (France, Italy, Spain, and Portugal), hosts may not speak more than a handful of English words, but they're almost always enthusiastic and welcoming.

Rural Guesthouses

A stay in the European countryside is an unforgettable experience—ideal for travelers more interested in being on vacation than being caught up in a sightseeing whirlwind. Rural guesthouses tend to clump in areas famous for their pastoral charm. For instance, Italy's *agriturismi* (farmhouse accommodations) are especially abundant in Tuscany and Umbria (technically a true *agriturismo* must generate more money from its farm activities than from tourism—ensuring that the land is worked and preserved.) You'll find *quintas* (countryside inns) in Portugal's Douro Valley region, haciendas (country estates) in Spain's Andalucía, agroturizams (farm stays) in Croatia's Istrian peninsula, and *turistične kmetije* (family-run farms) in the Slovenian countryside. In Britain, farmhouse B&Bs in the Lake District and other bucolic settings get you close to the land (and sheep).

Rural accommodations are generally family-run and often rent by the week. They can span the amenity scale: Some properties are simple and rustic, while others offer luxuries such as swimming pools and riding stables (but don't expect daily maid service). Most have clean and comfortable rooms for rent, often with a kitchen, a living room, and a bathroom or two. Some travelers with romantic dreams of *agriturismi* are turned off when they arrive to actual farm smells and sounds. These folks would be happier at a countryside B&B or villa that offers more upscale comfort. Another option is to rent out an entire farmhouse or cottage (described later, under "Short-Term Rentals").

You'll likely need a car to fully enjoy—or even reach—a rural guesthouse.

At some places, a half-pension rate—including a home-cooked lunch or dinner—may be an option (or built into the price, whether you want it or not). Most places serve tasty homegrown food, often organic, and many are gourmet.

To stay in the countryside, try a website that specializes in rural accommodations (see the "Resources for Rural Guesthouses" sidebar), or do an online search for the country-specific terms mentioned earlier. You can also try vacation rental resources such as Airbnb. Since location is a big part of the draw, glean as much objective information about the setting as you can—a place that looks secluded on its website may actually be set right next to the local garage.

Hotels

In any European city you can find big, Old World-elegant hotels with modern amenities, as well as familiar-feeling business-class hotels that are no different from what you experience at home. But you'll also find hotels that are more uniquely European.

Classic Splurges

When I want to spend a little extra money for a special experience, I put my dollars toward a stay in a small, elegant hotel in the charming center. Throughout Europe, boutique hotels in the old town offer tradition and class for the price of sleek, transplanted American niceties in a newer international-class hotel.

In Florence, for example, I sometimes stay in a stately former convent, crisp with elegance and history. Yes, it's a splurge—but it stokes Medici fantasies like you can't imagine. There's a creaky freestanding armoire for my clothes and a heavy wood-beamed ceiling fifteen feet overhead. Looking out the window, I've got a view of the first Renaissance building—designed by Brunelleschi. You don't get that at the Sheraton.

A few splurges on an extended trip can just feel nice (and romantic). If it's in your budget, pick a Parisian room with a view of the Eiffel Tower, a canalside room in Venice, or a Swiss guesthouse tucked into a mountainside. Many such hotels have been in the same friendly family for generations; have unique amenities such as wine cellars, reading rooms, or roof terraces; and enjoy great locations in the most appealing parts of town.

Old-Fashioned Budget Hotels

Europe has a class of budget hotels that's all but unknown in the US: Friendly, no-nonsense, quirky little places—usually family-run—offering good-enough-for-the-European, good-enough-for-me beds for an average of $100 a night (less in southern Europe, more in big cities north of the Alps). While these older, traditional hotels are becoming something of an endangered species, they're certainly out there, and not too hard to find, particularly in southern Europe (Italy, France, Spain, Portugal, and Greece).

The best of these places offers comfort and character at affordable prices in smartly renovated older buildings that still retain their Old World feel. You'll climb lots of stairs, as a hotel's lack of an elevator is often the only reason it can't raise its prices. And you'll be given a front-door key because the desk is not staffed all night.

At the very low-end range, you'll likely get a simple bed, a rickety old chair and table, a freestanding closet, a small window, and a view of another similar room across a tall, thin interior courtyard. In the cheapest places, you might have a TV, but likely not a telephone, and you'll share the toilet and shower or tub down the hall with a handful of other rooms (saving you a bundle of money).

This is hard-core Europe: fun, cheap, and characteristic. The hotel I'm describing may be appalling to many Americans; to others, it's charming, colorful, or funky. To me, "funky" means spirited and full of character(s): a caged bird in the TV room, grandchildren in the backyard, a dog sleeping in the hall, no uniforms, singing maids, a handwritten neighborhood history lesson on the wall, and different furniture in each room. An extra $40-50 per night will buy you cheerier wallpaper and less funkiness.

As Europe becomes more affluent, its big cities are gentrifying, and Europeans are coming to expect what were once considered "American" standards of plumbing and comfort. Centrally located, old-school hotels are being bought out, gutted, and turned into pricier modern places. But you can still find good values at the remaining budget hotel that structurally can't fit showers in every room or an elevator up its spiral staircase. Prices are regulated, and regardless of how comfy and charming it is,

A typical budget hotel room: tidy, small, affordable.

with no elevator and a lousy shower-to-room ratio, it is—and will remain—a cheap hotel.

Modern Chain Hotels

Difficult as it is for me to admit, soulless chain hotels can sometimes be a good option. You'll give up the charm and warmth of a family-run establishment, and breakfast probably won't be included, but the price may be right. They're never my first choice, but when more traditional accommodation pickings are slim—in peak season, or any time of year in pricey places like London—modern chain hotels can make up for a lack of character with reasonable rates and convenient locations.

Chains provide predictable comfort and amenities (elevators, 24-hour reception), and can be an especially good choice for families who need triple or quad rooms. And they can offer some of the best prices in town, especially if you snag an advance-booking discount or a last-minute deal. When demand is extra low, even fancier business-class chains (such as NH, Sorat, and Barceló) may offer prices far below their peak-season rates.

Here's a rundown of some of Europe's affordable hotel chains, roughly from bare bones to the plusher end of the budget range:

Hotel F1 (France): Stark, cheap rooms with bathrooms down the hall—like hosteling with privacy; often located on major roads outside city centers

EasyHotel: Tiny, super-efficient, no-frills rooms that feel popped out of a plastic mold, with low base rates and steep add-on charges; mostly located in big cities

B&B Hotel (Germany): Basic, playfully colorful rooms with a slightly institutional feel

Ibis: Reliable, good-value, colorful, modern rooms; "Ibis Budget" subset is basic but a step above F1 and EasyHotel

Travelodge (Britain, Ireland): Plain, serviceable rooms often at great prices

Premier Inn (Britain, Ireland): Nice-enough, family-friendly rooms; most are conveniently located and operated with industrial-strength efficiency

Motel One (Germany, Austria, Britain): Small but surprisingly chic rooms, usually in great locations; prices generally fluctuate

Europe's cheap, no-character hotels cater to business travelers interested in going home with some of their per diem still in their pockets.

between two levels (normal and peak) but are always affordable

Jurys Inn (Britain, Ireland): Reasonably priced, usually spacious rooms with American-hotel feel

Best Western: Rooms of varied cushiness and personality, but always with standard amenities; often located in older buildings with character

Holiday Inn: Corporate-feeling rooms akin to their US cousins; good family option

Mercure: Stylish and cushy business-class rooms

Novotel: Often large (but characterless) rooms with Mercure-level quality but more amenities

What to Expect at Guesthouses and Hotels

Whether staying at a characteristic European hotel or a three-room guesthouse, be prepared for some quirkiness.

Arrival and Check-In

In European cities, hotels and B&Bs (and their reception desks) are sometimes located on the higher floors of multi-purpose buildings. You may arrive to find the ground-floor entrance is locked; if so, look for the hotel's name on the buzzer plate. Someone at the front desk will buzz you in when you ring the bell.

The EU requires hotels to collect your name, nationality, and passport ID number. At check-in, the front desk staff will normally ask for your passport and may keep it for several hours. If you're not comfortable leaving your passport at the desk, bring a photocopy to give them instead.

Check-in is a good time to reconfirm the complete and final price of your room, including any discounts. Know what's included in the price and what taxes and other charges (breakfast, Wi-Fi, etc.) will be added. Once when checking out, I was given a bill that was double what I expected. (Dinners were required, and I was billed whether I

Check-in is a good time to clarify details, such as what time breakfast is served.

The 🔑 to Keys

The following "keys" will help you unlock the mystery of European hotel-room doors.

Like in the US, many European hotels use a **key-card system.** If there's no slot in which to insert the card, try touching it to your door's keypad. Once inside the room, you'll probably need to insert your card into a slot near the door to turn on the lights. (This "green" measure prevents guests from leaving the lights on when they're not in the room).

At places that have yet to switch to key cards, you may fumble with old **skeleton keys** in rickety hotel doors. The haphazard, nothing-square construction of old hotels means the lock may need babying: Always turn the key away from the doorframe to open it. Some locks take two key revolutions to open. If the key doesn't work at first, don't push it in all the way. Lift the door in or up. Try a little in, quarter turn, and farther in for full turn.

When leaving the hotel for the first time, ask the hotelier if you should take the key with you or drop it off at the desk (bulky keychains are generally an indication that a key is meant to be left behind, but it's good to check). It can be handy to leave the key behind, as you can split up with your travel partner without worrying about who will get back to the room first. Before you drop your key and walk out, confirm when reception closes. In some smaller places, you're expected to keep the key to the outside door with you, so you can get back in after hours.

ate them or not, or so I was told—in very clear Italian.) Avoid such mishaps by going over everything at check-in.

Before leaving the front desk, request the Wi-Fi network name and password. Find out when and where breakfast is served. And pick up the hotel's business card, which likely comes with a handy little "you are here" map. If you get lost while out sightseeing, armed with the hotel's card, you can hop into a cab and be home in minutes. Most hotels also give out free city maps.

If you're arriving in the morning, your room probably won't be ready. Check your bag safely at the hotel and dive right into sightseeing.

Getting to Your Room

In general, European accommodations have more stairs and fewer elevators than in the US. When climbing to your room, think of the exercise you're getting, and be glad you've packed light. Remember that the floors of buildings are numbered differently in Europe. The bottom floor is called the ground floor, and what we call the second floor is a European's first floor. So if your room is on the second floor (European), bad news—you're on the third floor (American). On the bright side, higher floors generally have better views and less street noise than lower ones.

Hotel elevators in Europe tend to be minuscule. Sometimes only one person with a backpack can fit at one time (couples can split up, sending bags up separately for the other person to retrieve). In the elevator, push whatever's below "1" to return to the ground floor.

In Your Room

As European hotels are likely to be in small, centuries-old buildings, be prepared for some idiosyncrasies. (For details on hotel-room bathrooms, see page 424.)

Beds: At many hotels—especially in northern and eastern Europe—a "double bed" is two twin beds pushed together, and each one gets its own twin-sized comforter. If you asked for separate beds and arrive to find one big one, check to see if it's actually two twins that you can pull apart.

Expect regional differences in bedding. In France, some beds have irregular pillows (shaped like a wedge or a log). In alpine areas and in northern Europe, many hotels use covered duvets instead of a top sheet; don't be confused if your top sheet is "missing." In warm climates, you may only have a sheet, and no comforter. To get an American-style pillow or extra blankets, look in the closet or ask at the desk.

Air-Conditioning and Heat: While not universal, air-conditioning is becoming more common in European hotels. Most units come with a remote control with a fan icon (for toggling through wind power), louver icon (for steady air flow or waves), sunshine and snowflake icons (cool in summer, heat in winter), two clock settings (to preset when the unit will turn on or off), and temperature control (20 degrees

LEFT A remote lets you cool off the room without getting out of bed.

RIGHT French hotels sometimes come with Lincoln Log pillows.

Celsius is comfortable). It's good form to turn off the air-conditioning when you leave your room for the day.

Be aware that local regulations may prohibit turning on the air-conditioning between October and May—if it's important to you, confirm that air-conditioning will be available during your stay (most hotels without air-conditioning provide fans upon request). Similarly, some hotels and guesthouses in warmer regions don't run their central heat before November and after March unless it's unusually cold—prepare for cool evenings if you travel in spring and fall.

Windows: Much of northern Europe favors clever "turn-tilt" windows that you operate by turning an L-shaped handle in one of three positions: Down is closed, horizontal allows you to swing the entire window wide open at its vertical hinges, and up lets you tilt it outward on top—perfect for airing out the room without letting in rain.

Safes: Many hotel rooms come with safes, but I've never bothered using one. (Years of tour guiding have taught me that the risk of accidentally leaving behind valuables stashed in a safe is far greater than the chance of theft.) But it's always smart to keep your most tempting items—cash, jewelry, electronics, cameras—out of sight (as maids may leave the doors open for long stretches during the day). In the rare case that something is stolen from your room, report your loss to the hotelier right away.

Wi-Fi: Don't be surprised if the Wi-Fi signal is less than robust in your room. The quirky configurations and often thick stone walls of older buildings can be too much of a hurdle for some routers. Try logging on near the front desk—or wait until late in the evening (or midday), when fewer guests are competing for bandwidth.

Televisions: Hotel rooms generally have TVs, while many guesthouse rooms don't—but this varies. European TVs differ from US ones only in that they usually take an extra button press to turn on (possibly on the TV itself). Once the power's on, press any channel number (or the channel-up or channel-down button) on the remote to bring the TV to life.

Hairdryers: All but the very cheapest hotels and guesthouses tend to provide hairdryers—if you don't see one on the bathroom wall or under the sink, ask at reception; they likely have one to lend.

Hotelier Help

Front-desk clerks can be a great help and source of advice.

Hoteliers and guesthouse hosts know their city well and can assist you with everything from public transit and airport connections to finding a good restaurant, the nearest launderette, or a late-night pharmacy. Staff at any full-service hotel will happily call a taxi for you, make restaurant reservations, telephone your next hotel, or give you driving instructions for your departure.

Hoteliers can offer valuable advice about visiting their city.

Guesthouse hosts might not have as much time to field these sorts of requests but asking nicely usually does the trick.

Many hoteliers can book bus tours and evening entertainment for you—just be wary that their recommendations may be biased, as they usually get a commission for these bookings. In general, it's a good idea to seek objective sightseeing advice and handle your own entertainment plans: You'll be less likely to find yourself in a tourist herd, and you may even save a little money.

Hotel Hassles

As at any hotel anywhere, the room you're assigned might not be exactly what you expected. Since it's easier to change rooms before you've settled in, consider potential headaches and report any problem with the room as soon as possible (noisy, too small, broken fixtures, moldy shower, etc.)—fixing it may be as simple as handing you the keys to a different room.

Disappointing Rooms: I always take a few minutes upon arrival to tweak my room to my tastes. If the furniture's arranged in a way that doesn't work for me, I move it (carefully). If the mattress has one of those protective rubber mats that causes me to sweat through the night, I take it off. If my weird pillow has "neck cramps" written all over it, I look in the closet for a different one—or ask at the front desk. Being proactive can make a huge difference.

That said, it's important to have a sense of what's normal—but not actually problematic—about your average budget European hotel room. European hotel bathrooms—especially showers—are often teeny by our standards, and the capacity of the hot-water tank is limited (for more on hotel bathrooms, see page 424).

It can be especially disappointing to arrive at a hotel and find that your room is in a less desirable annex or in a partner hotel. If you feel the hotel has misrepresented its offer, it can help to show the front desk a copy of their confirmation email and press them to change your room (if they don't accommodate you, you don't need to stay).

Noise: Europe seems to excel in thin-walled rooms, narrow streets that amplify traffic noise, and people who party until the wee hours in formerly romantic piazzas. If you suspect night noise will be a problem, ask for a room in the back or on an upper floor.

Mechanical Issues: These are a reality for any building—sinks leak, hot water turns cold, toilets may gurgle or smell, the Wi-Fi goes out, or the air-conditioning dies when you need it most. After you've (calmly) reported your concerns at the front desk, be patient. Don't expect instant results, especially if it's right after breakfast (when the staff is busy checking out other guests) or in a family-run place with a small staff.

Bugs: Now and then travelers encounter bedbugs, even at fine hotels. Make it a habit to check mattress seams for specks of blood before you unpack. Otherwise, your first sign of trouble will be small, itchy welts (similar to mosquito bites), which may not show up until a day or two after you've been bitten. These critters are a nuisance, but they don't spread disease. If you find evidence of bedbugs, it doesn't necessarily mean the hotel is overrun with them. Report the problem and see how it's dealt with. Changing rooms should be enough.

Unfortunately, European mosquitos like warm evenings just as much as their American cousins. If your hotel room's windows don't have screens, think twice before leaving your window open all day for ventilation.

Resolving Issues: If you're unhappy with something, let your hotelier know. Doing this doesn't make you an Ugly American. If you state your concern to your hotelier politely, you'll likely be dealt with kindly.

If your concerns aren't being addressed, be persistent; if you aren't getting anywhere with one staff member, try approaching a more sympathetic or capable employee. Generally, the hotel staff doesn't like to have complaints aired in earshot of other customers, so it can be effective to state your problems clearly and reasonably with witnesses around. The staff may accommodate you just to shut you up.

If you're in southern Europe and having trouble getting a problem solved, ask to see the complaint book, which the hotelier is legally required to show you on request.

Sometimes even just asking to see the complaint book will inspire the hotelier to address your concern. If you've had a good experience, jot a friendly note in the hotel's guest book; conscientious hoteliers love to show these off to arriving guests.

Unfriendly staff, malfunctioning equipment, uncomfortable mattresses, and other hotel annoyances can be a hassle, but don't let them take the joy out of your trip. If your hotel is a disappointment, spend more time out enjoying the place you came to see.

Departure and Check Out

While it's customary to pay for your room upon departure, it can be a good idea to settle your bill the day before, when you're not in a hurry and while the manager's in. That way you'll have time to discuss and address any points of contention.

If surprise charges do pop up on your bill, ask the hotelier to explain each item you're not sure about. It's every guest's right to understand their bill.

Some unexpected charges are legitimate. For example, in many touristy areas, hotels must charge a per-day city tax that may not be included in the official rates (usually about €1-5 per person per night).

It's smart to have extra cash on hand at checkout, just in case. I've seen credit-card readers mysteriously break just as guests are checking out, requiring them to pay in cash. Even if the hotel will happily take your card, they may request that you pay the city hotel tax in cash (to simplify their book-keeping). And it's always worth asking whether they'd give a discount for paying with cash.

If you're not heading directly to your next stop, hoteliers are almost always happy to store your bags for the day— either behind the desk or in a locked room near reception. I've never had anything stolen from a hotel's bag-storage room, but if you're worried, consider keeping your most valuable items with you for the day (and never leave your money belt behind).

SHORT-TERM RENTALS

A short-term rental—whether an apartment, a house, or a room in a private residence—is a popular alternative, especially if you plan to settle in one location for more than a few days. Rental options run the gamut, from French *gîtes* and Tuscan villas to big-city apartments and basic rooms in a local's home. You can usually find a rental that's comparable to—or even cheaper than—a hotel room with similar amenities. Prices vary depending on the season, size, location, and quality of the accommodation.

The rental route is a great way to experience Europe on its own terms, but it isn't for everyone. First off, you're generally on your own. While the apartment owner or manager might offer some basic assistance, don't expect all the services of a hotel reception desk. If you like daily access to a breakfast room, fresh towels, and a sheet change, stay in a hotel. In a rental, breakfast is up to you, and your apartment or room likely won't be serviced or cleaned during a one-week stay unless you pay extra.

Some rentals, especially rooms in a local's home, are very casual affairs, without the professionalism (or privacy) you'd expect in a more formal hotel environment. Rentals often require a minimum-night stay and long lead times on cancellations. Choose a hotel instead if there's a decent chance your plans might change.

Finding and Reserving Short-Term Rentals

Where to Look

Sources for rental accommodations include websites that put you in touch with the owners or managers of a range of properties (from a single room to a plush villa), and rental agencies, where a go-between facilitates your rental.

Aggregator Websites: Websites such as Airbnb, FlipKey, Booking.com, and VRBO let you browse a wide range of properties. TripAdvisor has an option for searching just vacation rentals, and each listing comes with TripAdvisor's voluminous user reviews. But keep in mind that, for the most part, the listings are unvetted. It's up to you to determine if a holiday house meets your particular needs in terms of location, features, and amenities.

Owners pay a fee to list their places and include photos and loads of other information (number of bedrooms and bathrooms, amenities, parking availability, nearby attractions and services, etc.) to help you make your decision. Reading reviews from previous guests can help identify trouble spots that may be glossed over in the official description.

These websites collect payment when you reserve but only release the funds to owners after you've checked in, a method of reducing fraud. A booking fee is generally built into the price. Most sites allow guests to rate hosts—and sometimes vice versa. To help renters feel safe, some sites require hosts and guests to be "verified" by providing a government-issued ID and connecting their profiles to online social networks. Hosts can gain elevated status, such as being "certified" or named a "superhost," through a track record of good service.

Rental Agencies: If you prefer to work from a curated list of accommodations, consider going through a rental agency for homes and apartments. Using an agency is convenient, the places they list have been screened, and their staff will work with you to find an appropriate accommodation. For instance, if you're traveling with a large group or aren't sure what neighborhood you want to be in, it might be easier to convey your needs to a rental agency and let them do the legwork. Agency-represented apartments typically cost more, but this method often offers more help and safeguards than booking direct.

Agencies such as InterhomeUSA.com and the more upscale RentaVilla.com list places all over Europe. Other agencies concentrate on a certain region or city. For example, Prague-stay.com focuses on apartments in Prague, while FranceHomestyle.com lists rentals throughout France.

Narrowing Your Options

Before you commit to a rental, be clear on the details, location, and amenities (for a list of questions to ask, see the "Short-Term Rental Questions" sidebar, later).

Check out the location on a map—one person's "close to downtown" is another's "boondocks." I like to virtually explore the neighborhood using Google Street View. Also consider the proximity to public transportation, and how well connected the property is with the rest of the city. Factor the cost of commuting to your sightseeing into the overall price. If you plan on driving, ask about parking.

Make sure you're aware of the property's amenities and quirks. Don't be afraid to ask questions. For example, what floor is the apartment on? Is there an elevator or is it a walk-up? Does the kitchen have a microwave, coffee maker, and so on? Is there a washer/dryer? How dependable is the Wi-Fi? If the owner or agency is anything but helpful, skip to the next place on your list.

Read reviews. If there's one complaint, you can ignore it as being from a grumpy renter. But if four or five posters

LEFT For groups of friends, renting an apartment or house is a fun, more sociable option.

RIGHT Remember that top-floor apartments—like this one in Prague—may come with a lot of stairs.

comment on the same problem, pay attention. Be aware that reviewers on aggregator websites are a diverse lot, ranging from high-maintenance travelers to rugged backpackers, so expectations—and resulting opinions—may vary. A booking agency's posted reviews are almost certainly curated to weed out particularly negative ones.

Think about the kind of experience you want: Just a key and an affordable bed...or a chance to get to know a local? Some hosts offer self check-in and minimal interaction; others enjoy meeting their guests. Read the description and reviews to help shape your decision.

Confirming and Paying

When you make a reservation, expect to pay a deposit, which can range from 10 to 50 percent of the rental cost. Many places require you to pay the entire balance before your trip or upon arrival (possibly in cash). The easiest and safest way to pay is through the listing site, which can process credit-card payments and offers some degree of fraud protection. Be wary of owners who want you to take your transaction offline to avoid fees charged by the rental site; this gives you no recourse if things go awry. Never agree to wire money—this is a key indicator of a fraudulent transaction in the making.

Before you finalize a booking, read the rental agreement, which usually includes the house rules and the cancellation policy. Rentals can have much more rigid cancellation policies than hotels (such as 30 or 60 days, and some portion of your deposit may be nonrefundable).

Rental Options

Apartments and Houses

Whether in a city or the countryside, renting an apartment, house, or villa can be a fun and cost-effective way to delve into Europe. In general, if you're staying in one location for several nights, it's worth considering an apartment or rental house (shorter stays aren't worth the hassle of arranging key pickup, buying groceries, etc.). This gives you an opportunity to really get to know a town. Renting an apartment can be a particularly good strategy if you're choosing a home-base city from which to take day trips (see the list of good home-base cities on page 56).

Apartment or house rentals can be especially cost-effective for groups. Two couples traveling together can share a two-bedroom apartment, which often ends up being less expensive than a pair of hotel rooms. Groups of backpackers find that splitting the price of a cheap apartment can cost even less than paying for several bunks at a youth hostel. Having a place to cook can further your savings. Stock your kitchen for breakfast and simple home-cooked meals, taking advantage of the colorful markets that pop up throughout European cities and towns.

For families, an apartment or house is a huge benefit. Kitchens make it easier and cheaper to feed picky eaters. Laundry machines are especially handy. With more than one room, parents of younger children can hang out and chat while their kids slumber (as opposed to being trapped in a hotel room with the lights out at 8 p.m.). Teenagers can stay at "home" while you go out to a restaurant: They'll feel independent, and you'll get a night on the town.

Rooms in Private Residences

Renting a room in someone's home is another alternative that can be much more affordable than a hotel, homier than a hostel, and just as comfortable as either. Most people informally renting out rooms are in it to make

Short-Term Rental Questions

Ask these questions when booking:
- What is the cancellation policy?
- What are check-in and check-out times?
- Whom do I contact if there is a problem?
- How do I get the key? (request multiples if needed)
- What floor is the unit on? Is there an elevator?
- What amenities are available?
- Is there reliable Wi-Fi?
- Is the kitchen fully equipped for cooking?
- Where can I park?
- Where is the closest public transportation?
- Where is the closest grocery store, pharmacy, playground?
- What is your cleaning policy/fee?

a few extra bucks, not to run a full-fledged lodging business with the infrastructure and expenses that drive up costs. If you're willing to accept a small space, a shared bathroom, or other "inconveniences," you'll be able to find remarkably affordable deals through services like Airbnb. Some places allow you to book for a single night.

Renting a room in someone's home is an especially good option for those traveling alone, as you're more likely to find true single rooms—with just one single bed, and a price to match. Some room-rental arrangements also include use of the house's kitchen and laundry facilities.

While you can't expect your host to also be your tour guide—or even to provide you with much info—some are interested in getting to know the travelers who pass through their home. (If you're interested in staying in locals' homes less as a lodger and more in the spirit of cultural exchange, see "Crashing with Locals for Free," later.)

Rural Rentals

Having an entire farmhouse, countryside cottage, or villa to yourself is a wonderful way to immerse yourself in rural Europe. Often the owners have renovated an original rambling farmhouse or medieval estate into a series of well-constructed apartments with private kitchens, bathrooms, living areas, and individual outdoor terraces. They usually share a common pool and other amenities, and breakfast may be included.

Many of these vacation properties (*casas rurales* in Spain, *Ferienhäuser* in Germany, *gîtes* in France) are available only for a traditional Saturday-to-Saturday rental. Especially for stays in July and August, when much of Europe is on vacation, it may be difficult to rent a place for a shorter time. Europeans often reserve their favorite spot a year in advance, so you may have to hunt around to find an opening. (Fortunately for Americans, the British are some of the most avid seekers of weekly rental property in Europe, so there's usually plenty of English-language info.) It's wise to book several months in advance for high season (late April to mid-October).

Although a week might seem like a long time, one of the joys of staying that long in one location is *il dolce far niente* (the "sweetness of doing nothing"). Settling in one spot gives you the chance to let the days unwind without a plan. A walk at sunrise may find you in the company of the local farmer as he trims his grape vines, or the neighboring grandmother who is lovingly tending her small garden. In the evening, breathe in the fresh air as you sip your wine, and perk your ears and nostrils to the sounds and scents of the countryside. This is your chance to slow down and enjoy.

Short-Term Rental Tips

Get directions. Make sure you nail down directions to the rental prior to your arrival. Apartments, especially those in big cities, can be tricky to find. House numbers often have no obvious correlation to one another (for example, in Italy, #28 may be directly across the street from #2).

Know how to get in. Some owners will send you a combination to a keypad door lock or a lock box where they keep the key. Others will want to arrange a time to meet in person so they can give you the keys and show you around. This is your opportunity to ask for neighborhood tips. But once the owners leave, you probably won't see them again.

Read the manual. The rental property usually comes with an "instruction manual" containing information on how to operate the appliances and suggestions for local restaurants, shops, and sightseeing. The property owner's suggestions can point you to authentic local restaurants and activities you may never stumble upon otherwise. Patronize nearby mom-and-pop grocery stores, butcher shops, pastry shops, and bakeries.

Leave it like you found it. When departing, leave the place clean and in good condition—or you may lose some or all of your security deposit. Some owners may ask you to do minimal cleaning before you leave (for instance, stripping off bed linens or emptying the fridge).

HOSTELS

While Europe is no longer the budget backpacker's paradise, shoestring travelers still have their pick of several thousand hostels, each providing cheap beds where you sleep alongside strangers for $20-40 per night. Travelers of any age are welcome if they don't mind dorm-style accommodations and meeting other travelers. Most hostels offer kitchen facilities, Wi-Fi, and a self-service laundry.

If cost is your main concern, hostels are a good way to go: You're paying just for what you need, and access to kitchen facilities can seriously trim your food budget. But millions of travelers—including many older adventurers who could afford a nice hotel—love hostels just as much for the chance to connect with fellow travelers from around the world. Hosteling is a philosophy. A hosteler trades service and some privacy for a chance to stay inexpensively, simply, and communally with people from around the world.

Don't rule out "youth" hostels just because, by every standard, you're older than young. If you're alive, you're young enough to hostel just about anywhere in Europe (hostels with age cutoffs are rare). Yes, the bulk of the hosteling crowd is 18 to 26 years old—but every year there are more seniors and families hosteling. As a reader posted on my website: "My partner and I stayed in a 'youth' hostel for the first time by Lake Como and thought we'd be the oldest people there. Not so! At our table was a 60-ish couple from Sydney and a 79-year-old British woman who was backpacking alone through Europe. All three were a delight, but especially the backpacker, who said she stays in hostels for the evening company."

For students, travelers on a budget, solo travelers, groups or families who can take a whole room, and those hoping to meet other travelers, hostels can be a great option.

The Hostel Experience

Hostels vary in size, quality, and character. If a hostel is an official member of the venerable Hosteling International organization, it's probably big, institutional, and a bit rule-laden, but predictably clean, well-organized, and family-friendly (it probably also takes in lots of school groups). Although you'll still find plenty of official HI hostels (especially north of the Alps), these days they're outnumbered by independently run hostels. Independent hostels tend to be more easygoing and colorful (or chaotic and ramshackle, depending on the place).

Amenities: In general, hostels offer no-frills accommodations in clean dormitories, which typically hold four to eight bunk beds (sometimes many more), possibly along with lockers and a sink. Mixed-sex dorms are standard (except at official HI hostels), but nearly all offer some female-only rooms. If single-sex dorms are unavailable—and a dormmate is making you feel unsafe—let the staff know, and they'll do their

One of Europe's hostels: $45 a night, your own kitchen, a million-dollar view of the Swiss Alps, and lots of friends.

best to accommodate you (by swapping your bunk assignment, or perhaps putting you in a private room at no extra charge). Hostels almost always provide bedding, but the towel's up to you (though you can usually rent one for a small fee). Bathrooms are usually just down the hall and likely have a room with a few toilet stalls, and another with showers. Most hostels provide free Wi-Fi, although it's sometimes limited to the ground floor.

Private Rooms: Most hostels offer a few well-priced private rooms. Four-bunk rooms are common and a great value for families, while couples who want privacy can find true doubles. Private single rooms are also available and a boon for solo travelers who aren't up for the dorm experience.

Location: Big-city hostels can be overrun by young backpackers, so if a party-hearty scene sounds more annoying than fun, pay special attention to reviews about the vibe when booking. Still, you should find plenty of urban hostels offering a more subdued atmosphere.

Rural hostels, far from train lines and famous sights, are usually quiet and frequented by a more mature crowd, with relaxed backpackers striking up intergenerational friendships with outdoorsy retirees. While most hostels are conveniently located within easy access of public transportation, those traveling by car are smart to use that mobility to enjoy some of Europe's overlooked hostels.

Upscale Hostels: As Europe has grown more affluent, the average hostel experience has gotten a little cushier. Many hostels have been remodeled to provide more plumbing and smaller rooms. In recent years, a slew of "boutique" hostels has sprouted up. These "poshtels" usually come with funky, design-oriented decor, often with equally stylish on-site bars and restaurants. Most offer more private rooms and en suite bathrooms than your average hostel, but still come with affordable smaller dorms, shared kitchens, and lots of common areas. Of course, all that flair comes at a price—a bed in an upscale hostel can easily cost more than one at a budget hotel.

Finding and Booking Hostels

HostelWorld is the dominant online resource for hostel reviews and bookings (although you may pay a bit less by reserving directly with the hostel). To reserve any official HI hostel, head to HIHostels.com. Both sites collect small nonrefundable deposits at booking.

When looking for hostels, keep the following in mind.

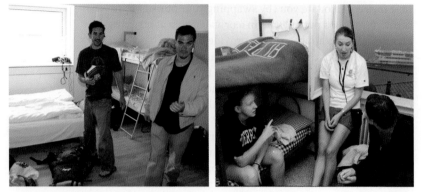

Consider factors other than price. You might save a few bucks by choosing a bunk in a big dorm, but you've wasted your money if it costs you a decent night's sleep. Pay attention to location and atmosphere. User reviews can be helpful, but I wouldn't pay much attention to ratings for cleanliness or helpfulness of the staff (these can be negatively influenced by first-time hostelers who unfairly hold their dorm room to hotel standards).

In some hostels, there are dorms for boys...and dorms for girls.

Be prepared for peak-season competition. The most popular hostels fill up every day; don't assume you can just show up and find a bed (especially if you want a private room). If possible, book a hostel stay as soon as your schedule is set. If you want to keep your itinerary flexible, try to book at least a day or two in advance. If a hostel shows as full online, call or email—they may be holding some beds for drop-ins. (For the best shot at nabbing a last-minute spot, arrive early in the morning, especially if the office closes at midday—otherwise you'll be just one among the scruffy gang lining up for the evening reopening, when remaining beds are doled out.)

Don't worry about HI membership. Although official HI hostels are technically for members only, nonmembers pay just a few dollars extra per night. Unless you plan to stay at a lot of HI hostels, membership probably isn't worth it, especially given the proliferation of independent hostels.

Hostel selectively. In some areas, budget hotels can make more sense than hostels. Especially if you're traveling as a couple, a cheap hotel room can beat the price of a private hostel room. This is more likely in southern Europe (Italy and Spain); the farther north you go, the bigger the price gap between hostels and the cheapest hotel rooms. (In Scandinavia, for example, locals know that hostels provide the best—and usually only—$30 beds in town...which explains all the Volvos you'll see in hostel parking lots.)

Look for unique hostel experiences. Some hostels are sightseeing destinations in themselves. For a small fraction of what you'd pay for a run-of-the-mill hotel room, you can enjoy a memorable stay in a hilltop castle (Bacharach, Germany), former stables (Nürnberg, Germany), moored ships and a converted jumbo jet (Stockholm), alpine chalets (Gimmelwald, Switzerland), a lakefront villa (Lugano, Switzerland), former prisons (Stockholm—again—and Ljubljana, Slovenia), a medieval manor house (Shropshire, England), a 400-person tent (Munich), vintage camper trailers (Bonn, Germany), white-washed cave houses (Santorini, Greece), retired train cars (Scottish Highlands), former choirboys' dorms (London), and a brothel-turned-hostel (Amsterdam, of course).

Europe is home to all sorts of unique hostels, such as this castle overlooking the Rhine River in Bacharach, Germany.

Hosteling Tips

When hosteling, it pays to pack smartly, use common sense, and take advantage of all that hostels have to offer.

Pack a few hostel extras. Bring a towel—lightweight, quick-dry towels are best—as few hostels include them with your stay (though most have towels for rent). A sleep mask and ear plugs (or headphones) help you sleep through bunkmates' late arrivals and early morning departures. Flip-flops come in handy in bathroom stalls, and a small power strip (so lots of gear can be charged at the same time) does wonders for dormmate relations. While lockers are common in dorm rooms, they're not universal, and often don't come with a built-in lock—bring your own. Hostelers who are used to bringing a sleep sack should check ahead before packing it—concerned about bedbugs, many hostels now require you to use their linens.

Get out of your social bubble. Travelers find new friends and travel partners in every hostel. A hostel's recreation and living rooms are my favorite hangouts. People gather, play games, tell stories, share information, read, write, and team up for future travels. Even if the lights go out at 11 p.m., bunk-bed conversation can rage on. You may well find yourself propped on your elbows staring intensely into the darkness, passing around travel tales like a bucket of popcorn.

Save money by eating in. A simple breakfast is usually included in the price of your bed. Additional hearty, super-cheap meals may be served (at an extra cost but generally the cheapest hot meals in town), often in cafeteria-style settings. A typical dinner is fish sticks and

Hostels: Meet, drink, and be merry.

mashed potatoes seasoned with conversation with new friends from Norway to New Zealand. Most hostels have a self-service kitchen, complete with utensils, pots, and pans. Larger hostels even have small grocery stores.

Seek sightseeing information. Most hostel lobbies are littered with brochures and bulletin boards alerting you to local tours, events, and public-transportation details; larger ones in bigger cities may also organize walking tours and pub crawls. Remember that your roommates or breakfast companions can also be great sources of advice.

Guard your valuables. Theft can be a problem in hostels. Wear your money belt (even while sleeping), and don't leave your phone—or anything else tempting—lying around. Don't worry—no one's going to steal your sneakers or journal. If the hostel doesn't offer lockers, consider securing your bag with a small combo lock, or at least clipping it to a bedpost. Any hindrance, no matter how small, makes it more likely that a thief will move on.

Note lockout hours. Institutional-feeling hostels may have midday lockout times (commonly 10 a.m. to 5 p.m.), when guests are required to vacate rooms (for cleaning and for safety's sake, if the office staff isn't around to keep an eye on things). Nighttime curfews and lockouts are even rarer—but check the hostel's policy before you go out for the evening. A curfew can be a big advantage: Hostels that don't have curfews are more likely to have drunk and rowdy hostelers returning at ungodly hours.

Exercise tolerance. The sounds you'll hear in bigger dorm halls just after everyone's turned in remind me of summer camp—giggles, burps, jokes, and strange noises in many languages. Snoring is permitted and practiced openly. School groups can turn a normally quiet HI hostel upside down, typically over school-year weekends and at any time in summer. Try to be understanding (remember, we were all noisy kids at one time).

CRASHING WITH LOCALS FOR FREE

There's no better way to get to know a new country than to stay in someone's home. There are several ways to do this for free, from swapping houses to couch-surfing to crashing on your neighbor's cousin's couch.

Staying with Europeans as a House Guest

Being a guest in a European home isn't all that different from being a guest in an American one. Before you arrange to stay with someone, though, consider the possible drawbacks of your free bed. At a hotel, B&B, hostel, or short-term rental you have no social obligations to your host, and it isn't perceived as rude to return late at night. There's also location to consider: If you're sleeping where others live, there's a decent chance you'll be in a workaday suburb, far from old-town charm or the sights you came to see. You'll probably be able to reach the city center on your own (thanks to Europe's great public transit), but that commute will cost you time and money. Nonetheless, for those aware of the trade-offs, crashing with locals can be a great option.

Volunteering and Cultural Exchanges: If you believe that travel is about community good and bringing people together, consider joining a cultural-exchange organization, which lets you stay with hosts in their home or finding volunteer work abroad (see page 481). Note that while travelers do get a free bed with their hosts, the focus is much less about providing accommodation than an opportunity to connect and contribute.

Bunking with Friends (or Friends of Friends)

Staying with a friend, relative, or common acquaintance not only stretches your budget (usually along with your belly), but your cultural horizons. Try and dig up some European relatives, friends, friends of relatives, or relatives of friends. No matter how far out on the family tree they are, unless you're a real jerk, they'll be tickled to have an American visitor in their nest. I email my potential host, telling them when I'll arrive and asking if they'd be free to meet for dinner while I'm there. They answer with "Please come visit us" or "Have a good trip." It's obvious from their response (or lack of one) if I'm invited to stop by and stay awhile.

Especially if you are traveling solo and reasonably extroverted, you're likely to make new friends on the road. When people meet, they invite each other to visit. Once

Alternative Budget Options

Hostels aren't the only places to find low-cost rooms in Europe. Consider these creative alternatives.

Convents and Monasteries: Around Europe, but particularly in Italy, convents and monasteries provide peaceful and often economical sleeping quarters. The beds are twins, the decor is spartan, and English can be in short supply—but it's quiet at night. MonasteryStays.com and GoodNightandGodBless.com are good starting points for finding places that take guests (most are in Italy, with scattered listings in Ireland, Spain, and Austria). Saint Patrick's Church in Rome maintains a list of such places in the city and beyond (StPatricksAmericanRome.org; select "Resources/Convent Accommodations"). It's best to email your reservation request (most convents don't have an English website), or book through one of the websites for a fee.

Dorms: Student housing is often rented out between terms. In London, for example, the University of Westminster, as well as several other colleges, opens its dorm rooms to travelers from June through mid-September. Located in several high-rise buildings scattered around central London, the rooms—some with private baths—come with access to well-equipped kitchens and big lounges. Try UniversityRooms.com for leads.

Turn-Key Camping: Many of Europe's campgrounds offer sites already set up with a tent, trailer, or mobile home and outfitted with linens and kitchen gear. Two British companies are a good place to start: Eurocamp.co.uk and CanvasHolidays.co.uk contract with campgrounds across continental Europe. For more on camping in Europe, see the end of this chapter.

invited to visit, I warn my new friends that I may very well show up some day at their house, whether it's in Osaka, Auckland, Santa Fe, or Dublin. When I have, it's been a good experience.

Don't be afraid to follow up with indirect contacts. You'll be surprised how many friends are potential hosts on the road.

If you're afraid of being seen as a freeloader, remember that both parties benefit. A Greek family is just as curious about you as you are about them. Armed with pictures from home and a bag of goodies for the kids, make a point of giving as much from your culture as you are taking from theirs. I insist on no special treatment other than to be treated simply as part of the family. If you ask for a favor, make it easy for your host to say no. Help with the chores, don't wear out your welcome, and follow up each visit with postcards or emails to share the rest of your trip. It's easy and thoughtful to reimburse your hosts for their hospitality with a bottle of wine, a bunch of flowers, or a thank-you note, possibly with photos of all of you together.

Couch Surfing

Couchsurfing.com and a handful of similar services can put you in touch with outgoing people happy to host fellow travelers in their homes for free. Most do this out of a sincere interest in meeting interesting people, and many are in it for the good karma, having couch-surfed themselves. This service is a boon for laid-

back, budget-minded extroverts who aren't too picky about where they rest their heads. Most surfers are in their 20s and traveling solo, but plenty are a decade or two older, or traveling in small groups.

Safety is a concern of any smart couch surfer. While the Couchsurfing service makes an effort toward this end (offering plenty of safety tips, listing references from travelers and hosts on member profiles, and allowing hosts to pay for name and address verification), travelers must still be on alert for creeps and scammers—they're certainly out there. My best tip for crashing with strangers: Always arrive with a backup hostel, hotel, or Couchsurfing host in mind. If you don't feel comfortable with your host, just leave (after all, it's free). Don't worry about hurting their feelings. Never let budget concerns make you put up with something that feels dangerous.

Tips for Staying with Locals

Not only are you a guest in someone's home, but you are a guest in their country. These tips can help ensure a pleasant experience.

Ask your host for guidance. People who are OK with welcoming guests in their home are usually friendly, interested in others, and eager to show off their town. You'll likely be greeted with genuine enthusiasm. Many hosts happily provide maps, sightseeing and transit information, and advice on how to make the most of your time.

Do your cultural home-work. Some awkwardness is

Staying with friends or relatives (this is my Norwegian cousin) gives you a spot at a local dinner table.

inevitable—expect to make a faux pas or two. Limit embarrassing blunders by researching, before you arrive, etiquette in the country you're visiting. Follow your host's lead—if they're not wearing shoes in the house, leave yours at the door. Be aware of what makes for touchy conversation, and do your best to get squared away on geopolitical basics— e.g., Scotland isn't in England, and Bratislava is no longer in "Czechoslovakia." To bridge a wide language gap, try to learn the elements of that country's nonverbal communication: What means "OK" in the US can mean something quite the opposite in some parts of Europe.

Communicate your plans. Clear communication and a focus on being considerate are critical when trying to bridge a linguistic or cultural divide. If you accept a bed from someone for free, it's polite to give your hosts plenty of advance warning of your arrival and not change plans at the last minute. Let your host know how long you expect to stay, whether you'll be there for dinner in the evening, and where to leave the key in the morning. If your host invites you to dinner, do your best to accept.

House Swapping and House Sitting

Many families enjoy this great budget option. They trade houses (sometimes cars, too—but most draw the line at pets) with someone at the destination of their choice. People who've tried house swapping rave about the range of places they've enjoyed for free, and about the graciousness and generosity of their swap-mates. Good places to start are HomeExchange.com, HomeLink-USA.org, Intervac Home Exchange, and LoveHomeSwap.com.

Swapping works best for people with an appealing place to offer and can live with the idea of having strangers in their home, touching their stuff (of course, you can always lock up your most valuable items and precious heirlooms). Unsurprisingly, those living in swanky Manhattan apartments and beachside villas have the best pick of options in Europe, but you don't need to live in an obvious vacation spot or a mansion to find a workable exchange. Your guests may appreciate the pace of a smaller town (especially if you offer your car) and may be less interested in luxury or location than in finding a suitable place that's available when they are.

Be open to serendipitous opportunities: If you get an inquiry from someone in an unfamiliar spot, you might end up discovering a great new place. Note that your swaps don't have to be simultaneous—for example, you might stay at their place while they're off on a cruise, while they visit your place months later when you're away visiting family for the holidays.

Many swappers who could easily afford pricey trip lodgings still prefer to take the deep culture dive that a home exchange provides. As one experienced swapper told me, "When exchanging, you feel as

With luck, you could swap for this Norwegian retreat.

though you are entering a neighborhood in a way a hotel cannot match. In addition to a car, you often have use of bikes, boats, toys, books, and even sometimes the exchanger's local relatives—all the comforts of home. Being stuck 'at home' on a rainy day doesn't feel like a vacation tragedy!"

Once you've found a potential host, expect to be in fairly close contact as you finalize the swap. Be very clear about your expectations, agree on how you'll handle worst-case scenarios, and get the details pinned down before you leave. Know where to find the key and how to open the door, find out beforehand how to get to the nearest grocery store, make sure your host family leaves instructions for operating the appliances, be sure you have needed passwords (for Wi-Fi, smart TVs, etc.), and ask about any peculiarities with the car you'll be driving. Veteran house swappers report that by the time these logistics are all worked out, it usually feels less like you'll be swapping with strangers, and more like you've made a new, conveniently located friend.

If you're not up for offering up your own place, look into house sitting, which offers many of the same upsides (and downsides). MindMyHouse.com and TrustedHousesitters. com have plenty of listings in Europe but may require pet sitting as well.

CAMPING EUROPEAN STYLE

Camping in Europe is more a social experience than a chance to retreat to nature. There, it's the middle-class family way to travel, and it's cheap. Relatively few Americans take advantage of the thousands of available campgrounds, but those who do give rave reviews. A tent, pillow, and sleeping bag are all you need.

In the US, we think of campgrounds as picturesque outposts near a lake or forest. By contrast, European "campings" (the international word for campgrounds) are often located within or on the outskirts of an urban center and can range from functional (like park-and-rides) to vacation extravaganzas, with restaurants, mini water-parks, and miniature golf. Many campgrounds have small grocery stores and washing machines. In general, European campgrounds are less private than American versions, and many forbid open fires.

Aside from the biggest cities, most tourist-friendly areas have a campground within a reasonable walk or bus ride from the town center or train station. And if you're camping outside a major city, the money you save on parking alone will likely pay for your campsite (leave your car at the campground and take the handy bus downtown).

Campgrounds generally mirror their surroundings: If the region is overcrowded, dusty, dirty, unkempt, and chaotic, you're unlikely to find an oasis behind the campground's gates. A sleepy Austrian valley will probably offer a sleepy Austrian campground.

Campgrounds can fill up. But if they do, the "Full" sign usually refers to motorhomes and trailers. A small tent can almost always be squeezed in somewhere. However, "weekend campings" are rented out on a yearly basis to local urbanites, and often are full or don't allow what they call "stop-and-go" campers (you). Camping guidebooks indicate which places are the "weekend" types.

Cost: Prices at European campgrounds vary according to facilities and style, but don't be surprised if you're asked to pay by the tent, the person, and the vehicle. A camper who bicycles in might pay $3, plus $5 for the tent; a couple driving into the same site might pay $6 for the two of them, $5 for their tent, and $4 for their car.

Registration and Regulations: Camp registration is easy. As with most hotels, you show your passport, fill out a short form, and learn the rules. Quiet is enforced beginning at 10 or 11 p.m., and checkout time is usually noon. English is the second language of campings throughout Europe, and most managers will understand the monoglot American.

Services: Not every campground will take tents; some are RV only. Most campgrounds have laundry

Resources for Camping

EuroCampings.co.uk: Searchable database and user reviews on more than 9,000 campgrounds

CoolCamping.com: "Glamping" and luxury campsites in the UK and France

McRent.eu: Motorhome rentals across Europe

AnywhereCampers.com: One-way RV rentals in Europe

Out of Options (or Money)?

This book is not a vagabonding guide, but things happen: You run out of money, you get into town too late to find a room, or volcanic ash strands you somewhere without a place to stay. I once went 29 out of 30 nights without paying for a bed. It's not difficult...but it's not always comfortable, convenient, clean, safe—or legal.

I no longer lug a sleeping bag around, but if you'll be vagabonding, bring a light bag—you'll find plenty of places to roll it out. Just keep your passport with you, attach your belongings to you so they don't get stolen, and use good judgment in your choice of a free bed. Faking it until the sun returns can become, at least in the long run, a good memory.

The Great Outdoors: Some large cities, such as Amsterdam and Athens, are flooded with tourists during peak season—and some of those tourists spend their nights dangerously in city parks. Most cities enforce their "no sleeping in parks" laws only selectively. Away from the cities, in forests or on beaches, you can pretty much sleep where you like. In my vagabonding days, I found summer nights in the Mediterranean part of Europe mild enough that I was comfortable with just my jeans, sweater, and hostel sheet.

Trains and Train Stations: Some rail-pass holders get a free if disjointed night's sleep by riding a train out for four hours and catching a different train back for another four hours. Assuming the station stays open all night, it can be a free, warm, safe, and uncomfortable place to hang your hat. Most popular tourist cities in Europe have stations with concrete floors that are painted nightly with a long rainbow of sleepy vagabonds. Some stations close for a few hours in the middle of the night, and everyone is always cleared out at dawn before the normal rush of travelers converges on the station. A train ticket or rail pass entitles you to a free night in a station's waiting room: You're simply waiting for your early train. For safety, store your pack in a station locker or check it at the baggage counter.

Airports: After a late landing, crash on an airport sofa rather than waste sleeping time looking for a place that will sell you a bed for the remainder of the night (for a guide to airport slumber, try www.sleepinginairports.com). A few large airports have sterile, womblike "rest cabins" that can be rented for as few as four hours or overnight, but they aren't cheap (for example, see www.yotel.com for London's Heathrow and Gatwick airports, Paris' Charles de Gaulle airport, and Amsterdam's Schiphol airport).

facilities and great showers with metered hot water—carry coins and scrub quickly. Larger campgrounds may have a grocery store and café (a likely camp hangout with an easy-going European social scene).

Equipment: You can bring your gear with you—or buy it in Europe. Tents, sleeping bags, and cooking supplies are cheaper at large European superstores than at specialty backpacking stores. European campers prefer a very light-weight "three-season" sleeping bag and a closed-cell sleeping pad. I'd start without a stove, keeping meals simple by

picnicking and enjoying food and fun in the campground café. If you don't want to bog down with equipment, consider a place that can set up a tent site for you (see "Turn-Key Camping" on page 248).

Safety: Campgrounds are remarkably low-theft. Campings are full of basically honest, middle-class European families, and someone's at the gate all day. Most people just leave their gear in their vans or zipped inside their tents.

Kids: A family can sleep in a tent, van, or motorhome a lot cheaper than in a hotel. Camping offers plenty to occupy children's attention, namely playgrounds that come fully equipped with European kids. As your kids make friends, your campground social circle widens. Campgrounds are filled with Europeans in the mood to toss a Frisbee with a new American friend.

RV Camping: David Shore, co-author of *Europe by Van and Motorhome* (along with Patty Campbell), gives consults on finding and renting the right camper vehicle and offers free shipping on his book for Rick Steves readers (www.roadtripeurope.com).

Each country has companies specializing in camper van and motorhome rentals. Look for one with a pickup and drop-off location that makes sense for your itinerary. McRent.eu has 50 rental depots across Europe; AnywhereCampers.com offers one-way RV rentals.

Another bonus to camper-van travel: Across Europe, with a camper van or motorhome, you can sleep overnight for free in any legal parking space, including rest stops on national motorways (look for a big blue and white *P* sign).

LEFT For a "room" with a view on a tight budget, pitch your tent in a secluded mountain valley.

RIGHT Some campgrounds offer bungalows with kitchenettes and four to six beds. Comfortable and cheaper than hotels, these are particularly popular in Scandinavia.

Eating

Eating in Europe is sightseeing for your taste buds. Every country has local specialties that are good, memorable, or both. Whether it's Wiener schnitzel in Vienna, salade niçoise in Nice, or wurst in Würzburg, a country's cuisine is as culturally important as its museums. But just as there are tricks for sightseeing, there are also ways to maximize your culinary journey.

Much of my experience lies in eating well cheaply. In most places, I find that I can eat well for an average of $50-60 a day by mixing picnics and quick, budget eats with atmospheric restaurant meals. This budget includes $15-20 for lunch (cheaper if you picnic or eat fast food), $30-35 for dinner at a good restaurant (more with wine or dessert), and $5 for chocolate, cappuccino, or gelato. This assumes that breakfast is included with your hotel room (if you have to buy breakfast, have a picnic lunch...or eat less gelato). If you splurge one day, go cheap the next; you can find a satisfying dinner for $20 or less anywhere in Europe. Galloping gluttons can survive on $25 a day by picnicking. If you have more money, of course, it's delightful to spend it dining well.

BREAKFAST BASICS

One time, I grabbed breakfast at a hotel in southern Spain. The only cereal available was a local version of frosted flakes. As there was no "mature" option, I was tickled to have a bowl. But the cereal milk was heated—apparently standard in this part of Spain—and my poor frosted flakes immediately turned to mush. Not so grrrrrrreat.

Soggy flakes or not, I find breakfast to be a fun part of my travel day, especially because the experience varies so much from one country's breakfast table to the next.

The farther north you go in Europe, the heartier the breakfasts. The heaviest is the traditional British "fry-up" or full English (or Scottish or Welsh) breakfast. This large, home-cooked meal is a fundamental part of the bed-and-breakfast experience, and generally included in your room price (for more on British breakfasts, see page 635).

A Scandinavian breakfast buffet is the perennial favorite for the "most food on the table" award. It pays to take advantage of breakfast smorgasbords when you can (generally included in the cost of your room). Even at $15, it's a deal by local standards and can serve as your best big meal of the day. This all-you-can-eat extravaganza generally consists of fresh bread, cheeses, yogurt, cereal, fruit, boiled eggs, herring, cold cuts, and coffee or tea. Grab a drinkable yogurt and go local by pouring it in the bowl and sprinkling your cereal over it. Some hosts provide a roll of foil so you can pack up a lunch from the breakfast spread. If that sounds like a good idea, just ask.

Throughout the Netherlands, Belgium, Germany, Austria, Switzerland, and most points east of there, breakfast is usually included with your room. Though you can expect a more modest buffet than in Scandinavia, you'll still have plenty of options, including rolls, bread, pastries, cold cuts, cheeses, fruit, yogurt, and cereal. If a buffet has eggs, they're most likely boiled (soft or hard); scrambled or fried eggs are relatively rare.

For breakfast, Germans prefer a sandwich with cold cuts and/or a bowl of Müsli (an oat cereal like granola, but less sweet). Try Bircher muesli, a healthful mix of oats, nuts, yogurt, and fruit that tastes far more delicious than it looks (most commonly available in Switzerland). If breakfast is optional, take a walk to the nearest bakery—every German, Austrian, and Swiss town has at least a few bakeries offering an enticing world of bread and pastry, pulled fresh from the oven that morning.

The continental breakfast: bread, jam, and coffee

As you move south and west (France, Italy, Spain, and Portugal), skimpier "continental" breakfasts are the norm. If breakfast is included with your room, it may be something basic, such as a roll with marmalade or jam, possibly a slice of ham or cheese, and coffee or tea.

Many places add items like yogurt, juice, cereal, cold cuts, cheese, fruit, sweet rolls, and eggs to the mix. If your breakfast is too sparse, supplement it with fruit or cheese from a local market.

In many hotels in Spain and France (and some in Italy, Portugal, and elsewhere), you'll have the option of paying extra for breakfast. If that's the case, I often skip the hotel breakfast and visit the corner café, which offers more atmosphere and is less expensive.

In Italy, do as the locals do: Stop into a bar or café to drink a cappuccino and munch a *cornetto* (croissant) while standing at the bar. In France, locals often grab a warm croissant and coffee on the way to work. Queue up with the French and consider the yummy options: croissants studded with raisins, packed with crushed almonds, or filled with chocolate or cream. In Spain, start your day at a corner bar or at a colorful café near the town market hall for the *desayunos* (breakfast special, usually available until noon), which can include coffee, a roll (or sandwich), and juice. Or sample a Spanish specialty, such as *chocolate con churros* (fritters served with a thick, hot chocolate drink), *pan con tomate* (toasted baguette rubbed with garlic and tomato), or a *tortilla española* (hearty slice of potato omelet).

If you're a big coffee drinker, note that breakfast is the only cheap time to caffeinate. Some hotels will serve you a bottomless cup of a rich brew only with breakfast. After that, the cups acquire bottoms and refills will cost you. Some Europeans—especially those from big coffee-drinking countries like France and Italy—have specific coffee etiquette (see "Know Your Joe," later in this chapter). Being a juice man, I keep a liter box of OJ in my room for a morning eye-opener.

Sure, you can find American-style bacon, fried eggs, and orange juice if you look hard enough, but they're nearly always overpriced and disappointing. Instead, come to the European breakfast table with an adventurous spirit. I'm a big-breakfast traditionalist at home, but when I feel the urge for a typical American breakfast in Europe, I beat it to death with a hard roll.

RESTAURANTS

Restaurant dining can lay waste to a tight budget, but it would be criminal to pass through Europe without sampling the specialties served in good restaurants.

For the most part, European restaurants are no more

expensive than American ones. The cost of eating is determined not by the local standard, but by your personal standard. Many Americans can't find an edible meal for less than $30 in their hometown, but their next-door neighbors enjoy eating out for half that. If you can enjoy a $15 meal in Boston, Chicago, or Seattle, you'll eat well in London, Rome, or Helsinki for the same price. Every year I eat about 100 dinners in Europe. My budget target is $15-20 for a simple, fill-the-tank meal; $30-35 for a good restaurant dinner; and $50-55 for a splurge feast.

Just like at home, lunch in Europe generally costs less than dinner. If you want to stretch your budget by mixing picnics and restaurant meals, your euros will go farther if you have lunch at restaurants and picnics for dinner. Drinks (except for wine in southern Europe) and desserts can be the worst value. Skipping those, you can enjoy some surprisingly good, affordable meals.

Keep in mind that restaurants and pubs don't usually serve meals continuously throughout the day. Restaurants often close in the late afternoon (about 2 p.m.) and then reopen at dinner; pubs stay open all day, but serve only drinks and snacks between lunch and dinner. For those in-between times, you'll find plenty of snack bars and cafés happy to feed you.

The Covid-19 pandemic has been particularly rough on the restaurant industry. During post-pandemic travels, be prepared for restaurants listed in guidebooks, articles, or review sites to be closed permanently. It's best to call or check ahead to make sure a place is open, to ask about reservations, and to learn about any regulations you may need to follow.

A fun neighborhood restaurant: no English menus, no credit cards, but good food, good prices, and a friendly staff

Finding a Restaurant

Average tourists are attracted—like moths to a light bulb—to the biggest sign on the most expensive square in town that boasts, *We speak English and accept credit cards.* This place also has an extensive printed menu with every item described in four languages. Though it might feel accessible, that's a place to avoid. It's a trap trying to snare naive, green, rich tourists.

Many European cities have a

bustling, colorful "restaurant row": a street or square lined with characteristic eateries, such as Rue des Bouchers in Brussels, Rue Mouffetard in Paris, Rua das Portas de Santo Antão in Lisbon, Leidsedwarsstraat in Amsterdam, Campo de' Fiori in Rome, Adrianou street in Athens, and Prijeko street in Dubrovnik. The restaurants on these streets usually have straightforward menus of tourist-pleasing dishes, superficial elegance, and gregarious hawkers out front trying to lure in diners. Some of these places have overpriced food and rotten service; others are frequented by locals and offer great ambience and decent value. Differentiate between the two with the help of a travel guidebook, a tip from a trusted local, or some good online research.

Another strategy is to leave the tourist center; there are trendy restaurants all over European cities with innovative, affordable food. You don't need Michelin stars or a crowd-sourced review to tell you what's hot—just stroll around until you find a restaurant with a happy crowd of locals. Look for gastropubs in Great Britain, tapas bars in Spain, and *enoteca* wine bars in Italy. After a few days on the ground, you'll have no trouble telling a genuine hangout from a tourist trap.

Here are some tips for finding a good place to eat.

Look for mom-and-pop restaurants. I search out family-run places serving local specialties made with seasonal ingredients. To find these places, I look for low-rent spots a few blocks off the famous square, with a small selection of dishes featured on a handwritten menu in the native language. The menu is small because they're just going to cook up what they can sell out for the day, it's handwritten because it's shaped by whatever was fresh in the market that morning, and it's in one language because they're targeting local return customers rather than tourists.

Consult a guidebook. A reliable travel guidebook can be a good resource for finding a great place to eat. Most

LEFT Many cities have a "restaurant row" like Rue des Bouchers in Brussels.

RIGHT A small, handwritten menu in the local language is a good sign.

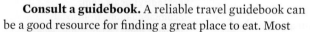

guidebooks list restaurants by neighborhood and locate them on a map, allowing you to peruse a selection of places near your hotel or a major sight. Guidebook listings can help you select a restaurant based on its specialty, ambience, or cost.

Get recommendations from locals. Ask your hotel receptionist, a shop owner, or even someone on the street for a good place—not a good place for tourists, but a place they'd take a friend. If you take a food tour (described near the end of this chapter), ask your guide for recommendations.

Peruse foodie publications and apps. You'll find guidebooks, blogs, and apps dedicated to food in specific destinations. For instance, *The Good Food Guide* prints annual reviews of restaurants, pubs, and cafés around the UK based on feedback received from thousands of readers.

The *Food Lover's Guide to Paris*, from admired French-food expert Patricia Wells, has recommendations for the city's best restaurants, cafés, and bistros (book and app). David Lebovitz, formerly a pastry chef at California's Chez Panisse, now lives in Paris and shares his latest finds and favorite bakeries on his blog (www.davidlebovitz.com). The Lost in Cheeseland website, by author and blogger Lindsey Tramuta, has tips on new hotspots, cooking classes, and more.

Eating & Drinking in Rome, by food journalist Katie Parla, features restaurant recommendations and Roman eating customs (ebook, blog, and app). Elizabeth Minchilli's Eat Italy app has picks for places to eat, drink, and food-shop in Rome, Venice, Florence, and Milan.

For Europe-wide resources, try websites such as TimeOut, with articles and food guides for many European cities, or Spotted by Locals, which features short restaurant write-ups and insider tips from a network of bloggers. And many US newspapers review European restaurants in their travel sections. (The New York Times "36 Hours" column is a good place to start.)

Check user-review sites and apps. Websites and apps such as Yelp, TripAdvisor, and even Google Maps can point you to recommendations based on reviews by other users. You can use these apps to find an eatery

Resources for Eating

SpottedByLocals.com: Recommendations from locals

TimeOut.com: Listings and reviews for restaurants, bars, and food festivals

TripAdvisor, Yelp: Uncurated user reviews

TravelingSpoon.com, BonAppetour.com, EatWith.com: Social dining sites

RickSteves.com/travel-talks: Rick's travel skills talks, including one on eating in Europe

nearby, or to search for a place with a certain price range or type of cuisine (for the pros and cons of user-review sites, see page 35).

Restaurant Etiquette

Your dining experiences will go much smoother if you know what to expect at European restaurants.

Go at the right time. Super-popular restaurants sometimes have two seatings, such as one at 7 p.m. and another at 9 p.m. In general, the early seating will include more tourists, and the late seating will have more locals. I've learned that if I go to a place at 7:30 p.m., it may seem like a tourist trap; but if I go back at 10 p.m., it can feel more like a local favorite. One's not better than the other, but the vibe will likely be different.

Splitting dishes is generally OK. While portions may be expensive, they're often huge and splittable. A key challenge of budget eating is ordering just enough to fill you, while leaving nothing on your plate. If a single main dish is enough for 1.5 people (as many are), split it between yourself and your travel partner, and supplement it with a bowl of soup or small first course. Servers are generally accommodating; the prices are high for Europeans, too. But be careful in France, where splitting meals at restaurants can be frowned upon; instead, head for a café, where it's perfectly acceptable to share meals or order just a salad or sandwich, even for dinner. At any place, it's fine to split a dessert. To save more money, order a carafe of house wine instead of a bottle of fine wine.

Slow service is good service. A lot of Americans complain about how long European meals take. In America, time is money, and restaurants are all about turning tables over. In Europe, the meal is routinely the event of the night. The restaurant expects that you're there for the evening. At good restaurants, respectful, quality service will seem slow to Americans. Dishes won't always come simultaneously—it's fine to start eating when served. Many Europeans will spend at least two hours enjoying a good dinner, and, for the full experience, so should you. Fast service is considered rude service. If you need to eat and run, make your time limits very clear as you order.

These days, Germans are splitting their bratwurst and kraut, too.

Know each country's dining quirks.
In Italy, it's common to be charged a *pane e coperto* ("bread and cover" charge) just to sit down. In Portugal, appetizers (olives, bread, etc.) that are automatically brought to your table are not free—if you touch them, you pay for them. If you see a *Stammtisch* sign hanging over a table at a German restaurant, it means that it's reserved for regulars. Spaniards eat very late—to adapt, eat lunch at 3 p.m. and dinner at 10 p.m., or go to a tapas bar, where you can get small dishes all day long.

Share fine things. Servers are happy to bring one dessert and as many spoons as needed.

Getting a table is a lot like at home.
When entering a restaurant without reservations, talk to the host or catch a server's eye and signal to be sure it's OK to sit at a table that isn't marked "reserved." Note that since European diners take their time with a meal, it's impossible to predict how quickly the tables will turn over. You may be asked to wait, or you may be turned away.

Make reservations when possible. For popular or higher-end places, it's smart to reserve a table in advance. For many restaurants, you can make reservations online. I find it just as easy to get on the phone and say, "A table for 4 people, we're coming at 8 p.m., my name is Ricardo." If you do that, you'll have a table waiting for you. Otherwise you're going to be roaming around, every place is going to be full, and you're going to be very frustrated.

Where there's smoke... No-smoking rules are in force in many European restaurants, but watch out if you're seated outdoors, where smokers congregate to light up.

Tips for Ordering

Finding the right restaurant is only half the battle. You also need to order smartly.

Check the menu first. Most European restaurants post their menus outside. Check the price and selection before entering. If the menu's not posted, ask to see one before you commit to a place. Be aware that in parts of Europe, the word *menu* means a fixed-price meal (menu in French, *menù* in Italian, *Menü* in German, and *menú* in Spanish); instead, to see an à la carte menu, you want *la carte* in French, *Speisekarte* in German, *la carta* in Spanish, and so on.

Roast suckling pig on a platter? When in Segovia...

Ordering in a foreign language can be fun, or it can be an ordeal. It's OK to ask for an English menu—if nothing else, you might get the server who speaks the most English. Many servers can give at least a very basic translation—"cheekin, bunny, zuppa, green salat," and so on. A phrase book or translation app is helpful for those who want to avoid ordering sheep stomach instead of lamb chops.

Order regional and seasonal specials. Learn what's in season (or ask your server). In the summer, French onion soup and cheese fondue (both winter dishes) are only served at tourist traps. White asparagus and porcini mushrooms are a treat for your palate in season...but come out of the freezer the rest of the year. Truffles, at the right time, are a beautiful thing. Whenever you can, order the daily special, which usually features what's seasonal. You'll get a better value and tastier food.

I also make it a point to try foods that are unique to a certain region—for instance, cassoulet in southwest France, *cochinillo asado* (roast suckling pig) in Segovia, Spain, or *bistecca alla fiorentina* in Florence (beef from the white Chianina breed of cattle grazing throughout Tuscany). Barnacles in Portugal are very expensive, but so worth it—the best seafood I've ever eaten.

Eat family style. I love cultures that highlight family-style eating, and wherever I can, I opt for sharing. A lot of Americans think it's bad style to share plates, but believe me—the chef is more than happy for you to share so you can sample more dishes.

To max out culturally, order and share two (or more) different meals with your travel partners: Choose at least one high-risk and one low-risk dish. At worst, you'll learn what you don't like and split the chicken and fries. Cut every meal into bits, and your table becomes a lazy Susan. If anything, the servers are impressed by your interest in their food and very often they'll run over with a special treat to sample—like squid eggs. With a gang of 10 travelers, I once ordered all 10 pizzas on the menu to come one after the other, each cut into 10 slices. We took our time, the servers had

Tap Water in Five Languages

Italian: *acqua del rubinetto*
French: *une carafe d'eau*
German: *Leitungswasser*
Spanish: *agua del grifo*
Portuguese: *água da torneira*

To get tap water in any language, do this international charade: Hold an imaginary glass in one hand, turn on the tap with the other, and make the sound of a faucet. Stop it with a click of your tongue and drink it with a smile.

Sample Fixed-Price Menu

Restaurant de la Château
17 Rue du Canard Rouge, Paris
♜ **MENU TOURISTIQUE €30** ♜
service compris

ENTRÉE
Salade de Saison
Escargots (6) au beurre d'ail
Soupe á l'oignon gratinée

PLAT
Moules marinières avec frites
Poulet Basquaise
Côte de veau à la Normande
Bouillabaisse (supp. € 5)
Plat du jour

DESSERT
Crème brûlée
Crêpe chocolat chaud
Glace maison

BOISSON
1/4 vin rouge ou blanc
ou eau minérale

Bon appétit!

A fixed-price menu makes ordering easy for travelers: Choose a first course *(entrée)*, second course *(plat),* dessert, and beverage *(boisson)*—all for a set price of €30. Note that some menu items (in this case the bouillabaisse) may have a supplement.

fun, we savored a great variety, and everything was hot...it was the cheapest 10-course meal in Rome.

Order small plates rather than entrées. Sometimes, rather than getting two main courses, my travel partner and I share a memorable little buffet of appetizers—they're plenty filling, less expensive, and more typically local than entrées. These small plates go by different names throughout Europe: tapas in Spain, *mezedes* in Greece, and *antipasti* in Italy. In Venice, *cicchetti* (small plates) are served in some bars.

Consider daily specials and fixed-price meals. Small eateries in most countries offer a fresh and economical daily special. Learn the native term (*menu del día* in Spain, *plat du jour* in France, *menù del giorno* in Italy, *dagens rett in Norway*). These are often limited to early seatings, with the time (usually before 7:30 p.m.) posted on the door and in the menu. Some classy restaurants in bigger cities in Britain and Ireland offer early-bird specials (order before 6:30 or 7 p.m.); having an early, nice dinner before attending a play or concert feels just right.

The fixed-price "tourist *menu*" (*menu touristique* in

France, *menù turistico* in Italy) is popular in restaurants throughout Europe's tourist zones, offering confused visitors a no-stress, three-course meal at a painless rate that usually includes service, bread, and a drink. You normally get a choice of several options for each course. The tourist *menu* can be a convenient way to sample some regional flavors for a reasonable, predictable price (even thrifty locals order it), although the cheapest ones can sometimes be bland and heavy.

Ask for recommendations or peek at your neighbors' plates. If you still don't know what to order, ask the server for recommendations or look for your dream meal on another table and order by pointing. People are usually helpful and understanding of the poor and hungry monoglot tourist. If they aren't, you probably picked a place that sees too many of them. Europeans with the most patience with tourists are the ones who rarely deal with them.

Travelers who agonize over each word on the menu season their whole experience with stress. If you're in a good place, you'll eat good food. Get a basic idea of what's cooking, have some fun with your server, be loose and adventurous, and just order something.

Drinks

If you're set on drinking the same way you do at home, restaurant drinks will likely add substantially to your expenses—and you can miss out on a key part of the culture. Cold milk, ice cubes, free water, and coffee with (rather than after) your meal are American habits. Insisting on any of these in Europe may get you a strange look and a reputation as an oddball American.

Water: Europeans are notoriously serious about their water and generally pay to drink bottled water with their meals—for taste, not health. At restaurants, your server just can't understand why you wouldn't want good bottled water to go with your good food.

Luckily, it's never expensive to order a half-liter of bottled water. It is served crisp and cold, either with or without carbonation. Some Americans don't like the bubbly stuff, but I do. Learn the local phrase for *con/avec/mit/con/*with gas or *senza/sans/ohne/sin/*without gas (in Italian, French, German, and Spanish, respectively), and you'll get the message across. Acquire a taste for *acqua con gas*. It's a lot more fun (and read on the label what it'll do for your rheumatism).

While it's possible to get tap water, to do so you may need to be polite, patient, inventive, and know the correct phrase. Availability of (and willingness to serve) tap water varies from country to country; you'll pay for it in Belgium (and in Denmark, too, unless you order an additional beverage), and it's not available in Greece. It's sometimes considered a special favor to provide free tap water. While a glass or carafe will normally be served politely, occasionally it just isn't worth the trouble.

German pubs don't serve minors beer—but many locals do.

Alcohol: In Europe, regionally produced alcohol is almost always cheaper than your favorite import (it's often even cheaper than juice and American soft drinks). A shot of the local hard drink in Portugal will cost a dollar, while an American drink would cost more than the American price.

More importantly, trying locally produced alcohol can be a great cultural experience. Ask for ordering advice at just about any bar in Scotland, for example, and you'll learn that Scots are passionate about finding and describing the whisky that fits their personality. All the locals at the pub have "their" whisky. And the flavors (fruity, peppery, peaty, smoky) are much easier to actually taste than their wine-snob equivalents.

In France, geography plays a big part in the country's liquid pride. *Terroir* (pronounced "tehr-wah") denotes "somewhere-ness," a combination of the macro- and microclimate, soil, geology, and culture (the accumulated experience of the people and their craft). The French don't call a wine by the grape's name. Two wines can be made of the same grape, but be of very different character because of their *terroir*. A real Chablis made from the Chardonnay grape is better than Chardonnays made elsewhere because of its *terroir*.

Drink the local stuff with local people in local bars; it's a better experience than having a Manhattan in your hotel bar. Drink wine in wine countries and beer in beer countries. Sample the regional specialties. Let a local person order you their favorite. You may hate it, but you'll never forget it.

Paying the Bill

To get the bill, you'll have to ask for it (catch the server's eye and, with raised hands, scribble with an imaginary pen on your palm). Before it comes, make a mental tally of roughly how much your meal should cost. The bill should vaguely resemble the figure you expected. (It should at least have the same number of digits.) If the total is a surprise, ask to have it itemized and explained. Some servers make the same "innocent" mistakes repeatedly, knowing most tourists are so befuddled by the money and menu that they'll pay whatever number is scrawled across the bottom of the bill.

If you pay with a credit card, your server will likely bring a mobile card reader to the table. These machines cut down on fraud since your card never leaves your sight. Be aware that you may have to enter the card's PIN rather than sign a receipt (see the Money chapter), and there may not be an opportunity to add a tip (see next section).

Tipping

Restaurant tips are more modest in Europe than in America. In Europe, servers are paid a living wage, and tips are considered a small bonus—to reward great service or for simplicity in rounding the total bill to a convenient number. In many countries, 5 percent is adequate and 10 percent is considered a nice tip. Locals just leave coins on the table, round up, or often don't tip at all.

Resist the urge to tip American-style in Europe. If your bucks talk at home, muzzle them on your travels. As a matter of principle—if not economy—the local price should prevail. Please believe me—tipping 15 or 20 percent in Europe is unnecessary, if not culturally ignorant. You're just raising the bar and messing up the local balance. And it's bad style.

Tipping is an issue only at restaurants with table service. If you order food at a counter (in a pub, for example), don't tip. At sit-down restaurants, the tipping etiquette and procedure vary slightly from country to country (see the "Tipping Standards by Country" sidebar).

In Mediterranean countries, the "service charge" (*servizio* in Italian, *service* in French, *servicio* in Spanish) can be handled in different ways. Sometimes the menu will note that the service is included (*servizio incluso*), meaning that the prices listed on the menu already have this charge built in. When the service is not included (*servizio non incluso*), the service charge might show up as a separate line item at the end of your bill. Most fixed-price tourist deals include service.

In northern and eastern Europe, the menu or bill is less likely to address the "service charge," but you can usually assume that it's included in the prices. Lately, some restaurants—especially those in well-touristed areas in Germany and Austria—have added a "Tip is not included" line, in

Tipping Standards by Country

Country	General Rule
Austria	Service is included, but it's common to round up (5-10 percent).
Belgium	Service is included, but it's common to round up (5-10 percent).
Croatia	At some touristy restaurants, a 10-15 percent "service charge" may be added (no additional tip is necessary). Otherwise round up 5-10 percent.
Czech Republic	Service is generally included, although it's common to round up after a good meal (5-10 percent). If you speak just a few Czech words to servers, you'll get better service and won't be expected to tip more than a local; if you greet servers in English, they'll want a 15 percent tip.
Denmark	The service charge typically included in your bill may not go to the server, so for good service, add 5-10 percent.
Estonia	Round up for good service (though never more than 10 percent).
Finland	The service charge typically included in your bill may not go to the server, so for good service, add 5-10 percent.
France	Prices include a 12-15 percent service charge, so locals only tip a little, if at all. For exceptional service, you could tip up to 5 percent—but don't feel obligated.
Germany	It's common to round up after a good meal, usually 10 percent.
Great Britain	It's not necessary to tip if a service charge is included (common in London—usually 12.5 percent). Otherwise, tip 10-12 percent for good service.
Greece	Service is generally included, but it's common to round up about 10 percent. It's considered bad form to leave a single euro, though; if a bill is €10, leave a €2 tip.
Hungary	Most Budapest restaurants tack on a service charge (typically 10-12 percent) that should be noted on the bill. If service isn't included, tip about 10 percent.
Iceland	Iceland is an emphatically no-tipping country. A side effect of the tipless culture is that servers in Icelandic restaurants are usually happy to split the bill for groups.
Ireland	Check the menu or your bill to see if service is included; if not, tip about 10 percent.

Country	General Rule
Italy	A 10 percent service charge *(servizio)* is usually built into your bill. If you wish, you can add an extra €1-2 for each person in your party (or about 5 percent). If *servizio* is not included, tip up to 10 percent.
Netherlands	Tipping is not necessary (15 percent service is usually included), but a tip of about 5-10 percent is a nice reward for good service. In bars, rounding up to the next euro ("keep the change") is appropriate if you get table service.
Norway	The service charge typically included in your bill may not go to the server, so for good service, add 5-10 percent.
Poland	Round up 5-10 percent. At tourist-oriented restaurants, a 10-15 percent service charge may be added to your bill, in which case an additional tip is not necessary.
Portugal	Service is generally included, but for good service, it's customary to leave an additional 5 percent (10 percent for upscale restaurants or if service is not included).
Slovenia	At touristy restaurants, a 10-15 percent "service charge" may be added to your bill, in which case an additional tip is not necessary. Otherwise tip 5-10 percent.
Spain	If you order at a counter—as you often will when sampling tapas at a bar—there's no need to tip, though you can round up with a few small coins. At restaurants with table service, if a service charge is included in the bill, add about 5 percent; if it's not, leave 10 percent.
Sweden	The service charge typically included in your bill may not go to the server, so for good service, add 5-10 percent.
Switzerland	Service is included with table service, but it's customary to round up the bill (no more than 5-10 percent).
Turkey	Tip about 10 percent. If you're not satisfied, tip less—or not at all. Some upscale restaurants may include a "service charge" on the bill; this goes to the owner, not the server—so still tip about 10 percent.

Interpreting the Bill

Examine this sample Italian restaurant bill to get used to the charges you'll see in Europe.

Check each line item. Be sure you understand what each charge was for. You don't have to speak fluent Italian to recognize *minestrone* or *spaghetti carbonara*. Even *insalata mista* isn't a stretch if you remember that you ate a mixed salad. But if it says *"4 birre"* and you don't remember drinking four beers, ask for an explanation (or an apology).

Pane e coperto ("bread and cover" charge) is a mandatory amount charged per customer just to sit down. Common in Italy, this is relatively rare in other countries (though you may also see it at touristy restaurants in popular destinations, such as Prague).

A legitimate **servizio** (service) charge of 10 percent has been added. You don't need to leave a big tip (but if you were pleased with the service, you could add

VIA GARIBALDI 37, ROMA

Ristorante Colosseo

DI RICARDO STEFANO

	IMPORTO
pane e coperto (x2)	4,00
insalata caprese	6,00
ins. mista	4,00
spaghetti carbonara	6,00
minestrone	8,00
frutta	4,00
tiramisú	5,00
vino rosso (bottiglia)	12,00
acqua min. (litro)	4,00
totale	53,00
servizio 10%	5,30
totale documento	**€58,30**

RICEVUTA FISCALE
COPIA PER IL CLIENTE

a euro or two for each person in your party). In many places, rather than adding the 10 percent at the end of the bill, the menu prices already include the service charge (in which case, the menu might say *"servizio incluso"*).

Note that Europeans use a comma as a decimal point—so €58,30 is the same as €58.30. For this meal, I'd hand over €60, smile, say *"grazie,"* and wave my hand to suggest the server should keep the change.

English, to the bottom of the bill. This is misleading, as the prices on any menu in these countries *do* include service. I wouldn't tip one cent more at a restaurant that includes this note on the bill.

Typically, it's better to hand the tip to the server when you're paying your bill than to leave it on the table, particularly in busy places where the wrong party might pocket the change. Servers prefer to be tipped in cash even if you pay with your credit card (otherwise the tip may never reach your server); in many cases, there isn't even a line on the credit-card receipt for a tip.

In Germanic countries, rather than leaving coins behind on the table (considered slightly rude), locals usually pay directly: When the server comes by with the bill, simply hand over paper money, stating the total you'd like to pay. For example, if paying for a €10 meal with a €20 bill, while hand-ing your money to the server, say "Eleven, please" (or "*Elf, bitte*" if you've got your German numbers down). The server will keep a €1 tip and give you €9 in change.

Don't stress about tipping in Europe. If you're unsure what to give, ask a local (but not a server) about the tipping norms for that country. Virtually anywhere in Europe, you can do as the Europeans do and (if you're pleased with the service) add a euro or two for each person in your party. In very touristy areas, some servers have noticed the American obsession with overtipping—and might hope for a Yankee-size tip. But the good news is that European servers and din-ers are far more laid-back about all this than we are. Any tip is appreciated, the stakes are low, and it's no big deal if you choose the "wrong" amount. Don't lose sleep over walking out of a restaurant in Europe without tipping.

DIETARY RESTRICTIONS

For vegetarians and those with allergies and food sensitivi-ties, life can be a little frustrating in Europe, but a little prep work can go a long way in giving you peace of mind (and body).

Vegetarians

Occasionally, Europeans think "vegetarian" means "no red meat" or "not much meat." If you are a vegan or strict vegetarian, you'll have to make things very clear. Those with dairy-free diets will find things more challenging, but doable. Write out the appropriate phrase (see sidebar), keep it handy, and show it to your server before ordering.

Vegetarians have no problem with continental break-fasts, which are normally meatless anyway. Meat-free picnic lunches are delicious, since bread, cheese, and yogurt are wonderful throughout Europe. Have some healthy snacks (such as nuts or fresh produce) on hand, in case you can't find a suitable meal.

In some restaurants your patience may be minced. For a good meal, seek out a vegetarian restaurant (most cities have them; look up

Salad bars are abundant and great for vegetarians.

recommendations online), or browse the menus at fine-dining restaurants, many of which offer at least one good vegetarian option. In my guidebooks, whenever possible, I list good vegetarian restaurants in each city.

Cafeterias (such as the bright, cheery, affordable ones you'll find on the top floor of major department stores) are a good option, since you can see exactly what you're getting and select foods that suit your diet.

Each country has its own quirks: Italy seems to sprinkle a little meat in just about everything. German cooking normally keeps the meat separate from the vegetables. Hearty German salads, with beets, cheese, and eggs, are a vegetarian's delight. Vegetarians enjoy *antipasti* buffets, salad bars, and ethnic restaurants throughout Europe.

Key Vegetarian Phrases

The phrases below communicate these points: "We are (I am) vegetarian. We (I) do not eat meat, fish, or chicken. Eggs and cheese OK."

German: *Wir sind (Ich bin) Vegetarier. Wir essen (Ich esse) kein Fleisch, Fisch, oder Geflügel. Eier und Käse OK.*

French: *Nous sommes (Je suis) végétarien. Nous ne mangeons (Je ne mange) pas de viande, poisson, ou poulet. Oeufs et fromage OK.*

Italian: *Siamo vegetariani (Sono vegetariano/a). Non mangiamo (Mangio) nè carne, nè pesce, nè polli. Uova e formaggio OK.*

Spanish: *Somos vegetarianos (Soy vegetariano/a). No comemos (No como) ni carne, ni pescado, ni pollo. Los huevos y el queso OK..*

Gluten and Allergy Concerns

For travelers with celiac disease, gluten sensitivity, or food allergies, travel has become easier—and tastier—in recent years. Bear in mind that bigger cities tend to have more options.

Though many Europeans also deal with these concerns, awareness levels vary from region to region, and even from restaurant to restaurant. Some countries, like Italy, are very accommodating. But even if you come armed with proper translations, locals won't always be familiar with terms such as "gluten." To avoid misunderstandings, explicitly name what you cannot eat. Keep the translation straightforward: "I am allergic to barley, wheat, and rye. I cannot eat bread, pasta, couscous, or other foods containing barley, wheat, or rye." Utilize a good phrase book and the Google Translate app. Digital translations designed for celiacs are available for purchase at www.legalnomads.com/gluten-free. Travelers with other

If you have dietary restrictions, write them out on a card. Flash it while ordering and you'll get what you want.

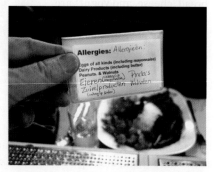

allergies can download free translated "chef cards" at www.
foodallergy.org/resources/food-allergy-chef-cards.

Plan ahead by finding eateries that offer alternatives
before your trip, and always confirm ingredients locally.
Many gluten-free travel bloggers have written reviews of restaurants throughout Europe. And restaurant menus increasingly include allergen information.

Researching health-food stores is also a good idea since
these almost always carry a range of gluten-free products.
Packaged foods in stores across Europe are required to
clearly state the presence or absence of gluten and other
common allergens.

If you plan to eat breakfast at your hotel, email ahead to
find out whether they'll have appropriate choices available.
Some places may stock up on supplies before you arrive. If
you know you'll be visiting destinations that are particularly
tricky for your dietary needs—or for those with extreme
intolerance—consider renting an apartment so you can
prepare your own meals. In some cases, it can make sense to
bring nonperishable food or snacks with you from home.

Bring any necessary medications, keep prescription
medication in its original packaging, and carry a copy of your
prescription should you need to visit a pharmacy. Two handy
resources are the Celiac Disease Foundation (lists celiac
associations around the world, https://celiac.org) and the
Food Allergy Research & Education network (downloadable
info on traveling with food allergies, www.foodallergy.org).

EUROPE'S CAFÉ SCENE

I'm not the cocktails-at-happy-hour type of traveler. But on
a recent trip to Italy, I savored a peaceful moment in Siena's
great square, Il Campo, sipping a glass of *vin santo* as the
early evening light bathed the red-brick stone. My five-euro
drink gave me a front-row seat at the best café table on the
square, and for a leisurely hour I soaked up the promenading
action that nightly turns Il Campo into "Il Italian Fashion
Show."

Public squares like Il Campo are the physical and
cultural heart of Europe's cities and towns. For Europeans,
these bustling squares proclaim "community." Defined by
stately architecture and ringed by shops and cafés, squares
are the perfect venue for café-sitting, coffee-sipping, and
people-watching. Promenaders take center stage, strolling
and being seen, while onlookers perch on the periphery.

To play your part, tether yourself to one of the café tables parked around any square, order a drink, and feel the pulse of the passing scene. Don't be in a hurry—spending endless hours sitting in an outdoor café is the norm. And don't worry about the price—I happily pay too much to enjoy a cup of coffee or a cocktail on the most expensive piece of real estate in a town and watch the scene go by. You're not paying for the drink. You're paying to be a part of the scene, and that is integral to a quality European experience.

LEFT A café on Siena's main square gives you a ringside seat to all the action.

RIGHT Be a part of the lively atmosphere in a Parisian sidewalk café.

Café Culture

The coffee scene is especially strong in Italy, France, Austria, Hungary, the Czech Republic, and Greece. Cafés provide a place for people to gather socially and spend hours catching up and discussing everything from politics to sports.

In Italy, cafés are commonly referred to as "bars." They serve coffee, wine, liquor, and light food such as mini pizzas and sandwiches. Italians tend to stop by their favorite bar in the morning for a coffee and pastry, then throughout the day for more coffee and eventually drinks. In fact, one of my favorite bar traditions in Italy has nothing to do with coffee. Around happy hour, many bars lay out an *aperitivo* buffet, which usually includes an array of meats, cheeses, grilled vegetables, and other antipasti-type dishes. If you pay for a drink, you're welcome to nibble to your heart's content. While this spread is intended as an appetizer course before a full dinner, light eaters could discreetly turn this into a small meal (typically served around 6 p.m. or 7 p.m. until 9 p.m.).

Historically, French cafés served as a second home to the great artists, writers, and political figures of the time, like Trotsky, Stravinsky, Hemingway, and Gertrude Stein. Today, the French still flock to cafés for business meetings, encounter sessions, political discussions, and romantic interludes.

But many cafés also serve a practical purpose: Unlike restaurants and bistros, which are only open at meal times, cafés serve light meals throughout most of the day. You're welcome to order just a salad, a sandwich, or a bowl of soup, even for dinner, making this a lighter and less formal option for dining out.

Viennese-style coffeehouses are another institution, found not only in Austria, but also in Prague, Budapest, Kraków, and other cities of the former Austro-Hungarian empire. Though coffee boomed as an aristocratic drink in the 18th century, later, during the Industrial Age, it became a hit with the working class, who were expected to put in 12-hour shifts. Neighborhood cafés allowed urbanites to escape their tiny flats and provided warmth for those who didn't want to pay to heat their homes during the day.

Today's Viennese coffeehouses still provide a living room down the street for locals, offering newspapers, pastries, sofas, quick and light lunches, elegant ambience, and "take all the time you want" charm for the price of a cup of coffee. Rather than read the news on your mobile device, relax with a cup of coffee and read the actual newspaper, Vienna-style, in a café.

If you do want to get online while you sip and relax, many cafés provide free Wi-Fi for customers; if you don't see a sign displaying the network and password, ask the server.

In European cafés, menus are two-tiered: cheaper at the bar, more expensive at a table.

Café Tips

Tourists are often stung by not understanding the rules at European cafés. In many countries, you'll pay more to sit at a table and less to stand at a bar. In general, if you're not planning to linger, it's cheaper to order and consume your drink at the bar. If you want to sit a while and people-watch, grab a table with a view, and a server will take your order. This will cost you about double what it would at the bar.

If you're on a budget, always confirm the price for a sit-down drink. While it's never high profile, there's always a price list posted somewhere inside—usually by the bar or cash register—displaying either a two- or three-tiered pricing system (cheap at the bar, more at a table, possibly even more at an outside table).

If ordering from the bar, you may have to pay the cashier first, then take your receipt to the bar, where the barista will make your drink. Lingering with your bar-priced drink on a nearby public bench or across the street on the beach is usually OK—just ask first.

If you pay for a seat in a café with an expensive drink, that seat's yours for the afternoon if you like. Note that at a French café, if the table is not set, it's fine to seat yourself and just have a drink. However, if it's set with a placemat and cutlery, you should ask to be seated and plan to order a meal.

As a traveler, you naturally want to take in as many sights as you can every day. But make time in your itinerary to simply drop yourself into a café chair for a few hours. Enjoying life like the Europeans do—watching the world go by—is one of the best and most relaxing ways to go local.

Europe is brimming with atmospheric, linger-a-while cafés.

Know Your Joe

If you're a coffee lover, it pays to know the ground rules in various caffeine-loving countries.

Two of the biggest coffee cultures in Europe are Italy and France (in fact, the espresso-based style of coffee so popular in the US was born in Italy). In either place, if you ask for *"un caffé"* (Italian) or *"un café"* (French), you'll get a shot of espresso in a little cup. Most coffee drinks begin with espresso, to which they add varying amounts of hot water and/or steamed or foamed milk. Milky drinks, such as a cappuccino, *caffè latte* (Italy), *or café au lait/café crème* (France), are served to locals before noon and to tourists any time of day. To a local, cappuccino is a breakfast drink, and drinking anything with milk or cream after a meal or later in the day is thought to upset your digestion (Italians also believe having milk after eating anything with tomatoes is a travesty). If they add any milk after lunch, it's just a splash, in a *caffè macchiato* (Italy) or *noisette* (France). You're welcome to order a milkier coffee drink later in the day, but don't be surprised if you get a funny look.

For the closest thing to brewed coffee, ask for a *caffè americano* (Italy) or *un café allongé* (France)—an espresso diluted with hot water. Cafés in Britain, Germany, and Scandinavia are more likely to serve brewed coffee, though there are plenty of espresso places across northern Europe these days.

Turkish coffee refers not to a type of coffee, but to the way the coffee is prepared: The coffee grounds float freely in the brew, leaving behind a layer of "mud" at the bottom of the cup. You'll also find this style of coffee in Greece (Greek coffee) and the Czech Republic (*turecká káva*). It's typically drunk as a digestive after dinner and sometimes after lunch. In these countries, if you take sugar, ask for it when you place your order (it's added while the coffee is being heated).

BUDGET AND ON-THE-GO OPTIONS

Europe offers a bounty of options for eating quickly and inexpensively. While cafeterias, street stands, chain restaurants, and "to go" meals are not high cuisine, they're cheap. And sometimes what you get is just as tasty as fine restaurant food. Some of my favorite and most memorable meals have been consumed at a market hall or a street-corner sausage stand. For an affordable, quality lunch, line up with the local office workers: They eat out every day and they know where the good values are.

Cafeterias and Institution-Affiliated Eateries

"Self-service" is an international word. You'll find self-service restaurants in big cities everywhere, offering low-price, low-risk, low-stress, what-you-see-is-what-you-get meals. All over Europe, towering department stores offer great cafeteria lunches—often with rooftop views for no extra charge (such as at the Galeria Kaufhof in Frankfurt). These places are designed for the shopper who has a sharp eye for a good value. At a salad bar, grab the small (cheap) plate and stack it like the locals do—high. Hungry sightseers also appreciate the handy, moderately priced cafeterias they'll find in larger museums.

In Italy, a fast and cheap

Cafeteria leftovers: even cheaper than picnics...

lunch option is a *tavola calda* ("hot table"), a point-and-shoot cafeteria with a buffet spread of meat and vegetables (it's sometimes called a *tavola fredda*, or "cold table," in the north). Don't be limited by what's displayed. If you'd like a salad with a slice of cantaloupe and a hunk of cheese, they'll whip that up for you. Belly up to the bar; with a pointing finger, you can assemble a fine meal.

If your wallet is as empty as your stomach, find a cheap, humble cafeteria that's associated with (and subsidized by) a local institution—such as a university, church, hospital, charity, senior center, fire station, union of gondoliers, retired fishermen's club, and so on. Profits take a back seat to providing good food at a good price—and many of these eateries welcome the public to pull up a chair. Options range from a cafeteria in Vienna serving Austria's Supreme Court of Justice, to student canteens in university towns (such as Salzburg, Austria), to Poland's dreary-looking but cheap-and-tasty "milk bars." Don't be afraid to take advantage of these opportunities to fill yourself with a plate of dull but nourishing food for an unbeatable price in the company of locals. University cafeterias (generally closed during summer holidays) also offer a surefire way to meet educated, English-speaking young people with open and stimulating minds. They're often eager to share their views on politics and economics, as well as their English, with a foreign friend.

Bakeries and Sandwich Shops

Bakeries are a good place to pick up basic sandwiches, tiny pizzas, or something equally cheap and fast but with more of a regional flavor (such as savory pasties in England or a *croque-monsieur* sandwich in France). The best (and often cheapest) lunch option in Iceland is a bakery's all-you-can-eat soup buffet, which usually includes unlimited fresh-baked bread. Britain's Pret à Manger, Norway's Deli de Luca, and Spain's Pans & Company are chains that sell good,

LEFT Local deli-like shops, such as this French traiteur, offer delicious to-go fare.

RIGHT Eat where the immigrants do, and you'll save plenty of money.

healthful sandwiches, salads, and pastries. Local deli-like shops are popular in many parts of Europe; try a *traiteur* in France or a *rosticceria* in Italy.

Street Food and Ethnic Eats

Every country has its own equivalent of the hot-dog stand or burger joint, where you can grab a filling bite on the go for cheap—French *crêperies*, Greek souvlaki stands, Danish *pølse* (sausage) vendors, Italian *pizza rustica* takeout shops, German sausage stands, British chippies (fish-and-chips), and Dutch herring carts.

Often the cheapest hot meals in town feature cuisine from another country. Ethnic eateries are more common in northern Europe than in southern countries like Italy or Spain. Throughout wealthy northern Europe, immigrant communities labor at subsistence wages. These people have very tasty food traditions, they have very small budgets, and they like to go out and eat. Rather than eat bland and pricey local food, they (along with savvy residents and travelers) go cheap and spicy at simple diners, delis, and takeaway stands serving Middle Eastern and Asian food.

Immigrant restaurants are a godsend for tourists, especially in pricey locales like Scandinavia or Great Britain. In fact, Indian food is considered "going local" in cosmopolitan, multiethnic Britain. You'll find Indian restaurants in most British cities and even in small towns. Take the opportunity to sample food from Britain's former colony.

Of all the ethnic options in Europe, the ubiquitous kebab stand is my favorite. Kiosks selling Turkish-style *döner kebab* (rotisserie meat wrapped in pita bread), falafel (fried chickpea patties), and other Middle Eastern dishes are popular in many places, including Germany, Florence, and Paris. The best stands have a busy energy, and a single large kebab draped in wonderful pita bread can feed two hungry travelers for €5. Don't miss the *ayran*—a healthy yogurt drink popular with Turks—which goes well with your kebab.

Market Halls

Europe's old Industrial Age glass-and-steel farmers markets seem to be celebrating their hundredth birthdays by getting a new lease on life as trendy food halls. These market halls still come with the farmers' market dimension (described later, under "Markets"), but they've been spiced up with great eateries, priced for local shoppers and serving the freshest

LEFT For good, affordable eats, join the locals at Frankfurt's Kleinmarkthalle.

RIGHT Market halls—such as Florence's venerable Mercato Centrale—are finding new life hosting chic eateries.

ingredients. At any stall where you see locals lining up, you know something exciting is being served.

Frankfurt's Kleinmarkthalle, a delightful, old-school market that was saved from developers by local outcry, is now an adventure in fine eating. Torvehallerne, an upscale Copenhagen food court housed in a pair of modern, glassy buildings, is a great place to try *smørrebrød* (open-face sandwiches topped with delicious fish, cheese, cold cuts, or interesting spreads). Lisbon's Mercado de Campo de Ourique is a 19th-century iron-and-glass market that has morphed into a trendy food circus with produce stalls, fishmongers, and bakeries that sell everything from pigs' ears to designer cupcakes.

One of my favorite market halls is Florence's Mercato Centrale. It's long been enjoyable as a thriving local market selling meat, fish, produce, and other staples to a mostly local clientele. The city recently renovated the market's long-neglected upper level, which now hosts a wonderful collection of quality eateries that are as busy as the ground-level produce stalls. The food artisans at work here serve pizza and pasta, but they also dish up regional treats. The food court is a real hit with the neighborhood's office workers during the day, and provides a good insight into local eating habits. Take a peek at what's on your neighbor's plate—Florentines eat just about every bit of the cow. Stay away from the *trippa* and *lampredotto* sandwiches if you can't stomach stomach meat.

If visiting a market hall, be sure to check the hours. Some are open in the evening while others are geared toward the working crowd and close early. It's best to go at lunch. These days, in nearly any European city, I find sitting down with local shoppers at the traditional market to be a great way to enjoy lunch and feel the pulse of everyday life.

European Chains

I know—you're going to Europe to enjoy characteristic little hole-in-the-wall places, so eating mass-produced food doesn't seem like a very authentic experience. But several excellent chains offer long hours, reasonable prices (especially in expensive big cities or countries like Norway), and reliable quality.

British chain Pret à Manger is the most pervasive of modern convenience eateries. In addition to Britain, you can find them in Denmark, France, Germany, and the Netherlands. Some are takeout only, and others have seating ranging from simple stools to restaurant-quality tables. The service is fast, the price is great, and the food is healthy and fresh. Their slogan: "Made today. Gone today. No 'sell-by' date, no nightlife." Similarly, Belgian chain Le Pain Quotidien, which has hearty meals in a thoughtfully designed modern-rustic atmosphere, can be found throughout Europe.

For pan-Asian cuisine (udon noodles, fried rice, and curry dishes), Wagamama is a noisy, organic slurpathon. Portions are huge and splittable. There's one in almost every midsize city in Britain and most major cities across Europe, usually located in sprawling halls filled with long shared tables and busy servers who scrawl your order on the placemat.

Throughout Scandinavia, Deli de Luca is a cheery convenience store chain that's a cut above other takeaway joints. Most are open 24/7, selling sandwiches, pastries, sushi, and to-go boxes of warm pasta or Asian noodle dishes.

McEurope

American fast-food restaurants are everywhere. Yes, the hamburgerization of the world is a shame, but face it—the busiest and biggest McDonald's in the world are in places like Tokyo, Rome, and Moscow. The burger has become a global thing. You'll find Big Macs in every language—it isn't exciting (and costs more than at home), but at least at McDonald's you know exactly what you're getting, and it's fast. A hamburger, fries, and shake can be fun halfway through your trip. You'll also see KFC, Subway, and Starbucks.

American fast-food joints are kid-friendly and satisfy the need

You'll find Big Macs in every language.

for a cheap meal and a tall orange juice. They've grabbed prime bits of real estate in every big European city. Since there's no cover charge, this is an opportunity to savor a low-class paper cup of coffee while enjoying some high-class people-watching (unless you're at Starbucks, where your paper cup will be high class, too). Many offer free Wi-Fi as well.

Each country also has its equivalent of the hamburger stand (I saw a "McCheaper" in Switzerland). Whatever their origin, they're a hit with youths and a handy place for a quick, cheap bite to eat.

PICNICS, MARKETS, AND SUPERMARKETS

The best way to feast like a European—enjoying tasty local specialties economically—is to picnic. You'll eat better while spending half as much as those who eat exclusively in restaurants. In my book, there's no better travel experience than a picnic sourced from local markets and grocers, eaten outdoors with a lively square, peaceful park, or rejuvenated harborfront as a backdrop.

I am a picnic connoisseur. While I'm the first to admit that restaurant meals are an important aspect of any culture, I picnic almost daily—and not just for budgetary reasons. It's fun to dive into a marketplace or corner grocery and interact with locals. Europe's colorful markets overflow with varied cheeses, meats, fresh fruits, vegetables, and warm-from-the-oven bread. Many of my favorite foods made their debut in a European picnic.

To busy sightseers and budget travelers, restaurants can be time-consuming and frustrating. After waiting to be served, tangling with a menu, and consuming a pricey meal, you walk away feeling unsatisfied, knowing your money could have done much more for your stomach if you had invested it in a picnic instead.

You can save on your food budget by visiting the corner bakery and picnicking on the grass or a bench.

To bolster your budget, I recommend picnic dinners every few nights. At home, we save time and money by raiding the refrigerator to assemble a pickup dinner. In Europe, the equivalent is the corner deli, bakery, produce market, or supermarket. You can also pick up a picnic from nearly anywhere

willing to pack a meal to go, such as a souvlaki stand, sausage truck, *crêperie*, pizza shop, or market hall. For ideas, see the "Budget and On-the-Go Options" section, earlier. For tips on shopping at markets and grocery stores, see "Markets," later in this chapter.

Only a glutton can spend more than $15 for a picnic feast. In a park in Paris, on a Norwegian ferry, high in the Alps, at an autobahn rest stop, or on your convent rooftop, picnicking is the budget traveler's key to cheap and good eating.

Picnic Tips

Here are some tricks for picnicking like a pro:

Picnic Supplies: Buy a good knife with a can opener and corkscrew in Europe (or bring it from home in your checked luggage). In addition to being a handy plate, fan, and lousy Frisbee, a plastic lid makes an easy-to-clean cutting board. Resealable plastic baggies (large and small) are great for containing messy food and packing up leftovers. Bring a reusable cup as well as a spoon and fork for eating takeout soups and salads.

Drinks: There are plenty of cheap ways to wash down a picnic. If you're tired of filling your water bottle, you can buy drinks in supermarkets and corner grocery stores. Liter bottles of soda are inexpensive, as is wine in most countries—and local wine gives your picnic a nice touch. Neighborhood wine shops have a great selection—and most will open your bottle if you forgot your corkscrew.

LEFT A quick dashboard picnic halfway through a busy day of sightseeing

Stretching Your Money: Bread has always been cheap in Europe. (Leaders have learned from history that when stomachs rumble, so do the mobs in the streets.) Cheese is a specialty nearly everywhere and is, along with milk and yogurt, one of the Continent's most affordable sources of protein. The standard low-risk option anywhere in Europe is Emmentaler cheese (what we call "Swiss"). Buy fruit and veggies that are in season; see what's inexpensive

RIGHT Throughout France, signs direct you to the most scenic places to *"pique-nique."*

and plentiful in the produce section or market. Anything American is usually pricey and rarely satisfying. Cultural chameleons eat and drink better and cheaper.

Site Selection: Proper site selection can make the difference between just another meal and *le pique-nique extraordinaire*. Since you've decided to skip the restaurant, it's up to you to create the atmosphere.

I might start the day by scouring the thriving market with my senses. Then I fill up my shopping bag and have breakfast on a riverbank. After sightseeing, I combine lunch and a siesta in a cool park to fill my stomach, rest my body, and escape the early afternoon heat. It's fun to eat dinner on a castle wall enjoying a commanding view and the setting sun. Some of my all-time best picnics have been lazy dinners accompanied by medieval fantasies in the quiet of after-hours Europe.

Punctuate a hike with a picnic. Food tastes even better on top of a mountain. Europeans are great picnickers. Many picnics become potlucks, resulting in new friends as well as full stomachs.

Picnicking in Your Hotel Room: I love taking off my shoes, stretching out, and having a simple, cheap meal while catching up on work or TV in my hotel room. I don't want an earth-shaking dinner every night. Every second or third night I just like to have a relaxing and cheap picnic in my home away from home.

When staying several nights, I cozy up my room by borrowing plates, glasses, and silverware from the breakfast room and making a pantry stocked with juice, fruits, vegetables, cheese, and other munchies. Some hoteliers dislike picnicking in rooms, as they worry about cleanliness, smells, and insects (this is especially true in France, where hoteliers uniformly detest it when guests bring food into bedrooms). If you can't picnic in your room, you'll find plenty of other atmospheric places to eat. If you do picnic in your room, be

LEFT This happy gang is living simply and well on the cheap: enjoying a picnic in Assisi, the hometown of St. Francis.

RIGHT Kick back and munch a picnic dinner in your hotel room.

tidy and considerate, and wrap up your garbage really well, or better yet, toss it out in a public waste bin.

Markets

I love the marketplaces of Europe. To me they're as important as the museums. Nearly every town, large or small, has at least one colorful outdoor or indoor marketplace. Find out when they are up and running, and make it a point to be there. You'll enjoy the local push and shove.

Assemble your picnic here; you'll probably need to hit several stalls to put together a complete meal. Make an effort to communicate with the merchants. Know what you are buying and what you are spending. Whether you understand the prices or not, act like you do (observe the weighing process closely), and you're more likely to be treated fairly. Gather your ingredients in the morning, as markets typically close in the early afternoon.

Learn the measurements. The unit of measure throughout the Continent is a kilogram, or 2.2 pounds. A kilo (kg) has 1,000 grams (g or gr). One hundred grams (a common unit of sale) of cheese or meat tucked into a chunk of French bread gives you about a quarter-pounder. If you don't know the local language, just point to the food you want and write the amount on a scrap of paper or type it into your phone's notepad or translation app.

Check how the item is priced. Watch the scale when your food is being weighed. It'll likely show grams and kilos. If dried apples are priced at €2 per kilo, that's $2.40 for 2.2 pounds, or about $1.20 per pound. If the scale says 400 grams, that means 40 percent of €2 (or 80 euro cents), which is nearly $1.

Farmers markets are a fun source for healthy picnic snacks.

Not everything is strictly priced by the kilogram. Read the little chalkboard price carefully: Particularly in the case of specialty items, you might see things priced by the ¼ kg, ½ kg, 100 g, 500 g, and so on. Or an item could be priced by the piece (*Stück* in German, *pièce* in French, *pezzo* in Italian), the bunch, the container, and so on. If the pâté seems too cheap to be true, look at the sign closely. The posted price is probably followed by "100 gr."

If no prices are posted, be wary. Travelers are routinely ripped off by market merchants in tourist centers. Find places that post the prices. Assume any stall without posted prices has a double price standard: one for locals and a more expensive one for tourists.

I'll never forget a friend of mine who bought two bananas for our London picnic. He grabbed the fruit, held out a handful of change, and said, "How much?" The merchant took the equivalent of $4. My friend turned to me and said, "Wow, London really is expensive." Anytime you hold out a handful of money to a banana salesman, you're just asking for trouble.

Point, but don't touch. Most produce stands and outdoor markets are not self-service: Tell the vendor (or point to) what you want, and let the merchant bag it and weigh it for you. It's generally considered rude for a customer to touch the goods. But if you see baskets laid out (as in some markets in France), you can select your own produce, then hand it to the vendor.

Want only a small amount? You'll likely need only one or two pieces of fruit, and many merchants refuse to deal in such small quantities. The way to get what you want and no more is to estimate what it would cost if the merchants were to weigh it and then just hold out a coin worth about that much in one hand and point to the apple, or whatever, with the other. Have a Forrest Gump look on your face that says, "If you take this coin, I'll go away." Rarely will they refuse the deal.

Appreciate the cultural experience. Shopping for groceries is an integral part of everyday European life for good reasons: People have small refrigerators (kitchens are tiny), value fresh produce, and enjoy the social interaction.

Not up for picnicking? You'll find competitive prices and characteristic seasonal food in the little eateries that always surround these markets.

Supermarkets and Grocery Stores

I prefer local markets, but American-style supermarkets, some of which hide out in the basements of big-city department stores, are a good alternative—and some of them are very upscale. Common European chains include Aldi, Carrefour, Co-op, Dia, Konzum, Lidl, Mercadona, Migros, Monoprix, Morrisons, Sainsbury's, Spar, and Tesco. Corner grocery stores give you more color but have a smaller selection.

If it's late in the day, you may be able to score some deals. One night in Oslo I walked into an ICA supermarket just before closing to discover that they'd marked down all the deli food by 50 percent. Back in my hotel room, I ate my cheapest meal in Norway—roast chicken and fries at almost US prices.

Ready-Made Food: Many supermarkets offer cheap packaged sandwiches, while others have deli counters where you can get a sandwich made to order—just point to what you want. Most supermarkets offer a good selection of freshly prepared foods, such as quiche, fried chicken, and fish, all for takeout.

At the supermarket, put your banana on the scale, push the banana button, rip off the price sticker, and stick it on your banana.

Produce: Don't be intimidated by the produce section. It's a cinch to buy a tiny amount of fruit or vegetables. Many have an easy push-button pricing system: Put the banana on the scale, push the picture of a banana (or enter the banana bin number), and a sticky price tag prints out. You could weigh and sticker a single grape. In Spain and Italy, if there is no one to serve you, the store provides plastic gloves for you to wear while picking out your produce (a bare hand is a no-no).

Drinks: Milk in the dairy section is always cheap and available in quarter, half, or whole liters. Be sure it's normal drinking milk. Strange white liquid dairy products in look-alike milk cartons abound, ruining the milk-and-cookie dreams of careless tourists. Look for local words for "whole," "half," or "light," such as *voll, halb,* or *lett.* Get refrigerated, fresh milk. Or look on the (unrefrigerated) shelves for the common-in-Europe but rarer-in-America "long life" milk. This milk—which requires no refrigeration until it's opened—will never go bad...or taste good.

European yogurt is delicious and can often be drunk right out of its container. Fruit juice comes in handy liter boxes (look for "100% juice" or "no sugar" to avoid Kool-Aid clones). If it's hot outside, don't expect soft drinks, beer, or wine to be chilled—most supermarkets sell these at room temperature.

Sweets: To satisfy your sweet tooth (or stock up on gifts for the folks back home), check out the dessert and candy section. European-style "biscuits" (cookies)—made by companies such as Lu, Bahlsen, or McVities—are usually a good value, as are candy bars that might cost twice as much at airport gift shops.

Supermarket Etiquette: Bring your own shopping bag, use your empty daybag, or expect to pay extra for the store's plastic bags. You may have to insert a euro to use a shopping cart—although you'll get your deposit back when you return the cart to its rack. Some stores' plastic shopping baskets have wheels and pull-out handles as a handy alternative.

If you're just grabbing some simple picnic items, it's easiest to pay cash at checkout. But for larger purchases, you can use your credit card—you may need to enter the PIN, or some machines may read your card as chip-and-sign (clerks may also ask for photo ID). No one will bag your groceries for you; expect to bag and pay at the same time. It's smart to start bagging immediately to avoid frustrating the shoppers behind you.

FOOD EXPERIENCES

My favorite way of becoming a temporary local is by joining a food tour or cooking class. Both are a big deal; you'll easily find many recommendations in guidebooks or online. A more recent trend is social dining—websites pair travelers with locals for a home-cooked meal.

Food Tours

All over Europe, guided food tours are trendy. I take many of them in hopes of finding the best ones to recommend in our guidebooks, and to learn fun new angles on the local food scene.

Typical food tours last about three or four hours, come with a mile or so of walking, and include four to eight stops. Eating styles vary: Some are mobile feasts, where you stand and share a plate of little bites, while others feature sit-down dining experiences. All will fill you up, and should be considered a meal and a tour wrapped up in one. During the tour, most guides are happy to recommend good restaurants and eating neighborhoods. It's smart to do food tours earlier in your trip, so you have time to try some of the recommended places or sample a favorite dish again.

I'd skip bigger tours. The best ones move at a brisk pace and max out at eight or ten people—that means you can squeeze into small shops and boutique restaurants. Some companies offer higher-end tours, which cost more, take longer, and usually include more stops where you linger and sample a greater variety of dishes. These are appreciated by foodies but may be overkill for others.

The best guides fluidly intersperse history, tradition, and local food culture while giving you a great glimpse into daily life in a characteristic neighborhood. For instance, I recently joined a food tour of Paris's historic Marais neighborhood.

Our first stop was a bakery that had just placed in the city's annual "best baguette" contest. As we tore into our just-out-of-the-oven bread, our guide made sure we heard the telltale "crrrrriiikkk" of a perfect crust breaking. Before this tour, I never knew that the shape of a croissant could tell me if it was made with butter. (Butter produces a croissant with more or less straight sides. The curvier *croissant ordinaire* is made with lowly margarine.)

Our next stop was a *traiteur*—a gourmet deli. Locals who don't feel like cooking (worn out by their 35-hour work week) pop in here for food to go. To dress up the bread, we were given some duck *rillette* (looks like tuna salad but tastes much better) and thinly sliced ham.

Next we followed our noses to a *fromagerie*, where the cheese mongers, standing white-coated like pharmacists, welcomed us in. How to choose from the wedges, cylinders, balls, and miniature hockey pucks of cheese? Our guide coached us through a selection of goat, sheep, and cow's milk cheeses to go with our growing picnic.

Finally, we settled in at communal tables at the local wine shop to consume our pungent spread, doing our best to imitate the way French people make the most out of eating. On the best food tours, you'll come away with a happy stomach, a new favorite dish or two, and a better understanding of the way locals live and eat.

Cooking Classes

A cooking class is another fine way to roll up your sleeves and dig into the local culture. If you're an efficiency fiend like I am, these are a great use of time: You're combining a unique opportunity (learning to cook, say, pasta from scratch) with a satisfying meal, all in a few hours.

In my experience, the best casual cooking classes are taught by trained chefs with actual restaurant backgrounds (rather than hobbyists or unemployed locals embarking on a second career), take place in a real kitchen environment (rather than a stuffy classroom or "show" kitchen), have a spirit of fun and interaction, involve small groups (allowing more personal interaction with the

With a cooking class, the kitchen is your classroom. Bon apétit!

instructor), and—perhaps most important—are hands-on rather than demonstration-based.

You'll typically spend a couple of hours cooking, and then sit down to a hard-earned (if not always flawlessly executed) meal. They'll send you on your way with the recipes you prepared that day. Some classes also include a shopping trip to the market.

Recently I joined one of my tour groups in Florence for a cooking class at a restaurant. Though it took a little time, it was really fun. The group made everything from the salad to the pasta to the tiramisu. Afterwards, with the chef proudly beaming over us, we sat down to eat it—and it was as good as what you'd get in a restaurant.

Social Dining

Similar to the way the "sharing economy" has enabled travelers to stay in locals' homes via Airbnb or VRBO.com, the concept of social dining is taking off in cities around Europe. Through sites like TravelingSpoon.com, BonAppetour.com, and EatWith.com, you can sign up to share a home-cooked meal at a local's home for a small price. Not only will you get a peek at your hosts' home and a taste of how they eat, but, they will probably be happy to share their thoughts about their city and country with you—a valuable insider perspective.

Staying Connected

One of the most common questions I hear from travelers is, "How can I stay connected in Europe?" The short answer? More easily and cheaply than you might think. The simplest solution is to bring your own device—phone, tablet, or laptop—and use it much as you would at home, following the tips below, such as getting an international plan or connecting to free Wi-Fi whenever possible. Another option is to buy a European SIM card for your US mobile phone. Or you can use European landlines and computers to connect.

Staying connected in Europe gets less complicated each year. This chapter details what you need to know to communicate on the go easily and cost-effectively. For a very practical one-hour lecture covering tech issues for travelers, see RickSteves.com/mobile-travel-skills.

USING A MOBILE DEVICE IN EUROPE

Traveling with a smartphone or tablet puts indispensable information at your fingertips—including audio tours, language translators, and transportation and mapping apps. Some people also bring a laptop for blogging, uploading or editing photos, or watching movies in their downtime.

Having an international calling and texting plan is useful, especially when you're traveling with a group—you can call or text if you get separated or if there's an emergency. I use my phone in Europe to call restaurants to check if they're open or to book a table, to confirm reservations with hotels and car-rental agencies, and so on. (For tips on communicating over the phone with someone who speaks another language, see page 402.)

Options for Connecting

If you plan to take your US device to Europe, start by assessing how (and how much) you will use it, whether making calls, sending and receiving text messages, or going online to check email, book reservations, get directions, or use other mobile apps.

Just like at home, you'll connect through a cellular network or via Wi-Fi. A **cellular network** is available wherever your mobile provider has service. **Wi-Fi i**s available wherever there's a wireless internet hotspot. Wi-Fi is typically free (or low cost); on a cellular network you're using your monthly data allotment, and may pay extra for data roaming.

Here are your basic options. More details on each option are given below.

1. Sign up for an international plan. For most travelers, who don't visit Europe as frequently or for as long as I do, it's easiest to set up your own phone with a basic international plan from your carrier. Most providers offer a simple bundle that includes calling, messaging, and data. And you get to travel with your US phone number, making it easy to connect with folks back home anytime, anywhere.

2. Do everything over Wi-Fi. More budget-conscious travelers can forego their carrier's international plan and use Wi-Fi for getting online, calling, and messaging.

3. Use a European SIM card. This option works best for travelers who'll be making lots of local calls or using lots of data. Buy a European SIM card to insert in your (unlocked) US phone—or buy a cheap mobile phone in Europe.

4. Leave the devices at home. There are still ways to communicate or get online without a mobile device. Some hotels have public computers, and you can make calls from your room at some hotels.

Setting Up International Service

Roaming on a cellular network overseas on a pay-as-you-go basis can add up (on average, about $1.80/minute for voice calls, 50 cents to send texts, 15 cents to receive them, and $2 per megabyte of data). Before your trip, call your provider or check online to confirm that your phone will work in Europe, and research your provider's international rates. Nearly all newer phones work fine abroad. To stay connected at a lower cost, sign up for your carrier's international service plan. Your normal plan may already include international coverage (T-Mobile's does).

International Rates and Plans

Rates and plan pricing varies by carrier. When researching your options, ask about the following:

Pay-As-You-Go: Ask about rates for pay-as-you-go calling, texting, and data for the countries you're visiting. If you turn off cellular data and stick to Wi-Fi and messaging apps, it may be cheaper to forego an international plan and simply pay the standard rates if you need to use your phone in an emergency.

Bundled Voice, Text, and Data Plans: Find out the cost for an international plan for the length of your trip. Plans usually offer a bundle of calling, messaging, and data, but it's wise to ask exactly what's included, especially when it comes to data allowances.

When assessing how much data you'll need, consider that 100 megabytes lets you browse online for about four hours, spend about 40 minutes on social media apps, send/receive about 100 emails, use navigation apps for about an hour, or stream about 30 minutes of standard-definition video or a

Sample International Plans

Each major mobile network has its own way of dealing with international travel. Here are the basic offerings as of this printing. Plans and rates change frequently; for the latest, check with your provider.

AT&T: AT&T's Passport option carries a one-time charge for a 30-day plan. It offers two data levels; both tiers include unlimited text and expensive per-minute talk rates. They also offer an International Day Pass, which charges you only for the days you use it. Just turn on your cellular data (usually under "Settings" on your phone) when you need it and pay $10/day for unlimited calling, texting, and the same data plan you have at home ($5 for each additional line on the same account).

Sprint: All Sprint plans include unlimited text and low-speed data, and reasonable per-minute talk rates. Daily and weekly supplements buy you reasonably priced high-speed data (for streaming videos or music).

T-Mobile: All T-Mobile plans include unlimited text and lower-speed data, plus reasonable per-minute talk rates. Daily and monthly supplements buy you high-speed data.

Verizon Wireless: One-month and pay-as-you go options are pricey. The pay-as-you-go TravelPass option allows you to keep all your normal talk, text, and data allowances for a daily fee ($10; remember to turn off cellular data and only turn it back on when you need it).

How to Dial

To make an international call, follow the dialing instructions below. Some European phone numbers begin with 0, but you must drop the 0 when dialing internationally (except when calling Italy). In some countries, phone numbers vary in length (for instance, a hotel can have a seven-digit landline and an eight-digit mobile number). I've used the phone number of one of my recommended Paris hotels in the dialing examples below (01 47 05 25 45).

From a Mobile Phone

It's easy to dial with a mobile phone. Whether calling from the US to Europe, country to country within Europe, or from Europe to the US—it's all the same. For international access, press zero until you get a + sign, then dial the country code (33 for France) and phone number, dropping the initial 0.

▶ To call the Paris hotel from any location, dial +33 1 47 05 25 45.

From a US Landline to Europe

Dial 011 (US/Canada access code), country code (33 for France), and phone number.

▶ To call the Paris hotel from home, dial 011 33 1 47 05 25 45.

From a European Landline to the US or Europe

Dial 00 (Europe access code), country code (33 for France, 1 for the US), and phone number.

▶ To call the Paris hotel from Spain, dial 00 33 1 47 05 25 45.

▶ To call my US office from France, dial 00 1 425 771 8303.

little over an hour of podcasts or music (these are ballpark figures; actual numbers vary greatly depending on which apps/websites you're using, your device, etc.). Keep in mind that if you stick to Wi-Fi you won't incur data charges.

Some plans have a 30-day duration or require you to set an end date when you sign up. If your international option is open-ended, remember to cancel any add-ons that you activated once you return home.

Wi-Fi and Data Roaming

Using Wi-Fi

Unless you have an unlimited-data plan, you're best off saving most of your online tasks for Wi-Fi, which is easy to find. You can access the internet, send texts, and make voice and video calls over Wi-Fi.

Most accommodations in Europe offer free Wi-Fi, but some—especially expensive hotels—charge a fee. If Wi-Fi is important to you, ask about it when you book and confirm

For a complete list of European country codes and more phoning help, see HowToCallAbroad.com.

Country Codes		Ireland & N. Ireland	353 / 44
Austria	43	Ireland & N. Ireland	353 / 44
Belgium	32	Italy	39
Bosnia-Herzegovina	387	Latvia	371
Croatia	385	Morocco	212
Czech Republic	420	Netherlands	31
Denmark	45	Norway	47
Estonia	372	Poland	48
Finland	358	Portugal	351
France	33	Russia	7
Germany	49	Slovakia	421
Gibraltar	350	Slovenia	386
Great Britain	44	Spain	34
Greece	30	Sweden	46
Hungary	36	Switzerland	41
Iceland	354	Turkey	90

that it'll be available in your room. In some hotels, Wi-Fi works great; in others, the signal is less reliable or doesn't work well (or at all) beyond the lobby (many European hotels are in old buildings with thick stone walls). Often it's good enough to shoot off an email, but too slow to stream movies or make a video call. (It's smart to download media and update apps before your trip, when bandwidth isn't an issue.)

When you're out and about, cafés are usually your best bet for finding free Wi-Fi. As in North America, most McDonald's and Starbucks in Europe offer free Wi-Fi. You'll likely also find Wi-Fi at tourist offices, in city squares, within major museums, at public-transit hubs, and aboard some trains and buses. You may need to register or accept terms of service to get online, and some networks limit browsing time. At cafés and restaurants, you may have to buy something to get the Wi-Fi password.

Using and Conserving Data
Using data roaming on your cellular network is handy when

you can't find Wi-Fi—but it's also potentially expensive. Make sure you know your plan's data rates to avoid sticker shock later. Budgeting your data is easy if you follow these tips:

Disconnect from your cellular network. The easiest way to avoid accidentally burning through data is to put your device on "airplane" or "flight" mode, then turn your Wi-Fi back on as needed (this disables phone calls and texts, as well as data). You can also manually turn off data roaming or cellular data (either works) whenever you're not using it—check under "cellular" or "network," or ask your service provider how to do it. Then, when you need to get online but can't find Wi-Fi, simply turn on your cellular network just long enough for the task at hand.

Save large-data tasks for Wi-Fi. Even with an international data plan, I wait until I'm on Wi-Fi to Skype or FaceTime, stream videos, or do any other megabyte-greedy tasks. Using a navigation app such as Google Maps over a cellular network can take lots of data, so do this sparingly or offline (for tips on using these apps while driving, see page 172; for details on using them to navigate a city on foot, see page 303).

Limit automatic updates in your email and other apps. By default, many mobile apps are set to constantly check for a data connection and update information. You can cut your data use by switching off this feature, or by setting updates to occur only when you're on Wi-Fi. Start with your email: Change the settings from "auto-retrieve" to "manual," or from "push" to "fetch." This means that you'll need to manually download (or "fetch") your messages. If you receive an email with a large photo, video, or attachment, wait until you're on Wi-Fi to view it.

Keep track of data usage. If you're concerned about bumping up against your data limits, keep track of your usage. On your device's settings menu, look for "cellular data usage" or "mobile data" and reset the counter at the start of your trip. Some carriers automatically send a text warning if you approach or exceed your limit and will let you upgrade your package without penalty.

Wi-Fi Calling and Messaging

A cheap way to stay in touch while traveling is to use a mix of calling/messaging apps. Just log on to a Wi-Fi network, then connect with any of your friends, family members, or local contacts who are also online and signed into the same service. (Avoid using these apps over a cellular network, which can burn through your data allowance, especially if using video.)

Apps such as Skype, WhatsApp (especially popular with Europeans), FaceTime, and Google Hangouts are great for making free or low-cost calls or sending texts over Wi-Fi worldwide. If you've never looked, check your phone—one or another app is often preloaded. (Most apps also work on tablets/laptops, too).

Internet calling makes it easy and cheap to keep in touch.

The biggest hurdle travelers face with Wi-Fi calling is signal strength. With a solid signal, the sound quality is better than a standard phone connection; but with a weak signal, the video and audio can be choppy and freeze up. If you're struggling with your connection, try turning off the video and sticking with an audio-only call.

With some of these services, if you buy credit in advance you can call anywhere outside the country for just pennies per minute. For example, I use Skype to call ahead from home and reserve hotels, or while I'm traveling to confirm tomorrow's reservation.

Some apps, such as Apple's iMessage, will use the cellular network for texts if Wi-Fi isn't available: To avoid this possibility, go to "Settings," then "Messages," and turn off the "Send as SMS" feature. See the "Resources for Wi-Fi Calling & Messaging" sidebar for options.

Using a European SIM Card

A mobile phone equipped with a European SIM card can be a good solution for travelers making a lot of local calls, or those who need a European phone number or faster connection speeds than their mobile carrier provides. This option gives you access to cheaper rates than you'll get through your US carrier, even with an international plan.

It's simple: Buy a SIM card in Europe to replace the one in your

Resources for Wi-Fi Calling & Messaging

Facebook Messenger: Messaging for mobile devices and computers

FaceTime: Video and voice calls between iOS devices

Google Hangouts: Video, voice, and messaging for mobile devices

iMessage: Messaging between iOS devices

Signal: Encrypted messaging for mobile devices

Skype: Video and voice calls for most devices

Snapchat: Video, messaging, and sharing photos for mobile devices

WhatsApp: Video, voice, and messaging for most devices

unlocked US phone or tablet (check with your carrier about unlocking it before your trip) or buy a basic cell phone in Europe.

You'll find SIM cards at department-store electronics counters, some newsstands, and even at vending machines. If you need help setting up your phone or determining the best option, buy your SIM card at a mobile-phone shop (you may need to show your passport). Costing about $5-10, SIM cards usually include a prepaid calling credit, with no contract and no commitment. Expect to pay about $20-40 more for a SIM with a gigabyte of data.

Mobile-phone stores can switch out your SIM card for you.

When you run out of credit, you can top your SIM card up at newsstands, tobacco shops, mobile-phone stores or many other businesses (look for your SIM card's logo in the window); some providers let you top up your SIM card online.

EU citizens using a domestic SIM card are not charged for roaming in other EU countries (although in some cases, data caps are applied). If you'll be traveling to multiple countries, inquire about this "roam-like-at-home" pricing at a mobile-phone shop.

Tips: Most European SIM cards expire after a certain period of inactivity (typically 3-12 months), so use up the credit or hand it off to another traveler. Note your new phone number so you can pass it on to friends and family. Also, be sure you've saved your contacts in the phone itself, rather than on the SIM card; otherwise, you'll lose access to them when you switch SIMs. When storing phone numbers, include the plus (+) sign (which fills in the international access code for you) and the country code to ensure that your calls will go through, regardless of where you're calling from.

Few phone booths remain in Europe... and those that do generally take phone cards rather than coins.

Untethered Travel

If you don't want to travel with your device, you can still stay connected. You can get online using public computers and make calls from your hotel.

Some hotels have **public computers** in their lobby for guests to use; otherwise you may find them at public libraries or tourist

Tech Prep Your Trip

Before you head to the airport, follow these tech-prep tips to ensure you'll have quick access to everything you need on your mobile device—in the air and when you land.

- Stock your device with any content and apps you will want on the road. Doing this from home avoids using data and dealing with slow Wi-Fi in Europe (or draining your battery on the go). Helpful tools include translators, mapping apps and journey planners, public transit apps, and sight-specific apps. Also download music, podcasts, or other audio files (including walking tours and interviews from my Rick Steves Audio Europe app—see page 17). If you have an ebook reader, load up on reading material.
- If you're accustomed to streaming content via a site such as Netflix, be aware that you'll most likely be denied access from Europe (most services have geographic content restrictions). Download movies and TV shows in advance (enough to get you through your trip). Some streaming services (such as Netflix and Amazon Prime) allow you to download select TV shows and movies to watch offline (not available on older devices or laptop browsers). Or purchase or rent movies and TV shows to download through iTunes, Google Play, and other paid services. (You may need to delete some apps or content you no longer use to make space.)
- To ensure photos from your device are backed up frequently, enable cloud backup or install an app such as Google Photos, which offers free storage (for tips, see the Photography & Sharing Your Trip chapter).
- Take photos or scan important documents—such as your passport—and save them to a password-protected file-hosting service like Dropbox, Google Drive, or Microsoft OneDrive. If you have a find-my-phone feature on your device, make sure it's enabled so you can track it down if it's lost or stolen (see the Theft & Scams chapter).

information offices (ask your hotelier for the nearest location). On European keyboards, most letters are familiar, but a few are switched around. To insert the extra symbols (such as brackets or accented characters) that appear on some keys, use the "Alt Gr" key to the right of the spacebar. If you can't locate a special character (such as the @ symbol), simply copy it from a web page and paste it into your document.

Most **hotels** charge a fee for placing calls—ask for rates before you dial. You can use a prepaid international phone card (usually available at newsstands, tobacco shops, and train stations) to call out from your hotel. Dial the toll-free access number, enter the card's PIN code, then dial the number. Since you're never charged for receiving calls, it's better to have someone from the US call you in your room (ask the hotel for the direct number to your room).

In some countries, you may still see **public pay phones,** but they're rare. You'll likely find them only in a few post offices and train stations. Most don't take coins but instead require insertable phone cards, which you can buy at a newsstand, convenience store, or post office.

INTERNET SECURITY ON THE ROAD

Whether you're getting online with your own device or at a public computer, using a shared network comes with increased security risks. Travelers who are too careless with their digital information can open themselves up to significant hassle and expense. Aim for a cautious middle ground, and protect your devices and personal information by heeding the following tips.

Security for Your Device

Gadget theft is an issue in Europe. Not only should you take precautions to protect your devices from thieves (see page 378 for tips), but you should also configure them so that your personal data stays private.

First, check that your device is running the latest versions of its operating system, security software, and apps. Next, consider tightening your security settings. At the very least, make sure your device is password-protected so thieves can't easily access your information.

For an extra layer of security, set up email and social-networking apps so they require a sign-in each time. It's best to use a different password for each app and log-in (a password manager can help you keep everything straight; some apps now use face recognition or fingerprint technology). Don't allow websites or apps—especially banking or shopping apps—to log you in automatically, and don't store passwords, PINs, account numbers, and other sensitive information directly on your mobile device. If your device is stolen and you use an app that accesses financial data, immediately alert your bank (as well as your mobile provider).

Once on the road, use only secure, password-protected Wi-Fi hotspots (an open network is more vulnerable). Ask the hotel or café staff for the specific name of their Wi-Fi network. Hackers sometimes create bogus hotspots with a similar or vague name (such as "Hotel Europa Free Wi-Fi") that shows up alongside a bunch of authentic networks. If you're not actively using a hotspot, turn off your device's Wi-Fi connection so it's not visible to others. Remember that even a legitimate Wi-Fi network can be hacked. Some people feel safer using a virtual private network (VPN), which encrypts your data.

Safety Tips for Using Public Computers

It's perfectly safe to check train schedules, maps, or museum hours on a public computer. The danger lies in accessing personal accounts that require a login and password.

If you do need to access personal accounts on a public computer, make sure that the browser you use doesn't store your login information. If you have the option of opening an "incognito" or "private" browser window, use it. When you sign into any site, look for ways to ensure that the browser forgets your username and password after you log out: For instance, click the box for "public or shared computer" or unclick any box that says "stay signed in" or "remember me." It's also a good idea to clear the browser's history after you're done, so fewer artifacts of your surfing session remain—especially if you've accessed sensitive information (under the browser's settings, look for a "Privacy" or "Security" category).

Accessing Financial Information Online

Financial institutions have invested heavily in security to ensure that your personal information remains secure during mobile banking—but it still pays to be careful.

While traveling, if you want to check your banking or credit-card statements, or take care of other personal-finance chores, use a banking app rather than signing into your bank's website via a browser (the app is less likely to get hacked).

Refrain from logging into personal finance sites on a public computer. When using your mobile device, a cellular network is safer than Wi-Fi, and a password-protected Wi-Fi network is safer than open Wi-Fi. Just like at home, don't click on links in unsolicited emails from your bank or respond to texts allegedly sent by your credit-card company.

If you need to enter your credit card information online, such as for booking museum or theater tickets, make sure the site is secure. Most browsers display a little padlock icon to indicate this; also check that the page's URL begins with "https" instead of "http." Never send a credit-card number (or any other sensitive information) over a website that doesn't begin with "https."

Be careful when emailing personal information. If there's not a secure website, it's better to relay a credit-card number by phone than in an email.

Getting Around in Cities

Shrink and tame big European cities by mastering subway and bus systems, hopping into the occasional taxi, and navigating smartly whether on foot or underground. By knowing where you're going and the best way to get there, you'll save time, money, and energy.

This chapter offers tips on navigation tools and on using subways, buses, taxis, and ride-booking services to get around Europe's cities. For information on using trains, long-distance buses, and ferries to link destinations, read the Trains, Buses & Boats chapter. For tips on biking, see the Outdoor Adventure chapter.

MAPS AND NAVIGATION TOOLS

In any big city, a map saves you endless time and frustration. Whether it's a detailed foldout paper map, the simpler map in your guidebook, the map on your phone—or some combination—a map is essential for efficient navigation.

To orient yourself, study your map before setting out. Familiarize yourself with the city's layout. Relate the location of landmarks on your map—your hotel, major sights, the river, main streets, the train station—to each other. When you're out sightseeing, use any viewpoint (such as a church spire, tower, or hilltop) to identify landmarks, understand the lay of the land, and see where you're going next.

Using Printed Maps

The map in your guidebook is likely small and intended as an overview. You'll want to also get a decent, detailed map of your destination. You can almost always get a decent foldout map free or cheaply at the local tourist office or your hotel.

When choosing a city sightseeing map, make sure the city

center is detailed enough, as that's where you'll spend most of your time. If you'll be relying on public transit, get a map that shows not just subway stations, but also bus and tram lines and stops. For an extended stay in a sprawling city, it can be worth paying for a sturdier, more detailed map. And if rain is in the forecast, a laminated map will hold up much better.

Resources for Navigation

Google Maps app: Best route planner for walking and public transit
City Maps 2 Go app: Easy-to-use maps that show your location offline
Here WeGo app: Extensive offline map library; provides driving, transit, and walking routes

Using Maps on Your Phone

Like many people, I've become accustomed to the convenience of having maps at my fingertips when I need to find an address or look up directions. It's amazing to pop out of a subway station, not knowing north from south, and find your location immediately on your phone.

If Using Data Roaming: If you have an international data plan, you can use data roaming on your phone to navigate. Those lucky enough to have unlimited data can roam freely, including using real-time turn-by-turn directions as you walk. Otherwise, use your data sparingly—just when you need to look up an address or get quick walking directions.

Without Data Roaming: Even without the real-time turn-by-turn walking directions that come with data roaming, there's plenty you can do. It just takes some planning.

With GPS activated, your smartphone always knows where you are—no data connection required. Even in airplane mode, when you call up a map you've previously downloaded, you'll see a dot marking your location. And since the GPS signal doesn't use the internet, it continues to track your location on the map as you move. You can even "pin" your destination on your map ahead of time so that you have a good idea of where you're headed.

Mapping apps that work well offline are Google Maps, City Maps 2Go, and Here WeGo. Download your city's map ahead of time, while online (using the Wi-Fi at your hotel, for example). Later, when you're on the street (and offline), just call up your map, and you're on your way.

If you want to rely on a specific walking route, look up the route on your phone while you're online at your hotel. Before setting out, punch in your start and end points, and select the route you want to take. After you leave your hotel (and go offline), the map remains available on your phone, so you can use it to navigate all day long. You can zoom in and out, and your location will be marked with a dot.

There are limitations: You can't adjust your route unless you go back online, and downloaded maps will eat into the available space on your phone—you'll want to delete maps once your trip is over.

PUBLIC TRANSPORTATION

Europe's public-transportation systems are so good that many urban Europeans go through life never learning to drive. Their wheels are trains, subways, trams, buses, and the occasional taxi. If you embrace these forms of transportation when visiting cities, you'll travel smarter. Nearly every European city has a fine public transportation network. Subways and trains are speedy and never get stuck in traffic jams. Buses and trams can give you a tour of the town on the way to your destination. With the proper attitude, taking public transit can be a cultural experience, plunging you into the river of workaday European life.

Tips for Riding Public Transit

Even if you've never used public transit in your hometown, these tricks can help you quickly master your transportation options in Europe's cities. You'll have the city by the tail, without having to shell out much for taxis.

Get a transit map or app. With a map, anyone can decipher the code to easy, affordable urban transportation. Paris and London have the most extensive—and the most needed—subway systems. Pick up a schematic map at the tourist office or subway ticket window, ask for one at your hotel, or print one off a website. Many city maps, even free ones, include a basic transit map.

To help you plot your travel, major transit systems offer online journey planners, and many sights list the nearest bus or subway stop on their websites and brochures. Apps for the London Tube, Paris Métro, and other transit systems have good trip-planning features and work offline. Some, such as Stockholm's SL transit app, let you purchase tickets in the app—a great

convenience when you don't have cash or can't find a ticket machine. Google Maps works as an all-around transit app in most European cities, and its route planner has a transit option that covers both subways and buses.

Learn what's covered by a ticket. In many cities, the same tickets are good on the subway, trams, and buses, and include transfers between systems; in other places, you'll need to buy a new ticket each time you transfer. If a ticket seems expensive, ask what it covers—$4 may seem like a lot until you learn it's good for a round-trip, two hours, or several transfers.

Consider your ticket options. Choices vary per city but generally include some mix of individual tickets, multiticket deals, passes, and reloadable cards. You'll pay the most per ride by buying individual tickets, but this can be the way to go if you'll be taking only a few rides or prefer to get around mainly on foot.

If you're committed to using public transit, the following options will cut your per-ride costs and save you time (because you won't have to stand in a ticket line every time you travel):

- Multiticket deals offer you a set number of tickets that you can use anytime and share with companions, even on the same ride (unlike passes and cards, which generally can be used by only one person at a time).
- Passes allow unlimited travel on all public transport for a set number of hours or days; a 24-hour pass usually costs less than four single fares. Some passes cover sights as well or offer admission discounts. Before you buy, plan how you'll get the most use out of your pass during its period of validity.
- Reloadable cards, such as London's Oyster Card, are prefunded with pay-as-you-go credit and can be topped

LEFT Public transit—the European treat

RIGHT With public transportation, you can zip quickly, effortlessly, and inexpensively around Europe's most congested cities.

off when the balance runs low (such cards may require a small initial fee).

You can buy tickets, passes, and cards at subway ticket machines or windows, and, depending on the city, on the bus (usually for exact change and at a slightly higher cost than the ticket-machine price), at newsstands, or in tourist offices. Ask about discounts if you're young, old, or traveling with children.

Don't try to travel for free. Many European subways, buses, and trams use the honor system. Ticket checkers (some in uniform, some incognito) patrol sporadically, and others check tickets as you exit the station—but all mean business. If you're caught without a valid ticket, even if you accidentally bought the wrong kind, you'll most likely have to pay a hefty fine, probably right on the spot.

If confused, ask for help. Europe's buses and subways are filled with people who are more than happy to help lost tourists locate themselves. Confirm with a local that you're at the right platform or bus stop before you board. If you tell the driver or nearby passengers where you're going, they will gladly tell you where to get off.

Expect pickpockets. While public transportation feels safe, savvy riders are constantly on guard. Per capita, there are more pickpockets on Europe's subway trains, trams, and buses than just about anywhere else. They congregate wherever there are crowds or bottlenecks: on escalators, at turnstiles, or at the doors of packed buses or subway cars as people get on and off. If there's a hubbub, assume it's a distraction for pickpockets—put a hand on your valuables. Be on the lookout, wear your money belt, and you'll do fine. (For tips on avoiding theft, see the Theft & Scams chapter.)

Follow local public-health rules. In order to prevent a recurrence of the coronavirus, destinations may enforce public-health regulations for transit riders (such as mask wearing and ridership limits). Check in advance for any restrictions at your destinations.

Subways

Most of Europe's big cities are blessed with an excellent subway system, and wise travelers know that learning this network is key to efficient sightseeing. European subways go by many

names: "Metro" is the most common term on the Continent, but Germany and Austria use "U-Bahn." For Scandinavia, it's the "T-bane" in Oslo, "T-bana" in Stockholm, and "S-tog" in Copenhagen. In London, it's the "Tube" (to the British, a "subway" is a pedestrian underpass).

Subways generally operate from about 6 a.m. until midnight. Trains rarely follow a specific schedule, but just pass by at frequent but irregular intervals. Most systems have electronic signs noting when the next train will arrive.

Here are tips for smooth sailing on Europe's subways:

Study your map. Subway maps are usually included within city maps and are posted prominently at the station and usually on board. A typical subway map is a spaghetti-like tangle of intersecting colorful lines. The individual lines are color-coded, numbered, and/or lettered (and even named, in the case of London); their stations, including those at either end of the line, are also indicated. These end stations—while probably places you'll never go—are important, since they tell you which direction the train is headed and appear (usually) as the name listed on the front of the train.

A few cities (like Rome) have just two or three subway lines, while London has more than a dozen. Some cities' subways share the tracks with express commuter trains (such as Paris' RER and Germany's S-Bahn), which make fewer stops and can usually get you across town faster.

Plan your route. Determine which line you need, the name of the end station in the direction you want to go, and (if necessary) where to transfer to another line. In the station, you'll use this information to follow signs to reach your platform. (See the sidebar for a step-by-step sample trip.) When in doubt, ask.

Validate your ticket. Once you buy a ticket, you may need to validate it in a turnstile slot (don't forget to retrieve it)—watch to see what others do. If you have an all-day or multiday ticket, you may need to validate it

As you'll constantly be reminded on London's Tube... mind the gap.

As you enter the subway station, insert your ticket into the slot to open the turnstile. After validating your ticket, remember to reclaim it.

Sample Subway Trip

Let's say you want to go from your hotel to the art museum on the other side of town. Your hotel is a five-minute walk from the Napoleon station on the A line. Note that the A line has two end stations: Outer Limits to the north and Suburb del Sud to the south. The art museum is on the B line, so you'll need to transfer at the station where these two lines intersect: Java Junction.

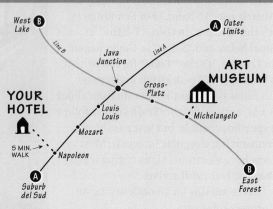

Here's how you'll do it:

1. Entering the subway at the Napoleon station, follow signs to trains going in the direction of Outer Limits (the northern end station).
2. Ride three stops to Java Junction, get off, and follow signs to transfer to line B (in the direction of East Forest).
3. Ride the train two stops to the Michelangelo station.
4. Use the neighborhood map in the station to choose the exit closest to the museum.

Congratulations—you've survived your first European subway trip!

only the first time you use it, or not at all (ask when you buy it). Don't throw away your ticket too soon—you may need to insert it in a turnstile to exit the system (the machine might keep your ticket if it's used up). Once you're out, toss or tear used tickets to avoid confusing them with unused ones.

Keep alert. Follow signage carefully as you navigate through the station. Confirm that you're at the right platform—heading in the right direction—before boarding. Subways can get packed during rush hour. Try to steer clear of crowds and commotion; there are usually fewer people in the first and last cars.

Stick together. If you're with a companion or group, make sure everyone knows the name of your final stop before boarding, stays close together, and agrees on a game plan in case you get separated. If a subway is about to depart as you arrive on the platform, don't rush to catch it and risk leaving behind your companions; trains run frequently, and it's far easier to wait for the next departure than to reconnect with your split-up group.

Get off at the right place. Once on the train, follow along with each stop on your map. Most cars have an electronic screen showing the next stop. Sometimes the driver or an automated voice announces the upcoming stop—but don't depend on this cue, as a foreign name spoken by a native speaker over a crackly loudspeaker can be difficult to understand. Keep an eye out the window as you pull into each station; the station name will be posted prominently on the platform or along the wall. If the train is crowded, move close to the doors one stop before you want to exit. When the train stops, the doors may open automatically, or you may need to open them yourself by pushing a button or pulling a lever. Don't panic—watch others and imitate.

If you need to transfer, follow the signs. Changing from one subway line to another can be as easy as walking a few steps to an adjacent platform—or a bewildering wander via a labyrinth of stairs and long passageways. Subway systems are clearly signed—just follow along (or ask a local for help).

Exit the station. When you arrive at your destination station, follow exit signs up toward street level, keeping an eye out for posted maps of the surrounding neighborhood to help you get your bearings. Bigger stations have multiple exits, signposted by street name or nearby landmarks. Choosing the right exit will help you avoid extra walking and unnecessary forays through busy intersections.

> ## Subway Etiquette
>
> - On escalators to and from platforms, stand on the right, pass on the left.
> - When waiting at the platform, stand to either side of the opening doors as people exit the train. Board only after everyone who wants to leave is off the train.
> - Talk softly on board. Listen to how quietly Europeans communicate and follow their lead.
> - On a crowded train, try not to block the exit (unless your stop is next). If you're at the door of a packed train when it reaches a stop, step out of the car and to the side, let others off, then get back on the train.

When using public transit, take full advantage of posted signs and maps. Neighborhood maps help you get oriented upon arrival.

Trams and Buses

Getting around town on city trams or buses is a little more complicated than using the subway, but has several advantages. Since you're above ground, it's easier to stay oriented, see the landmarks, and enjoy the vibrant street life out the window. In fact, some public bus routes

are downright scenic—Paris' bus #69 gives you a great sightseeing introduction for the cost of a transit ticket. Bus stops
are more closely spaced than subway stops—meaning the bus
is useful even for short hops and usually gets you closer to
where you need to go. And some buses go where the subway
can't.

Like subways, city trams and buses run frequently,
especially during peak hours (if a bus is packed, wait for
the next one). Although night buses run less frequently and
follow limited routes, they're useful for night owls who don't
want to spring for a taxi. The main disadvantage of trams
and buses is that they can be slowed down by traffic, so try to
avoid taking them during rush hour.

To travel smartly, follow these tips:

Plan your route. You can usually get a tram or bus map
and schedule from local tourist or transit offices, print them
off the system's website, or use a public-transit app. Many
stops have their routes and timetables posted, and some have
electronic signs noting how many minutes until the next
tram or bus arrives.

Confirm the essentials before you board. Find out if
you need a ticket in advance or if you can buy it on board (if
you buy it from the driver, you'll usually need exact change).
Make sure you're getting on the right tram or bus going in
the right direction. Before you get on, mention your destination to a local or the driver. Smile and ask, for example,
"Vaticano?"

Validate your ticket. Usually you enter at the front of

LEFT If your
destination is
obvious—such
as Florence's
Duomo—choos-
ing the right
stop is easy;
otherwise, ask
fellow passen-
gers for help.

RIGHT Posted
bus schedules
tell you when
the next bus
should be
coming...and
where it's going.

the tram or bus and show your ticket to the driver, or validate it by inserting it into an automated time-stamp box. Observe and imitate what the locals do.

Get off at the right stop. Tram and bus stops, like subway stops, are named (usually for a cross street or nearby landmark), but their signs are often difficult to see from a moving vehicle. Some trams and buses have on-board digital signs that announce the next stop. If they don't, it pays to stay alert. Have a sense of how long a ride should take, and know the names of the stops coming up right before yours (and the one right after yours, so you'll know if you've gone too far). If possible, sit near the door, so you can hop out easily. As you ride, follow along the route on your map, looking for landmarks along the way: monuments, bridges, major cross streets, and so on. If you're uncertain about your stop, get the attention of the driver or another passenger and ask, *"Prado?"* (For extra credit, preface your request with the local word for "please.")

In bike-friendly cities such as Amsterdam and Copenhagen, buses often let you off directly into busy bicycle lanes. Look carefully, in both directions, as you exit.

Signal for your stop. Some buses pull over at every stop, but more often they stop only by request. Look for a pull cord or a button with the local word for "stop," and use it to signal that you want to get off at the next stop.

TAXIS AND RIDE-BOOKING SERVICES

Taxis are scenic time savers that zip you effortlessly from one sight to the next (except during rush-hour traffic, when they're stuck like everyone else). While cabs are expensive for the lone budget traveler, a group of three or four people can often travel more cheaply by taxi than by bus or subway. Taxis are especially low-priced in Mediterranean countries and Eastern Europe. You can go anywhere by cab in downtown Lisbon or Athens for about $15.

I enjoy cab rides. Many of my favorite insider tips and most interesting conversations have come from chatting up taxi drivers. But don't trust their advice blindly; cabbies can get kickbacks for recommending (and delivering you to) a particular restaurant or attraction.

> ### Resources for Taxis and Ride-Booking
>
> **TaxiFareFinder.com, Ride.Guru:** Estimates fares and compares cabs to ride-booking costs
> **MyTaxi app:** Taxi-finder lets you book and pay for cabs in major cities
> **Uber:** Most popular ride-booking service

Many Americans are wired to assume that taxi drivers in other countries are up to no good. But I've found that most drivers are honest. Sure, scams happen. But with the right knowledge and a watchful eye, you'll get where you want to go without being taken for a ride.

These Sorrento cabbies hire by the hour and would love to show you around.

Hiring a Taxi

In some cities, it's easy to flag down a cab anywhere on the street; in any city, you can find cabs at a taxi stand. These stands are often listed as prominently as subway stations on city maps; look for the little Ts (or ask a local to direct you to the nearest one). When hiring a cab, make sure it has a big, prominent taxi-company logo and telephone number. Avoid using unmarked beaters with makeshift taxi lights on top.

Calling for a Taxi: When you need a ride from a hotel or restaurant, you can have the staff call a taxi for you—but be aware that in many places, the meter starts ticking from the time the call is received (and there may be an additional flat fee for calling a taxi). But if you have an early morning flight to catch, it'll save you some stress (and cost nothing beyond the usual supplements) to have your hotelier book a cab for you the day before.

Hiring Taxis at Airports and Train Stations: A taxi zipping you right to your hotel can be a relief after a long flight or train ride. But dishonest cabbies sometimes lurk at major transit points, ready to take advantage of travelers who are jet-lagged and travel-weary. To avoid problems, head for the official taxi stand and join the queue rather than flagging a taxi down.

Ordering a Taxi on Your Mobile Phone: There are several apps that work exactly like Uber (see below) but are for booking a licensed cab. One popular European app is MyTaxi, which operates in Great Britain, Germany, Austria, Poland, Spain, and Italy.

Using Ride-Booking Services in Europe

Uber is available in many European cities, and rides can be cheaper than taxis. (As of this printing, Lyft is not active in Europe.) The service works just as conveniently in Europe as it does in the States: You request a car via the Uber app on your phone (you'll need an internet connection or Wi-Fi), and the fare is automatically charged to your credit card. If you like Uber, check whether it's up and running in your destination.

Some countries—Germany, France, Italy, Spain, Belgium, Sweden, Norway, and the Netherlands—don't allow UberPop ride-sharing (unregulated drivers and cars), so you may find only the more expensive UberX or UberBlack (licensed cabs or limousine services).

Paying a Fair Rate (and Avoiding Scams)

It's usually best to make sure the cabbie uses the taxi meter. But for certain standard trips (such as to or from the airport), set prices are common. Learn the going rate for getting to your destination by asking your hotelier or at any tourist info point. You can check your guidebook, TaxFareFinder.com, or Ride.Guru for estimated taxi fares in larger cities (Ride Guru also compares taxi rates with services like Uber).

Sometimes tourists wrongly accuse their cabbies of taking the long way around or adding unfair extras. But what can seem like a circuitous route may still be the shortest, given pedestrianized zones and one-way streets. And many supplements are legit, based on the time of day (nights, early mornings, and weekends), amount of baggage, extra people, airport taxes, port fees, and so on.

In cities such as London, Paris, and Barcelona, meters are tamper-proof. That said, even cabbies with honest meters have ways of overcharging tourists. One common trick is for cabbies to select the pricier "night and weekend" rate on their meter during a weekday. An explanation of the different meter rates should be posted somewhere in the cab, often in English; if you're confused about the tariff, ask your cabbie to explain. If you suspect foul play, following the route on your map or conspicuously writing down the cabbie's license information can shame a cad into being honest.

At airports and train stations, look for the official taxi queue, where you'll wait in line to be assigned a taxi. Be wary of unofficial helpers who usher tourists out of line to a separate taxi area—this is often a scam that ends with your credit card number being stolen.

Paying and Tipping

Some European cab drivers only take cash, while others prefer only cards. Uber only takes credit cards, and some cities are following suit—London, for example, now requires all taxis to accept credit cards. But it's smart to be prepared to pay in cash.

Using small bills minimizes your chance of getting ripped off. If you only have a large bill, state the denomination out loud as you hand it to the cabbie. They can be experts at dropping your €50 note and then showing you a €20. Count your change. If, for whatever reason, I'm charged a ridiculous price for a ride, I put a reasonable sum on the seat and say good-bye. Don't be intimidated by a furious cabbie.

To tip, round up to the next euro on the fare (to pay a €13 fare, give €14); for a long ride, to the nearest 10 (for a €76 fare, give €80). If the cabbie hauls your bags and zips you to the airport to help you catch your flight, you might want to toss in a little more. But if you feel like you're being driven in circles or otherwise ripped off, skip the tip.

Taking a Taxi Between Cities

While a budget traveler may never think of hiring a taxi for a trip between cities, it can actually be a fairly good value. For example, if your next destination is a long train trip but a short drive away, a taxi can be an affordable splurge, especially if the cost is split between two or more people. Services such as Uber can be even cheaper in some places.

Consider the time you'll save over public transportation—for example, one hour of sweat-free, hotel-door-to-hotel-door service versus two sticky hours on stop-and-go public transit, including transfers to and from the train or bus station. Simply ask any cabbie what they'd charge (it could be an hourly rate or even an off-meter flat rate—they know you have a cheap public-transit alternative and could be willing to strike a deal). Or ask at your hotel if they have a line on any car or taxi services that do the trip economically. See if you can find a driver who's accustomed to taking tourists on these trips. While not technically guides, these drivers are often willing to provide some basic commentary on what you're seeing and may even suggest some interesting stops along the way.

Sightseeing

After months of planning, you're finally on the ground in Europe, and the real work—and joy— begins: sightseeing. This is when it pays to have a thoughtful plan. The pointers in this chapter will help you get oriented to your surroundings; make the most of your sightseeing time; navigate museums, churches, castles, and other sights smartly; and find your way off the beaten path.

GETTING ORIENTED

Whether tackling big cities or quaint villages, you don't want to feel like a stranger in a strange land (even though that's exactly what you are). Visitors who decide to wing it—especially in Europe's large cities—invariably waste time and miss out. Here are some useful resources for getting acclimated to a new place.

Maps: A good map (or navigation app) and a plan for getting around are essential. For details, see the previous chapter.

Guidebooks: Be sure to have a good, up-to-date guidebook. If you've arrived in Europe without one, you can often find English-language guidebooks at newsstands, major sights, and bookstores. For tips on selecting a guidebook, see page 36.

Tourist Information Offices: No matter how well I know a town, a quick stop at the tourist information office can be valuable. Nearly any place with a tourist industry has an information service for visitors on the main square, in the City Hall or public library, at the train station, or sometimes at airports or freeway entrances. You don't need the address—just follow the signs. A friendly and multilingual staff answers questions, hands out maps and sightseeing information, explains transit options, and sells sightseeing passes and concert or theater tickets. Some offices also offer guided walking tours, downloadable audio tours, and other resources.

Prepare a list of questions ahead of time. Write up a proposed sightseeing schedule. Find out if you've left out any important sights, and confirm closed and free-admission

Tourist information offices are ready to help you.

days. Ask about special events. Keep in mind that tourist-office advice can be biased (many offices are funded by fees and commissions from the places they recommend).

Entertainment Guides: Big European cities bubble with entertainment, festivities, and nightlife. But these events won't come to you. New in town and unable to speak the native language, travelers can be oblivious to a once-in-a-lifetime event erupting just across the bridge. An entertainment guide is the key. Every big city has one, either in English (such as *What's On* or *Time Out*, which has editions in many cities) or in the local language, but easy to decipher (such as SortiraParis.com, a weekly review of events).

Printed guides may be available at the tourist office (where they're often free), at newsstands, English-language bookstores, or at the front desk of big, fancy hotels (look like a guest and help yourself). Many guides are also available online or as apps. Events are posted on city walls everywhere. They may be in a foreign language, but that really doesn't matter when it reads: *Weinfest, Música Folklórica, 9 Juni, 21:00, Piazza Maggiore, Entre Libre*, and so on. Figure out the signs—or miss the party.

Other Resources: Seek out firsthand advice from your hotel's staff or other travelers. Glean hints from the couple seated next to you at breakfast, chat with the waiter who serves you lunch, or ask a shop owner for tips.

TOURS

Organized tours are a great way to acclimate to a new city and learn about its history and highlights. Tours not only provide a city overview, they also give you an idea of what you'll want to revisit later in your stay. Especially in big cities, you'll find tours of all kinds, from guided walks to bus rides that let you hop on and off at will. Audio tours are often

available for those who prefer
a DIY approach.

Guided Walking Tours

These are my favorite introduction to a city. Since walking tours focus on just a small
part of a larger whole (generally the old town center), they
are thorough. The tours are
usually conducted in English

Try a guided
walk to learn
about a town
that's probably
a thousand
years older than
your hometown.

by well-trained guides who are sharing their town for the
noble purpose of giving you an appreciation of its history,
people, and culture—not to make a lot of money. Walking
tours are personal, inexpensive, and a valuable education.
They're nearly always time and money well spent.

In major European cities, you'll also see advertisements
for "free" walking tours. While these tours are indeed free,
tipping is expected; in fact, the guides don't earn money
unless you tip. On these free tours, guides—generally expat
students who have memorized a script—tend to emphasize
stories over an academic approach, and are known to take
liberties with historical events and characters. And they may
take up your valuable time with heavy promotions for their
other (paid) tours. Personally, I'd rather pay up front for
hardworking guides whose goal is to make the city's history
come alive. But for travelers on a budget, these free tours
provide a cheap way to get to know a place.

Bus Orientation Tours

Many cities have orientation bus tours that take you around
the city on a double-decker bus. Riding in the open air atop a
two-story bus, you get a feel for the city's layout as the major
sights roll by; most buses include live or recorded narra-

You might even
go topless on
some hop-on,
hop-off buses.

tion. Many are structured as
hop-on, hop-off tours with a
circular route that connects
the top sights; with an all-day
pass, you can hop off to visit a
sight, then catch a later bus to
continue the route.

Bus tours usually cost
about $30-40. Some can be a
disappointing rip-off; others
are a great sightseeing tool. If

you're short on time, have limited mobility, or would appreciate an overview before diving into a city, they can be worth the money. If I had only one day in a big city, I might spend half of it on one of these tours.

Before you shell out for a ticket, consider a few key factors: route, quality of narration, and for hop-on, hop-off buses, frequency. The best-value hop-on, hop-off tours leave several times an hour, visit sights I actually want to see, and feature an engaging live guide (if the guide is good, I'll stay on for the entire route). Be wary of overcrowded buses—if the top fills up, you may have no choice but to cram into the (potentially hot and stuffy) lower level. It's worth waiting for the next bus to get space on an upper level, where views come from a higher vantage point and aren't obscured by fogged-up windows. The best scenario is enjoying the view from a topless bus on a sunny day.

Many cities also offer a public bus (such as Paris' bus #69) or boat route (Amsterdam has several; Venice has the Grand Canal) that connects the city's major sightseeing attractions; you can ride these as if they were low-cost (unguided) tour buses/boats. Tourists buy the one-day pass and make the circuit at their leisure (for more on city buses, see page 309).

Local Guides

For the price of four seats on a city bus tour with forgettable recorded narration, you can often hire your own private guide for a personalized city tour. This is most cost-effective if you're traveling with a group. In my research, I rely upon these experts and find them well worth the investment.

Nearly every city in Europe has great local guides who are independent businesspeople scrambling to fill their calendars and earn a living. A two- to four-hour tour with a private guide can cost from $100 to $300. Guides tend to charge more in big, touristy cities and in Western European countries. The farther east you travel, the cheaper they are. I strongly recommend hiring a guide in places like Prague or Kraków, where per-hour costs average $40 and guides often share fascinating personal stories of life in the not-so-distant past. Sure, hiring a private guide is a splurge. But so is a nice dinner. And if you can split the guide fee with a few other people, your cost goes down.

If you're spending several days in a destination, hire a guide early in your trip. You'll get an orientation to the city, and you'll learn about time- and money-saving tips. Guides can meet you wherever you like and tailor the tour to your interests. They can also give you advice on good restaurants, shopping, transportation, and sightseeing. It's basically like renting a friend who's really smart—I always learn something.

Local guides bring history to life.

Recently, my Portuguese guide Alex took me on a little scavenger hunt through Lisbon's castle town—built back when nobles needed a safe place within the castle walls—and showed me things I hadn't noticed in 20 years of visits to Lisbon.

In addition to sightseeing, I encourage travelers to use guides for cultural experiences. For example, after a two-hour Uffizi Gallery tour in Florence, take a coffee break in a café, and follow it with a guided old-town walk featuring Roman, medieval, and modern aspects of Florence. During a visit to Amsterdam, my guide and I spent an hour enjoying a Reypenaer cheese-and-wine tasting that was just as educational (and frankly, more fun) than a tour of the Rijksmuseum. Also consider food tours, which provide wonderful insight into this very important part of each country's culture (for details, see page 288).

Although it's possible to drop by the local tourist office when you're in town and book a guide, it's better to make arrangements in advance. Many tourist offices list local guides on their websites. You can also look for recommendations in guidebooks (when I meet particularly good independent guides, I list them in my books). In some cities, you can book a local guide—as well as meetups, walking tours, and excursions—through Airbnb. Other online resources include ToursByLocals (organized tours and private guides), and TravelLocal (small tour operators).

Self-Guided Walks and Audio Tours

If you don't want to join an organized tour or spring for a local guide, a self-guided walk or audio tour can provide direction and meaning to your wanderings through a new city or museum.

Many tourist offices offer do-it-yourself walking-tour leaflets that provide turn-by-turn directions for an orientation walk around town (some guidebooks offer similar self-guided walks). Tourist offices often offer audio tours to accompany their self-guided walks, and most major museums offer room-by-room audioguides. Sometimes you'll borrow or rent a device preloaded with the audio content at the tourist office or museum; in other cases you'll use free Wi-Fi to download the tour to your mobile device on the spot. Increasingly, destinations and museums are offering free downloadable apps that combine tours with other digital content. Remember to bring earbuds.

Audio tours are hard to beat: The price is right (free or low cost), the quality is reliable, and you can take the tour exactly when you like. With an audio tour, you can immerse yourself in a wonderful sight, enjoying its visual wonder while listening to information that gives it all meaning. Before you leave for Europe, it's worth looking for digital content you can download in advance to enhance your trip. For instance, the palace at Versailles offers helpful podcasts for touring its extensive palace grounds (www.chateauversailles.fr).

I've produced free, self-guided audio versions of my walking and museum tours throughout Europe (download the Rick Steves Audio Europe app; see page 17). These user-friendly, easy-to-follow, fun, and informative audio tours are available for museums (for instance, the Louvre and Orsay in Paris, Florence's Uffizi), churches (St. Paul's in London, St. Peter's in Rome, the Basilica of St. Francis in Assisi), ancient sites (Athens' Acropolis, Rome's Colosseum), my favorite neighborhoods (Edinburgh's Royal Mile, London's Westminster, Venice's Grand Canal), and much more.

Minivan Excursions

Some of Europe's top sights are awkward to reach by public transportation, such as the châteaux in the Loire, the *Sound of Music* sights outside Salzburg, the D-Day beaches of Normandy, the rural meadows of Cornwall, or the prehistoric cave paintings in France's Dordogne. For roughly $60-80 per

Minivan tours—such as this one, to the Rock of Gibraltar—can be an ideal way for nondrivers to reach certain sights.

half-day, an organized tour not only whisks you effortlessly from one hard-to-reach-without-a-car sight to the next, but gives you lots of information as you go.

If you have a choice between a big, 50-seat bus (a "coach") and a minivan, I'd generally recommend the minivan. With a smaller group, you're likely to have a more engaging, entertaining guide and more camaraderie as you roll.

SIGHTSEEING STRATEGIES

Westminster Abbey, the Eiffel Tower, the Sistine Chapel— these are the reasons you go to Europe. They're also the reason millions of other tourists go. Nothing kills a sightseeing buzz like waiting in line for hours to get into a popular sight, or being crammed shoulder to shoulder in front of a masterpiece painting. But if you plan ahead, the sights you dreamed of seeing won't disappoint.

Be Strategic and Selective

Set up an itinerary that allows you to fit in your must-see sights, but be realistic about what you can accomplish in a day. As you make your plan, note the specifics of the sights on your list, especially their closed days and any evening hours (which can help extend your sightseeing day). Be prepared for changes to hours or entry procedures as a result of the pandemic; call ahead to confirm details if it seems like the museum's website hasn't been updated recently. Check the weather report a few days out and plan your indoor/outdoor time accordingly. Arrange your sightseeing to cover a larger city systematically and efficiently, one neighborhood at a time.

Save yourself for the biggies. Don't overestimate your powers of absorption. Rare is the tourist who doesn't become somewhat jaded after several weeks of travel. At the start of my trip, I'll seek out every great painting and cathedral I can. After two months, I find myself "seeing" cathedrals with a sweep of my head from the doorway, and I probably wouldn't cross the street for another Rembrandt. Don't burn out on mediocre castles, palaces, and museums. Sightsee selectively.

When possible, visit major sights in the morning (when your energy is best), and save other activities for the afternoon. Don't put off visiting a must-see sight; even if you've double-checked hours, places can close unexpectedly for a strike or restoration. On holidays, expect reduced hours or

Medieval Sightseeing in a Modern World

Today's cities sprawl, but many, such as Florence (pictured), were once contained within medieval walls. Most of the walls were torn down long ago to allow the cities to expand beyond their historic centers. But in Paris, Kraków, Vienna, and others, you can still see the legacy of these walls in the shape of the modern ring roads that replaced them. To pare an otherwise overwhelming city down to size, remember that nearly everything worth your sightseeing time lies within this ring.

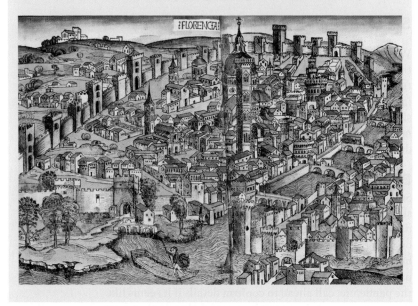

closures. In summer, some sights may stay open late. Off-season, many attractions have shorter hours.

For more spontaneous sightseeing, location-based apps such as Google Maps and Triposo point you toward sights and venues within walking distance. Google Maps provides hours and ratings along with navigation; Triposo lets you set a variety of filtering options, and works well offline.

Avoiding Lines and Crowds

Crowds and lines are a genuine nuisance at top European attractions, and too many people spend big chunks of their vacation time queueing up to buy tickets at popular sights. As far as I'm concerned, there are two IQs for travelers: those who queue...and those who don't. Smart tourists do whatever they can to minimize hassles and maximize their experience. With the right information, you can avoid nearly every line that tourists suffer through. The following tricks aren't secrets. They're in any good, up-to-date guidebook. Just read ahead.

Reservations and Advance Tickets

More and more travelers are taking the 21st-century version of a Grand Tour, bringing especially heavy crowds to major destinations such as Paris, London, Rome, Barcelona, and Prague. Certain sights—especially those that weren't built to accommodate mass tourism—are almost always jammed, all day long, most of the year. And some sell out early in the day, leaving those who arrive late disappointed.

To reduce these problems, many popular sights sell advance tickets that guarantee admission at a certain time (often with a small booking fee that's well worth it). Others have instituted mandatory reservations or limited occupancy to encourage social distancing during the pandemic, and may keep those changes even post-Covid.

Many museums offer convenient mobile ticketing. Simply buy your ticket online and send it to your phone, eliminating the need for a paper ticket.

Given how precious your vacation time is, I recommend getting reservations for any must-see sight that offers them—it's worth giving up some spontaneity. While hundreds of tourists are sweating in long ticket-buying lines, you'll show up at your reserved entry time and be assured of getting in.

In some cases, getting a ticket in advance simply means buying your ticket earlier on the same day. But for other sights, you should book as soon as your travel dates are set and tickets are released, often months in advance. These include sights such as the Eiffel Tower, Rome's Vatican Museums, the Anne Frank House in Amsterdam, Barcelona's Picasso Museum and Sagrada Família, and Florence's famous galleries—the Accademia (Michelangelo's *David*) and the Uffizi (Italian Renaissance art). When you're ready to commit to a certain date, book it.

Note that reservations are

Don't Miss Out! Book Key Sights in Advance

Europe's most popular sights are often crowded. To avoid wasting time in long ticket-buying lines or being shut out altogether, buy tickets or make reservations in advance whenever possible.

Most major sights sell tickets online in advance (Palace of Versailles, Tower of London, Anne Frank House, Vatican Museums). Some sights require a reservation (Berlin's Reichstag, Rome's Borghese Gallery). Either way, it's easy to do—and in some cases you'll get a price break.

Book as far in advance as possible for your must-see sights, and you won't be disappointed. Even if on-site, same-day tickets *may* be an option—why risk it?

required at some sights, such as the Reichstag in Berlin, Leonardo's *Last Supper* in Milan, Giotto's Scrovegni Chapel in Padua, and the Borghese Gallery in Rome. Check websites and guidebook listings for your must-see sights to learn if reservations are optional or mandatory.

It's Tuesday at Versailles, and these people now have time to read their guidebooks: "On Tuesday, many Paris museums are closed, so Versailles has very long lines."

Timing Is Everything

In many cities, several sights tend to be closed on the same day of the week (usually Sunday, Monday, or Tuesday). It follows that, in high season, any major sight that's open when everything else is closed is guaranteed to be crowded. For example, Versailles is packed on Tuesdays, when many big museums in Paris are closed.

Many museums are free one day a month—a great deal for locals. But for visitors, it's generally worth paying the entrance fee on a different day to avoid the hordes on the free day. In Rome, the Sistine Chapel feels like the Sardine Chapel when admission is waived once a month. Likewise, the Colosseum and Roman Forum are free...and a mob scene on their free days.

At popular sights, it can help to arrive early or go late. This is especially true at places popular with cruise excursions and big-bus tour groups. At eight in the morning, Germany's fairy-tale Neuschwanstein Castle is cool and easy, with relaxed guides and no crowds; come an hour later without a ticket and you'll either wait a long time, find that tickets are sold out, or both. Of course, there are exceptions: On my last visit to the Acropolis in Athens, I went around noon— which was perfect timing, since cruise-ship crowds tend to flock there first thing in the morning. They were heading out as I was heading in. A good guidebook will offer tips on the best times to visit a sight.

Many sights are open late one or two nights a week— another pleasant time to visit. For instance, London's Tate Modern stays open Friday and Saturday evenings, when you'll enjoy Dalí and Warhol in near solitude. Very late in the day—when most tourists are long gone, searching for dinner or lying exhausted in their rooms—I linger alone, taking

The Eiffel Tower comes with long lines for those who don't book online in advance. With my reservation in hand, I went directly to the elevator, while this long queue of tourists waited. (None of them had my guidebook.)

artistic liberties with some of Europe's greatest works in empty galleries.

Shortcuts

Even at the most packed sights, there's often a strategy or shortcut that can break you out of the herd, whether it's a side entrance with a shorter wait, a guided tour that includes last-minute reservations, a better place in town to pick up your ticket, or a pass with line-skipping privileges.

Sometimes getting in more easily is just a matter of picking the right door. Grand as the Louvre's main entrance is, that glass pyramid stops looking impressive as you wait—and wait—to get through security. You can't bypass security checks, but you'll encounter shorter lines if you use the less crowded underground entrance.

A pricier option for skipping lines at a sight is to take a guided tour. At the Vatican Museums, joining a guided tour gets you right in. In Milan, you can sign up a week ahead to take a bus tour that includes an easy stop at Leonardo's *Last Supper*, which normally books up more than a month in advance.

Self-service ticket kiosks, like those at the Louvre, Versailles, or the Prado, can provide a faster way in. On a recent trip to St. Petersburg I bought my ticket to the Hermitage at a kiosk and walked right past a ticket line bulging with cruise-ship travelers—and within minutes was enjoying the czars' grand art collection. Similarly, if you buy your ticket for the Tower of London at a souvenir stand on your way to the Tower, you can skip the long line at the sight itself.

At St. Mark's Basilica in Venice, you can either snake slowly through an endless line, or go instead to a nearby church to check a large bag or backpack—then walk right to the front of the basilica's line, show your bag-claim tag, and head on in (go figure). Check your guidebook for sight-specific, insider tips.

At the Acropolis in Athens, crowds and lines are an issue. To save time, buy a combo-ticket at one of the other sights covered by the ticket.

Sightseeing Passes and Combo-Tickets

Many tourist destinations offer a citywide sightseeing pass or tourist card, which includes free or discounted entrance to many or most sights for a certain amount of time (usually intervals of 24 hours). Such deals often include free use of public transit, a brief explanatory booklet, and a map.

In some places, passes can save you serious time and money; in others, you'd have to sightsee nonstop to barely break even. Do the math: Compare the price of the pass to the total of what you'd pay for individual admissions. Remember: Time is money. A pass is almost always worth-while if it allows you to bypass admission or ticket-buying lines. Plus, with a pass, you can spontaneously visit minor sights you otherwise might not want to pay to enter.

Combo-tickets combine admission to a larger sight with entry to a lesser sight or two that few people would pay to see. The bad news: You'll pay for multiple sights to visit one. The good news: You can bypass the ticket line at the congested sight by buying your ticket at a less-popular sister sight. For example, you can wait in line to buy a ticket for Venice's Doge's Palace or the Acropolis in Athens—or buy a combo-ticket at a participating (yet less crowded) sight and scoot inside.

Whether you have a combo-ticket or pass, never wait at the back of the line if there's any chance you can skip it. Don't be shy: March straight to the front and wave your pass or ticket. If you really do have to wait with everyone else, they'll let you know.

If You Can't Beat 'Em, Join 'Em

No matter how well-conceived your plans, it's inevitable that at some point you'll find yourself packed shoulder-to-shoulder with other visitors and their intercontinental B.O. Accept in advance that popular attractions, such as the Sistine

Chapel, come with a constant and raging commotion of tourists...but that doesn't mean you should stay away.

A few years back, I was unable to avoid lumbering through Versailles on one of the most crowded days of the year (a Sunday in July). It was an experience I'll never forget. A steady crush of visitors shuffled through the hot and muggy one-way route leading to the payoff: the magnificent Hall of Mirrors. Even with a mossy carpet of tourist heads, sights like these are a thrill to see—and worth every sweaty second.

At the Vatican Museums it's worth fighting through the gauntlet of crowds to see the Sistine Chapel.

Visiting Sights Smartly

Some people walk into Europe's major museums, churches, palaces, castles, and ancient sites, gawk for a few minutes, then walk out. But with a little preparation and know-how, your sightseeing will go more smoothly—and take on more significance. Here are some tips for navigating Europe's various sights.

Tickets: For high-profile sights, it's best to buy tickets in advance if possible (see "Reservations and Advance Tickets," earlier). When buying on-site, before you get to the ticket window, study the list of prices. You could have a choice of individual tickets, combo-tickets, or passes. You may be eligible for discounts if you're young, old, or with children (have proof of ID, student card, etc.). Be prepared to pay cash at some minor sights.

Museums may have special exhibits in addition to their permanent collections. Some special exhibits are included in the entry price, while others come at an extra cost (which you may have to pay even if you don't want to see the exhibit).

Your ticket may allow in-and-out privileges (say, for a lunch break outside the museum); if this is important to you, ask.

Getting Oriented: Entering a major sight is similar to arriving in a new town—you need to get oriented. Hit the information desk for a brochure or map, find out about any special events and tours, and ask about any temporary room or wing closures.

Security Check: Many sights have a security check, where you must open your bag or send it through a metal detector. Allow extra time for these lines in your planning. A few places will confiscate the same sharp items and full water bottles that you're not allowed to carry on board a plane.

Checkroom: Most sights offer a checkroom or lockers (usually free or with a small deposit), and some require you to check daypacks and coats. They'll be kept safely. If you have something you can't bear to part with, stash it in a pocket or purse. To avoid checking a small backpack, carry it under your arm like a purse as you enter. (From a guard's point of view, a backpack—which could bump against artwork—is generally a problem, while a purse is not.)

Stroll with a chatty curator through Europe's greatest art galleries, thanks to digital audioguides.

Touring the Sight: Many sights offer audioguides with recorded descriptions in English. If the audioguide isn't included with admission, ask to listen to it for a couple of minutes to gauge the quality before you pay. If you bring your own earbuds, you can enjoy better sound. If you don't mind being tethered to your travel partner, you'll save a little money by bringing a Y-jack and sharing one audioguide. Other sights offer downloadable audio tours that you'll listen to on your own mobile device. (See "Self-Guided Walks and Audio Tours," earlier.)

Guided tours in English are most likely to be available in peak season (generally at an extra cost, but sometimes included with admission). If you're interested, confirm in advance that your visit will coincide with a tour. Or hire your own guide to take you through the museum (see "Local Guides," earlier).

Some sights run short explanatory videos that are generally worth your time. I make it standard operating procedure to ask when I arrive at a sight if there is a video in English or with subtitles.

Once inside, hit the highlights first, then go back to other things if you have the time and stamina. Expect changes— items can be on tour, on loan, out sick, or shifted at the whim of a curator. If the painting you crossed the Atlantic to see isn't on the wall, ask a museum staffer if it's been moved to another location.

Most sights stop selling tickets and start shutting down rooms or sections 30 to 60 minutes before closing. Guards usher people out, so don't save the best for last. Get to the far end early, see the rooms that are first to shut down, and work your way back toward the entry.

My favorite time at a major sight is the lazy last hour, when the tourists clear out. On one of my visits to the Acropolis, I showed up late and had the place to myself in the cool of early evening. Other blockbuster sights such as St. Peter's Basilica and the Palace of Versailles can be magical just before closing.

Photography: Flash photography is often prohibited in museums but taking photos without a flash is usually allowed. Look for signs or ask. Flashes damage oil paintings and delicate artifacts, and distract others in the room. Even without a flash, a handheld camera or mobile device will take a decent picture (or buy postcards or posters at the museum bookstore). Think twice about bringing a selfie stick—they're banned at many sights.

Services: Bigger sights usually have a café or cafeteria (a good place to rejuvenate during a long visit). The WCs at sights are free and generally clean; they can be in short supply, though, so take advantage when you can.

AT THE SIGHTS

Museums

Europe is a treasure chest of great art and history. For some, visiting the world's greatest museums is the highlight of a European trip. For others, "museum" spells "dull." But you don't need to know how a Ferrari works to enjoy the ride. Paintings are like that. You can just stroll through a gallery and bask in the color scheme. That said, it doesn't hurt to keep in mind the following suggestions.

With a good guidebook, you stand a chance of finding Michelangelo's *Slaves* in the Louvre.

Learn about art and history. In my student days, I had to go to the great art galleries of Europe because my mom said it would be a crime not to. Touring places like the National Archaeological Museum in Athens, I was surrounded by people looking like they were having a good time—and I was convinced they were faking it. I thought, "How could anybody enjoy that stuff?" Two years later, after a class in classical art history, that same museum was a fascinating trip into the world of Pericles and Socrates, all because of some background knowledge.

Pretrip studying makes art and artifacts more fun. When you understand the context in which things were made, who paid for it and why, what the challenges of the day were, and so on, paintings and statues become the closest thing Europe has to a time machine.

A victim of the Louvre

My free online video clip library, Rick Steves Classroom Europe, is packed with more than 400 short clips excerpted from Rick Steves' Europe TV episodes. You can use it to understand what you'll see in Europe. Just enter a topic at Classroom.ricksteves.com to find everything I've filmed on a subject.

Don't miss the masterpieces. A common misconception is that a great museum has only great art. But only a fraction of a museum's pieces are masterpieces worthy of your time. You can't possibly cover everything—so don't try. With the help of a tour guide or guidebook, focus on just the top attractions. Most major museums provide brief pamphlets that recommend a greatest-hits plan. With this selective strategy, you'll appreciate the highlights while you're fresh. If you have any energy left afterward, you can explore other areas of specific interest to you. For me, museum going is the hardest work I do in Europe, and I'm rarely good for more than two or three hours at a time. If you're determined to cover a large museum thoroughly, try tackling it in separate visits over several days.

Find your favorites. Do some reconnaissance on the museum's website before your visit to line up your targets. Or, on arrival, look through the museum's collection handbook or postcard rack to make sure you won't miss anything of importance to you. For instance, I love Salvador Dalí's work. One time I thought I was finished with a museum, but as I browsed through the postcards...Hello, Dalí. A museum staffer was happy to show me where this Dalí painting was hiding. I saved myself the disappointment of discovering too late that I'd missed it.

Eavesdrop. If you're especially interested in a particular piece of art, spend a half-hour studying it and listening to each passing tour guide tell his or her story about *David* or the *Mona Lisa*. They each do their own research and come up with a different angle to share. Much of it is true. There's nothing wrong with this sort of tour freeloading. Just don't stand in the front and ask a lot of questions.

Take advantage of my free audio tours. My Rick Steves

Audio Europe app includes self-guided tours of the finest museums in many of Europe's greatest cities. These can make your museum going easier and more meaningful (see page 17).

Churches, Synagogues, and Mosques

England's Wells Cathedral offers a stunning interior and a moving evensong service.

European houses of worship offer some amazing art and architecture—not to mention a welcome seat and a cool respite from the heat. You may be there just to see the Caravaggio over the side altar, but others are there as worshippers. Be a respectful visitor.

A modest dress code (no bare shoulders or shorts) is encouraged at most churches, and actually enforced at some larger churches and most mosques. If you are caught by surprise, you can improvise, such as using maps to cover your shoulders and tying a jacket around your hips to cover your knees. (Throughout the Mediterranean world, I wear a super-lightweight pair of long pants rather than shorts for my hot and muggy big-city sightseeing.) At Turkish mosques, women must cover their heads and wear clothing that shields their legs and arms; everyone needs to remove their shoes.

At active places of worship, visitors may not be allowed inside for one or more time periods throughout the day. If you are already inside, you may be asked to leave so as not to disturb the congregation. Check your guidebook's listing to avoid showing up when a place is closed to tourists. But keep in mind that many churches welcome visiting worshippers. One of my favorite experiences in Great Britain is to attend evensong—a daily choral service—at a grand cathedral.

Some churches have coin-operated audio boxes that describe the art and history; just set the dial to English, insert your coins, and listen. Coin boxes near a piece of art illuminate the work (and present a better photo opportunity). I pop in a coin whenever I can. It improves my experience, is a favor to other visitors trying to appreciate a great piece of art in the dark, and is a little contribution to that church. Whenever possible, let there be light.

Castles

Castles send the imagination soaring. Fortresses perch on hilltops from Ireland to Istanbul, and from Sweden to Spain.

Boning Up on Europe's Relics

Centuries ago, displaying skeletal remains was a way of honoring the dead—and a reminder to all of their inevitable end. Storing human bones in ossuaries was handy, too, when burial space was otherwise scarce.

To drive home the point about human mortality, the bones of monks were sometimes even artistically arranged in crypts and chapels. In **Rome's** Capuchin Crypt, hundreds of skeletons decorate the walls to the delight—or disgust—of the always wide-eyed visitor. The crypt offers unusual ideas in home decorating, as well as a chance to pick up a few of Rome's most interesting postcards. A similar Capuchin Crypt is a highlight of many visits to **Palermo** in Sicily. In **Évora,** Portugal, osteophiles make a pilgrimage to the macabre "House of Bones" chapel at the Church of St. Francis, lined with the bones of thousands of monks.

TOP Even in death, Italians know how to look cool.
BOTTOM Head to Hallstatt's Bone Chapel.

Overcrowding in cemeteries has prompted unusual solutions. Austria's tiny town of **Hallstatt** is crammed between a mountain and a lake. Space is so limited that bones get only 12 peaceful buried years in the church cemetery before making way for the newly dead. The result is a fascinating chapel of bones in the cemetery. Hallstatt stopped this practice in the 1960s, about the same time the Catholic Church began permitting cremation.

Kutná Hora's ossuary (outside Prague) is decorated with the bones of 40,000 people, many of them plague victims. The monks who stacked these bones 400 years ago wanted viewers to remember that the earthly church is a community of both the living and the dead.

Some cities, such as Paris and Rome, have catacombs. Many cities opened up a little extra space by deboning the graveyards that used to surround medieval churches. During the French Revolution, **Paris** experienced a great church cemetery land grab. Skeletons of countless Parisians were dug up and carefully stacked along miles of tunnels beneath the city.

Seekers of the macabre can bone up on Europe's more obscure ossuaries, but any tourist will stumble onto bones and relics. Whether in a church, chapel, or underground tunnel in Europe, you might be surprised by who's looking at you, kid.

Storybook châteaux line the Loire River valley and walled strongholds guard harbors throughout the Mediterranean.

While some of Europe's castles are fairy-tale wonderful (such as Neuschwanstein in Bavaria), others are massive, crumbling hulks (Rheinfels on the Rhine).

Guédelon castle in Burgundy provides a fascinating look at medieval building techniques.

Relatively few castles are furnished; most of their original fixtures disappeared long ago. Some castles have little more than a ticket booth, while others (like England's Warwick) host jousting competitions, catapult demonstrations, museums of medieval armor and artifacts, and well-stocked gift shops. There are even entire towns built in and around medieval castles, such as Carcassonne in France.

Before visiting a castle, do your research; check to see if tours are offered. If you're visiting a ruined castle, wear good walking shoes. Bring a small flashlight if there are tunnels; claustrophobics beware. Learn the various parts of the castle; you'll appreciate your visit more if you can tell the difference between a dungeon and a donjon (a.k.a. the keep; the main tower that's the refuge of last resort if the castle is attacked).

Europe's castles generally fall into one of two categories: medieval fortresses (built to withstand sieges) and castle-palaces (residences and luxury châteaux for royalty and nobility).

With the advent of cannons, even the sturdiest medieval castles became obsolete. Many fell into ruin, used as quarries to build more practical things. You'll enjoy the best concentration of medieval ramparts and dark dungeons by touring the Rhine in Germany. To see a castle being built today with methods used in the 13th century, visit Guédelon in France (about two hours south of Paris).

Later, from the 16th century through the 19th-century Romantic era, the rich and famous built castle-palaces as residences, culminating in Europe's most opulent palace, Versailles, and its most fanciful, Neuschwanstein (Walt Disney made the Bavarian fairy-tale castle his trademark, and the rest is history). Whether a medieval bunker or a Romantic reinvention, these royal abodes make great sightseeing.

Europe's Coolest Castles

Visiting Europe can overwhelm you with too many castles to tour in too little time. To help you prioritize, here are my favorites.

Carcassonne (France): Europe's greatest Romanesque fortress-city, medieval Carcassonne is a 13th-century world of towers, turrets, and cobblestones—a walled city and Camelot's castle rolled into one.

Warwick Castle (England): The best castle in Britain, this 14th-15th-century fortified shell holds an 18th-19th-century royal residence surrounded by dandy gardens—a fairy-tale fortress that's entertaining from dungeon to lookout.

Burg Eltz (Germany): Lurking in a mysterious forest, this is my favorite European castle. Once the fortified home to three big landlord families, it retains its medieval furnishings and ambience.

Rheinfels Castle (Germany): This mightiest of Rhine castles, built in 1245, rumbles with ghosts from its hard-fought past—it withstood a siege by 28,000 French troops in 1692, but was destroyed by the French Revolutionary army a century later.

Storm Carcassonne early or late.

Warwick Castle—for kings and queens of any age

Even in ruins, Rheinfels is mighty.

Towering Eltz Castle, on Germany's Mosel River

Shimmering Château de Chillon

Reifenstein Castle, rugged inside and out

Sintra's hilltop ruins, where the winds of the past really howl

At the Ehrenberg ruins, grab a sword fern and unfetter your imagination.

Don't miss the Romantic-era interior of Hohenschwangau Castle.

Château de Chillon (Switzerland): This wonderfully preserved 13th-century castle is set romantically at the edge of Lake Geneva.

Reifenstein Castle (Italy): Situated below the Brenner Pass, Reifenstein once bottled up a strategic valley leading to the easiest way across the Alps—and features the best-preserved medieval castle interior I've ever seen.

Moorish Ruins of Sintra (Portugal): The desolate ruins of a 1,000-year-old Moorish castle is a medieval funtasia of scramble-up-and-down-the-ramparts delights and atmospheric picnic perches with vast territorial views.

King's Castles (Germany's Bavaria): The fairy-tale extravagance of Neuschwanstein Castle is proof that Bavaria's King Ludwig II was just "mad" about 19th-century Romanticism. Downhill, nestled near Alpsee lake, is the statelier Hohenschwangau Castle, Ludwig's boyhood home.

Ehrenberg Ruins (Austria): This ensemble of brooding ruins, connected by a valley-spanning suspension bridge, was once the largest castle complex in the Tirol region. Located near the town of Reutte, Austria, Ehrenberg offers a fascinating contrast to Ludwig's castles just across the border.

Neuschwanstein, the greatest of "Mad" King Ludwig's fairy-tale castles

Dusty rocks or busy ancient thoroughfare? The ruins at Hierapolis, Turkey, come to life with info and imagination.

Ancient Sites and Ruins

Climbing the Acropolis, communing with the druids at Stonehenge, strolling the Croatian shore in the shadow of Emperor Diocletian's palace in Split, tracing the intricate carvings on a Viking ship—the remnants of Europe's distant past bring a special thrill to those of us from the New World.

But the oldest sites are also the most likely to be initially underwhelming, especially if it's been a while since your last history class. On its own, the Roman Forum is just a cluster of crumbling columns and half-buried foundations. You've heard about it all your life, you've spent good money to get here, and your first thought upon entering is..."This is it?"

Ancient sites come to life with your imagination, aided by information. Bring a guidebook that's heavy on historical background and consider hiring a local guide. Eager local guides tend to cluster outside major ancient sites like Delos in Greece, and Pompeii and the Colosseum in Italy, but quality varies. I prefer to book a reputable guide in advance, but if you decide to choose a guide at a sight, first talk to potential candidates for a bit to make sure you connect.

For some well-known places you can get books that cleverly use overlays to visually mesh the present with the past. To fire up your imagination before your trip, watch a movie or read a book set in the time and place of any site you're excited to see. Once you're there, mentally reconstruct arches and repaint facades. Clad your fellow tourists in togas. Fill a ruined cathedral with the chants of cowled monks while inhaling imaginary incense.

Many major ancient sites (especially in Greece) have both an archaeological site and a nearby museum full of artifacts unearthed there. You can choose between first visiting the museum (to mentally reconstruct the ruins before seeing them) or the site (to get the lay of the ancient land before seeing the items found there). In most cases, I prefer to see the site first, then the museum. But if it's a blistering hot afternoon, tour the air-conditioned museum first, then hit the ruins in the cool of the early evening. Or, if rain clouds are on the horizon, do the archaeological site first, then duck into the museum when the rain hits.

Open-Air Folk Museums

Many people travel in search of traditional culture in action. But even while we're booking a ticket into the romantic past, much of Europe is squarely in the modern world. Often, the easiest way to see "traditional culture" is by exploring open-air folk museums. True, it's culture on a lazy Susan, with an often cleaned-up version of an area's preindustrial lifestyle. But these museums can be simultaneously fun and enlightening—a magic carpet ride through a culture's past. In more and more places they provide your only chance for a close-up look at the "Old World."

An open-air folk museum collects traditional buildings from every corner of a country or region, then carefully reassembles them in a park, usually near the capital or a major city. Log cabins, thatched cottages, mills, old schoolhouses, shops, and farms come complete with original furnishings and usually a local person dressed in the traditional costume who's happy to answer your questions. In the summer, these museums buzz with colorful folk dances, live music performances, and craft demonstrations by artisans doing what they can to keep the cuckoo clock from going the way of the dodo bird. Some of my favorite souvenirs are those I watched

LEFT Traditional culture is kept alive in Europe's open-air folk museums.

RIGHT At Stockholm's Skansen folk museum, you may be entertained by this rare band of left-handed fiddlers.

being dyed, woven, or carved by folk-museum artists. To get the most from your visit, start by picking up a list of the day's special exhibits, events, and activities at the information center, and take advantage of any walking tours.

Folk museums teach traditional lifestyles better than any other kind of museum. As our world hurtles past 300 billion McDonald's hamburgers served, these museums will become even more important. Of course, they're as realistic as Santa's Village, but how else will you see the elves?

BECOMING A TEMPORARY EUROPEAN

Many travelers tramp through Europe like they're visiting the cultural zoo. "Ooh, that guy in lederhosen yodeled! Excuse me, could you do that again in the sunshine so I can get a good picture?" It's important to stow your camera, roll up your sleeves, and enjoy the real thing.

By developing a knack for connecting with locals and their culture, we become temporary Europeans—approaching Europe on its level, accepting and enjoying its unique ways of life. When I'm in Europe, I strive to become a cultural chameleon—what I call a "temporary local." I consume wine in France, beer in Germany...and small breakfasts in Italy. While I never drink tea at home, after a long day of sightseeing in England, "a spot of tea" really does feel right. Find ways to really be there. Here are some ideas to consider:

Hit the back streets. Many people energetically jockey themselves into the most crowded square of the most crowded city in the most crowded month (St. Mark's Square, Venice, July)—and then complain about the crowds. If you're in Venice in July, walk six blocks behind St. Mark's Basilica, step into a café, and be greeted by Venetians who act as though they've never seen a tourist.

Play where the locals play. A city's popular parks and green spaces are filled with families, lovers, and old-timers enjoying a cheap afternoon or evening out. European communities provide their heavily taxed citizens with

Mass with the sun's rays, daily in St. Peter's

wonderful athletic facilities. In Britain, check out a public swimming pool, called a "leisure center." While tourists outnumber locals five to one at the world-famous Tivoli Gardens, Copenhagen's other amusement park, Bakken, is enjoyed purely by Danes. Disneyland Paris is great, but Paris' Parc Astérix is more French.

Take a stroll. Across southern Europe, communities relax with a *paseo*, or stroll, in the early evening. Stroll along. Join a *Volksmarch* in Bavaria to spend a day on the trails with people singing "I love to go a-wandering" in its original language. Mountain huts across Europe are filled mostly with local hikers. Most hiking centers have alpine clubs that welcome foreigners and offer organized hikes.

Go to church. Many regular churchgoers never even consider a European worship service. But any church would welcome a traveling American. And an hour in a small-town church provides an unbeatable peek into the community, especially if you join them for coffee and cookies afterward. I'll never forget going to a small church on the south coast of Portugal one Easter. A tourist stood at the door videotaping the "colorful natives" (including me) shaking hands with the priest after Mass.

Be an early bird. Throughout Europe—on medieval ramparts, in churches, produce markets, alpine farmsteads, and Riviera villages—the local culture thrives while the tourists sleep. In Germany, walk around Rothenburg's fortified wall at breakfast time, before the tour buses pull in and turn the town into a medieval theme park. Crack-of-dawn joggers and

Make your trip worth more by cranking up the experiences. Attending a sporting event anywhere in Europe—like this soccer match in Germany—puts you in touch with the local spirit for little money. If you're wearing a lei with colors, be sure you root for the right team. *Auf geht's Deutschland!*

Europe's Best Open-Air Folk Museums

Popularized in Scandinavia, these folk museums are now found all over the world, though the best are still those in the Nordic capitals.

Scandinavia and Iceland

Skansen (Stockholm): More than 100 buildings from all over Sweden, craftspeople at work, folk entertainment, and an Arctic camp complete with reindeer and Lapp dancing.

Funen Village (Den Fynske Landsby, near Odense): Life in 18th-century Denmark.

The Old Town (Den Gamle By, Aarhus): Slices of Danish town life from the 1700-1800s, 1920s, and 1970s.

Museum guides in traditional dress are eager to teach at The Old Town museum in Aarhus, Denmark.

Norwegian Folk Museum (Bygdøy, Oslo): Norway's first, with 150 old buildings and a 12th-century stave church.

Maihaugen Folk Museum (Lillehammer): Norway's best, with folk culture of the Gudbrandsdal Valley.

Seurasaari Open-Air Museum (near Helsinki): Reconstructed buildings from all over Finland.

Skógar Folk Museum (Iceland's South Coast): Rebuilt turf houses.

The Netherlands, Germany, and Switzerland

Netherlands Open-Air Folk Museum (Arnhem): Holland's first and biggest.

Zuiderzee Museum (Enkhuizen): Lively reconstruction of Dutch traditions lost forever to land reclamation.

Vogtsbauernhof Black Forest Open-Air Museum (Gutach): Farms filled with exhibits on traditional German dress and lifestyles.

Ballenberg Swiss Open-Air Museum (Lake Brienz): Fine collection of old Swiss buildings, arranged roughly as if in a huge map of Switzerland.

Hungary

Skanzen (Szentendre): Traditional architecture from around Hungary.

Hollókő (near Budapest): Time-capsule village that's a living hamlet and an open-air museum.

Great Britain and Ireland

Blists Hill Victorian Town (Ironbridge Gorge): Unrivaled look at the early days of the Industrial Revolution.

Beamish Museum (near Durham): Life in northeast England in 1900.

St. Fagans National Museum of History (near Cardiff): Traditional Welsh ways of life.

Ulster Folk and Transport Museum (near Belfast): Traditional Irish lifestyles and buildings from all over Ireland.

Muckross Traditional Farms (near Killarney): Three working farms, a schoolhouse, and other buildings from 1930s-40s Ireland.

Connect with people. Greeks and Turks love a game of backgammon.

walkers enjoy a special look at wonderfully medieval cities as they yawn and stretch and prepare for the daily onslaught of the 21st century. By waking up with the locals on the Italian Riviera in the off-season, you can catch the morning sun as it greets a sleepy village, breathe in the damp, cool air, and experience a rare Italian silence. Among travelers, the early bird gets the memories.

Root for your team. For many Europeans, the top religion is soccer. Getting caught up in a sporting event is going local. Whether enjoying soccer in small-town Italy or hurling in Ireland, you'll be surrounded by a stadium crammed with devout fans. Buy something with the hometown colors to wear or wave to help you remember whose side you're on.

Challenge a local to the national pastime. In Greece or Turkey, drop into a teahouse or *taverna* and challenge anyone to a game of backgammon. You're instantly a part (even a star) of the café or bar scene. Normally the gang will gather around, and what starts out as a simple game becomes a fun duel of international significance.

Contact an equivalent version of your club. If you're a member of an international service club, bridge club, professional association, or other organization, make a point to connect with your foreign mates.

See how the locals live. Residential neighborhoods rarely see a tourist; ride a city bus or subway into the suburbs. Browse through a department store. Buy a copy of the local *Better Homes and Thatches* and use it to explore that particular culture. Get off the map. In Florence, most tourists stick to the small section of the city covered by the

Connecting with the Culture

Generally speaking, Europeans enjoy getting to know Americans—all it takes to connect is a friendly smile and genuine curiosity. Take advantage of one of the many programs and organizations set up to help bridge the cultural divide.

Meet-the-Locals Programs: Several European cities have English-speaking volunteer greeters who belong to the Global Greeter Network (www.globalgreeternetwork.com). Greeters are screened extensively, but aren't trained historical experts. Instead, they introduce visitors to their city by spending a few hours sharing their insider knowledge—their favorite hidden spots, how to navigate public transit, where to find the best bargains, and so on.

A few bigger cities have more formal programs that put travelers in direct touch with locals. Dublin brings volunteers and first-time visitors together for a cup of tea or a pint (free, www.littlemuseum.ie, choose "City of a Thousand Welcomes"). In Paris, the group Meeting the French organizes dinners in private homes and workplace tours to match your interests or career (fee, www.meetingthefrench.com). Visitors to Copenhagen can enjoy a home-cooked meal with a family through Dine with the Danes (fee, www.facebook.com/dinewiththedanes).

Conversation Clubs: Most large European cities, and even many small towns, have informal English-language conversation clubs, usually meeting weekly or monthly in a public space (search online or ask at the tourist information office). You may well be the only native speaker there—if so, expect an especially warm welcome. For instance, in Rothenburg, Germany, the English Conversation Club meets on Wednesdays at Mario's Altfränkische Weinstube am Klosterhof. After 9 p.m., when the beer starts to sink in, the crowd grows, and everyone seems to speak that second language a bit more easily.

Casual Meetups: While primarily designed to connect travelers with overnight hosts, Couchsurfing.com also lists "day hosts" who are happy to just meet up with like-minded visitors and swap travel stories (see page 247). For another free means of finding people with shared interests in a given city, check Meetup.com. Sponsored events include picnics, museum tours, cocktail evenings, and more.

Cooking Classes: These give you not just a taste of the culinary traditions of the area you're visiting, but also a hands-on feel for what happens in European kitchens—along with a skill you can take home. For more on cooking classes, see page 289.

ubiquitous tourist maps. Wander beyond that, and you'll dance with the locals or play street soccer with the neighborhood gang. In Helsinki, rather than sweat with a bunch of tourists in your hotel's sterile steam room, ride the public bus into a working-class neighborhood to a rustic and woody sauna. Surrounded by milky steam, knotty wood, stringy blond hair, and naked locals, you'll have no idea which century you're in. But one thing is clear: You're in Finland.

Drop by a university. Mill around a university and

Blend into
Europe: Shop
at the town
market.

check out the announcement boards. Eat at the college
cafeteria. Ask at the English-language department if there's
a student learning English whom you could hire to be your
private guide. Be alert and even a little bit snoopy. If you
stumble onto a grade-school talent show—sit down and
watch it.

Join in. When you visit the town market in the morning,
you're just another hungry shopper, picking up your daily
produce. Traveling through the wine country of France
during harvest time, you can be a tourist taking photos—or
you can pitch in and become a grape picker. Get more than a
photo op. Get dirty. That night at the festival, it's just grape
pickers dancing—and their circle could include you.

If you're hunting cultural peacocks, remember they fan
out their tails best for people...not cameras. When you take
Europe out of your viewfinder, you're more likely to find it in
your lap.

Outdoor Adventure

Europe's fine art and rich history are major reasons to visit. But it's also a continent filled with natural beauty—often overlooked by tourists busy sprinting from sight to sight, or searching for the perfect souvenir. A day in the great outdoors can be just as culturally fulfilling as time spent in a church or museum—and much more invigorating.

If you're an energetic person, make a point to be active in Europe. Whether walking through the city core or speeding down an alpine luge, there are plenty of ways to get your heart pumping while savoring some of Europe's outdoor attractions.

HIKING AND WALKING

From casual city strolls to pleasant day hikes to multiday alpine treks, Europe is a walker's paradise.

City Walking (and Dodging)

It's easy to get in a lot of walking time in Europe's cities and towns. Skip public transport (or save it for the end of the day, when your feet are crying for mercy), and get a good feel for a place.

When putting together a walking itinerary, look for ways to splice in some top sights. In Rome, for example, winding up to the top of Gianicolo Hill rewards you with a lovely park and superb city views—and along the way you can stop at Bramante's Tempietto church, one of the jewels of the Italian Renaissance. In any city, a walking tour can help you get oriented (described on page 317).

Be prepared. Wear good, well-broken-in walking shoes, and keep blister remedies on hand. Pace yourself—concrete and cobblestones take their toll on feet much sooner than dirt trails do.

Be on your toes: Walking in cities can be dangerous, and jaywalking can have serious consequences (scores of people are run down each year on the streets of Paris, where drivers are notorious for ignoring pedestrians). Cross streets carefully, but if you wait for a break in the traffic, you may never make it to the other side. Look for marked crosswalks or—better yet—a pedestrian overpass or underpass. If you feel intimidated at a busy intersection, just shadow a local—one busy lane at a time—across that seemingly impassable street. Watch out for bikes as well as cars, particularly in cities with strong biking cultures, such as Amsterdam and Copenhagen.

Many cities have parks where you can stroll peacefully, away from the hubbub of humanity and the cacophony of cars. Many of Europe's urban parks are vast, thanks to their roots as royal hunting grounds. Henry VIII created what became London's Hyde Park to hunt deer in the 16th century; other expansive parks that began as sporting preserves include Berlin's Tiergarten, Munich's English Garden, and the Prater in Vienna. Likewise, the Tuileries Garden in Paris was once the private pleasure grounds of kings and queens; now everyday Parisians gather to stroll, sail toy boats, and turn their kids loose at a little trampoline park. No matter what city you visit, it's easy to join Europeans as they enjoy an afternoon of rambling, cycling, boating, or people-watching in their cities' public spaces.

Resources for Hiking, Biking & Climbing

ERA-EWV-FERP.com: European Ramblers' Association's country-specific advice and maps of Europe's walking paths

Ramblers.org.uk: Group walks all over Britain, from casual strolls to bracing treks

LDWA.org.uk: Long Distance Walkers Association in the United Kingdom

FI.is: Iceland Touring Association, with good general info about hiking in Iceland

CountryWalkers.com: Guided and self-directed hiking itineraries

TrailDino.com: Links to hiking trails around the world

EuroVelo.com: Long-distance cycling routes and all levels of guided and self-guided tours

EuropeBicycleTouring.com: Tips and tours from a longtime vet of cycling in Europe

Reading

Sunflower Books: Guidebooks for walking and touring

Cicerone Press: Reliable guidebooks for walkers, bikers, trekkers, and climbers

Explore Europe on Foot (Cassandra Overby, 2018). Comprehensive guide to planning hiking adventures in Europe.

Day Hiking

Beyond the city limits, outstanding national parklands are scattered throughout Europe, offering wonderful ways for visitors to commune with nature. Hikers enjoy nature's very own striptease as the landscape reveals itself in an endless string of powerful poses.

Europe has good hiking for all fitness levels, sometimes aided by a variety of "lifts"—including gondolas, funiculars, cable cars, and cogwheel trains—that take less-rugged explorers to the top in a sweat-free flash. Trails are generally well-kept and carefully marked, and detailed maps are readily available.

Hiking in the Alps

Europe's highest mountain range, the Alps extend for 750 miles and cross eight countries, each offering their own unique taste of alpine thrills. In Italy's Dolomites, for instance, a gondola whisks visitors to Europe's largest high-alpine meadow, Alpe di Siusi, where a dramatic mountainous rooftop high above the town of Bolzano serves up striking views with Italian sunshine. Within the park, buses take hikers to and from key points along the tiny road, all the way to the foot of the postcard-dramatic Sasso peaks. Meadow walks are ideal for flower lovers and strollers, while chairlifts provide springboards for more demanding hikes.

Thanks to well-maintained trails, hiking in the Swiss Alps can be a walk in the park—with more spectacular scenery.

The Swiss Alps are staggeringly beautiful and unforgettable when it's sunny. On one side of you, lakes stretch all the way to Germany. On the other stands the greatest mountain panorama in Europe—the peaks of the Eiger, Mönch, and Jungfrau. And up ahead you hear the long, legato tones of an alphorn, announcing that a helicopter-stocked mountain hut is open, it's just around the corner...and the coffee schnapps is on. That's the kind of magic that awaits anyone who makes the effort to get high in the Alps.

Alpine trail signs show where you are, the altitude in meters, and how long in hours and minutes it takes to hike to nearby points.

The Swiss Alps are great—but they're expensive. The French Alps above Chamonix—near the junction of France, Switzerland, and Italy—are a little more forgiving, and the

Lift Lingo

Europeans, and especially the Swiss, have come up with a variety of ways to conquer alpine peaks and reach the best viewpoints and trailheads with minimum sweat. Known generically as "lifts," each of these contraptions has its own name and definition.

Cogwheel Train: A train that climbs a steep incline using a gear system, which engages "teeth" in the middle of the tracks to provide traction. Also known as "rack-and-pinion train" or "rack railway." In German, it's a *Zahnradbahn* (*train à cremaillère* in French and *ferrovia a cremagliera* in Italian).

Funicular: A car that is pulled by a cable along tracks up a steep incline, usually counterbalanced by a similar car going in the opposite direction (meaning you'll pass the other car exactly halfway through the ride). Funiculars, like cogwheel trains, are in contact with the ground at all times. In German, it's a *Standseilbahn* (*funiculaire* in French and *funicolare* in Italian).

Cable Car: A large passenger car, suspended in the air by a cable. A cable car is generally designed for skiers and holds a large number of people (sometimes dozens at a time), who generally ride standing up. When a cable car reaches a station, it comes to a full stop to allow passengers to get on and off. In German, it's a *Seilbahn* (*téléphérique* in French and *funivia* in Italian).

Gondola: Also suspended in the air by a cable, but smaller than a cable car—generally holding fewer than 10 people, who are usually seated. Gondolas move continuously, meaning that passengers have to hop into and out of the moving cars at stations. Also, while cable-car lines usually have two big cars—one going in each direction—gondolas generally have many smaller cars strung along the same cable. In German, it's a *Gondel* (*télécabine* in French and *telecabine* in Italian).

lifts are more affordable. You can take a lift to one end, enjoy a relatively level hike known as the Grand Balcon Sud (Grand South Balcony) with wildflowers, glaciers, and a staggering view of Mont Blanc, and then ride the lift down from the other end, for a single round-trip fare.

Throughout the Alps, trail markers are both handy and humiliating. Handy, because they show hours to hike rather than kilometers to walk to various destinations. Humiliating, because these times are clocked by local senior citizens. You'll know what I mean after your first hike.

Other Hikes in Europe

England's Cotswolds are walkers' country. The English love to trace the peaceful footpaths that shepherds walked back when "polyester" meant two girls. A two-hour trek connecting two thatched-roof towns in the Cotswolds affords intimate backyard views of farms in action: rabbits popping up in fields, ducks butt-up in millponds, and black-and-white cows jostling for space at troughs.

Southern France's Cap Ferrat, near Nice, has well-maintained foot trails, perfect for short, view-struck walks above the Mediterranean. Traditional routes such as Spain's Camino de Santiago and Italy's Way of St. Francis link religious sights via paths used for centuries; pilgrims come for month-long walks while day-hikers can join in for just a short segment.

Iceland is a wonderland for hikers, whether you're taking an easy stroll from your car to a waterfall or geyser, or combining a hike with a natural thermal bathing experience or a volcano or lava tunnel tour. Glacier hiking is a quintessential Icelandic experience, and best on a guided excursion that includes spiky crampons for the crunchy climb up spooky-looking canyons of ice and black ash.

Perhaps my favorite place to hike is in Italy's Cinque Terre. The five towns that make up the Cinque Terre are strung together by a series of trails that form the backbone of a national park. Hiking these trails is one of the most exhilarating experiences in Italy. Take it slow...smell the cactus flowers and herbs, listen to birds, and enjoy spectacular vistas on all sides.

Hiking Tips

If you plan on hiking in Europe, look for walking and hiking books on your destination region. Ask for advice from the national tourist offices of the countries you will visit. Tourist offices often have booklets of nearby self-guided hikes. You can also look into local groups that offer walks to see if one of their scheduled hikes fits with your itinerary. For example, German groups routinely plan *Volksmärsche* and welcome participation. In Great Britain, the Ramblers extend guest privileges to nonmembers who want to try one of the group walks they lead every week.

Before setting out on any hike, check locally to be sure you've made the best match between your skills, gear, and trail conditions (snow can persist on alpine trails even into summer; Cinque Terre trails can be closed in bad weather or due to landslides). Wear sturdy shoes and carry the essentials: map, sun protection (sunscreen, hat, and/ or sunglasses), extra layer, first-aid kit, water, and snacks. To leave the route cleaner than you found it, bring a plastic bag and pick up a little trail trash along the way. It would be great if American visitors—who get so much joy out of European hikes— were known for this good deed. Note that while the trails themselves are public, outside of national parks the property to either side may be private (stick to posted routes).

Hard-core hikers invest in detailed maps (1:100,000 or 1:50,000)—look for OS Ordnance Survey (Britain), Michelin (throughout Europe), IGN's Blue series (good for France), and Touring Club Italiano (Italy). Make sure the map shows general elevation gain with contour lines and/or indicates the steepness of roads.

Resources for Hut Hopping

Sac-cas.ch: List of more than 150 hiker huts run by the Swiss Alpine Club

Aacuk.org.uk: Austrian Alpine Club English website, with links to other clubs and hut directories by country

MountainBothies.org.uk: Listing of free shelters for hikers in Great Britain

Reading

100 Hut Walks in the Alps (Kev Reynolds, 2014)

The Book of the Bothy (Phoebe Smith, 2015)

Hut Hopping

The hikers' shelters spaced along the continental European trail system make walking trips a simpler proposition: There's no need to carry a tent, stove, or cooking utensils. Hundreds of huts exist to provide food and shelter for hikers. Using a smart network of trails and mountain huts spaced one convenient day's hike apart, you could walk from France to Slovenia without ever coming out of the Alps. At mountain villages, you can replenish your food supply or enjoy a hotel bed and a restaurant meal.

Most alpine huts serve hot meals and provide bunk-style lodging. Older huts may not have showers or even hot water (you may find pay warm showers at more modern huts). It's smart to hut-hike with a travel sheet, sleeping bag liner, or hostel-style sleep sack, as many huts provide only an infrequently washed blanket. I'll never forget getting cozy in my top bunk while a German in the bottom bunk said, "You're climbing into zee germs of centuries."

Alpine huts can get booked up, especially in summer, so

it's smart to reserve ahead. In the Alps, look for the word *Lager* (that's German for warehouse), which means they have a co-ed loft full of $30-a-night mattresses. In Great Britain, a bothy is a basic shelter where hikers can spend the night for free.

BIKING

Europeans love bicycles, and are often genuinely impressed when they encounter Americans who reject the view from the tour-bus window in favor of huffing and puffing on two wheels. Your bike provides an instant conversation piece, the perfect bridge over a maze of cultural and language barriers. Riding a bike gets you close to the ground, and close to the people.

City Biking

While my schedule usually won't allow a week-long pedal in the Loire Valley, I'll often do day trips in or around cities. I feel local, efficient, and even smug with my trusty and well-fitted bike. Especially during rush hour, I can get across town faster on a bike than by taxi or tram.

Europe's cities are striving to become more bike-friendly. Dozens of them have joined a European Union initiative to make bicycles on par with cars as a form of urban transport. The progress is gradual. Some cities (such as Rome and Athens) are not yet set up well for bikers, but quite a few (particularly Stockholm, Amsterdam, Copenhagen, Lucca, Salzburg, Munich, and Bruges) are a delight on two wheels, offering an extensive network of well-marked bike lanes. In these cities, rather than relying on walking or public transportation, consider making a bike your mode of transport. Bikes cut transit times in half compared to walking, giving you more time to spend at the sights.

LEFT Bike tours are a fun, informative, and healthy way to see great cities with an entertaining guide.

RIGHT Use your bike lock correctly. I learned this lesson the hard way...and suffered the embarrassment of returning just one wheel to my bike-rental place.

Rental bikes are bargains at about $20 per day (the best deals are for multiple days); helmets aren't always available. Bike-rental shops generally provide strong locks. Always lock the frame (not the wheel) to the permanent rack. Bike thieves can be bold and brazen.

Many places (including Barcelona, Copenhagen, Dublin, London, Oslo, Paris, Stockholm, and Vienna) have citywide programs in which hundreds of free or cheap loaner bikes are locked to racks around town or freestanding (similar to LimeBikes in the US). While tourists can easily take advantage of these programs in cities like London and Vienna, in other places, the systems are designed mostly for residents (some require a membership or only take European credit cards). These bikes are usually very basic, sometimes in disrepair, and often plastered with ads. If you're serious about biking, rent a good one from a shop instead.

One of my favorite cities for a ride is Stockholm. Bike paths here are a city-planning priority, and they run along the entire harbor. On your bike you can join the urban paseo down Strandvägen—the harborfront of the trendiest neighborhood—to my favorite biking zone, Djurgården ("Animal Garden"), another former royal hunting preserve. Rolling down the garden-like lane past Rosendals Slott, the summer getaway minipalace of a 19th-century king, I marvel at how, on a bike, you see things that those on tour buses never would.

If you're hesitant to take a bike out on your own in an unfamiliar place, consider a bicycle tour. Guided bike tours are popular in cities throughout Europe, as well as many bike-friendly countryside areas. You'll get a young, entertaining, possibly foul-mouthed, sometimes informative guide who will give you a breezy introduction to the city and a close-up look at back streets few tourists ever see. The various companies are highly competitive, and come and go all the time. Tours are typically fun, reasonable (about $35), good exercise, and an easy way to meet other travelers as well as get a new angle on an old city.

Countryside Biking

Biking in the boonies (using a small town as a springboard) is extremely popular in Europe. Thanks to the law of supply and demand, you can generally count on finding bike-rental shops wherever there are good bike-tripping options: along the Danube, the Rhine, and other idyllic river valleys; around

Ireland's Dingle Peninsula; and in the Alps for mountain biking on service roads.

Biking is one of the most enjoyable ways to experience Austria's famous "Blue Danube." Bicyclists rule here, and you'll find all the amenities that make this river valley so popular with Austrians on two wheels. The best route starts west of Vienna in the village of Melk. From here, it's a three- to four-hour, gently downhill pedal to the riverside village of Krems. The best biking is on the south side of the river, which has a dedicated, paved bike path the whole way and plenty of vineyards and small inns (*Gasthöfe*) in the villages along the way.

In France's Loire River valley, cycling options are nearly endless since the elevation gain is generally man- ageable. Amboise, Chenonceaux, Azay-le-Rideau, and Chinon all make good biking bases and have places to rent cycles. The city of Blois is well-positioned as a start- ing point for biking forays into the countryside. You can cycle from Blois to Chambord—the monumental chateau of François I—in a level, one-hour, one-way ride along a well-marked, 10-mile route, much of it a bike-only lane that follows the river.

For the best short bike trip out of Bruges, pedal 4 miles each way to the nearby town of Damme—once a thriving medieval port, and then a moated garrison town, and now a tourist center. Along the way you'll enjoy a whiff of the Belgian countryside and see a working windmill while riding along a canal to a charming (if well-discovered) small market town. The route is a straight and level ride through Belgium's polder—a salt marsh that would flood each spring until it was reclaimed by industrious local farmers.

In many countries (especially France, Germany, Austria, Belgium, and the Netherlands), train stations rent bikes and sometimes have easy "pick up here and drop off there"

LEFT Wherever biking is fun, you'll find shops renting bikes and helmets.

RIGHT Anyone can enjoy a gentle pedal through some of Europe's flat and inviting countryside.

plans. If you ride the train into Amsterdam, rent a bike at the station for a few days to get around the city...and out into the tulip fields and windmills.

Longer Bike Trips

If you're interested in long-distance biking, figure out how much of Europe you want to see. With an entire summer free, you can cover a lot of ground on a bike. But with a month or less, it's better to focus on a single country or region.

Consider bringing your bike from home, but be sure to check your airline's baggage policies for fees and restrictions. It could cost you hundreds of dollars to bring your bike, and you may need to reserve a spot for it when you book your plane ticket. But if you're planning to ride a bike for more than a week, the cost of bringing your own may beat the cost of renting one in Europe, where bikes are more expensive than in the US. And having your own bike means you'll know that it works well for you. Carry along the tools you'll need to get your bike back into riding form, so you can ride straight out of the airport.

Don't be a purist. Taking your bike on a train can greatly extend the reach of your trip, and there's nothing so sweet as taking a train away from the rain and into a sunny place. Unless you love bike camping, it makes sense to stay in hostels, hotels, or B&Bs, since it frees you from lugging around a tent and sleeping bag. If you'd rather let someone else carry your gear, try a bike tour (offered by REI, EuroVelo partners, and many other companies). With a guide to figure out logistics, haul supplies, and handle emergencies, all you need to do is pedal and enjoy the ride.

You can find many good books and resources on cycling in Europe, such as at the site EuropeBicycleTouring.com.

WATER FUN

Summer days are perfect for a break at the beach or on the water. Opportunities to create memorable aquatic experiences in Europe abound, whether wading beneath the Roman aqueduct of Pont du Gard in Provence; frolicking on Venice's nearby lagoon beach, the Lido; or leisurely swimming laps in your B&B pool in Tuscany. Dive in!

Beaches and Swimming

Americans are sometimes disappointed or surprised by the quality of Europe's beaches. But as long as you know what to expect, you should have a perfectly enjoyable experience.

Beach quality and ambience vary. Some beaches are barren, pebbly or studded with spiny sea urchins, while some are equipped with fine sand, showers, and restaurants with outdoor seating. Some are family-friendly, others have a party vibe. Some have chairs and umbrellas for rent, others are BYO. Ask locals for the scoop. Throughout Europe, you'll find nude beaches, but keep in mind that any beach can be topless.

Some of Europe's best swimming might not be where you expect. Sandy beaches in Sweden's Archipelago are perfect for joining Swedes at play, while the French Riviera can be plagued with jellyfish in July and August. In Spain's South Coast, anything resembling a quaint fishing village has been bikini-strangled and Nivea-creamed (though there are still gems, such as the town of Nerja).

You'll find man-made beaches and pools in many cities, including (every summer) Paris' faux beaches on the Seine's Right Bank—with deck chairs, potted palm trees, beach volleyball, pools, Frisbee zones, and more; Barcelona's sandy beaches, complete with lounge chairs, volleyball, showers, WCs, bike paths, and inviting beach bars called chiringuitos; and Copenhagen's Harbor Baths, a former-industrial-area-turned-bathing complex.

Thermal Baths

Iceland's volcanic activity goes hand-in-hand with naturally heated water—which Icelanders have cleverly harnessed as thermal baths. Some bathing experiences cater primarily to tourists, chief among them the heavily advertised Blue Lagoon near Reykjavík and the similar (if smaller) Mývatn Nature Baths in North Iceland—a must for those doing the Ring Road. Icelanders are more likely to enjoy one of

LEFT Inviting beaches in Italy's Cinque Terre tempt you to take a vacation from your vacation.

RIGHT Punting takes practice but offers a waterside view of idyllic English towns like Cambridge.

An easy paddle along the Dordogne River in France delivers exceptional views of medieval castles.

the country's many community thermal swimming pools. In addition to being affordable, these provide a pleasantly authentic Icelandic experience.

Other well-known thermal baths include the Thermae Bath Spa in Bath, England, the Széchenyi Baths in Budapest, the Caracalla and Friedrichsbad baths in Baden-Baden, Germany, and Karlovy Vary in the Czech Republic. You can read about my visits to the baths in Budapest and Baden-Baden on pages 757 and 699.

Canoeing, Kayaking, and Punting

If you're near a lake or river, consider exploring the area by boat. Some of Europe's natural wonders and parks are best seen from the water.

In Český Krumlov, a small town in the Czech countryside, I enjoy renting a canoe or raft and paddling down to a medieval abbey (for details, see page 736). In France's unpretentious port town of Cassis, you can kayak to its exotic fjords of translucent blue water in the *calanques*—the narrow inlets created by the prickly extensions of cliffs that border the shore. These spiky pinnacles are located along the 13 miles of coast between Cassis and Marseille (you can get there by hiking or boat cruise, too).

When I'm in the Dordogne region of France, one of my rituals is exploring the riverside castles and villages by canoe. I can't think of a more relaxing way to enjoy great scenery while getting some exercise. Delights are revealed around each bend, and you can pop ashore whenever you like. There's always a place to stow the canoe, and plenty of welcoming villages. Two of the most picturesque are

La Roque-Gageac, a strong contender for "cutest town in France," and Beynac, a perfectly preserved medieval village that winds, like a sepia-tone film set, from the shore to the castle above. You can rent plastic boats—which are hard, light, and indestructible—from many outfits in this area for a reasonable price ($20 for two-person canoes, $25 for one-person kayaks). It's OK if you're a novice—the only white-water you'll encounter will be the rare wake of passing tour boats...and your travel partner frothing at the views.

In Madrid, head to majestic Retiro Park to rent a rowboat and traverse a big lake in its center (El Estanque). At midday on Saturday and Sunday, the area around the lake becomes a street carnival, with jugglers, puppeteers, and lots of local color. Other city parks offer rental rowboats at lakes (e.g., London's Hyde Park and Paris' Bois de Vincennes). Paddle boats are popular in many cities, too.

For a different type of experience and a little levity, try punting in Britain, in which you use a pole to maneuver a long, flat-bottom boat up and down (or around and around, more likely). This is one of the best memories towns like Cambridge, Oxford, and Canterbury have to offer. Though chauffeurs are sometimes available, the do-it-yourself crowd has more fun...even if you do end up a little wet.

MORE ACTIVITIES

Adventure travel continues to be a major trend in the tourism industry. While I'm not going to suggest you drop everything to climb the Matterhorn, Europe has plenty of thrills and chills to carbonate a stodgy vacation, from screaming down a mountain luge to marveling at Cappadocia's otherworldly landscape from the basket of a hot-air balloon. And for a firsthand account of one of the greatest outdoor thrills I've ever experienced—the *via ferrata* in Switzerland—see page 713.

Summer luges provide thrills for any age at any speed.

Riding a Luge
The *Sommerrodelbahn* ("summer toboggan run") is one of the most exhilarating alpine experiences. You

City Thrills

Surfing in Downtown Munich: Far from the nearest stretch of coast, surfers "hang ten" in Munich's English Garden, in the rapids of the city's little man-made river. While seeking their thrills, the surfers provide great entertainment for the ever-present crowd that gathers to watch from a bridge.

Zip Lining in Oslo: Outer Oslo hosts the Holmenkollen Ski Jump, with a tilted elevator that you can ride for an exciting view—and a zip line that you can rocket down for even more adrenaline. There's also a simulator (or should I say stimulator?) that lets you fly down the ski jump and ski in a virtual downhill race. My legs were exhausted after the five-minute terror.

Floating in Bern: In the summer heat, join the carp in a bracing float down Switzerland's Aare River. Hike upstream 5 to 30 minutes, then float back down to the excellent (and free) riverside baths and pools (Marzilibad) just below the Parliament building. Locals make it look easy, but the float can be dangerous—the current is swift. This is only for strong, experienced swimmers. For my first-hand account of this experience, see page 710.

take a lift up to the top of a mountain, grab a wheeled sled-like go-cart, and scream back down the mountainside on a banked course made of concrete or metal. Then you take the lift back up and start all over again.

Operating the sled is simple: Push the stick forward to go faster, pull back to apply the brake. Novices quickly find their personal speed limits. Most are cautious on their first run, speed demons on their second...and bruised and bloody on their third. A woman once showed me her travel journal illustrated with her husband's dried, five-inch-long luge scab. He had disobeyed the only essential rule of luging: Keep both hands on your stick. To avoid getting into a bumper-to-bumper traffic jam, let the person in front of you get way ahead before you start. You'll emerge from the course with a windblown hairdo and a smile-creased face.

You've got several luge options. In the French mountain resort of Chamonix, at the base of Mont Blanc, two concrete courses run side by side (the slow one marked by a tortoise and the fast one marked by a hare). In Austria, south of Salzburg on the road to Hallstatt, you'll pass two metal courses: one near Wolfgangsee (scenic with grand lake views) and one at Fuschlsee (half as long and cheaper).

A float above the surreal topography in Cappadocia, Turkey, is arguably the best hot-air balloon experience in the world.

In Germany and Austria, near "Mad" King Ludwig's Neuschwanstein Castle, you'll find two courses. One is in Austria, just beyond Biberwier (under Zugspitze, Germany's tallest mountain); the Biberwier *Sommerrodelbahn* is the longest in Austria at 4,000 feet. And just a mile from Neuschwanstein is Germany's Tegelberg course—because it's metal rather than concrete, it's often open when the other course has closed at the least sprinkle of rain.

Hot-Air Ballooning

A few years ago, I learned that even if I wasn't blessed with wings, I've got an abundance of hot air—and I can fly quite well with little more than that. I've always loved Cappadocia in central Turkey, so I took a majestic hot-air balloon ride over the fairy-chimney formations of that exotic landscape. From the moment our basket slipped from the land into the sky, I gazed in wonder, mesmerized at the erosion-shaped countryside and spectacle of colorful balloons gliding around me. As I stood in the basket of my balloon, the rhythmic bursts of flame punctuated the captain's jokes while warming my wide eyes. Illogically, the stripes on his epaulets made me feel safe as we lifted off.

You'll also find hot-air balloon companies in France's most popular regions (Burgundy, the Loire, Dordogne, and Provence are best suited for ballooning). These offer a bird's-eye view of France's sublime landscapes as you sail serenely over châteaux, canals, vineyards, Romanesque churches, and villages.

These trips aren't cheap (about $300), but they give lots of travelers a fine memory and stunning pictures.

Shopping

With each trip, I look for cultural souvenirs—
experiences and memories are the real gold
nuggets of travel. Shopping is never my priority,
but when I do shop, I find the best souvenirs often
come from local entrepreneurs and craftspeople.
Europe's modern shopping arenas are also good
spots to witness a slice of contemporary life.

It can be fun to immerse yourself in the retail culture
of Europe's grandest cities, but don't let it overwhelm your
trip. Slick marketing and clever displays can shift the focus
of your vacation toward things rather than experiences. On
one guided tour of the British Houses of Parliament I saw
half the group skip out on the tour to survey an enticing
array of plastic "bobby" hats, Big Ben briefs, and Union Jack
panties.

The thrill of where you bought something can fade long
before the item's usefulness does. Even thoughtful shoppers
go overboard. I have several large boxes in my attic labeled
"great souvenirs." On the other hand, a few well-chosen
items—a hand-painted tile from Siena, Provençal fabric from
Nice, a fine old print from Athens—can remind you of the
highlights of your travels for years to come.

WHERE TO SHOP

Avoid the souvenir carts outside of big monuments, where
the goods tend to be overpriced and low-quality. Do your
shopping in places that offer a fun cultural experience as
well.

Outdoor Markets

The most colorful shopping in Europe—and a fun way to feel the local vibe—is at its lively open-air markets. A stroll along Portobello Road, arguably London's best street market and one of the world's biggest antiques markets, has you rubbing elbows with collectors and people who brake for garage sales. In Florence, the sprawling San Lorenzo Market has stalls of garments, accessories, and leather jackets ranging from real to vinyl. Even a place as overrun with international visitors as Istanbul's Grand Bazaar has tourist-free nooks and crannies that offer a glimpse into the real Turkey. Jump into the human rivers that flow through these venues.

Other good markets are Amsterdam's Waterlooplein, Madrid's El Rastro, and Paris' Puces St. Ouen. In London, I like the East End's Broadway Market, with foodie delights and a few arts and crafts, and south London's Ropewalk (Maltby Street Market), featuring a festival of pop-up bars and artisan food carts.

Some markets are open daily, while others erupt only on weekends or a certain day of the week—make sure to check hours locally. Remember that markets anywhere have soft prices. Bargain like mad (see "Successful Haggling," later). Pickpockets love markets—wear your money belt and watch your day bag.

Artisan Shops

Try to experience some "creative" tourism when you travel. Seek out and appreciate a local craftsperson. In Orvieto, Italy, visit the young cobbler who's passionate about preserving the art of traditional shoemaking. In Rothenburg, Germany, admire the work of printmakers selling etchings made with the same copper-plate techniques that artist Albrecht Dürer used 500 years ago. The narrow streets near Vienna's cathedral are sprinkled with old-fashioned shops that seem to belong to another era—just the place to pick out an elegant dirndl.

Artisans, such as this Italian cobbler, help keep traditional crafts alive.

The artists who craft handmade guitars in Madrid, the family winemakers of Burgundy—these have all been fixtures for me in a lifetime of European travel. Before these local businesses are pushed out by the rising tide of cookie-cutter chains and synthetic conformity, seek out Europe's true artisans who are committed to doing things the old-fashioned way. You can find referrals to artisan shops through local tourist offices. In cities like Florence and Rome, tour companies offer guided excursions to private workshops. Engaging with these craftspeople is a memorable way to support local traditions and bring history and culture to life (and you can return home with a souvenir that reminds you of your experiences).

Christmas Markets

From the beginning of Advent through Christmas (and occasionally through January 6), Europe is peppered with festive Christmas markets serving up a healthy dose of holiday spirit and plenty of handmade and traditional nutcrackers, ornaments, and sweets. Bigger markets often host carolers and other musicians, ice-skating rinks, and carousels.

Especially in Germanic countries, Christmas markets dominate nearly every main square, from the smallest village to big cities. Nürnberg, famous for packaging its gingerbread in countless creative ways, has one of the best Christmas bazaars. In Austria, the cozy center of Innsbruck is the perfect setting for a memorable market, with the snowy Tirolean Alps hovering above medieval rooftops. Some bigger cities (Munich, Vienna, Berlin, Cologne, even smaller Salzburg) host multiple markets.

The best time to enjoy these convivial markets is in the evening, under the glow of cheerful lights. The sweet smell of *Lebkuchen* (gingerbread), *Stollen* (fruitcake-like bread), and roasting candied nuts wafts through the air. Hand-carved wooden ornaments and nativity scenes, festive wreaths, and aromatic candles line the booths. Look for nutcrackers made in the Erzgebirge region, where they originated. Seek out *Weihnachtspyriamide*—wooden structures that hold candles, often with a propeller that uses the candle's heat to spin part of the contraption.

Stroll around while sipping hot mulled wine, spiced with cinnamon, cloves, and citrus fruits. This quintessential Christmas market drink (*Gluhwein* in Germanic

In December, cities across Europe come alive with Christmas markets, such as this one in Nürnberg.

countries) is served in a holiday-themed ceramic mug, which itself makes a fun, affordable souvenir.

Department Stores

European department stores are generally laid out much like ours, providing an accessible and comfortable place to shop. Most are accustomed to wide-eyed foreign shoppers and have some English-speaking staff. The store directories often include English. Many department stores have a souvenir section, with standard local knickknacks and postcards at far lower prices than you'll find in cute little tourist shops. They can also be handy places to pick up necessities as you travel.

In Paris, visit Galeries Lafayette or Printemps. Harrods is London's most famous and touristy department store, but locals prefer Liberty on Regent Street. In Italy, an upscale department chain is La Rinascente, and in Spain, El Corte Inglés is everywhere. Berlin's Kaufhaus des Westens (KaDeWe) is mammoth, with two floors of food stalls. Though lacking the charm of artisan shops and markets, department stores are a quick and easy way to check souvenirs off your list.

Boutiques and Shopping Zones

The best shopping districts not only offer interesting stores, but also let you feel the pulse of the city. In Rome, an early evening stroll down Via del Corso takes you past affordable shops—and the city's beautiful people. For top fashion—and top people-watching—stroll the streets around the Spanish Steps.

London's best and most convenient shopping streets are in the West End and West London (roughly between Soho and Hyde Park). In Vienna, Mariahilfer Strasse combines a wealth of shops with lively people-watching.

In Paris, a stroll from the Bon Marché department store to St. Sulpice allows you to sample sleek clothing boutiques and clever window displays while enjoying one of the city's more attractive neighborhoods. You don't have to buy the glitz to feel *très* French (they call window shopping *lèche-vitrines*—"window licking").

In Europe's smaller shops and classy boutiques, follow local shopping etiquette, such as saying "hello" when you enter and asking before you touch an item.

Museum Gift Shops

Gift shops at major museums (such as the Picasso Museum in Barcelona or the Van Gogh Museum in Amsterdam) are a bonanza for shoppers. Consider picking up books, postcards, posters, decorative items, or clever knickknacks featuring works by your favorite artist or commemorating a historic event or sight. Museum gift shops are also a good source for books you may not see elsewhere. Before accumulating too much, keep in mind that many things (like prints and posters of universally loved art) can be purchased for a similar price online from home—saving you the hassle of traveling with your purchases.

SHOPPING TIPS

Here are some tips for shopping in Europe—from buying souvenirs and clothes to bargaining your way to the best price.

Souvenir Strategies

Shop smart, and remember that your most prized souvenirs are your memories.

Comparison shop at home. If you plan to buy a particular high-end item overseas, do some research first (and be aware that you can often find a similar item of better quality for a cheaper price at home). Before heading off to buy a Turkish carpet in Istanbul or leather coat in Florence, learn the going rate, types of materials, and signs of quality.

Beware street vendors selling knockoffs. Streetside vendors sell counterfeit designer goods everywhere in Europe—and in many cities, it's illegal. For these vendors, it's a game of cat-and-mouse with the police. Along the busy Ramblas zone in Barcelona, vendors lay out their merchandise on a sheet with ropes attached. When police officers arrive, the vendors scatter, quickly bundling their wares as they run. In some countries (such as Italy), buying from a street vendor is illegal and can cost you a hefty fine (anywhere from €1,000 to €10,000). Be cautious and ask an informed local before going for that fake Prada bag.

Know the origin of your souvenirs. The cheapest, mass-produced souvenirs are almost always imported. If the price seems too good to be true, it probably is. Stick

Boxloads of *Davids* await busloads of tourists.

to reputable, family-run shops to ensure you're getting an authentic product (and supporting a local business). Even at artisan Christmas markets, be wary of cheap trinkets labeled "handmade." Evaluate as you buy. Real Italian leather, for example, should feel soft and pliable without any chemical smell. When buying glass in Venice, look closely. Genuine Venetian glass is marked with the Murano seal.

Concentrate your shopping in countries where your dollar will stretch. You'll find the best bargains in Turkey, Morocco, Portugal, Spain, Greece, and Eastern Europe. For the price of a skimpy doily in Britain, you can get a lace tablecloth in Spain.

Be selective. Form an idea of what you want to buy in each country. I look for hand-knit sweaters in Ireland, glass in Sweden, painted beehive panels in Slovenia, or lace in Belgium. I also like books published in Europe; these are a great value all over the Continent, with many editions that are impossible to find in the US.

Lighten your load, or wait till the end. Larger stores can arrange shipping for you, or you can send packages yourself (see "Shipping Things Home," later). Or simply wait for the last country you visit to go hog wild and fly home heavy. One summer I had a 16-pound backpack and nothing more until the last week of my trip, when I hit Spain and Morocco and managed to accumulate two sets of bongos, swords, a mace, and a camelhair coat...most of which are now in boxes in my attic.

Remember the paperwork. If you intend to claim a Value-Added Tax (VAT) refund, you'll need to get the right documents from the merchant. For details on VAT as well as US customs regulations, see "VAT Refunds, Customs, and Shipping," later in this chapter.

Clothes Shopping

Many travelers enjoy shopping for wearable souvenirs in Europe, where the fashions can be quite different. Options range from hole-in-the-wall boutiques to grand department stores to colorful street markets.

Europe-wide chains such as Mango and C&A have stylish, affordable selections. They can offer good value, especially for designer-inspired clothing. In addition, each country has its own popular chains (such as Topshop in Britain). Fashions vary by store and by country, so if you see an item you like, grab it rather than wait to pick it up at a later stop—you might never see that style or color again.

Clothes Sizing Conversion

The US, the UK, and continental Europe all use different sizing conventions. European clothes are usually cut to fit more snugly than American clothes. When shopping for clothing, use the following rules as general guidelines (but note that no conversion is perfect). Be prepared to swallow your pride and go up a size or two. If you wear a size medium sweater back home, you might need a large or extra-large in Norway.

Women: For pants and dresses, women's sizes are the same across France, Belgium, Spain, Portugal, Croatia, and Slovenia. To figure your size, add approximately 32 to your US size (US 10 = French 42). In Italy, add 36 to your US size (US 10 = Italy 46). Sizes run slightly smaller in Germany, Austria, the Netherlands, Switzerland, Greece, the Czech Republic, and Scandinavia. In these countries, add 30 to your US size (US 10 = German 40). The UK operates on a different size system. Add 4 to your US size (US 10 = UK 14).

For blouses and sweaters, most of Europe uses the same system. Add 8 to your US size (US 32 = European 40). In the UK, add 2 (US 32 = UK 34).

To calculate your European shoe size, add about 31 to your US size (US 7 = European 37/38); in the UK, subtract 2½ (US 7 = UK 4½).

Men: Most of Europe uses the same size system for men. For shirts, multiply your US size by 2 and add about 8 (US 15 = European 38). For jackets and suits, add 10 (US 38 = European 48). For shoes, add 32-34 (US 9 = European 41). The UK uses the same men's clothing sizes as the US. For UK shoes, subtract about ½ from your US size (US 9 = UK 8½).

Children: Most of Europe's kids' clothing is sized by height—in centimeters (although some brands are sized by age). If you plan to do much shopping for children, convert their height to centimeters (1 inch = 2.5 cm). A US child size 8 roughly equates to 132-140 (cm). A US junior size 3 equals a European 152. For shoes up to size 13, add 16-18 (US 10 = European 26). For sizes 1 and up, add 30-32. To figure UK shoe size, subtract 1 from the US size.

Some women like buying high-quality underwear and camisoles in Italy or France; browse for them at any large department store.

Street markets also offer clothing. Remember that prices are often soft—especially if it's near the end of the day, you're paying cash, and you're buying multiple items (such as several scarves). Don't be afraid to bargain.

Successful Haggling

In some parts of the Mediterranean world, the price tag is only an excuse to argue. Bargaining is the accepted and expected method of finding a compromise between the wishful thinking of the merchant and the tourist. You can generally consider prices soft at flea markets, touristy souvenir

You can troll for quirky souvenirs at flea markets.

shops, and street stalls, but not at modern stores or shopping malls. (Note that bargaining applies to goods, not to food sold at stands or outdoor produce markets.)

Here are a few guidelines to help you get the best bargain.

Determine if bargaining is appropriate. It's bad shopping etiquette to "make an offer" for a hat in a London department store. It's foolish not to at a Greek flea market. To learn if prices are fixed, show some interest in an item but say, "It's just too much money." You've put the merchants in a position to make the first offer. If they come down even 2 percent, there's nothing sacred about the price tag. Haggle away.

Shop around to find out what locals pay. Prices can vary drastically among vendors at the same flea market, and even at the same stall. If prices aren't marked, assume there's a double price standard: one for locals and one for you. If only tourists buy the item you're pricing, watch to see what a tourist from elsewhere in Europe would be charged. I remember thinking I did well in Istanbul's Grand Bazaar, until I learned my Spanish friend bought the same shirt for 30 percent less. Merchants assume American tourists are rich, and they know what we pay for things at home.

Determine what the item is worth to you. Marked prices can distort your idea of an item's true worth. The merchants are playing a psychological game. Many tourists think that if they can cut the price by 50 percent they are doing great. So merchants quadruple their prices and tourists happily pay double the fair value. The best way to deal with crazy price tags is to ignore them. Before you even find out the price, determine the item's value to you, considering the hassles involved in packing it or shipping it home.

Determine the merchant's lowest price. Merchants hate to lose a sale. Work the cost down, but if it doesn't match with the price you have in mind, walk away. That last amount the merchants holler out as you turn the corner is often their best price. If *that* price is right, go back and buy. Prices often drop at the end of the day, when merchants are about to pack up.

Curb your enthusiasm. As soon as merchants perceive the "I gotta have that!" in you, you'll never get the best price. They assume Americans have the money to buy what they really want. Keep a poker face and don't settle for the first counter-offer.

Employ a third person. Use your friend who is worried about the ever-dwindling budget or who doesn't like the price or who is bored and wants to return to the hotel. This trick can work to bring the price down faster.

Impress merchants with your knowledge. You'll earn some respect—and be more likely to get good quality. For instance, if planning to buy a leather coat in Istanbul or Florence, talk to leather-coat sellers and do some research before your trip so you're better prepared to confidently pick one out.

Ask for a deal on multiple items. See if merchants will give you a better price if you buy in bulk (three necklaces instead of one). The more they think they can sell, the more flexible they may become.

Offer to pay cash at stalls that take credit cards. You

can expect to pay cash for most things at street markets, but some merchants who sell pricier goods (nice jewelry, artwork, etc.) take credit cards, too. They're often more willing to strike a deal if you pay cash, since they don't lose any profit to credit-card fees.

Show merchants your money. Physically hold out what you are willing to spend and offer "all you have" to pay for whatever you're bickering over. Salespeople might be tempted to just grab your money and say, "Oh, OK."

Obey the rules. Don't hurry. Bargaining is rarely rushed. Make sure you are dealing with someone who has the authority to bend a price downward. Bid respectfully. If a merchant accepts your price (or vice versa), you must buy the item.

If the price is too high, leave. Never worry about having taken too much of someone's time. Merchants are experienced businesspeople who know they won't close every deal.

VAT REFUNDS, CUSTOMS, AND SHIPPING

Included in the price of European products is a value-added tax (VAT)—a consumer tax on raw materials. You can't avoid paying this sales tax, but it is refundable on items that leave the country. For travelers making major purchases, the refund can be significant, so it's worth knowing how to get your refund and how to bring these items home (either in your luggage or by shipping them).

Claiming a Value-Added Tax Refund

Every year, tourists visiting Europe leave behind millions of dollars of refundable sales taxes. Though you aren't entitled to refunds on the tax you spend on hotels and meals, you can get back most of the tax you pay on merchandise. For some, the headache of collecting the refund is not worth the few dollars at stake. But if you do more extensive shopping, the refund is worth claiming. And the process is fairly easy: Bring your passport along on your shopping trip (a photo of your passport should work), get the necessary documents from the retailer, and file your paperwork at the airport, port, or border when you leave.

In Europe, the standard Value-Added Tax ranges from 8 to 27 percent per country (see sidebar). Exact rates and purchase minimums change; if you plan to take advantage

VAT Rates and Minimum Purchase Amounts

Country of Purchase	VAT Standard Rate*	Minimum Purchase Amount
Austria	20%	€75.01 ($90)
Belgium	21%	€125 ($150)
Bulgaria	20%	250 BGN ($150)
Croatia	25%	740 HRK ($115)
Czech Republic	21%	2,001 CZK ($90)
Denmark	25%	300 DKK ($45)
Estonia	20%	€38 ($46)
Finland	24%	€40 ($48)
France	20%	€100.01 ($120)
Germany	19%	€50 ($60)
Great Britain	20%	£30 ($39)
Greece	24%	€50 ($60)
Hungary	27%	63,001 HUF ($212)
Iceland	24%	6,000 ISK ($50)
Ireland	23%	€30 ($36)
Italy	22%	€155 ($186)
Netherlands	21%	€50 ($60)
Norway	25%	315 NOK ($35)
Poland	23%	200 PLN ($50)
Portugal	23%	€61.50 ($74)
Romania	19%	250 RON ($60)
Slovakia	20%	€100 ($120)
Slovenia	22%	€50.01 ($60)
Spain	21%	€90.16 ($108)
Sweden	25%	200 SEK ($20)
Switzerland	8%	300 CHF ($300)
Turkey	18%	118 TRY ($16)

* VAT standard rates are set by individual countries and can fluctuate. Your refund will likely be less than the rate listed above, especially if it's subject to processing fees.

of refunds, check online for the countries you'll be visiting before you go.

To get a refund, your purchase has to be above a certain amount, depending on the country. Typically, you must ring up the minimum at a single retailer—you can't add up purchases from various shops to reach the required amount—so if you're doing a lot of shopping, you'll benefit from finding one spot where you can buy big. You're also not supposed to use your purchased goods before you leave Europe—if you show up at customs wearing your new Dutch clogs, officials might deny you a refund. Refunds must be collected within three months of purchase.

Retailers choose whether to participate in the VAT-refund scheme. Most tourist-oriented stores do; often you'll see a sign in the window or on the check-out counter (if not, ask). For any significant purchase, even at a boutique shop, it's always worth asking about a VAT refund. The precise details of getting your money back will depend on how a particular shop organizes its refund process. In most cases, you'll present your refund documents at the airport on the way home (explained later). Some stores may offer to handle the process for you (if they provide this service, they likely have some sort of "Tax Free" sticker in the window). Some merchants will reimburse your credit card on the spot, or you may be able to take your paperwork to a nearby third-party agency to get an immediate cash refund (minus a commission for the quick service; these tend to be located at money-exchange counters near touristy shopping areas—think the Champs-Elysées). In either case, you will still need to get the documents stamped at the border, then mail them back; if the shop or agency doesn't receive the documents, they'll cancel your refund and charge the VAT amount to your credit card.

At the Merchant

The details on how to get a refund vary per country, but generally you'll need to do the following:

Have the merchant completely fill out the refund document; they'll need your passport (or a photo of it) to complete the form. Hang on to the paperwork and original sales receipt until you file it (see later). Note that you're not supposed to use your purchased goods before you leave Europe. (Some retailers, particularly those in Scandinavia, will staple and seal the shopping bag to keep you from cheating.)

If the store ships your purchase to your home, you won't be charged the value-added tax. But shipping fees and US duty can be pricey enough to wipe out most of what you'd save. Compare shipping costs to your potential VAT refund—it may be cheaper to carry the items home with you.

At the Border or Airport

Unless a merchant has processed the refund for you, you'll need to do it yourself before heading home. If you buy merchandise in a European Union country, process your documents at your last stop in the EU (most likely at the airport). So if you buy sweaters in Denmark, pants in France, and shoes in Italy, and you're flying home from Greece, get your documents stamped at the airport in Athens. (If the currencies are different in the country where you made your purchase and where you process your refund—say, euros and Czech koruna—you may have to pay a conversion fee.) And don't forget: Switzerland, Norway, the UK, and Turkey are not in the EU, so if you shop in one of those countries, get your documents stamped before you cross the border.

At some airports, you'll have to go to a customs office to get your documents stamped and then to a separate VAT refund service (such as Global Blue or Planet) to process the refund. At other airports, a single VAT desk handles the whole thing. Many customs offices are located before airport security; check before going through security. Customs agents may ask you to present your unused goods to verify that you are, indeed, exporting your purchase—if your purchases are inside your checked luggage, stop by customs before you check it. Allow plenty of extra time at the airport to deal with the VAT refund process.

Note that refund services typically extract a 4 percent fee, but you're paying for the convenience of receiving your money in cash immediately or credited to your card. The refund will be in the currency of the country from which you depart; if you want to be reimbursed in a different currency, such as US dollars, you'll be subjected to their (unfavorable) exchange rates. If a store or a refund agency has already reimbursed your VAT amount, you'll be required to mail the stamped documents back to them to prove that you obtained your customs stamp within the required three-month window (using a provided postage-free, preaddressed envelope—just drop it in a mailbox at the airport or border after getting your customs stamp).

Tips for Train Travelers: Be careful if you leave the EU by train. Bigger train stations handling international routes will have a customs office that can stamp your documents. But depending on your route, you may have to get off the train at the last station within the EU to get your stamp;

Hauling Home Heavenly Wines

Wine lovers wandering through Europe face a continual dilemma: Savor the memories or haul a few favorite bottles home?

Despite the global-goods-on-demand world we live in today, your neighborhood wine shop can't always track down the wine you enjoyed at that Parisian café or Spanish tapas bar. Some wineries only sell their wine within their country, which makes it tempting to bring a few bottles home.

The downside, of course, is the schlepping—the scary prospect of a bottle breaking in your suitcase or the weight of the box dragging you down as you trudge through the airport. You might be better off seeing wine like art—something to be enjoyed, marveled at, and remembered.

Before you purchase a bottle to carry home, ask the merchant whether the wine is exported to your home state. Or take a picture of the label—you can even email it to your hometown wine shop to find out if they can have the wine waiting for you when you return.

But if you can't resist bringing wine home, keep these tips in mind.

Pack softly and carry a hard suitcase. Per TSA regulations, if you purchase liquor from an airport duty-free shop and it's able to be screened (i.e., not in an opaque, metallic, or ceramic bottle) and is in a secure, tamper-evident bag (called a STEB), you can transport it in your carry-on (a STEB can also be used for transporting foods packed in liquid or oil—if purchased at the airport duty-free shop). If not, you'll have to pack your bottles carefully in checked luggage. This works most of the time if the bottles are thickly padded with clothing in a hard-sided suitcase (though bottles can still break); they'll also have to endure the extreme cold (or heat) of the cargo hold.

Divide and conquer. If you're traveling with a partner, divide the bottles among your bags (each bottle of wine weighs about three pounds, so five bottles means 15 extra pounds). Bring a spare fold-up tote bag or duffle for your clothes that get displaced by the wine.

Know your limits. A standard bottle of wine is 750 milliliters. If you bring back more than one liter, customs regulations require you to pay duty tax based on the percent of alcohol (generally $1-2 per liter for wine). Couples can get away with three standard bottles, adding up to 2¼ liters. There's also a small federal excise tax.

Tell the truth. Be up front if you're over the limit. You may even benefit—sometimes the special customs lines move faster than the nothing-to-declare ones. If your wine is for personal use, the agents might not even tax you. It won't happen all the time, but many wine-obsessed travelers report that this can be the case.

in some cases, a customs agent might board the train. Ask train station staff about the customs arrangement for your particular route.

Customs for American Shoppers

Customs regulations vary depending on whether you are bringing items home on the plane with you, or mailing them to a US address. To check US customs rules and duty rates, visit www.cbp.gov, click on "Travel," and then "Know Before You Go."

Bringing Items Home in Your Luggage

You can take home $800 worth of items per person duty-free in your luggage, once every 31 days (family members can combine their individual $800 exemptions on a joint declaration). The next $1,000 is taxed at a flat 4 percent. After that, you pay the individual item's duty rate. You can also bring in duty-free a liter of alcohol (slightly more than a standard-size bottle of wine; must be 21 or over), 200 cigarettes, and up to 100 cigars. Household effects intended for personal use, such as tableware and linens, are also duty-free.

Because food items can carry diseases or pests, they are strictly regulated. Many processed and packaged foods are allowed, including vacuum-packed cheeses, dried herbs, jams, baked goods, candy, chocolate, oil, vinegar, condiments, and honey. Fresh fruits and vegetables and most meats are not allowed, with exceptions for some canned items. Just because a duty-free shop in an airport sells a food product, it doesn't mean it will automatically pass US customs. Be prepared to lose your investment.

Of course, you'll need to carefully pack any bottles of wine, jam, honey, oil, and other liquid-containing items in your checked luggage, thanks to limits on liquids in carry-ons (though there's an exception for some foods and wine purchased at a duty-free shop; see the "Hauling Home Heavenly Wines" sidebar). For tips on bringing duty-free liquids onto the plane, see "What Can't I Carry On?" on page 106.

Shipping Things Home

If you buy more than you can comfortably carry, consider shipping your shopping bounty back home.

Customs regulations for items you ship amount to 10 or 15 frustrating minutes of filling out forms at a shipping office or post office. From Europe, you can mail one package per day to yourself in the US, worth up to $200 duty-free (mark it "personal purchases"). If you mail an item home valued at $250, you pay duty on the full $250, not $50. When you fill out the customs form, keep it simple and include the item's value (contents: clothing, books, souvenirs, poster,

value $100). For alcohol, perfume containing alcohol, and tobacco valued at more than $5, you will pay a duty. You can also mail home all the "American Goods Returned" you like (e.g., clothes you packed but no longer need) with no customs concerns—but note that these goods really must be American (not Bohemian crystal or a German cuckoo clock), or you'll be charged a duty. If it's a gift for someone else, it's subject to customs fees if valued at more than $100 (mark it "unsolicited gift").

If you accumulate a box's worth of dead weight, mail it home and keep on packing light.

It's fairly painless and convenient to use regular postal services, but it can be expensive. You can usually buy boxes and tape at the post office. Post offices in some countries, such as Great Britain, France, and Germany, have limits on how big or heavy your packages can be. For heavier packages, you may need to use their postal services' affiliated package services. The fastest way to get a package home from Italy is to use the Vatican post office—or take it home in your suitcase. Every box I've ever mailed from Europe has arrived—bruised and battered but all there—within six weeks. To send precious things home fast, I use DHL, with offices in every big city.

Theft & Scams

The odds are in your favor for enjoying a perfectly safe and incident-free trip to Europe. But anybody, whether at home or abroad, can experience unexpected problems, from inadvertently leaving a backpack on the train to getting pickpocketed in a crowd. By taking a few common-sense precautions, you'll greatly improve your chances of having a smooth trip.

PICKPOCKETING AND THEFT

While Europe has little violent crime, it does have its share of petty purse snatching, pickpocketing, phone grabbing, and general ripping off of tourists—especially in places where tourists gather. Thieves target vacationers—not because they're mean, but because they're smart. Travelers have all the good stuff in their bags and wallets. Loaded down with valuables, jetlagged, and bumbling around in a strange new environment, we stick out like jeweled thumbs. If I were a European street thief, I'd specialize in Americans—my card would say "Yanks R Us."

If you're not constantly on guard, you'll have something stolen. One summer, four out of five of my traveling companions lost cameras in one way or another. (Don't look at me.) But in more than 4,000 days of travel, I've been pickpocketed just once (on the Paris Métro, on a rare day I didn't wear my money belt) and mugged a single time (in a part of London where only fools and thieves tread). My various rental cars have been broken into a total of six times (broken locks, shattered windows, lots of nonessential stuff taken), and one car was hot-wired (and abandoned a few blocks away after the thief found nothing to take). Not one of my hotel rooms has ever been rifled through, and I simply don't let thoughts of

LEFT In Spain, just say *"No, gracias"* to women trying to thrust sprigs of rosemary on you for a tip.

RIGHT Outer backpack compartments are easy pickings for thieves.

petty crime—or the rare instance of it—spoil the fun of being abroad.

Many tourists get indignant when pickpocketed or ripped off. If it happens to you, it's best to get over it. You're rich and thieves aren't. You let your guard down and they grabbed your camera. It ruins your day and you have to buy a new one, while they sell it for a week's wages on their scale. It's wise to keep a material loss in perspective.

There probably aren't more thieves in Europe. We just notice them more because they target tourists. But remember, nearly all crimes suffered by tourists are nonviolent and avoidable. Be aware of the pitfalls of traveling, but relax and have fun. Limit your vulnerability rather than your travels.

Protecting Yourself from Theft

If you exercise adequate discretion, stay aware of your belongings, and avoid putting yourself into risky situations (such as unlit, deserted areas at night), your travels should be about as dangerous as hometown grocery shopping. Don't travel fearfully—travel carefully.

Here's some advice given to me by a thief who won the lotto.

Be prepared. Before you go, take steps to minimize your loss in case of theft. Make copies and/or take photos of key documents, and store them online (see page 69 for details). Consider getting theft insurance for expensive electronics (see page 76). Leave your fancy bling at home. Luxurious luggage lures thieves. The thief chooses the most impressive suitcase in the pile—never mine.

If your phone disappears, you're not just out the cost of the device—but also the photos and personal data stored on it. It's smart to take extra precautions before your trip: Make sure you've got a "find my phone"-type app, back up your data, and enable password protection. While traveling, use the Wi-Fi at your hotel to back up your phone and its photos each night. If you

If you need to access your money belt, just reach casually into your pants (ignoring the curious glances of onlookers) and pull it out.

don't know how to sync your stuff to the cloud, learn before your trip.

Wear a money belt. A money belt is a small, zippered fabric pouch on an elastic strap that fastens around your waist. I almost never travel without one—it's where I put anything I really, really don't want to lose. Wear it completely hidden from sight, tucked in like a shirttail—over your undies, under your pants or skirt. You can wear the pouch over your stomach for ease of access or slide it around to the small of your back.

Some people prefer to use a neck pouch, worn like a necklace but under a shirt; or a hidden pocket, which loops onto your belt, then tucks in behind it. Others use a Lycra running belt with secret storage or a growing range of specialty travel clothes—from blazers to yoga pants to scarves—with hidden pockets.

With a money belt or similar hidden, fastened storage, all your essentials are on you as securely and thoughtlessly as your underwear. Have you ever thought about that? Every morning you put on your underpants. You don't even think about them all day long. And every night, when you undress, sure enough, there they are, exactly where you put them. When I travel, my valuables are just as securely out of sight and out of mind, around my waist in a money belt. It's luxurious peace of mind. I'm uncomfortable only when I'm not wearing it.

But money belts don't work if you don't wear them properly. I once met an American woman whose purse was stolen, and in her purse was her money belt (that juicy little anecdote was featured in every street-thief newsletter). If you pull out your money belt to retrieve something, remember to tuck it back in. And don't use a fanny pack as a money belt—thieves assume this is where you keep your goodies.

Never leave your phone or money belt "hidden" on the

beach while you swim. Ideally, leave them locked up in your room; if that's not an option bring a small waterproof pouch or dry bag so your valuables can swim with you. In hostels or on overnight trains, wear your valuables when you sleep or store them safely in a locker. You can even shower with your valuables in a hostel (hang them in a waterproof bag from the nozzle or curtain rod). Keep your money-belt contents dry and sweat-free by slipping them into a plastic sheath or baggie before zipping them into the belt.

You don't need to get at your money belt for every euro. Your money belt is your deep storage—for select deposits and withdrawals. For convenience, carry a day's spending money in your pocket (a zipper, button-down flap, or Velcro strip sewn into your front or back pocket slows down fast fingers). Make sure it's an amount you're prepared to lose. I usually don't even carry a wallet. A few bills in my shirt pocket—no keys, no wallet—I'm on vacation!

Leave valuables in your hotel room. Expensive gear, such as a laptop, is much safer in your room than with you in a day bag on the streets. While hotels often have safes in the room (or at the front desk), I've never bothered to use one, though many find them a source of great comfort. (Some travelers leave their passports secured in the room safe while out for the day.) Theft from hotel rooms happens, of course, but it's relatively rare—hoteliers are quick to squelch a pattern of theft. That said, don't tempt sticky-fingered staff by leaving a camera or tablet in plain view; tuck your enticing things well out of sight.

Secure your bag, gadgets, and other valuables when you're out and about. Thieves want to quickly separate you from your valuables, so even a minor obstacle can be an effective deterrent. If you're sitting down to eat or rest, loop your day pack strap around your arm, leg, or chair leg. If you plan to sleep on a train (or anywhere in public), clip or fasten

Tour of a Money Belt

Packing light applies to your money belt as well as your luggage. Here's what to keep in it:

Passport: The item you least want to lose en route

Rail Pass: As valuable as cash

Driver's License: Necessary if you rent a car, and useful as collateral for rentals (bikes, audioguides, and so on)

Cards: Debit and credit cards

Cash: Larger bills

Plastic Sheath: Protective cover (a plastic baggie works) for keeping money-belt contents dry

your pack or suitcase to the seat, luggage rack, or yourself. Most zippers are lockable, and even a twist-tie, paper clip, or key ring is helpful to keep your bag zipped up tight. The point isn't to make your bag impenetrable, but harder to get into than the next guy's.

Never set down valuable items—such as a camera, phone, wallet, or rail pass—on a train seat or restaurant table, where they are easy to swipe. Keep these tucked away. When using your phone at a crowded café, don't place it on the bar: Put it in your front pocket (then return it to a safer place before you leave).

Some thieves can even be so bold as to snatch something right out of your hands. For instance, if you're holding up your phone to take a picture of the Eiffel Tower, a thief can grab it and run—and can navigate an escape route far better than you can. Be aware of who's around you.

One way to minimize this risk is to keep valuable devices attached to you or your bag (this also reduces the chance of accidentally leaving something behind). For instance, make sure your camera strap is looped around your chest or wrist, even when snapping a photo. Or use a lanyard to attach gadgets to your day pack (if there's no interior attachment point, feed straps through zipper pulls or a sturdy safety pin hooked to the inside of your bag).

Be discreet with your hiding places. If you're keeping valuables anywhere but a money belt or other secure pocket (I wouldn't), be as circumspect as possible. Thieves can easily identify the easiest mark—most likely the person with the bulging back pocket or the traveler who keeps patting a day bag to check that the money is still there.

Stay vigilant in crowds and steer clear of commotions. Go on instant alert anytime there's a commotion; it's likely a smokescreen for theft. Imaginative artful-dodger thief teams create a disturbance—a fight, a messy spill, or a jostle or stumble—to distract their victims. Crowds anywhere, but especially on public transit and at flea markets, provide bad guys with plenty of targets, opportunities, and easy escape routes.

Be on guard in train stations, especially upon arrival, when you may be overburdened by luggage and overwhelmed by a new location. A petite bump and a slight nudge getting off the Métro in Paris and…wallet gone. That's exactly what happened to me. Take turns watching the bags with your travel partner. Don't absentmindedly set down a bag while you wait in line; always be in physical contact with your stuff. If you check your luggage, keep the claim ticket or locker key in your money belt; thieves know just where to go if they snare one of these. On the train, tram, or subway, be hyper-alert at stops, when thieves can dash on and off with your bag.

City buses that cover tourist sights (such as Rome's notorious #64) are happy hunting grounds. Be careful on packed buses or subways; to keep from being easy pickings, some travelers wear their day bag against their chest (looping a strap around one shoulder). Some thieves lurk near subway turnstiles; as you go through, a thief might come right behind you, pick your pocket and then run off, leaving you stuck behind the turnstile and unable to follow. By mentioning these scenarios, I don't want you to be paranoid...just prepared. If you keep alert, you'll keep your valuables, too.

Establish a "don't lose it" discipline. Travelers are more likely to inadvertently lose their belongings than to have them stolen. I've known people to leave passports under pillows, bags on the overhead rack on the bus, and phones in the taxi. Always take a look behind you before leaving any place or form of transport. At hotels, stick to an unpacking routine, and don't put things in odd places in the room. Run through a mental checklist every time you pack up again: money belt, passport, phone, other electronic gear, charging cords, toiletries, laundry, and so on. Before leaving a hotel room for good, conduct a quick overall search—under the bed, under the pillows and bedspread, behind the bathroom door, in a wall socket...

Leave a clue for honest finders. Accidents happen, and even the most cautious traveler can leave something behind. Maximize your chances of getting it back by taping a tiny note with your email address or travel partner's phone number to any item you really don't want to lose, making it easy for a kind soul to return it. (For phones, you could use an "If Found Please Return To" note as your lock screen, or tuck your business card inside the case.)

Theft-Proofing Your Rental Car

Thieves target tourists' cars—especially at night. More than half of the work that European automobile glass shops do is repairing windows broken by thieves.

Don't leave anything even hinting of value in view in your parked car. Put anything worth stealing in the trunk (or, better yet, in your hotel room). Leave your glove compartment open so the thief can look in without breaking in. Choose your parking place carefully. Your hotel receptionist knows what's safe and what precautions are necessary.

Make your car look as local as possible. Leave no tourist information lying around. Put a local newspaper under the rear window. Before I choose where to park my car, I check to see if the parking lot's asphalt glitters. In Rome, my favorite hotel is next to a large police station—a safe place to park.

You can judge the safety of a European parking lot by how it glitters.

If you rent a hatchback, leave the trunk covered during the day. At night, roll back the cover so thieves can see there's nothing stored in the car. Many police advise leaving your car unlocked at night. "Worthless" but irreplaceable things (journal, memory cards full of photos, etc.) are stolen only if left in a bag. It's better to keep these things with you, or if need be, lay them loose in the trunk.

Be alert to "moving violations." In some urban areas, crude thieves reach into windows or even smash the windows of occupied cars at stoplights to grab a purse or camera. Also beware of other motorists trying to stop you. If you pull over, they may accuse you of hitting their vehicle. Police say it's best to keep driving.

SCAMS AND RIP-OFFS

Europe is a surprisingly creative place when it comes to travel scams. Many of the most successful gambits require a naive and trusting tourist. But it can happen to more sophisticated travelers, too. There are many subtle ways to be scammed—a cabbie pads your fare, a public computer records your password, or a waiter offers a special with a "special" increased price. Be smart: Know what you are paying for before handing over money, and always count your change. (For tips on avoiding taxi scams, see page 313.)

Scam artists come in all shapes and sizes. But if you're cautious and not overly trusting, you should have no problem. Here are some clever ways European crooks bolster their cash flow.

Such a Deal!

If a bargain seems too good to be true...it's too good to be true.

The "Found" Ring: An innocent-looking person picks up

a ring on the ground in front of you
and asks if you dropped it. When
you say no, the person examines
the ring more closely, then shows
you a mark "proving" that it's pure
gold and offers to sell it to you for a
good price—which is several times
more than the scammer paid for it
before dropping it on the sidewalk.

The "Friendship" Bracelet:
A vendor approaches and aggres-
sively asks if you'll help with a "demonstration." The vendor
proceeds to make a friendship bracelet right on your arm,
then asks you to pay a premium for it. And, since you can't
easily take it off on the spot, you feel obliged to pay up.
(These sorts of distractions can also function as a smokescreen for theft—an accomplice is picking your pocket as you
try to wriggle away from the pushy vendor.)

In Berlin, the police teach the public the latest shell-game scam. On the streets of Europe, anything that seems too good to be true...is.

Salesperson in Distress: A well-spoken, well-dressed
person approaches you and claims to be a leather jacket
salesperson, in need of directions. After chatting you up
("Oh, really? My cousin is from Chicago!"), the salesperson
reaches into the car and pulls out a "designer leather jacket"
to give to you as a thank you for your help. The salesperson
then claims their credit card isn't working, and asks you for
cash to pay for gas. Once you oblige, the salesperson takes off,
leaving you with your new, overpriced vinyl jacket.

Money Matters

In stores, restaurants, at ticket booths, everywhere—expect
to be cheated if you're not paying attention. Be alert any time
money changes hands, whenever you're withdrawing money
from an ATM, or if you're checking your bank balance (not a
good idea over public Wi-Fi). For more on keeping your debit
and credit cards safe, see page 198. When paying for things,
keep your cards in your sight and always count your change.

Slow Count: Cashiers who deal with lots of tourists
thrive on the slow count. They'll count your change back
with odd pauses in hopes the rushed tourist will gather up
the money early and say "*Grazie*."

Switcheroo—You Lose: Be careful when you pay with
too large a bill for a small payment. Clearly state the value
of the bill as you hand it over. Some cabbies or servers will
pretend to drop a large bill and pick up a hidden small one
in order to shortchange a tourist. Get familiar with the

currency and check the change you're given. Be alert for Asian coins that dishonest vendors try to pass off as €2 coins.

Talkative Cashiers: Be aware of shop cashiers who appear to be speaking on the phone when you hand over your credit card. But watch closely: They may surreptitiously take a picture of your card. Consider paying cash for smaller purchases, like I do.

Meeting the Locals

I want my readers to meet and get to know Europeans—but watch out for chance encounters on the street.

The Attractive Flirt: A single traveler is approached by a good-looking person on the street. After chatting for a while, the con artist invites the traveler for a drink at a nearby nightclub. But when the bill arrives, it's several hundred dollars more than expected—and there are now burly bouncers guarding the exits. There are several variations on this scam. Sometimes, the scam artist is disguised as a lost tourist; in other cases, it's simply a gregarious local person who (seemingly) just wants to show you around. Either way, be suspicious when invited for a drink by someone you just met; if you want to go out together, suggest a bar (or café) of your choosing instead.

Oops! You're jostled in a crowd as someone spills ketchup or fake pigeon poop on your shirt. The thief offers profuse apologies while dabbing it up—and pawing your pockets. There are similar schemes: Someone drops something, you kindly pick it up, and you lose your wallet. Or someone throws a baby into your arms as your pockets are picked. Treat any commotion (a scuffle breaking out, a beggar in your face) as fake—designed to distract unknowing victims. If an elderly person falls down an escalator, stand back and guard your valuables, then...carefully...move in to help.

Travel smart — keep what matters in your money belt.

www.ricksteves.com

50 EURO

In your wallet, you've got a fake 50-euro bill (with a funny note to the thief on the back—see next page). Cut it out and take it along.

Beggars: You'll meet a lot of people with beautiful eyes, beautiful children, and sad stories. They'll step right up and say, "Euro, please give me a euro." They don't want a euro; they want your wallet. Many beggars are pickpockets. Understand that.

The "Helpful" Local: Thieves posing as concerned locals will warn you to store your wallet safely—and then steal it after they see where you stash it. Or they may steal it first and then brazenly bring it back to you, saying they just found it on the ground. If someone wants to help you use an ATM, politely refuse (they're just after your PIN code). Some thieves put out tacks and ambush drivers with their "assistance" in changing the tire. Others hang out at subway ticket machines eager to "help" you, the bewildered tourist, buy tickets with a pile of your quickly disappearing foreign cash. If using a station locker, beware of "Hood Samaritans," who may have their own key to a locker they'd like you to use. And skip the helping hand from official-looking railroad attendants at the Rome train station. They'll help you find your seat...then demand a "tip."

Young Thief Gangs: These are common all over urban southern Europe, especially in the touristy areas of Milan, Florence, and Rome. Groups of kids with big eyes, troubled expressions, and colorful raggedy clothes politely mob unsuspecting tourists. As their pleading eyes grab yours, they hold up pathetic messages scrawled on cardboard, hoping to fool you into thinking that they're beggars. All the while, your purse or backpack is being expertly rifled. If you're wearing a money belt and you understand what's going on here, there's nothing to fear. In fact, having a street thief's hand slip slowly into your pocket becomes just one more interesting cultural experience.

In your wallet, you've got a little cash...and this funny note to the thief (with a fake 50-euro bill on back—see previous page). Cut it out and take it along.

DEAR THIEF...

ENGLISH: Sorry this contains so little money. Consider changing your profession.

ITALIANO: Mi spiace per te che ci siano così pochi soldi. Sara' meglio che cambi lavoro.

FRANCAIS: Je suis désolé d'avoir si peu d'argent. Considérez un changement de carrière.

DEUTSCH: Tut mir leid dass meine Geldbörse so wenig Geld enthält. Vielleicht sollten Sie sich einen neuen Beruf auswählen.

ESPAÑOL: Lamento que encuentre tan poco dinero. Vaya pensando en cambiar de trabajo.

Appearances Can Be Deceiving

The sneakiest pickpockets look like well-dressed businesspeople, generally with something official-looking in their hand. Some pose as tourists, with day packs, cameras, and even guidebooks. Don't be fooled by looks, impressive uniforms, or hard-luck stories.

Beware fake charity petitioners demanding cash donations.

Fake Charity Petition: You're at a popular sight when someone thrusts a petition at you. This person, sometimes pretending to be deaf, tries to get you to sign an official-looking petition, supposedly in support of a charity (the petition is often in English, which should be a clue). The petitioner then demands a cash donation. At best, anyone who falls for this scam is out some euros; at worst, they're pickpocketed while distracted by the petitioner.

Phony Police: Two thieves in uniform—posing as "Tourist Police"—stop you on the street, flash bogus badges, and ask to check your wallet for counterfeit bills, "drug money," or to establish your nationality. You won't even notice some bills are missing until after they leave. Never give your wallet to anyone.

Room "Inspectors": Two people claiming to be the hotel's room inspectors knock on your door. One waits outside while the other comes in to take a look around. While you're distracted, the first thief slips in and takes valuables left on a dresser. Don't let people into your room if you weren't expecting them. Call the hotel desk if "inspectors" suddenly turn up.

Broken Camera: While sightseeing, someone approaches with a camera or phone and asks that you take their picture. But the device doesn't seem to work. When you hand it back, the "tourist" fumbles and drops it, causing it to break. The scammer then asks you to pay for repairs (don't do it) or lifts your wallet while you are bending over to pick up the broken object.

LOSING IT ALL...AND BOUNCING BACK

You're winging your way across Europe, having the time of your life, when you make a simple mistake. You set your bag down next to your café chair, and before you know it...your bag is gone. Unfortunately, today's the day you tucked your passport, credit cards, and extra cash in your bag instead of in your money belt. That sinking feeling is the realization that you've lost everything but the euros in your pocket.

Odds are, this won't ever happen to you. But a little bit of advance preparation can make even this worst-case scenario a minor bump in your European adventure.

Don't panic. First of all, take a breath. Panic clouds your judgment. And don't beat yourself up: No matter how careful, any traveler can get ripped off or lose a bag. I once met a family in Amsterdam who managed to lose all their bags between the airport and their first hotel, but went on to have a very successful trip. A positive attitude is a great asset.

Ask for help. If you're in a country where little English is spoken, enlist the help of a local English speaker to assist you in making phone calls or explaining the situation to officials. Try your hotelier or someone at the tourist office: Even in the smallest towns, someone is likely to know at least a little English. Fellow travelers you've met and even family or friends back home can also be sources of help.

For emergency help (for any reason—police, medical, and fire), dial 112 from any phone. This toll-free number is the European Union's version of 911. In most cases, operators are able to answer in English.

File a police report. Find a police officer and report the theft or loss. Having a police report may help with replacing your passport and credit cards, and is a must if you file an insurance claim for a lost rail pass or expensive travel gear. The police may be able to direct you to a local travelers' aid office or Red Cross-like organization. And if you're lucky, someone may actually turn in your bag. That happened to me one time. My stolen bag showed up at the police station—turned in by a Good Samaritan who found it discarded after

If you get ripped off, find a police officer and report the loss.

the thief rifled through its contents. Thieves don't want your clothes or your bag. They want only what they can resell, and they discard the rest.

Gather critical information. In the best situation, you've got easy-to-access copies of important documents (either photocopies or electronic backups). If you don't have your bank or embassy's contact information, look it up. Your hotelier or a tourist-office staffer should be able to help you place necessary collect or toll-free calls. Retrieve information you've stored online, or solicit help from folks back home. Be careful about emailing passport and credit-card numbers.

Replace your passport. This is your top priority. Without a passport, you can't leave the country, and you may have problems checking into a hotel or receiving wired funds. First, it's smart to report that your passport has been lost or stolen at Travel.State.gov. To get a replacement, you'll need to go in person to the closest embassy or consulate (in the capital and sometimes major cities, too).

Every US consulate operates a US Citizen Services office, which aids Americans traveling abroad in coping with natural disasters, receiving money, and replacing passports (dial +1 202 501 4444; in the US, call 888 407 4747). You may be able to make an appointment at the embassy or consulate (often via its website; check embassy and consulate information at USEmbassy.gov), or you may need to show up during open hours and wait. If you can, save time by getting new passport photos and by filling out the required forms at Travel.State.gov before you go. Having a photo of your passport or other official ID can help; if you don't, embassy staff can look up your previous passport records, interview you and your travel partners, and even call contacts at home to verify your identity.

A replacement passport costs $145 and can generally

Lost It All? Follow These Steps

1. File a police report, either on the spot or within a day. You'll need it to file an insurance claim for a lost or stolen rail pass or travel gear, and it can help with replacing your passport or credit and debit cards.
2. Replace your passport at the nearest embassy or consulate; they're located in the country's capital and sometimes also in major cities (find locations at www.usembassy.gov for Americans, https://travel.gc.ca for Canadians).
3. Cancel and replace your credit and debit cards. With a mobile phone, call these 24-hour US numbers:

   Visa: +1 303 967 1096
   MasterCard: +1 636 722 7111
   American Express: +1 336 393 1111

   From a landline, you can call these US numbers collect by going through a local operator.
4. If your phone is gone, too, contact your mobile provider to suspend service. (If you use a security app, use the "locate, lock, and wipe" feature before you cancel service altogether.)

be issued within a few days, or faster if you make a good case that you need it right away. If you don't have the funds, the embassy will help you contact someone at home who can wire money directly to the embassy. If no one can wire money, the embassy may waive the fee or give you a "repatriation loan"—just enough funds to cover the new passport and get you back home.

If you're Canadian, you'll need to report the loss or theft to the local police, as well as the nearest embassy or consulate. Canadian authorities will conduct an investigation into the circumstances, which may delay the processing of your request. You must complete an application form and a statutory declaration concerning the lost/stolen passport, supply two passport photos and documentary proof of Canadian citizenship, and pay the fees (for details, see http://travel.gc.ca).

Cancel debit and credit cards. Within two days, cancel your lost or stolen debit and credit cards (meeting this deadline limits your liability to $50) and order replacements. Visa, MasterCard, and American Express all have global customer-assistance centers, reachable by collect call from anywhere. You'll need to verify your identity (with some combination of your birth date, mother's maiden name, your Social Security number, or answers to security questions you've set up—memorize these, don't carry a copy), and you may be asked for the name of the bank that issued the card, card type (classic, platinum, or whatever), card number, primary and secondary cardholders' names, cardholder's name exactly as printed on the card, billing address, home phone number, and circumstances of the loss or theft. If you are the secondary cardholder, you'll also need to provide the primary cardholder's identification-verification details.

Your bank can generally deliver a new card to you in Europe within two to three business days. Some may even be able to wire cash to keep you going or pay for your hotel room directly. Ask about these extra services.

If necessary, arrange for a wire transfer. A friend or relative can transfer money to you via Western Union's website or app (or they can call 800 225 5227). A "control number" is assigned to the transfer. If you have your passport, simply present it with the control number to a Western Union agent, who gives you cash. (Western Union has thousands of agents at banks, travel agencies, post offices, train stations, airports, currency-exchange offices, and supermarkets in Europe.) There's a hefty fee and a poor exchange rate, but the cash can be ready for pickup in a matter of minutes. If you don't have your passport, Western Union lets your financial angel set up a "secret question" that only you can answer to confirm your identity. Or you can use a slow US State Department service that wires money to an embassy or consulate for pickup during business hours (see www.travel.state.gov).

It's possible to transfer money from a bank in the US to a bank in Europe, but this may take several days (you'll probably have new cards faster). If your situation is dire and you can't get anyone to transfer or wire you money, ask the consulate about a "repatriation loan." Usually this is enough money to cover a night's lodging and a plane ticket home. Your passport will be stamped "Valid for Return to US Only" until your loan is repaid. If this happens to you, don't even think about stiffing Uncle Sam—after six months the State Department forwards the paperwork to the Treasury Department and the IRS.

Replace travel documents. Point-to-point rail etickets can often be reprinted from any computer or at the station, but tickets purchased at the station and printed on special ticket paper probably can't be replaced. Unfortunately, you can't replace a rail pass—you'll need to either purchase a new pass (most likely sent from home) or new tickets to complete your trip. (If you bought Rail Europe's Rail Protection Plan, you may be able to get a partial refund when you get home; be sure to file a police report within 24 hours to qualify.) There's no need to replace printed copies of airline, hotel, or car-rental reservations—once you have your new passport, these businesses can easily look up your reservation.

Rearrange travel plans. Depending on how long it takes to get your passport replaced—and how far you have to travel to reach an embassy or consulate—you'll probably need to rearrange your travel plans. Cancel and reschedule hotels and flights as soon as possible to avoid losing deposits or paying change fees (explaining the situation may help). If you're stuck without cash or credit cards for a few days, see if your bank or a family member back home can pay for your hotel stay.

Replace travel gear. Once you've started the process of replacing your passport and credit and debit cards, you can think about replacing travel gear such as your phone, camera, or tablet. Depending on your insurance policy, you may be able to get reimbursed for part of the replacement cost when you get home (see page 70). Decide which items are critical enough to your trip to replace immediately.

If you need to have something sent from home, have it addressed to you at a hotel you'll arrive at when it does; your hotelier will be happy to hold it for you. To speed things up, try second-day US-Europe services (such as DHL), though figure on four days for delivery to a small town. If you're not staying at a hotel (for instance, if you're camping or caravanning), you can have mail sent to any city's post office, addressed to you in care of "Poste Restante"; for convenience, pick a small town with only one post office and no crowds.

Refill prescriptions. Bring in a copy of your prescription to a pharmacy—if you don't have it, contact your doctor's office. They can usually fax or email a copy to you in Europe (see page 418 for more on filling prescriptions). Your optometrist can do the same for prescription eyewear.

Replace your rental-car key. If you lose the key to your rental car, call the car-hire company with your rental agreement number and your exact location. Be prepared for considerable expense and a delay: You will be charged $200 or more for a replacement key, and you may need to wait 24 to 48 hours for delivery of new keys or even a different vehicle.

Make the best of the situation. Getting everything straightened out can take a while. Be flexible and patient. It may not help at the time, but try to remember that your loss will make for a good story when you get home. Like a friend of mine says, "When it comes to travel, Tragedy + Time = Comedy."

Hurdling the Language Barrier

You're probably wondering: How can you connect with the locals if you can't communicate in their language? You'll be surprised at how easy it is. Over the years, I've collected tips and tricks that help travelers who speak only English step right over that pesky language barrier. In this chapter, you'll learn how to simplify your English and communicate creatively to get your points across and get what you need.

It always helps to be able to communicate—even just a few phrases—in the local tongue. Communication also goes beyond words: It also helps to know the meaning of various common gestures (and what to avoid doing).

A fear of the language barrier keeps many people (read: English speakers) out of Europe, but the "barrier" is getting smaller every day. Over the last few decades, an entire generation of Europeans has grown up speaking more English than ever. English is Europe's second language—more than half of all Europeans can speak at least some English. Historically, many European signs and menus were printed in four languages: German, French, English, and—depending on where you were—Italian, Spanish, or Russian. But there's been a shift. In the interest of free trade and efficiency, the European Union has established English as Europe's standard language of commerce. Now most signs are printed in just two languages: the native language for locals and English for

These signs in Amsterdam's airport don't even bother with Dutch.

everyone else. In some airports, signs are in English only.

Confessions of a Monoglot

While it's nothing to brag about, I basically speak only English. Of course, if I spoke more languages, I could enjoy a much deeper understanding of the people and cultures I visit. Still, speaking only English, I've enjoyed researching my guidebooks, leading tours, and making my TV shows, as well as navigating through wonderful trips—getting transportation, finding rooms, eating well, and seeing the sights. However, while you can manage decently with the blunt weapon of English, you'll get along in Europe better if you learn and use a few basic phrases and polite words.

Having an interest in the native language wins the respect of those you'll meet. Get a good language app or phrase book before your trip, and start your practical vocabulary growing right off the bat. My phrase books are the only ones on the market designed by a guy who speaks just English (that's why they're so helpful). They are both fun and practical, with a meet-the-people and stretch-the-budget focus. Mr. Berlitz knew the languages, but he never stayed in a hotel where he had to ask, "Do you have duct tape?"

Spend bus and train rides learning. Start studying the language when you arrive—or sooner. I try to learn five new words a day. You'd be surprised how handy it is to have a working vocabulary of even 50 words. Take advantage of everyday conversations to learn the language. You're surrounded by expert, native-speaking tutors in every country. Let them teach you.

Resources for Hurdling the Language Barrier

Consider these apps:

Bravolol: Basic phrases and vocabulary with translation and transliteration; also speaks phrases in the local language and lets you save favorites

Duolingo: Great for language learning, with short lessons, multiple-choice challenges, and levels to keep you progressing

Google Translate: Translates speech, handwriting, and images containing text, such as signs; save favorite words to access offline

Microsoft Translator: Translates text, speech, and photographed text; also translates conversations when multiple devices are connected

LEFT You don't have to speak Danish to understand these signs.

RIGHT If your taxi driver is going too fast, my phrase books will help you say, "If you don't slow down, I'll throw up."

While Americans are notorious monoglots, many Europeans are very good with languages. Make communication easier by choosing to speak with a multilingual person. Businesspeople, urbanites, well-dressed young people, students, and anyone in the tourist trade are most likely to speak English. Many Swiss grow up trilingual, and many young Scandinavians and Eastern Europeans speak several languages. People speaking minor languages (the Dutch, Norwegians, Czechs, Hungarians, Slovenes) have more reason to learn English, German, or French since their linguistic world is so small. All Croatians begin learning English in elementary school, and—since their TV programming is subtitled—they listen to Americans talk for hours each day. Scandinavian students of our language actually decide between English and "American." My Norwegian cousin speaks with a touch of Texas and knows more slang than I do.

We English speakers are the one group that can afford to be lazy, because English is the world's linguistic common denominator. When a Greek meets a Norwegian, they speak English. (What Greek speaks Norwegian?)

Imagine if each of our states spoke its own language. That's close to the European situation, but they've done a great job of minimizing the communication problems you'd expect to find on a small continent with such a Babel of Tongues. Most information a traveler must understand (such as road signs, menus, telephone instructions, and safety warnings) is printed either in English or as universal symbols. Europe's uniform road-sign system (see page 177)

Translating Foreign Websites

Many European websites offer English-language versions (usually accessed by clicking on a tiny British or American flag or the abbreviation "EN"). For web pages that are available only in the native language, a website translator is helpful.

Google's Chrome browser detects when a web page is in a foreign language and asks if you want it to be translated to English—or may even do so automatically. While less than perfect, this feature can open a whole new world of local information for travelers. For instance, you might find more interesting local eateries in Munich if you use a browser translator to read restaurant reviews written by German users. Even if you use Google via a different browser, you'll see a "Translate this Page" link in your search results next to foreign-language URLs. You can also cut and paste any text into Google Translate (translate.google.com) for an instant translation; click the speaker icon to hear the foreign words spoken aloud.

enables drivers to roll right over the language barrier. And rest assured that any place trying to separate tourists from their money will explain how to spend it in the necessary languages. English is always one of them.

Dominant as English may be, it's just good manners to know the most common polite words in the local tongue. The top 10 words in any language—mostly niceties like good day, please, thank you, and excuse me—are more important than the next 200 words combined. You should use these top words all the time. It's bad style for you to be in a country and not to know these "nice" words.

It's also a good idea to start every conversation by politely asking, "Do you speak English?" *"Parlez-vous anglais?"* *"Sprechen Sie Englisch?"* or whatever. If they say "No," then I do the best I can in their language. Usually, after a few sentences they'll say, "Actually, I do speak some English." One thing Americans can do well is put others at ease with our linguistic shortcomings.

COMMUNICATING WITH LOCALS

English may be Europe's lingua franca, but that doesn't mean everyone you encounter will be fluent. Below I've provided advice based on years of successful conversations (and amusing mishaps) while trying to talk to people for whom English is not their first language.

Use Simple English

If you have an upcoming trip to France and don't speak French yet, be realistic, and don't expect to become fluent by the time you leave. Rather than frantically learning a few more French words, the best thing you can do at this point is to learn how to communicate in what the Voice of America calls "Special English." Your European friend is doing you a favor by speaking your language. The least we can do is make our English simple and clear.

Speak slowly, clearly, and with carefully chosen words. Assume you're dealing with someone who learned English out of a book—reading British words, not hearing American ones. They are reading your lips, wishing it were written down, hoping to see every letter as it tumbles out of your mouth. For a better shot at being understood, talk like a Dick-and-Jane primer. Choose easy words and clearly pronounce each syllable (po-ta-to chips.) Try not to use contractions. Be patient—when many Americans aren't

International Words

As our world shrinks, more and more words leap their linguistic boundaries and become international. Sensitive travelers develop a knack for choosing words most likely to be universally understood ("auto" instead of "car"; "kaput" rather than "broken"; "photo," not "picture"). They also internationalize their pronunciation. "University," if you play around with its sound (oo-nee-vehr-see-tay), can be understood anywhere. Be creative.

Communication by analogy is effective. Anywhere in Europe (except in Hungary), "Attila" means "crude bully." When a bulky Italian crowds in front of you, say, "Scusi, Ah-tee-la" and retake your place. If you like your haircut and want to compliment your Venetian barber, put your hand sensually on your hair and say "Casanova." Nickname the hairstylist "Michelangelo."

Here are a few internationally understood words. Cut out the Yankee accent and give each word a pan-European sound ("autoboooos," "Engleesh").

Hello	Mobile (phone)	Communist
No	Wi-Fi	Amigo
Stop	Internet	Europa
Ciao	Google	Disneyland (wonderland)
Bye-bye	Facebook	Toilet
OK	Post (office)	WC
Mañana	Camping	Police
Pardon	Autobus	English
Bravo	Taxi	Telephone
Rock 'n' roll	Tourist	Photocopy
Mamma mia	Beer	Disco
No problem	Coke, Coca-Cola	Computer
Super	Tea	Sport
Sex/Sexy	Coffee	Central
Oo la la	Vino	Information
Momento	Chocolate	University
Bon voyage	Picnic	Passport
Restaurant	Self-service	Holiday (vacation)
Starbucks	Yankee, Americano	Gratis (free)
McDonald's	Hercules (strong)	America's favorite
Bank	Fascist	four-letter words
Hotel	Elephant (a big clod)	

easily understood, they tend to speak louder and toss in a few extra words. (Listen to other tourists talk, and you'll hear your own shortcomings.) For several months each year, I speak with simple words, pronouncing...very...clearly. When I return home, my friends say (very deliberately), "Rick, you can relax now, we speak English fluently."

Can the slang. Our American dialect has become a super-deluxe slang pizza not found on any European menu. The sentence "Can the slang," for example, would baffle the average European. If you learned English in a classroom for two years, how would you respond to the American who uses expressions such as "sort of like," "pretty bad," or "What's up?"

Keep your messages grunt-simple. Make single nouns work as entire sentences. When asking for something, a one-word question ("Photo?") is more effective than an attempt at something more grammatically correct ("May I take your picture, sir?"). Be a Neanderthal. Strip your message down to its most basic element. Even Neandertourists will find things go easier if they begin each request with the local "please" (e.g., "*Bitte*, toilet?").

Make an educated guess and go for it. Can you read the Norwegian: "Central Sick House"? Too many Americans would bleed to death on the street corner looking for the word "hospital."

Use internationally understood words. Some Americans spend an entire trip telling people they're on *vacation*, draw only blank stares, and slowly find themselves in a soundproof, culture-resistant cell. The sensitive communicator notices that Europeans are more likely to understand the word *holiday*—probably because that's what the English say. Then she plugs that word into her simple English vocabulary, makes herself understood, and enjoys a much closer contact with Europe. If you say *restroom* or *bathroom*, you'll get no relief. *Toilet* is direct, simple, and understood. If my car is broken in Portugal, I don't say, "Excuse me, my car is broken." I point to the vehicle and say, "Auto kaput."

Tips on Creative Communication

Even if you have no real language in common, you can have some fun communicating. Consider this profound conversation I had with a cobbler in Sicily:

"Spaghetti," I said, with a very saucy Italian accent.

"Marilyn Monroe," was the old man's reply.

"*Mamma mia!*" I said, tossing my hands and head into the air.

"Yes, no, one, two, tree," he returned, slowly and proudly.

By now we'd grown fond of each other, and I whispered, secretively, "*Molto buono, ravioli.*"

He spat, "Be sexy, drink Pepsi!"

Waving good-bye, I hollered, "*No problema.*"

"*Ciao*," he said, smiling.

Risk looking goofy. Even with no common language, rudimentary communication is easy. Butcher the language

Deciphering Signs

Öffnungszeiten

VOM 4. JULI AN

Montag:	08:30 - 13:00 u. 14:00 - 18:30
Dienstag:	08:30 - 13:00 u. 14:00 - 18:30
Mittwoch:	08:30 - 13:00 GESCHLOSSEN
Donnerstag:	08:30 - 13:00 u. 14:00 - 18:30
Freitag:	08:30 - 13:00 u. 14:00 - 18:30
Samstag:	08:30 - 13:00 u. 14:00 - 18:30

Hurdle the language barrier by thinking of things as multiple-choice questions and making educated guesses. This sign on a shop in Germany lists times. The top word can only mean "open times" or "closed times." I'd guess it lists hours open from (*vom* = from; if it rhymes, I go for it) the Fourth of July. Those six words on the left, most of which end in *tag*, must be days of the week (think *Guten Tag*). Things are open 8:30-13:00 *und* 14:00-18:30 (24-hour clock). On *Mittwoch* (midweek), in the afternoon...something different happens. Since it can only be open or closed, and everything else is open, you can guess that on Wednesday afternoons this shop is *geschlossen*!

if you must, but communicate. I'll never forget the clerk in the French post office who—long before email or Twitter— flapped her arms and asked, "Tweet, tweet, tweet?" I understood immediately, answered with a nod, and she gave me the airmail stamps I needed. At the risk of getting birdseed, I communicated successfully. If you're hungry, clutch your stomach and growl. If you want milk, "moo" and pull two imaginary udders. If the liquor was too strong, simulate an atomic explosion starting from your stomach and mushrooming to your head.

Be melodramatic. Exaggerate the native accent. In France, you'll communicate more effectively (and have more fun) by sounding less like an American and more like

The European Babel of Tongues

Most of Europe's many languages can be arranged into one family tree. Many of them have the same grandparents and resemble each other kind of like you resemble your siblings and cousins. But occasionally, an oddball uncle sneaks in whom no one can explain.

Romance Countries (Italy, France, Spain, Portugal): The Romance family evolved from Latin, the language of the Roman Empire ("Romance" comes from "Roman"). Few of us know Latin, but being familiar with any of the modern Romance languages helps with the others. For example, high school Spanish makes it easier to learn some Italian.

Germanic Countries (British Isles, Germany, Netherlands, Scandinavia, Iceland): The Germanic languages, though influenced by Latin, are a product of the tribes of northern Europe (including the Angles and Saxons)—people the ancient Romans called "barbarians" because they didn't speak Latin. German is spoken by all Germans and Austrians, and by most Swiss. The people of Holland and northern Belgium speak Dutch, a close relative to German. While Dutch is not *Deutsch*, a Hamburger or Frankfurter can almost understand conversations in Amsterdam. The Norwegians, Danes, and

Inspector Clouseau. The locals won't be insulted; they'll be impressed. Use whatever French you know. Even English spoken slowly with a sexy French accent makes more sense to the French ear. In Italy, be melodic and exuberant, and wave those hands. Go ahead, try it: *Mamma mia!* No. Do it again. *MAMMA MIA!* You've got to be uninhibited. Self-consciousness kills communication.

    Make logical leaps. Most major European languages are related, coming from (or at least being influenced by) Latin. Knowing that, words become more meaningful. The French word for Monday (our "day of the moon") is *lundi* (lunar day). The Germans say the same thing—*Montag. Sonne* is sun, so *Sonntag* is Sunday. If *buon giorno* means good day, *zuppa del giorno* is soup of the day. If *Tiergarten* is zoo (literally

Swedes can read each other's magazines and enjoy their neighbors' TV shows. But isolated Icelandic is different enough that other Germanic languages aren't much help.

Slavic Countries (Czech Republic, Poland, Slovakia, Slovenia, Croatia, etc.): Most Eastern European countries (except Hungary, Romania, and the Baltics) speak Slavic languages. While these languages are more or less mutually intelligible, spellings change as you cross borders; for example, Czech *hrad*, or castle, becomes Croatian *grad*. Farther east—in Serbia, Russia, Ukraine, Bulgaria, and elsewhere—the language sounds similar, but is written with the Cyrillic alphabet. The Baltic languages, Latvian and Lithuanian, are distantly related to Slavic tongues.

Finno-Ugric Countries (Hungary, Finland, Estonia): Hungarian, Finnish, and Estonian are more closely related to Asian languages than to European ones—likely hinting that the Hungarians, Finns, and Estonians share ancestors from Central Asia.

Multilingual Countries and Regions: Switzerland has four official languages—German, French, Italian, and Romansh (an obscure Romance tongue)—and most Swiss are at least bilingual. Because the region of Alsace, on the French-German border, has been dragged through the mud during several tugs-of-war, most residents speak both languages. Belgium waffles (linguistically), with the southern half (the Walloons) speaking French and the rest speaking Dutch.

Europe's Underdog Languages: Every year on this planet, a dozen or so languages go extinct. But thanks to Europe's determination to celebrate diversity, its underdog languages—once endangered—are thriving once more. The Basques, who live where Spain, France, and the Atlantic all touch, speak Euskara—mysteriously unrelated to any other European language. England is surrounded by a "Celtic Crescent." In Scotland, Ireland, Wales, and Brittany (northwestern France), the old Celtic language survives. Seek out these die-hard remnants in local shops, Gaelic pubs, and the Gaeltachts (districts, mostly in western Ireland, where the old culture is preserved by the government).

"animal garden") in German, then *Stinktier* is a stinky animal—a skunk—and *Kindergarten* is children's garden. Think of *Vater, Mutter, trink, gut, rapide, grand, económico, delicioso,* and you can *comprender mucho*.

Many letters travel predictable courses (determined by the physical way a sound is made) as related languages drift apart over the centuries. For instance, *p* often becomes *v* or *b* in the neighboring country's language. Italian menus always have a charge for *coperto*—a "cover" charge.

Read and listen. Read time schedules, posters, multilingual signs (and graffiti) in bathrooms and newspaper headlines. Develop your ear for foreign languages by tuning in to the other languages on a multilingual tour. It's a puzzle. The more you play, the better you get.

A Yankee-English Phrase Book

Oscar Wilde wrote that the English "... have really everything in common with America nowadays, except, of course, language." On your first trip to Britain, you'll find plenty of linguistic surprises. I'll never forget checking into a small-town bed-and-breakfast as a teenager on my first solo European adventure. The owner cheerily asked me, "And what time would you like to be knocked up in the morning?" I looked over at her husband, who winked, "Would a fry at half-eight be suitable?" The next morn-

Hmm... Where's the "exit"?

ing I got a rap on the door at 8 a.m. and a huge British breakfast a half-hour later.

Traveling through Britain is an adventure in accents and idioms. Every day you'll see babies in prams and pushchairs, sucking dummies as mothers change wet nappies. Soon the kids can trade in their nappies for smalls and spend a penny on their own. "Spend a penny" is British for a visit to the loo (bathroom). Older British kids enjoy candy floss (cotton candy), naughts and crosses (tic-tac-toe), big dippers (roller coasters), and iced lollies (popsicles), and are constantly in need of an Elastoplast or sticking plaster (Band-Aid).

It's fun to browse through an ironmonger's (hardware store) or chemist's shop (pharmacy), noticing the many familiar items with unfamiliar names. The school-supplies section includes sticky tape or Sellotape (adhesive tape), rubbers (erasers), and scribbling blocks (scratch pads). Those with green fingers (a green thumb) might pick up some courgette (zucchini), swede (rutabaga), or aubergine (eggplant) seeds.

In Britain, fries are chips and potato chips are crisps. A beefburger, made with mince (hamburger meat), comes on a toasted bap (bun). For pudding (dessert), have some gateau or sponge (cake).

The British have a great way with names. You'll find towns with names like Upper and Lower Piddle, Once Brewed, and Itching Field. This cute coziness comes through in their language as well. Your car is built with a bonnet and a boot rather than a hood and trunk. You drive on motorways, and when the freeway divides, it becomes a dual carriageway. And never go anticlockwise (counterclockwise) in a roundabout.

A notepad can work wonders. Words and numbers are much easier to understand when they're written rather than spoken (especially if you mispronounce them). My back-pocket notepad is my constant travel buddy. To repeatedly communicate something difficult and important (such as medical instructions, "I'm a strict vegetarian," "boiled water," "well-done meat," "your finest ice cream," or "I am rich and single"), have it written in the local language on your notepad.

Assume you understand and go with your educated

Gas is petrol, a truck is a lorry, and when you hit a tailback (traffic jam), don't get your knickers in a twist (make a fuss), just queue up (line up).

A two-week vacation in Britain is unheard of, but many locals holiday for a fortnight in a homely (homey) rural cottage, possibly on the Continent (continental Europe). They might pack a face flannel (washcloth), torch (flashlight), and hair grips (bobby pins) in their bum bag (never a fanny pack!) before leaving their flat (apartment). On a cold evening it's best to wear the warmest mackin-

Don't take British road signs personally.

tosh (raincoat) you can find or an anorak (parka) with press studs (snaps). If you ring up (call) someone who witters on (gabs and gabs), tell that person you're knackered (exhausted) and it's been donkey's years (ages) since you've slept. After washing up (doing the dishes) and hoovering (vacuuming), you can go up to the first floor (second floor) with a neat (straight) whisky and a plate of biscuits (cookies) and get goose pimples (goose bumps) just enjoying the view. Too much of that whisky will get you sloshed, paralytic, bevvied, wellied, popped up, ratted, or even pissed as a newt.

All across the British Isles, you'll find new words, crazy humor, and colorful accents. Pubs are colloquial treasure chests. Church services, sporting events, the Houses of Parliament, live plays, the streets of Liverpool, the docks of London, and children in parks are playgrounds for the American ear. One of the beauties of touring Great Britain is the illusion of hearing a foreign language and actually understanding it—most of the time.

Somehow, "Broken TV" just doesn't have the same ring to it.

guess. My master key to communication is to treat most problems as multiple-choice questions, make an educated guess at the meaning, and proceed confidently as if I understand. At the breakfast table the waitress asks me a question. I don't understand a word she says, but I tell her my room number. Faking it like this applies to rudimentary things like instructions on customs forms, museum hours, and menus. With this approach, I find that 80 percent of the time I'm correct. Half of the time that I'm wrong, I never know it, so it doesn't really matter. And 10 percent of the time, I really blow it. My trip becomes easier—and occasionally much more interesting.

Desperate Telephone Communication

Getting a message across in a language you don't speak requires some artistry. It takes something closer to wizardry on the phone, where you won't have any visual aids (your dynamic hand and facial expressions, for example). When attempting a phone conversation, speak slowly and clearly, pronouncing every syllable. Keep it very simple—don't clutter your message with anything more than what's essential. Many things are already understood and don't need to be said. (See? Those last six words didn't need to be written.) Use international or carefully chosen English words. When all else fails, let a local person on your end (such as a hotel receptionist) do the talking after you explain (with visual help, if needed) the message.

Let me illustrate with a hypothetical phone conversation. I'm calling a hotel in Barcelona. I just arrived at the train station here, read my guidebook's list of budget accommodations, and I like Pedro's Hotel. Here's what happens:

Pedro answers, "Hotel Pedro, grabdaboodogalaysk."

I ask, "Hotel Pedro?" (Question marks are created melodically.)

He affirms, already a bit impatient, "*Sí*, Hotel Pedro."

I ask, "*Habla* Eng-leesh?"

He says, "No, dees ees Ehspain." (Actually, he probably does speak a little English or will say "*momento*" and get someone who does. But we'll make this particularly challenging. Not only does he not speak English, he doesn't want to...for patriotic reasons.)

I remember not to overcommunicate—I don't need to tell him I'm a tourist looking for a bed. (Who else calls a hotel speaking in a foreign language?) Also, I can assume he's got a room available. If his place is full, he'll say "complete" or "no hotel" and hang up. If he's still talking to me, he wants my business. Now I must communicate just a few things, like how many beds I need and who I am.

I say, "OK." (OK is international for, "Roger, prepare for the next transmission.") "Two people"—he doesn't understand. I get fancy, "*Dos* people"—he still doesn't get it. Internationalize, "*Dos* pehr-son"—*no comprende.* "*Dos hombre*"—nope. Digging deep into my bag of international linguistic tricks, I say, "*Dos* Yankees."

"OK!" He understands that I want beds for two

Tongue-Twisters (or "Tongue-Breakers")

These are a great way to practice a language—and break the ice with the Europeans you meet. Here are some that are sure to challenge you and amuse your new friends.

GERMAN

Fischer's Fritze fischt frische Fische, frische Fische fischt Fischer's Fritze.

Fritz Fischer catches fresh fish, fresh fish Fritz Fischer catches.

Ich komme über Oberammergau, oder komme ich über Unterammergau?

I am coming via Oberammergau, or am I coming via Unterammergau?

ITALIAN

Sopra la panca la capra canta, sotto la panca la capra crepa.

On the bench the goat sings, under the bench the goat dies.

Chi fù quel barbaro barbiere che barberò così barbaramente a Piazza Barberini quel povero barbaro di Barbarossa?

Who was that barbarian barber in Barberini Square who shaved that poor barbarian Barbarossa?

FRENCH

Si ces saucissons-ci sont six sous, ces six saucissons-ci sont trop chers.

If these sausages are six cents, these six sausages are too expensive.

Ce sont seize cents jacinthes sèches dans seize cent sachets secs.

There are 1,600 dry hyacinths in 1,600 dry sachets.

SPANISH

Un tigre, dos tigres, tres tigres comían trigo en un trigal. Un tigre, dos tigres, tres tigres.

One tiger, two tigers, three tigers ate wheat in a wheatfield. One tiger, two tigers, three tigers.

Pablito clavó un clavito. ¿Qué clavito clavó Pablito?

Paul stuck in a stick. What stick did Paul stick in?

Excerpted from my phrase books—full of practical phrases, spiked with humor, and designed for budget travelers who like to connect with locals.

Americans. He says, "*Sí*," and I say, "Very good" or "*Muy bien*."

Now I need to tell him who I am. If I say, "My name is Mr. Steves, and I'll be over promptly," I'll lose him. I say, "My name Ricardo (ree-KAR-do)." In Italy I say, "My name Luigi." Your name really doesn't matter; you're communicating just a password so you can identify yourself when you

Happy Talk

English	French	Italian	German	Spanish
Good day.	Bonjour.	Buongiorno.	Guten tag.	Buenos dias.
Good morning.	Bonjour.	Buongiorno.	Guten Morgen.	Buenos días.
Good evening.	Bonsoir.	Buona sera.	Guten Abend.	Buenas tardes.
Good night.	Bonne soirée.	Buona notte.	Gute Nacht.	Buenas noches.
How are you?	Comment allez-vous?	Come sta?	Wie geht's?	¿Cómo está?
Very good.	Très bien.	Molto bene.	Sehr gut.	Muy bien.
Thank you.	Merci.	Grazie.	Danke.	Gracias.
Please.	S'il vous plaît.	Per favore.	Bitte.	Por favor.
Excuse me.	Excusez-moi.	Scusi.	Entschuldigung.	Perdone.
Do you speak English?	Parlez-vous anglais?	Parla inglese?	Sprechen Sie Englisch?	¿Hablas inglés?
Yes./No.	Oui./Non.	Si./No.	Ja./Nein.	Sí./No.
My name is John.	Je m'appelle Jean.	Mi chiamo Giovanni.	Ich heisse Johann.	Me llamo Juan.
What's your name?	Quel est votre nom?	Come si chiama?	Wie heissen Sie?	¿Cómo se llamas?
See you later.	Á bientôt.	A più tardi.	Bis später.	Hasta luego.
Good-bye.	Au revoir.	Arrivederci.	Auf Wiedersehen.	Adiós.
Good luck!	Bonne chance!	Buona fortuna!	Viel Glück!	¡Buena suerte!
Have a good trip!	Bon voyage!	Buon viaggio!	Gute Reise!	¡Buen viaje!
OK.	D'accord.	Va bene.	OK.	De acuerdo.
No problem.	Pas de problème.	Non c'è problema	Kein Problem.	Sin problema.
Everything was great.	C'était super.	Tutto magnifico.	Alles war gut.	Todo estuvo muy bien.
Enjoy your meal!	Bon appétit!	Buon appetito!	Guten Appetit!	¡Qué aproveche!
Delicious!	Délicieux!	Delizioso!	Lecker!	¡Delicioso!
Magnificent!	Magnifique!	Magnifico!	Wunderbar!	¡Magnifico!
Bless you! (after sneeze)	À vos souhaits!	Salute!	Gesundheit!	¡Salud!
You are very kind.	Vous êtes très gentil.	Lei è molto gentile.	Sie sind sehr freundlich.	Eres muy amable.
Cheers!	Santé!	Salute!	Prost!	¡Salud!
I love you.	Je t'aime.	Ti amo.	Ich liebe dich.	Te quiero.

walk through the door. Say something that will be easily understood.

He says, "OK."

You repeat slowly, "Hotel, *dos* Yankees, Ricardo, coming *pronto*, OK?"

He says, "OK."

You say, "*Gracias, adiós!*"

Twenty minutes later you walk up to the reception desk, and Pedro greets you with a robust, "Eh, Ricardo!"

EUROPEAN GESTURES

In Europe, while some gestures can help you communicate, others can contribute to the language barrier. For example, if you count with your fingers, in Europe remember to start with your thumb, not your index finger (if you hold up your index finger, you'll probably get two of something).

The "thumbs up" sign popular in the United States is used widely in most of Europe to say "OK" (it also represents the number one when counting). The "V for victory" sign is used in most of Europe as in the United States, but may get you a punch in the nose in parts of Britain, where it's an obscene gesture (if you make the "V" with your palm toward you.)

Some cultures also indicate "yes" and "no" differently: In Turkey, they shake their heads as Americans do, but someone may also signal "no" by tilting their head back. In Bulgaria and Albania, "OK" is indicated by happily shaking your head left and right—as if you were signaling "no" in the US.

Here are a few more common European gestures, their meanings, and where you're likely to see them.

Fingertips Kiss: Gently bring the fingers and thumb of your right hand together, raise to your lips, kiss lightly, and joyfully toss your fingers and thumb into the air. People in Italy, France, Spain, Greece, and Germany commonly use this gesture as a form of praise. It can mean sexy, delicious, divine, or wonderful. Be careful—tourists look silly when they overemphasize this subtle action.

Hand Purse: With palm facing up, bring together the tips of your fingers and thumb and point them upward. Place your hand about a foot in front of your face, and either hold it still or move it up and down a bit. This is a common and very Italian gesture for a query, such as "What do you want?" or "What are you doing?" or "What is it?" or "What's new?" It can also be used as an insult to say "You fool." In other countries the hand purse can also mean fear (France), a lot (Spain), and good (Greece and Turkey).

Very delicious!

Hand Shake: "Expensive" is often indicated by shaking your hand and sucking in like you just burned yourself.

Cheek Screw: Make a fist, stick out your index finger, and (without piercing the skin) screw it into your cheek. The cheek screw is used widely and almost exclusively in Italy to mean good, lovely, beautiful, or delicious. Many Italians also use it to mean clever. But be careful: In southern Spain, the cheek screw is used to call a man effeminate.

Eyelid Pull: Place your extended forefinger below the center of your eye and pull the skin downward. In France and Greece this means "I am alert. I'm looking. You can't fool me." In Italy and Spain, it's a friendlier warning, meaning "Be alert, that person is clever."

Forearm Jerk: Clench your right fist and jerk your forearm up as you slap your right bicep with your left palm. This is a rude phallic gesture that men throughout southern Europe use the way many Americans "give someone the finger." This jumbo version of "flipping the bird" says "I'm superior" (it's an action some monkeys actually do with their penises to insult their peers). This gesture is occasionally used by rude men in Britain and Germany as more of an "I want you" gesture about (but never to) a sexy woman.

Chin Flick: Tilt your head back slightly and flick the back of your fingers forward in an arc from under your chin. In Italy and France, this means "I'm not interested; you bore me," or "You bother me." In southern Italy it can mean "No."

Health & Hygiene

Understandably, two big concerns of American travelers are staying healthy and adjusting to European plumbing. Take comfort: Doctors, hospitals, launderettes, and bathrooms aren't that different in Europe. And dealing with them is actually part of the fun of travel. This chapter provides information on staying healthy while traveling, handling jet lag, and finding medical treatment, along with tips on hygiene—from doing your laundry to mastering European bathrooms.

STAYING HEALTHY

Before You Go

When getting organized before a trip, remember to also get your medical business in order. Your health is critical to your enjoyment of your vacation.

Read up on the latest travel advisories. Visit the Centers for Disease Control and Prevention's travel website (www.cdc.gov/travel) to get advice on preparing for and staying healthy during your travels. Current health and safety conditions, including any restrictions for your destination, are also available from the US State Department's international travel website (www.travel.state.gov).

Understand Covid-19 requirements. Travelers should expect new—and changing—health requirements for international travel. You'll likely need to carry proof of vaccination against the coronavirus and/or a recent negative Covid-19 test. Some countries are also requiring proof of medical insurance. Depending on when and where you travel, face masks may be required on planes, buses, trains, and other forms of public transportation or even more broadly at large public events. Consult the CDC and US State Department websites listed above for up-to-date requirements; US embassy websites are also good resources for individual countries.

As of this printing, anyone traveling to the US by air, including vacationers returning home, must present a negative Covid-19 test result before boarding a plane (for the latest requirements, see the CDC website). Know in advance where you'll get your test (must be performed 1-3 days before your flight). For testing sites abroad, see the country-specific listings at the US State Department website listed above. Major international airports have testing centers on-site, and most airlines list testing locations on their websites.

Get a checkup. Just as you'd give your car a good checkup before a long journey, it's smart to meet with your doctor before you depart if you have any medical concerns. Ask for advice on maintaining your health on the road. Obtain recommended immunizations and discuss proper care for preexisting medical conditions. If you have health concerns, keep a copy of your records accessible, including your latest EKG or X-rays (store them online). If you have a medical device such as an insulin pump or an implant such as an artificial knee or pacemaker, inform the TSA officer before airport screening begins. Bring along documentation of your condition or carry a TSA notification card (available at www.tsa.gov) to show the agent.

It's also a good idea to figure out if your health insurance covers you internationally or whether you might need to buy special medical insurance (see page 74).

Pack your prescriptions. If you take regular prescriptions—or have health problems that could flare up on your trip—bring a letter from your doctor describing the condition and any prescription medications you may need, including the generic names of the drugs. It's best to bring a big enough supply to cover your entire trip, along with a copy of your prescription in case you need more while you're abroad. Bring pharmaceuticals in their original containers (clearly labeled), and pack them in your carry-on bag (don't stow them in checked luggage, which could get lost).

Visit the dentist. Get a dental checkup well before your trip. Emergency dental care during your trip can be expensive, time consuming...and painful. I once had a tooth crowned by a German dentist who knew only one word in English, which he used in question form—"Pain?"

Take extra precautions for exotic locations. If you're heading to destinations outside western Europe, such as

Morocco, Russia, or Turkey, you may need immunizations beyond Covid-19. Ask your doctor about any shots or medicine you might need, or consult a travel-medicine physician. Only these specialists keep entirely up-to-date on health conditions for travelers around the world.

Tell the doctor about every possible destination on your vacation itinerary, confirmed or not. Then you can have the flexibility to take that impulsive swing through Turkey or Morocco knowing that you're prepared medically and have the required shots. Ask about vaccines against hepatitis A (food- or water-borne virus) and hepatitis B (virus transmitted by bodily fluids), antidiarrheal medicines, and any additional precautions.

Countries "require" shots in order to protect their citizens from you and "recommend" shots to protect you from them. If any travel vaccines or medications are recommended, take that advice seriously. The CDC offers current information on every country.

Conquering Jet Lag

Anyone who flies through multiple time zones will grapple with the biorhythmic confusion known as jet lag. Flying from the US to Europe, you switch your wristwatch six to nine hours forward. Your body says, "Hey, what's going on?" Body clocks don't reset so easily. All your life you've done things on a 24-hour cycle. Now, after crossing the Atlantic, your body wants to eat when you tell it to sleep and sleep when you tell it to enjoy a museum.

Too many people assume their first day will be made worthless by jet lag. But most people I've traveled with, of all ages, have enjoyed productive—even hyper—first days. You can't avoid jet lag, but by following these tips you can minimize the symptoms.

Leave home well rested. Flying halfway around the world is stressful. If you leave frazzled after a hectic last night and a wild bon-voyage party, there's a good chance you won't be healthy for the first part of your trip. An early trip cold was a regular part of my vacation until I learned this very important trick: Plan from the start as if you're leaving two days before you

Jet lag hits even the very young.

really are. Keep that last 48-hour period sacred (apart from your normal work schedule), even if it means being hectic before your false departure date. Then you have two orderly, peaceful days after you've packed so that you are physically ready to fly. Mentally, you'll be comfortable about leaving home and starting an adventure. You'll fly away well rested and 100 percent capable of enjoying the bombardment of your senses that will follow.

Use the flight to rest and reset. In-flight movies are good for one thing—nap time. With a few hours of sleep during the transatlantic flight, you'll be functional the day you land. When the pilot announces the European time, reset your mind along with your wristwatch. Don't prolong jet lag by reminding yourself what time it is back home. Be in Europe.

On arrival, stay awake until an early local bedtime. If you doze off at 4 p.m. and wake up at midnight, you've accomplished nothing. Plan a good walk and stay out until early evening. Jet lag hates fresh air, daylight, and exercise. Your body may beg for sleep, but stand firm: Refuse. Force your body's transition to the local time.

You'll probably awaken very early on your first morning. Trying to sleep later is normally futile. Get out and enjoy a "pinch me, I'm in Europe" walk, as merchants set up in the marketplace and the town slowly comes to life. This may be the only sunrise you'll see in Europe.

Consider jet-lag cures. The last thing I want to do is promote a pharmaceutical, but I must admit that the sleep aid zolpidem (commonly sold as Ambien) has become my friend in fighting jet lag. Managing a good seven hours of sleep a night in Europe (or after flying home) hastens my transition to local time. That way, I'm not disabled by sleepiness that first afternoon and can stay awake until a decent bedtime. Zolpidem can have side effects, and if misused, can be habit-forming; consult your doctor, and read and follow the directions carefully.

Other travelers rave about melatonin, a hormone that helps recalibrate your internal clock (available over the counter in the US, but illegal in some European countries).

Bottom Line: The best prescription is to leave home unfrazzled, minimize jet lag's symptoms, adopt European time, and enjoy your trip from the moment you step off the plane.

European Water

I drink European tap water and any water served in restaurants. Read signs carefully, however: Some taps, including those on trains and airplanes, are not for drinking. If there's any hint of nonpotability—a decal showing a glass with a red "X" over it, or a skull and crossbones—don't drink it. Many fountains in German-speaking countries are for drinking, but others are just for show. Look for *Trinkwasser* ("drinking water") or *Kein Trinkwasser* ("not drinking water").

The water at many European public fountains is safe to drink...unless your travel partner has dirty hands.

Unfamiliar water (or, just as likely, the general stress of travel on your immune system) may, sooner or later, make you sick. It's not necessarily dirty. The bacteria in European water are different from those in American water. We are capable of handling American bacteria with no problem at all, but some people go to London and get sick. Some French people visit Boston and get sick. Some Americans travel around the world eating and drinking everything in sight and don't get sick, while others spend weeks on the toilet. It all depends on the person.

East of Bulgaria and south of the Mediterranean, do not drink untreated water. Water can be sanitized by boiling it for 10 minutes or by using purifying tablets or a filter. Bottled water, beer, wine, boiled coffee and tea, and bottled soft drinks are safe as long as you skip the ice cubes. Coca-Cola products are as safe in Egypt as they are at home.

Staying Healthy While Traveling

Using discretion and common sense, I eat and drink whatever I like when I'm on the road. I've stayed healthy throughout a six-week trip traveling from Europe to India. By following these basic guidelines, I never once suffered from Tehran Tummy or Delhi Belly.

Take precautions on the flight. Long flights are dehydrating. I ask for "two orange juices with no ice" every chance I get. Eat lightly, stay hydrated, and have no coffee or alcohol and only minimal sugar until the flight's almost over.

Some people are susceptible to blood clots in their legs during long flights (factors include obesity, age, genetics, smoking, and use of oral contraceptives or hormone replacement therapy). You can reduce the risk by flexing your ankles and not crossing your legs while seated, taking short walks hourly, and staying hydrated; those at greatest risk can wear compression socks.

Eat nutritiously. The longer your trip, the more you'll be affected by an inadequate diet. Budget travelers often eat more carbohydrates and less protein to stretch their travel dollars. But protein helps you resist infection and rebuilds muscles. Supplemental super-vitamins, taken regularly, help me to at least feel healthy.

Use good judgment when eating out. Avoid unhealthy-looking restaurants. Meat should be well cooked (unless, of course, you're eating sushi, carpaccio, etc.) and, in some places, avoided altogether. If you're concerned, write the local equivalent of "well done" on a piece of paper and use it when ordering. Prepared foods gather germs (a common cause of diarrhea). Outside of Europe, be especially cautious. When in serious doubt, eat only thick-skinned fruit...peeled.

Keep clean. Wash your hands often, keep your nails clean, and avoid touching your eyes, nose, and mouth. Carry and use a hand sanitizer, such as Purell (must contain at least 60 percent alcohol to be effective against coronavirus). Remember that hand sanitizers are an adjunct to, not a replacement for, hand washing with soap and warm water.

Practice safe sex. While sexually transmitted diseases are not as widespread in Europe as they are in the US, they are still common. Take precautions. Condoms are readily available at pharmacies and from restroom vending machines.

Be active. Physically, travel is great living—healthy food, lots of activity, fresh air, and all those stairs! If you're a couch potato, try to get in shape before your trip by taking long walks. People who regularly work out have plenty of options for keeping in shape while traveling. Biking is a great way to get intimate with a destination while burning calories. Though running is not as common in Europe as it is in the US, it's not considered weird, either. Traveling runners can enjoy Europe from a special perspective—at dawn. Swimmers will find that Europe has plenty of good, inexpensive public swimming pools.

Whatever your racket, you'll find ways to keep in practice as you travel if you really want to. Most big-city private tennis and swim clubs welcome foreign guests for a small fee, which is a good way to make friends as well as stay fit.

Get enough sleep. Know how much sleep you need to stay healthy (generally 7-8 hours per night). If I go more than two nights with fewer than six hours' sleep, I make it a priority to catch up—no matter how busy I am. Otherwise, I'm virtually guaranteed to get the sniffles.

Give yourself a break. Europe can do to certain travelers what southern France did to Vincent van Gogh. Romantics can get the sensory bends, patriots can get their flags burned, and anyone can suffer from culture shock. Europe is not particularly impressed by America or Americans, and it will challenge many things you always assumed were above the test of reason.

On a longer trip, it can be refreshing to take a break from Europe every so often. Enjoy a long, dark, air-conditioned trip back to California in a movie theater. Loiter in the lobby of a world-class hotel, where the local culture is lost under a big-business bucket of intercontinental whitewash. Or simply stop at a Starbucks. A taste of home can do wonders to refresh the struggling traveler's spirit.

Women's Health Concerns

For advice on women's health, I turned to Rick Steves' Europe researcher Risa Laib, who wrote the following section based on her experiences traveling solo (and pregnant) through Europe.

Feminine Products: You can find whatever medications you need in Europe, but you already know what works for you in the US. It's easiest to B.Y.O. pills, whether for cramps, yeast infections, or birth control. Some health-insurance companies issue only a month's supply of birth control pills at a time; ask for a larger supply for a longer trip. Tampons and pads are sold at supermarkets, pharmacies, and convenience stores everywhere in Europe. But you may not see the range of brands and sizes typical in American supermarkets, so if you prefer a particular type, or to avoid having to buy more than you need, it can be simpler and cheaper to bring a supply from home.

Yeast and Urinary Tract Infections (UTIs): Women prone to yeast infections should bring their own over-the-counter medicine (or know the name and its key ingredient to show a pharmacist in Europe). Some women get an advance prescription for fluconazole (Diflucan), a powerful pill that cures yeast infections more quickly and tidily than creams and suppositories, though it's not recommended if you're pregnant.

If you get a yeast infection in Europe and need medication, go to a pharmacy. If you encounter a pharmacist who doesn't speak English, use an online translator to translate "yeast infection" to avoid an embarrassing charade.

Changes in your diet—especially increases in alcohol, coffee, or juice—can cause your bladder to react, leaving you with a UTI. If you experience UTI symptoms in Europe, it's best to see a pharmacist right away; you'll be prescribed an antibiotic.

Traveling when Pregnant: Some people want to time conception to occur in Europe so they can name their child Paris, Siena, or wherever. (Be thoughtful about this, or little Zagreb may harbor a lifelong grudge against you.) Consider bringing a pregnancy test from home if you're embarking on a longer trip.

Generally, health care providers consider it safe for women with healthy pregnancies to fly up until 36 weeks. Check with your doctor and confirm the airline's policies before booking your ticket. You'll want to plan around the timing of recommended prenatal screening tests, too.

Traveling in the first trimester can be rough: Morning sickness can make bus or boat rides especially unpleasant, and climbing all those stone stairs can be exhausting. Packing light is more essential than ever, though you'll want to bring motion-sickness remedies (tablets or acupressure wristbands) and snacks that relieve nausea. Many women find it easiest to travel in the second trimester, between weeks 14 and 28, when their body is used to being pregnant, they're not yet too big to be uncomfortable, and the risks of miscarriage and preterm labor are low.

Wear comfortable shoes with good arch support. Pack comfortable maternity wear to accommodate your changing body. Skip the constricting money belt for your valuables. Instead, look for a neck pouch or a cozy scarf with a hidden security pocket.

Pace yourself and allow plenty of time for rest. If problems pop up, go to a clinic or hospital (for more, see "Medical Care in Europe," later).

Seek out nutritious food, and stay hydrated. Pack baggies for carrying snacks. Bring prenatal vitamins and any other supplements you need from home.

It's actually pleasant to be pregnant in Europe. People are particularly kind. And when your child is old enough to understand, they'll enjoy knowing they've already been to Europe—especially if you promise to take them again.

Basic First Aid

It's tempting to go, go, go while you're in Europe—but if you're not careful you might push yourself to the point of

Fahrenheit and Celsius Conversion

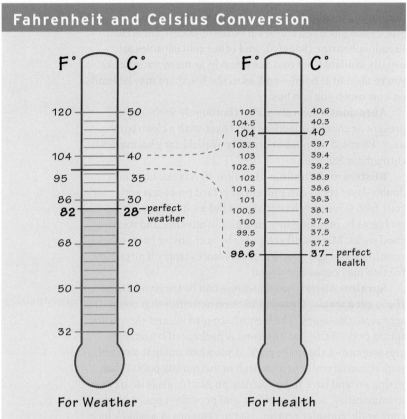

For Weather   For Health

Europe takes its temperature using the Celsius scale, while we opt for Fahrenheit. For a rough conversion from Celsius to Fahrenheit, double the number and add 30. For weather, remember that 28°C is 82°F–perfect. For health, 37°C is just right.

getting sick. Be proactive to stay well. If you do get sick, take action to regain your health. For a list of first-aid items to pack from home, see page 93.

Headaches and Other Aches: Try requesting "paracetamol" to get acetaminophen (Tylenol) when you need to soothe headaches, sore feet, bruises, Italian traffic, and other minor problems.

Fever: A high fever merits medical attention, particularly for children. A normal temperature of 98.6° Fahrenheit equals 37° Celsius. If your thermometer reads 40°C, you're boiling at 104°F. You can use acetaminophen to bring down a fever, along with putting cold washcloths on your forehead for relief.

Colds: If you're feeling run-down, get lots of sleep and force fluids. (My trick during the hectic scramble of TV production is to suck on tablets of vitamin C and zinc.) Stock each place you stay with boxes of juice upon arrival. Pseudoephedrine (Sudafed) and other cold capsules are usually available, but may not come in as many varieties as you're used to at home—and, as in the US, there may be limits on how much you can buy.

Abrasions: Clean abrasions thoroughly with soap to prevent or control infection, and cover with a clean bandage. First-aid supplies are readily available at pharmacies throughout Europe.

Blisters and Chafing: Moleskin, bandages, tape, or double-layer socks can prevent or retard problems with your feet. Cover any irritated area before it blisters. Avoid problems by breaking in your shoes in advance and wearing good socks. Many walkers swear by anti-blister balm sold in running shops and sporting-goods stores (apply it anywhere friction may cause a problem).

Sprains: All those cobblestones can be tough on ankles. If you get a sprain, try to cut back on activities that could aggravate the injury. The best advice is to ice and elevate any sprain periodically for 48 hours. A package of frozen veggies works as a cheap ice pack. If your foot or leg is swollen, soak it in cold water in a bathtub or swimming pool. When sitting around isn't an option, use an Ace bandage or air cast to immobilize, reduce swelling, and provide support. If you can't walk, consider renting a set of crutches or a wheelchair: Ask your hotelier for help. Take regular doses of an anti-inflammatory drug like ibuprofen (Advil, Motrin).

Motion Sickness: To be effective, medication for motion sickness—such as dimenhydrinate (Dramamine) or cyclizine (Marezine)—should be taken one hour before you think you'll need it. These medications can also serve as a mild sleep aid. Meclizine (Bonine) also treats motion sickness but causes less drowsiness. Acupressure bands worn on the wrists help some people.

Allergies: Even those immune to pollen or cat dander at home might come down with allergies when exposed to unfamiliar flora and fauna. You might not find Claritin in Europe, but you can get the generic equivalent, loratadine. For an antihistamine like Benadryl, request diphenhydramine.

Diarrhea: Get used to the fact that you may have diarrhea for a day. If you get the runs, take it in stride. It's simply not worth taking eight Pepto-Bismol tablets a day or brushing your teeth in Coca-Cola all summer long to avoid a day of

Good news for your health: Europe has become enthusiastic about not smoking. These days most countries prohibit smoking in enclosed public spaces. Cigarette packages make it really clear: "Smoking kills"; and Berlin's subway–like much of Europe–is now smoke-free.

the trots. I take my health seriously and, for me, traveling in India or Mexico is a bigger health concern. But I find Europe no more threatening to my stomach than the US.

I've routinely taken groups of 24 Americans through Turkey for two weeks. With adequate discretion, we eat everything in sight. At the end of the trip, my loose-stool survey typically shows that five or six travelers coped with a day of the Big D and one person was stuck with an extended weeklong bout.

If you get diarrhea, don't panic: It will run its course. Take it easy for 24 hours. Make your diet as bland and boring as possible for a day or so (bread, rice, boiled potatoes, bananas, clear soup, toast, weak tea). Keep telling yourself that tomorrow you'll feel much better. You likely will. But if loose stools persist, drink lots of water to replenish lost liquids and minerals.

Don't take antidiarrheal medications if you have blood in your stools or a fever greater than 101°F (38°C)—you need a doctor's exam and antibiotics. A child (especially an infant) who suffers a prolonged case of diarrhea also needs prompt medical attention.

I visited the Red Cross in Athens after a miserable three-week tour of the toilets of Syria, Jordan, and Israel. My intestinal commotion was finally stilled by a recommended strict diet of boiled rice and plain tea. As a matter of fact, after five days on that dull diet, I was constipated.

Constipation: With all the bread you'll be eating, constipation, the other side of the intestinal pendulum, is (according to my surveys) as prevalent as diarrhea. Get exercise, drink water, and eat food with lots of fiber (raw fruits, leafy vegetables, prunes, or bran tablets from home). Drinking herbal tea helps many people get moving again. If that fails, try laxatives or stool softeners, and everything will come out all right in the end.

Medical Care in Europe

Most of Europe offers high-quality medical care that's as competent as what you'll find at home. The majority of Europe's doctors and pharmacists speak at least some English, so communication generally isn't an issue.

Emergencies

If an accident or life-threatening medical problem occurs on the road, get to a hospital. In the European Union, for serious conditions (stroke, heart attack, bad car accident), summon an ambulance by calling 112, the universal emergency number for ambulance, fire department, or police. Most countries also have a 911 equivalent that works as well. Or you can ask your hotelier, restaurant host, or whoever's around to call an ambulance (or a taxi for less dire situations).

Be aware that you will likely have to pay out of pocket for any medical treatment, even if your insurance company provides international health care coverage. A visit to the emergency room can be free or cost only a nominal fee, or it can be expensive, depending on where you are and what treatment you need. Make sure you get a copy of your bill so that, when you return home, you can file a claim to be reimbursed. If you purchased travel insurance to serve as your primary medical coverage, call the company as soon as possible to report the illness or injury. They can usually work directly with the hospital to get your bills paid (for information on travel insurance, see page 70).

Minor Ailments

If you get sick on your trip, don't wait it out. Find help to get on the road to recovery as soon as possible. Here are your options if you have a non-emergency situation:

Pharmacies: Throughout Europe, people with a health problem go first to the pharmacy, not to their doctor. European pharmacists can diagnose and prescribe remedies for many simple problems, such as sore throats, fevers, stomach issues, sinus problems, insomnia, blisters, rashes, urinary tract infections, or muscle, joint, and back pain. Most cities have at least a few 24-hour pharmacies.

When it comes to medication, expect some differences between the way things are done in Europe and at home.

Certain drugs that you need a prescription for in the US are available over the counter in Europe. Some drugs go by different names. And some European medications can be stronger than their counterparts in the US, so follow directions and dosages carefully. Also, topical remedies are common in Europe; if you're suffering from body aches and pains, or any swelling, don't be surprised if a pharmacist prescribes a cream to apply to the problem area. If you need to fill a prescription—even one from home—a pharmacy can generally take care of it promptly. If pharmacists can't help, they will send you to a doctor or a health clinic.

Regardless of the local word for "pharmacy" (*farmacia* in Spanish), you can always look for the green cross.

Clinics: A trip to a foreign clinic is actually an interesting travel experience. Every few years I end up in a European clinic for one reason or another, and every time I'm impressed by its efficiency and effectiveness.

A clinic is useful if you need to be checked for a nonemergency medical issue, get some tests done, or if your problem is beyond a pharmacist's scope. Clinics in Europe operate just like those in the US: You'll sign in with the receptionist, answer a few questions, then take a seat and wait for a nurse or doctor.

A trip to a clinic may be free or cost a small fee. Expect to pay this fee up front, whether you're covered through your health insurance company or a special travel policy. Make sure you get a copy of the bill so you can file a claim when you return home.

House Calls: If you're holed up sick in your hotel room and would rather not go out, the hotel receptionist may be able to call a doctor who will come to your room and check you out. This option is generally more expensive than dragging yourself to a pharmacy or clinic.

Finding Medical Help

To locate a doctor, clinic, or hospital, ask at a pharmacy or at places that are accustomed to dealing with Americans on the road—such as tourist offices and large hotels. Most embassies and consulates maintain lists of physicians and hospitals in major cities (go to www.usembassy.gov,select your location, and look under the US Citizens Services section of that embassy's website for medical services information).

Travelers in need of assistance can also check with the Travel Doctor Network (https://traveldoctor.network).

LAUNDRY

I met a traveler in Italy who wore her T-shirt frontward, backward, inside-out frontward, and inside-out backward, all to delay laundry day. A guy in Germany showed me his take-it-into-the-tub-with-you-and-make-waves method of washing his jeans. But you don't need to go to these extremes to have something presentable to wear. Do laundry in your hotel room, find a launderette, or splurge on full-service laundry.

Washing Clothes in Your Room

One of my domestic chores while on the road is washing my laundry in the hotel-room sink. I keep it very simple, using hotel laundry bags to store my dirty stuff, washing my clothes with hotel shampoo, and improvising places to hang things. But you can pack a self-service laundry kit: a plastic or mesh bag with a drawstring for dirty clothes, concentrated liquid detergent (either in individual travel packs or a small, sturdy squeeze bottle wrapped in a sealable baggie to contain leakage), individual spot-remover wipes, and a stretchable travel clothesline (a double-stranded cord that's twisted, so clothespins are unnecessary).

To make things easier, I bring a quick-dry travel wardrobe that either looks OK wrinkled or doesn't wrinkle. (I test-wash my shirts in the sink at home before I let them come to Europe with me. Some shirts dry fine; others prune up.)

Most European hotels prefer that you not do laundry in your room. Some bathrooms even have a multilingual "no washing clothes in the room" sign (which, after "eat your peas," may be the most ignored rule on earth). Interpret hoteliers' reticence as "I have lots of good furniture and fine floors in this room, and I don't want your drippy laundry ruining things." As long as you wash carefully and are respectful of the room, go right ahead.

Whistler's laundry

Sometimes a hotel will remove the sink and tub stoppers to discourage washing. Bring a universal drain stopper from home, try using a wadded-up sock or a pill-bottle lid, or line the sink with a plastic bag and wash in it. Some travelers create their own washing machine with a large, two-gallon sealable baggie: soak in suds for an hour, agitate, drain, rinse.

Go ahead and ask! There's a good chance you can share the clothesline in the B&B's backyard or on the hotel's roof.

Wring wet laundry as dry as possible to minimize dripping. Other than a clogged toilet, there's little a hotelier likes seeing less than a pool of water on their hardwood floors. Rolling laundry in a towel and twisting or stomping on it works well (if you have an extra towel—remember that many accommodations don't provide new towels every day).

Account for drying time: Cotton needs much longer to dry than the lightweight performance fabrics often used in travel clothing. Hang clothes in a low-profile, nondestructive way. Suspend them over the bathtub or in a closet. Housekeeping hardly notices my laundry, as it's either hanging quietly in the bathroom or shuffled among my dry clothes in the closet. Separate the back and front of hanging clothes to speed drying time. (Some travelers pack inflatable hangers for this.) Don't hang your clothes out the window or on the balcony—hoteliers find it unsightly, and you might find it has blown away when you return from dinner. Laid-back hotels will let your laundry join theirs on the lines out back or on the rooftop.

Smooth out your wet clothes, button shirts, set collars, and "hand iron" to encourage wrinkle-free drying. If your shirt or dress dries wrinkled, hang it in a steamy bathroom or borrow an iron and ironing board from the hotel (nearly all have loaners). A piece of tape is a good ad hoc lint-brush. In very hot climates, I wash my shirt several times a day, wring it, and put it on damp. It's clean and refreshing, and (sadly) in 15 minutes it's dry.

Using a Launderette

For a thorough washing, ask your hotel to direct you to the nearest launderette. In Western Europe, nearly every neighborhood has one; in Eastern Europe, launderettes are less common. It takes about an hour and $10-15 to wash and dry an average-size load. (Some short-term rentals have laundry facilities, and many hostels have coin-op washers and dryers or heated drying rooms.)

Better launderettes have coin-op soap dispensers, change machines, English instructions, and helpful attendants. Others are completely automated—but many of these have pictogram instructions that usually aren't too hard to parse. Look around for a sign listing the "last wash" time, and stick to it. When it's closing time, an attendant might come by to evict you, or the machines may simply stop operating.

Many of Europe's launderettes are completely unstaffed—it's just you, sparse English instructions, and dirty clothes.

While the exact procedure varies, it usually includes the same steps you'd encounter at a launderette at home. If you're planning on visiting a launderette, you could pack one or two small detergent boxes, although you can typically buy some there at a dispenser. The soap compartments on most washers have three reservoirs: for prewash, the main wash cycle (normally at the top of the washer), and fabric softener. (Don't put your main soap into the prewash compartment, or it'll be washed away before its time.)

While you might be able to pay at the washer itself, more likely you'll have to insert your money at a central unit. Note the number of your machine, then type that number into the central unit and put in your coins (use exact change if possible—some machines don't give change). Sometimes a central unit dispenses tokens, which you then insert in the machine.

Select your cycle, either at the machine or at the central unit. Below I've listed some of the cycles you're likely to see. The first number is the temperature in Celsius for the first cycle (prewash), the second is the temperature for the second cycle (main wash), and the third is how long the whole process takes.

45° / 90° / 55 m	whites (very hot)
45° / 60° / 50 m	colors (hot)
45° / 45° / 40 m	permanent press (warm)
— / 30° / 30 m	nylon (lukewarm)
— / 20° / 25 m	delicates (cold)

Sample Laundry Instructions

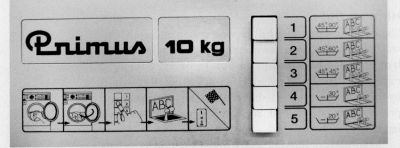

This laundry machine hurdles the language barrier with pictographic instructions: Insert your laundry, close the door, select the program, add the soap, and insert coins to start. The buttons on the right let you select from five washing options: The first water temperature (in Celsius) is for the prewash cycle, and the second is for the wash cycle. The pictures tell you where to put the soap and softener for each selection (the last two skip the prewash—no soap needed in compartment A).

Some washing machines have a built-in spin cycle, while others leave clothes totally soaked. In this case, you'll need to put your wet clothes in a special spin-dry machine (usually called a "centrifuge" or something similar) to wring out excess water before moving them to the dryer.

Some European clothes dryers are not vented to the outside, but instead collect the water from the clothes in an interior reservoir. The dryer will stop and an icon will light up when this reservoir is full and needs to be emptied. Ask an attendant if you can't figure out how.

Drying time is generally available in smaller units (5- or 10-minute increments) rather than as a full cycle. Most machines let you choose the drying temperature: low (cool and slow); medium (warmer but still slow); and high (speedy but shrinky). Because both washers and dryers at launderettes can be unpredictable, hand wash anything that you value dearly.

While waiting for your clothes, use the time to picnic, catch up on postcards and your journal, or chat with other customers. Launderettes throughout the world seem to give people the gift of gab. Most launderettes have Wi-Fi. If you ask attendants sweetly, they might be willing to transfer your clothes to the dryer, allowing you to slip out for some bonus sightseeing. (In these cases, it's appropriate to thank them by offering a small tip.)

Hiring It Out

Some launderettes offer full service, which means they'll wash, fold, and sometimes even iron your laundry. Just drop it off and come back later in the day. This service is more expensive than doing it yourself—you'll generally be charged by the kilo or by the item—but can save lots of time. Also pricey, but handiest of all: You can pay your hotel to do your laundry.

Regardless of the cost, every time I slip into a fresh pair of pants, I figure it was worth the hassle and expense.

EUROPEAN BATHROOMS

European bathrooms can be quirky by American standards. Your hotel's WC may come with luxurious heated towel racks—or a rattling fan, leaky sink, and shoebox-sized shower. My advice is to keep an open mind, wash up quickly, and get out and about in the place you came to enjoy. And remember that nothing beats a good bathroom story when you get home.

Your Hotel Bathroom

First, don't expect big spaces. Europe's hotel owners have carved out chunks of elegant bedrooms to shoehorn in prefab private bathrooms—and they can be very tight. Counter space is often limited, and showers can be surprisingly small. Be careful bending over to pick up a dropped bar of soap— you might just hit your head on the toilet or sink.

In some bathrooms, you may see a mysterious porcelain thing that looks like an oversized bedpan. That's a bidet. Tourists who aren't in the know use them as anything from a launderette to a vomitorium to a watermelon-rind receptacle to a urinal. Locals use them in lieu of a shower to clean the parts of the body that rub together when they walk. Go ahead and give it a try. Just remember the four S's—straddle, squat, soap up, and swish off.

When traveling in Europe, you may need to lower your washcloth and towel expectations. Most European hotels don't supply washcloths. If a washcloth is part of your bath ritual, bring a quick-drying one with you.

And, like breakfast and people, towels get smaller as you go south. In simple places, bath towels are not replaced every day, so hang them up to dry and reuse. This is also becoming common practice at bigger hotels—even fancy ones—in an effort to be eco-friendly. You may see a sign explaining that they'll replace towels left on the floor, but not those that are hanging to dry. In my experience, pricey hotels rarely stay true to this promise; your towels will probably be replaced no matter where you leave them. On the other end of the spectrum, dorm-style accommodations don't provide towels or soap at all, so bring your own quick-drying travel towel if you plan on staying in hostels.

Shower Strategies

Americans are notorious (and embarrassing) energy gluttons—wasting hot water and leaving lights on as if electricity were cheap. Who besides us sings in the shower? European energy costs are shocking, so many accommodations try to conserve where they can.

Hot-Water Hiccups: Most of the cold showers Americans take in Europe are cold only because they don't know how to turn on the hot water. You'll find showers and baths of all kinds. The red knob is hot and the blue one is cold—or vice versa. Unusual showers often have clear instructions posted. Study the system, and before you shiver, ask the receptionist for help.

There are some very peculiar tricks. For instance, in Italy and Spain, "C" is for *caldo/caliente*—hot. In Croatia, look for the switch with an icon of a hot-water tank (usually next to the room's light switch). The British "dial-a-shower" features an electronic box under the showerhead—turn the dial to select how hot you want the water and to turn on or shut off the flow of water (this is sometimes done with a separate dial or button). If you can't find the switch to turn on the shower, it may be just outside the bathroom.

No matter where you are in Europe, get used to taking shorter showers. Some places, especially modest accom-

European showers: Each has its own personality.

modations, furnish their bathrooms with little-bitty water heaters that are much smaller than the one in your house. After five minutes, you may find your hot shower turning very cold.

Handheld Showerheads: In Europe, handheld showers are common. Sometimes the showerhead is sitting loose in a caddy; other times

it's mounted low on the tub. Not only do you have to master the art of lathering up with one hand while holding the showerhead in the other, but you also have to keep it aimed at your body or the wall to avoid spraying water all over the bathroom. To avoid flooding the room, you may find it easier to just sit in the tub for your shower.

Throughout southern Europe, even the cheapest hotel rooms come with a bidet. Europeans use them to stay clean without a daily shower.

Strange Drains: Speaking of flooding, in some hotels, the line between shower and bathroom is nonexistent. There may not be a shower curtain or even a shower pan to contain the water. Instead, the water simply slides into a drain in the middle of the bathroom floor.

Emergency Cords: The cord that dangles over the tub or shower in some hotels is not a clothesline; only pull it if you've fallen and can't get up. (But if the cord hangs *outside* the tub or shower, it probably controls the light—good luck with this.)

Shared Showers: The cheapest rooms sometimes feature a shared toilet and shower "down the hall." To batholics, this sounds terrible. But you're unlikely to find a long line for the loo: Many budget hotels have modernized by adding private bathrooms to some of their rooms, leaving fewer guests to share the remaining communal bathrooms. You may even end up with what amounts to a private bath—down the hall.

Finding Places to Shower: If you are vagabonding or spending several nights in transit, you can buy a shower in "day hotels" at major train stations and airports, at some freeway rest stops, and in public baths or swimming pools. Most Mediterranean beaches have free, freshwater showers all the time. I have a theory that after four days without a shower, you don't get any worse, but that's another book.

Toilet Trauma

Every world traveler has one or two great toilet stories that give "going local" a very real meaning. Getting comfortable in foreign restrooms takes a little adjusting, but that's travel. When in Rome, do as the Romans do—and before you know it, you'll be Euro-peein'.

Flummoxing Flushers: In Europe, you may or may not encounter a familiar flushing mechanism. In older bathrooms, toilets may come with a pull string instead of a handle (generally with the tank affixed to the wall rather than the toilet itself). In modern bathrooms, you may see two buttons on top of the tank—one performs a regular flush, the other (for lighter jobs) conserves water. In Great Britain, you'll likely come across the "pump toilet," with a flushing handle that doesn't kick in unless you push it just right: too hard or too soft, and it won't go. (Be decisive but not ruthless.)

Toilet Paper: Like a spoon or a fork, this is another Western "essential" that many people on our planet do not use. What they use varies. I won't get too graphic, but remember that a billion civilized people on this planet never eat with their left hand. While Europeans do use toilet paper, WCs may not always be well stocked. If you're averse to the occasional drip-dry, carry pocket-size tissue packs (easy to buy in Europe) for WCs sans TP. Some countries, such as Greece and Turkey, have very frail plumbing. If you see a wastebasket near the toilet with used toilet paper in it, that's a sign that the sewer system isn't up to snuff. Put your used TP in the wastebasket instead of flushing it. (The rule of thumb in those places: Don't put anything in the toilet unless you've eaten it first.)

Paid Toilets: Paying to use a public WC is a European custom that irks some Americans. But isn't it worth a few coins, considering the cost of water, maintenance, and cleanliness? And you're probably in no state to argue, anyway. Pay toilets are the norm at highway rest areas, train stations, and even at some sights—hang onto your small change for WC stops. (Many coin-op WCs have self-cleaning toilet seats; stick around after you're done to watch the show.)

LEFT This high-tech public toilet offers a free, private place to do your business.

RIGHT Going local

Sometimes the toilet itself is free, but an attendant in the corner sells sheets of toilet paper. Most common is the tip dish by the entry. Caution: Many attendants leave only bills and too-big coins in the tray to bewilder the full-bladdered tourist. The local equivalent of about 50 cents is plenty. The keepers of Europe's public toilets have earned a reputation for crab-

One of Europe's many unforgettable experiences is the rare squat-and-aim toilet.

biness. You'd be crabby, too, if you lived under the street in a room full of public toilets. Humor them, understand them, and carry some change so you can leave them a coin or two.

Women in the Men's Room (and Vice Versa): The female attendants who seem to inhabit Europe's WCs are a popular topic of conversation among male tourists. Sooner or later you'll be minding your own business at the urinal, and the lady will bring you your change or sweep under your feet. Yes, it is distracting, but you'll just have to get used to it—she has. (Women may also see male employees attending to restroom maintenance.)

Gender-Neutral Bathrooms: Some European bathrooms have shared hand-washing facilities for women and men, with adjacent but separate toilet areas. And some restrooms make no distinctions for gender at all.

Squat Toilets: The vast majority of European toilets are similar to our own. But in a few out-of-the-way places, you may find a toilet that consists simply of porcelain footprints and a squat-and-aim hole. If faced with a squat toilet, remember: Those of us who need a throne to sit on are in the minority. Throughout the world, most humans sit on their haunches and nothing more. Sometimes called "Turkish toilets," these are more commonly found in, well, Turkey.

Finding a Public Restroom

I once dropped a tour group off in a town for a potty stop, and when I arrived to pick them up 20 minutes later, none had found relief. Locating a decent public toilet can be frustrating. But with a few tips, you can sniff out a biffy in a jiffy.

Restaurants: You can walk into nearly any restaurant or café, politely and confidently, and find a bathroom. Assume it's somewhere in the back, either upstairs or downstairs. It's easiest in large places that have outdoor seating—waiters will think you're a customer just making a quick trip inside. Some call it rude; I call it survival. If you feel like it, ask permission. Just smile and say, "Toilet?" I'm rarely turned down. Fast-food places usually have a decent and fairly accessible "public" restroom. Timid people buy a drink they don't want in order to use the bathroom, but that's generally unnecessary (although sometimes the secret bathroom door code is printed only on your receipt).

Even at American chains, be prepared for bathroom culture shock. At a big Starbucks in Bern, Switzerland, I opened the door to find an extremely blue space. It took me a minute to realize that the blue lights made it impossible for junkies to find their veins.

Public Buildings: When nature beckons and there's no restaurant or bar handy, look in train stations, government buildings, libraries, large bookstores, market halls, and upper floors of department stores. Parks often have restrooms, sometimes of the gag-a-maggot variety. Never leave a museum without taking advantage of its restrooms—they're clean and usually free. Sometimes you can access a museum's restrooms from the entry hall, without paying to go inside. Large, classy, old hotel lobbies are as impressive as many palaces you'll pay to see. You can always find a royal retreat here, and plenty of soft TP.

Street Toilets: Some large cities make it easy to answer nature's call while out and about. Paris' 400 free self-cleaning public toilets (sanisettes) open with the push of a button. In some other cities, you'll see similar coin-operated, phone booth-like WCs on street corners. London has coin-op street loos; WCs in a few key transit stations (including Cannon Street, Charing Cross, London Bridge, and Victoria) are free.

You may also see free, low-tech public urinals (called pissoirs) that offer just enough privacy for men to find relief... sometimes with a view. Paris unveiled uritrottoirs in high-profile locations in 2018, sparking some controversy—and protests from women who complained that public urinals are sexist. Munich had outdoor urinals until the 1972 Olympics and then decided to beautify the city by doing away with them. What about the people's needs? There's a law in Munich: Any place serving beer must admit the public (whether they're customers or not) to use the toilets.

Photography & Sharing Your Trip

Photographs and travel journals aren't just treasured mementos that spark memories of your journey. They're also the best way to tell others about the places you've been and what you've experienced, whether you share your pictures and thoughts online or collect them in scrapbooks. This chapter outlines some considerations for stand-alone and phone cameras, as well as backing up, editing, organizing, and sharing your photos and writing.

TRAVEL PHOTOGRAPHY

What to Bring

You'll be more relaxed and able to enjoy your trip if you're shooting with a camera you've practiced with beforehand. Phones with high-quality built-in cameras are the handiest way for travelers to take photos—and share them immediately. Many people travel with only a phone or tablet to document their trip and are perfectly happy with the results. But I prefer a dedicated camera that takes higher-quality photos that I can enlarge and print.

Even compact point-and-shoot cameras typically offer more settings and take better photos than phones. Serious photographers prefer digital SLR cameras, which are bulkier but produce more professional-looking images. In between are mirrorless cameras, which offer better image quality than point-and-shoots, but aren't as large as DSLRs. When deciding what to bring, weigh your preference for portability against your desire for better image quality.

Some people prefer to capture Europe in motion using an action camera, such as those from GoPro or Garmin. Many action cameras fit in your front pocket, and accessories make it easy to attach the camera to tripods, handlebars, helmets—you name it. Stick one to your bike helmet in Amsterdam, capture the Bavarian countryside as you glide down a hill on a luge, or create a stunning panorama video at the top of Florence's Duomo.

Consider which accessories you'll want (but, as always, be mindful of packing light):

Memory: Make sure your memory card or phone has plenty of storage space (also see "Managing Images on the Road," later). For video, you'll want higher-capacity storage.

Batteries and Chargers: A portable power bank is handy if you take a lot of pictures and video with your phone; for cameras, bring an additional battery, a battery charger and cable, and a plug adapter. Pack spare rechargeable batteries in your carry-on in a zip-lock bag or in their original packaging (note that lithium batteries aren't allowed in checked bags).

You can take remarkably clear low-light shots—like this serene twilight image of Moscow's Red Square—with the help of a mini-tripod.

Mini-Tripod: Because the flash on most cameras gives a harsh image, it's best to use existing light—which often requires a tripod. A mini-tripod screws into most cameras, sprouts three legs, and holds everything still for slow shutter speeds, timed exposures, and automatic shutter-release shots.

Lenses and Filters: No-frills photographers will stick with the midrange lens that comes with the camera; more serious shutterbugs can look into zoom, wide-angle, image stabilization lenses, and lens shades (to prevent "lens flare" and enhance color in daylight). Add-on lenses are also available for phones. Make sure all your lenses have a haze or UV filter.

Case and Lens Cleaner: If you're packing a separate camera, stow it in a small, padded case inside your day bag; lens-cleaning tissue and solution are wise additions. Steer clear of formal camera bags, which are bulky and attract thieves.

What Not to Bring: The selfie stick is banned in many European sights and marks you (whether you are or not) as one of a rising flood of mindless "bucket list" travelers who photograph themselves in front of famous sights like dogs pee on fire hydrants. I don't like them.

Managing Images on the Road

It's always wise to back up your images. One year, I took some of the best photos I can remember at Chartres Cathedral in France, when the setting sun brought life to the expressions on the delicately carved faces of the Gothic statues. Afterward, I celebrated with a *salade de gésiers* of bouncy lettuce and chicken innards, washed down with a life-is-good carafe of red house wine. Back at my hotel, as I sorted through my intimate moments with those statues through the viewing screen of my camera, I accidentally erased everything on my memory card. That night, I learned several important lessons: 1) Never cull photos with a wine buzz, and 2) be vigilant about backing up. You never know what might happen, from leaving your camera on a train to dropping your memory card in a puddle. Here are some tips for dealing with images while you travel.

Use the cloud. Many travelers back up their photos and video to an online cloud storage or photo-sharing service. Your content is stored safely on servers accessible from anywhere (see the sidebar for options).

Most phones have an automatic photo backup system built in. Activate the cloud settings on your phone to automatically send your latest photos to the cloud whenever you're at a Wi-Fi hotspot. You can also set it to sync your content to your other cloud-enabled devices (tablet, home computer, etc.) the next time they're connected to the internet.

While most cloud services offer a few gigs of online storage for free, expect to pay a small monthly fee for storing lots of photos.

Back up your back up. It's a good idea to back up your images in more than one place. If you travel with a tablet or laptop, you can transfer photos to that device via a card reader, cable, or Wi-Fi. For added safety, you can back up photos from a laptop to a high-capacity USB flash drive. Or

Resources for Photography and Trip Sharing

Digital-Photography-School.com, iPhonePhotographySchool.com: Free tips and tutorials for taking good photos

Apple iCloud, Microsoft OneDrive, Google Photos, Google Drive, Amazon Photos, Dropbox, Flickr: Cloud storage, organization, and photo sharing

Snapseed, VSCO, Adobe Photoshop Express: Photo editing

WordPress, Blogger, Tumblr: Blogging

Day One Journal, BonJournal, PolarSteps Tripcast, Travel Diaries: Travel journal apps

Shutterfly, Snapfish, Mixbook: Tools for creating high-quality photobooks

Wix, Weebly: Website builders for making digital scrapbooks

consider a Wi-Fi enabled memory card, which allows your phone or laptop to access it wirelessly. If you use a phone or tablet to take pictures or videos, a device like MediaShair Hub allows you to wirelessly transfer content to an external hard drive.

Be selective. Cull your images ruthlessly and often, keeping only the best shots. Get in the habit of doing this periodically to avoid bringing home an overwhelming number of photos. You may find it efficient to do some quick photo editing while you're purging your less-than-stellar shots (see "Editing Your Photos," later, for tips).

Tricks for a Good Shot

Whether you use a camera phone or higher-end camera, make sure you understand its features. Take experimental shots, make notes, and see what happens. If you don't understand f-stops or depth of field, you'll find tutorials online and in books (see https://digital-photography-school.com and https://iphonephotographyschool.com). Camera stores sell good books on photography in general and travel photography in particular. I shutter to think how many people are underexposed and lacking depth in this field.

Camera bugs are likely already well-versed in getting good shots, but phone photographers often have more shooting options than they think. Every new generation of camera phone enhances features, from zoom to panorama to video and more. The burst function takes multiple photos at once so you can choose the best; the HDR setting automatically takes several photos at different exposures to get the ideal lighting. Experiment!

Find a creative new angle.

A sharp eye connected to a wild imagination will be your most valuable piece of equipment. Develop a knack for what will look good and be interesting after the trip. The skilled photographer's eye sees striking light, shade, form, lines, patterns, texture, and colors. Try the following tips to get better shots.

Look for a new slant to an old sight. Everyone knows what the Eiffel Tower looks like. Find a unique or different approach to sights that everyone has seen. Shoot the bell tower through the horse's legs, or lay your camera on the floor to shoot the Gothic ceiling.

Capture the personal and intimate details of your trip. Show how you lived, whom you met, and what made each day an adventure (a close-up of a picnic, your favorite taxi driver, or the character you befriended at the launderette).

The Vatican Museum staircase: Have fun with composition.

Vary your perspective. You can shoot close, far, low, high, during the day, and at night. Don't fall into the rut of always centering a shot. Use foregrounds to add color, depth, and interest to landscapes.

Get close. Notice details. Eliminate distractions by zeroing in on your subject. Get so close that you show only one thing. Don't try to show it all in one shot. For any potentially great shot, I try several variations—then delete the ones that don't pan out. The famous war photographer Robert Capa once said, "If your pictures aren't good enough, you're not close enough." My best portraits are so close that the entire head can't fit into the frame.

People are the most interesting subjects. It takes nerve to walk up to people and take their picture. Ask for permission. (If you don't speak the language, point at your camera and ask, "Photo?") It can be difficult, but your subject will probably be delighted. Try to show action. A candid is better than a posed shot. Even a "posed candid" shot is better than a posed one. Give your subject something to do. Challenge your travel companion to juggle oranges in the market. Many photographers take a second shot immediately after the first portrait to capture a looser, warmer subject.

Buildings, in general, are not interesting. It doesn't matter if Karl Marx or Beethoven was born there—a house is as dead as its former resident. As travel photographers gain experience, they take more people shots and fewer buildings or general landscapes.

Maximize good lighting. Real photographers get single-minded at the "magic hours"—early morning and late afternoon—when the sun is very low, light is rich and diffused, and colors glow. Plan for these times. Grab bright colors. Develop an eye for great lighting; any time of day, you may luck into a perfectly lit scene. Some of my best photos are the result of great lighting, not great subjects. Take advantage of a tripod and shoot with longer exposures to create more light in an otherwise dark setting.

Even if your camera is automatic, your subject can turn out to be a silhouette. Get those faces in the sun or (even better) lit from the side. When shooting a portrait, the sun should be behind you. Have the sunlight hit the subject's face at an angle by making sure it's coming over your right or left shoulder. This creates dramatic highlights and shadows on the subject's face. Avoid shooting outdoor portraits during the lighting "dead zone," between 11 a.m. and 2 p.m. If you have to shoot then, use your camera's flash to fill the shadows that form in the eye sockets, under the nose, and under the chin.

The best people shots are up close and well lit, with a soft background.

I like to use a polarizer filter, which eliminates reflections, enhances color separation, and protects my lens. Don't use more than one filter at a time, and don't go cheap.

High-end cameras and camera phones have an adjustable power setting on the flash. Use it to get the right ratio of sunlight to fill light. Some camera phones also can add directional lighting and blur the background for portraits.

Don't be afraid to handhold a slow shot. Tripods enable you to take professional shots that could compete with those at the museum gift shop. But most major museums prohibit you from using a tripod or a flash (which ages paintings). Despite these restrictions, you can take good shots by holding your camera as still as possible or leaning against a wall or banister. Wait until you breathe out to take the picture (when you hold your breath, your body shakes more). Many cameras use "image stabilization" to help in these situations. (And if you still can't get that perfect shot, go to the gift store. Nearly every important museum has a

LEFT Vary your perspective—add extra depth with a foreground.

RIGHT Fill the lens with your subject.

LEFT Capture the magic with just the right light.

RIGHT Back lighting "puts an edge" on your subject.

good selection of top-quality cards and prints at reasonable prices.)

Bracket shots when the lighting is tricky. The best way to get good shots in difficult lighting situations is to "bracket" your shots (take several different pictures of the same scene, slightly varying the exposure and shutter speed settings for each one). You can simply delete the unsuccessful attempts. The HDR setting on camera phones does this automatically.

Editing Your Photos

Even the most skilled photographers edit their photos, improving variables such as contrast, color, and sharpness. You can do basic editing such as cropping right on your camera or phone; apps such as Snapseed, VSCO, and Adobe Photoshop Express provide more robust tools. More serious shutterbugs use Adobe Photoshop Elements (an easy-to-use program for novices), Adobe Lightroom, or Adobe Photoshop.

Editing your photos—cropping out distractions around the edges, tweaking colors, and enhancing lighting—before posting online or creating an album will improve their impact. Go easy though: If you can tell that a photo has been edited, you've edited too much.

SHARING YOUR TRIP

On my first trip to Europe at age 14, I collected and logged my journey in a file of several hundred numbered postcards, each packed with notes. Throughout the '70s and '80s, I eagerly shared my travel experiences through slideshows.

But now it's all about sharing travel tales through blogs, social media, and digital journals, slideshows, and scrapbooks.

Digital File Sharing

Sharing photos with friends and family is part of the joy of taking them. If you use an iPhone, you can wirelessly transfer photos to other nearby iPhone or iPad users via AirDrop, which is installed on Apple products. Apps (such as SHAREit) can provide the same functionality for Android, iOS, and PC.

To create and share albums, you can use the preinstalled photo editing tools on your phone or computer (see "Blogs and Journals," later, for more). You can also create shared albums on most cloud services, but some (like Apple's iCloud) are limited to sharing only with others using the same technology. Services such as Google Photos, Amazon Photos, or Dropbox are all good file-sharing options.

Social Media

While on the road and back at home, I interact with thousands of readers via my Facebook page. Each night, my favorite bedtime reading is the comments from my followers. It's become a fun way for us to experience Europe together.

Facebook offers easy photo uploading and albums to organize your photos. Twitter lets you share (or "tweet") pictures and text tidbits from your mobile device as you travel. With Instagram, you can post a string of pictures that document your travels. Pinterest lets you share your photos in albums (called "boards"). Many social media applications are compatible; for example, most allow simultaneous posting to two or more platforms, such as Facebook and Instagram.

Check the privacy settings for every application and device you use to be sure you aren't accidentally sharing your whereabouts with strangers or advertising that your home is unoccupied. Most applications are not automatically set to "private"; you'll have to activate the privacy settings yourself. Facebook and other social media sites allow you to share content to smaller groups within your list of "friends."

Blogs and Journals

While social media is optimal for quick updates, blogging is the best option for lengthy storytelling. Maintaining a blog or journal of your travels is the perfect way to document your journey, as well as entertain family and friends with your adventures.

Blog Hosts: WordPress, Tumblr, and Blogger all have basic free versions and are relatively easy to use, with templates and customization options. You can post text, photos, audio, video, slideshows, links, and more; set your blog to automatically publish at staggered times; and have multiple people contribute to one blog. You can also link your blog to your Facebook or Twitter account. These blogging platforms also have apps that let you post from your mobile device.

Digital Travel Journals: Apps such as Day One Journal, BonJournal, PolarSteps Tripcast, and Travel Diaries allow you to create a travel journal using a variety of tools. You can chart your route and add photos, videos, and stories to create a trip journal that you can share with others. Apps offer different options—for instance, automatic trip tracking, printable books, text dictation, or collaboration with other travelers in your group. Look around and test various apps to see what works best for your storytelling style.

A handwritten journal can become a cherished souvenir.

Whichever host you choose, here are some guidelines for creating a memorable blog:

- When posting stories online, think about interactive elements that combine entertaining, insightful text with engaging videos and photos.
- Consider embedding slideshows or links to related websites and resources. Slideshare.net is a helpful presentation-sharing site, but you must link it to your Facebook or LinkedIn account.
- Include amusing tidbits or interesting quotes to spice up your stories.
- If struggling for inspiration, consider implementing a theme or ongoing elements like a "picture of the day."

Pen-and-Paper Journals: For many, the best way to document your trip as you travel is to pick up a pen and put your experiences to paper. Even in my days as a vagabond backpacker, I was a keen and disciplined journal writer. Journaling the old-fashioned way has no limits, word counts, or caps on creativity.

Postcards from Europe

On my first solo trip to Europe, in 1973–just after high school graduation–I wrote postcards home nearly every day. I packed so much information onto each card it was a challenge to read them without a magnifying glass. Looking back on these exuberant little reports back to my family, I can see a travel writer in waiting.

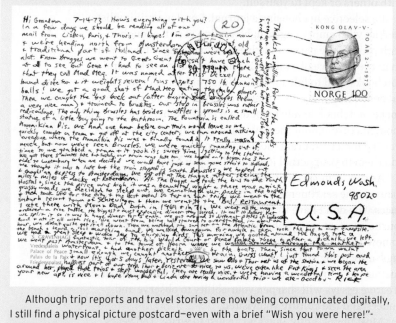

Although trip reports and travel stories are now being communicated digitally, I still find a physical picture postcard–even with a brief "Wish you were here!"-type message–a nice touch. It's fun for people back home to get a personal message that has traveled thousands of miles from another country.

If sending postcards, you may have to contend with a European post office. These can be handy and efficient or jam-packed and discouraging, depending on the country. In general, small-town post offices can be less crowded and more user-friendly. If possible, avoid the Italian male...I mean, mail. Service is best north of the Alps. Postcard stamps are often sold in machines at post offices, as well as at neighborhood newsstands, gift shops that sell cards, or your hotel's front desk. (Write your postcards before getting stamps–you may be in the next country by the time you're ready to mail them.)

To send your own photos as a postcard, try an app such as Postagram and SnapShot Postcard. For about $2 per card they will print and send custom postcards for you via snail mail. Just choose a photo from your phone along with a template, type a message, and the postcard will be on its way–all without stepping foot inside a post office.

Great travel journals describe both the inner and outer journey—your physical surroundings and sensory experiences as well as your emotions and thoughts at the time. Transcribing intimate details into your journal will allow you to revisit a place time and time again, whether shared with others or kept to yourself.

Be selective in choosing a journal. I prefer a minimalist booklet with empty pages, lightweight yet stiff enough to both protect the pages and give me something solid to write on in the absence of a table. Consider a bound book; spiral notebooks tend to fall apart. I write in black ink or mechanical pencil, allowing my simple words to be the focus. Keep a pocket notebook handy to jot down brief moments or fleeting thoughts throughout the day—such as while at a bus stop or waiting for a restaurant meal. You can expand on these and add them to your actual journal when you have time.

As you write, avoid guidebook-type data and instead focus on the sentimental effects and imagery of your experiences. You don't have to give a chronological account of your journey. In fact, you probably shouldn't. Consider just sitting somewhere interesting and writing about your surroundings or focusing an entry on a specific topic: strange cultural customs or a touching moment, for instance. Throwing in creative essays will sharpen your ability to observe and understand the culture you visited.

Most importantly, don't write just to write. Ten years from now, you won't feel the need to recall the mediocre meal you grabbed at that café or the quality of the hotel's complimentary breakfast. Leave out the boring stuff. You want to include details that define the character of a place as well as your personal response. Include sketches, mementos, little paper souvenirs like maps and old tickets—anything that takes you back to that moment. Combining these personal touches with candid accounts and reflective musings will create a travel souvenir you'll forever cherish.

Digital Slideshows, Galleries, and Scrapbooks

When it comes to showing off photos of your trip, you have many options, from making prints of your favorite photos to designing a printed photobook to creating a digital gallery or scrapbook.

Before displaying your photos, it's best to organize them. Apps such as Google Photos, Flickr, and Amazon Photos help you organize and share your images. Some websites offer more options—for example, Smilebox can help you create a slideshow story with music and captions. The de facto video-sharing site is YouTube, which offers high-quality, free video hosting with detailed privacy controls.

Photobooks and Scrapbooks: Creating a scrapbook online is simple—a few clicks and personal touches, and you've got your own coffee-table masterpiece. Snapfish and Shutterfly (owned by the same company), along with Mixbook are all easy-to-use sites where you can upload, view, organize, and edit photos, then order a printed photobook, prints, posters, and more. Or make a scrapbook the old-fashioned way, with photo archival paper...and a glue stick.

Your friends will enjoy seeing photos of the different characters you meet.

Free-Form Digital Scrapbooks: Using a website builder like Wix or Weebly, or one of the blogging or travel journal websites mentioned earlier, you can compile your trip notes and photos into a detailed and polished website, as a cherished tribute to your European adventure. Each year at Rick Steves' Europe, we hold a contest for our tour members to see who's created the best digital scrapbook of their recent trip with us (the top prize is a free tour). For lots of great inspiration, peruse the award-winning entries at RickSteves.com/tours/scrapbooks.

Let's Travel!

International travel can feel like a big step for anyone. More than logistics, travel is a deeply personal experience. It's reasonable to ask: How will my background, identity, and outlook resonate with those I meet? How can I embrace new experiences in a way that meshes with my individual needs? This chapter addresses the concerns and interests of solo travelers (including issues specific to women), LGBTQ travelers, travelers of color, families, students, seniors, and travelers with disabilities. Europe is waiting. Let's travel!

SOLO TRAVELERS

I've talked to many people who put off their travel dreams because they don't want to do it by themselves. If you want to go to Europe but don't have a partner, consider gathering the courage to go it alone. You'll meet plenty of people as you travel: Think of them as a montage of fun, temporary travel partners.

Traveling solo has its pros and cons—and for me, the pros far outweigh the cons. When you're on your own, you're independent and in control. You can travel at your own pace, do the things that interest you, eat where and when you like, and splurge where you want to splurge. You don't have to wait for your partner to pack up, and you never need to negotiate where to eat or when to call it a day. You go where you want, when you want, and you can get the heck out of that stuffy museum when all the

Traveling without a tour, you'll have the locals dancing *with* you—not for you.

Traveling alone immerses you in Europe.

Monets start to blur together. If ad-libbing, it's easier for one to slip between the cracks than two.

Of course, there are downsides to traveling alone: When you're on your own, you don't have a built-in dining companion. You've got no one to send ahead while you wait in line, help you figure out the bus schedule, or commiserate with when things go awry. And traveling by yourself is usually more expensive. With a partner, hotel accommodations cost less because they're shared. Other things become cheaper too when you're splitting costs, such as groceries, guidebooks, taxis, storage lockers, and more.

But when you travel with others, it's natural to focus on them—how you're getting along, whether they meant it when they said they weren't hungry—and tune out the symphony of sights, sounds, and smells all around you. Traveling on your own allows you to be more present and open to your surroundings. You'll meet more people—you're seen as more approachable. You're more likely to experience the kindness of strangers.

Solo travel can be intensely introspective. You may discover more about yourself at the same time you're discovering more about Europe. Traveling on your own is fun, challenging, vivid, and exhilarating. Realizing that you have what it takes to be your own guide is a thrill known only to solo travelers. Your trip is a gift from you to you.

Traveling Alone Without Feeling Lonely

For many people contemplating a solo trip, loneliness is their biggest fear. Big cities can be cold and ugly when the only person to talk to is yourself. And being sick and alone in a country where no one knows you can be a sad and miserable experience.

Fortunately, combating loneliness in Europe is easy. The continent is full of travelers and natural meeting places, especially in peak season. And the internet offers

Traveling with a Partner

Although I love trekking through Europe by myself, there's nothing like that special lifelong bond that forms between you and the person you've dined with, slept with, and trudged around in the rain with for two weeks straight in a foreign land.

A group of travel buddies defending Caesar's empire atop Hadrian's Wall in Britain

But your choice of travel partner is critical—it can make or break a trip. Traveling with the wrong partner can be like a bad blind date that lasts for weeks. I'd rather do it alone. One summer I went to Europe to dive into as many cultures and adventures as possible. I planned to rest when I got home. My partner wanted to slow life down, get away from it all, relax, and escape the pressures of the business world. Our ideas of acceptable hotels and how much time we wanted to spend eating were quite different. The trip was a near disaster.

Traveling together greatly accelerates a relationship—especially a romantic one. You see each other constantly and make endless decisions. The niceties go out the window. Everything becomes very real; you're in an adventure, a struggle, a hot-air balloon for two. The experiences of years are jammed into weeks. If you haven't traveled with your companion before, consider a trial weekend together before merging dream trips. Any shared trip is a good test of a relationship—often revealing its ultimate course. I'd highly recommend a little premarital travel.

Many people already have their partner—for better or for worse. Couples should take particular care to minimize the stress of traveling together by recognizing each other's need for independence. Too many couples do Europe as a three-legged race, tied together from start to finish. Have an explicit understanding that there's absolutely nothing selfish, dangerous, insulting, or wrong about splitting up occasionally. This is a freedom too few travel partners allow themselves. Doing your own thing for a few hours or days breathes fresh air into your togetherness, making those shared experiences all the more memorable.

connections with locals eager to welcome you to their home turf.

Meeting People: You'll run across vaga-buddies every day. If you stay in hostels, you'll have a built-in family (hostels are open to all ages). Or choose small pensions and B&Bs, where the owners and fellow travelers sharing breakfast have time to talk. At most tourist sights, you'll meet more people in an hour than you would at home in a day. If you're feeling shy, cameras are good icebreakers, even in our "selfie" era; offer to take someone's picture with his or her camera.

It's easy to meet people on buses and trains. When you meet locals who speak English, find out what they think—about anything. Take your laundry and a deck of cards to a launderette and turn solitaire into gin rummy. You'll end up with a stack of clean clothes and interesting conversations.

Learn how to say "pretty baby" in the local language. If you play peek-a-boo with a baby or fold an origami bird for a kid, you'll make friends with the parents as well as the child.

Take a group walking tour of a city (ask at the tourist office). You'll learn about the town and meet other travelers, too. Food tours, cooking classes, sports events, and excursions can also be great social experiences; search online or ask at your hotel or hostel. Airbnb, ToursByLocals, and TravelLocal offer good options. Likeminded individuals can find one another on Meetup.com, which has worldwide members who welcome visitors to diverse events such as photography walks, happy hours, and weekend ski trips.

Use your social media connections to find out if anyone you know has friends or family in the destinations that you'll be visiting, then drop them a note about your upcoming trip. Consider joining a hospitality-exchange network, which can help you find events and free accommodations (see "Lodging for Solo Travelers," later in this chapter). Facebook's events listings are as popular abroad as they are in the US.

Eating Out: Dining solo is as common in Europe as it is in the US, and you'll rarely stand out as you sit down alone at a restaurant. But some countries have special meals that are more fun to experience with others. You could invite someone to join you for, say, a *rijsttafel* dinner in the Netherlands, a *smorgasbord* in Scandinavia, a fondue in Switzerland, a paella feast in Spain, or a spaghetti feed in an Italian trattoria. Just say to someone whose company you might enjoy, "Would you like to meet up for dinner?" Wondering whom to ask? People with Rick Steves guidebooks are like an extended family in Europe. My readers are on the trail of the same travel thrills, and happy to share in the adventure.

If you're feeling sociable, eat in places so crowded and popular that all the tables are shared, or ask other single travelers if they'd like to join you.

Phrase book + big smile = plenty of friends

Eat in the members' kitchen of a hostel; you'll always have companions. Make it a potluck.

Or consider alternatives to formal sit-down meals. Try a self-service café, a local-style fast-food restaurant, or a small ethnic eatery. Visit a supermarket deli or food truck and get a picnic to eat in the square or a park. Get a slice of pizza from a takeout shop and munch it as you walk, people-watching and window-shopping.

If you prefer to eat alone, stay busy. Use the time to learn more of the language. Practice your verbal skills with the waiter or waitress (when I asked a French waiter if he had kids, he proudly showed me a picture of his twin girls). Read a guidebook, a novel, or the international edition of the *New York Times*. Do trip planning, draw in your journal, update your social media feed, or text a few photos to the folks back home.

For a writer like me, spending an afternoon at a café is a great way to get some writing done; for the cost of a beverage and a snack, you'll be granted more peace and privacy than at a public fountain or other open space.

Evenings: Experience the magic of European cities at night. Go for a walk along well-lit streets. With gelato in hand, enjoy the parade of people, busy shops, and illuminated monuments. You'll invariably feel a sense of companionship when lots of people are around. Take advantage of the wealth of evening entertainment: concerts, movies, and dance performances. Some cities offer tours after dark: You can see Paris by night on a river cruise or take a ghost walk in London.

If you like to stay in at night, get a room with a balcony overlooking a square. You'll have a front-row seat to the best show in town. Read novels set in the country you're visiting. Post travel news to your friends and family so you'll find friendly answers from another time zone in your notifications in the morning. Learn to treasure solitude. Go early to bed, be early to rise. Shop at a lively morning market for fresh rolls and join the locals for coffee.

Lodging for Solo Travelers

Solo travelers need to do some extra legwork to find hotel accommodations that offer a good value. Rarely is a single room just half the price of a double. If a double room costs $100, a single room will generally be about $80—making your stay $30 more expensive each night than if you were sharing the room and the cost. True single rooms are also relatively rare, so you may find yourself paying for a double more often than you'd like.

You can use websites such as Booking.com or Hotels.com to find hotels that offer accommodations for solo travelers. Filter your results for true singles with one twin bed in your price range. Once you've zeroed in on the best options, book directly with the hotel of your choice.

Hostels welcome travelers of all ages and are in the business of renting out single bunks. Not only is this an affordable option, it's an excellent way to meet others. Hostels also sometimes have private rooms, which may be cheaper than a single in a budget hotel.

Other alternatives include home-sharing services such as Airbnb, Servas, and Couchsurfing. Here you can find affordable accommodations ranging from a young city-dweller's sofa to a guest bedroom in a farmhouse to a studio apartment all your own. Servas and Couchsurfing, in particular, are focused on bringing hosts and visitors together for cultural exchange and camaraderie (see the "'Voluntourism' and Cultural Exchanges" sidebar later in this chapter for more info).

Safety for Solo Travelers

All travelers should exercise common sense and caution when it comes to personal security abroad (for general tips, see the Theft & Scams chapter). For solo travelers, this means greater self-reliance and being particularly aware of your surroundings.

Use street smarts. Be well prepared so that you don't need to depend on someone unless you want to—carry cash, a map, a guidebook, and a phrase book. Walk purposefully with your head up; look like you know where you're going. If you get lost in an unfriendly neighborhood, be savvy about whom you ask for help; seek out a police officer or a family, or go into a store or restaurant to ask for directions or to study your map.

Be proactive about public transportation. Use the same caution in taxis and on buses and subways that you would at home. Consider daytime departures and arrivals when you plan long-distance travel. You may want to visit the train or bus station the day before your departure, so you'll know where it is, how long it takes to reach it, if it feels safe, and what services it has. Reconfirm your departure time. If you're leaving late at night and the bus or train station is sketchy, hang out in your hotel's lounge or in a café until you need to head for the station.

Unless you're fluent in the language, accept the fact that you won't always know what's going on. Although it might seem worrisome, there's a reason why the Greek bus driver drops you off in the middle of nowhere. It's a transfer point, and another bus will come along in a few minutes. You'll often discover that the locals are looking out for you. However, a healthy dose of skepticism and an eagle eye in crowded and isolated places will help you stay safe.

Stay connected. Make it a habit to update family and friends back home about your itinerary. Talk over your plans with your hotelier before you head out, especially at night.

Trust your gut. If a situation or locale doesn't feel right, leave. It *is* better to be safe than sorry.

Tips for Solo Women Travelers

Thanks to my female staffers and their friends for assembling their top tips for women.

Theft and harassment are often concerns for women traveling alone. My female colleagues assure me that if you've traveled alone in America, you're more than prepared for Europe. In America, theft and harassment are especially scary because of their connection with violence. In Europe, you'll rarely, if ever, hear of violence. Theft is past tense (as in, "Where did my wallet go?"). As for experiencing harassment, you're far more likely to think, "I'm going to ditch this jerk ASAP" than, "This jerk is going to hurt me."

In general, use the same good judgment you use at home. Begin with caution and figure out as you travel what feels right to you. Here are some tips for a safe, smooth, enjoyable trip.

Plan carefully for overnight train travel. If you take an overnight train, avoid sleeping in empty compartments. Rent a *couchette* for a small surcharge, which puts you with roommates in a compartment you can lock, in a car monitored by an attendant. You may be assigned to an all-female compartment as a matter of course, but if not, ask for female roommates. Certain countries, such as Spain, are better about accommodating requests than others.

Seek out other female travelers to swap tales and advice

Books for the Woman Traveling Alone

Practical Advice

Gutsy Women: Stories, Advice, Inspiration (Marybeth Bond, 2012): Funny, instructive, and inspiring ideas for solo travelers

Kicking Ass on the Road: The Ultimate Guide for the Solo Woman Traveler (Sunni Dawson, 2016): Empowering guide covering everything from insurance to romance

The Solo Traveler's Handbook (Janice Leith Waugh, 2012): A how-to guide with lots of anecdotes

Women with Wanderlust: A Guide to Roaming (Melissa D. Jones, 2016): Tips and tricks gleaned from travel through 40 countries

Tales from the Road

The Best Women's Travel Writing: True Stories from Around the World (Lavinia Spalding, ed.): Anthologies of funny and inspirational tales, with a new edition every few years

Expat: Women's True Tales of Life Abroad (Christina Henry de Tessan, ed., 2002): A collection of stories about how the reality of life abroad matches up to the fantasy

Go Your Own Way: Women Travel the World Solo (Faith Conlon and others, eds., 2007): Cultural revelations mixed with advice for the female traveler

A Woman's Europe: True Stories (Marybeth Bond, ed., 2004): Europe from a totally female point of view

Humor

More Sand in My Bra: Funny Women Write from the Road, Again! (Jennifer L. Leo, ed., 2007): Travel shenanigans

The Unsavvy Traveler: Women's Comic Tales of Catastrophe (Rosemary Caperton, Anne Mathews, and Lucie Ocenas, eds., 2005): A collection of humorous and cathartic misadventures

Be prepared to interact with European men. If you never talk to men in Europe, you could miss out on a chance to learn about the country. So, by all means, talk to men. Just choose the man and choose the setting.

In northern Europe, you won't draw any more unwanted attention from men than you do in America. In southern Europe, particularly in Italy, you may get more attention than you're used to, but it's usually in the form of the "long look." Be aware that in the Mediterranean world, when you smile and look a man in the eyes, it can be considered an invitation for conversation (or more). Wear dark sunglasses and you can stare all you want.

Create conditions that are likely to turn out in your favor. Standards of dress and modesty vary across Europe; take your cues from local women. Avoid walking alone at night, particularly in unlit areas with few people around. Don't be overly polite if you're bothered by someone; it's your prerogative to set boundaries that feel comfortable. If a man comes too close, say "no" firmly and loudly in the local language. That's usually all it takes.

If you feel like you're being followed or hassled, don't worry about overreacting or seeming foolish. Yell if the situation warrants it. Or head to the nearest hotel and chat up the person behind the desk until your unwanted companion moves on. Ask the hotelier to call a cab to take you to your own hotel, hostel, or B&B.

There's no need to tell anyone that you're traveling alone or to disclose your relationship status. Lie unhesitatingly. You're traveling with your husband. He's waiting for you at the hotel. He's a professional wrestler who retired from the sport for psychological reasons.

If you're arranging to meet someone, choose a public place. Tell them you're staying at a hostel: You have a 10 p.m. curfew and 29 roommates. Better yet, bring a couple of your roommates along to the meeting. After the introductions, let everyone know where you're going and when you'll return.

By using common sense, making good decisions, and above all else, having confidence in yourself and your ability to travel on your own, you'll be rewarded with rich experiences—and great stories to tell your friends.

LGBTQ TRAVELERS

Gabe Gunnink is a former educator on LGBTQ issues and a current travel consultant at Rick Steves' Europe. A long-distance runner, he has represented the US in gay sporting events across Europe and enjoys uncovering the queer history hidden in every city.

Today's lesbian, gay, bisexual, transgender, and queer

Resources for LGBTQ Travelers

Equaldex.com: Thorough database of country-specific laws/policies regarding sexual orientation and gender identity

Travel.state.gov: Find tips under the "International Travel/Before You Go/Travelers with Special Considerations" tab

IGLTA.org: LGBTQ-friendly hotels, travel agents, and tour companies recommended by the International Gay and Lesbian Travel Association, as well as a comprehensive LGBTQ events calendar

ManAboutWorld.com: Digital magazine and free city guides for gay travelers; their exemplary *LGBTQ Guide to Travel Safety* covers considerations for female, nonbinary, and transgender travelers

PurpleRoofs.com: LGBTQ-owned/-friendly hotels and B&Bs; also hosts a variety of LGBTQ travel blogs

TSA.gov/transgender-passengers: Airport security guidelines for transgender passengers

TransEquality.org/issues/travel: Transgender rights advocacy group's exhaustive guide to US airport security

RefugeRestrooms.org: Searchable global database of handicap-accessible, unisex, and family restrooms; also available as a free app

Quist: Free app that plots LGBTQ and HIV points of interest on an interactive map

(LGBTQ) travelers planning a trip to Europe will find increasingly progressive European countries and a burgeoning pool of travel agents, tour guides, and local businesses that cater directly to the LGBTQ community. And while some companies stereotype LGBTQ vacationers as glittery partygoers, there are opportunities for all types of LGBTQ travelers. Whether you're looking for a classic European grand tour or a uniquely queer experience, it's important to know your rights and realize that gender and sexuality are not barriers to enriching adventures overseas.

Happily, Europe has been at the vanguard of LGBTQ rights for several decades: The European Union began combatting sexual orientation discrimination in 1999; Amsterdam hosted the world's first gay marriages in 2001; and Iceland, Belgium, Luxembourg, Ireland, and Serbia have all elected openly LGBTQ heads of state. However, as in the US, certain regions of Europe are more welcoming to LGBTQ people than others, and ideologies shift between urban and rural communities. Central, northern, and western Europe are almost universally embracing of LGBTQ people, as are large cities throughout the Continent. In contrast, rural regions of eastern and southern Europe often operate under an unspoken "don't ask, don't tell" policy and occasionally exhibit outright hostility. Russia has made headlines for its anti-gay laws and attitudes, sentiments which ripple through other nations of the former Soviet bloc.

Tips for LGBTQ Travelers

Know your destinations. To research the laws and policies in any country, consult Equaldex.com, which provides helpful maps and summaries on issues ranging from same-sex marriage to changing gender to employment discrimination. You can also sign up to receive general travel alerts for your destination from the US State Department at Travel.state.gov.

Understand the risks. Be aware of the risks of visiting less-welcoming regions and consider how "out" you want to be. Balancing safety and values can be a challenge. While some LGBTQ people have bodies and personal styles that allow them to conform to "normative" expectations, LGBTQ travelers who value androgyny or public displays of affection are more visible—and assume greater risk. Travelers in regions with anti-gay laws or attitudes should be especially wary of using gay dating apps, which have been utilized by police and others to entrap gay men.

"Pink money" talks. As LGBTQ people have become more visible and accepted, the collective purchasing power of "pink money" has grown. Many businesses are happy to cater to LGBTQ travelers. Hotels, resorts, cruises, tour companies, and entire destinations brand themselves as gay-friendly paradises to capitalize on this valuable market. Notable examples of "gaycation" hot spots include Sitges near Barcelona, Brighton near London, and the Greek island of Mykonos.

Seek out diverse options. The side effect of "pink money" is gay tours, events, and resorts that are overwhelmingly targeted at white, male, affluent travelers. A growing number of local guides and travel companies are striving to include the full diversity of the LGBTQ community. Walking tour groups such as The Gay Locals in Paris, Quiiky in Italy, and Original Berlin Walks balance LGBTQ points of interest with traditional sights and actively seek to include all travelers, regardless of race, gender, or ability. And online resources like Man About World and the International Gay and Lesbian Travel Association (IGLTA) provide recommendations to a wide spectrum of travelers.

Navigate safely. If you're considering taking a cab in an area where you aren't completely comfortable, consider using Uber, which has an international support line where you can easily report issues in English. The Uber app allows drivers to see a photo before picking you up, so it's wise to check that it matches your current appearance.

Find a home away from home. The best launch pads for meaningful European exploration are locally operated hotels and B&Bs that put you in the heart of a city. My guidebooks are full of accommodation listings with kind, open-minded owners. If you prefer specifically LGBTQ-owned options, online directory PurpleRoofs.com can connect you with quaint, queer-friendly establishments across Europe. Big chain hotels such as Marriott, Hilton, and Hyatt can also provide peace of mind to nervous LGBTQ travelers.

Paris, like many major European cities, has an array of gay-themed festivals and sporting events.

Celebrate Pride worldwide. It's fun to time your trip to coincide with local Pride celebrations, which flood the streets of Europe's major cities with polychromatic parades. Europe offers many other gay-friendly festivals and events to consider. L Fest invites lesbian, bisexual, and trans women to Wales for a weekend of music, art, and social events. The EuroGames welcome LGBTQ athletes to compete in dozens of sporting events each summer. Front Runners clubs invite runners and walkers of all ages and abilities to join weekly workouts followed by dinner or drinks. Even the winter months offer festivals such as the Heavenue gay Christmas market in Cologne and Arosa Gay Ski Week in Switzerland. Find a calendar of LGBTQ events around the world at IGLTA.org/Events.

Transgender Travelers

Transgender travelers face unique—but far from prohibitive—challenges. Two of the largest issues that disproportionately affect transgender travelers are packing and airport security, especially for those who regularly use prostheses or medications. It's smart to leave extra time for the airport security process, and follow these tips to reduce hassle and stress.

Make sure your documents match. When you purchase your airline tickets, remember that TSA agents will not let you through security if the names on your passport and airline ticket do not match exactly. If you have legally changed your name since your passport was issued, you'll either need to update it or use your former name when purchasing airline tickets. However, according to the National Center for Transgender Equality, your physical appearance and gender presentation are not required to match the picture on your passport, and security agents should not comment on it.

Although many major US airlines now offer multiple gender options for tickets—male (M), female (F), unspecified (X), and undisclosed (U)—US passports currently allow only male and female options (though lawmakers are working to change this). When traveling internationally, it's best to have the sex markers on your tickets and your passport match. Check Travel.State.Gov for the most current information: See the "Change or Correct a Passport" page for information on name changes, and the "Change of Sex Marker" page for information on sex markers and transitional passports.

Practice smart packing. Remember that medically necessary liquids and gels are exempt from the usual carry-on luggage volume limits. You'll need to notify a TSA agent if you have items exceeding these limits and remove them from your luggage. If you are checking a bag, consider placing all nonessential medications, hormones, syringes, and prostheses in your checked luggage. Otherwise, place all these items in one bag near the top of your carry-on, along with your prescriptions and doctors' notes. This way you can smoothly remove the items and present them to the TSA agent. Also, bring multiple copies of any medical documents. To expedite screening, the TSA website offers downloadable medical notification cards which you can fill out in advance, then discreetly hand to a TSA agent.

Plan for the scan. Full-body scanning machines compare travelers to a generic human outline to identify anomalies or areas of unusual density. If significant deviations from the generic outline are detected, you'll likely be pulled aside for a pat-down. Be aware that bulky clothing and prostheses increase the likelihood of a pat-down. These pat-downs are thorough and may feel invasive, but you should never be asked to expose or remove a prosthetic. You can request a private screening with a witness of your choice and a TSA agent who matches your gender presentation—just ask. Consider registering with TSA Precheck to speed up your security check (see page 68).

The TSA has a toll-free hotline that you can call with any questions at 855-787-2227. If you believe you have been mistreated by airport security, file a complaint with the

Aviation Consumer Protection Division on their website at Transportation.gov/AirConsumer.

Finally, remember that European airport workers are likely to reflect the values of the regions they work in: Consider organizing your trip to fly into a less tolerant region and out of a more tolerant region.

Find accommodating relief. Unlike the US, European nations have not felt the need to legislate transgender people's bathroom access. However, transgender travelers should research a country's laws governing gender change and monitor local attitudes around LGBTQ issues to gauge their safety in various regions. Helpfully, unisex and single-stall WCs are common in Europe, and the Refuge Restrooms app can help you track down WCs in many major European cities. For more tips on finding (and using) public restrooms, see Rick's advice on page 426.

TRAVELERS OF COLOR

People who are not of European descent may wonder how they'll be treated abroad. I've collected the following advice from a wide range of people of color who have lived or traveled extensively in Europe. By and large, the travelers I heard from felt safe and comfortable in Europe. But they did report some issues.

For context, it helps to be mindful of the cultural and historical differences between Europe and the US. On the whole, Europe is more homogenous than the US, with non-white diversity coming mainly in the form of transplants from former colonies or more recent immigrants. Some parts of Europe are home to many people of color, often part of immigrant communities, which face their own challenges; other areas are as white as it gets (and can be pretty clueless when it comes to race).

All of that said, in general, your Americanness will probably be more notable to the Europeans you meet than the color of your skin. (Most Europeans can spot Americans a mile away.) Any stereotypes Europeans might have about your race are likely informed by American culture. For example, Black travelers have told me that they sensed a new respect and appreciation in Europe during

the Obama presidency. But this can cut both ways: A Black woman who taught school in Europe told of a student who freely used language he'd heard in hip-hop music, not realizing how offensive it was.

Travelers of color and mixed-race couples report that their most common source of discomfort in Europe is being stared at. While impolite, these long glances are typically rooted not in disapproval or hostility, but in what one traveler termed "benign curiosity." Put simply, for some Europeans, you're just not who they're used to seeing. Another traveler suggested that this isn't racism so much as "rarism"—Europeans reacting to you as a novelty. Several Black travelers described a more invasive variation on this: Europeans wanting to touch their hair. (Um, no.)

By American standards, Europeans can be opinionated and blunt. What's considered polite conversation in Europe can be shockingly different from our own unwritten rules. Some travelers note they find this weirdly refreshing ("at least it's out in the open") and appreciate the opportunity to do a little educating. Most Europeans are as interested in learning about you as you are in learning about them.

Some travelers of color report feeling more comfortable in cosmopolitan areas and multicultural cities (London, Paris, Amsterdam, Berlin, etc.) than in smaller towns or provincial areas, where there can be more staring or inappropriate comments. On the other hand, in certain areas—for example, cities in southern France where immigration has become an issue—you may feel caught up in someone else's racial tensions. Across Europe, authorities are under pressure to keep out undocumented arrivals—and often that means targeting non-white travelers at border crossings and airport security. Be prepared for the possibility of being closely scrutinized before continuing on your way.

If you're wondering about a specific destination, ask fellow travelers about their experiences. An excellent resource for Black Americans, including destination-specific reports, is the website I'm Black and I Travel (www.imblacknitravel. com). Or seek out a travel writer or blogger who matches your background and travel style.

Will you encounter unfriendliness in your travels? Definitely—and racism may be behind some of it. But several travelers of color noted the importance of not always attributing grumpiness to racism. One told me: "I think we're more likely to interpret bad behavior from non-Americans as being racist because of our history with white Americans.

Often Europeans' impatience is just because we're American, and we're clueless about other people's cultures."

TRAVELING WITH KIDS

When parents tell me they're going to Europe and ask me where to take their kids, I'm sometimes tempted to answer, "to Grandma and Grandpa's on your way to the airport." It's easy to make the case against taking the kids along: A European vacation with kids in tow is more about playgrounds and petting zoos than world-class art and evocative ruins. Out of exhaustion and frustration, you may opt for spendy conveniences like taxis and the first restaurant you find with a kid-friendly menu. Two adults with kids spend twice as much to experience about half the magic of Europe per day than they might without.

But if you can afford it and don't mind accomplishing less as adult sightseers, traveling with your children can be great family fun. Moreover, it's great parenting, as it helps get kids comfortable with the wider world. Taking the kids along changes how you'll experience Europe—in ways that may surprise you.

With kids, you'll live more like a European and less like a tourist. Prioritizing neighborhood parks and public swimming pools over tourist-jammed museums and dim churches opens you up to a slower-paced, more locally grounded approach to a foreign culture. Your children become your ambassadors, opening doors to new experiences and relationships. Your child will be your ticket to countless conversations. Some of your best travel memories may be of your kids floating a wooden boat alongside Parisian *enfants* in the great pond at Luxembourg Garden, or kicking a soccer ball with other *niños* at a park in Madrid. Let them race their new

Conquering peaks on your rental mountain bike (as my proud son Andy did here in Switzerland) and connecting with local families can leave your own family with the most important souvenirs—life-long memories of times shared together.

Italian friends around Siena's main square, the Campo, while you sip your Campari.

And lucky for you, European families enjoy traveling, too. You'll find kids' menus, hotel playrooms, and kids-go-crazy zones at freeway rest stops all over Europe. Parents with a babe-in-arms will generally be offered a seat on crowded buses and sometimes ushered to the front of the line at museums.

The key to a successful European family vacation is to slow down and to temper expectations. Don't overdo it. Tackle one or two key sights each day, mix in a healthy dose of pure fun, and take extended breaks when needed. If you do it right, you'll take home happy memories to share for a lifetime.

What's the Right Age for Europe?

My children are young adults now. But after taking them to Europe every year for their first 20 years, it's fun to think back about our European trips during their childhood. When they were grade-schoolers, our trips were consumed with basic survival issues, such as eating, sleeping, and occupying their attention. By the time they entered their teens, the big challenge became making our trips educational and fun.

Some parents won't take their kids abroad until they are old enough to truly enjoy the trip. My rule of thumb is that children should be able to stand a day of walking, be ready to eat what's in front of them, and be comfortable sleeping in strange beds. They should be able to carry their own daypacks with some clothes, a journal, and a couple of toys. I've found that children are ready for an international trip at about the same age they're ready for a long day at Disneyland.

Grade-school kids are often the easiest travelers, provided you schedule some kid-friendly activities every day. They're happiest staying in rural places with swimming pools and grassy fields to run around in, or in small towns where the crowds, chaos, and must-see sights are manageable.

Tweens and teens feel that summer break is a vacation they've earned. If this European trip is not their trip, you become the enemy. Make it their trip, too, by asking for their help. Kids can quickly get excited about a vacation if they're involved in the planning stages. Give each kid a location to research (a good place to start is the main tourist information website for that destination). Consider your teen's suggestions and make real concessions. Spending some time in cities is essential, and a day of shopping or at the beach could be more fun than another ruined abbey.

If you'd rather remove the stress of planning and have some energy to enjoy adult company, consider taking your kids on an organized tour designed for families. For example, kids as young as eight are welcome on my Family Tours and "My Way" unguided tours. At 12, they can accompany their parents on any Rick Steves tour. Especially in summer, your kids will often find friends in the group, and you'll be able to relax with other adults.

Prepping Your Kids

Before you leave home, get your kids enthusiastic about what they'll be seeing in Europe. Encourage them to learn about the countries, cities, sights, and people they'll be visiting. Look online for articles, photos, and video clips to pique their curiosity.

Read books, both fiction and nonfiction, set in the place you're going, such as *The Diary of a Young Girl* by Anne Frank for Amsterdam, *The Thief Lord* for Venice, or *All the Light We Cannot See,* about a blind French girl and German boy during World War II. For younger kids, check out M. Sasek's delightfully illustrated *This Is* series on various European destinations (*This is Venice, This is Edinburgh,* and so on). Watch movies, such as *Paddington* and *Paddington 2* for London, *The Sound of Music* for Salzburg, *The Red Balloon* or *Hugo* for Paris, or *The Secret of Roan Inish* for Ireland. Your hometown library can be a great resource for age-appropriate books and movies. LittlePassports.com offers suitcase-shaped boxes with maps, games, and activities designed to spark children's interest in going abroad (subscribe for about $25 a month).

For a fun sneak peek into the destinations you'll be visiting, you can stream full-length *Rick Steves' Europe* TV episodes on my website. Or for specific subjects, try my free online video library, Rick Steves Classroom Europe, with a searchable database of short video clips on European history, art, culture, and geography

Resources for Family Travel

NatGeoKids.com/uk: Find fun facts galore on the British version of National Geographic's site for children

FamilyVacationCritic.com and **CiaoBambino.com:** Trip-planning resources and reports for travel with babies and kids

TravelforKids.com: Comprehensive listing of fun things to do with kids worldwide

TravelswithBaby.com: Baby and toddler travel tips from author Shelly Rivoli

Reading

Kids' Travel Guide series (Flying Kids): Combo travel guide/activity books for major cities and countries; full list at TheFlyingKids.com

Scavenger Hunt Adventures series (Catherine Aragon): Explore Europe's great cities on a scavenger hunt for art, culture, and landmarks; titles include *Mission London, Mission Barcelona, Mission Amsterdam,* and others

City Trails series (Lonely Planet): Two young explorers find weird and wonderful secrets in destinations including London, Paris, and more

100 Tips for Traveling with Kids in Europe (E. Ashley Steel and Bill Richards, 2016): Practical tips and places to go based on the authors' travels in more than 40 countries with two kids

Travels with Baby: The Ultimate Guide for Planning Travel with Your Baby, Toddler, and Preschooler (Shelly Rivoli, 2014): Award-winning manual for managing with the youngest of travelers

(classroom.ricksteves.com). Kids might also enjoy reading my blog (blog.ricksteves.com), where they can search for posts about the places and sights on your itinerary.

Get a jump on foreign phrases. Type out the top 20 or so and put them on the fridge for everyone to learn. Get the *10 Minutes a Day* language book for your destination, which comes with sticky word labels that your kids will enjoy plastering around the house. My phrasebooks are also accessible and fun to use. Kids might especially enjoy language-learning game apps like Duolingo (see page 392).

Try to relate your children's hobbies or favorite games to the place you're visiting (draw pictures of the Eiffel Tower, play dominoes saying the numbers in Italian). Give your kids the chance to try out foreign specialties in advance by eating at ethnic restaurants, or download some recipes and make meals together at home. Many US cities host celebrations of different cultures—look for festivals held by local communities of Greeks, Italians, Hungarians, or whatever group might be vibrant in your town or relevant to your travels.

Travel Documents for Kids

You'll need the proper documents—even babies need

passports (see the Paper Chase chapter for specifics on passports, visas, and Covid entry requirements). For children of any age, bring an official copy of their birth certificate, in addition to their passport (and a photocopy of their passport). For parents of adopted children, it's a good idea to bring their adoption decree as well. These documents are especially important if you have a different last name than your child. Keep these documents separate from your passports, as they'll be a huge help if you end up needing to get a replacement passport for your child.

If you're traveling with a child who isn't yours (say, a niece or grandkid), bring along a signed, notarized document from the parent(s) to prove to authorities that you have permission to take the child on a trip. Even a solo parent traveling with children must demonstrate that the other parent has given approval. Specifically, the letter should grant permission for the accompanying adult to travel internationally with the child. Include your name, the name of the child, the dates of your trip, destination countries, and the name, address, and phone number of the parent(s) at home. Before flying, prepare young children for passport-control questions: For example, officers may ask children their names and the whereabouts of the nonaccompanying parent(s).

You may want to bring extra passport photos with you. Since infants and toddlers change so quickly, carry pictures that were taken for the passport, as well as ones taken close to your departure date. Most parents hold onto their kids' passports, but if you have older children who'll be out on their own, you could get them a money belt or neck pouch for carrying their cash and ID.

Outfit younger kids with ID wristbands or lanyards holding emergency contact information. You can update your hotel name and contact info as you go. Or improvise by writing your phone number on a piece of paper to tuck into a pocket or shoe. In a pinch, you could write your contact number—gently—on your child's arm with a pen.

What to Bring

The amount and type of gear you need depends on the age of your child. Since a baby on the road requires a lot of equipment, the key to happiness is a rental car or a long stay in one place, especially one that offers baby gear. If you're visiting friends or family or planning a home stay, your hosts may be able to provide a car seat, stroller, and travel crib so you won't have to pack them. If you have older kids, let them know they'll be hauling their own luggage through airports and down cobblestone streets. Pack as light as you can, and think hard about what you'll really need.

With little kids, I found having the best gear was sometimes more important than packing light. We would rent a car because lugging everyone and everything on trains would have been miserable. Once the kids were older, however, I insisted

A sturdy, lightweight stroller is essential for sightseeing with a tot in tow.

on being mobile, and we had a family ethic whereby everyone carried their own stuff...so everyone packed light. (This book's packing tips apply to teens just as much as to adults.)

Infants and Toddlers: It's helpful to have a stroller and a baby carrier. Bringing both will maximize sightseeing: When the bambino gets bored in one you can switch to the other, and then back. Spend a little extra on a solidly built but lightweight stroller that can easily navigate cobblestones. Make sure it has a basket underneath for storing overflow items. A stroller that can recline and has a hood over which to drape a dark blanket allows you to create a good napping environment anywhere. Baby carriers are great for keeping your hands free, and are easier than a stroller on subways and buses.

Prepare to tote more than a tot. A good backpack makes an ideal combo purse/diaper bag that's hands-free and comfortable to carry all day. You can always stow it in your stroller's basket, but be on guard: Purse snatchers target parents (especially while busy, as when changing diapers).

Most hotels in Europe can provide an extra crib—often called a cot—or can give you cushions or bumpers to make a safe sleeping environment on a regular bed. For years, we packed along a travel crib and it worked great—providing a safe and familiar zone for our toddler even in iffy hotel rooms. Look for a lightweight pop-up tent or travel crib that fits in a small carry bag. At a minimum, bring your child's sleep sack or blanket, which can be a comforting reminder of home. If all else fails, get creative: Make a kid-sized nest on the floor from pillows or couch cushions and get your young adventurer excited about indoor "camping."

In addition to being required safety equipment while driving, a car seat can be a stress-saver when traveling by plane, train, or bus. Although it makes for a bulky carry-on, your child's car seat from home is a dose of familiarity and a familiar place for a nap.

Be aware that car-seat attachment points can be different in European cars: If you bring your own seat, pack a car-seat clip in case you need to secure the seat to the shoulder-strap seat belt. You can also arrange a safety seat through your car-rental company (usually an expensive option).

If your child drinks formula, do some research before packing it along: Your usual formula may be available in Europe, but under a different name. Before you fly away, be sure you've packed acetaminophen (easy-dissolving tabs are best), diaper rash cream, a thermometer, and any special medications your baby may need (medically necessary liquids including formula and breast milk are exempted from the volume limit for carry-on liquids, but make sure they are labeled and declare them to the screener).

Older Kids: Technology can make the difference between a dream trip and a nightmare. A tablet or portable gaming device can fill long hours traveling between destinations and soak up time when dinner drags on. Load up on kid-friendly apps, ebooks, movies, and TV shows before you leave. Get a Y-jack so two kids can listen with earbuds. There's nothing like a favorite show to help calm your kids before bedtime. Consider giving each kid their own camera so they can take pictures and make movies from their own perspective. (Back home, encourage older kids to organize and edit photos and video clips.)

Toys: Too many toys can take up lots of suitcase space (though a small toy or stuffed animal from home can be comforting). You can easily buy toys and sports equipment in Europe. The cheapest toy selection is often in large department stores. For the athletic child, a soccer ball guarantees hours of amusement with newfound friends on foreign turf.

A trip to a European toy store can be a fun outing. For quiet time in the hotel room, buy a set of Legos, coloring books, stickers, dolls, or other toys, which can be excitingly different from those found in the US.

Flying with Kids

Deciding whether to buy a separate plane ticket for your child under age two is a matter of what you can endure in the air: That cute gurgling baby might become the airborne hellion as soon as the seat-belt light goes on. If you elect to keep your child on your lap, you'll still pay the tax on the ticket cost for an international flight. The child doesn't get a seat, but many airlines have baby perks for moms and dads who request them in advance—roomier bulkhead seats, bassinets, and baby meals.

Kids age two and up are required to have their own seat. Some airlines offer a child's fare, which is typically 85-90 percent of the adult fare. Other airlines simply charge the full fare—a major financial owie. Children's fares may not appear when booking tickets online, so it's worth calling a travel agent to see if they can get you a discount. Generally, kids 12 and up pay full fare.

Watching the in-flight movie can help pass a few hours in the air.

As soon as you buy your plane tickets, immediately grab seat assignments so your family has a better chance of being seated together. (This may cost extra on bargain carriers.) Inquire about food service on your flight; most international flights still offer a complimentary meal, but be prepared to bring snacks for your crew.

Pick flights with few connections; if your child is able to sleep on planes, a red-eye can work well. Decide if you want your child to sit near the aisle or window. A window seat gives an active child only one escape route, plus the added entertainment of the window. However, a toddler who needs frequent diaper changes and sits quietly may be more comfortable by the aisle. (Note that if you're using a car seat on the plane, it must be placed in a window seat so it won't block the escape path in an emergency.)

At the airport, you'll have to clear security with your brood. It's easier for you (and everyone else in line) if you're ready before entering the security line: Children under 12 can leave their shoes, light jackets, and caps on, but older children must remove them. Pull out liquids and be ready to declare medications, formula, or breast milk. All of your carry-ons, including children's bags, toys, and blankets, must go through the X-ray machine. Children who can walk without assistance are expected to go through the metal detector separately from their parents; babies can be carried through. You may encounter a full-body scanner; you and your children can opt out of this type of screening. You may be subjected to a pat-down instead, but TSA has modified screening procedures for families to reduce that likelihood.

Programs such as TSA Precheck (which lets you keep your shoes on your feet—and your liquids and laptops in your bags—as you go through security on your way out of the country), or the US Customs Global Entry (which provides Precheck benefits and lets you bypass passport control on your return) can be a major help to harried parents. Children 12 and under can accompany a prescreened parent or guardian through Precheck, but teenagers must register

separately. For more details, see page 68.

Some airlines have phased out early boarding for families or charge for the privilege. If your carrier doesn't offer early boarding, approach the gate agent at a quiet moment and ask for help. Tire out your tykes before boarding the plane. Some airports have play spaces—if you can't find one, take over an empty gate area. If you fly at night, consider having your child skip that afternoon's nap. While you're waiting to board, get your kids up and moving as much as possible. Finally, when you're on the plane and it's time for sleep, follow normal bedtime routines. Change your kids into pajamas, tuck them in with a blanket, and read a story or two.

Be prepared. Have at least one change of clothes and plenty of diapers and wipes for your baby or toddler (Mom and Dad might want to have an extra shirt, too, just in case). Make sure your electronics are fully charged before boarding. Don't forget to pack earbuds for tablets and gaming devices (others on the plane will thank you). For younger kids, have lots of activities and surprises, such as books they haven't seen before, stickers, paper, washable markers, activity books, and Mad Libs.

Jet lag can be kiddie purgatory. If you can tolerate some—OK, maybe a lot of—crankiness on the first day, keep young children awake until a reasonable bedtime. After Junior passes out from exhaustion, hopefully the whole family will sleep through the night and wake up when the locals do. Take it easy at the beginning (maybe even starting with a rural destination), allowing a couple of low-impact days to get over jet lag (for more on dealing with jet lag, see page 409).

Family-Friendly Lodging

Instead of picking up and moving every few days, some families prefer settling down in an apartment or house, using it as their home base, then side-tripping to nearby destinations.

In very tight European hotel rooms, you might have to stow your kids in the closet...or, better yet, ask for an extra bed.

If you're traveling with school-age kids, staying in one place for two to three nights is a good bet. Self-catering flats rented by the week, such as *gîtes* in France and villas in Italy, give a family a home on the road. To cut costs, try home-sharing services that let you swap houses with a European family. Not only is it cheaper, but you get to spend time together cooking, watching movies, and just hanging out. It's a cultural experience just to see European TV together. But be aware that European standards on televised sex and nudity are more relaxed than in the US; you might stumble on some uncensored movies, or even unbridled porn, right next to the Nickelodeon channel.

Renting or swapping a house or a flat can facilitate traveling with another family, a strategy that can make your trip easier and more fun. You'll have other adults around to help orchestrate things, and your kids will have built-in playmates.

If you're traveling with older kids, consider hostels. Families can hostel very cheaply (especially in high-priced Scandinavia). Family membership cards are inexpensive, and there's no age limit. Hostels typically have member kitchens where the family can cook and eat for the price of groceries. Some hostels offer family rooms with enough beds for all of you.

If your kids love camping, rent a camper van or small RV. Kids and campgrounds—with swings, slides, and plenty of friends—mix wonderfully. Suddenly your family and the Spanish kids over at the next tent are best amigos.

Most hotels, especially those catering to business travelers, have large family rooms. Many big, budget chain hotels allow two kids to sleep for free in their parents' room. Bonus:

They'll sometimes have a swimming pool. Bigger hotels are also more likely to have entertaining public spaces, such as lobbies with glass elevators or casual terraces with foosball tables. Some European chains, such as Kinderhotels, appeal to families by providing playrooms, baby equipment, and professional babysitters.

In some countries, you may need to know the necessary phrases to communicate your needs. If you're a family of four and your children are young, request a triple room plus a small extra child's bed. Traveling with teenagers, you may need two rooms: a double (one big bed) and a twin (a room with two single beds). In much of Europe, a "double" bed is actually two twins put together. These can easily be separated.

Be careful about staying in small hotels or B&Bs with a baby. If your child wakes up in the middle of the night, you're going to wake up everybody else. Some B&Bs won't take children, or impose an age limit (such as no kids under age 8); ask before booking.

Choosing lodging close to your daytime activities is smart if your little traveler needs to return for a nap or supplies. Two adjoining rooms can be smart for dealing with sleep issues: One jet-lagged person won't keep everyone else up, and napping will be easier. Request quiet rooms away from the street and bar. If you're all in one room but your kids are used to sleeping in their own space, ask for a room with a partition, large closet, or other area that you can separate when it's bedtime (safely snuggled in a portable crib or enough blankets, baby can even sleep in the bathroom).

If you have young children, childproof the room on arrival. A roll of duct tape makes quick work of electrical outlets (outlet guards from home won't work). Place anything breakable out of reach. Proprietors are generally helpful to considerate and undemanding parents.

With a toddler, budget extra to get a bathtub in your room—a practical need and a fun diversion. If the shower has a high lip, you can at least create a kid-friendly bathing puddle.

For more information on the types of accommodations mentioned above, see the Sleeping chapter.

Feeding Kids on the Road

Start the day with a good, substantial breakfast (at hotels, kids sometimes eat free), and plan for snack breaks. Buying bread, cheese, fruit, and drinks in the morning means you can picnic anytime, anywhere. Foreign grocery stores are an adventure for kids, so bring them along to help shop.

Find the most scenic perch for your picnic.

In each country, grocery stores have different kinds of kids' treats, some of which may end up being a real hit—sparking both a country-specific passion and great memories. Another fun (and cheap) option is to get takeout food, such as bratwurst, pizza by the slice, crepes, or sandwiches, from a street stand. You can eat your meals on a square, at a park, or on the top deck of a tour bus.

Sample gelato, croissants, or chocolate every day (gelato should be twice a day)—whatever is a "specialty" treat of the country you're in. It's a great way to get off your feet and take a break. At home, you may try to avoid bribes, but the promise of a treat can make a huge difference to everyone's cooperation when you're out and about—and don't have space for a "time out."

Seek out kid-pleasing local dishes wherever you go, including crepes and *croque monsieurs* (grilled ham-and-cheese sandwiches) in France, *pasta bianca* (plain pasta) and *frullati* (smoothies) in Italy, *tortillas* (omelets) in Spain, and fish-and-chips in England.

Quality chain restaurants—including many local varieties you won't have seen before—provide some good go-to options that will please young palates. An occasional Big Mac or Whopper between all the bratwurst and kraut helps keep the family happy. (And, at European fast-food joints, parents can often enjoy their own treat of a beer.)

Eating at full-service European restaurants is a social event, but it can get stressful with small children, since service is much slower than at home. Dinner can easily take two hours, so bring something to occupy the kids while lingering. You may want to skip the white-tablecloth places and hit self-service cafeterias, relaxed cafés, or bars (kids are welcome, though sometimes restricted to the restaurant section or courtyard area). Sidewalk cafés allow parents to dine

Since many restaurants don't have high chairs, you might have to do a little juggling at mealtime.

The Steves Kids Vote on Britain's Best and Worst

Imagine being a teenager forced to spend a big part of your summer vacation with robo-tourist Rick Steves (alias "Dad"). Jackie and Andy did that a while ago. What were the highlights? Here are the results of the post-trip interview:

Best City: Blackpool—England's white-knuckle ride capital! The Big One (one of the world's fastest and highest roller coasters) is still the best. A tip: Avoid the old wooden-framed rides. They're too jerky for parents.

Best Nature Experience: Horseback riding through the Cotswolds with a guide who'll teach you to trot. Wear long pants. One hour is plenty.

Types of Tours: Open-deck bus tours are good for picnic lunches with a moving view. At museums, audioguide tours are nice because you can pick and choose what you want to learn about.

Worst Food: The "black pudding" that so many B&B people want you to try for breakfast...it's a gooey sausage made of curdled blood.

Best New Food: Chocolate-covered digestive biscuits and vinegar on chips (that's British for "French fries").

Most Boring Tour: The Beatles tour in Liverpool: Most kids couldn't care less about where Paul McCartney went to grade school or a place called Strawberry Fields.

Funniest Activity: The Bizarre Bath walking tour is two hours of jokes and not a bit of history. It's irreverent and dirty—but in a way that parents think is OK for kids.

Best Activities: Leisure (LEZH-ur) Centres in almost every town have good swimming pools.

Best Theater: Shakespeare's Globe in London. First tour the theater to learn about how and why it was built like the original from 1600. Then buy cheap "groundling" tickets to see the actual play right up front, with your elbows on the stage. The actors involve the audience...especially the groundlings.

Most Interesting Demonstrations: The precision slate-splitting demonstration at the slate mines in North Wales. The medieval knight at the Tower of London who explained his armor and then demonstrated medieval sword fighting tactics—nearly killing his squire.

alfresco while well-behaved youngsters explore nearby. Eat by 7 p.m. to miss the adult crowd. Don't expect high chairs to be available; use your stroller in a pinch.

If your kids find certain condiments make anything palatable (I'm looking at you, ketchup), pack a small bottle of the kind they like to help make unfamiliar foods more appealing. If your kids love peanut butter, bring it from home for food emergencies—it can be hard to find or could taste different in Europe. But note that both ketchup and peanut butter fall under TSA's "liquids" category, so you're limited to 3.4 ounces in your carry-on—you'll need to stow larger quantities in checked baggage.

In restaurants (or anywhere), if your infant is making a disruptive fuss, apologetically say the local word for "teeth" (*dientes* in Spanish, *dents* in French, *denti* in Italian, *Zähne* in German), and annoyed people will become sympathetic.

If you crave a leisurely, peaceful evening out, splurge on a babysitter. Hotels often can get sitters, usually from professional agencies. The service is expensive but worth it. With older kids, we enjoyed an adult break in a nicer, romantic restaurant by giving our teenagers enough money for dinner at a diner and turning them loose for the evening. It was an adventure for them, a welcome break for all involved, and we all shared our stories back at the hotel before bedtime.

Kid-Friendly Sightseeing

Review the day's plan at breakfast with the family. Let your kids make some decisions: choosing lunch spots or deciding which stores to visit. Turn your kid into your personal tour guide and navigator. If you use my guidebooks, deputize your child to lead you on my self-guided walks and museum tours.

Since a trip is a splurge for the parents, the kids should enjoy a larger allowance, too. Provide ample money and ask your kids to buy their own treats, *gelati*, postcards, and trinkets within that daily budget. Expect older kids to carry and use the currency. If you don't want your younger child to carry cash, you can be the "banker" and keep a tally of expenses.

Before buying sightseeing passes for your family, consider how many of the covered attractions will be top choices

What's more fun: a museum or the Eiffel Tower?

for your kids. It's not worth setting an exhausting whirlwind pace to race to every attraction just to make the pass pay for itself. Instead, make a short list of the places you and your kids really want to see, and calculate whether a pass makes sense; if not, buy individual admissions. And remember that some museums are free for kids under a certain age.

Make getting somewhere as much fun as the destination. Kids love subway maps, train schedules, and plotting routes. Even the automated ticket kiosks are entertaining. Allow time for all of this, rather than just rushing onto a subway train or bus. After a teaching run, let your child lead the family on subway journeys—kids love the challenge. An added perk: Train rides are free for infants and toddlers (and sometimes even for school-age children).

Hands-on activities, such as this candlemaking demonstration, bring museums to life for kids.

Boat and bus tours can also be a hit. Your kids might not care about the Crown Jewels, but they may go nuts riding the double-decker bus getting there. Open-top, double-decker, hop-on-hop-off tour buses are great for young sightseers and provide easy transportation to the biggest sights. You can even have a picnic on top while you race through city streets. Boats are also memorable, such as a ride on a Venetian *vaporetto* or a glide down Amsterdam's canals.

Try a guided walking tour. Some parents are leery of group tours because they're afraid their kids will be the most disruptive members. But your kids will listen to a guide more

European amusement parks—such as Denmark's Legoland—are fun for kids of all ages.

than they will listen to you. Being in a group of adults can tone down even the wildest child.

Hands-on tours, from cheesemaking to chocolate factories, keep kids engaged. Go to sports or cultural events, but don't insist on staying for the entire event.

European parks provide a wonderland of fun, including puppet shows, pony rides, merry-go-rounds, small zoos, or playgrounds. One of my favorite places to mix kid business with pleasure is Luxembourg Garden in Paris. They have cafés and people-watching for parents, and a play area full of imaginative slides, swings, jungle gyms, and chess games for kids. You'll also find a merry-go-round, pony rides, toy rental sailboats in the main pond, and *guignols* (French marionette shows). On summer evenings, visit Paris's carnival at the Jardin des Tuileries to ride bumper cars and giant swings, try a ring toss, and eat barbe à papa ("Papa's beard," cotton candy).

Copenhagen's Tivoli Gardens is like a Hans Christian Andersen fairy tale, with games, marching bands, shows, and rides ranging from vintage cars to roller coasters, as well as a playground and family amenity center.

Many cities have public swimming pools, and bigger cities also have recreation centers or water parks (check out Paris' Aquaboulevard). For family adventures and fun memories, rent bikes, paddle boats, or rowboats. Local tourist offices can help you dig up these treats.

On days when your troop will need lots of staying power, don't wear them out with too much walking. It's worth taking a taxi to the Louvre to conserve leg strength for getting to the *Mona Lisa*. At least every other day, take an extended break. Return to your hotel or apartment after lunch for a couple of hours to nap, read, or listen to music. What you lose in sightseeing time, you will gain in energy levels.

Consider visiting an amusement park as an end-of-trip reward—the promise of Legoland in Denmark, Blackpool in England, or Disneyland Paris can keep your kids motoring through the more mundane attractions. Europe's open-air folk museums are a bonanza for families; it's worth a detour if your itinerary takes you near one (see page 340).

Big-Sight Survival with Kids

Europe is rich with amazing museums, churches, and art. But unlike you, kids may not appreciate the magnificence of a Michelangelo statue or the significance of an ancient temple frieze. Still, there are ways to liven up big sights. And

whenever possible, go early or book ahead for key sights to avoid long lines (see my crowd-beating tips on page 324).

Ask at the information desk for activity packets designed for children; you'll find these most often at museums in Great Britain. Museum audioguides are great for older children. My kids liked them because they could choose what they wanted to learn about. Bigger sights often have audioguides tailored to school-age children. For younger children, hit the gift shop first so they can buy postcards and have a scavenger hunt to find the pictured artwork. When boredom sets in, try "I spy" games or have them count how many babies or dogs they can spot in all the paintings in the room.

Seek out kid-friendly museums. London's Natural History Museum offers a wonderful world of dinosaurs, volcanoes, meteors, and creepy-crawlies. There are no "do not touch" signs at Florence's two Leonardo da Vinci museums, where kids can use their own energy to power modern re-creations of Leonardo's inventions. For less kid-focused museums, limit visits to 45 minutes—period! Kids will accept a little culture if it's short and focused, with plenty of breaks. If you choose your destination carefully, everyone can enjoy, or at least tolerate, a museum visit.

Indulge your kids' interest in climbing and seeing the world from different angles. Kids love being on such a lofty perch, face-to-face with a gargoyle. A trip up Pisa's Leaning Tower or across the see-through glass walkway of London's Tower Bridge may be a much better use of time and money than another museum visit.

Precautionary Measures

Even well-behaved kids can wander off or get separated from you in a crowd. Whenever you're traveling with children in an unfamiliar place, have a go-to procedure in place in case something happens.

When visiting crowded public venues like markets or

LEFT
Audioguides keep kids engaged and entertained on bus tours.

RIGHT
Art comes alive at the Louvre with kid-friendly audioguides.

Tips for Traveling with Teens

Watching young adults discover a wider world and engage with a new culture can be uniquely gratifying. But helping teens get excited for your trip and stay happy on the road can take some work. The more you can let them travel on their own terms, the better. Here are some ideas for harmonious travel.

Give Them a Choice: Have your teens flip through the guidebook or destination websites and point out things they want to see or do. Ask them to plan the details of a visit, such as how to get there, whether advance tickets are needed, and what everyone should know about the sight ahead of time.

Be Fashionably Secure: Teens may find travel-specific accessories and clothes, such as money belts and fast-drying fabrics, to be "lame." Send them looking for stylish alternatives, such as underwear, hoodies, belts, and scarves with hidden pockets. Athletic wear such as yoga or running pants often have theft-deterring zippered pockets.

Keep a Low Profile: Reading a walking tour aloud while leading the family down the sidewalk is a major faux pas—to a teen. Download my free audio tours to let your teen listen to the narration via earbuds instead.

Cut Them Loose: Teens are usually eager to explore independently. Set a time and place to meet when you arrive at a museum or other sight so they can experience it on their own, perhaps with an audioguide. Then compare notes when you reconvene.

Stay in Touch: Your teens can connect with friends at home and European pals they meet on their trip with apps such as WhatsApp, Snapchat, Instagram, FaceTime, or Skype. (And messaging apps are great for keeping you and your teen in touch if they venture out on their own.) Readily available Wi-Fi helps keep online habits affordable if your plan doesn't include unlimited data. Otherwise, consider buying an international data plan (for more on using phones in Europe, see the Staying Connected chapter).

Be Present: Set limits for tech time while traveling—and abide by them yourself. Putting down the screen opens you up to more experiences and memories.

Decide About Drinking: The drinking age varies between 16 and 18 across Europe. Be ready for your kids to point this out (and settle on the family policy before they do). Ordering a glass of wine with dinner at a European restaurant may be a thrilling experience for an American teen.

Enjoy a Taste of Home: When homesickness sets in, take your teenager to see a movie—American movies are commonplace (make sure your screening is presented in English or subtitled). Or give in to a visit to a McDonald's or Starbucks for familiarity's sake.

bustling museums, pause before entering and agree on a place to meet if you get separated. If you haven't established a meeting place, your kids should know to inform any nearby uniformed or official-looking person that they're lost, and to stay close to where they last saw you. In a crowded situation, having a unique family noise (a whistle

or call, such as a "woo-woop" sound) enables you to easily get each other's attention. If the worst happens, get local authorities involved quickly.

For handy identification your kids can carry, see "Travel Documents for Kids," earlier in this chapter. Before leaving the hotel for a day of sightseeing, give your kids your hotel's business card and your mobile phone number. If you're bringing phones from home, make sure your plan allows you to text each other in Europe; it's the easiest way to keep track of everyone. Consider purchasing cheap pay-as-you-go phones once you arrive in Europe (explained on page 293). Show your kids how to make calls in each country you visit. If your child won't have a mobile phone, make sure they know to ask to use a phone if they are lost.

When using public transportation, make sure everyone knows the destination stop, and have a backup plan for what to do if you lose each other (for example, plan to meet at your final stop or reconvene at your hotel).

Europe is not the United States of Litigation. Europeans love children, but their sense of childproofing public spaces is vastly different from ours. You may find a footbridge across a raging river has child-sized gaps between the railings. Windows in fourth-floor hotel rooms may be easy to open and unscreened. The hot water may scald you in about 30 seconds. Pay attention.

Reflecting and Connecting

Help your kids collect and process their observations. Buy a journal at your first stop, and it becomes a fun souvenir in itself. Kids like cool books—pay for a nice one. The journal is important, and it should feel that way. Encourage kids to record more than just a trip log: Collect feelings, smells, tastes, reactions to cultural differences, and so on. Grade-school kids enjoy pasting in ticket stubs (bring a glue stick)

LEFT Journaling trip experiences is fun for kids—and lets them create a personalized souvenir..

RIGHT Taking photos is a great way for a child to remember a trip.

or drawing pictures of things they've seen (for more on journaling, see page 438).

It can be hard for kids to hang around grown-ups all day, so help them connect with other children. In hot climates, kids gravitate toward the squares (in cities and villages alike) when the temperature begins to cool in the late afternoon, often staying until late in the evening. Take your children to the European nightspots to observe—if not actually make— the scene (such as the rollerbladers at the Trocadéro in Paris or the crowd at Rome's Trevi Fountain).

Just a few phrases spoken by your kids will open many doors. Make a point of teaching them "thank you," "hello," and "goodbye" in the country's language. You'll find nearly everyone speaks English, but small phrases out of the mouths of babes will melt the cool of surly museum guards or harried shop clerks.

During the trip, your kids may complain about being parted from their friends or having to visit yet another museum. But don't lose heart—sometimes the payoff comes years down the road. Your child may surprise you one day by mentioning a painting in Madrid's Prado or recalling a fact about Rome's Colosseum. Besides building memories, your investment in a trip now is a down payment on developing a true citizen of the world.

STUDENT TRAVELERS

When people study abroad, they become students of life. While there are valuable lessons to be learned in foreign classrooms, the real education takes place in sleek Swiss

From Padova, Italy (left) to Coimbra, Portugal (right), for students abroad the real education takes place outside the classroom.

trains and on blaring Istanbul streets. Out in the world, American students forge new friendships, discover fresh solutions to familiar problems, and gain an appreciation for diverse perspectives. Such immersive learning can be as exhausting as it is exciting, and there will be plenty of lows to balance out the highs. But studying abroad creates young people that are more independent individuals, more capable professionals, and more connected global citizens. Students who study abroad quite literally learn a new way to live.

How to Choose Your Own Adventure

Choosing the best program requires establishing clear goals and priorities for your time abroad, gathering a short list of possibilities, and asking a lot of questions. Remember that there isn't one perfect choice; many programs and places will allow you to learn and grow.

Brainstorm your goals. Before you begin researching programs, decide what you want to learn and how you want to grow from an experience abroad. Do you want to master a language? Visit a wide variety of countries? Make a deep connection with a host family? Whatever your preferences, begin by drafting a list of general criteria to guide you during your search.

Use your school's resources. Take your list to your high school counselor or university's study abroad office. These offices are packed with resources and staffed with people whose job is to help you find the best program overseas. If your school offers a program that interests you, prioritize it. Universities help students fit overseas programs to their academic schedules, ensure credits will transfer correctly, and, in some cases, assist with the logistics. Ask your program coordinator to connect you with an alumnus who has already completed the program you're considering.

Investigate other opportunities. A bevy of independent

organizations are happy to help coordinate experiences abroad. Nonprofit groups such as AFS (www.afs.org) facilitate study abroad programs for high schoolers lasting one month to one year; the Council on International Educational Exchange (www.ciee.org) provides opportunities for college students. Organizations such as GoOverseas.com and GoAbroad.com allow you to choose from hundreds of programs for studying, working, and teaching abroad for people of all ages.

Consider every angle. Regardless of where you search for a program, weigh the many details.

Academics: How does the program fit with your home school's academic plan? Can you fulfill any academic requirements while abroad? Will your credits transfer? Will you receive grades, or will the courses be pass/fail? Do the offered courses interest you? How many hours a week will you be in class?

Destination: Is the program located in a big city or a small town? Are there good flight and rail connections for weekend excursions? How is the public transportation? Will you have access to parks and outdoor recreation?

Population: How does the city's size compare to your hometown? How big is the student population? Is the city demographically diverse? How diverse is the student body, and will it be representative of the region or country you're visiting?

Culture: What language is spoken? What are the general political attitudes? What are the popular opinions on gender, race, age, and sexuality? How different is the culture?

Lodging: How close will you live to the university or to the city center? Will you live with a host family, with roommates, or on your own? Will you be expected to find your own lodging, or will the program arrange it?

Cost: What is and isn't included in the program's price? What is the cost of living? Could you actually save money by studying abroad? Is financial aid available?

Timing: How long is the program? Will you need a student visa? What time of year is the program? What is the weather generally like at that time? Are there any local events or festivals you want to attend (or avoid)?

Put the "Study" in "Study Abroad"

The greatest lessons you'll learn abroad are taught outside the classroom. But it would be a mistake to discount academics as just a distraction. The courses offered at your host school or university can deepen your understanding of the local culture and offer opportunities you'd never find at home.

Consult your advisor. Before you commit to a program, meet with your academic advisor to carefully fit your time abroad into your academic plan. If you study abroad through your high school or university, a credit transfer system should ensure that your foreign courses transfer over smoothly. Ask about taking courses abroad for credit rather than for a grade, meaning your GPA isn't in jeopardy.

Feed your curiosity. View your program abroad as an opportunity to take classes that spark your curiosity or wouldn't have as much resonance back home. A class in creative writing can be liberating when you're not focusing on a grade, and a course on World War II history is much more powerful when you're a short train ride from Normandy.

Prepare for academic differences. Recognize that other countries have different academic practices. A 72 on an essay is considered a great score in England. In Spain, some instructors post spreadsheets of students' grades on their office doors for anyone to see. Contact the host school in advance to ask for tips for American students, and connect with your new professors early in the term.

Make Yourself at Home

Many students studying abroad share living spaces with a host family or roommates. Approached thoughtfully, this can be a powerful way to forge lasting relationships and immerse yourself more deeply in a culture.

Learn the language. If English will not be the primary language in your host city, take the time to learn at least a few crucial words and phrases. Even if many people there speak English, a few simple greetings can make a good impression, and knowing basic vocabulary words for foods, buildings, and transportation can go a long way.

Come bearing gifts. It's a nice touch to bring your host family or roommates a gift that represents your hometown—coffee from Seattle, bourbon from Kentucky, a gold brick from San Francisco. This starts the relationship on a positive note and serves as a good conversation starter.

Set expectations. Acknowledge cultural differences, set boundaries, and open up channels of communication as quickly as possible. Discuss house rules and expectations clearly and directly. If living with a host family, ask them to give you a tour of the home. Tell your host family if you have any dietary needs or health conditions. Opening communication early will ensure that any issues that arise can be resolved smoothly.

Adjust if necessary. Don't stay in an uncomfortable situation that will ruin your time abroad. Contact your program coordinator to discuss any unresolvable problems and arrange a new placement. Be aware that discomfort can run both ways, so be considerate: If you struggle to live by others' rules, crawl home drunk every other night, or insist on eating frozen pizza for every meal, reevaluate why you're studying abroad.

Maximize Your Experience

It can be tempting to insulate yourself from culture overload by retreating into your room or surrounding yourself with other Americans. Other students go to the opposite extreme and find it hard to focus on homework with so many cultural experiences so close (and parents so far). Make a point of finding the right balance for you.

Adjust to your new city. A good way to get comfortable quickly is to make a list of places and services you'll need in your new home, such as the train station, grocery store, pharmacy, laundromat, and post office. Add a few social spots like a go-to coffee shop, a welcoming restaurant, and a nice park for picnicking. Include resources at the university such as the international student office, counseling office, or student activities office. Hit the streets with your list and track down each place. Get lost...and find yourself again. Better yet, take a classmate with you so that you can build a new friendship while exploring the city.

Create a community. While it's natural to gravitate toward other American students, you didn't travel halfway around the world to re-create your life back home. Expand your circle to include students from other countries, local students, and local people of different ages from beyond the university campus. To establish relationships beyond the university, ask the neighborhood library about upcoming events, join an athletic club, frequent an open-mic night at a nearby pub, volunteer at a festival or food bank, attend a local church, or peruse Meetup.com for hundreds of social groups based on common interests.

Go local. For many students, the most formative experiences abroad are unique to a locale: Scottish dancing at a local church gym, marching through Spanish streets in a Good Friday processional, hunting for truffles in France. A

"Voluntourism" and Cultural Exchanges

For some travelers, making the world a better place is the driving focus of their trip. Combining a cause you really care about with a place you've always wanted to see can make your trip especially rewarding. Various organizations sponsor "volunteer vacations," work camps, and other service projects in needy countries, including Global Volunteers (www.globalvolunteers.org), Volunteers for Peace (www.vfp.org), and Service Civil International (www.sciint.org). If you've got more time and stamina than money, consider Workaway.info, which connects you with families or small organizations offering room and board in exchange for volunteer work (usually manual labor such as gardening, carpentry, or paint-

Talking with young people in Ethiopia

ing). For more resources, search online for "volunteer vacation" or "volunteer travel." And if you're wondering whether a charitable organization is reputable, a good place to start is CharityNavigator.org, a nonprofit organization that rates US-based charities on their accountability and transparency.

Or, consider taking an educational tour. For an American to gain a new perspective through one of these tours can be a powerful service in itself to struggling people. While not explicitly service-oriented, these tours can do a brilliant job of broadening horizons. I traveled to Central and South America three times with the Center for Global Education and Experience (at Augsburg College in Minneapolis), and those trips are among the most vivid and perspective-stretching travel experiences I've ever enjoyed (www.augsburg.edu/global). For trip journals of my CFGE experiences in El Salvador and Nicaragua, see Ricksteves.com/centam, and for a free PDF of my book *Hunger and Hope: Lessons from Ethiopia and Guatemala*, go to RickSteves.com/hunger.

Culturally curious travelers can sign up with one of several hospitality exchange organizations. These groups connect travelers with host families with the noble goal of building world peace through international understanding. Guests sightsee less but engage more in everyday life with their hosts—talking, sharing, and learning. You'll arrive as a stranger at new destinations but leave as a friend. Although no money changes hands, these exchanges aren't for people simply out to travel cheap—the logistics involved aren't worth it. Most organizations screen members (with varying degrees of stringency) and set ground rules about length of stay. Opening your own home to visitors is encouraged, but not required.

Servas is the oldest and largest of these organizations (www.usservas.org). Couchsurfing.com is newer and popular for locating hosts and events worldwide. London-based Globetrotters Club runs a similar network of hosts and travelers (www.globetrotters.co.uk), as do several groups that are free to join, such as the Hospitality Club (www.hospitalityclub.org). Friendship Force International organizes homestay tours for small groups with a goal of fostering international goodwill (www.thefriendshipforce.org). Many travelers swear by these exchanges as the only way to really travel, and they treasure their global list of friends.

good place to find such opportunities is at the university's international student or student activities offices. They can tell you about on-campus clubs, student excursions, and university events.

Get out of town. Take advantage of Europe's generous public transportation to explore beyond your host city and country. Traveling between countries in Europe is often faster and easier than traveling between states in the US. As a result, many Americans who study in Europe leap at the opportunity to jet to Prague for the weekend or take a bullet train to Paris for the day. Many overseas programs don't hold classes on Fridays, catering to these extracurricular adventures. Use this book to learn how to purchase train tickets, secure lodging, organize your weekend getaway sightseeing, and save money doing it.

Travel intentionally. With access to so many exciting destinations, it's tempting to forget the culture around you. As you prepare for your term abroad, consider your priorities: Do you want to get to know your host city or country deeply, or would you prefer to get quick glimpses of a wide variety of places? There is no right or wrong way to allot your time—just do so intentionally so that you don't leave wishing you had hopped on that flight to Helsinki or regretting that you never had that dinner party with your neighbor.

Stay safe. No matter where you roam or who you are with, use the same good judgment abroad that you use at home: Always carry your phone, and keep it well charged. If there's an emergency, call 112. Save the phone numbers of local friends, program coordinators, or university employees in case you get lost or need help navigating a difficult situation. Meet dates in a public place and let others know your plans. For many American students, a major pitfall is the drinking age: Students unable to legally drink in the US can waltz into the local pub without anyone batting an eyelash. Plan ahead (have a designated sober person even if no one is driving), pace yourself, and pay attention.

SENIOR TRAVELERS

Looking for a fountain of youth? I've long noticed that older travelers seem younger than average in their appearance, attitudes, and energy levels. Travel is an excellent way to stay young in spirit—and many senior adventurers are proclaiming, "Age matters only if you're a cheese" as they plan their next trip (and the one after that).

When to Go: If you can travel whenever you want, it's smart to aim for shoulder season (April and October). Traveling in early spring and late fall allows you to avoid the most exhausting things about European travel: crowds and the heat of summer, and it saves money, too.

Travel Insurance: Seniors pay more for travel insurance—but are also more likely to need it. Find out exactly whether and how your medical insurance works overseas. (Medicare is not valid outside the US except in very limited circumstances; check your supplemental insurance coverage for exclusions.) When considering additional travel insurance, pay close attention to evacuation insurance, which covers the substantial expense of getting you to adequate medical care in case of an emergency—especially if you are too ill to fly commercially. For more on travel-insurance options, see page 70.

Packing: When you pack light, you move effortlessly through Europe. To lighten your load, take fewer clothing items and do laundry more often. Fit it all in a roll-aboard suitcase or a carry-on that converts to a backpack. Figure out ways to smoothly carry your luggage, so you're not wrestling with a big bag or several bulky items. For example, if you bring a second bag, make it a small one that stacks neatly (or attaches) on top of your wheeled bag.

A small notebook or your phone's notes app is handy for jotting down facts and reminders, such as your hotel-room number or Metro stop. (Your phone's camera can take visual notes, too.) Recording these things will help keep your mind clear and uncluttered. If you wear eyeglasses, carry an extra pair, and bring along a magnifying glass if it'll help you read detailed maps and small-print schedules.

LEFT Their fountain of youth is Europe!

RIGHT Seniors can travel as footloose and fancy-free as their teenage grandkids.

Medications and Health: It's best to take a full supply of any medications and to leave them in their original containers. Finding a pharmacy and filling a prescription in Europe isn't necessarily difficult, but it can be time-consuming. Plus, nonprescription medications (such as vitamins or supplements) may not be available abroad in the same form you're used to. Pharmacists overseas are often unfamiliar with American brand names (for example, atorvastatin instead of Lipitor), so before you leave, ask your doctor for the precise generic names of your medications and the names of equivalent medications. For more on getting medical help in Europe, see page 418.

If you wear hearing aids, be sure to bring spare batteries—it can be difficult to find a specific size in Europe. If your mobility is limited, see "Travelers with Disabilities," later in this chapter, for tips and resources.

Flying: If you're not flying direct, you might consider checking your bag to avoid lugging it to a connecting flight through a huge, busy airport. (Be sure to keep medications and other important items in a smaller carry-on bag for the plane and any layovers.) If you're a slow walker, request a wheelchair or an electric cart when you book your seat so you can easily make any connecting flights. Since the lack of legroom on an airplane can cramp your style, book early to reserve aisle seats (or splurge on roomier "economy plus," or first class). Stay hydrated during long flights and take short walks hourly to minimize the slight chance of getting a blood clot.

Accommodations: Hotels vary widely in their amenities and layouts, so think about your needs before you book. Ask about any accessibility quirks for the hotel you're considering—find out whether it's at the top of a steep hill, has an elevator or stairs to upper floors, and so on. If stairs are a problem, request a ground-floor room. Location matters, too: If you stay near the train station at the edge of town, you'll minimize carrying your bag on arrival; on the other hand, staying in the city center gives you a convenient place to take a break between sights (and you can take a taxi on arrival to reduce lugging your bags).

With the advantage of a more flexible schedule, older travelers can often find good alternative accommodations for longer stays. You can rent a house or apartment, or even swap houses for a week or more with someone in an area you're interested in. The swap needn't be simultaneous, and can sometimes include cars and recreational equipment like bikes and canoes (for more on rentals and house swapping, see the Sleeping chapter). Travelers' cultural exchange organizations offer you the chance to stay in local homes for a minimal courtesy fee and to learn about your destination from those who live there.

Getting Around: Subways involve a lot of walking and stairs (and can be a pain with luggage if they're crowded). They also have relatively few stops; just getting to the station can be a journey on its own. If you want to do less walking, consider using city buses or taxis instead. City buses stop frequently, and with a little planning you can align your sightseeing itinerary with convenient routes. If you're renting a car, be warned that some countries and some car-rental companies have an upper age limit: To avoid unpleasant surprises, mention your age when you reserve (for details, see the Driving & Navigating chapter).

Senior Discounts: At some sights, senior discounts are reserved for European citizens, but at other sights—and even some events such as concerts—just showing your gray hair or identification can snag you a discount. Always ask about discounts, even if you don't see posted information about one—you may be surprised. (The British call discounts "concessions"; look also for "pensioner's rates.") In non-English-speaking countries, memorize the phrase for requesting a senior discount or write it down on a card to hand over at the admissions desk.

Most rail passes are about 10 percent cheaper for seniors age 60 and up. And seniors can get deals on point-to-point rail tickets in many countries, such as Austria, Belgium, Great Britain, Finland, France, Germany, Italy, Spain, Sweden, and Norway. Qualifying ages range from 60 to 67 years old. But to get many of those discounts—including in Austria, Britain, Germany, Italy, and Spain, and a second tier of discounts in France—you must purchase a senior card at a local train station (valid for a year, prices range from €6 in Spain to €115 in Germany). Note that advance-purchase discounts are usually as good as or better than the senior card offers.

Sightseeing: Go late in the day for fewer crowds and

cooler temperatures. Many museums have elevators, and even if these are freight elevators not open to the public, the staff might bend the rules for older travelers who'd appreciate a lift. Many larger museums offer loaner wheelchairs. Take bus tours (usually two hours long) for a painless overview of a city's highlights. Boat tours—of the harbor, river, lake, or fjord—are a pleasure. Hire an English-speaking cabbie to take you on a tour of a city or region (if it's hot, spring for an air-conditioned taxi). Or participate in the life of local seniors, such as joining a tea dance in England or playing boules in France. If you're traveling with others but need a rest break, set up a rendezvous point. Some people—of all ages—find that one day of active sightseeing needs to be followed by a quiet day to recharge the batteries. Europe needn't be nonstop museums and markets: Grab a table at a sidewalk café for a drink and people-watching.

Pilgrims of all ages hike from France to Santiago de Compostela in northwest Spain.

Educational, Exchange, and Volunteer Opportunities: For a more meaningful cross-cultural experience, consider going on an educational tour such as those run by Road Scholar (formerly Elderhostel), which offers study programs around the world for those over 50 (trips from several days to several months, www.roadscholar.org). For more ideas see "'Voluntourism' and Cultural Exchanges," earlier.

Long-Term Trips: Becoming a temporary part of the community can be particularly rewarding. Settle down and stay a while, doing side trips if you choose. If you're considering retiring abroad, two good resources are ExpatExchange.com, where you'll find tips and resources for expatriates, and InternationalLiving.com, with extensive reporting by North Americans who have moved overseas. The *Living Abroad* series (Moon Travel Guides) offers a look at the challenges and rewards of life in European destinations including France, Italy, London, and Paris.

More Tips: The AARP (formerly the American Association of Retired Persons) provides an extensive library of travel-related articles and advice at Travel.AARP.org, including destination guides, budget travel recommendations, and an interactive trip finder. The AARP also offers info on retiring abroad.

TRAVELERS WITH DISABILITIES

The creaky, cobblestoned Old World has long had a reputation for poor accessibility. It's the very charm of Europe—old and well preserved—that often adds to its barriers. But Europe has made some impressive advances toward opening its doors to everyone, including travelers with limited mobility.

I'm inspired by the fact that, wherever I go in Europe, I see locals with disabilities: On the streets, in museums, in restaurants, and on trains, you'll see people using wheelchairs, scooters, walkers, and canes to get around. If people with disabilities can live rich and full lives in Europe, then travelers with disabilities can certainly have an enjoyable and worthwhile vacation there, too.

Anyone with adventure in their soul can take advantage of all Europe has to offer. Levels of personal mobility vary tremendously from person to person. Consider your own situation thoughtfully in choosing which attractions to visit, which hotels to sleep in, which restaurants to dine at...and which things you might want to avoid.

Trip Planning for Travelers with Disabilities

John Sage owns Sage Traveling, which plans and books accessible travel to Europe for senior and disabled travelers. John has taken his wheelchair to more than 120 European cities and has run into his share of challenges during his travels—but he also says that the obstacles can almost always be overcome. Here, I've included excerpts, in John's own words, from his top tips for traveling in Europe.

Do your research. I often hear that "Venice is not wheelchair accessible" or "Paris has poor accessibility." While there are certainly some accessibility challenges, the truth is that the more research you do, the more accessible your trip will be. Avoiding bridges in Venice and hills in Paris is entirely possible. Did you know that Herculaneum's ruins are nearly identical to Pompeii's, but are wheelchair-friendly? And that cruise passengers with disabilities can enjoy incredible experiences such as reaching the top of the Acropolis in Athens or entering the Sistine Chapel in Rome by using specially designed wheelchair lifts? Your vacation doesn't need to be a struggle. Do your homework and your trip can be filled with fully accessible hotel accommodations, accessible routes between accessible tourist attractions, and wonderfully accessible travel experiences.

Book hotels far in advance. It is almost always cheaper to book your accessible hotel accommodation far in advance. And it is also necessary! Many hotels in European city centers have only one or two accessible rooms. The best ones get booked very early. For travel in the summer, make your reservations in December. Remember, a hotel's accessibility status does not only depend on its interior features such as elevators, grab bars and roll-in showers. The location is just as important.

Carefully plan your route. If you know what you're getting into before you arrive in Europe, you'll have a much easier and enjoyable time on your trip. There'll likely be numerous ways to get to the tourist attractions you're so eager to see. Some routes will have wheelchair ramps, smooth pavement, and flat terrain; others may have steep hills, bothersome (and even dangerous) cobblestones, and flights of stairs. Research the accessibility of sidewalks, bus routes, subway stations, and the location of accessible building entrances before your trip. Check for accessibility information in the online visitors guides for your destinations—but be aware that not all guides will offer this type of information and some of them may be outdated as access features change all the time.

Stay in the most accessible parts of town. This is one of the hardest parts of planning your trip. You may have found a great accessible hotel, but what will you find when you walk (or roll) out the front door? Are there hills and stairs in all directions? Will you have to roll over cobblestones? Are there accessible restaurants nearby? It's crucial to research the hotel's neighborhood. You can use street view in Google Maps to get the lay of the land, then email the hotel with your questions.

Figure out accessible public transportation options. When choosing a hotel, don't forget to factor in the price of transportation. If you have to pay for a taxi to get to accessible restaurants, accessible shopping, and the tourist attractions, that hotel "deal" you found won't feel like such a good deal after all. In cities such as London, Paris, and Barcelona, stay near an accessible bus stop. In Berlin, Istanbul, and Venice, stay near an accessible metro, tram, or boat stop.

In Florence, Cambridge, and Edinburgh, stay right in the middle of town so you can walk/roll everywhere.

Rely on the experience of other travelers with disabilities. You're certainly not the first person with disabilities to visit Europe. Find out what accessibility challenges other travelers encountered and how they got around them. Check recent posts at travel forums such as TripAdvisor.com, CruiseCritic.com, and RickSteves.com to find previous travelers' experiences. Or seek out a travel agent who specializes in accessible travel. You can also find accessibility reviews of multiple European destinations on SageTraveling.com.

Have a backup plan. Even on the most perfectly planned accessible vacation, something can go wrong. If it does, how will you deal with it? If you prepare for all the possible issues, travel with someone who can help you during your trip, and remain flexible, unexpected events won't turn into potential trip-ruining problems. What will you do if a part on your wheelchair breaks? If a train strike occurs in Italy, how will you get from Florence to Rome? With backup plans (such as packing vital spare parts for your wheelchair), you won't have to put your vacation on hold.

Consider a tour. A company that specializes in accessibility will lead you on the flattest, smoothest, shortest tour routes.

Before you take a tour or hire a guide, ask these questions:

- Is the tour guide a licensed professional? How much training has the guide received?
- What route will the guide use? Does it involve curbs, steps, steep hills, or cobblestones? Where are the accessible bathrooms located? Will the guide physically assist you if needed (for example, push a manual wheelchair)?
- Is this a private tour, or will you be with other travelers? Are you expected to keep up with able-bodied tour members?
- How many people with disabilities have they guided in the past year? (You want a guide who is active enough to be aware of the latest regulations or updates regarding accessibility.)

Anticipate your trip! You've done as much planning as you can. You've relied on the experience of other travelers with disabilities, and you're prepared for the unexpected. Now it's time to get excited about your trip. Majestic cities, beautiful art and architecture, fascinating history, exquisite food, and wonderful experiences await you.

Tips for Travelers with Wheelchairs

Susan Sygall is the CEO and cofounder of Mobility International USA (www.miusa.org), a nonprofit that links people with disabilities with work, study, teaching, volunteer, exchange, and research opportunities. It also offers a blog, resource library, and database of disability organizations. Sygall has been traveling the "Rick Steves way" for decades. Here, she shares some of her best tips for traveling in Europe with a wheelchair. Thanks to MIUSA's staff for help with this advice.

People who use wheelchairs, like so many of our nondisabled peers, want to get off the tourist track and experience the real France, Italy, or Portugal. Don't accept other people's notions of what is possible—I have climbed Masada in Israel and made it to the top of the Acropolis in Greece. Whether you travel alone, with friends, or with an assistant, you're in for a great adventure.

Pack light. I use a lightweight manual wheelchair with pop-off tires. I take a backpack that fits on the back of my chair and I store my daypack underneath my chair in a net bag. Since I usually travel alone, if I can't carry it myself, I don't take it.

Plan for eventualities. I keep a bungee cord with me for the times I can't get my chair into a car and need to strap it in the trunk or when I need to secure it on a train. Bike shops are excellent for tire repairs if you get a flat.

Check your chair at the gate. I always insist on keeping my own wheelchair up to the airline gate, where I then check it. When I have a connecting flight, I again insist that I use my own chair.

Susan Sygall, in Italy's Cinque Terre

Don't let bathroom access stop you. Bathrooms are often a hassle, so I have learned to use creative ways to transfer into narrow spaces. To be blatantly honest, when there are no accessible bathrooms in sight, I have found ways to pee discreetly just about anywhere. You gotta do what you gotta do. Bring along an extra pair of pants and a great sense of humor.

Look for freight elevators. If a museum lacks elevators for visitors, be sure to ask about freight elevators. Almost all have them somewhere, and that can be your ticket to seeing a world-class treasure.

Let wheelchairs help you. People who

Accessibility in Europe

This section was contributed by Carole Zoom, who has traveled to more than 30 countries with her scooter-style electric wheelchair and ventilator.

The concept of accessibility varies by culture. In the US, access means that an individual can use elevators, lifts, doors, entrances, and other features without any assistance. Individual autonomy is central to the American concept of access, as enshrined in the Americans with Disabilities Act (ADA).

Europe, on the other hand, subscribes to a medical rather than political model of disability. Policy tends to be focused on helping people with disabilities navigate a society built for nondisabled individuals—instead of helping society find ways to accommodate their needs. For example, in Europe an entryway with one step is considered accessible: The law assumes that disabled people will use manual wheelchairs that can be rolled up a step and/or will have family members assisting.

In the US it's illegal to discriminate based on what kind of mobility device a wheelchair user chooses. But in Europe, mobility scooter users have fewer rights than wheelchair users; scooters are seen not as a medical necessity, but as a convenience item for people who can still walk to some extent. Scooter-style wheelchairs are not allowed in some museums and other public facilities—you may be asked to walk if you can or to transfer to a manual wheelchair. If those are not options for you, be persistent in explaining your situation to museum staff.

Due to the age of many buildings in Europe, elevator access is not a given. A US citizen would assume a hotel is accessible upon hearing that it has an elevator. But many older European elevators are not large enough for American-style electric wheelchairs and scooters. Before you book a room, ask the hotel concierge for photos and exact measurements to ensure your style and size of wheelchair will fit. A hotel that hesitates to provide the info or photos you request is unlikely to be accommodating; in that case, move on and choose another.

Unlike in the US, European transit companies that operate planes, ships, trains, and buses may require advanced documentation of disability. If you need specific assistance, have your doctor fill out forms attesting to your needs before you travel, then contact the transit provider's medical desk at least 72 hours before your departure to ask how to submit them. Always confirm and reconfirm your reservations for assistance on all modes of advanced-ticketed transport.

We have an increasingly barrier-free world. But Americans going abroad need to be more aware and vigilant about accessibility than they are used to at home.

have difficulty walking long distances may want to bring a lightweight wheelchair or borrow or rent one when needed.

Insist on your rights. Don't confuse being flexible and having a positive attitude with settling for less than your rights. I expect equal access and constantly let people know about the possibility of providing access through ramps or other modifications. When I believe my rights have been violated, I do whatever is necessary to remedy the situation,

Resources for Travelers with Disabilities

Tours

Accessible Journeys: Wheelchair-accessible trips, travel-planning, tips, and resources (www.accessiblejourneys.com)

Accessible Tour Operators: Companies such as Rome and Italy Tourist Services (www.romeanditaly.com), Bespoke France (www.bespokefrance.com), and Christianakis Travel (Greece, www.christianakis.gr) provide accessible visits to their home turf

DisabilityHorizons.com: UK-based online magazine with travel section covering a range of accessible tourism topics

The Opening Door, Inc.: Extensive listings of disability travel organizations, access guides, tour operators, and other resources (www.travelguides.org)

SageTraveling.com: European trip-planning for people with disabilities, with guides for hire and accessibility reviews of European destinations

Reading

Accessibility Disabled World Travels: Travel Tips for People with Disabilities (Tracey Ingram, 2014): An occupational therapist writes on how to travel with a wheelchair or with other mobility issues

Barrier-Free Travel: A Nuts and Bolts Guide for Wheelers and Slow Walkers (Candy B. Harrington, 2012): A handy compilation of information for mobility-limited travelers

Go Where You Wanna Go: Using GPS on the iPhone (Judith Dixon): Tips and tricks for apps to help you find your way (available in Braille and other formats from National Braille Press, www.nbp.org)

so that the next traveler or disabled person in that country won't have the same frustrations.

Break down barriers. Try to learn some of the language of the country you're in. It cuts through the barriers when people stare at you (and they will), and also comes in handy when you need help going up a curb or a flight of steps.

Learn from locals. Remember that you are part of a global family of people with disabilities. Always get information about disability groups in the places you are going. See the "Resources for Travelers with Disabilities" sidebar in this chapter for a number of helpful organizations. They have the best access information, and many times they'll become your new traveling partners and friends.

Tips for Travelers with Impaired Vision

Carmen Papalia, who began to lose his vision in his early twenties, is a self-described "social-practice artist and nonvisual learner" who leads eyes-closed city walking tours and museum visits and has served as artist-in-residence at London's Victoria and Albert Museum.

When you travel, trust the senses that are available to you. Use them to be curious. Let them lead your exploration.

Carmen Papalia, leading an eyes-closed city walking tour

As a nonvisual traveler, I find what's interesting for me in a place. For example, I'm not a churchgoer but I went to Mass at St. Paul's in London just so I could spend time in that acoustic space. It was amazing, hearing the choir fill up the dome. In Strandhill, Ireland, I had a profound sensory experience soaking in a seaweed bath, followed by the quintessentially Irish taste of fish-and-chips for lunch. I relished pausing on a bridge over the Garavogue River in Sligo, Ireland, letting the rich waves of texture and sound consume me as the water beneath rushed out to the Atlantic.

Here are some other tips from my time traversing Europe:

Set your own terms. You can define your access and support needs and preferences, even in an unfamiliar place. Advocate for yourself; make your access considerations known, and only accept support that is consistent with your personal disability politics. Doing so gives you agency as a traveler. For example, when I am traveling alone, airline staff often ask me to sit in a wheelchair so they can push me instead of guiding me on foot to my connecting gate or to baggage claim. I always refuse. You can too; be firm about your limits.

Connect with people. The best support comes from relationships. In Europe, people are generally helpful and have a good respect for physical boundaries. Find out if the city you're visiting has a blind society or other support organization. Hostels are also great places to make friends.

Ask what museums offer. Many museums have programming such as touch tours and audioguides to help nonvisual visitors engage. I often prefer to have a friend describe the material to me. Always ask if museums offer concessions to disabled travelers and their companions. In Paris, my friend and I were able to skip the line and get free admission to many museums.

Accept help when necessary. Transit workers are usually approachable and willing to guide you to your platform, as well as radio ahead to your transfer point or destination to arrange for someone to meet you. In the London Tube, for example, such help is routine and friendly. Rely on hotel concierges, who can call cabs and coordinate other assistance. Menus are never accessible, but waitstaff are always happy to tell you about the food.

This 3-D map of Cambridge with a Braille description helps sight-impaired travelers in England's famous university town.

Learn to navigate cities. Many cities in Europe have tactile paving and various types of signals at crosswalks. For example, some intersections in the UK have a small, ridged cone underneath the signal box. The cone rotates when you can cross the street; touch it or listen for its spin. Research the places you're going so you know what to expect.

Employ all your senses. Nonvisual learners have the interesting opportunity of using other senses to initiate learning experiences. But to do this, we must actively choose to let our nonvisual senses guide our choices. It's a way of approaching the world from which even seeing travelers can benefit. I encourage all travelers to do it—your time abroad will take on much greater richness.

Bus Tours & Cruises

This book is all about mastering individual, self-directed travel. But while I advocate independent travel, I'm not against organized travel. Far from it—for more than 30 years, I've been organizing tours, taking thousands of travelers to Europe's best destinations. For many people, a bus tour or cruise is the best way to scratch their travel itch. Having someone else navigate for you, arrange transportation and hotels, and make the decisions takes the stress and work out of travel. Whether you join a bus tour or sign up for a cruise, a good organized tour can create plenty of memorable experiences.

A tour can also be the most economical way to see Europe: Large tour companies book thousands of rooms and meals year-round, and with their tremendous economic clout, they can get prices that no individual tourist can match. Similarly, the base price of mainstream cruises beats independent travel by a mile. For people looking to travel comfortably and cheaply, bus tours and cruises can be a good option, especially if you use the tips in this chapter to help you travel smartly—and through the Back Door.

During the coronavirus pandemic, organized travel by bus and by cruise ship effectively shut down. Companies will be up and running again once travel restrictions ease. The information in this chapter is geared toward the post-pandemic era. If you do book a group tour, expect cancellation policies to be more flexible, health protocols to be ramped up, and group sizes to be smaller, at least initially. Book early, as pent-up travel demand may fill tours and ships quickly. For current health and safety guidelines, see the US State Department's international travel website (www.travel.state.gov).

TOURING EUROPE BY BUS

Taking a bus tour can be a good choice if your European vacation time is limited—but you'll want to carefully consider your options before signing up. Offerings range from luxury we-handle-everything bus tours for smaller groups to comfortable midrange tours (like mine, which are also for smaller groups) to low-end, pack-'em-in, big-bus operators for large groups. In nearly all cases, a bus tour includes a professional and multilingual guide, a comfy bus, decent hotels with mass-produced comfort, and some meals. The cheapest tours can cost less than $150 a day.

Choosing a Tour

Would you rather travel with a group of 48 or 28? Change hotels every night or enjoy two-night stays? There are plenty of variables to consider when comparing the fully guided tours offered by travel companies.

There are hundreds to choose from, covering a wide price range. The big names are dependable. Abercrombie & Kent, Maupintour, and Tauck are high-end expensive. Cosmos and Globus are solid budget options. In between are Insight, Trafalgar, Collette—and my own tour company, Rick Steves' Europe.

Start by browsing your options online, asking friends, or talking to a travel agent for advice. The tour company may be very big, booking rooms by the thousands; it may even own

Comparing Bus Tours

When you're selecting a bus tour, the cost you're quoted isn't the only factor to consider. Investigate how many people you'll be traveling with as well as what extras you'll be expected to cover. Most tour companies include customer feedback on their websites so you can read what previous tour members have to say. When comparing prices, remember that airfare is not included. The chart below illustrates what to expect from a range of tour companies.

	High-End	Rick Steves Tours	Low-End
Price per day	$400-1,050	$200-375	$130-230
Group size	18-40	24-28	40-50
Meals	50-75% included	50% included	35-50% included
Sightseeing	All included	All included	Most cost extra
Tips	All included except guide/driver	All included	None included

the hotels it uses. While these hotels fit American standards—large, not too personal, with double rooms and good plumbing, they're often on the outskirts of town. Keep in mind that the goal of most tour companies is to fill every seat on that bus. On the biggest tours, groups are treated as an entity: a mob to be fed, shown around,

profited from, and moved out. If money is saved, it can be at the cost of real experience.

Many who take an organized bus tour could have managed fine on their own.

When considering tours, remember that some of the best sellers are those that promise more sightseeing than is reasonable in a given amount of time. No tour can give you more than 24 hours in a day or seven days in a week. What a wide-ranging "blitz" tour can do is give you more hours on the bus. Choose carefully among the itineraries available. Do you really want a series of one-night stands? Bus drivers call tours with ridiculous itineraries "pajama tours." You're in the bus from 8 a.m. until after dark, so why even get dressed?

The cheapest bus tours are impossibly cheap. There's literally no profit in their retail price. They can give you bus transportation and hotels for about what the tourist-off-the-street would pay for just the hotels alone. But there's a catch: These tours tend to charge extra for sightseeing, and make money by taking you to attractions and shops from which they receive kickbacks. However, savvy travelers on a tight budget can take advantage by thinking of them as a tailored bus pass with hotels tossed in. Skip out on the shopping,

The standard European guide does the leading... and you do the following.

don't buy any of the optional tours, equip yourself with a guidebook, and do your own sightseeing every day. Just apply the skills of independent travel to the efficient, economical trip shell that these kinds of organized coach tours provide.

Having learned long ago what doesn't work when it comes to bus tours, I've made it a priority to give people taking my Rick Steves tours the best possible experience at a midrange price. I keep my groups small (24-28 travelers), stay at least two nights in most locations (at centrally located hotels), and visit the important sights while also seeking out authentic cultural experiences. I offer a variety of itineraries—Europe-wide, regional, and city tours—and a variety of tour styles: fully guided tours, family-oriented tours, winter tours, and My Way vacations, which let you set the sightseeing itinerary (we provide the transportation, hotels, and a tour manager).

Here's my advice for choosing a bus tour and getting the most value for your money:

Go with the smallest possible group. A small group can sightsee, dine, and sleep at places that mainstream groups can only dream of. The bigger the group, the more you're cut off from Europe's charms. When 50 tourists drop into a "cozy" pub, any coziness is trampled.

Avoid one-night stands. Frequent one-night stops can really wear you out. To help you feel settled for a good night's rest, the best tours let you sleep for at least two nights in the same hotel whenever possible.

Ask where your hotels are located. Hotels set in the historic heart of a city, within walking distance of major sights, make for a far more memorable trip—but some tour companies save money by parking guests in the middle of nowhere. If the tour brochure says you'll be sleeping in the "Florence area," that could be halfway to Bologna—and you'll spend half your sightseeing time on transportation to and from the city center. *Arrivederci, Firenze.* Get explicit locations before you decide.

Look for authentic eating experiences. Pick a tour that offers a generous taste of the best local dishes. A common complaint among travelers is that tour meals don't match the country's cuisine. Avoid a tour that offers too many forgettable buffets in big, impersonal hotel restaurants. I also like tours that don't cover too many meals, as that gives you the freedom to explore restaurants on your own.

Find out about the guide. The quality of your guide can make or break your travel experience. Ask if your tour guide is salaried, or paid through tips and/or commission. Guides from most tour companies make the bulk of their income from tips and merchant kickbacks. A salaried guide can focus on creating memorable travel experiences for you—not on selling you an optional sightseeing or shopping excursion.

Take a close look at

Some tours deliver exactly what they promise.

what's included—and what's not.
Many budget tours expect you to
shell out additional cash during your
trip to cover "optional" sightseeing,
charging as much as $50 or $100
extra for each excursion.

Confirm which sights you'll see.
Do you at least recognize them? Don't
assume that every famous museum
or castle will be included in your
itinerary. Some companies choose
sights for their convenience rather
than merit. For instance, the Lion
Monument in Luzern, Switzerland is
mediocre. What makes it "great" for
tour companies is its easy tour-bus
parking. Meanwhile, Leonardo da
Vinci's *Last Supper* in Milan may be
passed over because it's expensive to
visit and its mandatory reservation
system is inconvenient.

**Ask if the tour price is locked
in once you make your deposit.**
Some tour outfits reserve the right to
increase the price after you've signed
up (depending on how many travelers
sign up and/or currency fluctuations).
Choose a company that guarantees
the price will not change.

Read the fine print. What are
the company's policies regarding
cancellations, transfers, and refunds?

Bus Tour Self-Defense

Once you're on board with a bus tour,
you'll be part of a group dynamic,
but that doesn't mean you can't have
control over your trip. Here are some
suggestions to help make sure the
good times roll for you while you're on the road:

Be informed. A good guidebook and map are your keys
to travel freedom. Get maps and tourist information from
your hotel or a tourist information office. If your accommodations are located outside the city center, ask your
hotelier how to take public transportation downtown. Taxis

Questions to Ask Tour Companies

Nail down the price:
- How many nights and meals are
  included in the price?
- Does the price cover entry fees
  for sights?
- Do singles pay a supplement? Can
  singles save by sharing rooms?
- Are optional excursions offered?
  Average cost?
- Will the guide and driver expect a
  tip? Approximately how much?
- Are there any other costs?
- Does a deposit lock in the adver-
  tised price?

Run a reality check on your dream trip:
- How many travelers will be on the
  tour?
- Roughly what is the average age
  and singles-to-couples ratio?
- Are children allowed? What is the
  minimum age?
- Which sights are on the itinerary?
- What is the driving time between
  destinations?
- How many nights are planned at
  each destination?
- Are hotels located downtown, or
  are they on the outskirts?
- Does each room have a private
  bathroom? Air-conditioning?
- How many meals are eaten at the
  hotel?
- What are the cancellation and
  refund policies?
- Can I see tour evaluations from
  past customers?

and Uber can be affordable if you split the cost with other travelers.

Remember that it's your trip. Don't let bus tour priorities keep you from what you've traveled all the way to Europe to see. If your Amsterdam guide schedules a trip to the diamond-polishing place instead of the Van Gogh Museum (no kickbacks on Van Gogh), feel free to skip out and sightsee on your own. Your guide may warn you that you'll get lost and the bus won't wait. Keep your independence—and remember the name of your hotel.

Discriminate among optional excursions. Some tour companies include certain activities in the price (such as half-day city sightseeing tours), then offer optional special excursions or evening activities for an additional cost. While you are capable of doing plenty on your own, optional excursions can be a decent value—especially when you factor in the time and energy it requires to plan and execute logistics independently. But don't feel pressured to join. Guides may promote excursions because they get a commission. Compare prices by asking your hotelier or checking a guidebook for the going rate for a gondola ride, Seine River cruise, fado show, or whatever.

You'll find that some options are a better value through your tour than from the hotel concierge, but others aren't worth the time or money. While illuminated night tours of Rome and Paris are marvelous, I'd skip most "nights on the town." On the worst kind of big-bus-tour evening, several bus tours come together for an evening of "local color." Three hundred tourists drinking watered-down sangria and watching flamenco dancing on stage to the rhythm of their camera clicks is big-bus tourism at its worst.

If you shop...shop around. Many people make their European holiday one long shopping spree. This suits your guide and the local tourist industry just fine. Guides are quick to say, "If you haven't bought a Rolex, you haven't really been to Switzerland," or, "You can't say you've experienced Florence if you haven't bargained for and bought a leather coat."

Don't necessarily reject your guide's shopping tips; just keep in mind that the prices you see often include a

A well-chosen tour can be a fine value, giving you a great trip and a table filled with new friends.

10-20 percent kickback. Do some comparison shopping, and don't let anyone rush you. Never swallow the line, "This is a special price available only to your tour, but you must buy now."

Keep your guide happy. Leading a tour is a demanding job with lots of responsibility, paperwork, traveler hand-holding, and miserable hours. Very often, guides are tired. They're away from home and family—often for months on end—and are surrounded by foreigners having an extended party that they're not always in the mood to join. Most guides treasure their time alone. Each traveler has personal demands, but don't insist on individual attention when the guide is being hounded by others. Wait for a quiet moment to ask for advice or offer feedback.

Some guides feel threatened by independent-type tourists, but it's possible to maintain your independence without alienating your guide. Use your guide as a resource, and consider their insider advice when planning your solo sightseeing.

Seek out unjaded locals. The locals most tour groups encounter are hardened businesspeople who put up with tourists because they have to—it's their livelihood. Spending a "Bavarian evening" with 40 Americans at a touristy beer hall in Munich, you'll meet all the wrong Germans. But if you make it a quest to find your own beer hall, it won't be long before you're clinking mugs with friendly locals. Break away. One summer night in Regensburg, Germany, I skipped out. While my tour was still piling off the bus, I enjoyed a beer—while overlooking the Danube, and under shooting stars—with the great-great-great-grandson of the astronomer Johannes Kepler.

CRUISING IN EUROPE

I once spoke to the CEO of a cruise line, who, in a previous career, sold children's snacks. As bizarre as that connection may seem, he explained how adults retain a natural, childlike impulse to explore, coupled with the need for a safe home to return to. While travelers love to get out of their comfort zones, doing so

Cruising offers a comfortable, efficient way to see Europe—if you do it smartly.

leads many of us to yearn all the more for a refuge or nest. Cruise ships cater to this expertly, by greeting passengers with a welcome table, cold drinks, and friendly smiles from crew members. On my first cruise, even I remember thinking, as I returned to my ship, "Whew...we're back home now."

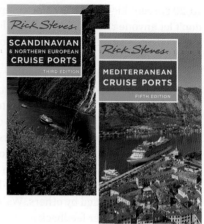

Taking a cruise can be a fun, affordable, time-efficient, low-hassle, and comforting way to experience Europe—provided you do it smartly. Cruise lines have no incentive to help you have a good time on your own in port—they'd rather you buy an organized excursion or stay on the ship to spend more money. So it's not only important to choose the right cruise, but also to keep your extra expenses to a minimum and equip yourself with good information to make the most of your time in port. (These strategies are covered in detail by my *Mediterranean Cruise Ports* and *Scandinavian & Northern European Cruise Ports* guidebooks, which teach cruisers how to use their precious shore time to their best advantage.)

A smart, informed cruiser can have a meaningful and culturally engaging experience while taking advantage of the economy and efficiency of cruising. Here are a few insights and suggestions for deciding whether or not to cruise, and how to pick the right one and make the best of your experience.

Is Cruising for You?

Short of sleeping on a park bench, I haven't found a more affordable way to see certain parts of Europe than cruising. On a Mediterranean cruise that includes room, board, transportation, tips, and port fees, a couple can pay as little as $100/person per night—that's as much as a budget hotel room in many cities.

Cruising also works well for travelers who prefer to tiptoe into Europe, rather than dive right in. Cruising can serve as an enticing sampler of bite-sized visits, helping you decide where you'd like to return and spend more time.

It's also great for retirees, particularly those with limited mobility. Cruising rescues you from packing up your bags and huffing to the train station every other day. And some cruise lines offer excursions specifically designed for those who don't walk well, making it possible to access sights that might be difficult to get to on your own. A cruise aficionado who had done the math once told me that, if you know how to find the deals, it's theoretically cheaper to cruise indefinitely than to pay for a retirement home.

Enjoy the scenery as the ship drifts away from shore.

Of course, independent, free-spirited travelers may not appreciate the constraints of cruising. For many, seven or eight hours in port is way too short, a tantalizing tease of a place where they'd love to linger for the evening—and the obligation to return to the ship every night is frustrating. If you're self-reliant, energetic, and want to stroll the cobbles of Europe at all hours, cruising probably isn't for you. Even so, some seasoned globetrotters find that cruising is a good way to travel comfortably on a shoestring budget.

There are different types of cruisers. Some travelers cruise because it's an efficient way to experience many ports of call. They appreciate the convenience of traveling while they sleep, waking up in an interesting new destination each morning, and making the most out of every second they're in port. This is the "first off, last on" crowd that attacks each port like a footrace. You can practically hear their imaginary starter's pistol go off when the gangway opens.

Other cruisers come to enjoy the cruise experience itself. They enjoy basking by the pool, taking advantage of onboard activities, dropping some cash at the casino, running up a huge bar tab, and watching ESPN on their stateroom TV.

Or you can aim for somewhere in the middle: Experience the ports that really tickle your wanderlust, but give yourself a "day off" every now and again in the less enticing ports to sleep in or hit the beach.

How Cruises Operate

Understanding how the cruise industry makes money can help you take advantage of your cruise experience...and not the other way around. In order to compete for passengers and fill megaships, cruise lines offer fares that can be astonishingly low. In adjusted dollars, the price of cruises hasn't risen for several decades. Your cruise fare covers accommodations, all the meals you can eat in the ship's main dining room and buffet, and transportation from port to port. You can have an enjoyable voyage and not spend a penny more on board (though you'd still have some expenses in port). But the cruise industry is adept at enticing you with extras that add up quickly: alcohol, gambling (at onboard casinos), and cruise-company-run excursions. Other temptations include specialty restaurant surcharges, duty-free shopping, Wi-Fi access, fitness classes, spa treatments, and photos.

It's very easy to get carried away—a round of drinks here, a night of blackjack there. First-timers are often astonished when they get their final onboard bill, which can easily exceed the original cost of the trip. But with a little self-control, you can limit your extra expenditures, making your supposedly cheap cruise *actually* cheap. You always have the right to say, "No, thanks" to these additional expenses.

Resources for Cruising

CruiseLine.com: Consumer reviews, cruise search engine, and advice forum

CruiseCritic.com: Consumer reviews of cruises and ports, cruise ship deck plans, and cruise search engine

CruiseCompete.com: Comparison quotes from multiple travel agencies, including special deals

CruiseReport.com: Consumer reviews and professional editorial reviews, cruise news, and special deals

AvidCruiser.com: Informative blog, port profiles, and cruise videos

Ship Mate app: Cruise and excursion planning, ship information, connect with other cruisers

Choosing a Cruise

Selecting a cruise that matches your travel style and philosophy is critical. Each cruise line has its own distinct personality, quirks, strengths, and weaknesses. Cruise lines fall into four basic price categories: mass-market (Royal Caribbean, Norwegian, Carnival, MSC, and Costa), premium (Celebrity, Cunard, Disney, Holland America, and Princess), luxury (Azamara Club, Oceania, Star Clippers, Viking, and Windstar), and ultra-luxury (Crystal, Regent Seven Seas, Seabourn, SeaDream, and Silversea). River cruises offer the same range of prices and quality, but with smaller boats, fewer people, and a more intimate atmosphere (see the "River Cruises" sidebar in this chapter).

Here are a few factors to keep in mind:

Price: In addition to the base fare, you'll pay taxes and port fees (which can be hundreds of dollars per person), and an auto-tip of around $15/day for each person will be added to your bill. Also remember to budget for all the aforementioned "extras" you might wind up buying onboard.

River Cruises

From the Rhine to the Danube, river cruises are a fun and relaxing way to see Europe from a different angle. Open-water sea cruises highlight many of Europe's metropolises, but they exclude the charming, smaller cities set along the Continent's historical river trade routes. River cruises fill this niche, bringing travelers closer to the true nature of a place and its people.

Budapest on the Danube is a popular river cruise destination.

River trips usually last one to two weeks. The most popular itineraries flow down the Danube, Rhone, Rhine, and Mosel (the Rhine's peaceful little sister), but routes are emerging elsewhere, such as along Portugal's Douro and Italy's Po. There are also specialty itineraries, such as Christmas markets, food and wine, and family cruises. Riverboats are notably smaller than cruise ships, which mean fewer people and a more laid-back atmosphere. Expect to share a ship with only 100 or 200 other passengers, and few children. Major operators include Avalon Waterways, Viking, Tauck, AmaWaterway, Crystal, and Uniworld.

You'll typically pay more per person for a river cruise than you would on a big cruise ship. Usually included in the price are some additional perks such as excursions, and beer and wine. Take advantage of included town walking tours—they are a valuable service that most sea-going cruises don't provide. Onboard activities aren't as heavily promoted as on sea cruises, but the focus on dynamic scenery and local culture is well worth the tradeoff.

Most river itineraries offer a pleasant balance of major tourist destinations and Back Door-type towns. You won't spend nights out on the open water, and you'll dock in the center of activity, with walk-off-the-ship access to everything, usually spend about three to eight hours in port before setting sail for the next destination. It's typical to visit at least one destination per day; a 10-day cruise, for example, will include stops in eight or more towns.

For major cities such as Paris or Prague, many cruise agencies offer packages that give you a few days ashore at the beginning or end of your voyage. Carefully examine the cost of such add-ons; you can likely extend your travels more economically by booking a hotel on your own.

Destinations: If you have a wish list of ports, use it as a starting point when shopping for a cruise.

Time Spent in Port: If exploring European destinations is your priority, look carefully at how much time the ship spends in each port; this can vary by hours from cruise line to cruise line. Be aware that certain cruise ports are in industrial zones miles away from the sights you want to see.

You may need to take public transportation into the center of town, reducing your sightseeing time.

Ship Size: The biggest ships offer a wide variety of restaurants, activities, entertainment, and other amenities (such as resources for kids)—but they can also foster a herd mentality and crowded shore experience for their 3,000-some passengers. Smaller ships offer fewer crowds, access to out-of-the-way ports, and less hassle when disembarking, but they also have fewer onboard amenities and generally cost much more.

Onboard Amenities: Decide which features matter to you most, including food (both quality and variety of restaurants), entertainment, athletic facilities, children's activities, and so on.

Booking a Cruise

While you can book directly with the cruise line, it's worth considering a travel agent, who can guide you toward picking the right cruise and cabin, and can sometimes get you upgrades or other perks. There are two types of cruise-sales agencies: a travel agency, where you can get in-person advice, or a giant cruise agency, which sells most of its inventory online or by phone. Several big cruise agencies have comparison-shopping websites, such as CruiseLine.com, CruiseCritic.com, and CruiseCompete.com.

Most cruise lines post their schedules a year or two in advance. The earlier you book, the more likely you'll have your choice of sailing and of cabin type—and potentially a better price (cruise lines typically offer discounts for booking at least 6-12 months before departure). While last-minute deals (usually within 90 days of departure) are fairly common on Caribbean cruises, they're relatively rare for European ones—and last-minute airfares to Europe can be much more expensive, too.

Like cars or plane tickets, cruises are priced flexibly. In general, for a mass-market cruise, you'll rarely pay the list price. (Higher-end cruises are less likely to be discounted.) It's common to see sales and other incentives, such as two-for-one pricing, free upgrades, onboard credits, or other extras.

While most cruise lines are willing to arrange your airfare to and from the cruise, you'll typically save money (and gain flexibility) by booking flights on your own. Allow plenty of time—ideally an overnight—before meeting your cruise; if

Excursion Cheat Sheet

This simplified roundup shows which Mediterranean ports are best by organized excursion and which are doable on your own. For details, see my *Mediterranean Cruise Ports* guidebook, dedicated to helping people cruise "through the Back Door." (Baltic cruisers should look for my *Scandinavian & Northern European Cruise Ports*.)

Destination (Port)	Excursion?
Barcelona Shuttle bus from terminal drops you right in town	No
Provence (Marseille/La Seyne-sur-Mer) Wide range of worthwhile destinations far from the ports; an excursion can hit several of these with ease	Yes
French Riviera (Nice/Villefranche/Monaco) Entire region is easy to navigate by train or bus	No
Florence, Pisa, Lucca (Livorno) These cities are cheap and reasonably easy to reach by public transportation, but excursions offer a no-hassle connection that also includes tours of major sights	Maybe
Rome (Civitavecchia) Easy, direct train trip into town, but an excursion could help you navigate this big city	Maybe
Amalfi Coast (Naples/Sorrento) Narrow roads of the Amalfi Coast are often snarled by traffic; an excursion gives you peace of mind	Yes
Naples, Pompeii (Naples) Within Naples, everything is easy to reach by foot or bus; the ruins at Pompeii are a quick train ride away	No
Venice Getting downtown is easy by public transportation; even walking there is delightful in this unique city	No
Dubrovnik Very compact and easy on your own	No
Athens (Piraeus) Getting downtown is relatively easy, but sights benefit from a good guide, and an excursion offers easy connections	Maybe

your flight is delayed and you miss your ship, you'll have to figure out how to meet it at the next port.

Cruising Tips

Food and Drink: Most cruise lines offer a wide range of onboard restaurants, including traditional dining rooms (with a semiformal dress code and assigned seating), casual buffet restaurants, room service whenever you want it, and a variety of specialty restaurants. Avoid this last kind of restaurant if you're on a budget—besides the $10-50 cover charge, certain entrées incur a "supplement" ($10-20). A couple ordering specialty items and a bottle of wine can quickly run up a $100 dinner bill.

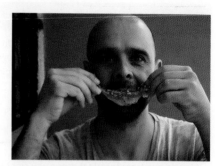

A local guide—such as my Portuguese friend Ricardo, with his "fishy" smile—makes your shore excursion memorable and fun.

In general, water, coffee, tea, milk, iced tea, and juice are included. Other drinks cost extra: alcohol of any kind, name-brand soft drinks, fresh-squeezed fruit juices, and premium espresso drinks. (Certain luxury lines include beer and wine.) To encourage alcohol sales, many cruise lines limit how much alcohol guests can bring on board, or prohibit them from bringing any at all.

Internet Access: While available, on-ship Wi-Fi can be expensive and slow. For the most part, you're often better off waiting until you're in port to get online. Find a café on shore where you can sit and download your email or log into social media over Wi-Fi while enjoying a cup of coffee—at a fraction of the shipboard cost.

Excursions vs. Independent Sightseeing: Whether it's better to sightsee on your own or with an organized excursion depends on the destination and your own level of comfort navigating Europe independently. A shore excursion efficiently takes you to a carefully selected assortment of sights, with a vetted local guide to explain everything, and is guaranteed to get you back to the ship in time (if an excursion is late, the ship will wait—but not if you're on your own). If you don't want to hassle with logistics, excursions can be a great option. But they are expensive, ranging from $40-60/person for a three-hour town walking tour to $100-150/person for an all-day bus tour.

Particularly in a place where it's easy to get into the city center on public transportation, you can have a similar experience for far less money. If you decide to go it alone, use a good guidebook or visit the local tourist information office in port. Other options are to hire a private guide to meet you at the ship and take you around or to join a scheduled walking tour of the town. As long as you keep a close eye on the time, it's easy to enjoy a very full day in port and be the last tired but happy tourist back onto the ship.

Shopping: At every stop, your cruise line will give you an information sheet highlighting local specialties and where to buy them. But be aware that cruise-recommended shops commonly give kickbacks to cruise lines and guides. This doesn't mean that the shop (or what it sells) isn't good quality; it just means you're probably paying top dollar. Many stores—not just the places working with cruise lines—jack up their rates when ships arrive, knowing they're about to get hit with a tidal wave of rushed and desperate shoppers. Before spending big money at the obvious tourist shops, be sure to check out local shopping venues, too.

Perspectives

Beyond all the practical considerations of preparing for your trip, there is another vital task: calibrating your mind for your European experience. When you travel—whether to Europe or beyond—your best souvenir can be a global perspective. This chapter covers a range of ideas, including using travel to broaden your perspective, understanding the European political landscape, and recognizing the challenges facing Europe today (and some of Europe's creative solutions). Consider this chapter pre-trip reading...a way to organize the baggage in your mind.

BROADENING YOUR PERSPECTIVE THROUGH TRAVEL

Every traveler's experience is shaped by who they are. Along with being a traveler, I'm a historian, Christian, parent, carnivore, musician, capitalist, minimalist, board member of NORML, and a workaholic. And, yes, I'm a privileged, white, upper-class American male. Growing up in the era of Leave It to Beaver, I was raised thinking the world was a pyramid with the US on top and everyone else trying to get there. I believed our role in the world was to help other people get it right...American-style. If they didn't understand that, we'd get them a government that did.

But travel changed my perspective. I met intelligent people—nowhere near as rich, free, or blessed with opportunity as I was—who wouldn't trade passports even if they could. They were thankful to be Nepali, Estonian, Turkish, Nicaraguan, or whatever. I was perplexed. I witnessed stirring struggles in lands that found other truths to be self-evident and God-given. I learned of Nathan Hales and Patrick

Henrys from other nations who only wished they had more than one life to give for their country. I discovered that considering my work ethic to be "the" work ethic was ethnocentric (and it was actually only "a" work ethic that could fall anywhere on a sliding scale of family values). I saw national pride that wasn't American. It was a challenging adjustment to my way of thinking—

but it opened my mind to a whole new world of experiences I otherwise likely would have ignored or derided.

You may be coming at your trip with more wisdom and worldliness than I did as a teenager. But no matter how much you think you know, travel has ample lessons to teach...if you're open to them. And the first step (note that I'm writing this chapter with my fellow citizens in mind) is checking your Americanness at the door.

What a difference perspective makes. When I bragged about how many gold medals our American Olympians were winning, my Dutch friend replied, "Yes, you have many medals, but per capita, we Dutch are doing five times as well."

Attitude Adjustment

When American tourists are unhappy abroad, I believe it's usually because of a stubborn desire to find the United States wherever they go. Meanwhile, the happiest travelers I meet are truly taking a vacation from America—immersing themselves in different cultures and fully experiencing different people, outlooks, and lifestyles. Here are some tips for being a thoughtful, open-minded traveler.

Embrace the differences. Even if you believe American ways are better, your trip will go better if you don't compare. Things are different in Europe—that's why you go. And European travel is a package deal. Accept the good with the "bad." If you always require the comforts of home, then that's where you'll be happiest. On the other hand, if you're observant and tune into the little differences, you may find great wisdom in how Europeans do things. For example, a three-hour dinner at a French restaurant doesn't mean the service was "slow." To the French, slow service is actually good and thoughtful. Only a rude server would rush you by dropping off the bill before you ask for it.

Don't be an "Ugly American." Years ago, the Ugly American stereotype painted US citizens as boorish travelers with a habit of putting shoes on train seats, chilling grapes in the bidet, talking loudly in restaurants, taking flash photos during Mass, hanging wet clothes out the hotel window, and consuming energy like it's cheap and theirs to waste. It's not that these travelers were bad people— just ethnocentric. Over time, I've observed that Americans are better behaved and more respectful than they once were. But a few bad apples—snapping selfies at somber memorial sites, complaining about wimpy air-conditioning—are doing their

best to carry on the Ugly American tradition.

Fortunately, fears of being perceived as an Ugly American are overblown. That's because Europeans judge you as an individual, not by your nationality. If you respect their culture and their way of doing things, I've found that Europeans love to get to know you. (When Americans find less than a warm welcome, it's likely not because they are Americans, but because they're acting out their ethnocentrism...or, simply, because that particular European is having a bad day.) If anything, my Americanness has been an asset in Europe.

Learn about current issues. Look beyond the pretty pictures and flowery tourist brochures: A few months before your trip, begin paying attention to political and economic news in your destination. If you've studied up on an area's politics, you'll get the most out of opportunities to talk with involved locals. At a Paris bistro, ask your neighbors how they think President Emmanuel Macron is handling his job. Or, at a London pub, share a pint with a few Brits and get their take on the "Brexit" saga. And be prepared to share your take on American politics, which many Europeans are fascinated—or baffled—by. (A good, tight definition of the Electoral College can come in handy.) Universities can be the perfect place to solve the world's problems with an open-minded local over a cafeteria lunch. By plugging directly into the present and listening to the European take on things, a traveler gets beyond traditional sightseeing and learns "today's history."

Go as a guest. I once asked a Parisian shopkeeper about the many social rules in her culture, such as always saying hello and goodbye, asking permission before touching any wares, and so on. "This shop is like my home," she explained. "I simply want people to behave as they would if I invited them into my living room." Act like a respectful guest, and

The Thoughtless Traveler vs. the Thoughtful Traveler

While thoughtless travelers slog through a sour Europe, mired in a swamp of complaints, thoughtful travelers fully experience their surroundings.

Thoughtless Travelers...	Thoughtful Travelers...
...criticize "strange" customs and cultural differences. They don't respect the devout Spanish Catholic appreciation of a town's patron saint, or the sense of community expressed by the evening promenade in southern Europe.	...seek out European styles of living and try new ways of thinking and doing things. They are genuinely interested in the people and cultures they visit. They accept and try to understand differences.
...demand to find America in Europe. They throw a fit if the air-conditioning breaks down in a hotel. They insist on orange juice and eggs (sunny-side up) for breakfast, long beds, English menus, ice in drinks, punctuality in Italy, and cold beer in England. They measure Europe with an American yardstick.	...are positive and optimistic. They don't dwell on problems or compare things to "back home," instead focusing on the good points of each country. As a guest in another land, they are observant and sensitive. If 60 people are dining with hushed voices in a Belgian restaurant, they know it's not the place to yuk it up.
...use money as a shield against a genuine experience. They throw money at the locals instead of trying to engage with them.	...don't flash signs of affluence, especially in poorer countries. They don't joke about the local currency or overtip. Their bucks don't talk.
...invade a country while making no effort to communicate in the local language. They don't bother to learn even the basic survival phrases ("please" and "thank you") and get angry when the Europeans they meet "refuse to speak English." Traveling in packs, they talk at and about Europeans in a condescending manner.	...make an effort to bridge the flimsy language barrier. They enjoy rudimentary communication in any language. On the train to Budapest, they might enter a debate with a Hungarian over the merits of a common European currency—despite only a 20-word shared vocabulary. They don't worry about making mistakes—they communicate!

you'll be treated like one. That's good advice no matter where you travel.

10 Ways to Travel as a Political Act

Ever since 9/11—now some 20 years ago—I've devoted a lot of time and energy to thinking about travel as an invaluable tool for learning to fit more thoughtfully into our ever-smaller world. For me, the great value of travel is the opportunity to pry open my hometown blinders and bring home a broader perspective. And when we implement that worldview as citizens of our great nation, we make travel a political act. (In fact, I wrote a book by that title—see page 38.) Here are my top 10 practical tips for doing just that:

1. Get out of your comfort zone. Choose Tangier over St. Tropez, or Turkey over Greece. When visiting Israel, make time to also explore the West Bank. You can enjoy far richer experiences for far less money by venturing away from the mainstream.

2. Connect with people—and try to understand them. Make itinerary decisions that put you in touch with locals who are also curious about you. Stay in people's homes (via Couchsurfing.com, for example) and spend time with your hosts. Hire local guides to take you around. Seek answers for cultural riddles: Why do many Muslim women wear head coverings? Why do some Americans fiercely defend their right to own a gun? Why do Norwegians willingly pay such high taxes? If America has separation of church and state, why does it say "in God we trust" on all its coins?

3. Celebrate diversity and be a cultural chameleon. When encountering a cultural difference, embrace it with joy rather than with judgment...and actually join in: Dip your fries in mayonnaise in Belgium, eat with your fingers in Moroccan restaurants that have no silverware, smoke a hookah in Turkey, and go to a hurling match in Ireland. Rather than gawking at the pilgrims, become one. Climb Rome's Scala Santa (Holy Stairs) on your knees, feeling the pain while finding comfort in the frescoes of saints all around you.

4. Understand the contemporary context. While traveling, get caught up on local news. Go to a political rally in Scotland. Listen to expat radio on Spain's Costa del Sol. Think about how all societies are on parallel evolutionary tracks. Imagine how the American approach to common and persistent societal problems might work in other places—and (more importantly) vice versa.

5. Empathize with the other 96 percent of humanity. Just as Americans have the American Dream, others have their own dreams. Make a point to put yourself in the shoes (or sandals, or bare feet) of the people you meet. Find out why Basque people are so passionate about their language... and then find a parallel in your society. As you travel, learn to celebrate the local Nathan Hales and Ethan Allens—Turkey's Atatürk, Italy's Garibaldi, and so on.

6. Identify—and understand—other societies' baggage. The US was preoccupied with terrorism for decades, although in recent years civil rights and racism have risen to the forefront. Other nations have their own, sometimes even heavier, baggage. Ponder societal needs even more fundamental than freedom and democracy. Why is Putin so popular in Russia? Why would a modern and well-educated Egyptian be willing to take a bullet for the nation's military dictator (as my friend in Cairo told me)? Why, in some struggling countries, does stability one-up democracy?

7. Accept the legitimacy of other moralities. Be open to the possibility that controversial activities are not objectively "right" or "wrong." Consider Germany's approach to prostitution or the Netherlands' marijuana policy, which are both based on pragmatic harm reduction rather than moralism. Get a French farmer's take on force-feeding his geese to produce foie gras. In Istanbul, skip the touristy versions and attend an authentic Whirling Dervish ritual. Ask a Spaniard why bullfighting still thrives as the national pastime—and why it's covered not in the sports pages, but in the arts section of the local newspaper. You don't have to like the answer, but at least try to understand it.

Thank You	
Arabic	*shukran*
Bulgarian	*blagodarya*
Croatian	*hvala*
Czech	*děkuji*
Danish	*tak*
Dutch	*dank u wel*
Estonian	*tänan*
Finnish	*kiitos*
French	*merci*
German	*danke*
Greek	*efharisto*
Hebrew	*todah*
Hungarian	*köszönöm*
Icelandic	*takk*
Italian	*grazie*
Polish	*dziękuję*
Portuguese	*obrigado*
Russian	*spasiba*
Slovak	*d'akujem*
Slovene	*hvala*
Spanish	*gracias*
Turkish	*teşekkür ederim*

8. Sightsee with an edge. Seek out political street art… and find out what it means. Read local culture magazines and attend arts and political events. Take an alternative tour to learn about heroin maintenance clinics in Switzerland or Copenhagen's Christiania commune. Explore the poorer parts of town with the help of a local friend or guide. And, when you meet struggling people living with a spirit of abundance, ponder how so many rich people live with a mindset of scarcity.

9. Make your trip an investment in a better world. Our world has a lot of desperation, and travelers are the privileged few who can afford to experience what's outside their own hometowns. Travel with a goal of good stewardship—the idea that each traveler has a responsibility to be an ambassador to, and for, the entire planet. Think of yourself as a modern-day equivalent of the medieval jester: sent out by the king to learn what's going on outside the walls, and then coming home to speak truth to power...even if it is annoying.

10. Make a broader perspective your favorite souvenir. Back home, be evangelical about your newly expanded global viewpoint. Travel shapes who you are. Weave favorite strands of other cultures into the tapestry of your own life. Live your life as if it shapes the world and the future... because it does. Believe that you matter. Then make a difference.

UNDERSTANDING THE EUROPEAN UNION

Over several generations, the countries of Europe have gone from being bitter rivals to member states in one of the world's biggest economies: the European Union. Peacefully bringing together such a diverse collection of separate nations—with different languages and cultures—is unprecedented.

Essentially, the EU is a free-trade zone with its own currency (the euro, used in most member countries). While not quite a "United States of Europe," the EU has an elected Europe-wide parliament with real power and a substantial budget that passes laws on economic policy and some social and foreign policy issues.

Today, the European Union includes most of Western Europe (except Switzerland and the United Kingdom), and a large chunk of Eastern Europe and Scandinavia. But the union is not a perfect marriage; most notably, the UK left the EU in 2020 (after a national referendum supported Britain's exit—"Brexit").

Everyone has an opinion on how well the EU works. "Eurocrats" and other optimists see it as a bold and idealistic experiment in unity, mutual understanding, and shared priorities. "Euroskeptics" view it as a bloated, overly bureaucratic monster that threatens to wring the diversity and charm out of the Old World. They especially resent the rising power of corporate lobbyists (to essentially write Europe's new laws) and the way the EU has lashed economically healthy countries to troubled ones. One fascinating dimension of traveling in today's Europe is finding out how the people you meet feel about the EU. There are as many opinions as there are Europeans.

EU Nations

FINLAND
SWEDEN
ESTONIA
North
Sea
LATVIA
DENMARK
LITHUANIA
IRELAND
POLAND
NETH.
GERMANY
Atlantic
Ocean
Brussels☆
LUX.
BELGIUM
CZECH.
SLOVAKIA
FRANCE
AUST.
HUNG.
SLOVENIA
CROATIA
ROMANIA
PORTUGAL
ITALY
BULGARIA
SPAIN
Mediterranean
Sea   GREECE
MALTA→
CYPRUS→
North Sea

The EU: Past and Present

World War II left 40 million dead and a continent in ruins, and convinced Europeans that they had to work together to maintain peace. Poised between competing superpowers (the US and the USSR), they also needed to cooperate economically to survive in an increasingly globalized economy.

Just after the war ended, visionary "Eurocrats" began the task of persuading reluctant European nations to relinquish elements of their sovereignty and merge into a united body. Starting in 1949, European states gradually came together to form the Common Market (also known as the European Economic Community). In 1992, with the Treaty of Maastricht, the 12 member countries of the Common Market made a big leap of faith: They created a "European Union" that would eventually allow capital, goods, services, and labor to move freely across borders. The by-products would be a common currency, softened trade barriers, EU passports, and the elimination of border checks between member countries (the "Schengen Agreement").

In 2002, most EU members adopted the euro as a single currency, and for all practical purposes, economic unity was a reality. Over the next two decades, membership grew quickly, mainly through the addition of formerly communist countries in Central and Eastern Europe. As of 2021, EU membership stands at 27 nations, encompassing a vast swath of the Continent. The EU is now the world's seventh largest "country" (1.7 million square miles), with the third largest

As Europe unites, historically subjugated peoples are enjoying more autonomy. Dissolved by England in 1707, the Scottish Parliament returned in 1999, meeting in its modern Edinburgh digs (above). A statue, just outside the European Parliament in Brussels, holds the symbol of the euro (right).

population (about 450 million people). Its annual GDP (around $17 trillion) makes its economy second only to the US (roughly $21 trillion), with China in third place (about $14 trillion).

The EU is governed from Brussels and administered through a complicated network of legislative bodies, commissions, and courts that attempt to complement each country's government while minimizing encroachment on individual nations' sovereignty. The EU cannot levy taxes (that's still done through national governments), and it cannot deploy troops without each nation's approval. Unlike America's federation of 50 states, Europe's member states retain the right to opt out of some EU policies. For example,

US vs. EU by the Numbers

	US	EU
Population	332.6 million	450 million
Land area	3.8 million square miles	1.7 million square miles
Gross domestic product (GDP)	$19.5 trillion	$17.3 trillion
Life expectancy	80.3 years	80.9 years
Infant mortality rate	5.3 deaths/1,000	3.7 deaths/1,000
Mobile phones	408.5 million	625 million
Annual military budget	3.42% of GDP	1.5% of GDP

Sources: CIA World Factbook, 2020

LEFT The vast and shiny EU headquarters in Brussels welcomes visitors on guided tours to take a peek at Europe at work.

RIGHT New roads are bringing the infrastructure in Europe up to speed. These EU-funded projects (such as this one in Ireland) come with a billboard and an EU flag reminding drivers where the funding came from.

several countries (such as Denmark, Croatia, and Romania) belong to the EU but have retained their traditional currencies.

It's a delicate balance trying to develop laws and policies for all Europeans while respecting the rights of nations, regions, and individuals. An oft-quoted EU slogan is "promoting unity"—that is, economic and political—"while preserving diversity." But the European responses to the Yugoslav Wars in the early 1990s, the economic bailout of Greece, the refugee crisis, and the coronavirus pandemic have demonstrated that Europe isn't always prepared to speak with a single voice.

Like any bold experiment, the EU has hit some snags as it's evolved. On the positive side, France and Germany have woven their economies together to such a degree that there likely will never again be a huge war in Europe. And by creating a vast free-trade zone, the EU economy is better able to compete with other giant markets (like the US and China). But momentum toward further integration and expansion has hit a wall. Nativist, isolationist movements are on the rise across Europe (much as they have been in the US); this culminated in the UK's departure from the EU in 2020. Later in this chapter, the "European Challenges (and Solutions)" section considers some of these topics in depth.

What Is European Socialism?

As the limits of unbridled American capitalism have grown more evident in recent years—with our shrinking, struggling middle class and growing gap between the haves and the have-nots—we're hearing more and more about "European-style socialism." What is European socialism, exactly?

To understand the European approach to government, it helps to consider the different philosophies that influence life on either side of the Atlantic—and specifically, the different ways we approach what philosophers call "the Social Contract": the community-wide agreement about what personal liberties each citizen gives up in order to live peaceably together. The Enlightenment philosophers John Locke and Jean-Jacques Rousseau are famed for their opposing takes.

The US, which celebrates rugged (white, male) individualism, is closer to John Locke's idea: People should be free to do anything, as long as it doesn't impinge on their neighbor. This is reflected throughout our history and our contemporary politics: "Don't Tread on Me," the cowboys of the Old West, "Get the government off my back," the push for lower taxes and less regulation, an ethic of self-reliance ("pull yourself up by your bootstraps"), and so on.

Europe (with a denser population and a longer history) is more on the side of Rousseau—embracing the idea that giving up more than you get is a fair trade in order to live well together as a society. The result is bigger government, more taxes, and more restrictions. Rousseau believed this approach allows people to live more efficiently together as a society...and, ultimately, enjoy more freedoms. (Thomas Jefferson, so instrumental in writing the US Constitution, was a fan of Rousseau.)

But socialism is not binary, it's a spectrum: How much socialism will you employ to create your society? American voters are presented with two options: big, bad government or good, small government. Europe offers a third option: big, good government. Like us, Europe is enthusiastically capitalistic. But unlike us, it's also enthusiastically socialist. Most Europeans continue to favor their high (and highly progressive) tax rates—and the social programs those taxes fund. That's because they believe that collectively creating

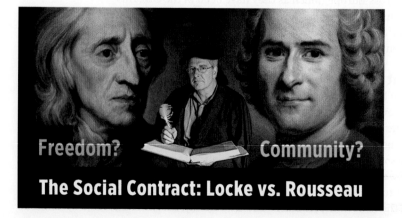

Freedom?   Community?

The Social Contract: Locke vs. Rousseau

the society of their dreams is more important than allowing individuals to create personal empires.

In Scandinavia—the most highly taxed, socialistic, and humanistic corner of Europe—you won't find a church with a steeple on the main square. Instead, you'll find a city hall with a bell tower. Inside, a secular nave leads not to a pulpit, but to a lectern. Behind that lectern, a grand mosaic tells epic stories—not from the Bible, but stories celebrating heroic individuals who contributed mightily to their community.

In Europe's most socialistic corner, city halls rather than churches dominate the town center.

Europeans pay high taxes to buy big, good government... and they expect results. Those results include an extensive social-welfare network that puts the financial burden of childcare, health care, education, and retirement on the collective shoulders of society, rather than on individuals. I once asked Olle, my Swiss friend, "How can you Swiss people be so docile about paying such high taxes?" Without missing a beat, he replied, "Well, what's it worth to live in a society where there is no homelessness, no hunger, and where every child—regardless of the wealth of their parents—enjoys equal access to quality health care and education?"

The benefits are widespread. A Slovenian friend of mine who had a baby was guaranteed a year's maternity leave at near-full pay...and was given a state-subsidized "starter kit" with all the essential gear she needed to care for her newborn. Higher education in Europe is subsidized; in many countries, it's entirely free, and students even get "pocket money" while they are learning. (Europeans consider a well-educated society fundamental to their notion of national security and pay for it as readily as Americans invest in military hardware.) Hundreds of thousands of students and professors travel to other EU countries to study and teach, building a sprawling network of intra-European relations through the EU-funded Erasmus Program.

Another major example is health care. While specifics vary from country to country, all of Europe has some form of socialized medicine. Anecdotally, it's clear to me that—while they may complain from time to time—Europe is satisfied with their system. In fact, I have never met a single European, of any walk of life or socioeconomic status (and I know hundreds from across the Continent), who would trade their socialized health care for our private-insurance system. And American travelers who find themselves needing a doctor while in Europe report a high level of care and a very small bill...if they ever even see the bill.

Don't get me wrong: Europeans grumble about paying sky-high taxes as much as anyone, and tax evasion is a national pastime for many. But philosophically, they understand that when it comes to taxes, the necessity outweighs the evil. European politicians don't have to promise tax cuts to win elections. Many European voters support high taxes and big government because they like what they get in return.

When I shudder at Switzerland's high taxes, my friend Olle explains it's simply the cost of living in a country with equal access to healthcare and education.

Is the American approach "wrong" and Europe's approach "right"? As a taxpayer and a job creator, I see pros and cons to both systems. (And I'll delve into some of the challenges Europe faces in the next section.) But one thing's clear: We can all benefit by comparing notes.

EUROPEAN CHALLENGES (AND SOLUTIONS)

While I'm clearly a fan of the EU, I recognize that it's not all smooth sailing. Understanding the challenges that face the EU today can add a new dimension to your trip, and give you something to chat about with new friends. Many of these challenges are similar to those facing the US; seeing how another culture grapples with difficult issues can help put our own struggles in a new light.

Economic Issues

Since World War II, Europe has been, by and large, an economic success story. But global trends over the past several years have revealed some vulnerabilities in the unified European economy.

Europe's generous approach to entitlements (such as health care and education) was conceived in a postwar baby boom society with lots of people working, fewer living to retirement, and those living beyond retirement having a short life span. That was sustainable...no problem. But the consequence of that success—a healthy, well-educated, and affluent society—is fewer babies and longer lifespans. Now the demographic makeup of Europe has flipped upside down: relatively few people working, lots of people retiring, and those who are retired living a long time. With less tax revenue and more expenses, the arithmetic just isn't there to sustain the generous entitlements Europeans have come to expect. As taxes necessarily go up and benefits necessarily go down, Europe will be struggling with this recalibration for years to come.

These challenges are exacerbated by the disparity in economic success among the EU's various members. When Europe united, its less-affluent countries (such as Ireland, Portugal, and Greece) received lots of development aid from the rich ones (mostly Germany and France). I remember when there were no freeways in any of the poor countries. Now they are all laced with German-style (and mostly German-funded) superhighways. These countries traded in their lazy currencies for the euro (which is, in a way, the mighty Deutsche mark in disguise, as the European economy is driven and dominated by Germany).

The 2008 global economic crisis brought those disparities to the fore. It became clear that, by earning wages in euros and getting aid in euros, Europe's poorer nations had enjoyed a false prosperity that they might not have merited—and the bursting real estate bubble made it worse. Before unity, if a nation didn't produce much and slid into debt, the economy could be adjusted simply by devaluing that nation's currency. Today, there's no way to devalue the currency of a particular country on the euro, so this fix is not an option.

As this reality set in, the EU's wealthier nations grew impatient with shoring up the poorer ones. In the mid-2010s, many Germans became resentful at seeing some of their taxes sent south to bail out Greece's failing economy. The two countries debated whether Germany had a right to make those funds provisional. While the conflict was resolved diplomatically—without resorting to the much-feared "Grexit"—it highlighted an ongoing tension within the EU. During the 2020 coronavirus pandemic, German Chancellor Merkel and French President Macron—representing the EU's wealthiest nations—supported an $850 billion bailout benefitting the entire union. Pundits asked: Was this simply a band-aid on the inevitable unraveling of the EU economy? Or a sign that EU leaders are doubling down on this idealistic experiment—and determined to keep the European economy woven together?

Facing these economic challenges, Europeans who worked diligently with the expectation of retiring at 62 are now being told they'll need to work an extra decade—and even then, a generous retirement may not be waiting for them. Any austerity programs strong enough to put a society back on track is also tough enough to get people marching in the streets. I expect we'll continue to see marches and strikes in Europe as it continues to sort out its economy. Europeans demonstrate: It's in their blood and a healthy part of their democracy. When frustrated and needing to vent grievances, they hit the streets. I've been caught up in huge and boisterous marches all over Europe, and it's not scary; in fact, it can be exhilarating. "*La Manifestation!*" as they say in France.

I'm sometimes asked whether struggling economies within the EU are safe to visit. When assessing the seriousness of any civil unrest, remember that commercial TV news is there both to report and to make a profit. Producers will always grab video footage that makes a demonstration appear as exciting as possible. Unrest is generally localized—frightening in a zoom lens' tight focus but much less so with a wide-angle shot. As a traveler, you'll scarcely be aware of these problems. Expect a few demonstrations and a few strikes. They bring far more inconvenience than risk.

Diversity and Immigration

One thing I love about Europe is its diversity—how many different countries and cultures you can encounter in a relatively compact area. On a global scale, Europe's "diversity" may be subtle: To a casual observer, a Spaniard, a Pole, a Greek, and a Scot may come across basically the same. But they recognize worlds of difference between themselves, such as language, food, culture, customs, history, and so on.

Diversity means something different in Europe (where, historically, its nations' populations have been largely homogenous) than in the US (a nation of immigrants with a heritage of slavery and indigenous genocide). People of non-European descent are a relatively recent addition to the European cultural tapestry. While most Europeans did not directly own slaves, they participated in (and greatly benefitted from) the African slave trade of the 16th through 19th centuries. Colonial powers such as Portugal, Spain, the Netherlands, Belgium, France, and Great Britain built their wealth on the exploitation of people and resources on the far side of the globe. (What they call the "Age of Exploration"

could just as easily be called the "Age of Exploitation.")
Some transplants from these overseas holdings eventually
made their way to Europe, which is why you'll meet people
of African, Caribbean, Indian, and Bangladeshi descent in
Britain, dine at Indonesian restaurants in Amsterdam, hear
Brazilian music in Portugal, explore a Congolese neighborhood in Brussels, and notice a large Tunisian population in
parts of France. Some of these minority groups have been
oppressed and excluded from mainstream society; others
have found opportunities to assimilate and thrive. (Great
Britain considers chicken tikka masala its "national dish.")

Another wave of new arrivals began as Europe rebuilt
after World War II. The local population had been depleted,
and able-bodied workers were needed. For example, in the
postwar years, many Turkish people came to Germany
to help rebuild the country while building new lives for
themselves. The German term Gastarbeiter—guest worker—
become pan-European jargon for immigrant labor.

But even taking these non-native European groups into
account, Europe remains predominantly white. According
to the European Network Against Racism, only about 10
percent of Europe identifies as non-white (compared to about
25 percent of Americans). This may be why travelers of color
find different challenges when visiting Europe (see page
455).

The Black Lives Matter movement that swept the United
States during the summer of 2020 also spread across the
Atlantic. In much of Europe, people were forced to grapple
with questions of diversity and racism that had long been
brushed aside. Statues of European "heroes" instrumental in
the slave trade were toppled into rivers, and long-overlooked
minority groups were, in many cases, seen and heard for
the first time by white Europeans. The EU parliament voted
to declare "Black Lives Matter," to condemn racism, and to
denounce the slave trade as a crime against humanity. As in
the US, Europe has a long way to go in combatting racism.
But progress is being made.

At the same time, the past several years have also seen
a rise in anti-immigrant sentiment across much of Europe.
With the EU's financial success has come a wave of people
from around the world seeking to take part. And as immigrants from every corner of the world come to Europe, many
white Europeans struggle to adapt.

Some whites say they are frustrated by large numbers
of immigrants—and their European-born children—who,

critics claim, stick together in tight communities, cling to their homeland traditions, and are slow to adopt European culture. (Immigrants would likely counter that they've found few opportunities to integrate with their European neighbors and are in some cases held back by systemic racism.)

As in the US, immigrants are sometimes perceived as challenging lifelong residents for jobs, or overburdening an already strained welfare system. Yet many experts see immigrants as a solution to Europe's economic woes: As the native-European population ages and the birth rate declines (as explained in the previous section), Europe will need an influx of labor to keep up. Others ask whether European culture might in fact be strengthened more by diversity than assimilation. It seems that, like it or not, Europe is poised to grow more and more diverse.

Another thorny issue is friction between European Christianity and the Islamic faith of many immigrants. Europe's population is now approximately 5 percent Muslim, having increased sharply over the past several years. Europe has a long history of seeing itself as the bulwark of Christianity against a rising tide of Islam—from the Moors in Spain to the Crusades of the Holy Land to the Ottomans from present-day Turkey. While many Europeans are secular progressives who pride themselves on accepting all faiths, others worry about the Muslim impact on their traditional culture.

In the last decade, warfare and failed states in areas nearby (especially in Syria) have sent a wave of refugees toward Europe. In 2015, the Continent saw more than a million refugees arrive from war-torn countries in the Middle East, Asia, and Africa; hundreds of thousands more followed over the next few years.

These refugees are leaving miserable and dangerous worlds, taking huge risks in the process. (And much of today's tragic chaos in countries like Libya, Syria, and Iraq can be attributed to the nonsensical borders drawn by Europeans a century ago that ignored tribal and ethnic realities while building colonial empires.) Thousands have died trying to cross the Mediterranean to Europe. And terrible hardships are being experienced at Europe's borders. But many Europeans feel it's simply too many people, coming too fast, to constructively join a society already facing other challenges.

The coronavirus pandemic—and resulting closure of borders—took the steam out of the refugee debate. But it will also increase the desperation of people seeking better lives in Europe. These questions will likely loom large on the European scene for quite some time to come.

Nativism

Concerns about immigration and refugees have contributed to the rise of nativist, anti-EU movements. Brexit is the best-known example of this trend, but each European country has its own version. In some countries, nativists remain on the fringe, while in others, they've had great success. In Germany, white supremacist groups continue to exist despite concerted efforts to root them out. Two of the most influential (and alarming) nativist movements are Hungarian Prime Minister Viktor Orbán's Fidesz party and the "Law and Order" party in Poland. Nativist movements are even more active at the edges of Europe. In Russia, Vladimir Putin has devised ways to stay in power for more than 20 years—providing a blueprint for would-be despots everywhere. And in Turkey, Recep Tayyip Erdoğan took power in 2014 and has aggressively moved his country away from Europe and from its own moderate, pluralistic, and democratic roots—and toward fundamentalism.

In each place, upon being democratically elected, the nativists act quickly to expand their power, politicize their judicial systems, silence and delegitimize critics, and stir up their base with fearmongering, bold lies, and empty promises. Once in power, a nativist movement often marches toward authoritarianism. (If any of this sparks déjà vu, that's because our own Donald Trump took a page from the nativist playbook—even enlisting several advisers who had aided nativist movements in Europe.) Nativism poses an existential threat to representative democracy, to open society, and to the EU itself. (Believing history is speaking to us and it's important to listen, I produced a one-hour public television special about the rise of fascism in Europe in the lead up to WWII to help viewers identify these trends; you can watch it for free at www.ricksteves.com/fascism.)

The European political pendulum is always swinging. A decade ago, left-leaning social democratic parties dominated; today, nativism is in vogue. For those who appreciate the EU, the hope is that the pendulum will swing back toward the cooperative, open-minded center sooner rather than later. But in the meantime, learning—and asking your new European friends—about the political situation in the country you're visiting adds a fascinating dimension to your trip...and, potentially, some new insights about how things are going politically back home.

Drug Policy: Pragmatic Harm Reduction

In both the US and Europe, the abuse of drugs—whether "soft drugs" (such as marijuana, alcohol, and tobacco) or "hard drugs" (including opioids and methamphetamines)—is a serious problem. However, while the US tends to view drugs through a lens of crime prevention and eradication (the "war on drugs"), Europe takes a more pragmatic view, focusing on harm reduction. And, while Europe certainly doesn't have all the answers, their results have been compelling. I've traveled with an appetite for learning why Europe has fewer drug-related deaths, less drug-related violence, and less drug-related incarceration, while having less drug consumption per capita than the United States. In short, Europe is not "hard on drugs" or "soft on drugs"—they're simply smart on drugs.

There is no Europe-wide agreement on drug policy. But what most European countries have in common is an emphasis on education and prevention rather than arrests and incarceration. They believe that by handling drug abuse more as a public health problem than as a criminal one, they are better able to reduce the harm it causes—both to the individual (health problems and antisocial behavior) and to society (health-care costs, policing costs, and drug-related crime).

Generally, Europeans employ a three-pronged strategy for dealing with hard drugs: law enforcement, education, and health care. Police zero in on dealers—not users—to limit the supply of drugs. Users generally get off with a warning and are directed to get treatment. Anti-drug education programs work hard to credibly warn people (particularly teenagers) of the dangers of drugs. And finally, the medical community steps in to battle health problems associated with drug use (especially HIV/AIDS and hepatitis C) and to help addicts reclaim their lives.

The casual American observer who sees more junkies on the streets of Europe than in the US may conclude they have a bigger drug problem. In fact, according to UN figures, the percentage of Western Europeans who use illicit drugs is about half that of Americans. The difference is that theirs are out and about while receiving treatment and trying to get their lives back on track. Ours are more often either dead or in jail.

For example, consider a society that, a generation ago,

suffered a severe opioid epidemic (and resulting crime wave): Switzerland. The Swiss have made remarkable progress in combating that social ill with progressive and compassionate policies. Today, when a Swiss addict needs a fix, they go to a heroin-maintenance clinic, where they get access to clean and safe needles, the drug their body craves, a safe environment in which to shoot up, and—crucially—the services of a nurse and a counselor. With these provisions, you still have an addict. But you remove crime, violence, money, and disease from the equation, so you can treat it for what it is: a health problem for people who are hurting themselves. Swiss society wants to help addicts stay alive, get off welfare, and rejoin the workforce.

When it comes to soft drugs, policies in much of Europe are also more creative and pragmatic than America's. For example, take the Netherlands, with its famously permissive marijuana laws. The Dutch are known for their practice of gedogen—toleration. They believe that as soon as you criminalize something, you lose any ability to regulate it. So, just as we tolerate and regulate alcohol and tobacco, they tolerate and regulate recreational pot smoking. But Dutch tolerance has its limits. The moment you hurt or threaten someone else, the crime is no longer victimless—and no longer tolerated. Dutch laws against driving under the influence—whether alcohol or marijuana—are extremely tough. (For more on Amsterdam's marijuana trade, see "Cannabis and Coffeeshops" on page 677.)

Meanwhile, while attitudes are changing, much of the US still seems afraid to grapple with this problem openly and innovatively. Rather than acting as a deterrent, the US criminalization of marijuana drains precious resources, disproportionately convicts and imprisons people of color for simple possession, clogs our legal system, and distracts law enforcement attention from more pressing safety concerns. Of the many billions of tax dollars we invest annually fighting our war on drugs, more than half is spent on police, courts, and prisons. On the other hand, European nations—seeking a cure that isn't more costly than the problem itself—spend a much larger portion of their drug policy funds on nurses, counselors, and clinics. This idea—under the (unfortunate) name "defunding the police"—remains controversial in the US. But in Europe, it has a proven track record. European policymakers estimate that they save 15 euros in police and health-care costs for each euro invested in drug education, addiction prevention, and counseling.

In recent years, American legislators and voters have finally taken Europe's lead: Starting with my home state of Washington in 2012, more and more parts of the US are decriminalizing marijuana. Inspired by my experiences seeing how Europe has successfully tackled this program, I have personally campaigned for legalization in many states. And as of this writing, more than half of US states have some form of legal or decriminalized marijuana. For more on this complicated topic, I've written an entire chapter on European drug policy in my book *Travel as a Political Act* (or go to www.ricksteves.com/marijuana).

Global Climate Change

During a heat wave several years ago in Italy, I switched hotels because it was too hot to sleep without air-conditioning. It was the first time I had done that, and it was a kind of personal defeat—since I've always prided myself on not needing air-conditioning.

There's no doubt in Europe (and among Europeans) that things are warming up. Nearly everywhere in the Alps, summer skiing is just a memory, and—even in the winter—ski resorts are in desperate straits for lack of snow. (These days, new ski lifts in Europe routinely come with plumbing for snowmaking equipment.) Eating outdoors in formerly cool-climate Munich or Amsterdam now feels like a tradition. With each visit to Germany, more and more hoteliers tell me that they've needed to install air-conditioning to cope with sweltering summer heat. Dutch kids wait years for a frozen canal to skate on. Scandinavia is seeing a spike in summer-time visitors from Spain and Italy seeking a break from the heat.

Europeans don't have to be convinced that climate change is real. And they are rising to the challenge—both in responding to its impact and in adopting "green" policies to slow the frightening warming of our planet.

Everywhere I go in Europe, I see the results of hundreds of billions of dollars being invested in infrastructure changes that will allow Europe to survive in the future that we are creating. For instance, the German city of Hamburg—situated just up a big river from the sea, and therefore in danger of storm surges—has raised 60 miles of embankments...and artfully designed the ones in the city center to be inviting people zones. In England's Portsmouth, floodgates are being built on medieval streets that never needed them before. And the Dutch—famously smart, famously frugal, and famously below sea level—are spending billions of euros to shore up their dikes and prepare for a rising sea.

Europe also legislates in a way that minimizes its carbon footprint. High-speed (and energy-efficient) trains have replaced long drives and polluting flights, wind farms dot the landscape, and industries are held to rigid emissions standards. In particularly green Denmark, residents must pay for the disposal of a car when they first buy it, while entire towns are competing to see which will be the first to become entirely wind-powered. Cities such as London, Stockholm, and Milan levy a congestion charge on drivers entering the city center during peak hours. This cuts down on both pollution and traffic, and the money generated helps fund the cities' public transportation systems.

As they've sweltered through summer after summer, Europeans (and their visitors) have long embraced the "inconvenient truth" that things are heating up.

To reduce reliance on cars, many European cities have become aggressively bike-friendly, with well-groomed bike lanes and even free or very cheap loaner bikes for quick rides within town. Next to Amsterdam's central train station stands a high-rise garage—not for cars, but for bicycles. While these ideas sound laughably idealistic to some oil-addicted American cynics, Europeans are making them a reality, and environmentally conscious travelers can take advantage of them, too.

I believe a day of reckoning will soon come, when honest travelers will recognize that flying to Europe pumps more carbon into the atmosphere than our earth can handle. Europeans are starting to impose "carbon taxes" that force consumers to pay for the negative impact their purchases have on the environment. But the US government lags behind Europe on these measures.

That's why, at my travel company (Rick Steves' Europe, Inc.), we're committed to giving back some of our profit—with a kind of self-imposed carbon tax—to mitigate the impact our European bus tours have on our environment. Rather than purchase "carbon offset credits," we've innovated an approach that invests in climate-smart agriculture and agroforestry projects in the world's poorest countries. As of 2020, our donations have totaled $1.5 million, which is what experts estimate we need to spend annually to make up for the carbon footprint of our tour members' flights to Europe (that's $30 per traveler). The money has been

Green Travel Tips

Europe is taking the lead on protecting our fragile environment. As travelers—who burn fossil fuels with every intercontinental flight and bus tour—we need to do our part to address climate change, too. Here are a few "green" travel tips to consider on your next trip:

- Make sure your home isn't bleeding energy while you're away—turn down the thermostat, unplug appliances, and suspend print subscriptions.
- Once in Europe, travel by train, which is energy-efficient and generally fast, easy, and comfortable.
- If you rent a car, pick the most fuel-efficient option, and decline offers to upgrade to a model that's bigger than you need.
- In cities, take advantage of Europe's excellent public transportation rather than relying on taxis. (For example, Europe's airports are all well-served by easy, frequent public transit.) Enjoy the thrill of getting around by bike if you can.
- Be conscious of your energy consumption in hotels. Turn off the lights and air-conditioning whenever you leave. (Many European hotel rooms already help you do this: The power turns on only when your key is in a slot.) On warm days, close the window shutters or curtains before you leave in the morning, and you won't need to blast the air-con when you return.
- Because room service generates needless laundry, I hang the "do not disturb" sign on my door and reuse my towel.
- Most of Europe is flowing with great tap water, often available from fountains in towns and cities. By reusing a plastic water bottle or bringing a refillable bottle, you save money and reduce demand for plastic bottles that are shipped by trucks and trains.
- Reduce your use of disposable items with a little prep: Pack a lightweight shopping bag to keep in your day bag, and bring a set of reusable picnic ware. Don't pick up brochures, maps, or other materials that you don't plan to keep—get your info online instead. (The fewer brochures you pick up at tourist offices, the fewer they'll print next year.) Avoid using the individually packaged toiletries found in hotel rooms—a single bar of soap and squeeze bottle of shampoo from home can last an entire trip.
- Eat locally: Food that hasn't been trucked long distances is easier on the environment (and tastier). Do your picnic shopping at farmers markets, and avoid chain restaurants. Look for restaurants that use mainly local and organic ingredients (more likely at smaller, family-run places; "bio" is shorthand for "organic" in many European languages).
- Use hotels and travel companies that promote and practice sustainable travel.
- Europeans seem to live more while consuming less, and live as if their choices can shape a better future. Take home a little of that sensibility as a souvenir. Even in small ways, we can make a difference.

invested in non-profit organizations working in three areas: building cleaner and more efficient "smart stoves" for off-the-grid communities; introducing environmentally friendly farming practices that help smallholder farmers increase their yield, reduce erosion and deforestation, and improve their quality of life; and lobbying the US government to support climate-smart policies. To learn more about our initiative and the thinking behind it, go to www.ricksteves.com/climate.

The COVID-19 Pandemic

Europe, the US, and the rest of the planet came to a standstill in early 2020 as Covid-19 spread across the globe. I was struck by the difference between the American and European responses. The initial European response was more communal-minded, launching strict lockdowns and forfeiting a higher degree of personal freedom to "flatten the curve." The US, with its "don't fence me in" individualism, was reluctant to sacrifice quite so much; businesses reopened sooner (or never closed) and masking guidelines met with resistance. The result was that Europe got their initial outbreak under control much more quickly and decisively than the US.

When another Covid wave hit both sides of the Atlantic in late 2020 and early 2021, Europe was swift to lock down, while the US politicized commonsense measures (like mask-wearing). And as the pandemic peaked, Covid had killed well over half a million Americans—about a 50 percent higher per capita death rate than in Europe.

With the rollout of vaccines in 2021, the US had the advantage—our new leadership vaccinated the population faster than Europe's less efficient, patchwork approach. By early summer, jabbed Americans were raring to go, but Europe was still getting its act together to let us back in.

What will post-pandemic travel in Europe look like? As of this printing, much is still not known. Proof of vaccination, mask-wearing, and some degree of social distancing are likely to be part of the European travel experience for a while. But I'm hoping that, as "herd immunity" is reached, we can get back to normal. For extroverts like me, the beauty of travel is the opposite of social distancing. It's having my cheeks kissed in Paris, packing the piazza in Rome, doing the paseo in Spain, and clinking glasses in an Irish pub where they like to say "strangers are just friends who've yet to meet."

Terrorism

Times change. But, it seems, terrorism is always with us—whether in the US (9/11 and too many mass shootings to count) or in Europe (Norway's 2011 Utøya Island massacre and more recent attacks in Paris, Brussels, Nice, Vienna, and

Heavy security at major attractions, such as the Duomo in Florence, is a common sight.

so on). Every superpower is seen by angry people beyond its borders as an evil empire. All have had insurgents nipping at them, sometimes from within. Romans had what they called "barbarians." Habsburgs had "anarchists." And today, Americans and Europeans have terrorists.

Most of the time, travelers can be blissfully oblivious of terrorism. But there's always a chance that terrorists will strike just before, or during, your trip.

If that happens, take a deep breath. Survey the situation. Get a grip on the odds...the statistical risk. According to START, a research group that studies terrorism, 615 Americans died worldwide from 1995 through 2017 as victims of terrorism (apart from 9/11, when nearly 3,000 Americans died). Compare that to the 612,310 people killed by guns on US soil from 1999 to 2017 (Centers for Disease Control and Prevention). Each year, more than 37,000 Americans die of gun violence in the US (Brady Center). So if you understand the actual statistics and if you really care about your loved ones...you'd take them to Europe tomorrow.

Paris' see-through garbage cans give terrorists one less place to hide a bomb.

The US State Department issues travel advisories for foreign countries (www.travel.state.gov). Consider these, but don't follow them blindly. Certain warnings (for example, about civil unrest in a country that's falling apart) could be grounds to scrub my mission. But I travel right through most advisories. A threat against the embassy in Rome doesn't affect my sightseeing at the Pantheon. For other perspectives, check the British (www.fco.gov.uk) and Canadian (www.travel.gc.ca) government travel warnings.

Sure, terrorist threats can have a tangible impact on your travels, usually in the form of increased security lines, disrupted flight plans, and other inconveniences. You may have to go through extra security to get on a train or into a great museum. It's harder to find a place to check your bags—and you may pay more when you do—because of concern about bombs. If something unusual is happening in the world, carefully confirm flight schedules and local information, and allow plenty of time to get where you're going and through security. If I get stuck in a long security line, I use the extra time to meditate on the fundamental causes of terrorism.

Security on Europe's premium trains can be tight. At this London train station, the police keep a close eye on who boards the Eurostar for Paris.

Having been in Europe during some high-profile terrorist events, I've been impressed by the local response. Europe is on guard: They have a lot of challenges, and a lot of soft targets. They also have a knack for bouncing back and carrying on. Europeans don't surrender their emotions and politics to sensational news coverage. They keep the risk and tragedy of terrorism in perspective. As a matter of principle, it seems, they refuse to be terrorized by terrorists. Inspired by Europe, I believe it's critical that we not confuse fear with risk, that we not overreact, and that we see travel as a way to get to know our neighbors and contribute to peace.

In a world of easy access to firearms, explosives, and vivid media, terrorism is likely here to stay. And our challenge to maintain a free and open society is here to stay, as well. Europe is strong. It will pursue both safety and the bad guys. And, as a matter of principle, its people will continue to embrace freedom. If we overreact to a terrorist event, we empower the terrorist and become part of the problem. As a matter of principle, I will keep on traveling. If we refuse to be terrorized, the terrorists lose—and we win.

Union or Divorce?

When I first traveled to Europe, it was a hodgepodge of border crossings and currencies. Today I can seamlessly travel from Madrid to Munich to Mykonos with one currency and virtually no passport control.

But with all of the challenges facing Europe over the past decade or so, the ties that bind the EU are feeling frayed.

Britain has Brexited. Nations that have long had open borders are building fences with razor wire and high-tech cameras. (The political dynamic behind Trump and his passion for a wall is not unique to America.) In certain regions, forces want to break apart nations that have been united for centuries. In Belgium, tension between the country's Dutch- and French-speaking halves recently led to effectively no government for nearly two years. Although Scottish voters rejected an independence referendum in 2014, post-Brexit polling suggests that a similar referendum would pass today by a wide margin. (And if Scotland leaves, where does that leave Northern Ireland?)

If there's a silver lining, it's that these conflicts are political rather than military. After an almost 50-year and, at times, violent struggle for independence, the ETA, a Basque separatist group, dissolved in 2018, laying down its weapons. More recently, it's Catalunya that's in the news, with its own bold independence movement, and Spain, for its hard line against Catalan separatists.

I remain a staunch supporter of the European Union. But with Brexit, I'll admit that my idealism took a serious blow. I've long said that the EU, despite its cumbersome political correctness and almost comically excessive regulations, has become an entrenched part of Europe's fabric. After all, it has created a free-trade zone big enough to compete with the US and the emerging economies of China and India, and it has helped keep Europe at peace. Brexit shrank the EU from 28 to 27 member nations, losing 17 percent of its economic clout. The question going forward, in regard to the EU, is what is the right size?

Thoughtfully considering these dimensions of travel—and embarking upon your trip hoping to grow and learn—may just be the greatest way to add value to your vacation. History is unfolding all around us. Societies everywhere are struggling with the same challenges. The world is filled with good people. Americans are not exceptional. And those of us who travel with a humble and curious mindset, intent on getting out of our comfort zones, and seeing our trips as an opportunity to gain perspective, find that travel is indeed transformational. We fly home changed...and changed for the better.

Back Doors

Europe is your playground...and it's time for recess.

Traveling Through the Back Door

The travel skills covered in the first half of this book enable you to open doors most travelers don't even know exist. Now I'd like to introduce you to some of my top European destinations, where you'll have a chance to put those skills to work. I'm the matchmaker, and you and the travel bug are about to get intimate. By traveling vicariously with me through this selection of places and sights, you'll get a peek at my favorite parts of Europe. And, just as important, by internalizing this lifetime of memorable travel moments, you'll develop a knack for finding your own.

Europe's Top Destinations

Europe Through the Back Door is the first book I ever wrote. In the early days, Back Doors to me were Europe's undiscovered nooks and undeveloped crannies: all-day walks on an alpine ridge, sword-fern fantasies in a ruined castle, and untrampled towns that had, for various reasons, missed the modern parade (like Gimmelwald, Dingle, Salema, and the Cinque Terre). But with ever more sophisticated travelers armed with ever-better guidebooks, places I "discovered" 30-some years ago are now undeveloped and noncommercial only in a relative sense. And certain places that I really raved about now suffer from Back Door congestion.

Europe's Top Destinations

So now, rather than isolate a few locations and call them "Back Doors," I'm giving you a country-by-country rundown of my favorite destinations throughout Europe and sharing some of my most unforgettable experiences...in the hope that they will inspire you to travel and fill your own journal with

Ratings & Map Legend

I use the following symbols to rate destinations in this book:

▲▲▲ Don't miss
▲▲ Try hard to see
▲ Worthwhile if you can make it

I've written these chapters to give you the flavor of each country, not for you to navigate by. My various guidebooks provide all the details necessary to splice your chosen Back Doors into a smooth trip (see page 37).
Bon voyage!

⌂ Castle	·········	Ferry/Boat Route
▪ Point of Interest	‐‐‐‐‐	Trails & Paths
▲ Mountain Peak	⊛	Capital City
)(Mtn. Pass	🌲	National Park

your own memories. This approach is less about finding the undiscovered places and more about demonstrating how thoughtful Back Door travel—anywhere you go—can get you beyond tourist traps, broaden your perspective, and enrich your travel experience. This is my niche—teaching people how to be travelers (as opposed to tourists).

Each corner of Europe has a unique and genuine charm. A destination is worthy simply because it exists, with people who proudly call it home. With a Back Door angle, you can slip your fingers under the staged culture of any destination and actually find a pulse. It's clear to me that the more you understand a region, the more you appreciate and enjoy it.

Italy

When travel dreams take people to Europe, Italy is often their first stop. There's something seductively charming about this country, its people, and *la dolce vita*. I always feel at home in Italy, whether struggling onto a crowded bus in Rome, navigating the fun chaos of Naples, sipping a cocktail in a Venetian bar, or sitting on the banister of Florence's Ponte Vecchio for a midnight street-music concert.

Italy is the cradle of European civilization. As you explore, you'll stand face-to-face with iconic images from its 2,000-year history: the Colosseum of ancient Rome, the medieval Leaning Tower of Pisa, a cornucopia of Renaissance achievement (Michelangelo's *David* and the Sistine Chapel, for example), and the playful exuberance of the Baroque, perhaps best seen in the Bernini-designed fountains and squares of Rome.

Italy has it all—romantic hill towns, peaceful lakes lined with 19th-century villas, sun-baked Sicily, the business center of Milan, Mediterranean beaches (like the Cinque Terre), German-flavored Alps, and the art-drenched cities of Venice, Florence, and Rome. The country is reasonably small and laced with freeways and train lines, so you're never more than a day's journey from any of these places. And everywhere you can enjoy Italy's famous cuisine and wine.

I love Italy for its idiosyncrasies—the fun, the unpredictability, and the serendipity. And that comes with frustrations and complications. Precision in Italy seems limited to the pasta (which is exactly and reliably *al dente*). The country bubbles with emotion, traffic jams, strikes, and irate Italians shaking their fists at each other one minute and walking arm in arm the next. Have a talk with yourself before you cross the border. Promise yourself to relax, and remember it's a package deal.

From fragments of once grandiose Roman statues to bobbing gondolas ready for romance, Italy has sightseeing treats for everyone.

Accept Italy as Italy. Savor your cappuccino, dangle your feet over a canal, and imagine what it was like centuries ago. Ramble through the rabble and rubble, and mentally resurrect those ancient stones. Get chummy with the winds of the past—and connect with the pleasures of the moment. Travel memories here are low-hanging fruit: They're yours to harvest.

FAVORITE SIGHTS AND MEMORABLE EXPERIENCES IN ITALY

Swept Away in Rome

Not long ago in Rome, I spent an entire sunny afternoon in my hotel room, tinkering with changes to the next edition of my guidebook. I had time for just a quick break, but stepping outside was dangerous. There's a strong current of distractions in this city. Just by turning the corner from my hotel, I was swept out into a Roman sea, teeming with colorful and fragrant entertainments. I didn't make it back for hours.

I flowed downhill to the Pantheon, the influential domed temple that served as the model for Michelangelo's dome of St. Peter's and many others. I stopped at the portico—nicknamed "Rome's umbrella," a fun, local gathering spot in a rainstorm—from where I saw a symphony of images: designer shades and flowing hair backlit in the magic-hour sun; a flute section of ice-cream lickers sitting on a marble bench in the spritz of a fountain; strolling Romanian accordion players who refused to follow their conductor; and the stains of a golden arch on a wall marking where a McDonald's once sold fast food. The entire scene was corralled by pastel walls, providing the visual equivalent of good acoustics.

As I let go of the Pantheon's columns, the current swept

me past siren cafés and out onto Via del Corso, which since ancient times has been the main north-south drag through town. On my swim through the city, this was the deep end. The rough crowd from the suburbs comes here for some cityscape elegance. Today they'd gooped on a little extra grease and were wearing their best leggings, heels, and T-shirts.

Veering away from the busy pedestrian boulevard, I came upon Fausto, a mad artist standing proudly amid his installation of absurdities. While eccentric, he seemed strangely sane in this crazy world. He's the only street artist I've met who personally greets viewers. After surveying his tiny gallery of hand-scrawled and thought-provoking tidbits, I asked for a card. He gave me a handmade piece of wallet-sized art, reminding me that his "secretary" was at the end of the curb: a plastic piggy bank for tips.

Fast Facts

Biggest cities: Rome (capital, 2.7 million), Milan (1.3 million), Naples (1 million)

Size: 116,000 square miles (similar to Arizona), population 61 million

Locals call it: Italia

Currency: Euro

Key dates: 5th century AD, the fall of the Roman Empire; 15th century, the birth of the Renaissance

Biggest festivals: Carnevale (usually February, especially big in Venice), Palio horse races (July 2 and August 16, Siena)

Handy Italian phrases: *Buongiorno* (good day; bwohn-**jor**-noh), *Per favore* (please; pehr fah-**voh**-ray), *Grazie* (thank you; **graht**-see-ay), *Mi fanno male i piedi!* (My feet hurt!; mee **fah**-noh **mah**-lay ee pee-**eh**-dee)

Tourist info: Italia.it

Next came the market square Campo de' Fiori, which usually creates its own current in the hours after the fruit and vegetable vendors have packed up. But today the square felt like a punished child. After a Roman teenager drank herself into a coma, police banned the consumption of alcohol in outdoor public spaces. It's like someone turned on the lights at a party before midnight.

I passed a homeless man, tattered but respectfully dressed, leaning against a wall. He was savoring a cigar and a bottle of wine while studying Rome's flow as if it held a secret. Next, I chatted with twins from Kentucky, giddy about their Roman days as they celebrated their 40th birthday together. Their Doublemint smiles and high energy made a great case for embracing the good life.

Moving on to Piazza del Popolo, the vast oval square known for its symmetrical design and art-filled churches, I ducked into the Church of Santa Maria del Popolo just as the ushers closed the doors for Mass. Inside, the white noise of Roman streets became the incense-scented hum of a big church with a determined priest—and not enough people. With my hands folded as if here to worship, I slipped

down the side aisle to catch a glimpse of a Caravaggio, that late-16th-century thriller of Italian painting.

Stepping back outside, I found myself at the north entrance of the ancient city. Determined to swim back to my hotel and my work, I passed the same well-dressed bum with the cigar and the buzz, still intently caught up in the city. I imagined being in his pickled head for just a moment.

Near him, guys from Somalia launched their plastic fluorescent whirlybirds high into the twilight sky. These street trinkets keep African immigrants from starving. They make me wish I had made a museum from all the goofy things people have sold on the streets of Rome over the years—from flaming *Manneken-Pis* lighters to five-foot-tall inflatable bouncing cigars to twin magnets that jitter like crickets when you play with them just so.

Finally, with a struggling stroke, I made it back to the safety of my hotel, where none of that Roman current is allowed in. The problem: While taking a break from writing, I came home with even more to write about. In Rome, one thing leads to another, and if you're trying to get on top of your notes, it can be perilous to go out.

The charms of Rome have a current like a river, and being swept away—from the Pantheon to the Trevi Fountain—is part of the experience.

Tuning in to Tasty Italy

Tuscany is a region fiercely proud of its Chianina beef, from white cows. Recently, while in the town of Montepulciano, I sank my teeth into a carnivore's dream come true. In a stony cellar, under one long, tough vault, I joined a local crowd for dinner. The scene was powered by an open fire in the far back of the vault. Flickering in front of the flames was a huge hunk of red beef, lying on the counter like a corpse on a gurney. Like a blacksmith in hell, Giulio—a lanky man in a T-shirt—hacked at the beef with a cleaver, lopping off a steak every few minutes.

In a kind of mouth-watering tango, he pranced past the

boisterous tables of customers, holding a raw slab of beef on butcher's paper as if handling a tray of drinks. Giulio presented the slabs to each table of diners, telling them the weight and price (the minimum was about $40) and getting their OK to cook it. He'd then dance back to the inferno and grill the slab: seven minutes on one side, seven on the other. There was no asking how you wanted it done; *this* was the way it was done.

Eating a steak at Giulio's place—Osteria dell'Acquacheta— is just one of my many memorable Italian dining experiences. And over the years, I've come up with some observations about food and Italy.

If America's specialty is fast food, Italy's is slow food: locally grown ingredients, in season, bought daily, prepared with love, and enjoyed in social circumstances with friends and family. While American food often has to look good, travel well, and be available all year, Italian food does none of that—it just has to taste good.

A perfect example is *vignarola*, a holy trinity of artichoke, peas, and fava beans. It's only available during a brief perfect storm of seasonality in spring, when everything is bursting with flavor. Italian chefs and home cooks religiously prep the vegetables—trimming the artichokes, cleaning the peas, and shelling the fava beans—to create this traditional dish that signals spring at its fullest.

While I've never liked putting up with TV noise when grabbing a simple meal in Italy, I now see that when an eatery has the TV playing, it's often because it's where the local workers drop by to eat—and that indicates a low price and a good value.

To go gourmet and not go broke, I go to a small, classy *enoteca* (wine bar). The bars are owned and operated by food evangelists who thoughtfully design the food menu to

LEFT In Tuscany, enthusiastic carnivores can have the meal of a lifetime at a rustic steakhouse.

RIGHT For many Italians, "a good marriage" is the relationship between their favorite wine and what's on the plate.

Italy's Top Destinations

Rome ▲▲▲   allow 3-5 days

Italy's capital, studded with ancient architectural remnants, floodlit fountain squares, and Vatican opulence

Top Sights

Colosseum Huge stadium where gladiators squared off
Pantheon Antiquity's best-preserved domed temple
Roman Forum Ancient Rome's main square, with ruins and grand arches
St. Peter's Basilica World's most influential church, with Michelangelo's *Pietà* and dome
Vatican Museums Western civilization's finest art, including the Sistine Chapel
Borghese Gallery Bernini sculptures plus paintings by Caravaggio, Raphael, and Titian

Florence ▲▲▲   2-3 days

Walkable Renaissance wonderland and Tuscan capital with iconic Duomo (and other grand churches), palaces, museums, and Italy's best gelato

Top Sights

Accademia Michelangelo's *David* and powerful (unfinished) *Prisoners*
Uffizi Gallery Greatest collection of Renaissance paintings anywhere
Bargello Sculpture museum of Renaissance greats
Duomo Museum Original sculptured masterpieces from Florence's cathedral
Duomo Imposing Gothic cathedral with bell tower, baptistery, and Renaissance dome

Nearby

Pisa Leaning Tower and surrounding Field of Miracles
Lucca Charming city with walled old center
Volterra and San Gimignano Stony, characteristic hill towns

Venice ▲▲▲   1-3 days

Romantic island-city famous for St. Mark's Square and Basilica, the Grand Canal, and singing gondoliers

Milan ▲▲   1 day

Powerhouse city of commerce and fashion, with spiny Duomo, prestigious opera house, and Leonardo's *Last Supper*

Lake District ▲   1-2 days

Low-key resort towns with majestic alpine vistas and aristocratic Old World romance on **Lake Como** and **Lake Maggiore**

Cinque Terre ▲▲▲   1-3 days

Picture-perfect Riviera hamlets strung along a rugged coastline laced with hiking trails

Hill Towns of Central Italy ▲▲   1-3 days

Postcard villages of the Italian heartland: cathedral-capped **Orvieto,** minuscule **Civita,** wine-soaked **Montalcino** and **Montepulciano,** Renaissance-perfect **Pienza,** and classically Tuscan **Cortona**

Assisi ▲▲   1 day

St. Francis' hillside hometown, with a divine basilica decorated by Giotto

Siena ▲▲▲   1 day

Italy's ultimate hill town, with grand square and strikingly striped cathedral

Naples ▲▲   1-2 days
Gritty port city featuring vibrant street life and a top archaeological museum

Nearby
Pompeii Famous ruins of the ancient town buried by Mount Vesuvius' eruption
Sorrento and Capri Seaside resort port and jet-set island getaway
Amalfi Coast String of seafront villages tied together by scenic mountain road

With more time, consider visiting
Dolomites Italy's rugged rooftop, with alpine meadows and a Germanic flair
Padua University town with Giotto's gloriously frescoed Scrovegni Chapel
Verona Town with Roman amphitheater plus Romeo and Juliet sights
Ravenna Coastal town known for its top Byzantine mosaics

complement the wine list. A great wine costs about $10 a glass. Rather than bog down on an expensive entrée, I order top-end on the *antipasti* (starter) and *primi piatti* (first course) list. By doing that, I usually end up with the freshest meats and cheeses and the chef's favorite pasta dish of the day.

I've realized I should stay away from restaurants famous for inventing a pasta dish. Alfredo (of fettuccini fame) and Carbonara (of penne fame) are both Roman restaurants—and they're both much more famous than they are good.

One of my favorite Italian specialties isn't even on the menu: good conversation. In Rome, I talked about dessert with a man at a nearby table. He told me how his grandfather always said, in the local dialect, "The mouth cannot be finished until it smells of cows." In other words, you must finish the meal with cheese.

Another time, I shared a delightful dinner with a local guide, Giuseppe, and his wife, Anna. She greeted each plate with unbridled enthusiasm. Suddenly Giuseppe looked at me and said, "My wife's a good fork." Misunderstanding him, I blushed. My face said, "Come again?" And Giuseppe clarified, saying *"un buona forchetta*...a good fork—that's what we call someone who loves to eat."

To me, Italian cuisine is a symphony—the ingredients are the instruments. The quality is important, and the marriage of ingredients is what provides the tonality. When things are in tune, you taste it.

The Long Italian Meal

For many Italians, dinner is the evening's entertainment. Italians eat in courses, lingering over each one; a three-hour meal is common. A typical meal might start with *antipasti* (such as *bruschetta* or a plate of cold cuts and veggies). Next comes the *primo piatto* (first dish—such as a pasta, risotto, or soup), then the *secondo piatto* (usually meat or seafood), and finally, *dolce* (dessert). For most travelers, the full multi-course meal is simply too much food. A good rule of thumb is for each person to order any two courses, such as an *antipasto* and *primo piatto* (sharing is perfectly acceptable). When you want the bill, you'll have to ask for it (possibly more than once). For Italians, the meal is an end in itself, and only rude servers rush you. To "eat and run" is seen as a lost opportunity.

Florence: The Cultural Capital of Europe

Geographically small but culturally rich, Florence is home to some of the greatest art and architecture in the world. It was in Florence, in about 1400, that the Renaissance began.

After wallowing for centuries in relative darkness, Western civilization was suddenly perky, making up for lost centuries with huge gains in economics, science, and art. And Florence was at the center of it all.

Wealthy merchant and banking families—like the Medici, who ruled Florence for generations—demonstrated their civic pride (and showed off) by commissioning great art. Because of them, in a single day I can look Michelangelo's *David* in the eyes, fall under the seductive sway of Botticelli's *La Primavera*, and climb the modern world's first dome, which caps the cathedral and still dominates the skyline.

In Florence, great art is everywhere—even my hotel. I enjoy staying at Loggiato dei Serviti—a former monastery, crisp with elegance and history. The hotel's entrance is on a quintessentially Florentine square, with a beautifully arcaded building— the first designed by Brunelleschi (the man who engineered the cathedral's famed dome). The building, once an orphanage, now shelters the local down-and-outs on its elegant porch. While these well-worn people used to get me down, now I realize that for 500 years, vagabonds and street people who couldn't afford a bedroom like the one I call home in Florence could still enjoy the architecture (or at least the shade). Since the days of the Renaissance greats, they have set up camp for free, under the loggia eave of my fancy front door.

From my room, I can look across the way to the Accademia Gallery and its art school. The courtyard in between is gravelly with broken columns and stones set up for students to carve. All day long I hear the happy pecking and chirping of chisels gaining confidence as they cut through the stone. If they need inspiration, students only need to dip into the Accademia's exhibition space.

Entering that gallery is like

Ticket Tricks

Italy's most popular museums and churches can have long lines and lots of crowds. Here are some tips for avoiding lines at the most congested sights.

- Book tickets ahead of time if visiting the Uffizi Gallery or the Accademia Gallery in Florence, or the Colosseum or Vatican Museums (including the Sistine Chapel) in Rome. It's also worth considering advance tickets for Pompeii.
- Some sights require a reservation, including the Scrovegni Chapel in Padua, the Borghese Gallery in Rome, Leonardo's *Last Supper* in Milan, and the Brancacci Chapel and the Duomo's dome in Florence.
- Consider sightseeing passes and combo-tickets, which can sometimes save you time waiting in lines. For instance, in Venice, a combo-ticket covers the popular Doge's Palace (with long lines) and a few less crowded sights, such as the Correr Museum—guess where you should buy the ticket?
- Avoid free-entry days at Italy's state museums, which take place once or twice a month, usually on a Sunday (check the museum websites to find out when they are). Free days are actually bad news— they attract crowds.

walking into a temple of humanism. At the high altar stands Michelangelo's colossal statue of *David,* the slingshot-toting giant slayer. This perfect man represents humankind finally stepping out of medieval darkness. Clothed only in confidence, his toes gripping the pedestal, *David* sizes up his foe, as if to say, "I can take this guy." The statue was an apt symbol for the city, inspiring Florentines to tackle their Goliaths.

Until 1873, *David* lived not in the Accademia, but in the city's great square, Piazza della Signoria. A replica *David* marks the spot where the original once stood. With goony eyes and a pigeon-dropping wig, the fake *David* seems a bit dumbfounded, as tourists picnic at his feet and policewomen clip-clop by on horseback.

One edge of Piazza della Signoria opens into the long arcaded courtyard of the Uffizi Gallery, the museum that once housed the offices of the Medici. A permanent line of tourists waits patiently in the shade to see this best-anywhere collection of Italian paintings. Lounging between the columns, enterprising artists sketch the tourists and display their work. And filling the niches all around are life-size statues of Leonardo, Dante, Lorenzo de' Medici, and a dozen other Renaissance greats—Florentines, every one of them.

My favorite Florentine painter—Botticelli—has a few special paintings inside the Uffizi. His *Primavera* shows the personification of Spring—and the Renaissance in full bloom. Botticelli painted a splendid innocence, where a maiden can walk barefoot through a garden scattering flower petals from a fold in her dress and call it a good day's work—and where the Three Graces can dance naked with no more fanfare

Botticelli's *Primavera,* a highlight of the Uffizi Gallery

than the happy do-si-do of butterflies. To me, the delicate face of Botticelli's Spring is the purest expression of Renaissance beauty in Florence.

In Florence, Brunelleschi's dome towers above much of the finest art in Europe. Yet cross the Arno River, and you're in a rustic zone of traditional artisans.

Today, Florence's artistic legacy lives on across the Arno River, in the Oltrarno neighborhood—home to small shops featuring handmade furniture, enameled jewelry, marbled papers, and finely glazed pottery. One artisan drew me into his shop as if inviting me on a journey. Under a single dangling light bulb, he hammered gold leaf into a dingy halo, breathing life back into a faded statue that had originally been crafted by a neighbor of his—five centuries ago. Hundreds of years after the Renaissance, the spirit of creation remains alive and well in Florence.

The Cinque Terre: Italy's Riviera

"A sleepy, romantic, and inexpensive town on the Riviera without a tourist in sight." That's the mirage travelers chase around busy Nice and Cannes. Pssst! Although hardly free of tourists, the most dream-worthy stretch of the Riviera rests in Italy just across the border, between Genoa and Pisa. It's Italy's Cinque Terre.

Leaving the nearest big city, La Spezia, your train takes you into a mountain. Ten minutes later, you burst into the sunlight. Your train nips in and out of the hills, teasing you with a series of Mediterranean views. Each scene is grander than the last: azure blue tinseled in sunbeams, carbonated waves hitting desolate rocks, and the occasional topless sunbather camped out like a lone limpet.

The Cinque Terre (pronounced **chink**-weh **tay**-reh), which means "five lands," is a quintet of villages clinging to this most inaccessible bit of Riviera coastline. Each is a variation on the same theme: a well-whittled pastel jumble of

homes filling a gully like crusty sea creatures in a tide pool.
Like a gangly clump of oysters, the houses grow on each
other. Residents are the barnacles—hungry, but patient. And
we travelers are like algae, coming in with the tide.

The rugged villages of the Cinque Terre, founded by Dark
Age locals hiding out from marauding pirates, were long
cut off from the modern world. Only with the coming of the
train was access made easy. Today, the villages draw hordes
of hikers, and the castles protect only glorious views. To
preserve this land, the government has declared the Cinque
Terre a national park. Visitors hiking between some of the
towns pay a small entrance fee, which stokes a fund designed
to protect the flora and fauna and keep the trails clean and
well-maintained.

The government, recognizing how wonderfully preserved these towns are, has long prohibited anyone from
constructing any modern buildings. For that reason, today
there are no big, comfortable hotels in the area—great news
for Back Door travelers because it keeps the most obnoxious
slice of the traveling public—those who need big, comfortable hotels—from spending the night. But rugged travelers,
content to rent a room in a private home or simple *pensione,*
enjoy a land where the villagers go about their business as if
the surrounding vineyards are the very edges of the earth.

Overseen by a ruined castle, with the closest thing to
a natural harbor, Vernazza is my Cinque Terre home base.
Only the occasional noisy slurping up of the train by the
mountain reminds you there's a modern world out there
somewhere.

From Vernazza's harbor, wander through the jumble of
a tough community living off the sea...or living off travelers
who love the sea. The church bells dictate a relaxed tempo.
Yellow webs of fishing nets, tables bedecked with umbrellas,
kids with plastic shovels, and a flotilla of gritty little boats
tethered to buoys provide splashes of color. And accompanying the scene is the soundtrack of a dream...a celebrate-the-
moment white noise of children, dogs, and waves.

Vernazza's one street connects the harbor with the train
station before melting into the vineyards. Like veins on a
grape leaf, paths and stairways reach from Main Street into
this watercolor huddle of houses. All of life is summer reruns
in this hive of lazy human activity. A rainbow of laundry
flaps as if to keep the flies off the roly-poly grandmothers
who fill the ancient doorways.

Residents spend early evenings doing their *vasche* (laps),

strolling between the station and the breakwater. Sit on a bench and study this slow-motion parade.

Today, at the top end of town, Vernazza's cruel little road hits a post. No cars enter this village of 600 people. Like the breakwater keeps out the waves at the bottom of the town, the post keeps out the modern storm at the top. But Vernazza's ruined castle no longer says "stay away." And its breakwater—a broad, inviting sidewalk edged with seaside boulders—sticks into the sea like a finger beckoning the distant excursion boats.

The five pastel ports of Italy's Cinque Terre were established as hideouts from pirates in the Middle Ages. Today, villagers will eagerly rent you a room and drizzle pesto on your pasta.

Barefoot in Venice

When you know where to look, there's so much to see in Venice. Stepping ashore after a boat ride from the airport, I noticed everything seemed particularly vivid in this beautifully decrepit cityscape: the pilings rotten at the water line; a funeral boat with an iron casket-rack lashed to the center of the hull; chandeliers lighting a mansion's ceiling frescoes; white marble inlay lining the edges of the stairs over a bridge. In Venice, always look both ways when you pass over a bridge, as lovely views can hit you from any direction.

But there are times when the magic suddenly stops. I needed to check out the parking situation at the edge of the city, and the traffic appalled me. As I dodged the crazy Italian drivers, the contrast between mainland and island was clear. What a charming world the Venetians enjoy—it's free of traffic noise and, as pedestrians, they completely own their byways.

A boat ride took me to the nearby island of Burano, which is famous for humble fishermen's houses and squinting lacemakers. I noticed how the pastel colors of the homes are getting more and more vibrant. The place is just darling (an adjective I've never used to describe a town before).

But the rising sea has forced Burano to raise its canal-side pavement. I could see a strip of fresh bricks above the water line. Houses that could be made higher have had their ground floors raised, leaving them with shorter ceilings.

Venice has been battling rising water levels since the fifth century. Venice now floods about 100 times a year—usually from October until late winter—a phenomenon called *acqua alta*. During these floods, some high-end hotels lend wading boots to their customers. Wooden benches are placed end-to-end in St. Mark's Square to create elevated sidewalks. But these turn into total gridlock, as the square-sized crowds jostle for space on the narrow wooden walkways.

On this trip, St. Mark's Square was as dry as ever. At Caffè Florian, the most venerable café on the square, the manager lamented how, in the last decade, the café's elegance has been trampled by poorly dressed tourists (not unlike me, I must admit). Still, I love this place, with its smoke-stained mirrors, white-tuxedoed waiters, and finicky piano and string quartet, which somehow gets called an "orchestra."

While you can enjoy a romantic drink here with live music and all the tourists, I opted for a quiet cup of coffee in the morning, when the square was empty. Surrounded by the patina of faded elegance, I marveled at how the history popped with the architecture and without the modern tourism. The Gothic was so lacy, and the Renaissance so capable. It looked like a pure, computer-generated Venetian cityscape—only it was real. In so many ways, when you get up early and stay out late, you enjoy a different, and it seems, more authentic Venice.

Likewise, on the vaporetto water buses, there's a stark

Venice is awash with wonders—from the cultural grounding that comes with going barefoot on the flooring *"alla veneziana"* to the surge of the gondolier's oar as you glide under the Bridge of Sighs.

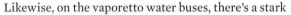

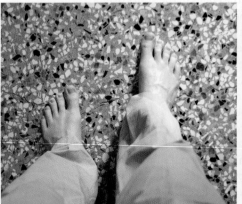 

contrast between the midday/rush-hour mobs and the easy-going joy of riding at quiet times. Venice is two cities: one garishly touristic and the other so romantic and tranquil that it makes you go *fortissimo* in describing it.

In Venice, I spend my evenings visiting restaurants to consider for my guidebooks, then return to my favorite for dinner. This dining derby is my nightly ritual in Italy. Tonight, when the waiter asked me how I liked my wine, I said, *"Complicato"*—and he served up his house Amarone, a local red. I drank it like a monkey climbs a tree. Just when the branches were getting pretty bendy, he capped the meal with a glass of Sgroppino, a Venetian after-dinner slushy of lemon juice, lemon gelato, Prosecco, and vodka. It's my new favorite taste treat.

Done with dinner, I retreated to my hotel room. The speckled "Venetian pavement"—the city's characteristic floor made of a broken hodgepodge of marble fragments and then polished—greeted my bare feet. While some might mistake it for cheap linoleum, it's far from that—it's treasured here and quite expensive. It flexes with the settling of the buildings and is costly to maintain, but it's so characteristic. My feet connected with that floor in a way my feet have never before connected with flooring—happily grounding me in Venice.

Bella Tuscany

After checking in to my Tuscan *agriturismo*, my host, Signora Gori, takes me on a welcome stroll. Our first stop is a sty dominated by a giant pig. "We call him Pastanetto—'the little pastry.'" While the scene through my camera's viewfinder is pristine and tranquil, the soundtrack is not. As a horrendous chorus of squeals comes from a rustic slaughterhouse on the horizon, she says, "This is our little Beirut." I stow my camera, deciding to simply absorb the attention I'm enjoying from a host who is both old-money elegant and farmhouse-tough. The Gori family estate is Tuscany in the rough.

The Italian landscape is dotted with *agriturismi* like this one—traditional family farms renting out spare rooms to make ends meet. To qualify officially as an *agriturismo*, the farm must still generate more money from its farm activities—whether growing olives, making wine, or producing prosciutto—and most sell or serve the food they produce to guests. Don't confuse these with farmhouse B&Bs, which aren't actual farms, though they can be fine places to stay. If you want the real thing, make sure the owners call their place an *agriturismo*.

Hiking to the slaughterhouse, we enter a room dominated by a stainless-steel table piled with red sides of pork. Signora Gori says, "Here begins prosciutto." Burly men in aprons squeeze the blood out of hunks of meat the size of dance partners. Then they cake the ham hocks in salt to begin a curing process that takes months. While the salt helps cure the meat, a coating of pepper seals it. In spooky but great-smelling rooms, towering racks of ham hocks age. A man, dressed and acting like a veterinarian, tests each ham by sticking it with a horse-bone needle and giving it a sniff.

Back outside, Signora Gori takes me into the next barn, where fluffy white lambs jump to attention in their hay, kicking up a sweet-smelling golden dust. Backlit by stray sunbeams, it's a dreamy, almost biblical scene. Picking up a baby lamb, she gives it an Eskimo kiss—nose to nose. She explains, "I must really know my sheep." Their milk is turned into Pecorino cheese.

Strolling down another lane, we observe the family's team of vintners just as Signora Gori's brother empties a bucketful of purple grapes into a dump truck. The load tumbles from the truck into a grinder, which munches through the bunches, spitting stems one way and juice with mangled grapes the other. As the juice flows through pipes into a cellar, the brother explains that wine-making is labor-intensive, "but right now the grapes are doing all the work."

And as the new grapes ferment, we taste the finished product. A key word for your Tuscan travels is *corposo*—full-bodied. Lifting the elegant glass to my lips, I sip the wine while enjoying the pride in the eyes of those who made it. Satisfied, I say, "*Corposo.*" They say, "*Si, bello.*"

That night at dinner, we're joined by the rest of the Gori family. The two sons dress and act like princes home on break from some Italian Oxford. Sitting down to a classic Tuscan table—where things are simple, harmonious, and unhurried—with a glass of good red wine, I nod to my hosts, knowing I've found the art of Tuscany.

After dinner, full and content, we sip port and enjoy a backgammon board that has provided evening fun for 200 years in this very room. Surrounded by musty portraits putting faces on this family's long lineage, I realize that this—a special moment for me—is just another night on the farm here in the Gori home.

Naples: Just Do It

All my life, Naples has been the symbol of chaos, stress, and culture shock for European travel. I remember my first visit as a wide-eyed 18-year-old. I stepped off the train into the same vast Piazza Garibaldi that many years later still strikes everyone who visits it as a big, paved hellhole. On that first visit, a man in a white surgeon's gown approached me and said, "Please, we need blood for a dying baby." I made a U-turn, stepped back into the station, and made a beeline for Greece.

The city is calmer now, but Naples remains uniquely thrilling. One of my favorite sightseeing experiences anywhere in Italy is simply wandering Spaccanapoli, the long, straight, narrow street that runs through the historic center and bisects the city. Living in the streets is quintessentially Neapolitan—people here seem perfectly adept at enjoying life with their domestic worlds tumbling right out onto the gritty pavement. Naples may be an urban jungle, but it's a warm and welcoming place. Like Cairo or Bombay, it's appalling and appealing at the same time, the closest thing to "reality travel" you'll find in Western Europe. But this tangled mess still somehow manages to breathe, laugh, and sing—with a captivating Italian accent.

An essential stop on any Naples visit is the Archaeological Museum, which offers the closest possible peek into the

Lurking deep in old Naples, you know you can't be a local...but you can imagine.

artistic jewelry boxes of Pompeii and Herculaneum. The actual archaeological sites, while impressive, are barren—the best frescoes and mosaics ended up here. The Secret Room displays R-rated Roman "bedroom" art. A highlight is the Farnese Collection—a giant hall of huge, bright, and wonderfully restored statues excavated from Rome's Baths of Caracalla. You can almost hear the *Toro Farnese* snorting. This largest intact statue from antiquity (a third-century copy of a Hellenistic original, showing a tangled group of people with a raging bull) was carved out of one piece of marble and later restored by Michelangelo.

Take time to explore Naples. This living medieval city is its own best sight. Couples artfully make love on Vespas, while surrounded by more fights and smiles per cobblestone than anywhere else in Italy.

Paint a picture with these thoughts: Naples has the most intact ancient Roman street plan anywhere. Imagine life here in the days of Caesar, with streetside shop fronts that close up to form private homes after dark. Today is just one more page in a 2,000-year-old story of city activity: all kinds of meetings, beatings, and cheatings; kisses, near misses, and little-boy pisses.

For a peek behind the scenes in the shade of wet laundry, venture down a few narrow streets lined by tall apartment buildings. Black-and-white death announcements add to the clutter on the walls. Widows sell cigarettes from plastic buckets. Buy two carrots as a gift for the woman on the fifth floor if she'll lower her bucket down to pick them up.

In search of cheap eats (near major sights) that I can recommend to my guidebook readers, I walk behind the Archaeological Museum and meet exuberant Pasquale, the owner of a tiny deli. Rather than do the cheapskate "how much?"

question, I just let fun-loving and flamboyant Pasquale surprise me.

He turns making a sandwich into a show, and I watch, enthralled. After demonstrating the freshness of his rolls as if squeezing the Charmin, he lays a careful pavement of salami, brings over the fluffy mozzarella ball as if performing a kidney transplant, slices a tomato with rapid-fire machine precision, lovingly pits the olives by hand before hanging them like little green paintings on a tasty wall, and then finishes it all off with a celebratory drizzle of the best olive oil. Five euros and a smile later, I have my cheap lunch and a new guidebook listing.

After saying goodbye to Pasquale, I step outside to look for a bench upon which to enjoy my lunch and watch the spirit of Naples roll by.

Civita: A World Apart

The hill towns of central Italy hold their crumbling heads proudly above the noisy flood of the 21st century and offer a peaceful taste of what eludes so many tourists. Sitting on a timeless rampart high above the traffic and trains, hearing only children in the market as the rustling wind ages the weary red-tile patchwork that surrounds me, I find the essence of Italy.

Of all the hill towns, Civita di Bagnoregio is my favorite. People who've been here say "Civita" (chee-**vee**-tah) with warmth and love. This precious chip of Italy is a traffic-free community with a grow-it-in-the-valley economy.

Civita teeters atop a pinnacle in a vast canyon ruled by wind and erosion. Over the years its population has dropped, but the town survives to serve a steady stream of tourists. The saddle that once connected Civita to its bigger and busier sister town, Bagnoregio, eroded away. Today a bridge connects the two towns. A man with a Vespa does the same work his father did with a donkey—ferrying the town's goods up and down the umbilical bridge that connects Civita with a small, distant parking lot and the rest of Italy. Rome, just 60 miles to the south, is a world away.

Entering the town through a cut in the rock made by Etruscans 2,500 years ago, and heading under a 12th-century Romanesque arch, you feel history in the huge, smooth cobblestones. This was once the main Etruscan road leading to the Tiber Valley and Rome. Inside the gate, the charms of Civita are subtle. Those searching for arcade tourism wouldn't know where to look. There are no lists of attractions, orientation tours, or museum hours. It's just Italy.

Civita is an artist's dream, a town in the nude. Each lane and footpath holds a surprise. The warm stone walls glow, and each stairway is dessert to a sketch pad or camera.

Smile and nod at each passerby. It's a social jigsaw puzzle, and each person fits. The old woman hanging out in the window monitors gossip. A tiny hunchback lady is everyone's daughter. And cats, the fastest-growing segment of the population, scratch their itches on ancient pillars.

Explore the village. The basic grid street plan of the ancient town survives—but its centerpiece, a holy place of worship, rotates with the cultures: first an Etruscan temple, then a Roman temple, and today a church. The pillars that stand like bar stools in the square once decorated the pre-Christian temple. The heartbeat and pride of the village, this is where festivals and processions start, visitors are escorted, and the town's past is honored.

Just around the corner from the church, on the main street, is La Cantina de Arianna, a family-run wine cellar, trattoria, and bruschetteria. Pull up a stump and let the family serve you *panini* (sandwiches), wine, and a cake called *ciambella*. The white wine has a taste reminiscent of dirty socks. But it's made right here. After eating, ask to see the cellar with its traditional winemaking gear and provisions for rolling huge kegs up the stairs. Grab the stick and tap on the kegs to measure their fullness.

Explore further through town. At Antico Frantoio Bruschetteria, venture into their back room to see an interesting collection of old olive presses. This local equivalent of a

Somehow keeping its head above the flood of the 21st century, the hill town of Civita di Bagnoregio survives and welcomes the adventurous traveler.

lemonade stand sells bruschetta to visitors. Bread toasted on an open fire, drizzled with the finest oil, rubbed with pungent garlic, and topped with chopped tomatoes—these edible souvenirs stay on your breath for hours and in your memory forever.

At the end of town, the main drag shrivels into a trail that leads past a chapel (once a jail) and down to a tunnel—now barred to entry—that was cut through the hill under the town in Etruscan times. Tall enough for a woman with a jug on her head to pass through, it may have served as a shortcut to the river below. It was widened in the 1930s so farmers could get between their scattered fields more easily.

Civita has only a few restaurants, which cluster near the piazza. At Antico Forno Trattoria ("Antique Oven"), you eat what's cooking. Owner Franco slices and dices happily through the day. Spaghetti, salad, and wine on the Antico Forno patio, cuddled by Civita—I wouldn't trade it for all-you-can-eat at Maxim's.

Spend the evening. After dinner, sit on the church steps and observe the scene. They say that in a big city you can see a lot, but in a small town like this you can feel a lot. The generous bench is built into the long side of the square, reminding me of how, when I first discovered Civita back in the 1970s and 1980s, the town's old folks would gather here every night. Children play on the piazza until midnight. As you walk back to your car—that scourge of the modern world that enabled you to get here—stop under a lamp on the donkey path, listen to the canyon...distant voices...a clicking chorus of crickets.

More Italian Experiences

In Assisi with St. Francis: I have a personal ritual of enjoying a quiet picnic on the rampart of a ruined castle high above Assisi, the town of St. Francis. I look down at the basilica dedicated to the saint, then into the valley, where a church stands strong in the hazy Italian plain. It marks the place where Francis and his friars started the Franciscan order, bringing the word of God to people in terms all could embrace. Hearing the same birdsong that inspired Francis, and tasting the same simple bread, cheese, and wine of Umbria that sustained him, I calm my 21st-century soul and ponder Francis' message of love, simplicity, and sensitivity to the environment.

A Dove on a Zipline: One spring day, I couldn't resist joining a multitude that had gathered in front of Orvieto's cathedral. For generations, citizens of this small Umbrian town have celebrated the Pentecost—the descent of the Holy Ghost upon the Apostles—in this spot. The anticipation built and built, and then, suddenly, it happened: A dove in a little plastic tube rocketed down a zipline and into a nest of fireworks at the front of the church, setting it all ablaze. After the fireworks exploded, a fireman climbed up to see if the dove was OK. It was. And that was great news, as it brings good luck to the town and fertility to the last couple married in Orvieto.

The Allure of Lake Como: Sleepy Lake Como is a good place to take a break from the obligatory turnstile culture of central Italy. It seems that half the travelers I meet here have tossed their itineraries into the lake and are actually relaxing. The town of Varenna offers the best of all lake worlds. On the quieter side of the lake, with a tiny harbor, narrow lanes, and its own villa, Varenna is the right place to munch a peach and ponder the place where Italy is welded to the Alps. Other than watch the visitors wash ashore with the landing of each ferry, there's wonderfully little to do here. Varenna's volume goes down with the sun. At night, it whispers *luna di miele*—honeymoon. And a good place to enjoy that romance is on its lakefront promenade, the *passerella*. After dark, it's adorned with caryatid lovers pressing silently against each other in the shadows.

Siena Soul: Unlike its rival, Florence, Siena is a city to be seen as a whole rather than as a collection of sights. While memories of Florence consist of dodging Vespas and pickpockets between museums, Siena has an easy-to-enjoy Gothic soul: Courtyards sport flower-decked wells, churches modestly hoard their art, and alleys dead-end into red-tiled rooftop panoramas. Climb to the dizzy top of the 100-yard-tall bell tower and reign over urban harmony at its best. At twilight, first-time poets savor that magic moment when the sky is a rich blue dome no brighter than the medieval towers that seem to hold it high.

Siena is famous for hosting the frantic Palio horse race, held every year on July 2 and August 16. Dirt is brought in and packed down over the pavers of Il Campo, the town's main square, to create the track's surface, and mattresses are strapped onto the sharp corners of surrounding buildings. On the big day, the horses are taken into church to be blessed (it's considered a sign of luck if a horse leaves

droppings in the church). The snorting horses and their nervous riders—each representing a Sienese neighborhood—line up to await the starting signal. Then they race like crazy, while spectators, hungry for victory, wave the scarves of their district. After the winning horse crosses the line (with or without its rider), the prevailing neighborhood goes berserk with joy. If you go, you won't see much—but you'll feel it. It's a real medieval moment.

On My Knees in Rome: All of my Protestant life I've watched hardscrabble pilgrims and frail nuns climb Rome's Scala Santa on their knees. These are the "Holy Stairs" of Pontius Pilate's palace that Christ climbed the day he was condemned. One year, a voice inside me said "Do it!" So I picked up the little pilgrim's primer explaining what holy thoughts to ponder on each step, knelt down, and—one by one—began climbing. Knees screaming, weathered faithful struggling up the staircase with me, I climbed the 28 wooden steps. In my pain, the frescoed art surrounding the staircase snapped into action, goading me on. And, while my knees would never agree, the experience was beautiful.

Whether pondering wisteria villas on Lake Como (left), screaming for your favorite rider in Siena's Palio (center), or struggling on your knees up the steps Jesus climbed on the day he was condemned (right), sightseeing in Italy has an impact on the traveler.

CULTURE AND TRADITIONS: EVERYTHING'S SO...ITALIAN

Style Matters

For Italians, it's very important to exhibit a positive public persona—a concept called *la bella figura*. While some Americans don't think twice about going to the supermarket in sweats, Italians dress well anytime they leave the house—and they'd rather miss their bus than get all sweaty and mussed-up rushing to catch it. An elderly woman will do her hair and carefully put on makeup for her monthly doctor's appointment, and no matter how hot it gets, Italian men wear long pants—never shorts (except at the beach).

Communicating with Italians

Because they're so outgoing and their language is so fun, Italians are a pleasure to communicate with. They are animated and even dramatic. You may think two people are arguing when in reality they're agreeing enthusiastically. Body language is an important part of communicating, especially hand gestures. For instance, the "cheek screw" (pressing a forefinger into their cheek and rotating it) is used to mean good, lovely, or beautiful. A chin flick with the fingers bunched up means "I'm not interested; you bore me." Italians have an endearing habit of speaking Italian to foreigners, even if they know you don't speak their language—and yet, thanks to gestures and thoughtfully simplified words, it somehow works.

Social Time

Italian families and communities are more close-knit than many others in the modern world. Many Italians, especially in rural regions and small towns, still follow the traditional siesta schedule (called *reposo* in Italy). At about 1 p.m., shops close and people go home for a three-hour break to have lunch, socialize with friends and family, and run errands.

Early evening is the time for the ritual promenade called the *passeggiata*, when shoppers, people watchers, families, and young flirts on the prowl all join the scene to stroll arm in arm and spread their wings like peacocks. In a more genteel small town, the *passeggiata* comes with sweet whispers of *"bella"* (pretty) and *"bello"* (handsome). In Rome, the *passeggiata* is actually a cruder, big-city version called

In Italy, the temptations are on parade—in the streets and in the gelato shops. Any town... any evening... *la vita è bella.*

the *struscio* (meaning "to rub"), and people utter the words "*buona*" and "*buono*"—meaning, roughly, "tasty."

Gelato

Gelato is an edible art form. While American ice cream is made with cream and has a high butterfat content, Italian gelato is made with milk. It's also churned more slowly, making it denser. With less air and less fat than American-style ice cream, gelato is more flavorful. To find the best *gelateria*, look for the words *artiginale, nostra produzione*, and *produzione propia*, meaning it's made on the premises. Seasonal flavors and pastel hues (not garish colors) are also good signs. Gelato displayed in covered metal tins (rather than white plastic) is more likely to be homemade. To avoid having your request for a cone turn into a €10 "tourist special," survey the size options and be very clear in your order. My advice is to get plenty of vitamin G. Italy is best explored with long, meandering walks, and nothing refuels the body and spirit like cones of gelato.

Is the Pope Catholic?

Italy, home of the Vatican, is still mostly Catholic. Although Italians will crowd into St. Peter's Square with rock-concert energy to catch a glimpse of "il Papa," they're not particularly devout. And while most people would never think of renouncing their faith, they don't attend church regularly. They baptize their kids at the local church (there's one every few blocks), but they hold modern opinions on social issues, often in conflict with strict Catholic dogma. Italy is now the land of legalized abortion, a low birth rate, nudity on TV, socialist politics, and a society whose common language is decidedly secular. The true dominant religion is life: motor scooters, soccer, fashion, girl-watching, boy-watching, good coffee, good wine, and *il dolce far niente* (the sweetness of doing nothing).

Coffee, Italian-Style

Italians are religious about their coffee. Every coffee drinker has a certain style and a favorite place to buy it. If that place is closed, many would rather skip their coffee altogether. According to Italians, you can tell if coffee is good just by looking at it. When the beans are ground correctly, it comes out of the machine first a creamy brown color, then darker.

Italians tend to drink their coffee with less water than Americans (as one friend put it, "If we are so thirsty, we have a Coke"). In fact, the espresso-based style of coffee that's popular in the US was born in Italy. Most Italian drinks begin with espresso, to which the barista adds varying amounts of hot water and/or steamed or foamed milk. *Un caffè* is just a shot of espresso in a little cup; the closest thing to American-style drip coffee is a *caffè americano*—espresso diluted with hot water. Milky drinks, like

cappuccino or *caffè latte*, are served to locals before noon... and to tourists any time of day. (Italians believe that milk can be properly digested only in the morning.) If Italians add any milk after lunch, it's just a splash, in a *caffè macchiato*—coffee "marked" or "stained" with milk.

Italy Travel Resources from Rick Steves

Guidebooks

Check out Rick's guidebooks covering all of Italy; Rome; Venice; Florence & Tuscany; Sicily; Naples & the Amalfi Coast; the Cinque Terre; Milan & the Italian Lakes District; and Central Italy's hill towns; plus his Italian phrase book

Audio Europe

Download Rick's free Audio Europe app, with interviews about Italy and self-guided audio tours of sights and neighborhoods in Rome (Vatican Museums, Pantheon, St. Peter's Basilica, Forum, Colosseum, Sistine Chapel, Trastevere, Jewish Ghetto, Heart of Rome Walk), Florence (Accademia Gallery, Uffizi Gallery, Bargello Museum, Museum of San Marco, Renaissance Walk), Venice (Frari Church, St. Mark's Basilica, St. Mark's Square, Grand Canal), Siena (City Walk), Assisi (Basilica of St. Francis, Town Walk), Naples (Archaeological Museum, City Walk), Milan (Duomo Neighborhood), and the ancient sites of Ostia Antica and Pompeii

TV Shows

The quintessence of Italy with Rick as your host, viewable on public television and at RickSteves.com. Episodes cover Rome, Florence, Venice, Venice day trips (Verona, Padua, and Ravenna), Assisi, Siena, Tuscany, Italian Alps, Cinque Terre, Amalfi Coast, Naples and Pompeii, Italy's hill towns, Milan, Lake Como, and Sicily

Organized Tours

Small group tours, with itineraries planned by Rick: Italy in 17 Days; Village Italy in 14 Days; Tuscany in 12 Days; South Italy in 13 Days; Sicily in 11 Days; Heart of Italy in 9 Days; Venice, Florence & Rome in 10 Days; Rome in 7 Days; My Way Italy in 13 Days; Family Europe: London to Florence; My Way Europe, My Way Alpine Europe, Best of Europe (all include stops in Italy)

For more on all of these resources, visit RickSteves.com. For Italy trip-planning tips, see RickSteves.com/europe/italy.

France

France is Europe's most diverse, tasty, and, in many ways, most exciting country to explore. With luxuriant forests, forever coastlines, grand canyons, and Europe's highest mountain ranges, France has cover-girl looks. You'll also discover a dizzying array of artistic and architectural wonders—soaring cathedrals, chandeliered châteaux, and museums filled with the cultural icons of the Western world.

Moving from region to region, you feel as if you're crossing into different countries. Paris is in the heart of France. To the west is Normandy, with the historic D-Day beaches and the ethereal island-abbey of Mont St-Michel. To the south is the Loire river valley, filled with luxurious châteaux, and the Dordogne region, with prehistoric caves, medieval castles, and hill-capping villages. Near Spain is Languedoc, crowned by castles, from the fortress town of Carcassonne to remote Cathar ruins. Closer to Italy, sunbaked and windswept Provence nurtures Roman ruins and rustic charm, while the Riviera celebrates sunny beaches and yacht-filled harbors. And to the east, travelers encounter the villages of Germanic Alsace, the vineyards of Burgundy, and Europe's highest snow-capped Alps.

In France, *l'art de vivre* is something every traveler can aspire to learn.

In France, *l'art de vivre*—the art of living—is not just a pleasing expression; it's a building block for a sound life. With five weeks of paid vacation, plus every Catholic holiday ever invented, the French have become experts at living well. It's no accident that France is home to linger-longer pastimes like café lounging, fine dining, and

barge cruising. The French insist on the best-quality crois-sants, cheese, mustard, and sparkling water; they don't rush lunch; and an evening's entertainment is usually no more than a lovingly prepared meal with friends. France demands that the traveler savor the finer things.

As you travel through this splendid country, slo-o-o-ow down. Spend hours in cafés dawdling over *un café*, make a habit of unplanned stops, and surrender willingly to *l'art de vivre*.

FAVORITE SIGHTS AND MEMORABLE EXPERIENCES IN FRANCE

Circling in on the Arc de Triomphe in Paris

I have a funny ritual I follow whenever I'm in Paris. I ask my taxi driver to take me around the Arc de Triomphe—two times. My cabbie plunges into the grand roundabout where a dozen boulevards converge on this mightiest of triumphal arches. Like referees at gladiator camp, traffic cops are sta-tioned at each entrance to this traffic circus, letting in bursts of eager cars. As marble Lady Liberties scramble up Napo-leon's arch, heroically thrusting their swords and shrieking at the traffic, all of Paris seems drawn into this whirlpool. Each time, being immersed in the crazy traffic with my cabbie so in control makes me laugh out loud.

In the mid-19th century, Baron Haussmann set out to make Paris the grandest city in Europe. The 12 arterials that radiate from the Arc de Triomphe were part of his master plan for a series of major boulevards that would intersect at diagonals. At the crisscross points, he had monuments (such as the Arc de Triomphe) erected as centerpieces. As we zip around the circle, it's obvious that Haussmann's plan did not anticipate the automobile.

My cabbie explains to me, "If there is an accident here, each driver is considered equally at fault. This is the only place in Paris where the accidents are not judged. No matter what the cir-cumstances, insurance companies split the costs fifty-fifty. In Paris, a good driver gets only scratches, not dents."

Fast Facts

Biggest cities: Paris (capital, 2.2 million), Marseille (1.5 million), Lyon (1.5 million)

Size: 215,000 square miles (roughly twice the size of Colorado), population 65 million

Currency: Euro

Key date and biggest festival: July 14, Bastille Day, the start of the French Revolution in 1789

Per-capita snail consumption: 500 per year

Handy French phrases: *Bonjour* (good day; bohn-zhoor), *S'il vous plait* (please; see voo play), *Merci* (thank you; mehr-see), *J'aime le fromage* (I like cheese; zhehm luh froh-mahzh)

Tourist info: US.France.fr

The commotion of cars fights to get to the arch at the center as if to pay homage to the national spirit of France. Cars entering the circle have the right-of-way; those in the circle must yield. Parisian drivers navigate the circle like a comet circling the sun—making a parabola. It's a game of fender-bender chicken. This circle is the great equalizer. Tippy little Citroëns, their rooftops cranked open like sardine lids, bring lumbering buses to a sudden, cussing halt.

While we're momentarily stalled on the inside lane, I pay and hop out. As the cabbie drives away, I'm left feeling small under Europe's ultimate arch. Here the flame of France's unknown soldier—flickering silently in the eye of this urban storm—seems to invite me to savor this grandiose monument to French nationalism.

The Arc de Triomphe affords a great Paris view, but only to those who earn it—there are 284 steps to the top. At the top, I look down along the huge axis that shoots like an arrow all the way from the Louvre, up the Champs-Elysées, through the arch, then straight down the Avenue de la Grande-Armée to a forest of distant skyscrapers around an even bigger modern arch in suburban La Défense. I love the contrast between the skyscrapers in the suburbs and the more uniform heights of buildings closer to the arch. The beauty of Paris—basically a flat basin with a river running through it—is man-made. There's a harmonious relationship between the width of its grand boulevards and the standard height and design of the buildings. This elegant skyline is broken only by venerable historic domes and spires—and the lonely-looking Montparnasse Tower, which stands like the box the Eiffel Tower came in. The appearance of this tower served as a wake-up call in the early 1970s to preserve the historic skyline of downtown Paris.

Paris is a capital of grand monuments and grand boulevards.

France's Top Destinations

Paris ▲▲▲ allow 3-5 days

World capital of art, fashion, food, literature, and ideas, offering
historic monuments, grand boulevards, and corner cafés

Top Sights
Notre-Dame Cathedral Paris' most beloved church
Sainte-Chapelle Gothic cathedral with peerless stained glass
Louvre Europe's oldest and greatest museum, starring *Mona Lisa* and *Venus de Milo*
Orsay Museum Nineteenth-century art, including Europe's best Impressionist collection
Eiffel Tower Paris' soaring exclamation point
Arc de Triomphe Triumphal arch with viewpoint marking start of Champs-Elysées

Nearby
Versailles The ultimate royal palace
Chartres Cathedral Best example of Gothic architecture, statues, and stained glass
Giverny Monet's flowery gardens, which inspired many of his paintings

Normandy ▲▲ 2-3 days

Pastoral mix of sweeping coastlines, half-timbered towns, and intriguing cities,
including **Rouen** (Joan of Arc sights and soaring Gothic cathedral), artistic
seaside **Honfleur,** historic **Bayeux** (famous tapestry), stirring D-Day beaches and
museums, and pretty-as-a-mirage island abbey of Mont St-Michel

Brittany ▲ 1 day

Windswept and rugged peninsula, with a gorgeous coast, Celtic ties, and two
notable towns: medieval **Dinan** and the beach resort of **St-Malo**

Loire Valley ▲▲ 1-2 days

Lushly romantic area of picturesque towns (**Amboise** and **Chinon**) and hundreds
of castles and palaces

Dordogne ▲▲ 2 days

Region of prehistoric cave paintings (including Lascaux), lazy canoe rides past
medieval castles, market towns **(Sarlat),** and, for wine lovers, nearby **St-Emilion**

Languedoc-Roussillon ▲ 1-2 days

Sunny southern region, highlighted by **Albi**'s Toulouse-Lautrec museum,
Carcassonne's perfectly preserved city walls, and the seaside village of **Collioure**

Provence ▲▲▲ 2-3 days

Home to Van Gogh sights in **Arles,** the famed medieval bridge and Palace of the
Popes in **Avignon,** Roman history (including a pair of amphitheaters and the Pont
du Gard aqueduct), rock-top villages (including **Les Baux**), the **Côtes du Rhône**
wine road, and the quintessentially Provençal hill towns of the **Luberon**

French Riviera ▲▲▲ 2-3 days

A string of coastal resorts, including cosmopolitan and art-crazy **Nice,** beachy
Villefranche-sur-Mer, glitzy **Monaco,** easygoing **Antibes** (with a Picasso
museum), and hill-capping **Eze-le-Village**

French Alps ▲   2 days

Spectacular mountain scenery featuring the scenic, lakeside city of **Annecy;** Europe's highest peak, Mont Blanc; and the world-famous **Chamonix** ski resort (with lift to Italy)

Burgundy ▲▲   1-2 days

Region of bountiful vineyards, rustic cuisine, and age-old spirituality, with the compact wine capital of **Beaune** (and nearby wine roads), France's best-preserved medieval abbey **(Fontenay),** and a magnificent Romanesque church **(Vézelay)**

With more time, consider visiting

Reims and Verdun Historic cathedral, champagne cellars, and WWI battle sites
Alsace Franco-Germanic region dotted with wine-road villages
Lyon Metropolitan city with Roman ruins and delicious cuisine

The grandest of boulevards emanating from the arch, the Champs-Elysées, used to be even grander. From the 1920s through the 1960s, it was lined with top-end hotels, cafés, and residences—pure elegance. Parisians actually dressed up to come here. Then, in 1963, the government pumped up the neighborhood's commercial metabolism by bringing in the RER (commuter train). Suburbanites had easy access, McDonald's moved in, and *pfft*—there went the neighborhood. Still, the Champs-Elysées remains the country's ultimate parade ground, where major events all unfold: the Tour de France finale, Bastille Day parades, and New Year's festivities. With its monumental sidewalks, stylish shops, venerable cafés, and glimmering showrooms, this is Paris at its most Parisian.

Joyride in a Loire Valley Restaurant

French cuisine is sightseeing for your taste buds. You're not just paying for the food. A meal can be a three-hour joyride for the senses—as rich as visiting an art gallery and as stimulating as a good massage.

Not long ago, I dined at a fine restaurant in Amboise, in the midst of France's château-rich Loire Valley, with Steve Smith, the co-author of my France guidebook. Aurore, our waitress, was enchanting. She smiled as I ordered escargot for my first course. Getting a full dozen escargot rather than the typical six snails doubles the joy. Eating six, you're aware that the supply is very limited, but with twelve, there's no end to your snail fun. Add a good white wine, and you've got a full orchestral accompaniment.

My crust of bread lapped up the homemade garlic-and-herb sauce. I asked Aurore how it could be so good. With a sassy chuckle she said, "Other restaurateurs come here to figure that out, too." Then she added, "It's done with love." While I've heard that line many times, here it seemed believable.

In France, slow service is good service. After a pleasant pause, my main course arrived: tender beef with beans wrapped in bacon. Slicing through a pack of beans in their quiver of bacon, I let the fat do its dirty deed. A sip of wine, after a bite of beef, seemed like an incoming tide washing the flavor farther ashore.

My crust of bread, a veteran from the escargot course, was called into action for a swipe of sauce. Italians brag about all the ingredients they use. But France is proudly the land of sauces. If the sauce is the medicine, the bread is the

In France, luxuriate over a dinner, as if taking your palate out to a spa. And, when it comes to the cheese course, don't hold back.

syringe. Thanks to the bread, I enjoyed one last encore of the meat and vegetables I'd just savored.

Shifting my chair to stretch out my legs, I prepared for the next course—a selection of fine cheeses. It sounds like a lot of food, but portions are smaller in France, and what we cram onto one large plate they spread out over several courses.

Aurore brought out her cheese platter on a rustic board, the vibrant-yet-mellow colors promising a tantalizing array of tastes. As cheese needs wine, I checked my wine bottle like I would my gas tank before driving home. Noticing the restaurant crowd thinning, I reminded myself that there was no rush. I liked hearing the quiet murmur of other diners, as eating among appreciative patrons is part of the sensory experience.

Finished with the cheeses, I leaned back to stifle a burp, just as Steve announced, "And here comes dessert." Mine was a tender crêpe papoose of cinnamon-flavored baked apple with butterscotch ice cream, garnished with a soft slice of kiwi. That didn't keep me from reaching over for a snip of Steve's lemon tart with raspberry sauce.

Our entire meal cost about $60 each. You could call it $20 for nourishment and $40 for three hours of bliss. Even if you're not a foodie, I can't imagine a richer sightseeing experience, one that brings together an unforgettable ensemble of local ingredients, culture, pride, and people.

Well-Fed Geese in the Dordogne

With elbows resting on a rustic windowsill on a farm in France's Dordogne region, I'm watching Denis grab one

In France, the geese run free on the farm and are force-fed to fatten their livers for foie gras. Being high on the food chain is always nice, but never so nice as when eating in France.

goose at a time from an endless line of geese. In a kind of peaceful, mesmerizing trance, he fills each one's gullet with corn. Like his father and his father and his father before him, Denis spends five hours a day, every day, all year long, sitting in a barn surrounded by geese.

Denis rhythmically grabs a goose by the neck, pulls him under his leg and stretches him up, and slides the tube down to the belly. He pulls the trigger to squirt the corn in, slowly slides the tube up the neck and out, holds the beak shut for a few seconds, lets that goose go, and grabs the next.

Many of my friends express disgust when I tell them I've witnessed geese being force-fed—the traditional way farmers fatten the livers to make foie gras, a prized delicacy in the Dordogne. Some people want to boycott French foie gras for what they consider inhumane treatment of the geese. That's why I was on the goose farm—to learn more about la gavage, the force-feeding process.

Elevage du Bouyssou, a big homey goose farm a short drive from the market town of Sarlat, is run by Denis and Nathalie Mazet. Their geese are filled with corn three times a day for the last months of their lives. They have expandable stomachs and no gag reflex, so the corn stays there, gradually settling as it is digested and making room for the next feeding. Watching Denis work, I wonder what it must be like to spend so much time with an endless cycle of geese. Do geese populate his dreams?

While Denis takes care of the geese, Nathalie meets tourists—mostly French families—who show up each evening at 6 p.m. to see how their beloved foie gras is made. The groups stroll the idyllic farm as Nathalie explains that they raise a thousand geese a year. She stresses that the key to top-quality foie gras is happy geese raised on quality food in an unstressed environment. They need quality corn and the same feeder.

The Mazets sell everything but the head and feet of their geese. The down feathers only net about 30 cents a goose. The serious money is in the livers. A normal liver weighs a quarter-pound. When done with the force-feeding process, the liver weighs about two pounds. (With a thousand geese, they produce a ton of foie gras annually—Nathalie says, "Barely enough to support one family.")

Like other French supporters of *la gavage*, Nathalie points out that their free-range animals are in no pain and live six months. By contrast, most American chickens live less than two months in little boxes and are plumped with hormones. Who's to say which system is better or worse?

In the Dordogne, farmers in the markets pass out petite goose-liver sandwiches as they evangelize about their foie gras, and every meal seems to start with a foie-gras course. After a few days of this rich eating, I leave with a strong need for a foie gras detox and a plate of vegetables.

On Top of Provence's Pont du Gard

The south of France offers many sightseeing treats. And when it comes to something stony and ancient, it's hard to beat the Roman aqueduct called the Pont du Gard.

This region is named Provence because it was the first "foreign" conquest as ancient Rome set about building its vast empire. Since it wasn't Rome proper, they called it "Provincia Romana" (province of Rome)—and the name stuck.

The Romans left behind some impressive examples of engineering in their first province, including the Pont du

The Pont du Gard is the most famous and scenic stretch of a 30-mile-long Roman aqueduct.

Gard, one of the most striking—and most visited—sights in all of France. This impressively preserved Roman aqueduct was built in about 19 B.C. Throughout the ancient world, aqueducts were like flags of stone that heralded the greatness of Rome.

Although most of the aqueduct runs on or below ground, at Pont du Gard it spans a canyon on a massive bridge—one of the most remarkable surviving Roman ruins anywhere. Even after many visits, I'm forever in awe of the ability of the ancient Roman engineers. This structure, built with perfectly cut stones fitted together without mortar, was designed to slope ever so slightly—less than an inch every hundred yards—as part of a 30-mile canal system that let water flow effortlessly into the city of Nîmes, supplying nine million gallons of water per day (about 100 gallons per second) to one of ancient Europe's largest cities.

The classic view of the aqueduct, from the river, is something every visitor sees. But recently, I joined a tour that took me through the water channel at the top of the Pont du Gard. Following a guide, I actually walked the length of this ancient bridge—a much more memorable experience.

I love to cap my Pont du Gard visit in Nîmes, where you can see what is considered the best-preserved arena of the Roman world and a stunning temple that rivals Rome's Pantheon as the most complete and splendid building that survives from the Roman Empire.

And at a small excavation site, sitting next to the street, is the castellum: a modest-looking water distribution tank that was the grand finale of the 30-mile-long aqueduct. Looking at the spout marking the end of that amazing structure, I imagine the jubilation locals felt when water gushed freely (with nobody having to carry it) into their city. And then, looking down into the castellum's collection tank, I marvel at a bit of social compassion those ancient

In summer, you can actually hike through the water channel at the top of the Pont du Gard.

Romans engineered into their water system: The lowest water pipes powered the public wells that graced neighborhood squares. The higher pipes—which got water only when the supply was plentiful—routed water to the homes of the wealthy, to public baths, and to decorative but nonessential fountains. I guess losing to the Roman Empire wasn't all bad—even if you lived in the provinces.

Contemplating the Toll of World War II in Normandy

On a small square in a Normandy town, an elderly French-man approaches me, singing "The Star-Spangled Banner." In 1944, British, Canadian, and American troops invaded this area, beginning the end of World War II—and the French apparently haven't forgotten. But of course, reminders are still abundant. Seventy-five miles of France's north coast are littered with WWII museums, monuments, cemeteries, and battle remains left in tribute to the courage of the armies that successfully carried out the largest amphibious military operation in history: D-Day.

Wandering the beach of Arromanches—ground zero for the D-Day invasion—I take in the remnants of the Allied-built man-made harbor, Port Winston, which gave the Allies a foothold in Normandy, allowing them to begin their victorious push to Berlin and the end of the war. Several rusted floats—once supports for hastily built pontoon roads—are mired on the sand. I can just make out what's left of an anti-aircraft gun on a concrete block in the sea. I'm thankful that, instead of the sound of artillery, all I hear are birds and surf.

Later, I visit Omaha Beach, the eye of the D-Day storm. In the cemetery, a striking memorial with a soaring statue represents the spirit of American youth. Around the statue, giant reliefs of the Battle of Normandy and the Battle of

To remember the heroes of Normandy, visit the American Cemetery above Omaha Beach.

Europe are etched on the walls. Behind is the semicircular Garden of the Missing, with the names of 1,557 soldiers who were never found.

Nearly 10,000 brilliant white marble tombstones glow in memory of the Americans who gave their lives to free Europe. Wandering among the peaceful, poignant sea of headstones, I read the names, home states, and dates of death inscribed on each, and think of the friends and families affected by each lost life. It's a struggle to reconcile the quiet beauty of the setting with the horrible toll of that battle.

Not just in Normandy, but all over France, I'm reminded of the gratitude the French feel for what American troops did for their country. I remember filming one of my public-television shows at a charming little mom-and-pop château. When I'm filming, I'm on a mission—the sun's going down, and we've got work to do. But the aristocratic couple whose family had called that castle home for centuries insisted, "We must stop and have a ceremony because we have an American film crew here working in our castle." They cracked open a fine bottle of wine and brought out—with great ceremony, as if it were a precious relic—the beautiful 48-star American flag they had hoisted over their château on that great day in 1944 when they were freed by American troops. They implored us, "Please go home and tell your friends that we will never forget what America did for us."

Medieval Carcassonne

Before me lies Carcassonne, the perfect medieval city. Like a fish that everyone thought was extinct, Europe's greatest Romanesque fortress-city somehow survives.

Located in southeastern France, medieval Carcassonne is a 13th-century world of towers, turrets, and cobblestones. It's a walled city and Camelot's castle rolled into one, frosted with too many day-tripping tourists. At 10 a.m., the sales-people stand at the doors of their main-street shops, their gauntlet of tacky temptations poised and ready for their daily ration of customers. But an empty Carcassonne rattles in the early morning or late-afternoon breeze. Enjoy the town early or late, or off-season. Spend the night.

I was supposed to be gone yesterday, but it's sundown and here I sit—imprisoned by choice—curled in a cranny on top of the wall. The moat is one foot over and 100 feet down. Happy little weeds and moss upholster my throne. The wind blows away many of the sounds of today, and my imagination "medievals" me.

Twelve hundred years ago, Charlemagne stood below with his troops, besieging this fortress-town for several years. As the legend goes, just as food was running out, a cunning townswoman had a great idea. She fed the town's last bits of grain to the last pig and tossed him over the wall. Splat. Charlemagne's restless forces, amazed that the town still had enough food to throw fat party pigs over the wall, decided they'd never succeed in starving the people out. They ended the siege, and the city was saved. Today, the walls that stopped Charlemagne open wide for visitors.

Carcassonne, in the south of France, is Europe's greatest fortress city.

Paris' Ultimate Market Street

I grew up thinking that cheese was no big deal. It was orange, and the shape of bread was square: slap, fwomp... sandwich. Even though I'm still far from a gourmet eater, my time in Paris—specifically in the Rue Cler street market—has substantially bumped up my appreciation of good cuisine (as well as the French knack for good living). Rue Cler, lined with shops spilling out into the street, feels like village Paris—in the skinny shadow of the Eiffel Tower.

Parisians shop almost daily for three good reasons: Refrigerators are small (tiny kitchens), produce must be fresh, and shopping is an important social event. Strolling down Rue Cler, I soon spot a friend, Marie-Alice. She beckons me to the strawberry display. "You must shop with your nose," she says, burying hers in a basket of lush fruit.

We follow our noses to a long, narrow, canopied cheese table. Marie-Alice bounces her finger over a long line of cheeses: wedges, cylinders, balls, and miniature hockey pucks all powdered white, gray, and burnt marshmallow—it's a festival of mold. *Oh là là* means you're impressed. If you like a cheese, show greater excitement with more *las*. *Oh là là là là.* She holds the stinkiest glob close to her nose, takes a deep, orgasmic breath, and exhales, "Yes, this smells like zee feet of angels."

Inside the shop, we browse through some of the several hundred types of French cheese. A cheese shop

Visiting the Eiffel Tower

A stroll along Rue Cler works well with a visit to the nearby Eiffel Tower. There are two ways to get up the tower: smart or stupid. Get a reservation—those who just show up waste lots of time waiting in line. Book an entrance time in advance (www.toureiffel.paris) and scoot right in. Just be sure to reserve well ahead in peak times such as summer; tickets go on sale a couple of months in advance and can sell out within hours.

(known as BOF, for *beurre, oeuf, fromage*) is the place where people go for butter, egg, and cheese products. In the back room are *les meules*, the big, 170-pound wheels of cheese. The "hard" cheeses are cut from these. Don't eat the skin of these big ones—they roll them on the floor. But the skin on most smaller cheeses—like Brie or Camembert—is part of the taste. As Marie-Alice says, "It completes the package."

Across the street we pause at a table of duck, pigeon, quail, and rabbit. Marie-Alice sorts through the dead. With none of the tenderness shown in the cheese shop, she hoists a duck. Rubbing a thumb toughly on its rough and calloused feet, she tells me that well-used feet indicate that the birds ran wild on a farm instead of being confined in an industrial kennel.

The ruddy-faced butcher, wearing a tiny plaid beret and dressed in a white apron over a fine shirt, is busy chopping. He's the best-dressed butcher I've ever seen. A battalion of meat hooks hang in orderly lines from the ceiling. The white walls bring out the red in the different cuts of meat.

At the nearby bakery, French women, thick and crusty after a lifetime of baguette munching, debate the merits of the street's rival boulangeries. It's said that when bakers do good bread, they have no time to do good pastry. If the baker specializes in pastry, the bread suffers. But this shop bucks the trend—the women and Marie-Alice agree that this baker does both equally well.

A man with working-class hands steps out the door, cradling a bouquet and a baguette in his arms—and heads off to gather the rest of his daily meal. If you want to learn the fine art of living, Parisian-style, Rue Cler is an excellent classroom.

More French Experiences

Inside the Lascaux Caves: In France's Dordogne region, proud guides compare the prehistoric paintings in the Lascaux caves to Michelangelo's frescoes in the Sistine Chapel. Hyperbole, I thought—until I saw Lascaux IV. It's a painstakingly created copy of the actual cave, which the public is no longer allowed to visit. Swept away by its grandeur, I soon forget it's a replica.

The vast cave looks amazingly like my (healthy) colonoscopy scan. Main difference: The cave is covered with paintings made 17,000 years ago, when mammoths and saber-toothed cats roamed the earth. This was a sophisticated project executed by artists from the impressive Magdalenian culture. In the museum, filled with original Magdalenian artifacts, I begin to feel a connection with these people. Looking at the oil lamps, I can imagine the wonder of wandering under flickering flames that lit the Sistine Chapel of the prehistoric world.

Magnificence on a Mudflat: I love to scamper far from shore at low tide, shoes in my hands, across the mud flat in the vast Bay of Mont St-Michel in northwestern France. Splashing across black sand and through little puddles, I head for a dramatic abbey reaching to heaven from a rock surrounded by a vast and muddy solitude, where hermit monks sought seclusion since the sixth century. The silhouette of the Gothic Mont St-Michel sends my spirits soaring today, just as it did the spirits of weary pilgrims in centuries past. Though a dreamscape from a distance, Mont St-Michel can be a human traffic jam until late afternoon. It's some consolation to remember that, even in the Middle Ages, the abbey-town was a commercial gauntlet, with stalls selling souvenir medallions, candles, and fast food. I prefer to ramble on the ramparts after dark, when the tourists are gone and the island is magically floodlit. At night, it's easy to

The sights and experiences of France range from caves painted 17,000 years ago, to medieval island abbeys, to cable cars zipping you to thin-air alpine summits.

ponder the promise of desolation and the simple life of solitude that attracted monks to this striking spot so long ago.

Getting High in Chamonix: Europe's ultimate mountain lift
towers high above the tourist-choked French resort town of
Chamonix. Ride the Aiguille du Midi *téléphérique* (gondola)
to the dizzy 12,600-foot-high tip of a rock needle. Chamonix
shrinks as trees fly by, soon replaced by whizzing rocks, ice,
and snow, until you reach the top. Up there, even sunshine is
cold. The air is thin. People are giddy (those prone to altitude
sickness are less giddy). Fun things can happen if you're not
too winded to join locals in the halfway-to-heaven tango.

The Alps spread out before you. In the distance is the
bent little Matterhorn. You can almost reach out and pat the
head of Mont Blanc, the Alps' highest point.

Next, for Europe's most exciting border crossing, get into
the tiny red gondola and head south to Italy. Dangle silently
for 40 minutes as you glide over glaciers and a forest of peaks
to Italy. Hang your head out the window; explore every corner of your view. You're sailing a new sea.

At Helbronner Point, you'll descend into Valle d'Aosta in
Italy, the land of cappuccino, gelato, and *la dolce vita*.

Chamonix, the Aiguille du Midi, and the Valle d'Aosta—
surely a high point in anyone's European vacation.

CULTURE AND TRADITIONS: EVERYTHING'S SO...FRENCH

Play the Markets

Market days have been a central feature of life in rural
France since the Middle Ages. No single event better symbol-
izes the French preoccupation with fresh products and their
strong ties to the soil than the weekly market. Many locals
mark their calendars with the arrival of prized seasonal produce, such as truffles in November.

Most markets take place once a week in the town's main
square and, if large enough, spill onto nearby streets. Markets combine fresh produce; samples of wine and locally produced brandies or ciders; and a smattering of nonfood items,
like knives, berets, kitchen goods, and cheap clothing. The
bigger the market, the greater the overall selection—particularly for nonperishable goods.

Market day is as important socially as it is commercially—it's a weekly chance to resume friendships and get

the current gossip. Neighbors catch up on the butcher's barn renovation, see photos of the florist's new grandchild, and relax over *un café*. Dogs sit beneath café tables while friends exchange kisses. Tether yourself to a bench and observe: Three cheek-kisses are for good friends (left-right-left); a fourth kiss is added for friends you haven't seen in a while.

Wine Talk

The French sum up the unique natural conditions where a wine is produced in one word: *terroir* (pronounced "tehr-wah"). It means "somewhere-ness," a particular combination of macro- and microclimate, soil, geology, and the accumulated experience of the winemakers. Two wines can be made from the same grape but be of very different character because of their *terroir*. The best vintners don't force their style on the grape. They play to the wine's strength, respecting the natural character of the sun, soil, and vine—the *terroir*.

Grapevines are creepers, with roots going through the topsoil and into the geology deep down. The roots are commonly 150 feet long and deep. While topsoil can be influenced by the vintner, the deep geology cannot, and this gives the wine a distinct character. The French do not allow irrigation, thus forcing the grapes to search deep for water. A good grape, in the French view, must suffer.

Dealing with the French in French and English

French people value politeness, and take pride in their culture, tradition, and language. You'll get better treatment if you learn and use the simplest of French pleasantries. Begin every encounter with "*Bonjour* (or *S'il vous plaît*), *madame* (or *monsieur*)," and end it with "*Au revoir* (or *Merci*), *madame* (or *monsieur*)."

The French are language perfectionists—they take their language (and other languages) seriously. Often they speak more English than they let on. This isn't a tourist-baiting tactic, but timidity on their part about speaking another language less than fluently. If you want them to speak English, say, "*Bonjour, madame* (or *monsieur*). *Parlez-vous anglais?*" They may say "*non*," but if you continue talking and butchering their language, they'll soon say, "Well, actually, I do speak some English."

Bowling *Boules*

In small squares in every Provençal village and city, you're likely to find the local gang playing *boules,* the horseshoes of southern France. Every French boy grows up playing *boules* with Papa and *Ton-Ton* (Uncle) Jean. It's a social-yet-serious sport, and endlessly entertaining to watch—even more so if you understand the rules.

Boules (also known as *pétanque*) is played with heavy metal balls (*boules,* about the size of oranges) and a small wooden target ball (*le cochonnet*—"piglet," about the size of a ping-pong ball). Whoever gets their *boule* closest to the *cochonnet* scores.

I like to pause and watch old-timers while away the afternoon tossing shiny silver balls on gravelly courts—and if I feel like creating a memory, I give it a try myself.

Persnickety Perceptions

The good life in France—music, culture, an appreciation of fine wine and food—is seductive but intimidating to Americans. No one wants to make a "mistake" when picking a wine, croissant, or cheese. For a long time, I thought there was something affected and pseudo-sophisticated about all this finicky Frenchness. I once asked a wine merchant in Paris to suggest a good bottle to go with snails, and he wanted to know how I planned to cook them. I had envisioned a good Chardonnay, but *mais non*—not "flinty" enough—only a Chablis would do.

I felt inept for making the wrong pairing and annoyed by the wine seller's hair-splitting choosiness. But then I thought of the way I catalogue the nuances of baseball—it's taken me a lifetime of slowly absorbing the game's rules and situations to simply "know" the game the way the Frenchman "knows" wine. All the stuff that matters to me—how far the runner is leading off first base, who's on deck, how a batter does against left-handed pitchers, when to put in a pinch runner—would be nonsense to a French person. The next time I mortify my French friend by putting a little ketchup on my meat, I'll just remember that with two outs and a full count, he'll have no idea why I know the runner's off with the pitch.

France Travel Resources from Rick Steves

Guidebooks

Check out Rick's guidebooks covering all of France; Paris; Provence & the French Riviera; the Loire Valley; Normandy; and Basque Country Spain & France; plus his French phrase book

Audio Europe

Download Rick's free Audio Europe app, with interviews about France and self-guided audio tours, including walks through historic Paris and Rue Cler, and tours of the Louvre, Musée d'Orsay, Père Lachaise Cemetery, and Versailles Palace

TV Shows

The quintessence of France with Rick as your host, viewable on public television and at RickSteves.com. Episodes cover Paris, Paris side trips, the Loire Valley, the French Alps, Lyon, Burgundy, Alsace, Dordogne, Normandy, Provence, and the Riviera

Organized Tours

Small group tours, with itineraries planned by Rick: Paris & the Heart of France in 11 Days; Loire to the South of France in 13 Days; Paris in 7 Days; Eastern France in 14 Days; Basque Country of Spain & France in 9 Days; My Way France in 13 Days; My Way Europe, My Way Alpine Europe, Family Europe: London to Florence, Best of Europe (all include stops in France)

For more on all of these resources, visit RickSteves.com. For France trip-planning tips, see RickSteves.com/europe/france.

Spain

For the tourist, Spain means many things: bullfights, massive cathedrals, world-class art, Muslim palaces, vibrant folk life, whitewashed villages, bright sunshine. You'll find all of this, but the country's charm really lies in its people and their unique lifestyle. From the stirring communal *sardana* dance in Barcelona to the sizzling rat-a-tat-tat of flamenco in Sevilla, this country creates its own beat amid the heat.

Spain is in Europe, but not *of* Europe, thanks largely to the Pyrenees Mountains that physically isolate it from the rest of the Continent. For more than 700 years (711-1492), Spain's dominant culture was Muslim, not Christian. And after a brief Golden Age in the 16th century (financed by New World gold), Spain retreated into three centuries of isolation. Spain's seclusion contributed to the creation of its distinctive customs—bullfights, flamenco dancing, and a national obsession with ham. Even as other countries opened up to one another in the 20th century, the fascist dictator Francisco Franco virtually sealed off Spain from the rest of Europe's democracies. But since Franco's death in 1975, Spaniards have swung almost to the opposite extreme, becoming wide open to new ideas and technologies.

Spain's spread-out geography makes it less a centralized nation than a collection of distinct regions. In the central plain sits the lively urban island of Madrid. Just south is holy Toledo, a medieval showpiece and melting-pot city with Christian, Muslim, and Jewish roots. Farther south is Andalucía, home to sleepy, whitewashed hill towns and three great cities: Granada (topped with the Alhambra palace), Córdoba (with a massive mosque and pretty patios), and Sevilla (where Holy Week is celebrated as if God were watching). Spain's south coast offers a palm-tree jungle of beach resorts along the

Costa del Sol, a taste of British fish-and-chips in Gibraltar, and a laid-back launch pad to Morocco (from Tarifa).

To Spain's far north is San Sebastián and the Basque Country, which combine sparkling beaches, cutting-edge architecture, and the *pintxo* (a local—and often gourmet—take on tapas). Nearby is Pamplona, where bulls and tourists run for their lives. Gregarious pilgrims hike through the town on their long journey across northern Spain to the cathedral town of Santiago de Compostela. Along the Mediterranean coast (to the east), Spain has an almost Italian vibe. Trendy Barcelona, where Antoni Gaudí's architecture makes waves, keeps one eye cocked toward trends sailing in from the rest of the Continent.

The Alhambra in Granada, the last Moorish stronghold on the Iberian Peninsula, is a vivid reminder of the splendor of the Muslim society that ruled Spain for centuries.

FAVORITE SIGHTS AND MEMORABLE EXPERIENCES IN SPAIN

Good Morning in Santiago

I'm tucked away in Santiago de Compostela, in the northwest corner of Spain. I have a three-part agenda: to see pilgrims reach their goal in front of the cathedral, to explore the outdoor market, and to buy some barnacles in the seafood section—then have them cooked for me, on the spot, in a café.

Whenever I'm here, I make a point to be on the big square at the foot of the towering Cathedral of St. James around 10 in the morning. That's when scores of well-worn pilgrims march in triumphantly from their last overnight on the Camino de Santiago (Way of St. James)—a 30-day, 500-mile hike from the French border.

Humble hikers have trod these miles since the Middle Ages to pay homage to the remains of St. James in his namesake city. (I love the idea that the first guidebook ever written talked up "going local, packing light, and watching out for pickpockets" for pilgrims traveling the Camino a thousand years ago.) Arriving in the church square, they step on a scallop shell symbol embedded in the pavement in front of the cathedral. I witness joy and jubilation sweep over those who finish this journey.

Pilgrims often ask me to take a photo for them. Then

they say, "I've got to go meet with St. James," and—as has been the routine for a thousand years—they head into the cathedral.

Two blocks away, the market is thriving, oblivious to the personal triumphs going on over at St. James' tomb. There's something fundamental about wandering through a farmers market early in the morning anywhere in the world: Salt-of-the-earth people pull food out of the ground, cart it to the city, and sell what they've harvested to people who don't have gardens.

Dried-apple grandmothers line up like a babushka cancan. Each sits on a stool so small it disappears under her work dress. At the women's feet are brown woven baskets filled like cornucopias—still-dirty eggs in one; in the next, greens clearly pulled this morning, soil clinging to their roots. One woman hopes to earn a few extra euros selling potent homebrews, her golden bottles stoppered with ramshackle corks.

> ## Fast Facts
>
> **Biggest cities:** Madrid (capital, 3.3 million), Barcelona (1.6 million)
> **Size:** 195,000 square miles (roughly twice the size of Oregon), population 48 million
> **Locals call it:** España
> **Currency:** Euro
> **Key date:** November 20, 1975, Prime Minister Francisco Franco dies, ending nearly four decades of dictator rule
> **Languages:** You'll find four—Castilian (what we call Spanish, spoken country-wide), Catalan (NE Spain), Galego (NW Spain), Euskara (Basque region)
> **Biggest festivals:** Semana Santa (Holy Week, before Easter, best in Sevilla), Running of the Bulls (July, Pamplona)
> **Handy Spanish phrases:** *Hola* (hello; **oh**-lah), *Por favor* (please; por fah-**bor**), *Gracias* (thank you; **grah**-thee-ahs), *Soy rico y soltero* (I'm rich and single; soy **ree**-koh ee sohl-**teh**-roh)
> **Tourist info:** Spain.info

Babushkas sit behind rickety card tables filled with yellow cheeses shaped like giant Hershey's Kisses...or, to locals, breasts. This local cheese is called *tetilla* to revenge a prudish priest who, seven centuries ago, told a sculptor at the cathedral to redo a statue that he considered too buxom. Ever since, the townsfolk have shaped their cheese exactly like what the priest didn't want them to see carved in stone. You can't go anywhere in Santiago without seeing creamy, mild *tetilla*.

In vendors' stalls, spicy red chorizo hangs in sausage chains, framing merchants' faces. Chickens, plucked and looking as rubber-like as can be, fill glass cases. A selection of pigs' ears, mixed with hooves going nowhere, fills a shoebox. The ears, translucent in the low rays of the morning sun, resemble neatly flattened conch shells. At the best stalls, short ladies with dusty, blue-plaid roller carts jostle for deals.

The sound of cascading clams and castanet shrimp—red, doomed, and flipping mad—greet me as I enter the seafood

hall. Fisherwomen in rubber aprons and matching gloves sort through folding money. From one vendor I buy my barnacles (*percebes*)—at about $16 a pound, they're one-third the price I'd pay in a bar. I get a little less than a half-pound and hustle my full bag over to the market café called Churro Mania. There, Ramon and Julia boil them up for a few dollars. Feeling quite like a local—sipping my beer so early in the morning—I wait for my barnacles to cook.

Then comes the climax of my morning: Julia brings my barnacles, stacked steaming on a stainless steel plate, as well as bread and another beer. I'm set. Twist, rip, bite. It's the bounty of the sea condensed into every little morsel: edible jubilation in Santiago.

Gaudí's Barcelona Dreaming

Barcelona's most famous architect, Antoni Gaudí, speckled the city with his Art Nouveau fantasies at the beginning of the 20th century. His buildings bloom with flowery shapes, race with galloping gables, and bend with organic curves. A prime example, the apartment building called La Pedrera, has walls of wavy stone and an undulating rooftop, where 30 chimneys play volleyball with the clouds. At Casa Batlló, a green-blue ceramic facade, tibia-esque pillars, and shell-like balconies are inspired by nature, while the humpback roofline suggests a cresting dragon's back.

But Gaudí's best-known and most persistent work is the Sagrada Família church. I've long said that if there's one building I'd like to see in Europe, it's the Sagrada Família... finished. The church, an epic work-in-progress for more than a hundred years, promises to be the most exciting church built in our lifetimes. If there is a miracle anywhere in the world of architecture, it is this church. Climb up stairs between the melting ice-cream-cone spires for a

If there's one building I'd like to see completed, it's Gaudí's wondrous Sagrada Família church in Barcelona. And it's well on its way.

gargoyle's-eye perspective of a living, growing, bigger-than-life building. Local craftspeople often finish up their careers by putting in a couple of years working on the project. The hope: to finish it by 2026—the 100th anniversary of Gaudí's death. By then, it's my bet that Gaudí will be sainted.

Gaudí fans also enjoy the artist's magic in the colorful, freewheeling Park Güell, a 30-acre hilltop garden once intended to be a high-end housing project. Carpeted with fanciful mosaics, dotted with sculptures (including a famous tiled lizard), and offering grand views of the city and the glittering Mediterranean beyond, this park is a great place to cap a day of Barcelona dreaming.

Strolling Córdoba's Back Streets

The Andalusian town of Córdoba has a glorious Moorish past. The town's centerpiece is its massive Mezquita. Magnificent in its grandeur, this huge mosque dominates the higgledy-piggledy old town around it. A wonder of the medieval world, the Mezquita is remarkably well-preserved, giving visitors a chance to appreciate the glory days of Muslim rule. But like most big sights, the Mezquita is surrounded by a touristy zone of shops and tour-group-friendly restaurants.

To separate from the crush of tourists, I wander the back streets. Exploring the residential lanes of old Córdoba, I'm quickly all alone with the town. Away from modern-day tourism, it's easy to catch an evocative whiff of the old.

I keep an eye out for colorful patios, framed by decorative ironwork gates. A common feature of houses throughout Andalucía, patios are taken very seriously here. The Romans used them to cool off, and the Moors added lush, ornate

Córdoba, in the south of Spain, comes with exquisite patios *(left)* and the biggest mosque Europe ever saw *(right)*.

touches. The patio functioned as a quiet outdoor living room, an oasis from the heat. Inside the see-through gates, roses, geraniums, and jasmine spill down whitewashed walls, while fountains play and caged birds sing.

I continue wandering after dinner. It's almost midnight—everyone's out, savoring a cool evening. I'm drawn to a commotion on a square. Short men with raspy tobacco voices and big bellies—called *curvas de felicidad* (happiness curves)—jostle and bark as a dozen little school girls rattle a makeshift stage with flamenco flair, working on their sultry.

Well after midnight, the city finally seems quiet. I return to my hotel and climb into my bed. Just as I doze off, a noisy and multigenerational parade rumbles down the cobbled lane. Standing in my underwear and wrapped in the drapes, I peer secretively out my window. Below, a band of guitars and castanets funnels down my narrow alley. Grandmothers—guardians of a persistent culture—make sure the children pick up their Andalusian customs. Finally, one woman looks up at me, catches my eye, and seems to nod, as if satisfied that I am witnessing the unwavering richness of their traditional way of life.

Feeling the Heat in Madrid

Changing cultures is always fun. I love to feel disoriented, as I am when I first arrive in a new place. Recently, following a stint in Austria, I switched to Madrid. I felt myself going from crisp rationality to casual disorganization.

When I'm in Madrid, I try to book a room with a balcony overlooking the Times Square of Spain, Puerta del Sol.

Spain's Top Destinations

Barcelona ▲▲▲   allow 3 days

Catalan capital with atmospheric Gothic old town, elegant new town, and striking art and architecture by resident artists Antoni Gaudí, Pablo Picasso, and Joan Miró

Top Sights
Picasso Museum Works from the artist's early years
Ramblas Colorful, touristy pedestrian zone with thriving market
Barri Gòtic Old town maze of streets with towering cathedral
Gaudí's Architecture Sagrada Família Church, La Pedrera, and Park Güell
Catalan Art Museum World-class showcase of this region's art

Nearby
Figueres and Cadaqués Salvador Dalí sights
Montserrat Dramatic mountaintop monastery
Sitges Beach resort

Madrid ▲▲▲   3 days

Spirited Spanish capital, boasting top-notch art treasures, stately squares, a lively tapas scene, and urban Spain at its best

Top Sights
Royal Palace Sumptuous national palace
Prado Museum Masterpieces by Velázquez, Goya, and El Greco
Centro de Arte Reina Sofía Modern art, including Picasso's epic *Guernica*
Thyssen-Bornemisza Museum Especially good Impressionist collection

Nearby
El Escorial Palace and mausoleum of Spanish royalty
Segovia Storybook town with a towering Roman aqueduct

Toledo ▲▲   1 day

Hill-capping former capital, with a colorfully complex history, a magnificent cathedral, and works by hometown boy El Greco

Salamanca ▲   1 day

Spain's quintessential university town, with the country's finest main square

Sevilla ▲▲▲   2 days

Soulful cultural capital of Andalucía, with a spectacular cathedral (the world's largest Gothic church), the Alcázar (labyrinthine Moorish palace), tangled former Jewish Quarter, teeming evening paseo, and fantastic flamenco

Andalucía ▲▲   2-3 days

Classic heartland of southern Spain, home to **Córdoba** (with Spain's top surviving Moorish mosque, the Mezquita) and whitewashed hill towns (including **Arcos de la Frontera** and **Ronda**)

Granada ▲▲▲   1 day

Grand Moorish capital with the magnificent Alhambra palace and Spain's best old Moorish quarter

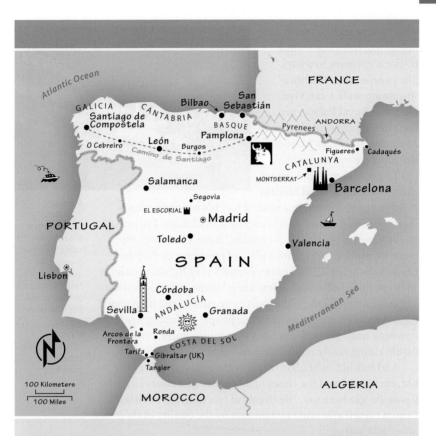

Basque Country ▲▲   3-4 days

Anchored by the culinary capital of **San Sebastián** and the more workaday
Bilbao (home to the dazzling Guggenheim Museum), with sleepy seaside retreats
and colorful villages scattered through the green countryside

Camino de Santiago ▲   4-5 days

Centuries-old pilgrimage route running across the top of Spain from France to
Santiago de Compostela in green Galicia, with stops along the way at big cities
(Pamplona, Burgos, León) and charming villages **(Puente la Reina, O Cebreiro)**

With more time, consider visiting

Cantabria Rustic northern coast with high-mountain scenery and prehistoric
cave art

Tarifa Charming beach-resort town and handy base for day trip to Morocco

Gibraltar A slice of Britain on a giant rock

This square, like so many in Europe, has gone from a traffic nightmare to a park-like people zone. Within a 10-minute walk I can visit the great Royal Palace; my favorite paintings in the Prado Museum; and Plaza Mayor, the ultimate town square.

To get acclimated, I get up early. Walking around Madrid at 8 a.m., people seem in a kind of fog. It's not clear who is starting their day and who is ending it. As for me, I'm intent on crossing off my rituals for Spain (I have a list for every place I travel): digging into a plate of *pimientos de Padrón* (these lightly fried, little green peppers play Russian roulette with my taste buds...only a few are jalapeño-spicy); savoring a slice of *jamón ibérico*—the most expensive cured ham, made from acorn-fed, black-hooved pigs; people-watching while downing a tall glass of *horchata*, that milky, nutty, refreshing drink; eating really really late; and being really, really hot.

And it is hot in Madrid. Even in the evening, things are so hot, they've moved the times of bullfights two hours later—to 9 p.m. People here say, "Be thankful you're not in Sevilla." I catch myself assessing restaurants by the quality of their air-conditioning.

But despite the heat, Madrid is vibrant. Even the living-statue street performers have a twinkle in their eyes. As always, Spain is a festival of life.

Anywhere in southern Europe, enjoy the relative cool of summer evenings by joining the festival of locals out and about. Each summer evening, Madrid's plazas become community gathering places.

Queen of the White Hill Towns

Arcos de la Frontera smothers its hilltop, tumbling down all sides like the train of a wedding dress. While larger than most other Andalusian hill towns, it's equally atmospheric. The labyrinthine old center is a photographer's feast. Viewpoint-hop through town. Feel the wind funnel through the narrow streets as drivers pull in car mirrors to fit around tight corners.

Residents brag that only they see the backs of the birds as they fly. To see why, climb to the viewpoint at the main square high in the old town. Belly up to the railing—the town's suicide jumping-off point—and look down. Ponder the fancy cliffside hotel's erosion concerns, orderly orange groves, flower-filled greenhouses, and the fine views toward Morocco.

The thoughtful traveler's challenge is to find meaning in the generally overlooked tiny details of historic towns such as Arcos. On one visit, I discovered that a short walk from Arcos' church of Santa María to the church of St. Peter is littered with fun glimpses into the town's past.

The church of Santa María faces the main square. After Arcos was reconquered from the Moors in the 13th century, this church was built—atop a mosque. In the pavement is a 15th-century magic circle: 12 red and 12 white stones—the white ones marked with various constellations. When a child came to the church to be baptized, the parents would stop here first for a good Christian exorcism. The exorcist would stand inside the protective circle and cleanse the baby of any evil spirits.

Small towns like Arcos come with lively markets. On my last visit, I was encouraged by the pickle woman to try a *banderilla*, named for the bangled spear that a matador sticks into a bull. As I gingerly slid an onion off the tiny skewer of pickled olives, onions, and carrots, she told me to eat it all at once. Explosive!

Near the market is a convent. The spiky security grill over the window protects cloistered nuns. Tiny peepholes allow the sisters to look out unseen. I stepped into the lobby to find a one-way mirror and a blind, spinning, lazy Susan-type cupboard. I pushed the buzzer, and a sister spun out some boxes of freshly baked cookies for sale. When I spun back the cookies with a *"No, gracias,"* a Monty Python-esque

Arcos de la Frontera perches on its cliff.

voice countered, "We have cupcakes as well." I bought a bag of these *magdalenas,* both to support their church work and to give to kids on my walk. Feeling like a religious Peeping Tom, I actually saw—through the not-quite one-way mirror—the sister in her flowing robe and habit momentarily appear and disappear.

Walking on, I passed street corners plastered with recycled Roman columns—protection from reckless donkey carts. The walls are scooped out on either side of the windows, a reminder of the days when women stayed inside but wanted the best possible view of any people-action in the streets.

Arcos' second church, St. Peter's, really is the second church. It lost an extended battle with Santa María for papal recognition as the leading church in Arcos. When the pope finally recognized Santa María, pouting parishioners from St. Peter's even changed their prayers. Rather than say, "María, mother of God," they prayed, "St. Peter, mother of God."

The tiny square in front of the church—about the only flat piece of pavement around—serves as the old-town soccer field for neighborhood kids. I joined the game and shared my cupcakes, savoring this idyllic slice of village Spain.

Holy Week in Sevilla

Holy Week (Semana Santa)—the week between Palm Sunday and Easter—is celebrated with intense fervor in Spain. All over the country, Semana Santa processions clog the streets. But nobody does Holy Week better than Sevilla.

Even if all you care about on Easter is chocolate, it's inspiring to witness the intense devotion of Sevillians during Holy Week. The scene is a holy spectacle. Paraders in purple-and-white cone hats shuffle past me, carrying crusader swords and four-foot candles. Like American kids scrambling for candies at a parade, Spanish kids collect dripping wax from religious coneheads, attempting to amass the biggest ball on a stick for their Easter souvenir. In bars, all eyes are fixed on the TVs, watching not soccer or bullfighting...but live coverage of their town's Holy Week procession.

The bell tower of Sevilla's cathedral

When you meet Spaniards, it's common to ask which football team they support. But in Sevilla, you also ask which Virgin Mary they favor. The top two in town are La Virgen de la Macarena and La Esperanza de Triana (same Mary, different churches). On Thursday during Holy Week, it's a battle royale of the Madonnas, as Sevilla's two favorite virgins are paraded through the streets simultaneously.

The procession squeezes down narrow alleys. Legions of drums crack eardrums in the confined space. Kids sit wide-eyed on parents' shoulders. A gilded, candlelit

Gilded and glittering floats are parked in churches until they are paraded through the streets on holy days.

float rumbles by, edging bystanders against rustic ancient walls. I look up, and high in the sky I see what Good Friday is all about: An extremely Baroque Jesus lurches forward under the weight of that cruel cross, symbolically climbing to his crucifixion. Later, it occurs to me that he floated not on wheels, but on boys. Unseen and unheralded, bent under all that tradition, a team of boys had been trudging for hours through the throngs.

The Running of the Bulls in Pamplona

Like a cowboy at a rodeo, I sit atop my spot on the fence. A loudspeaker says, "Do not touch the wounded. That's the responsibility of health personnel." A line of green-fluores-cent-vested police sweeps down the street, clearing away drunks and anyone not fit to run. Cameras are everywhere—on robotic arms with remote controls vise-gripped to windowsills, hovering overhead on cranes, and in the hands of nearly every spectator that makes up the wall of bodies pressed against the thick timber fence behind me.

I'm at the Festival of San Fermín in Pamplona. Each July, a million revelers come to this proud town in the Pyrenees foothills for music, fireworks, and merrymaking. But most of all, they come for the Running of the Bulls, when fearless (or foolish) adventurers thrust themselves into the path of six furious bulls each day for a week.

The street fills with runners. Nearly everyone is wearing the standard white pants, white shirt, and red bandana. San Fermín, patron of this festival, was beheaded by the Romans 2,000 years ago, martyred for his faith. The red bandanas evoke his bloody end.

The energy surges as 8 a.m. approaches. The street is so full, if everyone suddenly ran, you'd think they'd simply trip over each other and all stack up, waiting to be minced by angry bulls. Then it's eight, and the sound of a rocket

During Pamplona's famed Running of the Bulls, the mark of a good run is to feel the breath of the bull on the back of your legs.

indicates that the bulls are running. The entire half-mile-long scramble takes about two and a half minutes. The adrenaline surges in the crowded street. The sea of people spontaneously begins jumping up and down like hundreds of red-and-white human pogo sticks—trying to see the rampaging bulls to time their flight.

For serious runners, this is like surfing—you hope to catch a good wave and ride it. A good run lasts only 15 or 20 seconds. You know you're really running with a bull when you feel his breath on your pants.

Like a freak wave pummeling a marina, the bulls rush through. It's a red-and-white cauldron of desperation. Big eyes, scrambling bodies, the ground quaking, someone oozing under the bottom rail. Then, suddenly, the bulls are gone, people pick themselves up, and it's over. Boarded-up shops open up. The timber fences are taken down and stacked. The nine-day cycle of the festival, built around the Running of the Bulls, is both smooth and relentless.

Soaking Up San Sebastián Sunshine

Jostling with enthusiastic eaters at the bar, I munch on my last spider crab open-face sandwich. A tiny plate of toothpicks is all that's left of my meal. I keep them because the bartender will count them to tally the bill.

I'm in the beach resort of San Sebastián, just over the French border in Spain. This is the Basque Country, where bright white chalet-style homes with patriotic red-and-green shutters dot lush, rolling hills. The Pyrenees Mountains soar high above the Atlantic. And surfers and sardines share the waves. Insulated from mainstream Europe for centuries, this plucky region has maintained its spirit while split between Spain and France.

Shimmering above the breathtaking bay of La Concha,

The Basque resort of San Sebastián is a hit for its crescent-shaped beach and its gourmet tapas.

elegant and prosperous San Sebastián has a favored location, with golden beaches bookended by twin peaks and a cute little island just offshore. With a romantic setting, a soaring statue of Christ gazing over the city, and a late-night lively old town, San Sebastián has a Rio de Janeiro aura.

The highlight of the old town is its incredibly busy and colorful tapas bars—though here, these appetizers are called *pintxos*. Local competition drives bars to lay out the most appealing array of petite gourmet snacks. The selection is amazing. Just wander the streets (Calle Fermín Calbetón is best) and belly up to the bar in the liveliest spot.

The bartender insists I drink one more glass of *txakolí*—the local sparkling white wine. It's on the house...and nearly from the ceiling, as he theatrically pours from as high as he can reach to aerate the drink. No one but me marvels as the house wine high-dives expertly into my glass.

Toledo's grand cathedral

More Spanish Experiences

Toledo's Magnificent Cathedral: Just 30 minutes by train from Madrid, Spain's former capital crowds 2,500 years of tangled history onto a high, rocky perch protected on three sides by a natural moat, the Tajo River. Toledo's highlight is its Gothic cathedral, which is shoehorned into the old center, with an exterior that rises brilliantly above the town's medieval clutter. The cathedral's spectacular altar—real gold on wood—is one of the country's best pieces of Gothic art. The sacristy is a mini Prado Museum, with masterpieces by the likes of Francisco de Goya, Titian, Peter Paul Rubens, Diego Velázquez, Caravaggio, and

Giovanni Bellini, not to mention 18 El Grecos. The interior is so lofty, rich, and vast that visitors wander around like Pez dispensers stuck open, whispering "Wow."

Granada at Sunset: Granada's magnificent Alhambra was the last stronghold of the Moorish kingdom in Spain. At the end of the day, I head to my favorite viewpoint in the city—the San Nicolás terrace—and enjoy the breathtaking vista over the palace. It comes with great Roma (Gypsy) music nearly all day long. Pop a few euros into the musicians' hat, sit down with a nice picnic, and enjoy an open-air concert as good as any you might pay for. And the view can't be beat, as the setting sun makes the Alhambra glow red.

A Taste of Britain in Spain: I can't resist popping into the British colony of Gibraltar whenever I'm in southern Spain. Gibraltar is hardly signposted in Spain, as if Spain wishes the British colony didn't exist. But when you see that famous "Rock of Prudential" standing boldly above the sea, you know it's here to stay. The place is quirkily and happily British: They have big three-pronged English plugs, their own Gibraltar pound currency, and an Anglican church headquarters. The food is a throwback to the days when English food really was as bad as its reputation. Hotels are twice as expensive as those across the border in Spain (and not as comfortable). The imported macaque monkeys might try to steal your bananas. Nevertheless, tourism is booming. Midday, the pedestrian-friendly main street is a human traffic jam. Twice as many planes are landing in the colony every day. When you walk across the airstrip that marks the border between Spain and what's left of the British Empire, it's more important than ever to look left, right—and up.

LEFT The Alhambra glows at sunset.

RIGHT Gibraltar's famous rock

CULTURE AND TRADITIONS: EVERYTHING'S SO...SPANISH

Bullfighting

The Spanish bullfight is as much a ritual as it is a sport. Originally a form of military training, with refined knights fighting the noble beast from horseback, bullfighting today consists of a series of six bulls facing off against a matador and his team of fighters. Each ritual killing lasts 20 minutes. Then another bull romps into the arena.

While controversial to many for its brutality, aficionados insist that bullfighting is an art form. The Catalunya region banned the practice in 2012, but it remains popular in places such as Sevilla, Madrid, and Ronda, the birthplace of modern bullfighting. Personally, I find the spectacle rather pathetic and cruel, and prefer to get my bullfight "culture" by popping into a bull bar. My favorite is La Torre del Oro, right on Madrid's Plaza Mayor. Its interior is a temple to bullfighting, festooned with gory decor. For many people, a quick sangria or beer in a bar like this is more than enough nasty for their Spanish vacation.

Flamenco

Although flamenco is performed throughout Spain, this music-and-dance art form has its roots in the Roma (Gypsy) and Moorish cultures of Andalucía. And even if flamenco concerts in Sevilla, Granada, and other Andalusian towns are designed for tourists, they are still real and riveting. For a more local-feeling experience, be at a bar (such as La Carbonería in Sevilla) after midnight, when spirited flamenco singing erupts spontaneously.

At any flamenco performance, sparks fly. The men do most of the flamboyant machine-gun footwork. The women often concentrate on the graceful turns and smooth, shuffling step of the *soléa* version of the dance. I always watch the musicians. Flamenco guitarists, with their lightning-fast finger-roll strums, are among the best in the world. The intricate rhythms are set by castanets or the hand-clapping (called *palmas*) of those who aren't dancing at the moment. In the raspy-voiced wails of the singers, you'll hear echoes of the Muslim call to prayer.

Tapas

Tapas bars are everywhere in Spain. Serving small portions of seafood, salad, meat-filled pastries, and deep-fried tasties, they offer a casual, cheap, and very local way of eating.

Chasing down a particular bar nearly defeats the purpose and spirit of tapas—they are impromptu. Just drop in at any lively place. I look for noisy bars with piles of napkins on the floor (go native and toss your trash, too), lots of locals, and the TV blaring.

You'll generally eat standing up in tapas bars. Standing makes sense if you're on a budget because food and drinks are usually cheapest served at the *barra* (counter). To get started with a basic glass of red wine, you can ask for *un tinto*. But by asking for *un crianza*, you'll get a better aged wine for only a little extra money.

When you're ready to order your food, be assertive or you'll never be served. *Por favor* (please) grabs the server's attention. Then quickly rattle off what you'd like (pointing to other people's food if necessary). Don't worry about paying until you're ready to leave (your server is keeping track of your tab).

The Spanish Eating Schedule

Spaniards eat late. Lunch is anywhere between 1 and 4 p.m., and dinner doesn't even cross their minds until at least 9 p.m. To get by in Spain, you'll either have to adapt to the Spanish schedule and cuisine, or scramble to get food in between. You can have an early, light lunch at a tapas bar. Or do as many Spaniards do and have a *bocadillo* (baguette sandwich) at about 11 a.m. to bridge the gap between their coffee-and-roll breakfast and late lunch (hence the popularity of fast-food *bocadillo* chains). Then, either have your main meal at a restaurant around 3 p.m. followed by light tapas for dinner; or reverse it, having a tapas meal in the afternoon, followed by a late restaurant dinner.

Night Owls

Spain comes to life in the cool of the evening, when it's prime time. Whole families pour out of their apartments to stroll through the streets and greet their neighbors—a custom called the paseo. Even the biggest city feels like a rural village. The whole town strolls—it's like "cruising" without cars. Streets are polished nightly by the feet of families licking ice cream; buy an ice-cream sandwich and join the parade. Some people duck into bars for a drink or to watch a big soccer match on TV. They might order a bite to eat, grazing on tapas. Around 10 p.m. in the heat of summer, it's finally time for a light dinner. Afterward, even families with young children might continue their paseo or attend a concert. Spaniards are notorious night owls. Many clubs and restaurants don't even open until after midnight. Dance clubs routinely stay open until the sun rises, and young people stumble out bleary-eyed and head for work. The antidote for late nights? The next day's siesta.

Spain Travel Resources from Rick Steves

Guidebooks

Check out Rick's guidebooks covering all of Spain; Barcelona; Madrid & Toledo; the Basque Country; and Sevilla, Granada & Southern Spain; plus his Spanish phrase book

Audio Europe

Download Rick's free Audio Europe app, with interviews about Spain and self-guided audio tours, including walks through Barcelona and Madrid

TV Shows

The quintessence of Spain with Rick as your host, viewable on public television and at RickSteves.com. Episodes cover Madrid, Barcelona and Catalunya, northern Spain and the Camino de Santiago, Andalucía, Sevilla, the Basque Country, Toledo and Salamanca, Granada, Córdoba, and the Costa del Sol

Organized Tours

Small group tours, with itineraries planned by Rick: Best of Spain in 14 Days; My Way Spain in 11 Days; Best of Andalucía in 10 Days; Best of Barcelona & Madrid in 8 Days; Basque Country of Spain & France in 9 Days

For more on all of these resources, visit RickSteves.com. For Spain trip-planning tips, see RickSteves.com/europe/spain.

Portugal

Portugal has an appealing mix of hardscrabble cities, sweet port wine, wistful blue tiles, heartfelt ballads, and weather-beaten faces. Tucked into a corner of the Iberian Peninsula, Portugal seems somewhere just beyond Europe—prices are a bit cheaper, and the pace of life is noticeably slower. The traditional economy is still based on fishing, cork, wine, and textiles.

Portugal isn't showy—even its coastal towns lack glitzy attractions. The beach and the sea are enough, as they have been for centuries. They were the source of Portugal's seafaring wealth long ago, and are the draw for tourists today. The country's long coastline has some tucked-away gems that feel authentic—the beach towns of Salema (on the south coast) and Nazaré (on the west).

Portugal is more diverse than its neighbor Spain, as it's inhabited by many people from its former colonies in Brazil, Africa, and Asia. Especially in Lisbon, Portugal's Old World capital, you are as likely to hear lively African music as wistful Portuguese fado. The town of Fátima attracts devout pilgrims, while the university towns of Coimbra and Èvora have a youthful vibe.

With a rich culture, affordable prices, and a salty setting on the edge of Europe, Portugal understandably remains a popular destination. If your idea of travel includes friendly locals, exotic architecture, windswept castles, and fresh seafood with chilled

The birthplace of port wine, Portugal's Douro Valley is famed for its vineyards.

wine on a beach at sunset, you'll love this rewarding corner of Europe.

FAVORITE SIGHTS AND MEMORABLE EXPERIENCES IN PORTUGAL

Lisbon Gold

When I first came to Lisbon in the 1970s, the colorful Alfama neighborhood—then the shiver-me-timbers home of Lisbon's fisherfolk—was one of the places that charmed me into becoming a travel writer. But 30-some years later, I noticed that much of the area's grittiness has been cleaned up. Old fishermen's families have been replaced by immigrant laborers. Widows no longer wear black after their husbands die. Once-characteristic fish stalls have moved off the streets and into more "hygienic" covered shops.

But the Alfama, which tumbles down from the castle to the river, remains one of the most photogenic neighborhoods in all of Europe. Wandering deep into this cobbled cornucopia of Old World color, I always get lost. Little streets squeeze into tangled stairways and confused alleys. Bent houses comfort each other in their romantic shabbiness, and the air drips with laundry and the smell of fresh clams and raw fish.

Like its salty sailors' quarter, Lisbon is a ramshackle but charming mix of now and then. Its glory days were the 15th and 16th centuries, when Vasco da Gama and other explorers opened new trade routes, making Lisbon the queen of Europe. Later, the riches of colonial Brazil boosted Lisbon even higher. Then, in 1755, an earthquake (estimated at 9.0) leveled two-thirds of the city. Within a month, a new city

LEFT A typical Alfama street and resident

RIGHT Lisbon's vintage trolleys are perfect for a joyride.

was designed, and downtown Lisbon was quickly rebuilt on a progressive grid plan, with broad boulevards and square squares.

Following the quake, Portugal's rattled royalty chose to live out in suburban Belém, in wooden rather than stone buildings. Five miles from downtown, this district is now a stately pincushion of important Golden Age sights such as the Monastery of Jerónimos, with Vasco da Gama's tomb. The area is guarded by the ornate Belém Tower, which has kept an eye on Lisbon's harbor since 1520. It was the last sight sailors saw as they left, and the first thing they'd see when they returned—loaded down with gold, diamonds, and venereal diseases.

The more modern-feeling Baixa is the rebuilt center of Lisbon. This flat shopping area features grid-patterned streets and utilitarian architecture (buildings are uniform, with the same number of floors and similar facades). The Baixa's pedestrian streets, inviting cafés, bustling shops, and elegant old storefronts give the district a certain magnetism. I find myself doing laps up and down the pedestrians-only main boulevard in a people-watching stupor.

On my must-do list in Lisbon is stopping at a bar to have *pastel de bacalhau*, a fried potato-and-cod croquet. Bacalhau (salted cod) is Portugal's national dish. Imported from Norway, it's never fresh, and kids think it's a triangular fish because of the way it's sold. I think that Portugal must have the only national dish that's imported from far away—strange, and yet befitting of a nation known for seafaring explorers.

Another quintessential Lisbon experience is to take a trolley ride. The city's trolleys—many of which are vintage models from the 1920s—shake and shiver through the old parts of town, somehow safely weaving within inches of parked cars, climbing steep hills, and offering breezy views

Fast Facts

Biggest cities: Lisbon (capital, 564,000), Porto (238,000), Coimbra (102,000)

Size: 35,000 square miles (slightly smaller than Indiana), population 10.5 million

Currency: Euro

Key dates: November 1, 1755, a severe earthquake and tsunami nearly destroy Lisbon and coastal communities; April 25, 1974, the Carnation Revolution marks the last gasp of the Salazar dictatorship and the beginning of Portuguese democracy

Biggest festivals: Fátima Pilgrimage (May 13 and October 13), Semana Santa (Easter Holy Week)

Major export: Half the world's cork comes from Portugal

Handy Portuguese phrases: *Olá* (hello; oh-**lah**), *Por favor* (please; poor fah-**vor**), *Obrigado/Obrigada* (thank you—said by male/female; oh-bree-**gah**-doo/dah), *Fala inglês?* (Do you speak English?; **fah**-lah een-**glaysh**)

Tourist info: VisitPortugal.com

of the city (rubberneck out the window and you will die). They're perfect for a Rice-A-Roni-style Lisbon joyride. I enjoy hopping off the trolley for the hilltop viewpoint near São Jorge Castle—a good starting point for touring the Alfama district since you'll stroll down rather than hike up.

To complement all your Lisbon sightseeing, be sure to get out and be with the locals. One summer evening I found myself at a fairground watching Portuguese families at play. I ate dinner surrounded by chattering locals ignoring the ever-present TVs, while great platters of fish, meat, fries, salad, and lots of wine paraded frantically in every direction. A seven-year-old boy stood on a chair and sang hauntingly emotional folk songs. With his own dogged clapping, he dragged applause out of the less-than-interested crowd and then passed his shabby hat. All the while, fried ducks dripped, barbecues spat, dogs squirted the legs of chairs, and somehow local lovers ignored everything but each other's eyes.

Sunny Salema

The Algarve, in southern Portugal, is my favorite stretch of Iberian coastline. I fantasize about being here on a real vacation—nursing a drink in a still-wet bathing suit, hauling in octopus pots, hiking to the beach, and exposing skin that's never seen the sun.

Warm and dry, the Algarve was once known as Europe's last undiscovered tourist frontier. But it's well discovered now, and if you go to the places featured in most tour brochures, you'll find it paved, packed, and pretty stressful. Still, there are a few great beach towns left along the coast, perfect for soaking up rays in the summer.

My favorite hideaway is the little fishing town of Salema. It's at the end of a small road just off the main drag between the big city of Lagos and the rugged southwest tip of Europe, Cape Sagres. Here the tourists and fishermen sport the

Portugal's Top Destinations

Lisbon ▲▲▲   allow 2-3 days
Lively, hilly port and capital, with historic trolleys, grand squares, fado clubs, fine art, and distinctive neighborhoods

Top Sights
  Bairro Alto and Alfama Golden Age and medieval districts
  Belém Waterfront district with Monastery of Jerónimos
  Gulbenkian Museum Fine art from Ancient Egypt to Art Nouveau

Nearby
  Sintra Fairy-tale castles set in verdant hills

Algarve ▲▲▲   2-3 days
Sunny southern coast, with fishing village **Salema,** end-of-the-road **Cape Sagres,** and beach-party town **Lagos**

Nazaré ▲▲   1-3 days
Traditional fishing village turned surfing capital, and a springboard for nearby sights: **Batalha** (grand monastery), **Fátima** (famous pilgrimage site), **Alcobaça** (huge Gothic church), and **Óbidos** (walled hill town)

Porto and the Douro Valley ▲▲   1-2 days
Gritty hillside port city with charming old town, near the scenic Douro Valley, birthplace of port wine

Évora ▲▲   1 day
Whitewashed little college town with big Roman, Moorish, and Portuguese history encircled by its medieval wall

Coimbra ▲▲   1 day
Portugal's Oxford, home to an Arab-influenced old town and bustling with students from its prestigious university

---

same stubble. It's just you, a beach full of garishly painted boats, your wrinkled landlady, and a few other globetrotting experts in lethargy.

When I first came here, in the late 1970s, the road into town wasn't paved. I turned up in the early evening, driving a group of eight tour members in a minivan and with no reservations. I parked at one end of the town, flagged down some locals, and asked for rooms: *"Quartos?"* Eyes perked, heads nodded, and I got nine beds in three homes for 20 bucks each.

While the main street looks pretty much the same today, the character of the town is changing. Nowadays, beach towns like Salema are becoming the playgrounds of an international crowd of retirees and vacationers, who stay in newly built gated communities and golf clubs on the inland

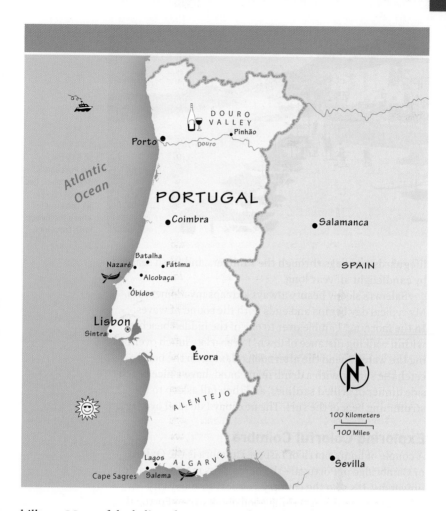

hilltops. Many of the ladies who once rented out rooms have disappeared, chastened by stricter government regulations (necessary, as southern Europe learns to pay its taxes). There are fewer shoestring-budget backpackers to keep them in business anyway.

Salema is still a fishing village—but just barely. It has a split personality: The whitewashed old town is for locals, and the other half was built for tourists—both groups pursue a policy of peaceful coexistence on the beach. Tourists laze in the sun, while locals grab the shade.

In Portugal, restaurateurs are allowed to build a temporary, summer-only beachside eatery if they provide a lifeguard for swimmers and run a green/yellow/red warning-flag system. The Atlântico restaurant, which dominates Salema's beach, takes its responsibility seriously—providing

In Salema, on Portugal's south coast, two worlds merge as fishermen share the beach with travelers.

lifeguards and flags through the summer...and fresh seafood by candlelight all year long.

Salema's sleepy beauty always kidnaps my momentum. My typical day begins and ends with the sound of waves. In the morning, I amble over to one of the hidden beaches within walking distance of town. I grab a late lunch overlooking the water, spend the afternoon relaxing on the beach, catch the sunset with a drink in my hand, have a nice beach-side dinner of grilled sardines, and then fall asleep to the strumming beat of the surf. The next day I do it all over again.

Exploring Colorful Coimbra

A couple of hours north of Lisbon, Coimbra is the Oxford or Cambridge of Portugal—the home of its most venerable university. It's also the country's easiest-to-enjoy city—a mini-Lisbon, with everything good about urban Portugal without the intensity of a big metropolis. I couldn't design a more delightful city for a visit.

Any stroll through Coimbra comes with lots of color. I love wandering the inviting, Arab-flavored old town—a maze of narrow streets, timeworn shops, and tiny *tascas* (budget eateries). A pedestrian street divides the old town into the lower part (Baixa) and the upper (Alta). Historically, only the rich could afford to live within the protective city walls of the Alta. Even today, the Baixa remains a poorer section, with haggard women rolling wheeled shopping carts, children running barefoot,

At Coimbra's colorful market, the character of the vibrant town shines through.

and men lounging on squares as if wasting time is their life's calling.

A favorite old-town stop of mine is the Mercado Municipal. Though nearly every city in Europe has a vibrant farmers market, in many cases, the character has been lost thanks to the EU asserting itself and raising hygiene standards. But in Coimbra, the color and twinkle survive. I appreciate that I can still feel the wrinkled and fragrant pulse of the town and see the "salt of the earth" in the faces of the women selling produce while their men are off in the fields—or in their beloved "little chapels" (a.k.a. bars).

Coimbra's university is the city's leading attraction, highlighted by one of Europe's best surviving Baroque libraries, which displays 55,000 books in 18th-century splendor. The zealous doorkeeper locks the door at every opportunity to keep out humidity, so you need to buzz to get into this 300-year-old temple of books.

The interior is all wood. Even the "marble" on the arches is painted wood, since real marble would add to the humidity. The resident bats—who live in the building, but not the library itself—are well cared for and appreciated. They eat insects, providing a chemical-free way of protecting the books, and alert the guard to changing weather with their "eee-eee" cry.

Whenever I'm visiting a university, I try to eat at its on-campus cafeteria if open to tourists. Generally, that's where I find the cheapest meals and the most interesting crowd of fellow diners in town (and usually the locals most likely to speak English well). During busy times here in

Coimbra gives travelers a taste of urban Portugal without the big-city intensity.

Coimbra, all seats are taken, and you're very likely to find yourself munching with law students and their professors.

At the end of the day, it's worth seeking out fado. Though this folk music is generally performed by Portuguese women, in Coimbra, men sing the fado. Rather than the songs about love, loss, and hopelessness that are common in Lisbon's fado, songs here tend to be literary translations or follow themes students can relate to. Singers are accompanied by the Coimbra-style Portuguese guitar. A modern statue of a guitar, which morphs into the slinky and nubile body of an inviting woman, graces an old town lane. It's a reminder of the local belief that a good musician plays his guitar with art and passion, as if loving a woman.

You can watch fado at various clubs, though my favorite performances are by the roving bands of students, dressed in their signature black capes and serenading around town for tips—and the hearts of their admirers. For me, listening to this unique, mournful music, performed in its unique Coimbra style, feels like just the right way to end a day in this distinctive city.

More Portuguese Experiences

Our Lady of Fátima: In 1917, three kids encountered the Virgin Mary near the central Portugal village of Fátima and were asked to return on the 13th of each month for six months. The final apparition was witnessed by thousands of locals. Ever since, Fátima has been on the pilgrimage trail—mobbed on the 13th of each month through the spring and summer.

Wandering around today's modern town, I'm impressed by how it mirrors my image of a medieval pilgrim gathering place: oodles of picnic benches, endless parking, and desolate toilets for the masses. On my last visit, the vast esplanade leading to the site of the mystical appearance was quiet, as only a few solitary pilgrims slowly shuffled on their knees down the long, smooth approach. In the basilica, a forest of candles dripped into a fiery trench that funneled all the melted wax into a bin—to be resurrected as new candles. Just beyond the basilica, 30 stalls lining a horseshoe-shaped mall awaited the 13th. Even without any business, old ladies still manned their booths, surrounded by pilgrim trinkets—including gaudy wax body parts and rosaries that would be blessed after Mass and taken home to remember Our Lady of Fátima.

Nazaré Dreaming: I got hooked on the Atlantic village of Nazaré back when colorful fishing boats littered its beach. Now the boats moor comfortably in a modern harbor outside town, and the beach is packed with sunbathers and surfers. But I still like the place. This fishing town turned resort is both black-shawl traditional and beach-friendly. The back streets are good for a wander and a fine look at Portuguese family-in-the-street life. Older ladies wear skirts made bulky by traditional petticoats, and men stow cigarettes and fish hooks in their stocking caps. Laundry flaps in the wind, kids play soccer, and fish sizzle over tiny curbside hibachis. Squadrons of salted fish are crucified on nets pulled tightly around wooden frames and left to dry under the midday sun. Locals claim they are delightfully tasty—but I'll take their word for it. Off-season Nazaré is almost empty of tourists— inexpensive, colorful, and relaxed, with enough salty fishing- village atmosphere to make you pucker.

The Alentejo Plain: Deep in the heart of Portugal, sur- rounded by cork trees and the vast, bleak beauty of the Alen- tejo region, I drive toward the walled city of Évora. It sits on lots of history. Outside of town stand 92 stones—2,000 years older than Stonehenge—erected by long-ago locals to make a celestial calendar. Évora's old center is crowned by the gran- ite Corinthian columns of a stately, ruined Roman temple. Tourists wander wide-eyed through the town's macabre 16th-century chapel, decorated with human bones meant to remind worshippers of their mortality.

The people of the Alentejo are uniformly short, look at tourists suspiciously, and are the butt of jokes in this corner of Europe. Libanio, my Évora guide, said it was the mark of a people's character to laugh at themselves. He asked me, "How can you tell a worker is done for the day in Alentejo?" I didn't know. He said, "When he takes his hands out of his pockets." My guide continued more philosophically: "In your land, time

Portugal's top experiences include witness- ing pilgrims at Fátima *(left)*, savoring the beach at Nazaré *(center)*, and hanging out with locals in Évora *(right)*.

is money. Here in Alentejo, time is time. We take things slow and enjoy ourselves." I'm impressed when a region that others are inclined to insult has a strong local pride.

CULTURE AND TRADITIONS: EVERYTHING'S SO...PORTUGUESE

Fado

The songs of fado, the folk music of Portugal, reflect the country's bittersweet relationship with the sea. Fado, which means "fate," originated in the mid-1800s in Lisbon's rustic neighborhoods. These mournfully beautiful and haunting ballads are usually about lost sailors, broken hearts, romance gone wrong, and the yearning for what might have been if fate had not intervened. Fado, like a musical oyster, is sexy and full of the sea.

The singer (*fadista*) is accompanied by a 12-string *guitarra portuguesa* (with a round body like a mandolin) or other stringed instruments unique to Portugal. Fado singers typically crescendo into the first word of the verse, like a moan emerging from deep inside. The singers rarely overact—they plant themselves firmly and sing stoically in the face of fate.

One of my favorite fado bars is A Baiuca, in Lisbon's Alfama district. Here mustachioed mandolin pluckers hunch over their instruments, lost in their music, while the kitchen staff peers from a steaming hole in the wall, backlit by their flaming grill. There's not a complete set of teeth in the house. The waiter delivers plates of fish and pitchers of cheap cask wine to tables. Then, doubling as a Portuguese

At Portugal's fado bars, patrons sip wine while tuning in to the mournful melodies.

Ed Sullivan, he stops to introduce the star, who wears blood-red lipstick, big hair, and a black mourning shawl over her black dress—with a revealing neckline that promises that there is life after death.

Convent Sweets and Monks' Treats

Many of Portugal's pastries are called "convent sweets." During its days as a trading powerhouse, Portugal had access to more sugar than any other European country. Even so, sugar was so expensive that only the upper classes could afford it routinely. Historically, the daughters of aristocrats who didn't marry into suitably noble families ended up in high-class convents, bringing precious sugar with them. Over time, the convents became famous as keepers of wondrous secret recipes for exquisite pastries, generally made from sugar and egg yolks (the whites were used to starch the nuns' habits). *Barriga de freira* ("nuns' belly") and *papo de anjo* ("angel's double chin") are two such traditional fancies that you'll see in sweets shops.

While nuns baked sweets, the monks took care of quenching thirsts with *ginjinha,* a sweet liquor made from the sour cherry-like ginja berry, sugar, and brandy. Try it with or without berries (*com elas* or *sem elas*) and *gelada* (if you want it poured from a chilled bottle). The oldest *ginjinha* joint in Lisbon is a colorful hole-in-the-wall in the Baixa district, which sells shots for about a buck. In Portugal, when people are impressed by the taste of something, they say, "*Sabe que nem ginjas*" (It tastes like ginja).

Beware of Appetizers

In Portugal's restaurants, there's no such thing as a free munch. If the server puts appetizers on your table before you order, they'll appear on your bill. If you don't want them, push them to the side—you won't be charged if you don't touch the food (which ranges from olives, bread, and pâtés to a veritable mini-buffet of tasty temptations). Simple appetizers usually cost about €1 each, so even if you eat a couple of olives, it won't break the budget.

In Portugal you can discover a new favorite pastry *(left),* or make a pilgrimage to Porto's harbor—where port wine ages *(right).*

Barnacles!

Gooseneck barnacles (*percebes*) are a salty delicacy. These little taste treats are expensive because they're so dangerous to harvest—they grow on rocky promontories in narrow inlets where the waves and currents are fierce. (Connoisseurs know that they are fresh only from April through September—otherwise they're frozen.) Merchants in coastal towns sell the crustaceans on the street as munchies. They'll happily demonstrate how to eat them and give you a sample, figuring if you try just one briny morsel, you'll buy a kilo. Local bars serve *percebes* with beer, like corn nuts.

Port Party

Much of the world's port wine comes of age in Porto, in northern Portugal. The grapes are grown about 60 miles upstream in the Douro River Valley. A young port is produced, which sits for a winter in silos before being shipped downstream to Porto's Vila Nova de Gaia district. There it ages for years in wooden barrels stored in "lodges" on the cool, north-facing bank of the Douro. For wine connoisseurs, touring a port-wine lodge (*cave do vinho do porto*) and sampling the product is a must-see attraction.

For most people, "port" means a tawny port, which is aged for 10 to 40 years. But there are multiple varieties of port. Wood ports are aged in wooden vats or barrels, and vintage ports are aged in bottles. *Reserva* on the label means it's the best-quality port (and the most expensive). As for me, I'm not choosy. As I always say, "Any port in a storm..."

Portugal Travel Resources from Rick Steves

Guidebooks
Check out Rick's guidebooks covering all of Portugal; Lisbon; plus his Portuguese phrase book

Audio Europe
Download Rick's free Audio Europe app, with interviews about Portugal and self-guided audio tours, including a walk through Lisbon

TV Shows
The quintessence of Portugal with Rick as your host, viewable on public television and at RickSteves.com. Episodes cover Lisbon, the Algarve, and Portugal's heartland (Nazaré, Fátima, and Coimbra)

Organized Tours
Small group tours, with itineraries planned by Rick: Heart of Portugal in 12 Days

For more on all of these resources, visit RickSteves.com. For Portugal trip-planning tips, see RickSteves.com/europe/portugal.

Great Britain

From the grandeur and bustle of London, to a rich and royal history that inspired Shakespeare, to some of the quaintest towns you'll ever experience, Great Britain is a delight. Stand in a desolate field and ponder a prehistoric stone circle. Do the Beatles blitz in Liverpool, and walk in the Lake District footsteps of Wordsworth. Discover your favorite pub and have a pint of beer with the neighborhood gang. Tackle some Welsh words, relax in a bath in Bath, and shake paws with a Highland sheepdog. There's something unparalleled yet familiar about traveling in Great Britain.

Three very different countries—England, Wales, and Scotland—make up Great Britain (add in Northern Ireland, and you've got the United Kingdom). England is the center in every way: the seat of government, the economic powerhouse, the bastion of higher learning, and the cultural heart. Anchored by thriving London, England has everything from castles to cathedrals and sheep-speckled hillsides to dark-wooded pubs.

Humble, charming little Wales is a land of stout castles, salty harbors, slate-roofed villages, stunning mountains, and lusty men's choirs. Traditional and beautiful, Wales sometimes feels trapped in another century. But soon you'll awaken to the distinctive, poetic vitality of this small country.

And then there's rugged, feisty, colorful Scotland—the yin to England's yang. Whether it's the laid-back, less-organized nature of the people, the stony architecture, the unmanicured landscape, or simply the haggis, go-its-own-way Scotland stands apart. Its sights are subtle, but the misty glens, brooding castles, hardy bagpipers, and warm culture are engaging.

I love traveling in Great Britain. It hosts the heritage of the greatest empire the world has ever lived under, yet bears the humiliation of a struggling economy, with remnants of its former empire owning much of its capital city. Its pomp, which seems to serve as a quaint reminder of former grandness, feels almost designed for tourists. Still, a visit here connects you with people, nature, heritage, and culture, all of which combine to make Great Britain such a rewarding destination.

FAVORITE SIGHTS AND MEMORABLE EXPERIENCES IN GREAT BRITAIN

Edinburgh's Royal Mile

There's no better introduction to Edinburgh—the historical, cultural, and political capital of Scotland—than a walk straight down the spine of the old town. Stretching from a hill-topping castle to a queen's palace, this ramble is appropriately called the Royal Mile. Despite being crammed with tourists, it's one of Europe's best sightseeing walks.

I begin my stroll on the bluff where Edinburgh was born and where a castle now stands. Over the centuries, this mighty fortress was home to many of Scotland's kings and queens. Today it's well worth touring to see the old buildings, stunning views, and crown jewels.

As Edinburgh grew, it spilled downhill along the tight, sloping ridge that became the Royal Mile. Back in the vibrant 1600s, this was the city's main street, bustling with breweries, printing presses, and banks. With tens of thousands of

Edinburgh's Royal Mile entertains from top to bottom, from connoisseur's whisky at Cadenhead's shop to St. Giles Cathedral, where John Knox preached the Reformation.

citizens squeezed into the narrow confines of the old town, there was nowhere to go but up. So builders lined the street with multistory residences (called tenements)—some 10 stories and higher.

Truth be told, these days much of the Royal Mile is a touristic mall—all tartans, sightseers, and shortbread. But it remains packed with history, and intrepid visitors can still find a few surviving rough edges of Auld Reekie, as the old town was once called (for the smell of smoke and sewage that wafted across the city). Exploring back alleys and side lanes, it's easy to imagine Edinburgh in the 17th and 18th centuries, when out-of-towners came here to marvel at its "skyscrapers," and thousands of people scurried through these alleyways, buying and selling goods and popping into taverns.

Scotland is a proud nation, and everywhere I turn, the Royal Mile is littered with symbols of that pride— from a statue of philosopher David Hume, one of the towering figures of the Scottish Enlightenment of the mid-1700s, to its very own Church of Scotland, embodied by St. Giles Cathedral. Filled with monuments, statues, plaques, and stained-glass windows dedicated to great Scots and moments in history, St. Giles serves as a kind of Scottish Westminster Abbey.

St. Giles is also the home church of the great reformer John Knox, whose fiery sermons helped turn once-Catholic Edinburgh into a bastion of Protestantism. Knox's influence was huge. His insistence that every person should be able to read the word of God firsthand helped give Scotland an educational system 300 years ahead of the rest of Europe. Just down the road from St. Giles is the John Knox House, featuring atmospheric rooms and period furniture.

But I'm eager to get to one of my favorite stops along the Mile: Cadenhead's Whisky Shop. Founded in 1842,

Fast Facts

Biggest cities: London (capital, 7.8 million), Birmingham (1 million), Glasgow (600,000), Liverpool (450,000)

Size: 95,000 square miles (about the size of Michigan), population 61.5 million

Currency: British pound

Key date: 1533, King Henry VIII breaks with the Catholic Church and establishes himself as the head of the Church of England, setting the English Reformation in motion

Biggest festivals: Chelsea Flower Show (May, London), Edinburgh International Festival (August, music, dance, and theater)

Language: Predominantly English, but also Scottish Gaelic and Welsh Cymraeg

Handy British phrases: *I'm bloody knackered* (I'm so exhausted), *Don't get your knickers in a twist* (Don't get all upset), *Bob's your uncle* (obviously), *Sod off* (Screw off), *That's a load of bollocks* (That's a bunch of nonsense)

Tourist info: VisitBritain.com

Great Britain's Top Destinations

ENGLAND

London ▲▲▲   allow 3-5 days

Thriving metropolis packed with world-class museums, monuments, churches, parks, palaces, theaters, pubs, Beefeaters,
double-decker buses, and all things British

Top Sights

Westminster Abbey Britain's most important church
British Museum World's greatest chronicle of Western civilization
National Gallery European paintings from Leonardo, Botticelli, Van Gogh, and more
British Library Top literary treasures of the Western world
Tower of London Castle, palace, and prison housing the crown jewels
St. Paul's Cathedral Christopher Wren's domed masterpiece

Nearby

Greenwich Maritime center with famous observatory
Windsor Queen's primary residence
Cambridge England's classic university town

Bath ▲▲▲   2 days

Genteel Georgian city, built around the remains of an ancient Roman bath

Nearby

Glastonbury New Age mysticism, abbey ruins, and a holy hill
Stonehenge and Avebury Prehistoric stone circles
Wells and Salisbury Serene Gothic cathedrals

Cotswolds ▲▲   1-2 days

Quaint villages—cozy market town **Chipping Campden,** popular hamlet **Stow-
on-the-Wold,** and handy transit hub **Moreton-in-Marsh**—scattered over a hilly
countryside and near one of England's top palaces, Blenheim

Lake District ▲▲   1-2 days

Idyllic lakes-and-hills landscape, with enjoyable hikes and joyrides, time-passed
valleys, William Wordsworth and Beatrix Potter sights, and the charming home-
base town of **Keswick**

Durham and Hadrian's Wall ▲   1-2 days

Youthful working-class university town with magnificent cathedral, within an easy
drive of the Roman ruins of Hadrian's Wall

York ▲▲▲   1-2 days

Walled medieval town with grand Gothic cathedral, excellent museums (Viking,
Victorian, railway), and atmospheric old center

WALES

North Wales ▲▲   1-2 days

Scenically rugged land filled with evocative castles, the natural beauty of Snowdonia National Park, and the tourable slate mines at **Blaenau Ffestiniog,** all
accessible from the cute castle town of **Conwy**

SCOTLAND

Edinburgh ▲▲▲   2 days
Proud Scottish capital, with an imposing castle on a bluff, attraction-studded
Royal Mile, and Georgian New Town with trendy shops and eateries

Nearby
St. Andrews Famous golf town and Scotland's top university

Highlands ▲▲   1-2 days
Traditionally Scottish mountainous region, with the handy hub of **Inverness**
(near Loch Ness and Culloden Battlefield) in the north, and the home-base town
of **Oban** in the south, with boat trips to the historic isles of **Mull** and **Iona**

With more time, consider visiting
Liverpool Gentrified English port city and the Beatles' hometown
Stratford-upon-Avon Shakespeare's home and fine theater
Glasgow Workaday but revitalized city with fun nighttime scene

Cadenhead's prides itself on bottling good whisky without watering it down or adding cosmetic coloring. Popping in, I'm shown a shelf of aged wooden casks. The shop owner explains that distillers prefer to drink their whisky rough, from casks like these: "It's like getting your milk straight from the farmer." But this is not a tourist sight—so I pay for my whisky. He draws a dram for me, and I taste it. Whoa! Then he pours a little spring water on it. Squinting into the glass, he coaches me along: "Look at the impurities gathering in a happy little pool there on top. The water is like a spring rain on a garden—it brings out the character, the personality." Sipping this whisky with an expert, I see how Scotland's national drink can become, as they're fond of saying, "a very good friend."

Fortified, I walk on to the Royal Mile's next attraction: the modern Scottish parliament building. After three centuries of being ruled from London, the Scots regained a parliament of their own in 1999, and a few years later built this striking, eco-friendly home for it. In the distance is the craggy summit called Arthur's Seat, and this soaring building, mixing wild angles and bold lines, seems to be surging right out of the rock.

My very last stop is the Palace of Holyroodhouse, one of Queen Elizabeth's official residences and a long-time home to Scottish royalty, including James IV and Mary, Queen of Scots. The Scottish monarchs also kept a home at the top end of the Mile, but they preferred the cushier Holyroodhouse to the blustery castle up on the rock.

I've soaked up plenty of Scottish history on my walk from castle to palace. But no Royal Mile walk is complete without popping into a pub—and there's no shortage of them—where a bit of live music and whisky await.

History Comes Alive at Westminster Abbey

Eddie the Verger is posted in his red robe with a warm smile at the exit of London's Westminster Abbey. His responsibility: to sort through those visitors who want to enter the abbey to worship, and those who are masquerading as worshippers in order to sidestep the high entrance fee.

Westminster Abbey is the most famous English church in Christendom, where royalty has been wedded, crowned, and buried since the 11th century. A thousand years of English history—3,000 tombs, the remains of 29 kings and queens, and hundreds of memorials to poets, politicians, scientists, and warriors—lie within its stained-glass splendor, making it a must-see on any London trip. Dropping by, I tell Eddie I'm working on the Rick Steves book, and he says, "I'd like a word with that Rick Steves. He implies in his guidebook that you can pop in to worship in order to get a free visit."

I tell him who I am, and we sort it out. Really charmed by Eddie, I agree that I'll encourage visitors to attend the free worship service for the experience of it, not to dodge the admission fee. (I highly recommend a sung evensong, which takes place six days a week.)

Eddie deposits me in the abbey, and I visit like any other tourist—enjoying the great audio tour narrated by Jeremy Irons. Listening to the actor's soothing voice, I have some private time with great history: the marble effigy of Queen Elizabeth I, modeled after her death mask in 1603—considered the most realistic likeness of her; the coronation chair that centuries of kings and queens sat upon right here on their big day; the literary greats of England gathered as if conducting a posthumous storytelling session around the tomb of Geoffrey Chaucer (Mr. *Canterbury Tales*); the poppies lining the Grave of the Unknown Warrior, an ordinary soldier who lost his life in World War I; the statue of Martin Luther King Jr., added above the west entrance in 1998 as an honorary member of this now heavenly English host; and so much more.

Then Eddie takes me into a place that no tourist goes—the Jerusalem Chamber, where long-ago monks set up shop to translate the Bible from ancient Greek into English, creating the King James Version (finished in 1611). These reformers faced real danger in getting the word of God into the people's language, and knowing the importance of their heroic steps back then, I got shivers and chills (much as I

London on the Cheap

London is one of Europe's most expensive cities. Here are some tips for stretching your pennies and pounds:

- Gorge on London's many free museums: the British Museum, British Library, National Gallery, National Portrait Gallery, Tate Britain, Tate Modern, and Victoria and Albert Museum.
- Go to a free evensong service at (the otherwise expensive) Westminster Abbey or St. Paul's.
- Look for free performances such as lunch concerts at St. Martin-in-the-Fields Church, the Changing of the Guard at Buckingham Palace, rants at Speakers' Corner in Hyde Park, and the legislature at work in the Houses of Parliament.
- Join an inexpensive London Walks tour. Or, cheaper yet, take advantage of the free guided London walks in the Rick Steves Audio Europe app.
- Get discounted same-day tickets at theater box offices or from the official TKTS booth at Leicester Square.
- Consider hosteling (www.yha.org.uk) or staying in dorms (June to mid-September; the University of Westminster is one option with doubles, www.westminster.ac.uk/summeraccommodation).

With Eddie the Verger *(left)* at Westminster Abbey *(right)*

did at Germany's Wartburg Castle, where I saw the room in which Martin Luther did essentially the same thing for the German-speaking world).

I thank Eddie on my way out; we part as friends. He's glad that tourists will be less likely to try to sneak into the abbey for free. And for me, it's been worth the visit to look back in time, remembering the writers, reformers, royalty, and soldiers who put the "great" in Great Britain.

The Quaint and Quirky Cotswolds

For three decades, I've said it's a temptation for a travel writer to overuse the word "quaint." I reserve my use of it for describing England's Cotswold villages, in the gentle, hilly region northwest of London. By quaint, I don't mean just thatched cottages and charming teahouses. There's a quirkiness here—a sort of impoverished nobility and provincial naiveté that has something to do with being time-passed. Whatever it is, it charms me to no end.

I like the north Cotswolds best. Two of the region's coziest towns are Chipping Campden, featuring what the great British historian G. M. Trevelyan and I call the finest High Street in England; and Stow-on-the-Wold, with good pubs, antique stores, and cute shops draped seductively around a big town square. Both are close to Moreton-in-Marsh, which has good public transportation connections and lacks the touristic sugar of the other towns. Any of these villages makes a fine home base for your exploration of the thatch-happiest of Cotswold towns and countryside.

Between Stow and Chipping Campden, the tiny hamlets of Snowshill, Stanton, and Stanway get my nomination for the cutest Cotswold destinations. Sweet as marshmallows in hot chocolate, they nestle side by side, each spiced with eccentric characters and odd bits of history.

Snowshill, a little bundle of delight, has a photogenic triangular square. On one corner stands Snowshill Manor. This dark, mysterious old palace is filled with the lifetime collection of the long-gone Charles Paget Wade. It is one big, musty celebration of craftsmanship, from finely carved spinning wheels to frightening samurai armor to tiny elaborate figurines carved by long-forgotten prisoners from the bones of meat served at dinner. It's clear that Wade dedicated his life and fortune to fulfilling his family motto: "Let Nothing Perish."

The sister villages of Stanton and Stanway are separated by a great oak forest and grazing land, with parallel waves in the fields echoing the furrows plowed by medieval farmers. It's my selfish tradition here to let someone else drive so I can hang out the window, enjoying a windy flurry of stone walls and sheep, all under a canopy of ancient oaks.

In Stanton, flowers trumpet, door knockers shine, and slate shingles clap. It's as if a rooting section is cheering me up the town's main street. The church, however, betrays a pagan past. Stanton is at the intersection of two ley lines (which some new-age types consider a source of special power) connecting prehistoric sights. Many churches such as Stanton's were built on pagan holy ground and are generally dedicated to St. Michael—the Christian antidote to pagan mischief. Michael's well-worn figure, looking down at me from above the door, seems to say, "It's all clear now—good Christians may enter." Sitting in the back pew, fingering grooves worn into the wooden posts by sheepdog leashes (at a time when a man's sheepdog accompanied him everywhere), I'm reminded that it was wool money that built this church.

Stanway, while not much of a village, is notable for its venerable manor house. The Earl of Wemyss (pronounced "Weemz"), whose family tree charts relatives back to 1202, occasionally opens his melancholy home to visitors. Musty

England's Cotswold villages are made to order for the word "quaint."

and threadbare, it feels like a trip back in time. You'll often find his lordship roaming about. The manor dogs have their own cutely painted "family tree," but the earl admits that his last dog, C.J., was "all character and no breeding." Once, while I was marveling at the 1780 Chippendale exercise chair in the great hall, the earl surprised me. Jumping up onto the tall leather-encased spring, and with the help of the high armrests, he began bouncing. A bit out of breath, he explained, "In grandmama's time, half an hour of bouncing on this was considered good for the liver."

The earl's house has a story to tell. And so do the docents—modern-day peasants who, even without family trees, probably have relatives in this village going back just as far as their earl's. If you probe cleverly, talking to these people gives a rare insight into this quirky, authentic slice of England.

A Day in Regal Bath

Shaking off my umbrella, I walked up to my B&B and climbed the stairs to my room, exhausted after a long day exploring Bath. When I blew my nose, I noticed a spray of red dirt on the Kleenex—and I remembered the snuff.

At the Star Inn, the most characteristic pub in town, the manager Paul keeps a tin of complimentary snuff tobacco on a ledge for customers. Earlier that evening I tried some, questioning Paul about it while a drunk guy from Wales tried to squeeze by me holding two big pints of local brew over my head. Paul said that English coal miners have long used it because cigarettes were too dangerous in the mines, and they needed their tobacco fix. He wanted me to take the tin. I put it back on the ledge and said I'd try it again the next time I stopped by.

From the hospitality of its people to its architectural beauty and aristocratic charm, Bath is one of those places that seems made for tour-ists. Just 90 minutes west of London by train, the city is known for its grand abbey (the last great medieval church erected in England), stately Georgian-era buildings, and restorative thermal baths (said to have cured Queen Mary of infertility and Queen Anne of gout). Despite its

In Bath, you'll enjoy a lazy picnic surrounded by Georgian elegance.

flood of sightseers, I still find Bath to be one of the most enjoyable cities in Britain.

I started my day joining a gang of curious visitors in front of the abbey, where volunteer guides divide up the tourists for a free walk around town. My guide, a retired school-teacher, explained that the volunteer-touring tradition started in 1930, when the mayor—proud of the charms of his historic town—took the first group gathered here on a walk. The mayor's honorary guide corps has been leading free walks daily ever since.

For 2,000 years, Bath's mineral spa has been attracting those in need of a cure.

The musical highlight of my day was a worship service at Bath Abbey. The service was crisp, eloquent, and traditional. I was struck by the strong affirmation of the worshippers' Catholic heritage, the calls for sobriety, and the stress on repentance (including repeated references to how we are such wretched sinners).

The Anglican worship ritual is carefully shuttled from one generation to the next. That continuity seemed to be underlined by the countless tombs and memorials lining walls and floors—worn smooth and shiny by the feet of worshippers over the centuries. With the living and the dead all present together, the congregation seemed to raise their heads in praise as sunlight streamed through windows. This bright church is nicknamed the "Lantern of the West" for its open, airy lightness and huge windows.

The church was packed with townsfolk—proper and still. As I sat among them at offering time, the pastor caught me off-guard with his gentility. He said, "If you're a visitor, please don't be embarrassed to let the plate pass. It's a way for our regular members to support our work."

Later that night, heading home from the Star Inn, I was surrounded by young kids partying. English girls out clubbing wiggled down the street like the fanciest of fish lures—each shaking their tassels and shimmying in a way sure to catch a big one.

The rock star Meatloaf was playing a big concert in the park, and during his performance, much of Bath rocked with him. Although the concert was sold out, I gathered with a hundred freeloaders, craning our necks from across the river for a great view of the stage action.

Bath's an expensive town in an expensive country. The young couple hired to manage the elegant Georgian guest-house I was staying in told me they took the gig just to live in Bath. As they put it, "Workaday English can't really afford to live here." They have an apartment in the basement, but they go through the grand front door just to marvel at the elegant building they live in. I don't blame them. The grandeur of Bath—wonderfully accessible to a tourist—is simply unmatched.

Highlands Magic

Years ago, I met a dear man on a deserted roadside in the Scottish Highlands. I was scrambling to make a TV show about the area, and as if placed there by heaven's Central Casting, this tender giant of a man was bagpiping to the birds, the passing clouds, and the occasional motorist. He had picked a spot that seemed intentionally miles from nowhere. We stopped, and he graciously demonstrated his pipes, giving us a tour of that fascinating symbol of Scottish culture. I've never forgotten that wonderful chance meeting.

The Scottish Highlands are filled with magic and mystery. In the northernmost reaches of Scotland, the Highlands feature a wild, severely undulating terrain that's punctuated by lochs (lakes) and fringed by sea lochs (inlets) and islands. Whenever I want a taste of traditional Scotland, this is where I come.

About two hours north of Edinburgh, the tiny village of Kenmore—little more than the fancy domain of its castle, a church set in a bouquet of tombstones, and a line of humble houses—offers a fine dose of small-town Scottish flavor. One day a year, it hosts its Highland Games festival—and one year I was lucky enough to be there, mixing it up with the locals. The open field was filled with families having a fun day out

watching tug-of-wars, little kids' sprints, gunnysack races, bands of marching pipers, and Highland dancing. While the girls impatiently and anxiously awaited their time with the bagpiper on stage, the big boys took turns tossing big things: Stones, hammers, and the caber (a log the size of a small telephone pole) were sent end-over-end to the delight of those gathered.

Loch Tay, near Kenmore, is a fascinating place. All across Scotland, archaeologists know that little round islands on the lochs are evidence of crannogs—circular lakefront houses built by big shots about 2,500 years ago. In the age before roads, people traveled by boat, so building houses on waterways made sense. There are 18 such crannogs on Loch Tay, and one is now the Crannog Centre, a museum dedicated to demonstrating the skills every crannog homeowner needed, such as making fire by rubbing sticks.

There can be very few Scots whose ancestors were not connected to working the land. And sheepdogs have a long rural lineage, too. The dogs herding sheep today are the direct descendants of a long-ago breed domesticated in the British Isles. In the Highlands, the best way to get a taste of this aspect of farm culture is at a good sheepdog show.

Recently, on a remote Highlands farm, I drove up a long rutted drive with one of my tour groups. As we stepped onto the grass, a dozen eager border collies scampered to greet us. Then came the shepherd, whom the dogs clearly loved and followed like a messiah. He proceeded to sit us down in a natural little amphitheater in the turf and explain all about his work. With shouts and whistles, each dog followed individual commands and showed an impressive mastery over the sheep. Then, with good, old-fashioned shears, we each got our chance to shear a sheep—who took it calmly, as if at a beauty salon.

The Highlands' past is written all over its landscape. Perhaps no other place is as evocative as the memorial battlefield of Culloden, near Inverness. In 1746, Jacobite troops (most of them Highlanders) gave it their all to put the Catholic Bonnie Prince Charlie on the English throne... and failed. While only about 50 English soldiers died, the Highlanders lost about 1,500 men. Bonnie Prince Charlie declared, "Every man for himself!" as he galloped away. The Highlanders were routed.

The victorious English pushed an aggressive campaign of cultural assimilation. After Culloden, they banned the wearing of kilts, the playing of bagpipes, and even the Gaelic language—effectively spelling the end of the clan system.

Near Culloden is another fascinating sight—the Clava Cairns. I always knew about England's famous stone circles, but I hadn't realized that Scotland had fancy-pants, over-achieving knuckle draggers, too. At Clava Cairns, set in a peaceful grove of trees, are the remains of three stone burial mounds, each cleverly constructed 4,000 years ago with a passageway that the sun illuminates, as if by magic, with each winter solstice. Wandering through these thought-provoking cairns, knowing they're as old as the pyramids, is a highlight of a Highlands visit.

When in Britain, Take a Hike

After decades of visits to Britain, I finally took some time to slow down and do some real hiking. One thing I learned: Even if you only have two or three hours, taking a hike is about the best time you can invest in places of outstanding natural beauty. Every day has a few hours to spare. What else is so important between 4 o'clock and dinnertime? Because of these walks, I took home vivid memories.

In the Lake District, I struggled up and over Catbells, a 1,480-foot hill above the lake called Derwentwater. The weather had almost kept me in, but I was glad I ventured out. I welcomed the comedic baaing of sheep, and the wind "blowing the cobwebs out" (as my B&B host warned). On previous visits, when I'd stayed down by the lake, I'd look up to see hikers silhouetted like stick figures on this ridge. Now I was one of those sky-high figures myself. With the weather storming overhead like a dark army, the wind buffeting in

Hiking in England's Lake District, you can find your own majestic perch overlooking a scenic valley *(left)* or stumble upon a surprise view of Derwentwater *(right)*.

my ears, and 360-degree views commanding my attention—I wanted to turn cartwheels.

Anywhere in Britain, blustery weather is just a part of the scene. Most "bad weather" comes with broken spells of brightness, and it doesn't pay to get greedy for more (like outright sunshine). You wish for and are thankful for brightness. As they say here, there's no bad weather, just inappropriate clothing.

And, oh, the joy of a pub after a good hike. Studying the light on ruddy faces while munching hearty pub grub has always been part of the magic of travel in Britain. When your skin is weather-stung and your legs ache happily with accomplishment, the pub ambience takes on an even more inviting glow.

Dartmoor Calling

A fine way to mix Neolithic wonders and nature is to explore one of England's many turnstile-free moors. You can get lost in these stark and sparsely populated time-passed commons, which have changed over the centuries about as much as the longhaired sheep that seem to gnaw on moss in their sleep. Directions are difficult to keep. It's cold and gloomy, as nature rises like a slow tide against human constructions. A crumpled castle loses itself in lush overgrowth. A church grows shorter as tall weeds eat at the stone crosses and tilted tombstones.

Windswept and desolate, Dartmoor National Park in southwest England is one of the few truly wild places you'll find in this densely populated country. With more Bronze Age stone circles and huts than any other chunk of England,

The stone circles at Dartmoor National Park are as old as the pyramids.

Dartmoor is perfect for those who dream of experiencing their own private Stonehenge sans barbed wire, police officers, parking lots, tourists, and port-a-loos.

On one visit, I trekked from the hamlet of Gidleigh through a foggy world of scrub brush and scraggy-haired goats on a mission to find a 4,000-year-old circle of stone. Venturing in the pristine vastness of Dartmoor, I sank into the powerful, mystical moorland—a world of greenery, eerie wind, white rocks, and birds singing but unseen. Climbing over a hill, surrounded by sleeping towers of ragged, moss-fringed granite, I was swallowed up. Hills followed hills followed hills—green growing gray in the murk.

Then the stones appeared, frozen in a forever game of statue maker. For endless centuries they waited patiently, still and silent, as if for me to come. I sat on a fallen stone, observing blackbirds and wild horses. My imagination ran wild, pondering the people who roamed England so long before written history, feeling the echoes of druids worshipping and then reveling right here.

More British Experiences

My Favorite Welsh Town: In North Wales, miles of green fields are dotted with grazing sheep. My preferred home base for exploring this region is the town of Conwy. Built in the 1280s to give the English king Edward I a toehold in Wales, it also served as a busy port, back when much of Europe was roofed with Welsh slate. Today it boasts the best medieval walls in Britain, a protective castle dramatically situated on a rock overlooking the sea, and a charming harbor that locals treat like a town square. Facing the harbor is the Liverpool Arms pub, a salty and characteristic hangout built by a captain who ran a ferry service to Liverpool in the 19th century. On summer evenings, the action is on the quay. It's a small town, and everyone comes out to enjoy the local cuisine—chips, ice cream, and beer—and to savor that great British pastime: tormenting little crabs. If you want to do more than photograph the action, rent gear from the nearby lifeboat house. Mooch some bacon from others for bait, and join in. It's catch-and-release. The scene is mellow, multigenerational, and perfectly Welsh.

Hunting Ghosts in York: Just two hours north of London by express train, York has a rich history—from its Roman origins to its role as a Viking trading center. It's got the largest Gothic church in Britain, and, as locals love to add, "a giant bell." Just as a Boy Scout counts the rings in a tree, you can count the ages of York by the different bricks in the city wall: Roman on the bottom, then Danish, Norman, and the "new" addition—from the 14th century. With all this history, joining a walking tour makes for a wonderful introduction to the city. Charming old Yorkers volunteer their time to give energetic, entertaining, and free two-hour walking tours every day of the year. Or, for a little more gore, you can pay to join one of the many ghost walks advertised all over town. While generally I find ghost walks to be little more than goofy entertainment, if any city can claim to be legitimately haunted, it would be York. At night, the old town center is crawling with creepy, black-clad characters leading wide-eyed groups of tourists around on various ghost walks. On my last trip, I spent an evening sampling several different walks—and woke up screaming at 2 a.m.

Scotland's Second City: Lately, I've been appreciating what I consider to be the "second cities" of Europe. These places— from Marseille to Porto, Antwerp to Belfast, Hamburg to Bilbao—often have a rough, Industrial Age heritage and a rust-belt vibe that keeps them honest, unvarnished, and nonconformist. Take Glasgow: Even though it is Scotland's largest city, it takes second place to Edinburgh (which wins out for its impressive sights and capital status). Nonetheless, Glasgow has a wonderful energy and plenty of sights, including Art Nouveau architecture from Charles Rennie Mackintosh and fine museums. But the highlight is the city's street scene, which percolates in places like the Golden Zed, a Z-shaped pedestrian shopping zone that zigzags through town. Just strolling up its lanes—listening to buskers, enjoying the people-watching, and remembering to look up at the architecture above the modern storefronts—is a treat. And rather than letting graffiti artists mess up the place with random or angry tagging, the top street artists are given

Britain offers a fine set of experiences: from English garrison towns like Conwy, built seven centuries ago to keep down the Welsh *(left)*, to ghost tours that really grab you in York *(center)*, to fun and spirited public art on the streets of Glasgow *(right)*.

entire walls to paint. These murals are almost sightseeing destinations in themselves.

Walking Hadrian's Wall: For years I've visited Hadrian's Wall, the remains of the 73-mile fortification the Romans built nearly 2,000 years ago. It marked the northern end of their empire, where Britannia stopped and where the barbarian land that would someday be Scotland began. The Romans got all the way up here, and then they said, "OK, this is good enough; let's call it an empire. We don't want to mess with the Picts. We'll just build a big wall right here." But until recently, I never ventured beyond the National Trust properties, the museums, and the various parking lot viewpoints.

This time, cameraman in tow, I grabbed a sunny late afternoon to actually hike the wall. When you're scrambling along Roman ruins, accompanied by the sound of the wind, surveying vast expanses of Britain from rocky crags that seem to rip across the island—like a snapshot that has frozen some horrific geological violence in mid-action—you need to take a moment and simply absorb your setting. As my cameraman did his work, I did just that. I imagined I was a legionnaire on patrol in dangerous and distant Britannia, at the empire's northernmost frontier...with nothing but this wall protecting me from the terrifying, bloodthirsty Picts just to the north. It was a goose-pimple experience, as the Brits would say.

CULTURE AND TRADITIONS: EVERYTHING'S SO...BRITISH

Pubs and Beer

Pubs are a basic part of the British social scene, and whether you're a teetotaler or a beer guzzler, they should be a part of your travel here. A pub is where the whole neighborhood goes to meet people. If you sit at a table you might get some privacy; if you sit at a stool at the bar, you'll have all sorts of friends.

Whenever I'm in London, I make it a point to savor a pint at the Anglesea Arms in South Kensington. In my mind, this place is everything a British pub should be: filled with musty paintings and old-timers, beautiful people backlit, dogs wearing Union Jack vests, a long line of tempting tap handles advertising the beers and ales available, and flower boxes spilling color around picnic tables—perfect for a warm summer evening.

Britain's pubs still provide the best places to hang out with the locals.

Brits take great pride in their beer, and many think that drinking beer cold and carbonated, as Americans do, ruins the taste. At pubs, long-handled pulls are used to literally pull the traditional, rich-flavored "real ales" up from the cellar. These are the connoisseur's favorites: fermented naturally, varying from sweet to bitter, often with a hoppy or nutty flavor. Short-handled pulls at the bar mean colder, fizzier, mass-produced, and less interesting (at least to Brits)—keg beers. Pubs are also a fine (and economical) place to sample traditional dishes, like fish-and-chips, roast beef, bangers and mash (sausages and mashed potatoes), and meat pies—though increasingly, "gastropubs" are raising the culinary bar, with menus that mingle updated English and international fare. For me, eating in a fine pub under ancient timbers is the best and most atmospheric way to dine in Britain.

B&Bs and the British Breakfast

No one does bed-and-breakfasts better than the Brits. You'll find these small, quaint, family-run accommodations everywhere in Great Britain. Besides the company of charming hosts, the best part of staying at a B&B is the huge, home-cooked breakfast, called a "fry-up," a "full English/ Scottish/Welsh breakfast," or a "heart attack on a plate." Most B&B owners take pride in their breakfasts. Each morning, you sit down at an elegant and very British table setting in an intimate dining room. You can order whatever parts of the fry-up you desire: Canadian-style bacon, sausage, eggs, broiled tomatoes, mushrooms, greasy pan-fried toast, sometimes potatoes, and coffee or tea. Or, rather than a big plate of cardiac arrest, you can go to the buffet table and help yourself to cereal, juice, yogurt, and fruit.

B&Bs are not without drawbacks. Because they're often housed in older buildings, rooms are commonly smaller and more cramped than hotels. They can have thinner walls and creaky floorboards, so you might hear other guests creeping around at night. And while most rooms have an "en suite" (attached) bathroom, some rooms come with a "private bathroom" instead, which can mean that the bathroom is all yours, but it's across the hall. Yet I happily make the trade-off for the personal touches that B&Bs do offer—whether it's joining my hosts for tea in the afternoon or relaxing by a communal fireplace at the end of the day. Compared to hotels, B&Bs give you double the cultural intimacy for half the price.

Evensong

One of my top experiences in Britain is to attend evensong at a great church. During this evening worship, a singing or chanting priest leads the service, and a choir—usually made up of both men's and boys' voices—sings the responses. The most impressive places for evensong include Westminster Abbey and St. Paul's Cathedral in London, King's College Chapel in Cambridge, Canterbury Cathedral, Wells Cathedral, York Minster, and Durham Cathedral.

Wherever you attend, arrive early and ask to be seated in the choir. You're in the middle of a spiritual Oz as 40 boys sing psalms—a red-and-white-robed pillow of praise, raised up by the powerful pipe organ. You feel as if you have elephant-size ears, as the beautifully carved choir stalls—functioning as giant sound scoops—magnify the thunderous, trumpeting pipes. If you're lucky, the organist will run a

In Britain, some things never change: The breakfasts are as traditional and hearty as ever *(left)*, and the Brits love their afternoon tea *(right)*.

spiritual musical victory lap as the congregation breaks up. Thank God for evensong. Amen.

Afternoon Tea

The best way to experience this most British of traditions is to attend an afternoon tea. This ritual generally takes place around 3 p.m. and is something to be savored over a couple of hours. Menus include several options. "Cream tea" is simply a pot of tea and a homemade scone or two with jam and thick clotted cream. "Afternoon tea" usually comes with a three-tiered platter of dainty sandwiches, scones, and small pastries. Don't confuse afternoon tea with "high tea," which to Brits generally means a more substantial late-afternoon or early-evening meal, often served with meat or eggs.

Depending on where you go, afternoon tea can get pricey, especially in London. You can save money by tucking in at a department store or bookstore café. Still, for maximum opulence and ambience, it can be worth raising a pinky in one of Britain's grand tea rooms, such as the Wolseley or Fortnum & Mason in London, Bettys Café Tea Rooms in York, or my favorite—the Pump Room in Bath, a classy Georgian hall just above the Roman baths.

Great Britain Travel Resources from Rick Steves

Guidebooks

Check out Rick's guidebooks covering London; England; Scotland; Edinburgh; Scottish Highlands; and all of Great Britain (including England, Scotland, and Wales)

Audio Europe

Download Rick's free Audio Europe app, with interviews about Great Britain and self-guided audio tours, including walks through Westminster and the City of London; tours of the British Museum, British Library, and St. Paul's Cathedral; and a walk down Edinburgh's Royal Mile

TV Shows

The quintessence of Great Britain with Rick as your host, viewable on public television and at RickSteves.com. Episodes cover England (London, Bath, York, Lake District, Cornwall, Southeast England, Heart of England, West England), Wales, and Scotland (Edinburgh, Glasgow, Highlands, Scotland's Islands)

Organized Tours

Small group tours, with itineraries planned by Rick: England in 14 Days; London in 7 Days; South England in 13 Days; Scotland in 14 Days; Heart of Scotland in 8 Days; Family Europe: London to Florence in 13 Days

For more on all of these resources, visit RickSteves.com. For Great Britain trip-planning tips, see RickSteves.com/europe.

Ireland

One of the many reasons I love traveling in Ireland is that it gives me the sensation I'm understanding a foreign language. The Irish have that amazing gift of gab—a passion for conversation. And they're experts at it. Ireland is a sparsely populated island of hardscrabble communities. And along with lush, unforgettable vistas and an endearing heritage, it's the people that make the Emerald Isle such a delight to visit.

This 300-mile-long island, ringed with some of Europe's most scenic coastal cliffs, is only 150 miles across at its widest point—no matter where you go in Ireland, you're never more than 75 miles from the sea. Ireland is dusted with prehistoric stone circles, cliffside fortresses, burial mounds, and standing stones—some older than the pyramids.

Given its small size and geographic isolation, Ireland has had an oversized impact on the world. It was Ireland's Christian monks who tended the flickering flame of literacy through the Dark Ages, and Ireland later turned out some of modern literature's greatest authors (from Jonathan Swift and W. B. Yeats to James Joyce and Oscar Wilde). In the 1800s, great waves of Irish emigrants sought new opportunities abroad, making their mark in the US, Canada, New Zealand, and Australia.

Politics and religion divide Ireland. The Republic of Ireland, to the south, encompasses 80 percent of the island and is an independent nation of 4.6 million predominantly Catholic people. Northern Ireland, with 1.8 million people (roughly half Protestant and half Catholic), remains a part of the United Kingdom—like Scotland or Wales—and pledges allegiance to the Queen.

I'd say no trip to Ireland is complete without a visit to both the North and the Republic. Wherever you venture—from Dublin to Dingle, or from the Aran Islands to the Antrim Coast—you'll find an engaging culture and plenty of locals ready and eager to help you experience and enjoy it firsthand.

FAVORITE SIGHTS AND MEMORABLE EXPERIENCES IN IRELAND

Dublin Spirit

Years ago, I spent a week in Dublin vacationing with my then-teenaged kids. I had a hunch that Dublin would deliver on family fun...and it was grand.

The city is safe, lively, easy, and extremely accessible. Each night we enjoyed spirited and affordable entertainment. Both kids connected with their Irish heritage. We were all pretty wide-eyed at the thriving late-night scene in Temple Bar, Dublin's beer-drinking hotspot. While run-down through most of the 20th century, this now-trendy center feels like the social heart of booming Dublin and is great for people-watching. The girls are wrapped up like party favors, and the guys look like they're on their way home from a rough-and-tumble hurling match.

Nowadays, except for baked beans at breakfast, forget "eating Irish" in Dublin. Going local here is going ethnic. A multinational food court we visited took diversity to extremes: Chinese were cooking Mexican, Poles were running the Old Time American diner, a Spaniard was serving sushi,

Fast Facts

Biggest cities: Dublin (capital of Republic, 1.3 million), Belfast (capital of Northern Ireland, 300,000), Cork (119,000)

Size (entire island): 32,595 square miles (about the size of Indiana), population 6.6 million

Locals call it: Éire

Currency: Euro (Republic of Ireland), British pound (Northern Ireland)

Key date: December 6, 1921, Ireland wins independence from Britain before plunging into a year-long civil war that ends up dividing the country

Biggest festival: St. Patrick's Day (March 17)—although it's a bigger deal for Irish Americans than for people who still live in Ireland

Leprechauns per square mile: 1.7

Handy Irish phrases: *Dia duit* (hello; **jee**-ah gwitch), *Conas atá tú?* (How are you?; cun-us ah-**taw** too), *Go raibh maith agat* (thank you; guh rov mah **ug**-ut), *Pionta Guinness, le do thoil* (A pint of Guinness, please; pyun-**tah** Guinness leh duh hull), *Slainte!* (Cheers!; **slawn**-chuh)

Tourist info: Ireland.com

and Irish were running the Thai concession. Save your craving for pub grub for the small towns.

We went to Croke Park, the longtime stadium for Gaelic sports, joining 50,000 screaming Irish football fans. (Irish football is a kicking, tackling, running game.) Tickets were $40. I got to talking with a man seated next to us, telling him we went to the Abbey Theater the night before to see a play by Oscar Wilde. He asked me the cost, and I said $40 per person. He said to his wife, "Imagine paying $40 just to see a play." She said that, to a theatergoer, spending $40 to see a football game would be just as strange.

We'd spent another $40 outside the stadium so that my kids and I would each have a scarf or hat with the correct team colors (gold and green—we were rooting for Donegal). I thought back to a game I'd attended here 20 years earlier, when the "colors" were cheaply dyed crepe-paper hats that sold for a buck. In the rain, my colors ran from my paper hat down onto my face, gold and green...I was for Donegal even back then. During both games I recall being careful—for my own safety—to sit with Donegal fans and cheer at the right times. I'll never forget the creative cursing. My vocabulary grew like never before.

Pouring out of the stadium with what seemed like half of Dublin, it occurred to me that we were the only tourists in sight.

In Ireland, make a point to connect with the Irish—whether on the streets, at the stadiums, or in the nightlife zones.

Belfast: The Troubles and the *Titanic*

Wandering through energetic downtown Belfast, it's hard to believe that the bright and bustling pedestrian center was once a subdued security zone. That precaution was necessitated by the Troubles (1968 to 1998), the long and violent struggle to settle Northern Ireland's national identity. The Unionist majority (mostly Protestant) wanted to remain part of the United Kingdom, and the Nationalist minority (mostly Catholic) wanted to become part of the Republic of Ireland.

As a young tour guide back in the 1970s, I had a passion for getting my travelers beyond their comfort zones. In those days, a trip to Ireland was made meaningful by seeing towering stacks of wood in Belfast destined to be anti-Catholic bonfires and talking with locals about sectarian hatred. Now, after a 1998 power-sharing agreement brought an end to on-the-streets fighting, security checks are a thing of the past.

But evidence of the old challenges remains. In downtown Belfast, I hired a cabbie to take me on a guided tour of the original home bases of the Troubles—the Catholic working-class neighborhood of Falls Road, and the Protestant ones of Shankill Road and Sandy Row.

Our first stop was a sad structure called a "peace wall," which separated the Catholics from the Protestants in the former no-man's-land between the Shankill and Falls roads. It's one of a number of walls erected in Belfast when the Troubles started. Now 40 feet high, the wall started as 20 feet of concrete, was extended with 10 feet of corrugated metal, and finally topped with 10 feet of wire mesh—all with the intent of stopping projectiles from sailing over it. Although meant to be temporary, barriers like this stay up because of lingering fears among the communities on both sides.

My cabbie also brought me past Belfast's Felons' Club— where membership is limited to those who've spent at least a year and a day in a British prison for political crimes. At the Milltown Cemetery, I hopped out of my guide's old black cab to see a memorial to Bobby Sands and nine other hunger strikers, who starved themselves to death for the cause of Irish independence.

To get an up-close dose of the Unionist perspective, I walked along Sandy Row—a working-class-Protestant street.

Sightseeing in Northern Ireland ranges from political murals remembering a titanic political struggle to exhibits describing the birthplace of a *Titanic* disaster.

Ireland's Top Destinations

REPUBLIC OF IRELAND

Dublin ▲▲▲ — allow 2 days

Bustling Irish capital, with fine museums, fascinating walking tours (history, pubs, literature, music), a passionate rebel history along with the trappings of now long-gone British rule, and a rambunctious pub district

Top Sights

National Museum: Archaeology Interesting collection of ancient Irish treasures
Kilmainham Gaol Historic political prison-turned-museum
Trinity College Home of illuminated Book of Kells manuscript from the Dark Ages

Nearby

Brú na Bóinne Boyne Valley's ancient pre-Celtic burial mounds
Battle of the Boyne Site Location of the pivotal battle that established Protestant rule
Trim Castle Biggest Norman castle in Ireland
Glendalough Evocative Dark Ages monastic ruins set in the Wicklow Mountains

Kilkenny ▲▲ — 1 day

Inland medieval town, just an hour from the hilltop church ruins known as the Rock of Cashel

Waterford ▲ — 1 day

Historic port town with famous Waterford Crystal Visitor Centre

County Cork ▲▲ — 1-2 days

Two quaint harbor towns: gourmet capital **Kinsale** and emigration hub **Cobh**—the *Titanic's* last stop

Ring of Kerry ▲▲ — 1-2 days

Mountainous, lake-splattered region with famous loop drive, prehistoric ring forts, and sweet home-base town of **Kenmare**

Dingle Town and Peninsula ▲▲▲ — 2 days

Fishing village, traditional Irish-music pub paradise, and launch pad for gorgeous peninsula loop drive with plenty of mysterious stone forts and a possible trip to the desolate yet evocative Blasket Islands

County Clare ▲▲ — 1 day

Rugged western fringe, with the stunning Cliffs of Moher, stone landscape of the Burren, and trad music crossroads of **Doolin**

Galway ▲ — 1 day

University city with thriving pedestrian street scene and great pubs

Aran Islands ▲▲▲ — 1 day

Three windswept islands (**Inishmore** is best) laced with rock walls, crowned by Iron Age ring forts, and inhabited by hardy fisherfolk

Connemara and County Mayo ▲▲ — 1 day

Green, hilly outback of cottages, lakes, and peaks

NORTHERN IRELAND

Belfast ▲▲   1-2 days
Industrial Revolution metropolis with stirring political murals and *Titanic* museum, near the charming Victorian seaside town of **Bangor**

Antrim Coast ▲▲   1 day
Scenic area embracing the beach resort of **Portrush,** geologic wonderland of the Giant's Causeway, and cliff-edge ruins of Dunluce Castle

Derry ▲   1 day
Walled city that ignited Ireland's "Troubles"—with an insightful city history museum and access to the rugged beauty of County Donegal

Along the way I passed murals filled with Unionist symbolism, such as a depiction of William of Orange's victory over the Catholic King James II in the Battle of the Boyne.

With more peaceful times, the character of these murals is slowly changing. Paramilitary themes are gradually being covered over with images of pride in each neighborhood's culture. A recurring motif is the *Titanic* ocean liner, built by a predominantly Protestant workforce in Belfast's shipyard. (A typical souvenir T-shirt reads, "Titanic—it was OK when it left here.")

In fact, Belfast has turned its ties to the ill-fated ship into a $155-million touristic landmark. Titanic Belfast, a high-tech, six-story museum, rises adjacent to the dry dock where the *Titanic* took shape. It's part of the quiet optimism that's taken hold in Belfast. Perhaps one day visitors will associate the city more with its proud shipbuilding industry than with political and religious conflict.

Money Matters

The Republic of Ireland uses the euro currency. Northern Ireland, part of the United Kingdom, uses the pound sterling, the same currency in circulation in England, Scotland, and Wales. The pound notes issued by banks in Northern Ireland look slightly different from the British pound sterling, but they are worth the same and are technically interchangeable. Nonetheless, if you're also traveling to Great Britain, note that "Ulster" pounds are considered "undesirable" in England. Banks in either region can exchange them for English pounds at no charge. Don't worry about the coins, which are accepted throughout Great Britain and Northern Ireland.

The Dingle Peninsula

Be forewarned: Ireland is seductive. I fell in love with the friendliest land this side of Sicily. It all happened in a Gaeltacht—an area of traditional culture where the government protects the old Irish ways and Irish is spoken. But Irish culture is more than just the ancient language. You'll find it tilling the rocky fields, singing in the pubs, and lingering in the pride of the small-town preschool that brags "all Irish." Signposts feature Irish Gaelic, and some even come with the old Irish lettering.

Green, rugged, and untouched, the Dingle Peninsula is my favorite Gaeltacht. For more than 30 years, my Irish dreams have been set here, on this sparse but lush peninsula where residents are fond of saying, "The next parish is Boston."

Of the peninsula's 10,000 residents, 1,500 live in Dingle town (An Daingean). Its few streets, lined with ramshackle but gaily painted shops and pubs, run up from a rain-stung harbor. During the day, teenagers—already working on ruddy

On Ireland's Dingle Peninsula, humble farms feel haunted with memories of the Great Potato Famine *(left)* and villages seem built to weather great storms *(right)*.

beer-glow cheeks—roll kegs up the streets and into the pubs in preparation for another tin-whistle night.

Fishing once dominated Dingle, and the town's only visitors were students of old Irish ways. Then, in 1970, the movie *Ryan's Daughter* introduced the world to Dingle, followed in 1992 by *Far and Away*. The trickle of fans grew to a flood, as word spread of Dingle's musical, historical, gastronomical, and scenic charms.

Dingle town sits on the Dingle Peninsula, which makes a perfect 30-mile loop for a bike ride (or drive). While only tiny villages lie west of Dingle town, the peninsula is home to half a million sheep. Cycling around the peninsula feels like a trip through an open-air museum. The landscape is littered with monuments left behind by Bronze Age settlers, Dark Age monks, English landlords, and Hollywood directors.

Talk with the chatty Irish you'll encounter along the roadside. I once met an elfish, black-clad old man in the little town of Ventry (Ceann Tra'). When I asked if he was born here, he breathed deeply and said, "No, 'twas about six miles down the road." I asked if he'd lived there all his life. He said, "Not yet." When I told him where I was from, a faraway smile filled his eyes as he looked out to sea and sighed, "Aye, the shores of Americy."

The wet sod of Dingle is soaked with medieval history. In the darkest depths of the Dark Ages, peace-loving, bookwormish monks fled the chaos of the Continent and its barbarian raids. They sailed to this drizzly fringe of the known world and lived their monastic lives in lonely stone igloos or "beehive huts," which you'll see dotting the landscape.

Parts of the peninsula are bleak and godforsaken. Study the highest fields, untouched since the planting of 1845, when the potatoes never matured and rotted in the ground. You can still see the vertical ridges of the potato beds—a reminder of that year's Great Potato Famine, which eventually, through starvation and emigration, cut Ireland's population by one-quarter.

Rounding Slea Head, the point in Europe closest to America, the rugged coastline offers smashing views of deadly black-rock cliffs and the distant Blasket Islands (Na Blascaodai). The crashing surf races in like white horses, while long-haired sheep—bored with the weather, distant boats, and the lush countryside—couldn't care less.

The tip of the peninsula is marked by a chalky statue of a crucifix. It faces the sea, but about half the time, it seems it's actually facing an impenetrable cloud and being whipped by sheets of rain. It rains with gusto here. I imagine that Dingle cows have thicker eyelids, evolved over the centuries to survive sideways rain. The Gallarus Oratory, a 1,300-year-old church made only of stone, is famously watertight—unless the rain is hosing in sideways. I've been splattered inside. I've driven over Conor Pass with the visibility at zero, ragamuffin sheep nonchalantly appearing like ghosts in the milky cloud. I've huddled, awaiting a chance to step out, in farmhouses abandoned in the Great Famine. Yes, the weather is a force on the peninsula. But when the sun does come out, everything rejoices.

More Irish Experiences

Slog on the Bog: One of the simple pleasures of Ireland's landscape is bouncing on a springy peat bog. Walk a few yards onto the spongy green carpet. (On wet days, you might squish into a couple of inches of water.) Find a dry spot, and jump up and down to get a feel for it. Have your companion jump; you'll feel the vibrations 30 feet away.

These bogs once covered almost 20 percent of Ireland. As the climate got warmer at the end of the last Ice Age, plants began growing along the sides of the many shallow lakes and ponds. When the plants died in these waterlogged areas, there wasn't enough oxygen for them to fully decompose. Over the centuries, the moss built up, layer after dead layer, helping to slowly fill in the lakes and eventually becoming peat. Peat was Ireland's standard heating fuel for centuries—sliced out of bogs, stacked to dry, and then burned like presto logs in fireplaces and stoves. In the old days, four or five good men could cut enough peat in a day to keep a family warm through the cold Irish winter. Today, a few locals—nostalgic for the smell of a good turf fire—still come to desolate bogs to cut their own fuel.

LEFT On the far west coast of Ireland, mighty cliffs plunge into the sea while locals gaze out and say, "Ah, the next parish over...is Boston."

RIGHT On the northern coast, the hexagonal basalt pillars of the Giant's Causeway offer a stony playground for visitors.

Bleak and Beautiful Inishmore: Strewn like limestone chips hammered off the jagged west coast, the three Aran Islands confront the wild Atlantic with stubborn grit. The largest, Inishmore, is nine miles of rock with one sleepy town, a few fishing hamlets, and a weather-beaten charm. The landscape is harsh, with steep, rugged cliffs and wind-swept rocky fields stitched together by stone walls. So barren is this landscape that fishermen had to collect seaweed, sand, and manure to create tiny patches of soil for growing vegetables. This blustery island's stark beauty alone is worth a visit, but the blockbuster sight is Dún Aenghus, an Iron Age stone fortress that hangs spectacularly and precariously on the edge of a sheer cliff 200 feet above the ocean. You'll feel like the westernmost person in Europe, lying down on the rock—your head hanging over the cliff-edge—high above the crashing Atlantic.

Giant's Causeway: With camera handy, explore this stretch of Northern Ireland's coastline, famous for its bizarre basalt columns. The shore is covered with largely hexagonal pillars, sticking up at various heights. It's as if the earth were offering God his choice of 37,000 six-sided cigarettes.

Geologists claim the Giant's Causeway was formed by volcanic eruptions more than 60 million years ago. As the surface of the lava flow quickly cooled, it contracted and crystallized into columns (resembling the caked mud at the bottom of a dried-up lakebed, but with deeper cracks). As the rock later settled and eroded, the columns broke off into the many stair-like steps that now honeycomb the Antrim Coast.

Of course, in actuality, the Giant's Causeway was made by a giant Ulster warrior named Finn MacCool, who knew of a rival giant living on the Scottish island of Staffa. Finn built a stone bridge over to Staffa to spy on his rival and found out that the Scottish giant was much bigger. Finn retreated back to Ireland and had his wife dress him as a sleeping infant, just in time for the rival giant to come across the causeway to spy on Finn. The rival, shocked at the infant's size, fled back to Scotland in terror of whomever had sired this giant baby. Breathing a sigh of relief, Finn knocked down the bridge. Today, proof of this encounter exists in the geologic formation that still extends undersea and surfaces at Staffa. For cute variations on the Finn story, as well as details on the ridiculous theories of modern geologists, drop by the Giant's Causeway Visitors Centre.

In Ireland I enjoy the feeling of understanding a foreign language. And the people you meet love to talk. Whether on a harborside stroll or in a pub between sets of traditional music, try striking up a conversation.

CULTURE AND TRADITIONS: EVERYTHING'S SO...IRISH

Gaelic and the Gift of Gab

Want to really get to know the Irish? Ask for directions to your next destination. It's almost always a rich experience and a fast way to connect with locals. Nearby friends often chime in with additional tidbits that may or may not be useful, and soon it's a communal chitchat session.

That legendary Irish "gift of gab" has its roots in the ancient Celtic culture. With no written language (until the arrival of Christianity), the ancient Celts passed their history, laws, and folklore verbally from generation to generation. Even today, most transactions come with an ample side-helping of friendly banter (called *craic* in Irish). As a local once joked, "How can I know what I think until I hear what I say?"

Traditional Irish Music

The Irish seem born with a love of music. At social gatherings, everyone's ready to sing his or her "party piece." Performances are judged less by skill than by uninhibited sincerity or showmanship. Nearly every Irish household has some kind of musical instrument on a shelf or in a closet.

Live traditional music is a weekly (if not nightly) draw at any town pub worth its salt. There's generally a fiddle, flute or tin whistle, guitar, bodhrán (goat-skin drum), and maybe an accordion. Occasionally the fast-paced music stops, the band puts down their instruments, and one person sings a heartfelt lament—a sad story of lost love or emigration to a faraway land. This is the one time when the entire pub will stop to listen. Spend a lament studying the faces in the crowd.

A session can be magic, or it can be lifeless. If the chemistry is right, it's one of the great Irish experiences. The tunes churn intensely while the drummer dodges the fiddler's playful bow. Sipping their pints, they skillfully maintain a faint but steady buzz. The floor on the musicians' platform is stomped paint-free, and servers scurry artfully through the commotion, gathering towers of empty, cream-crusted glasses. Make yourself right at home, "playing the boot" (tapping your foot) under the table in time with the music.

Eating and Drinking in an Irish Pub

Pub is short for "public house"—an extended living room where, if you don't mind the stickiness, you can feel the pulse of Ireland. Today the most traditional, atmospheric pubs are in Ireland's countryside and smaller towns.

In much of Ireland, when you say "beer, please" at a pub, you'll get a pint of "the tall blonde in the black dress"—Guinness, Ireland's king of beers. If you want a small beer, ask for a "glass" (a half-pint). Never rush your bartenders when they're pouring a Guinness. It takes time—almost sacred time. If you don't normally like Guinness, try it in Ireland; it doesn't travel well and is better in its homeland.

Pub grub is Ireland's best eating value, but don't expect high cuisine. This is comfort food: Irish stew (mutton with mashed potatoes, onions, carrots, and herbs), soups and chowders, coddle (stewed layers of bacon, pork sausages, potatoes, and onions), fish-and-chips, boxty (potato pancakes filled with fish, meat, or veggies), and champ (potato mashed with milk and onion). In coastal areas, mackerel, mussels, and Atlantic salmon join the menu. Irish soda bread nicely rounds out a meal.

Ireland Travel Resources from Rick Steves

Guidebooks
Check out Rick's guidebooks covering all of Ireland (including the Republic of Ireland and Northern Ireland); Dublin; and Northern Ireland

Audio Europe
Download Rick's free Audio Europe app, with interviews about Ireland and self-guided audio tours, including walks through Dublin (South Bank and O'Connell Street)

TV Shows
The quintessence of Ireland with Rick as your host, viewable on public television or at RickSteves.com. Episodes cover the best of Northern Ireland (including Belfast) and the Republic of Ireland, including Dublin, Waterford, the Ring of Kerry, Dingle, Galway, and the Aran Islands

Organized Tours
Small group tours, with itineraries planned by Rick: Ireland in 14 Days; Heart of Ireland in 8 Days

For more on all of these resources, visit RickSteves.com. For Ireland trip-planning tips, see RickSteves.com/europe/ireland.

Scandinavia

Scandinavia is Western Europe's most prosperous, pristine, and progressive corner. For the tourist, it is the land of Viking ships, brooding castles, fishy harbors, deep green fjords, medieval stave churches, and quaint farmhouses—juxtaposed with the sleek modernism of the region's cities. A visit here connects you with immigrant roots, contemporary European values, and the great outdoors like nowhere else.

Denmark is by far the smallest of the Scandinavian countries (although it once ruled Norway and part of Sweden). Danes are proud of their mighty history, and yet they're easygoing, with a delightfully wry sense of humor. Denmark's capital, Copenhagen, is freewheeling and modern, while the country's cozy islands seem set in a century gone by.

Norway is stacked with superlatives—it's the most mountainous, most scenic, and, thanks to its offshore oil fields, most wealthy of the Scandinavian countries. Perhaps above all, Norway is a land of epic natural beauty, its steep mountains and deep fjords carved out and shaped by an ancient ice age. The country's capital, Oslo, is wonderfully walkable, its museums reflect its seafaring heritage, and its parks are unforgettable.

Sweden, far bigger than Denmark and far flatter than Norway, is graced with vast forests, countless lakes, and picturesque islands. Its sleek capital, Stockholm, is as appealing as its archipelago, perfect for cruising. This family-friendly land is home to Ikea, Volvo, WikiLeaks, ABBA, and summer vacations at red-painted, white-trimmed cottages.

Residents of the Scandinavian countries are, for the most part, confident, happy, and healthy. They speak their minds frankly, even about subjects others might find taboo, like sex. They're well-educated and well-traveled. Though reserved and super-polite at first, they're quick to laugh and don't take life—or themselves—too seriously.

FAVORITE SIGHTS AND MEMORABLE EXPERIENCES IN SCANDINAVIA

Cozying Up to Ærø

The Danish word for "cozy," *hyggelig*, perfectly describes the little island of Ærø. Few visitors to Scandinavia even notice this sleepy, 6-by-22-mile isle on Denmark's southern edge. But Ærø has a salty charm. It's a peaceful and homey place, where baskets of strawberries sit for sale on the honor system in front of farmhouses. Its tombstones are carved with sea-inspired sentiments such as: "Here lies Christian Hansen at anchor with his wife. He'll not weigh until he stands before God."

Ærø's main town, Ærøskøbing, is a village-in-a-bottle kind of place. I wander down cobbled lanes right out of the 1680s, when the town was the wealthy home port to more than 100 windjammers (today the harbor caters to German and Danish holiday yachts). Stubby little porthole-type houses, with their birth dates displayed in proud decorative rebar, lean on each other like drunken sailors. It's OK to peek through the windows into living rooms. (If people want privacy, they shut their drapes.) I notice, mounted to several old houses, angled "snooping mirrors" that afford someone seated inside a wide view of the entire street. Antique locals are following my every move—a thought that fills me with comfort rather than paranoia.

On the Danish isle of Ærø, the town of Ærøskøbing is a ship-in-a-bottle place.

The post office dates to 1749, and cast-iron gaslights still shine in the night. On summer evenings, you can hang out with the locals in the town's one pub or, even better, join the night watchman, who takes anyone who is interested on a historic stroll through town. That's the only action going on after dark. During midnight low tides it can be so quiet, you can almost hear the crabs playing cards.

A strong social ethic permeates Danish society, and I really feel that on Ærø. Here, you're welcome to pick berries and nuts, but historically the limit has been "no more than would fit in your hat." For years I recommended Mrs. Hansen's bike-rental depot next to the gas station at the edge of town. One day, a big hotel in town (with far more economic clout) decided to rent bikes, too. I saw Danish communalism in the reaction of a local friend: "They don't need to do that—that's Mrs. Hansen's livelihood." In Denmark, looking out for Mrs. Hansen's little bike-rental business is a matter of neighborly decency.

And Ærø's subtle, breezy charms are best enjoyed on a bike. Pedaling into the idyllic countryside, I find myself saying "cute" more than I should as I roll past sweet little hamlets and traditional U-shaped farms (designed to block the wind and protect cows, hay, and people). After struggling uphill to the island's 2,700-inch-high summit—a "peak" aptly named Synnes Hoej ("Seems High")—I wind past a fine 12th-century church, a cliffside viewpoint, a 6,000-year-old burial place, and a little brewery.

Then, as I coast back into Ærøskøbing as the sun is setting, I roll right on through to Urehoved beach—where a row of tiny huts lines the strand, and Danes gather to barbecue

Fast Facts

Biggest cities: Copenhagen (capital of Denmark, 1.2 million), Stockholm (capital of Sweden, 910,000), Oslo (capital of Norway, 658,000)

Size: Denmark—16,600 square miles (twice the size of Massachusetts), population 5.5 million; Norway—148,900 square miles (slightly larger than Montana), population 5 million; Sweden—174,000 square miles (a little bigger than California), population 9.6 million

Locals call it: Danmark (Denmark), Norge (Norway), Sverige (Sweden)

Currency: Danish crown (krone, officially DKK), Norwegian crown (krone, NOK), Swedish crown (krona, SEK)

Key date: A.D. 793, the Viking Age begins

Biggest festival: Midsummer Eve (summer solstice celebrations—with feasting, music, and dancing around the maypole in Sweden, and with bonfires, picnics, and processions in Norway and Denmark)

Handy Danish phrases: Goddag (hello; goh-**day**), Tak (thank you; tack), Ingen ko på isen (no worries, no problem; literally, "No cow on the ice"; ing koh paw **ees**-ehn)

Handy Norwegian phrases: God dag (hello; goo dah), Takk (thank you; tahk), Det regner trollkjerringer! ("It's raining troll hags!"; deh **ray**-nehr **trohl**-shehr-ring-ehr)

Handy Swedish phrases: God-dag (hello; goh-**dah**), Tack (thank you; tack), Fartkontroll (speed trap; **fahrt**-kohn-trohl)

Tourist info: VisitDenmark.com, VisitNorway.com, VisitSweden.com

shrimp and sing songs. The huts are little more than a picnic table with walls and a roof—each carefully painted and carved—stained with generations of family fun, sunsets, and memories of pickled herring on rye bread. It's a perfect Danish scene where a favorite word, *hyggelig*, takes cozy to enjoyable extremes.

Cool, Calm Copenhagen

Copenhagen has always impressed me. Its improbable aspects just work so tidily together. Where else would Hans Christian Andersen, a mermaid statue, Europe's first great amusement park, and lovingly decorated open-face sand-wiches be the icons of a major capital?

For the tourist, Copenhagen is compact, with its key sights radiating out from the Rådhuspladsen (City Hall Square), the bustling heart of the city. This used to be the fortified west end of town. In 1843, the king cleverly quelled a revolutionary-type thirst for democracy by giving his people a place to gather in Tivoli Gardens—just beyond the walls.

Tivoli, the granddaddy of amusement parks, is still going strong, but the walls and moats of medieval Copenhagen are long gone. They've been replaced by a ring of lush parks and tranquil lakes that are appreciated by the nearly naked sunbathers who savor the short Danish summer—oblivious to the history all around them.

From Rådhuspladsen, a series of lively pedestrianized streets and inviting squares called Strøget bunny-hops through the old town. Established in 1962, Strøget was Europe's first major pedestrian boulevard, and it's become the model for people zones throughout the world.

A leisurely stroll down Strøget leads to Nyhavn harbor, which lounges comfortably around its canal. Here in the old sailor's quarter, a few lonely tattoo parlors and smoky

Copenhagen's Nyhavn (New Harbor) is no longer a rol-licking quarter of prostitutes and sailors' bars. But it does come with good-looking Danes showing off their tattoos.

taverns stubbornly defend their salty turf against a rising tide of expensive cafés. Glamorous sailboats fill the canal, where any historic all-wood sloop is welcome to moor.

While tattoos were once the mark of crusty old seadogs, today they are Danish chic. Young bodybuilders, showing off muscles, tans, and tattoos, clog the harborside promenade as they down bottles of local beer. While all this public beer-drinking is off-putting to some, it's perfectly legal. Many young Danes can't afford the highly taxed alcohol sold in bars, so instead they buy their beers at a convenience store and "picnic drink" in squares and along canals. The outdoor beer drinking in Denmark is pretty much the same as consuming a brew in a British pub...just without the building.

For a quick meal, locals grab a *pølse*—a local hot dog—and wash it down with chocolate milk. Sold from sausage wagons (*pølsevogne*) throughout the city, the Danish *pølse* has resisted the onslaught of our global, Styrofoam-packaged, fast-food culture. What the locals call the "dead man's finger" is fast, cheap, tasty, and, like its American cousin, almost worthless nutritionally.

Another option is Denmark's tasty open-face sandwich (*smørrebrød*), overflowing with a variety of toppings and sold wrapped and ready to go in many corner shops. There's no more Danish way to picnic; a favorite spot is the waterfront park where the *Little Mermaid*—of Hans Christian Andersen fame—sits demurely on her rock. The tradition calls for three sandwich courses: herring first, then meat, then cheese, washed down with a local beer. *Skål!*

For the Danes, small really is beautiful.

Delightful, Surprising Oslo

When I was a 14-year-old kid, I traveled through Europe with my parents. One of my best memories from this trip is of sleeping on a ship from Copenhagen to Oslo, and waking up to the pristine Oslofjord. Sitting on the deck and for the first time enjoying the Norwegian scenery—the land of my grandparents—was a thrill. Years later, sailing down the same fjord to Oslo—this time on a giant cruise ship—was a wonderful travel déjà vu.

I love Norway—probably because I'm Norwegian. Three of my grandparents grew up in Norway. (Two homesteaded in Edmonton. One was a relatively famous and often-drunk ski jumper in Leavenworth, Washington.) On a previous TV shoot in Oslo, I told my producer, "Everyone here looks like my brother." He was shocked (having traveled with me for

Scandinavia's Top Destinations

DENMARK

Copenhagen ▲▲▲   allow 2-3 days

Canal-laced, fun-loving Danish capital city with fine museums, well-presented palaces, hordes of bikes, and a flourishing culinary scene

Top Sights
Tivoli Gardens Classic Danish amusement park
National Museum History of Danish civilization
Rosenborg Castle and Treasury Renaissance castle of "warrior king" Christian IV
Christiania Colorful counterculture squatters' colony

Nearby
Roskilde Noteworthy Viking ship museum, plus cathedral packed with royal tombs

Central Denmark ▲▲   2 days

Peaceful, bike-perfect isle of **Ærø,** with Denmark's best-preserved 18th-century village, and the busy town of **Odense,** with Hans Christian Andersen museum

Jutland ▲   1 day

Family-friendly region with Legoland park and Denmark's second-largest city, **Aarhus,** with traffic-free core, modern art museum, and open-air folk museum

NORWAY

Oslo ▲▲   2-3 days

Norway's businesslike capital city, with stately fjordside setting, innovative architecture, grand palaces and museums, and enjoyable parks

Top Sights
City Hall Palace of good government, slathered with symbolic murals
National Gallery Norway's cultural and natural essence, captured on canvas
Vigeland Park Sprawling park strewn with nudes by sculptor Gustav Vigeland
Bygdøy Neighborhood of excellent museums about seafaring, Vikings, and folk culture

Sognefjord ▲▲▲   1-2 days

Norway in a Nutshell, a trip through fjord country—by train, bus, and boat—passing waterfalls, forests, and spectacular vistas, with functional towns **Flåm** and **Aurland** along the way

Gudbrandsdal and Jotunheimen Mountains ▲   1-2 days

Lush green valley with touristy **Lillehammer** and access to a rugged mountain range with fine hikes and drives

Bergen ▲▲   2 days

Salty port city and medieval capital of Norway, with bustling fish market, colorful Hanseatic quarter (Bryggen), and a funicular to great views over town

South Norway ▲   1-2 days

Harborside **Stavanger** (with its Norwegian Emigration Center, Petroleum Museum, and nearby Pulpit Rock), time-passed and remote Setesdal Valley, and resort town of **Kristiansand**

SWEDEN

Stockholm ▲▲▲   2-3 days

Sweden's stunning capital, scattered over 14 islands and bubbling with energy and history

Top Sights
Skansen Europe's first and best open-air folk museum
Vasa Museum Marvelous showcase for a once-sunken 17th-century warship
Nordic Museum Fascinating peek at 500 years of traditional Swedish lifestyles
Gamla Stan Picturesque, cobbled old-town island
Royal Palace Grand collections and pomp-filled changing of the guard

Nearby
Stockholm Archipelago Scenic island chain stretching into the Baltic Sea

Southeast Sweden ▲   1-2 days

Densely forested region punctuated by worthwhile emigration and glass museums in **Växjö;** a 12th-century castle in **Kalmar;** the holiday island of **Öland;** and "Glass Country," famous for its glassworks

12 years) and said, "I didn't know you had a brother." I don't. But if I did, he'd look like the guys around me. It's more than how they look. It's how they are. A fun part of travel is to feel a kinship with people from the land of your forefathers.

Oslo is the smallest of the Nordic capitals, but this brisk little city is a scenic smorgasbord of history, sights, art, and Nordic fun. On May 17, Norway's national holiday, Oslo bursts with flags, bands, parades, and pride. Blonde toddlers are dressed up in colorful ribbons, traditional pewter buckles, and wool. But Oslo—surrounded by forests, near mountains, and on a fjord—has plenty to offer the visitor year-round.

Norway is traditionally a seafaring nation, so it's no surprise that Oslo's most popular sights, like the Viking Ship Museum, tell an exciting story of Viking spirit. Rape, pillage, and plunder were the rage a thousand years ago. Back then much of a frightened Western Europe closed every prayer with, "And deliver us from the Vikings, amen." When I gazed up at the prow of one of the museum's sleek, time-stained vessels, I could almost hear the shrieks and smell the armpits of those redheads on the rampage.

Today, Oslo is full of Norwegians rich on oil money. It's an expensive place—so expensive that people share their drinks and munch sandwiches on park benches. I find myself chewing slower and ordering smaller quantities here. The city also has its share of down-and-outers: prostitutes and needle junkies. While wasted people seem to rot on Oslo's curbs, the lack of violent crime here is impressive by any standard.

Overall, I am always struck by how peaceful Oslo feels. A congestion fee keeps most cars out of the town center, while

The rooftop of Oslo's gleaming marble opera house slopes into the harbor and is a popular venue for outdoor concerts.

tunnels take nearly all the rest under the city. The waterfront, once traffic-choked and slummy, has undergone a huge change. With vehicles sent underground, upscale condos and restaurants are taking over.

When the sun's out, Oslo's parks are packed. A common ailment here is *solstikk*, or sunstroke—literally, "sun sting." Wandering through a sunny Vigeland Park, where sculptor Gustav Vigeland's 192 bronze and granite nudes strut their stuff, I can't miss the real-life nudity. All of Scandinavia has a casual approach to nakedness (I'm not talking just mixed saunas—many Americans are amazed at what's on prime-time TV here). Women unabashedly sunbathe topless, and parents let their kids run naked in city parks and fountains. It's really no big deal.

Oslo's Vigeland Park is a showcase for the work of Gustav Vigeland. Its centerpiece is a towering monolith of life.

For years, I've told the story about my Eureka moment when I was that 14-year-old kid in Vigeland Park. I knew my parents loved me very much, and I looked around and saw a vast park speckled with other families—parents loving their children just as much. Right then it occurred to me how our world is filled with equally lovable children of God. I've traveled with this wonderful truth ever since.

As much as I love Norway, goat cheese, and my blonde cousins, sometimes I need to inject some color into my days here. Oslo, too, seems to relish the fact that there's more to life than white food and fair hair. The city's rough-and-tumble immigrant zone—a stretch of street called Grønland—is where Turks, Indians, Pakistanis, and the rest of Oslo's growing immigrant community congregates. Colorful greengrocers' carts spill onto sidewalks and ethnic restaurants literally add spice to the otherwise pretty tame cuisine. The area's a hit with locals and tourists, and I love dining streetside here. It's relatively cheap—and seeing a rainbow of people and a few rough edges makes the city feel less Wonder Bready.

And that's the beauty of Oslo. Just when you think you have it figured out, it gives you a taste of something different.

Norway's Fjordland Beauty

If you go to Norway and don't get out to the fjords, you should have your passport revoked. The country's greatest claim to scenic fame is its deep and lush fjords. Sognefjord,

Norway's longest (120 miles) and deepest (more than a mile), is the ultimate natural thrill Norway has to offer.

For the best one-day look at Sognefjord, I like to do "Norway in a Nutshell." This package of well-organized train, ferry, and bus connections lays this beautiful natural feast before you on a scenic platter. Ambitious travelers can see the whole shebang in one very full day, but slowing down and spending the night is more relaxing.

Every morning, northern Europe's most spectacular train ride leaves from Oslo toward fjord country. Cameras smoke as this train roars over Norway's mountainous spine. The barren, windswept heaths, glaciers, deep forests, countless lakes, and a few rugged ski resorts create a harsh beauty. The railroad is an amazing engineering feat. Completed in 1909, it's 300 miles long and peaks at 4,266 feet—which, at this Alaskan latitude, is far above the tree line. You'll go under 18 miles of snow sheds, over 300 bridges, and through 200 tunnels along the way.

When the train reaches the mountain plateau station of Myrdal, a 12-mile spur line drops you 2,800 breathtaking feet to the village of Flåm, on an arm of the Sognefjord. This is a party train. The engineer even stops it for a photo op at a particularly picturesque waterfall along the way.

From Flåm, ardent "Nutshellers" zip immediately from the train to catch the most scenic of fjord cruises. The boat takes you up one narrow arm of the Sognefjord—the Aurlandsfjord—and down the next—the even narrower

On the Sognefjord, Norway shows off its scenic beauty.

Nærøyfjord. For 90 minutes, camera-clicking tourists scurry on the drool-stained deck like nervous roosters, scratching fitfully for a photo to catch the magic. Waterfalls turn the black-rock cliffs into a bridal fair. You can nearly reach out and touch the sheer, towering walls. The ride is one of those fine times when a warm camaraderie spontaneously combusts among strangers, all of whom traveled from the farthest reaches of the globe to share this experience.

At the end of Nærøyfjord, the boat docks at the town of Gudvangen, where waiting buses shuttle passengers back to the main train line n Voss. From here you can continue to Bergen to spend the night, or loop back to Oslo. Take a late train, and you'll sleep through all the scenery you saw on the way out.

While the "Nutshell" trip is fast-paced bliss, if you want to dig deeper into the Sognefjord—just like the glaciers did during the last ice age—spend the night. There's something poetic about summer evenings on a fjord. The mellow, steady, no-shadow light hardly changes from 8 p.m. until 11 p.m.

When settled in a village in a Victorian-era fjordside hotel, I spend lots of time sitting on the porch, mesmerized by Norwegian mountains. Rather than jagged, they're bald and splotchy, with snow fields on top and characteristic cliffs plunging into inky fjords.

After dinner, I stroll through the village enjoying the blonde cherubs running barefoot through the stalled twilight. Cobbled lanes lead past shiplap houses to rock cliffs—their gullies and cracks green with trees.

I sit on a lonely pier and look up. Half the sky is taken up by the black rock face of the mountain. The steady call of gulls and the lazy gulping of small boats taking on little waves provide a relaxing soundtrack. As I feel my pulse slow, I am thankful to be in Norway.

Stockholm's Island Getaways

One-third water, one-third parks, one-third city, Stockholm is built on an archipelago of 14 islands woven together by 50 bridges. And the islands don't stop at the city limits—they keep going for 80 miles into the Baltic Sea.

The local name for this archipelago is "Skärgården"—literally "garden of skerries." The skerries—meaning rocks—are leftover granite, carved out and deposited by glaciers. The area closer to Stockholm has bigger islands and more trees. Farther out, the glaciers lingered longer, slowly grinding the granite into sand and creating smaller islands.

For years I've simply flown over this famed archipelago,

or glided by it on a big cruise ship heading for Helsinki. Finally, I filmed one of my TV shows in Stockholm, diving into the scenic daisy chain stretching out from its downtown. Locals love to brag that there are 34,000 islands (but they must be counting every mossy little rock). A hundred are served by ferries. Even if an island isn't an official stop, ferries will dock on request...or to plop down the day's mail.

With so many islands to choose from, every Swede seems to have their favorite. Don't struggle too hard with the "Which island?" decision. Get a quick look on a half- or full-day package excursion from Stockholm's harbor. Or, do it on your own by ferry and overnight on an island.

Vaxholm, the nearest island, is practically a suburb, as it's connected by bridge to Stockholm. Skip past it to the more appealing (and traffic-free) Grinda. It's a rustic isle—half-retreat and half-resort—made to order for strolling through the woods, paddling a kayak, savoring an oh-so-Swedish meal in the rustic-chic lodge, or just chilling out in the floating sauna that bobs in the harbor.

Svartsö ("Black Island"), a short hop beyond Grinda, is the "Back Door" option of these isles. Unlike Grinda, Svartsö is home to a real community of just 80 year-round residents. Leafy and green Svartsö is less trampled than other islands (just one B&B and a top-notch steak house run by Stockholm foodies), but it is reasonably well-served by ferries. There's little to do—walk, bike, eat steak.

Out on the distant fringe of the archipelago—the last stop before Finland—sits the proud village of Sandhamn, on the island of Sandön. Literally "Sand Harbor," the town has a long history as a posh center for boating life—it's Sweden's answer to Nantucket. The headquarters of the Royal Swedish Yacht Club is here, making Sandhamn an extremely popular

The archipelago that stretches from Stockholm to the Baltic Sea is an idyllic and watery wonderland for nature-loving Swedes.

stop for boaters—from wealthy yachties to sailboat racers. A long sandy beach, perfect for families, stretches out on one side of the island.

But honestly, I wouldn't mind if I never get off the ferry. For me, the real highlight of an archipelago trip is the ride itself. Perched on the breezy rooftop sundeck with the Swedes, I position my lounge chair to catch just the right view and sun. It's a pleasure to key in to the steady rhythm of the ferries lacing this beautiful world together. Seeing the contentment of people savoring nature and quality time together, I'm convinced that the journey truly is the destination.

More Scandinavian Experiences

Copenhagen's Alternative Village: In the middle of Copenhagen, you'll find an unlikely hippie commune called Christiania. Surrounded by all that Danish perfection and orderliness, it's a funky enclave of squatters and rebels who operate their own little idealistic society. While hard drugs are emphatically forbidden (that's one of Christiania's rules), marijuana is sold as openly as the current political climate will tolerate—and sellers routinely press whatever boundaries are in place. Somehow, despite the best efforts of developers and the city government, Christiania has survived for more than 40 years. On my last visit, as I entered Christiania, I saw a huge mural that pretty much sums up the spirit of the place: "Only dead fish drift with the current."

Remarkably, Christiania has become one of the most popular sights among tourists in Copenhagen. Move over, *Little Mermaid*. Some visitors see dogs, dirt, and dazed people. Others see a haven of peace, freedom, and no taboos. But watching parents raise their children with Christiania values of peace and freedom, I've come to believe more strongly than ever in this do-your-own-thing haven.

Hobnobbing in Norway: Not long ago, I was at a cousin's dinner party with a dozen people in Oslo. Because I was there, everyone simply spoke English. I felt like it was an inconvenience, but it fazed no one. Topics were fascinating. One man, an author who had just completed a book on FDR, talked with me about the intricacies of American post-WWII politics like no one I've ever met. Someone else suggested that the international phone prefix system must have originated in America, as the US is no. 1—and Norway is a lowly 47. Another guest observed that Midwest Americans

speak louder than other Americans, and wondered if it was for the same reason that West Coast Norwegians talk louder than people from Oslo: They are always trying to be heard above the constant wind. Two new parents gently debated the various ways to split their paid maternal and paternal leave. People seemed very content—these Norwegians were just loving their salmon, shrimp, and goat cheese.

LEFT In Copenhagen's Christiania, a banner proclaims, "Live life artistically. Only dead fish drift with the current."

Revealing National Galleries: In the space of a week, I visited national galleries in Oslo, Stockholm, and Copenhagen. Each museum was a little palace of culture, showing off the nature of the land and the psyche of its people. In Scandinavia, paintings don't celebrate kings and popes. Instead, artists focus on the tumultuous symphonies of nature, exaggerating its power and awesomeness. When country folk do appear, they're the piccolo section—tiny but in sharp focus, barely surviving, but with grace. Many Scandinavian paintings are people's art—featuring bridal voyages (with traditional jewelry and formal wear), low church devotion (featuring renegade Lutherans who would not follow state dictates, until they ran out of patience and moved to Wisconsin), and solid families at work and play. The slice-of-life scenes seem to just as often be slice-of-death scenes: In one canvas, a stoic family fills their rowboat, carrying the coffin of a dead daughter, her sister clutching the funeral flowers through the bitter ride. And there's evidence of struggles with a puritanical 19th-century Protestant society and the psychological problems that resulted—leading artist Edvard Munch to let out a silent, bloodcurdling *Scream*.

CENTER Edvard Munch's *Scream* at Oslo's National Gallery

RIGHT The traditional *smörgåsbord* is a grand buffet and your chance to feast on many Scandinavian specialties in one sitting.

All Aboard the *Smörgåsbord*: Nobody visits Scandinavia for the cuisine, but there's one culinary tradition I never miss: the Swedish *smörgåsbord* (known in Denmark and Norway as the *store koldt bord*). With so much wholesome Nordic food spread out in front of me, I must pace myself. Thinking of the *smörgåsbord* as a five- or six-course meal, I take small portions, making several trips to the buffet. I start with the herring dishes, boiled potatoes, and *knäckebröd* (Swedish crisp bread); then, I sample the other fish dishes (warm and cold) and more potatoes; next, it's on to salads, egg dishes, and various cold cuts; and after that, the meat dishes—it's meatball time! I pour on some gravy and plop on a spoonful of lingonberry sauce, and have more potatoes—while other roast meats (hey, is that reindeer?) and poultry tempt me. With a few empty pockets still to fill in my stomach, I sample the Nordic cheeses, delicious seasonal fruits, and bread, and then raid the racks of traditional desserts, cakes, and custards. Stuffed, I cap the meal with coffee to keep from passing out.

CULTURE AND TRADITIONS: EVERYTHING'S SO...SCANDINAVIAN

Mamma Mia!

Sweden spent years trying to find a place for a museum to honor its national treasure, the disco group ABBA. And now there is one—ABBA: The Museum, in Stockholm. For a time, ABBA was a bigger business than Volvo. And even though the group disbanded in 1982, its songs are still on plenty of playlists. They've sold more than 380 million records, and the musical *Mamma Mia!* (based on their many hits) has been enjoyed on screen and in theaters by millions of people. The museum, like everything about ABBA, is slickly promoted and aggressively commercial, with pricey tickets (about $30). But if you like ABBA, it's lots of fun. The museum has plenty of actual ABBA artifacts, re-creations of the rooms where the group did its composing and recording, lots of high-energy video screens, and plenty of interactive

LEFT At Stockholm's popular ABBA museum, any tourist can hang out with the band.

RIGHT Medieval stave churches are a reminder that Christian Vikings employed their ship-building skills for the Church.

stations. The best part is the "digital key" included with admission: You get to record a music video, karaoke-style, as a fifth member of the group, then pick up the production from the museum website.

Stave Churches

Stave churches are the finest architecture to come out of medieval Norway. These medieval houses of worship—tall, skinny, wooden pagodas with dragon's-head gargoyles—are distinctly Norwegian and palpably historic, transporting you right back to the Viking days. Wood was plentiful and cheap, and locals had an expertise with woodworking (from all that boat-building). In 1300, there were as many as 1,000 stave churches in Norway. Today, 28 remain. See two or three, and they start to look the same—but exploring at least one of them is a must. The fairest stave church in Norway? Two near the Sognefjord are tops: Hopperstad (overlooking a fjord) and Borgund (in a valley with an adjacent excellent museum). These time-machine churches take you back to early Christian days, when there were no pews and worshippers stood through the service. The churches are extremely vertical: The beams inside and the roofline outside lead your eyes up, up, up to the heavens.

Coffee Breaks

When sightseeing your way through Stockholm, be sure to join in the local tradition of the *fika*—Sweden's ritual coffee break. People in Sweden must drink more coffee per capita than in just about any other country. The *fika* is to Swedes what the *siesta* is to Spaniards. While typically a morning or afternoon break in the workday, it can happen any time, any day.

Cheap-ish Eats

There are ways to take a bite out of Scandinavia's high cost of dining. First, take full advantage of your hotel's bountiful breakfast buffet. When out sightseeing, grab lunch from a street vendor or a food market, or at a restaurant offering a daily special.

In Copenhagen, get a *pølse* (hot dog) from the sausage wagon. In Oslo, hit a *gatekjøkken* (fast-food joint), such as Deli de Luca, for a sandwich, salad, or a classic *pølse med brød* (hot dog in a bun). In Norway you'll save money by getting takeaway food from a restaurant rather than eating inside, as the tax on dine-in food is higher than on takeout. In Stockholm, dine at a restaurant advertising *dagens rett*, a cheap lunch special.

Anywhere in Scandinavia you can save money by going to a grocery store and shopping for a picnic. In Norway, I've even cooked up my own dinner using an *engangsgrill* ("one-time grill"), a disposable foil barbecue that costs just a few bucks at a supermarket. On balmy evenings, Oslo is perfumed with the smoky fragrance of one-time grills as the parks fill up with Norwegians eating out on the cheap.

Fika fare includes coffee along with a snack or pastry—usually a cinnamon bun. You can get your *fika* fix at just about any café or *konditori* (bakery) in Stockholm. The coffee (drip-style, usually with a refill) and a cinnamon bun cost about what you'd pay at a Starbucks back home.

Dane Mellow

Danes (not to mention Swedes and Norwegians) like to joke about the flat Danish landscape, saying that you can stand on a case of beer and see from one end of the country to the other. Denmark's highest point, in Jutland, is only 560 feet above sea level. But I find Denmark to be simply cute, cute, cute. The place feels like a pitch 'n' putt course sparsely inhabited by blonde Vulcans. Poll after poll lists Danes as the most content and happy people on the planet.

Legoland, a wildly popular amusement park built from millions of Lego bricks, crawls with adorable little ice-cream-licking children. Even fueled by piles of sugar, the place is so mellow. Kids hold their mothers' hands and learn about the Lego buildings, or smile contentedly as they whip around on the carousel.

Throughout the countryside, newly paved roads are lined by perfectly smooth bike lanes—one for each direction. Even in the country, there are more bikes than cars. No one's uptight. When there's a little traffic jam, everyone takes it in stride. Damn those Danes.

Scandinavia Travel Resources from Rick Steves

Guidebooks
Check out Rick's guidebooks covering Scandinavia (including Denmark, Norway, and Sweden); Stockholm; Copenhagen & Denmark; and Norway

Audio Europe
Download Rick's free Audio Europe app, with interviews about Scandinavian culture and sightseeing

TV Shows
The quintessence of Scandinavia with Rick as your host, viewable on public television and at RickSteves.com. Episodes cover Denmark (Copenhagen, Ærø Island, Jutland), Norway (fjords, Bergen, Oslo), and Sweden (Stockholm)

Organized Tours
Small group tours, with itineraries planned by Rick: Scandinavia in 14 Days

For more on all of these resources, visit RickSteves.com. For Scandinavia trip-planning tips, RickSteves.com/europe and click on "Denmark," "Norway," or "Sweden."

The Netherlands

Windmills, wooden shoes, cheese, tulips, and lots of bicycles: These images conjure up the traditional view of the Netherlands, a.k.a. Holland. (While North and South Holland are just two of the country's 12 provinces, they're so dominant that people use the names Holland and the Netherlands interchangeably.) But dig deeper and you will discover that the country also has high-tech culture, far-out architecture, and no-nonsense people with a global perspective.

For many Americans, this is a great place to start your first European vacation. The Dutch generally speak English, pride themselves on their frankness, and like to split the bill. As connoisseurs of world culture, they appreciate Rembrandt paintings, Indonesian cuisine, and the latest French films, but with a nonsnooty, blue-jeans attitude.

The capital, Amsterdam, is a laboratory of progressive living, bottled inside Europe's most 17th-century city. Like Venice, this city is a patchwork quilt of canal-bordered islands, anchored upon millions of wooden pilings. But unlike its dwelling-in-the-past cousin, Amsterdam sees itself as a city of the future, built on good living, cozy cafés, great art, street-corner jazz, and a spirit of live-and-let-live.

Because the Netherlands is compact and flat, it's easy to do day trips from Amsterdam (or nearby Haarlem, which also makes a good home base). The slick, efficient train system gets you anywhere in just hours. Choose from an array of activities and sights: the market in cozy Haarlem, the

open-air folk museum in Arnhem, cheese in Edam, porcelain in Delft, or a trip through polder country out to the sea.

Approach the Netherlands as an ethnologist observing a fascinating and unique culture. A stroll through any neighborhood is rewarded with things that are commonplace here but rarely found elsewhere. Carillons chime quaintly in neighborhoods selling sex, as young professionals smoke pot with impunity next to old ladies in bonnets selling flowers.

FAVORITE SIGHTS AND MEMORABLE EXPERIENCES IN THE NETHERLANDS

Amsterdam Street Scenes

Unlike any city in Europe, Amsterdam opens like a fan out of its central train station. It just seems right for a trading center to open up from that lifeline to the world.

Stepping from the train station, I look down Damrak, the main drag, which flushes visitors past cheers of commercial neon into the old center. It's always been this way. After all, long before there was a station, this was a mighty port with a waterway cutting through the center of town, following the route of today's Damrak.

Outside the station, trams glide and canal-boat hustlers hawk their offerings. Street people wearing stocking hats over matted hair, black boots, and heavy coats in the sun choose the most public places in town to snooze. Children pedal to school as if in a small town, and pairs of police officers add no stress to the laid-back scene. Tourists pop out of the station, eager to explore.

First-time sightseers leaving the station carry a predictable checklist of sights. The Anne Frank House is on the right, the Red Light District is on the left, and Damrak leads right through the middle toward two great museums—the Rijksmuseum (filled with works by Rembrandt and Vermeer) and the Van Gogh Museum—standing like cultural bulldogs on the opposite side of town.

Fast Facts

Biggest cities: Amsterdam (capital, 820,000), Rotterdam (615,000), The Hague (500,000)
Size: 16,000 square miles (about twice the size of New Jersey), population 16.8 million
Locals call it: Nederland
Currency: Euro
Key date: July 26, 1581, the Dutch declare their independence from Habsburg Spain
Biggest festival: King's Day (April 27)
Bikes per Dutch citizen: 1.3
Handy Dutch phrases: *Hallo* (hello; hol-**loh**), *Alstublieft* (please; **ahl**-stoo-bleeft), *Dank u wel* (thank you; dahnk yoo vehl), *Nou breekt mijn klomp!* (Well, I'll be damned!; literally, "That breaks my wooden shoe"; now brayk men kloomp)
Tourist info: Holland.com

But to me, Amsterdam's unpredictable street scenes—crude one moment, then charming the next—are at least as rewarding as the city's fine museums. Walking down Damrak, I find it a crass perversion of traditional Dutch culture. Wooden shoes hang forlornly on a wall between a bank and a McDonalds. Nearby, a sex museum known as the temple of Venus promises a look at "sex through the ages," including the Sado Club, the Torture Tower, and the oldest sex shop in Amsterdam. Visitors are stopped first by the poster of Marilyn Monroe fighting a randy gale, then lured in by a sultry mannequin wearing a provocative dress and a huge smile as she rides a bicycle with a single, hardworking piston.

But slices of Holland survive. Just past a gimmicky torture museum, the sound of an old-time barrel organ revives traditional Amsterdam and cheers me up. It's a two-man affair. While grandpa works the crowd, the boss is in the back spinning the wheel and feeding tunes punched into a scroll, as if feeding bullets into a musical machine gun.

The street organ is a mini carnival, painted in candy-colored pastels and peopled with busy figurines. Whittled ballerinas twitch to ring bells while Cracker Jack boys crash silver dollar-sized cymbals. Playing his coin-tin maracas and wearing a carved-on smile, the old man looks like an ornamental statue that has just leapt to life. While shoppers trudge by, two tourists break into a merry waltz. Another hugs a day bag between her knees and winks into her camera's viewfinder.

Nearby, the Vlaamse Frites kiosk is painted with take-offs on great art. This art has a purpose: to make you hungry for Flemish-style French fries. On one side of the kiosk, God gives Adam the cone of fries (a variation on this decorates the Sistine Chapel). On the opposite side is Van Gogh's famous "French Fried Potato Eaters." The peasants, for whom Vincent always had an affinity, are shown solemnly sitting down to a bountiful platter of bright yellow fries. All they need is mayonnaise, the Dutch choice over ketchup.

Warming my hands around my cone of salty fries, I wander down a back street to a charming canal lined with tipsy houses. As their foundations of pilings rot or settle, they lean on each other, looking as if someone has stolen their crutches. Suddenly, away from the tourists and street-scene bustle, I'm in 17th-century Amsterdam, seeing the Dutch Golden Age reflected in the quiet canal.

Seeing Red in Amsterdam

With just a slight swing off Dam Square, I start walking down Warmoesstraat, one of Amsterdam's oldest streets. Lining the street are sex shops, a condom shop with a vast inventory, men-only leather bars, and a smartshop selling "100 percent natural products that play with the human senses." There's no doubt I've entered into Amsterdam's famous Red Light District.

The Red Light District is located in the old sailors' quarter. In fact, the city seems to have taken everything sailors did, put it in a jar, and let it germinate for 200 years. Today that jar is open, and browsers are welcome.

The Dutch have a similarly practical approach to prostitution as they do to the recreational use of marijuana. Rather than criminalize it, they control it with a policy they call "pragmatic harm reduction." Generally, prostitutes (or "sex workers") pay rent for their space and run an independent business with no need for pimps. They are unionized and get their business license only if they are periodically checked by a doctor and are not spreading diseases. If a prostitute has a

Red lights reflect on the canals in Amsterdam, where, as in much of Europe, prostitution is legal.

The Netherlands' Top Destinations

Amsterdam ▲▲▲   allow 2-3 days
Canal-laced city filled with cozy cafés, great art, Golden Age history, and progressive people

Top Sights
- **Rijksmuseum** Premier collection of Dutch Masters art
- **Van Gogh Museum** 200 paintings by the angst-ridden artist
- **Canal Boat Tours** Best cruise through city's fabled waterways
- **Anne Frank House** Young Anne's hideaway during the Nazi occupation
- **Dutch Resistance Museum** Powerful and insightful look at years under Nazi occupation

Haarlem ▲▲   1 day
Classic Dutch town (and handy home base) highlighted by a landmark market square, towering church, Corrie ten Boom House, and the Frans Hals Museum

Delft ▲▲   1 day
Charming, canal-lined hometown of Vermeer and the Delftware pottery factory

Edam ▲▲   1 day
Adorable cheese-making village with peaceful canals

Arnhem ▲▲   1 day
Unremarkable city but for Holland's top open-air folk museum and a first-rate modern-art museum

The Hague ▲   1 day
Big-city seat of Dutch government offering the excellent Mauritshuis Gallery and Golden Age art

With more time, consider visiting
Rotterdam Europe's busiest port, with soaring architecture and 21st-century buzz
Alkmaar Friday-morning cheese market, near Zaanse Schans Open-Air Museum
Utrecht Bustling student city with charming central zone and top rail museum

---

dangerous client and needs help, she pushes a button to summon not a pimp, but the police.

By the time I reach the area around De Oude Kerk, the oldest church in Amsterdam, I've hit the neighborhood's most dense concentration of prostitution. The church is the holy needle around which the unholy Red Light District spins. Rooms with big windows under red neon lights line the narrow alleys. In window after window, I see women in panties and bras winking at horny men, rapping on the window to attract attention, or looking disdainfully at sightseers. As the steeple chimes, women from Jamaica holler, "Come on, dahling."

Rubbing shoulders with a hungry gaggle of Dutch boy regulars, I rubberneck my way to the most popular window on the street. There, framed in smoky red velvet, stands a sultry blonde. Her ability to flex and shake her backside brings the slow, gawking pedestrian flow to a stuttering stop. And it

makes me just one of the faceless, rutting masses. Next up: an exotic woman wearing a black lace power-suit and enough lipstick to keep a third grader in crayons. Just making eye contact leaves me weak—and ready to rejoin the cute and quaint Holland back in the sunshine.

The Dutch remind me that a society has to make a choice: Tolerate alternative lifestyles or build more prisons. And they always follow that up by reminding me that Americans—so inclined to legislate morality—lock up seven times as many people per capita as Western Europeans do. Either Americans are inherently more criminal people, or we need to reconsider some of our laws.

By the end of my walk, I've seen a lot—from prostitutes to the ghosts of pioneer lesbians to politically active druggies with green thumbs. This is Amsterdam's hardcore, nonstop, live-couples, first-floor-straight, second-floor-gay paseo. The kid in me delights in the spectacle. The tour guide in me jumps at this opportunity to give readers such a unique memory as this red light ramble. But the father in me cringes at the sight of a 10-year-old schoolgirl, book bag on her back, studying a window full of vibrators, whips, and sex toys.

In truth, the Red Light District seems to have something to offend everyone. Whether it's in-your-face images of graphic sex, exploited immigrant women, whips and chains, passed-out drug addicts, the pungent smells of pot smoke and urine, or just the shameless commercialism of it all, it's not everyone's cup of tea. Amsterdam is a bold experiment in 21st-century freedom: It may box your Puritan ears. And, although I encourage people to expand their horizons, it's perfectly OK to say, "No, thank you."

Now, it's time to go back to my hotel and take a shower.

Haarlem with Herring Breath

A Dutch Masters kind of town, Haarlem is an easy place to start a European trip. While mighty Amsterdam is just a 20-minute train ride away, cute Haarlem provides a comfy base and a more genteel experience.

The centerpiece of Haarlem is its delightful Grote Markt (main square), where 10 streets converge. A noisy traffic circle in the 1960s, the now-car-free area has become the town's social and psychological hub—Haarlem's civic living room.

Today I'm standing on the square under the towering church spire, tempted to eat a pickled herring. The sign atop the mobile van reads: "Jos Haring—Gezond en Lekkerrr" (healthy and deeeeeelicious).

I order by pointing and ask, *"Gezond?"*

Jos hands me what looks more like bait than lunch, and says, *"En lekkerrr."*

I stand there—not sure what to do with my bait—apparently looking lost. Jos, a huge man who towers over his white fishy counter, mimes swallowing a sword and says, "I give you the herring Rotterdam style. You eat it like this. If I chop it up and give you these"—he points to the toothpicks—"this is Amsterdam style."

As I take a bite he asks, "You like it?"

Even with three "r"s on the delicious, "It's salty" is the only polite response I can muster.

"Yes. This is not raw. It is pickled in salt. Great in the hot weather. You sweat. You need salt. You eat my herring."

It's Saturday—market day, when Haarlem's main square bustles like a Brueghel painting. The scene cheers me with

a festival of flowers, bright bolts of cloth, evangelical cheese pushers, and warm, gooey syrup waffles. Gazing at the church, I'm appreciating essentially the same scene that Dutch artists captured centuries ago in oil paintings that now hang in museums. The carillon clangs with an out-of-tune sweetness only a medieval church tower can possess.

Savoring the merry dissonance, and taking tiny Amsterdam-style bites of my Rotterdam herring, I wander deeper into the market, happy that Jos is piling chopped onion on herring, contributing to the amazing ambience of this scene. Dodging flower-laden one-speed bikes, I feel like part of the family here. I'm immersed in Holland—with herring breath.

Haarlem's main square is a community gathering point. And there, like in nearly every Dutch town, you'll find a stand selling pickled herring. Locals declare the fish to be *gezond en lekker* (healthy and delicious).

The Dutch Made Holland

Today my long-time Dutch friends, Hans and Marjet, are driving me to polder country—the vast fields reclaimed from the sea where cows graze, tiny canals function as fences, and only church spires and windmills interrupt the horizon.

Hans is behind the wheel. He injects personality-plus in all he does, whether running a B&B or leading tours for Americans. And bouncy Marjet, with a head of wispy strawberry-blonde hair, red tennis shoes, and a knack for assembling a Salvation Army-chic outfit for under $20, is the sentimental half of this team.

On each of my visits, they show me a new slice of Holland, renewing my belief that the more you know about Europe, the more you'll uncover what's worth exploring.

It's early summer, and the landscape is streaked with yellow and orange tulip fields. Hans points out a quaint windmill along a dreamy canal.

"Every time I take a tour group through Holland's

countryside," I say, "someone in the back of the bus marvels, 'Everything's so Dutch.'"

The windmills were used to pump the polders dry. An area that was once a merciless sea is now dotted with tranquil towns. Many of the residents here are older than the land they live on, which was reclaimed in the 1960s. All this technological tinkering with nature has prompted a popular local saying: "God made the Earth, but the Dutch made Holland."

We motor past sprawling flower mogul mansions, then through desolate dunes. The tiny road dwindles to a trailhead. Hans parks the car, and we hike to a peaceful stretch of North Sea beach. Pointing a stick of driftwood at a huge seagoing tanker, Hans says, "That ship's going to the big port at Rotterdam. We're clever at trade. We have to be. We're a small country."

Holland welcomes the world's business, but Holland is not designed for big-shots. Hans explains, "Being ordinary is being prudent. If you grow above the grains, you'll get your head cut off. Even our former queen prefers to do her own shopping."

While Hans and I talk, Marjet collects shells with the wide-eyed wonder of a 10-year-old. "Cheap souvenirs," Hans teases. One cliché the Dutch don't dispute is their frugality. Hans quizzes me: "Who invented copper wire? Two Dutch boys fighting over a penny."

Marjet scuffs through the sand, her pockets full of

Charming Dutch villages sit on land reclaimed from the sea by pumping excess water into canals.

seashells, her scarf flapping in the wind like a jump rope. Under big, romping white clouds, we're surrounded by Holland.

More Dutch Experiences

Wartime Hideaways: Through the ages, the Dutch have given refuge to the persecuted. But they couldn't protect their citizens from the Nazis—more than 100,000 Dutch Jews died in the Holocaust. In Amsterdam, Anne Frank's House gives the cold, mind-boggling statistics of Nazi cruelty some much-needed intimacy. Even bah-humbug types who are dragged in because it's raining and their partners read the diary find themselves caught up in Anne's story. And the small town of Haarlem has Corrie ten Boom's "Hiding Place," which gives the other half of the Anne Frank story—the point of view of those who risked their lives to hide Dutch Jews during the Nazi occupation. During the war, Corrie and her family hid Jews and resistance fighters in their apartment above a clock shop. One night, with six people hiding behind a wall in Corrie's bedroom, the Nazis raided the house. Though they didn't find the hiding place, they did come across a suspiciously large number of ration coupons and sent the ten Boom family to a concentration camp. Only Corrie survived and later wrote her inspirational book, *The Hiding Place*.

Cannabis and Coffeeshops: Having been decriminalized decades ago, marijuana causes about as much excitement in the Netherlands as a bottle of beer. People can grow their own—cannabis seed sets are even sold in garden centers. Or they simply drop by a coffeeshop—a café that sells marijuana. For tourists, the open use of marijuana can feel either somewhat disturbing or exhilaratingly liberating.

Coffeeshops sell marijuana and hashish both in prerolled joints and in little baggies. They loan out bongs and inhalers, and dispense rolling papers like toothpicks. Pot, while sold openly in coffeeshops, is tightly regulated here. It's not sold to minors, and you can only buy a little at a time—and a new law may make it illegal to sell to tourists altogether. Because they're not allowed to advertise marijuana, you may have to ask to see the cannabis menu. In some coffeeshops, you actually have to push and hold down a button to see an illuminated menu—the contents of which look like the inventory of a drug bust. If you are able to buy it, coffeeshop baristas may warn you to try a lighter leaf. If you overdo it, the key is to eat

or drink something sweet to avoid getting sick. Cola is a good fast fix, and coffeeshops keep sugar tablets handy.

Charming Delft: Delft is a typically Dutch, "I could live here" town. An hour southwest of Amsterdam, it boasts an intelligent exhibit on hometown boy Johannes Vermeer, two grand churches squirreling away royal tombs, and the factory that produces Delft Blue earthenware. But despite some fine sights, Delft is best enjoyed by simply wandering around, watching people, munching local syrup waffles, and daydreaming on canal bridges. Looking out, you'll see reflections in canals that would inspire Monet to set up his easel. On a summer day, the entire town twinkles and ripples like water lilies.

Netherlands in Bloom: The Dutch love plants. And the granddaddy of the European flower festivals is Keukenhof, the greatest bulb-flower garden on earth. Open only for two months in spring, Keukenhof blossoms with seven million tulips, hyacinths, and daffodils that conspire to thrill even the most horticulturally challenged visitor. Located near the city of Leiden, this place is packed with tour groups daily—go in the late afternoon for the fewest crowds and the best light on all those happy flowers. If you can't get out to Keukenhof, try Amsterdam's De Hortus Botanical Garden, with 4,000 varieties of plants spread throughout several greenhouses and a tropical palm house. One of the oldest botanical gardens in the world, it dates from 1638, when medicinal herbs were grown here. Even today, no mobile phones are allowed in its café or terrace because "our collection of plants is a precious community—treat it with respect."

CULTURE AND TRADITIONS: EVERYTHING'S SO...DUTCH

Dutch Cheese

Cheese is a staple of the Dutch culture and economy. Cows have always proven to be more reliable than crops in this marshy landscape. And because cheese offered similar nutritional value to milk, but lasted much longer without refrigeration, it was taken on long sea voyages. Holland was the first country to export cheese, and today this small country remains one of the world's biggest cheese exporters.

The Netherlands' most famous cheeses are Edam (covered with red wax) and Gouda. Gouda can be young or old—*jong* is mellow while *oude* is salty, crumbly, and strong, sometimes seasoned with cumin or cloves. To sample Dutch cheese in Amsterdam, try the Reypenaer Tasting Rooms, whose delightful shop offers an hour-long cheese tasting (smart to reserve ahead). Or, for the real deal, head to the town of Alkmaar, Holland's cheese capital, with its bustling Friday-morning cheese market in spring and summer. Early in the morning, cheesemakers line up their giant orange wheels in neat rows on the square. Prospective buyers (mostly wholesalers) examine and sample the cheeses and make their selections. Then the cheese is sold off with much fanfare, as an emcee narrates the action (in Dutch and English). To close the deal, costumed cheese carriers run the giant wheels on something resembling a wooden stretcher back and forth to the Weigh House, just as they have for centuries.

Netherlands Clichés

What do windmills, canals, wooden shoes, and tulips have in common? Where did all of these Dutch icons come from?

Dutch clichés abound in the Netherlands, where cheese shops dot every corner and classic windmills still churn in the breeze.

It's all about the land. After diking off large tracts of land below sea level (*Netherlands* means "low lands"), the Dutch used windmills to harness wind energy to pump the excess water into canals. This drained the land, creating pockets of dry ground upon which to build. Wooden shoes (*klompen*) allowed farmers to walk across soggy fields, and since they could float, the shoes were easy to find if they came off in high water. Then in the mid-1500s, the Holy Roman Emperor's ambassador to Constantinople sent some tulip bulbs westward. The people here found that these hardy flowers grew well in the sandy soil near dunes, and tulips have become synonymous with Dutch culture ever since.

Ethnic Eats

The tastiest "Dutch" food isn't actually Dutch—it's Indonesian. As a former Dutch colony, Indonesia has had a mighty influence on the Dutch cuisine scene. Find any *Indisch* restaurant and experience a rijsttafel (literally, "rice table"). A rijsttafel features an assortment of dishes that shows off the varied cuisines of the

Going Dutch on a Bike

If you rent a bike in the Netherlands, you'll need to learn the rules of the road. Use arm signals, follow the bike-only traffic signals, stay in the obvious and omnipresent bike lanes, and yield to traffic on the right. Fear oncoming trams and tram tracks. Carefully cross tracks at a perpendicular angle to avoid catching your tire in the rut. Obey all traffic signals, and walk your bike through pedestrian zones. Use the bell to warn other bikers and pedestrians, and be sure to lock your bike.

If you are a pedestrian, look carefully both ways before crossing the brick-colored pavement on the side of the road—this is for bikes. As the Dutch believe in fashion over safety, no one here wears a helmet.

different Indonesian islands. You'll get as many as 30 spicy dishes ranging from small sides to entrée-sized plates and a big bowl of rice or noodles. These feasts can be split and easily fill two people.

Surinamese cuisine is also popular in the Netherlands. This mix of Caribbean and Indonesian influences features dishes like *roti* (spiced chicken wrapped in flatbread) and rice (white or fried) served with meats in sauces (curry and spices). Why Surinamese food in Amsterdam? In 1667, Holland traded New York City ("New Amsterdam") to Britain in exchange for the small South American country of Suriname. When Suriname gained independence in 1975, 100,000 Surinamese immigrated to Amsterdam, sparking a rash of Surinamese fast-food outlets.

Biking

The Netherlands' flat land makes it a biker's dream. And in Amsterdam, bikes are by far the smartest way to travel. Everyone—bank managers, students, pizza delivery boys, and police—use bikes to get around town, and much of my own Amsterdam experience is framed by my black bike handlebars: the shiny wet cobbles, powering up a bridge to coast down it and halfway to the next bridge, getting pinged by passing bikes and pinging my bell to pass others.

The Dutch average four bikes per family. Many people own two: a long-distance racing bike and an in-city bike, often deliberately kept in poor maintenance so it's less enticing to the many bike thieves. The Dutch appreciate the efficiency of a self-propelled machine that travels five times faster than walking, without pollution, noise, parking problems, or high fuel costs. A speedy bicyclist can traverse Amsterdam's historic center in 10 minutes. Meanwhile, pedestrians enjoy the quiet of a people-friendly town where bikes outnumber cars.

Netherlands Travel Resources from Rick Steves

Guidebooks
Check out Rick's guidebooks covering Amsterdam & the Netherlands

Audio Europe
Download Rick's free Audio Europe app, with interviews about the Netherlands and self-guided audio tours, including walks through the old center of Amsterdam, the Red Light District, and the Jordaan neighborhood

TV Shows
The quintessence of the Netherlands with Rick as your host, viewable on public television and at RickSteves.com. Episodes cover Amsterdam and Dutch side-trips

Organized Tours
Small group tours, with itineraries planned by Rick: Heart of Belgium & Holland in 11 Days; Best of Europe in 21 Days (which includes a stop in the Netherlands)

For more on all these resources, visit RickSteves.com. For Netherlands trip-planning tips, RickSteves.com/europe/netherlands.

Belgium

Belgium falls through the cracks. Nestled between Germany, France, and the Netherlands, it's famous for waffles, sprouts, and a statue of a little boy peeing. But visitors find Belgium to be one of Europe's more underrated destinations. After all, Belgium produces some of Europe's best beer, creamiest chocolates, and tastiest French fries. From funky urban neighborhoods to tranquil convent courtyards, from old-fashioned lace to high-powered European politics, from cows mooing in a pastoral countryside to gentrified medieval cityscapes bristling with spires...little Belgium entertains.

It's here in Belgium that Europe comes together: where Romance languages meet Germanic languages; Catholics meet Protestants; and nations meet in Brussels—the capital of the European Union. Its crossroads location has made Belgium strong: Belgians are smart businesspeople, excellent linguists, and savvy chefs who've learned how to blend delicious culinary influences from various cultures.

When I asked a local, "What is a Belgian?" he answered, "We are a melting pot. We're a mix culturally: one-third English for our sense of humor, one-third French for our love of culture and good living, and one-third German for our work ethic."

Bruges, a wonderfully preserved medieval gem, and Brussels, one of Europe's great cities, are the best two first bites of Belgium. Historic, well-preserved Ghent and big, bustling Antwerp are also worth a visit. To round out your Belgian experience, spend a few hours in the Flemish countryside around the town of Ypres—both for the pastoral scenery and to visit World War I's Flanders Fields.

Don't shortchange Belgium. Most travelers who squeeze in a day or two for Belgium wish they had more time. Like sampling a flavorful praline in a chocolate shop, that first enticing taste just leaves you wanting more. Go ahead, it's OK—buy a whole box of Belgium.

FAVORITE SIGHTS AND MEMORABLE EXPERIENCES IN BELGIUM

Bewitched by Bells in Bruges

With Renoir canals, pointy gilded architecture, vivid time-tunnel art, and stay-awhile cafés, Bruges is a joy. Where else can you bike along a canal, quench your thirst with gloriously good beer, savor heavenly chocolate, and see a Michelangelo statue, all within 300 yards of a bell tower that rings out "Don't worry, be happy" jingles?

Whenever I'm in Bruges, I visit the tall bell tower that has shaded the city's Market Square since 1300. With its medieval crenellations, pointed Gothic arches, round Roman arches, flamboyant spires, and even a few small flying buttresses, the tower is a sight in itself. Carillon concerts are played on its bells a few evenings each week. You can hear the tunes ringing out from anywhere in the town center, but to catch the performance while sitting in the tower courtyard is a ritual for me.

One evening I arrived early for the concert, so I had time to climb the tower's 366 steps. Just before the top is the carillon room. On each quarter hour, its 47 bells—tuned to 47 different notes—ring mechanically.

Fast Facts

Biggest cities: Brussels (capital, 1.1 million), Antwerp (508,000), Ghent (249,000)

Size: 12,000 square miles (slightly smaller than Maryland), population 10.4 million

Locals call it: België (Dutch), Belgique (French)

Currency: Euro

Key date: 1830, Belgium declares independence from the Netherlands

Languages: Dutch (to the north; Flemish is the local Dutch dialect), French (to the south)

Biggest festivals: Carnival (Mardi Gras celebrations), Ommegang Pageant (July, Brussels, medieval festival)

Handy Dutch phrases: *Hallo* (hello; **hal**-loh), *Alstublieft* (please; **ahl**-stoo-bleeft), *Dank u wel* (thank you; dahnk oo vehl)

Handy French phrases: *Bonjour* (good day; bohn-zhoor), *S'il vous plaît* (please; see voo play), *Merci* (thank you; mehr-see)

Tourist info: VisitFlanders.com, WalloniaBelgiumTourism.co.uk, Visit.Brussels

It's *bellissimo* at the top of the hour. During concerts, the bells are played by a *carillonneur* on a manual keyboard.

After my carillon close-up, I took a seat in the courtyard and gazed up at the lofty brick tower. The *carillonneur* popped his head out a window, and like a kid who checks in with a parent before going down a playground slide, he gave his audience a wave. Then he disappeared and began hammering—literally hammering. A carillon keyboard looks like the foot pedals of a big organ, but it is played by the little-finger sides of bare, clenched fists.

After the concert, the gathered audience clapped, and the *carillonneur* appeared again—his tiny head

jutting out the little window to happily catch our applause. The crowd dissipated, but I waited at the tower base to personally thank him. A few minutes later, he was at street level, in his overcoat, looking like any passerby. I shook his hand and found myself gripping a freakishly wide little finger. A lifetime of pounding the carillon had left him with a callus that had more than doubled the width of his pinky.

In a town with a knack for excellence, I'd met just one more artist perfecting his craft.

Carillon concerts are played on the bells of the tower overlooking the Market Square in Bruges.

Bruges Brews

In Bruges, pubs are not just pubs, they're destinations. Belgians appreciate a pub that's not owned by a single brewery, freeing them up to sample from the hundreds of microbrews made in their country. Pubs in the old center—places you'd think would be overrun by tourists—are the proud domain of locals. The fact that monasteries have historically brewed the finest Belgian beers aligns perfectly with their personal theology.

During one visit, I plunked myself down on a stool at a local pub with an Old Masters ambience. Wanting to check the material I had in my guidebook on Belgian beers, I planned to pick the bartender's brain, but I found myself surrounded by beer experts—all happy to clue me in on the 300 available choices. They advised me to forego my standard procedure of ordering what's on tap. Because the selection of specialty beers is so vast, no single brew can be consumed quickly enough to keep kegs from going old and stale. Those in the know prefer their beer from the bottle.

Different beers, depending on their taste temperament, are served cold, cool, or at room temperature. A critical part of the beer culture here is that the glass must fit the beer (to best bring out the beer's character). The better pubs have shelves lined with dozens of slightly different glasses, each marked with a beer's insignia. If the pub runs out of the right glass, the bartender will check to see if you'd like to change your order. Many Belgian connoisseurs will switch beers rather than use the wrong glass.

Soon I had a chemistry lab of four different beers in front of me. My selection included Brugse Zot, or "the fool"—the top beer brewed in Bruges and considered one of Belgium's best. Kriek beer is made bitter with cherry. I was told that raspberry-flavored Lambic is what you order if you "don't like beer." My favorite was a complex and creamy Chimay, brewed by Trappist monks. Licking my lips, I thought that Chimay would almost make celibacy livable.

Brussels' Grand Place

There's no better place to take in Brussels' ambience than its spectacular main square, the Grand Place. This colorful cobbled courtyard, encircled by fanciful facades, is the heart

Brussels has perhaps the grandest square in Europe—La Grand Place—and perhaps the silliest tourist attraction in the world—the Manneken-Pis. With each visit, you'll see the little guy peeing through a different outfit.

Belgium's Top Destinations

Bruges ▲▲▲   allow 1-2 days

Perfectly pickled Gothic city with charming cobbles, cozy squares, dreamy canals, divine chocolate, and unbeatable beer

Top Sights

Market Square 14th-century landmark square and bell tower

Groeninge Museum Top-notch 15th-century paintings

Sint-Janshospitaal Memling Collection Glowing Flemish Primitives masterpieces housed in medieval hospital

Nearby

Damme Charming market town a bike-ride away through the countryside

Flanders Fields Infamous WWI battlefields

Brussels ▲▲   1-2 days

Urbane capital of Belgium, the European Union, and NATO, with one of Europe's grandest squares, colorful urban zones, and a beloved statue of a little boy peeing

Top Sights

Grand Place Cobbled main square lined with medieval guild halls and chocolate shops

Royal Museums of Fine Arts Old Masters, huge Art Nouveau collection, and three floors of Magritte

Antwerp ▲▲   1 day

Gentrified port city with excellent museums, Belgium's best fashion, and an engaging mix of urban grittiness and youthful trendiness

Ghent ▲   1 day

Pleasant, lively university city with historic quarter and breathtaking Van Eyck altarpiece in its massive cathedral

of heart-shaped Brussels. The site where farmers and merchants once sold their wares in open-air stalls today hosts shops and cafés selling chocolates, waffles, beer, mussels, fries, and lace. It's the perfect backdrop for concerts, flower markets, and sound-and-light-shows—and there's always good people-watching.

The Town Hall's 300-foot-tall tower dominates the square, topped by a golden statue of St. Michael slaying a devil. Fancy smaller buildings—former guild halls—give the Grand Place its majestic medieval character.

Just three short blocks away is Brussels' most famous attraction and the most obvious example of Bruxellois irreverence: the *Manneken-Pis*, a 17th-century statue depicting a little boy urinating. Visiting VIPs have a tradition of bringing an outfit for the statue; he can be costumed as anything from a Beefeater to Elvis as his steady stream carries on.

There are several different stories behind this little

squirt: He was a naughty boy who peed inside a witch's
house so she froze him. Or the little tyke loved his beer,
which came in handy when a fire threatened the wooden
city—he bravely put it out. Want the truth? The city com-
missioned the statue to show the freedom and joie de vivre
of living in Brussels, where happy people eat, drink...and
drink...and then pee.

More Belgian Experiences

Antwerp's Ode to Industrialism: I can't think of a more
visit-worthy train station than the Industrial Age-meets-Art
Nouveau marvel in Antwerp, giddy with steel and glass. Built
at the turn of the 20th century, the station is a work of art and
a loud-and-clear comment on a confident new age. Its main
facade is like a triumphal arch on a temple of time, crowned
by a grand clock. Imagine the station's debut: Just a generation earlier, people thought you might die if you traveled at

more than 30 miles per hour. Timetables didn't need to be exact. Now, journeys that previously took days could be done in hours—and things ran according to the clock.

Life and Death in Flanders Fields: In far western Belgium, in the desolate WWI battlefield known as Flanders Fields, poppies were the first flowers to bloom once the dust (and mustard gas) cleared. Hundreds of thousands of soldiers took their last breaths here. Today, the poppy, representing sacrifice and renewal, is the symbol of Flanders Fields.

When touring in this area, I have to remind myself that everything I see—every building, every tree—dates from after the war's end in 1918. The devastation was monumental. You can't drive through this part of Flanders without passing countless artillery craters, monuments and memorials, stones marking this advance or that conquest, and war cemeteries standing stoically between the cow-speckled pastures. Local farmers routinely pull rustic relics of World War I from the earth when they till their fields. Every local has a garage collection of "Great War" debris fished out of the troubled earth.

European Union Headquarters in Brussels: This sprawling complex of glass skyscrapers is a cacophony of black-suited politicians speaking 23 different Euro-languages. It's exciting just to be here—a fly on the wall of a place that charts the future of Europe. The high-tech Parlamentarium, a fun and informative exhibit, is designed to let you meet the EU and understand how it works. And you can get inside the European Parliament itself by joining a free tour. The grand finale is the vast Hemicycle, where the parliament members sit. It's the largest multilingual operation on the planet. Yes, there are now some Euroskeptics sitting in this hall, but somehow things get done "with respect for all political thinking...consolidating democracy in the spirit of peace and solidarity."

Tiny Belgium's attractions range from a mighty Industrial-Age train station in Antwerp *(left)*, to the vast and evocative WWI cemeteries of Flanders Fields *(center)*, to the glassy headquarters of the European Union in Brussels *(right)*.

CULTURE AND TRADITIONS: EVERYTHING'S SO...BELGIAN

World Capital of Chocolate

With a smile, the shop owner handed me a pharaoh's head and two hedgehogs and said that her husband was busy downstairs finishing off another batch of chocolates. Happily sucking on a hedgehog, I walked out of the small chocolate shop with a 100-gram assortment of Bruges' best pralines.

Belgium—home to Godiva, Neuhaus, and Leonidas—is one of the world's largest exporters of chocolate, and produces some of Europe's creamiest confections. The two basic types are pralines (what we generally think of as "chocolates"—a hard chocolate shell with various fillings) and truffles (a softer, crumblier shell, often spherical, and also filled). Which is better? It takes a lot of sampling to judge. Locals swear by their personal chocolatier and buy with a concern for freshness—yesterday's chocolate just won't do. This can be disastrous for chocoholics during heat waves: If the weather's too hot, the chocolate makers close down.

Belgian Waffles

Waffles are a famous Belgian treat. There are two kinds: Liège-style (warm, dense, and very sweet—with a sugary crust), and Brussels-style (light and fluffy, dusted with powdered sugar). Although Americans think of Belgian waffles for breakfast, Belgians generally have them as a late-afternoon snack—though the delicious Liège-style waffles are sold 'round the clock to tourists as an extremely tempting treat. You'll see little windows, shops, and trucks selling these *wafels*, either plain (for Belgians and purists) or topped with fruit, jam, chocolate sauce, ice cream, or whipped cream (for tourists).

A Belgian waffle just tastes better in Belgium. And if you're one to gild the lily, there is a world of toppings from which to choose.

Just Say No...to Ketchup

Belgium has some of the tastiest "French" fries in Europe. Get a paper cone of warm fries at a *frituur* (fry shop) or a *frietkot* (fry wagon). One time a local chef took me into his kitchen to witness the double frying that makes the fries taste so good. (The first pass is to cook the potatoes; the second is to brown them.) My friend picked up a single fat fry, gave it a waggle, and then dipped it into its second hot-oil bath. Something about his nervous giggle reminded me of the kid who showed me my first dirty magazine. Belgians dip their fries in mayonnaise or other flavored sauces, not ketchup. But don't worry; most places provide ketchup for Americans.

No Tap Water at Restaurants

I'd rather drink free tap water than pricey bottled water in a European restaurant. But forget about it in Belgium—it can't be had. Belgian restaurateurs are emphatic about that. Tap water may come with a smile in the Netherlands, France, and Germany, but that's not the case in Belgium, where you'll either pay for water, enjoy the beer, or go thirsty.

Belgium Travel Resources from Rick Steves

Guidebooks
Check out Rick's guidebook covering Bruges, Brussels, Antwerp & Ghent

Audio Europe
Download Rick's free Audio Europe app, with interviews about Belgian culture and sightseeing

TV Shows
The quintessence of Belgium with Rick as your host, viewable on public television and RickSteves.com. Episodes cover Bruges and Brussels

Organized Tours
Small group tours, with itineraries planned by Rick: Heart of Belgium and Holland in 11 Days

For more on all of these resources, visit RickSteves.com. For Belgium trip-planning tips, see RickSteves.com/europe/belgium.

Germany

Germany is a young nation (united in 1871) with a long history. It's as modern as it is traditional. You can experience all the cultural clichés you want, from enjoying strudel at the bakery, to shopping for a cuckoo clock, to chugging a stein of beer while men in lederhosen play oompah music. The countryside is dotted with half-timbered villages like Rothenburg, looking as medieval as ever. But despite its respect for traditions, Germany truly is a 21st-century country. Laced together by bullet trains, its cities gleam with futuristic architecture, world-class museums, rejuvenated waterfronts, and people-friendly parks.

The country is blessed with spectacular scenery, and the nature-loving Germans know how to enjoy it: taking lifts to jagged peaks, hiking through the Black Forest, and cruising on rivers such as the moseying Mosel and the raging, castle-lined Rhine. The country boasts hundreds of castles, some ruined and mysterious, and others right out of a Disney fairy tale.

In contrast to its beautiful image, the country has a troubled 20th-century past. In the capital of Berlin and throughout Germany, you'll see respectful acknowledgment of this tumultuous era, with thought-provoking documentation centers, somber monuments, and haunting concentration camps.

Traditionally—and in some ways even today—German culture divides at a sort of North-South Mason-Dixon Line. Northern Germany was barbarian, is predominantly Protestant (thanks to Martin Luther), and tackles life aggressively, while southern Germany (Bavaria) was Roman, is largely Catholic, and enjoys a more relaxed tempo (think of soaking in spas). Americans' nostalgic image of Germany is

beer-and-pretzel Bavaria, probably because that was "our" sector after the war.

Germany is a country of paradoxes. From modern skyscrapers to medieval castles, speedy autobahns to meandering back roads, Nouveau German cuisine to old-fashioned *Wurst*, Germany truly offers something for everyone.

Germany ranges from half-timbered medieval cuteness (Rothenburg) to towering skyscraper zones (Berlin).

FAVORITE SIGHTS AND MEMORABLE EXPERIENCES IN GERMANY

Cruising the Rhine River

Jostling through crowds of Germans and tourists in the Rhine River village of Bacharach, I climb to the sun deck of the ferry and grab a chair. With the last passenger barely aboard, the gangplank is dragged in and the river pulls us away.

I'm captivated by the Rhine. There's a rhythm to the mighty river that merges with its environment: black slate cut from plains above, terraced vineyards zigzagging up hills, husks of crumbling castles, and stoic spires of stone churches slicing vertically through townscapes. While the Rhine is more than 800 miles long, the 36 miles from Mainz to Koblenz are by far the most interesting. This is the Romantic Rhine, a powerful stretch of the river slashing a deep and scenic gorge. And the best way to see it is to cruise it.

On the romantic Rhine River gorge, cafés at castles offer grand views of busy river traffic.

Passengers' parkas flap in the cool wind as the rugged hillscape gradually reveals castles both ruined and restored. All along the Rhine, it seems each castle and every rock comes with a story. Many of the castles were "robber-baron" fortresses built by petty princes and two-bit rulers back when there were several hundred independent little states in what is today's Germany. The castle owners raised heavy chains across the river when boats came—and lowered them only when the merchants had paid their duty. We sail close by one of the many scenic fortresses— Pfalz Castle—which was built on an island in the middle of the river.

As the cliffs get steeper, the rocks darker, and the river faster, the scenery becomes more dramatic. With the boat's sun deck filled mostly with beer-sipping, ice-cream-licking Germans, our collective pulse quickens as we approach the mythological climax of this cruise. Over the ship's blow horns comes the story of the Loreley—a rocky bluff where a maiden seduced sailors into shipwrecks—followed by a lusty rendition of the Loreley song. Parents point to the bluff, featured in the fairy-tale memory of every German schoolkid.

According to legend, a thousand years of skippers have dreaded the Loreley. Because of the reefs just upstream, many ships never made it beyond the bluff. Sailors (after days on the river) blamed their misfortune on the legendary siren, with her long blonde hair almost covering her body, who'd lured boatloads of drooling sailors to her river bed.

Our boat survives the Loreley and docks in St. Goar, a classic Rhine tourist town. Its massive ruined castle overlooks a half-timbered shopping street and leafy riverside park, busy with sightseeing boats and contented strollers. Sitting like a dead pit bull above St. Goar,

Fast Facts

Biggest cities: Berlin (capital, 3.4 million), Hamburg (1.8 million), Munich (1.5 million)

Size: 138,000 square miles (about half the size of Texas), population 81 million

Locals call it: Deutschland

Currency: Euro

Key date: October 3, 1990, two Germanys become one after the fall of the Berlin Wall (November 1989)

Biggest festivals: Oktoberfest (early autumn, Munich), Christmas markets (late November through Christmas Eve, Nürnberg and elsewhere)

Handy German phrases: *Guten Tag* (hello; **goo**-tehn tahg), *Bitte* (please; **bit**-teh), *Danke* (thank you; **dahn**-keh), *Noch ein Bier!* (Another beer!; nohkh īn beer)

Tourist info: Germany.travel

Of all the Rhine castle ruins to tour, Rheinfels is the mightiest.

Rheinfels Castle—the single best Rhineland ruin to explore—rumbles with ghosts from its hard-fought past.

The Rhine Valley is storybook Germany, a world of legends and medieval castles. Through it all, the quiet, deep-gray power of the river flows as steadily as time itself, a dance floor where ferries, barges, and sightseeing boats do their lumbering do-si-do past fabled and treacherous rocks.

Celebrating Democracy at Berlin's Reichstag

In Berlin, a must-see for any traveler is the Reichstag, the country's parliament building. Topped with a glass cupola that visitors can climb, this building is more than just the meeting place for parliament—it's also a symbol of German democracy.

From 1933 to 1999, this historic building—upon whose rooftop some of the last fighting of World War II occurred—sat a bombed-out and blackened hulk, overlooking the no-man's-land between East and West Berlin. After unification, Germany's government returned from Bonn to Berlin. And, recognizing this building's cultural roots, they renovated it—incorporating modern architectural design and capping it with a glorious glass dome.

This old-meets-new building comes with powerful architectural symbolism. The glass dome is designed for German citizens to climb its long spiral ramp to the very top and literally look down (through a glass ceiling) over the shoulders of their legislators to see what's on their desks. The Germans, who feel they've been manipulated by too many self-serving politicians over the last century, are determined to keep a closer eye on their leaders from now on.

I was in Berlin in 1999 during the week that the renovated Reichstag reopened to the public. That day, I climbed to the top of the dome and found myself surrounded by teary-eyed Germans. Anytime you're surrounded by teary-eyed Germans, something exceptional is going on. It occurred to me that most of these people were old enough to remember the difficult times (either during or after World War II), when their city lay in rubble. For them, the opening of this grand building was the

The glassy dome of Berlin's Reichstag welcomes German citizens as well as tourists.

symbolic closing of a terrible chapter in the history of a great nation. No more division. No more communism. No more fascism. They had a united government and were entering a new century with a new capitol filled with hope and optimism.

Castle Day in Bavaria and Tirol

Three of my favorite castles—two famous, one unknown—can be seen in one busy day. If you tackle "Castle Day," you'll visit Germany's Disney-like Neuschwanstein Castle, the more stately Hohenschwangau Castle at its foot, and the much older Ehrenberg Ruins, across the Austrian border in Reutte.

Reutte makes a fine home base. From here, catch the early bus across the border to touristy Füssen, the German town nearest Neuschwanstein. From Füssen, you can walk, pedal a rented bike, or ride a bus a couple of miles to Neuschwanstein.

Neuschwanstein is the greatest of King Ludwig II's fairy-tale castles. It's one of Europe's most popular attractions, so reserve ahead online (otherwise, arrive by 8 a.m. to buy a ticket). If you choose a combo-ticket, you'll first visit Ludwig's boyhood home, Hohenschwangau Castle, and then the neighboring Neuschwanstein on the hill. If you arrive late, you'll spend a couple of hours in the ticket line and may find all tours booked.

Ludwig's extravagance and Romanticism earned this Bavarian king the title "Mad" King Ludwig...and an early death. After Bavarians complained about the money Ludwig spent on castles, the 40-year-old king was found dead in a lake under suspicious circumstances.

Hohenschwangau Castle, where Ludwig grew up, offers a good look at his life. Like its more famous neighbor, it takes about an hour to tour. Afterward, head up the hill to Ludwig's castle in the air.

Neuschwanstein Castle, which is about as old as the Eiffel Tower, is a textbook example of 19th-century Romanticism. After the Middle Ages ended, people disparagingly named that era "Gothic," or barbarian. Then, all of a sudden, in the 1800s it was hip to be square, and Neo-Gothic became the rage. Throughout Europe, old castles were restored and new ones built—wallpapered with chivalry. King Ludwig II put his medieval fantasy on the hilltop not for defensive reasons, but simply because he liked the view.

The lavish interior, covered with damsels in distress,

Germany's Top Destinations

Berlin ▲▲▲   allow 3-5 days
Vibrant and reunified capital, featuring state-of-the-art museums, cutting-edge architecture, and trendy neighborhoods, along with evocative monuments of the Wall that once divided the city and country

Top Sights
   Reichstag Historic parliament building with a modern glass dome
   Brandenburg Gate Gateway at the former border of East and West
   Memorial to the Murdered Jews of Europe Compelling monument
   German History Museum Narrative of the country's tumultuous past
   Berlin Wall Memorial Exhibits at the lone surviving stretch of intact Wall
   Pergamon and Neues Museums Classical and Egyptian antiquities
   Gemäldegalerie Top collection of Old Master European paintings

Nearby
   Potsdam Frederick the Great's palace playground
   Sachsenhausen Concentration camp museum and memorial

Munich ▲▲▲   2 days
Lively, livable city with a traffic-free center, good museums, Baroque palaces, stately churches, rollicking beer halls, and sprawling parks

Top Sights
   Marienplatz Main square with glockenspiel show
   Hofbräuhaus Famous beer hall
   Residenz Opulent palace and treasury of Bavarian royalty
   Art Museums Alte Pinakothek, Neue Pinakothek, and Pinakothek der Moderne

Nearby
   Dachau First Nazi concentration camp, now a museum
   Andechs Monastery Monk-brewed beer in bucolic setting

Bavaria ▲▲▲   2-3 days
Alps-straddling region boasting the fairy-tale castles of Neuschwanstein, Hohenschwangau, and Linderhof (with Ehrenberg across the Austrian border); inviting villages such as the handy home base **Füssen** and adorable **Oberammergau;** and the towering Zugspitze and its high-altitude lifts

Rothenburg and the Romantic Road ▲▲   1-2 days
Well-preserved medieval city with half-timbered buildings, cobbled lanes, and walkable walls; a popular stop on the Romantic Road scenic route through lovely countryside and time-passed towns

Rhine Valley ▲▲   2 days
Mighty river steeped in legend, where storybook villages (including charming home-base towns **Bacharach** and **St. Goar**) cluster under imposing castles, such as Rheinfels and Marksburg

Mosel Valley ▲▲   1-2 days
Peaceful meandering river lined with tiny wine-loving cobbled towns, such as handy **Cochem** and quaint **Beilstein,** plus my favorite European castle, Burg Eltz

Baden-Baden and the Black Forest ▲   1-2 days
High-class resort/spa town of **Baden-Baden,** with pampered bath experiences and a grand casino; lively university city of **Freiburg** and cozy village of **Staufen;** and forested countryside rife with healthy hikes, folk museums, and cuckoo clocks

Nürnberg ▲▲   1 day
Old town core and great museums, along with thoughtful reminders of Nazi past and a huge Christmas market

With more time, consider visiting
Dresden Baroque palaces, WWII history, and delightful riverside scene
Erfurt and Wittenberg Martin Luther's stomping grounds
Frankfurt Skyscrapers and modern-day urban Germany
Cologne Riverside city highlighted by spectacular Gothic cathedral
Hamburg Rejuvenated port city with infamous nightlife
Leipzig Bach and Cold War sights in the former East Germany
Trier Roman monuments, including the Porta Nigra gate

dragons, and knights in gleaming armor, is enchanting. (A little knowledge of Wagner's operas goes a long way in bringing these stories to life.) Ludwig had great taste for a mad king. Read up on this political misfit—a poetic hippie king in the realpolitik age of Bismarck. After the tour, climb farther up the hill to Mary's Bridge for the best view of this crazy yet picturesque castle.

This is a busy day. By lunchtime, catch the bus to Reutte and get ready for a completely different castle experience. With picnic and directions in hand, walk 30 minutes (or take a taxi) out of town to the Ehrenberg Castle Ensemble, the brooding ruins of four castles. If Neuschwanstein was the medieval castle dream, Ehrenburg is the medieval castle reality. The 13th-century rock pile provides a super opportunity to let your imagination off its leash.

The impressive castle ensemble (once consisting of four buildings) was built to defend against the Bavarians and to bottle up the strategic Via Claudia trade route, which cut through the Alps as it connected Italy and Germany. For centuries, the castle was the seat of government, which ruled an area called the "judgment of Ehrenberg" (roughly the same as today's district of Reutte). When the emperor came by, he stayed here. In 1604, the ruler moved downtown into more comfortable quarters, and the castle was no longer a palace. After several battles, the castle eventually fell into disrepair, leaving only this evocative shell and a whiff of history.

You can see Ehrenberg's castles reconstructed on Reutte's restaurant walls. Ask at your hotel where you can find a folk evening full of slap-dancing and yodel foolery. A hot, hearty dinner and an evening of Tirolean entertainment

Fanciful castles decorate the foothills of the Alps along the German-Austrian border. King Ludwig's Neuschwanstein is less than a century older than the castle it inspired at Disneyland.

is a fitting way to raise the drawbridge on your memorable "Castle Day."

Getting Naked in Baden-Baden

Since the Roman emperor bathed in the mineral waters of Baden-Baden, this Black Forest town has welcomed those in need of a good soak. In the 19th century, it was Germany's ultimate spa resort, and even today the name Baden-Baden is synonymous with relaxation in a land where the government still pays its overworked citizens to take a little spa time.

It's long been a frustration for me that Americans won't go to a European spa because they're too self-conscious to get naked with a bunch of strangers. For me, enjoying the baths at Friedrichsbad in Baden-Baden is one of Europe's most elegant experiences. If you come here, don't miss out.

My experience kicked off with a weight check—92 kilos. The attendant led me under the industrial-strength shower—a torrential kickoff, pounding my head and shoulders and obliterating the rest of the world. He then gave me slippers and a towel, ushering me into a dry-heat room with fine wooden lounges—slats too hot to sit on without the towel.

Finally, it was time for my massage. I climbed gingerly onto the marble slab and lay belly-up. The masseur held up two mitts and asked, "Hard or soft?" In the spirit of wild abandon, I said "hard," not even certain what that would mean to my skin. I got the coarse, Brillo-Pad scrub-down, but it was still extremely relaxing. Finished with a Teutonic spank, I was sent off into the pools. Nude, without my glasses, and not speaking the language, I was gawky, careening between steam rooms and cold plunges.

In the end, it all led to the mixed section. This is where Americans get uptight. The parallel spa facilities intersect, bringing men and women together to share the finest three pools. Here, all are welcome to glide under exquisite domes in perfect silence, like aristocratic swans. Germans are nonchalant, tuned into their bodies and focused on solitary relaxation. Tourists are tentative, trying to be cool, but more aware of their nudity. Really, there's nothing sexy about it. Just vivid life in full flower.

The climax is the cold plunge. I'm not good with cold water—yet I absolutely loved this. You must not wimp out on the cold plunge.

Finally, the attendant escorted me into the quiet room and asked when I'd like to be awoken. I told him closing time.

He swaddled me in hot sheets and a brown blanket and laid me down warm, flat on my back, among 20 hospital-type beds. Only one other bed was occupied; he seemed dead. I stared up at the ceiling and some time later was jolted awake by my own snore.

Leaving, I weighed myself again: 91 kilos. I had shed 2.2 pounds of sweat. Stepping into the cool evening air, I was thankful my hotel was a level two-block stroll away. In my room, I fell in slow motion onto my down comforter, the big pillow puffing around my head like the Flying Nun. Wonderfully naked under my clothes, I could only think, "Ahhhh. Baden-Baden."

Standing at the Top of the World

One of my favorite places to be in Europe is atop the Zugspitze—the highest point in Germany. Standing on this 9,700-foot peak, you can't help but marvel at the thought that you are above everyone else in the entire country—number one out of 82 million. From here, facing south, I feel like a maestro conducting a symphony of snow-capped peaks, as the mighty Alps stretch seemingly forever to the right and left.

The Zugspitze also marks the border between Germany and Austria. There are two separate terraces—Bavarian and Tirolean—connected by a narrow walk that once served as the border station. Before Europe united, you had to show your passport just to walk across the mountaintop. Crossing was a big deal—you'd get your passport stamped at a little blue house and shift your currency from shillings to marks.

The Zugspitze marks the border of Germany and Austria. Although Germany's highest peak, it's just a wannabe among Austria's mightier Alps.

Lifts from both countries meet at the top. As if waging an epic battle of alpine engineering, just a few years after the Austrians built a cable car to their Zugspitze station, the Germans drilled through the mountain (in 1931) so that a cogwheel train could deposit nature lovers on a glacier just below their side of the summit.

Today, whether you ascend from the Austrian or German side, this is one of the few opportunities to straddle the border between two great nations while enjoying an incredible view. Once you're done admiring the mountains, you can head to the restaurant

that claims—irrefutably—to be the "highest *Biergarten* in Deutschland."

Medieval Rothenburg

Thirty years ago, I fell in love with Rothenburg in the rough. At that time, the town still fed a few farm animals within its medieval walls. Today its barns are hotels, its livestock are tourists, and Rothenburg has turned into a medieval theme park.

But Rothenburg is still the best-preserved medieval town in Germany—and possibly all of Europe. Many also consider it a horrible tourist trap. The place is stampeded midday with visiting tour groups, eager to buy faux traditional Christmas ornaments. The town even created its own traditional pastry—the *Schneeball* (a powdered-doughnut-like "snowball"). Yet when I pass through its medieval gates, I feel like a kid who just got a three-day pass for all the rides at Disneyland. I simply love Rothenburg.

In Rothenburg, medieval life comes alive in its cobbled alleys. The ramparts are intact, still walkable, and come complete with arrow slits for notching an imaginary crossbow. The fish tanks next to the water fountains continue to evoke the days when marauding armies would besiege the town, and the townspeople would survive on the grain in its lofts and the trout in its tanks. The monastery garden still has its medicinal herbs. And the Medieval Crime and Punishment Museum shows graphically how people were disciplined back when life was nasty, brutish, and short. Some travelers react with horror; others wish for a gift shop.

But beyond the medieval ambience, it's the local residents who bring the town to life. Hans-Georg, the night watchman, stokes his lamp and walks wide-eyed tourists through the back lanes telling stories of hot oil and great plagues.

In Rothenburg, Germany's best-preserved medieval walled town, you can skip the "snowballs" (*Schneeballen*, a "tradition" kept alive for tourists), but don't miss spending a delightful hour touring with the night watchman.

Spry Klaus, who runs a B&B above his grocery store, takes travelers jogging with him each evening at 7:30. Another B&B owner, Norry, plays in a Dixieland band, loves to jam, and has invented a fascinating hybrid saxophone/trombone called the Norryphone.

At the English Conversation Club, held every Wednesday night at a town pub, locals enjoy a weekly excuse to get together, drink, and practice their fanciest English on each other and on visiting tourists. Once Anneliese, who runs the Friese shop (my favorite souvenir store in town), invited me to join her. So I meandered into the pub through candlelit clouds of smoke and squeezed a three-legged stool up to a table already crowded with family and friends.

Anneliese poured me a glass of wine, then pulled a *Schneeball* from a bag. Raising a cloud of powdered sugar as she poked at the name on the now empty bag, she said, "Friedel is the bakery I explained you about. They make the best *Schneeball*. I like it better than your American doughnut. Every day I eat one. But only at this bakery."

For years, Anneliese has playfully tried to get me to write good things about *Schneeballen*. I put *Schneeballen* (which originated in a hungrier age as a way to get more mileage out of leftover dough) in that category of penitential foods—like lutefisk—whose only purpose is to help younger people remember the suffering of their parents. Nowadays these historic pastries are pitched to the tourists in caramel, chocolate, and other flavors unknown in feudal times.

Shoving a big doughy ball my way, Anneliese said, "You like to eat this?"

I broke off a little chunk, saying, "Only a teeny-weeny *bisschen*."

After I left the pub for the night, I passed Hans-Georg, the night watchman dressed in medieval garb, finishing up his spiel in the town square with his group: "Now I must call the 'all's well.' You, my friends, should hurry home. Bed is the best place for good people at this hour."

Heading toward my hotel, I heard him calling, "All's well!"

More German Experiences

My Favorite Castle: Nestled in an enchanted forest just above the Mosel River, Burg Eltz is my favorite castle in all of Europe. The castle avoided wars and was never destroyed, remaining in the Eltz family for more than eight centuries. The current owner, an elderly countess who enjoys flowers, always has grand arrangements adorning the public rooms.

The castle is furnished throughout basically as it was 500 years ago. That's unusual in castles. For your best approach, start from the Moselkern train station on foot. After hiking for more than an hour through an ancient forest where you'd expect Friar Tuck or Martin Luther to be hiding out, the castle of your fantasies suddenly appears.

Paying Homage in Berlin: Germany's capital city is speckled with touching memorials that honor victims of past sins. The Memorial to the Murdered Jews of Europe, consisting of 2,711 gravestone-like pillars, was the first formal, government-sponsored Holocaust memorial. Using the word "murdered" in the title was intentional, a sign that Germany, as a nation, was officially admitting to a crime. The Monument to the Murdered Sinti and Roma of Europe remembers the roughly 500,000 Sinti and Roma (Gypsy) victims of the Holocaust. The Memorial to Politicians Who Opposed Hitler is a simple row of slate slabs dedicated to the 96 members of the Reichstag who were persecuted and murdered because they didn't agree with Chancellor Hitler. One place with little to see is the site of the bunker where Hitler committed suicide in 1945. It's just a rough parking lot with an information plaque.

Simple, Unspoiled Erfurt: Long ago I gave up looking for an untouristy, half-timbered medieval German town. But recently, I stumbled upon it in the sleepy town of Erfurt. The capital of the German region of Thuringia, Erfurt has history swinging from its eaves. It's the rare city in the center of Germany that emerged relatively unscathed from World War II, after which it became stuck in the strange cocoon of East German communism for half a century. Erfurt is most notable as the place where Martin Luther studied and became a monk, essentially planting the seeds from which grew the Protestant Reformation in 1517. Without the pivotal accomplishments of the Reformation, the Bible would still be read in Latin and

LEFT Burg Eltz, on the Mosel River, is my favorite castle to tour in Germany.

CENTER The Memorial to Politicians Who Opposed Hitler in Berlin is a reminder of the hell Germany lived through in the 1930s and 1940s.

RIGHT For Luther fans, Erfurt is a must-see.

interpreted for us by priests. For me, as a Lutheran, coming to Erfurt is a bit like a Catholic going to Rome.

CULTURE AND TRADITIONS: EVERYTHING'S SO...GERMAN

Beer and *Biergartens*

One of the most satisfying sounds you'll hear in Germany is a big *whop!* as they tap a classic old wooden keg of beer. Hearing this, every German knows they're in for a good, fresh mug.

Germans are serious about their beer. It's regulated by the Reinheitsgebot (Purity Decree) of 1516—the oldest food and beverage law in the world—which dictates that only four ingredients may be used: malt, yeast, hops, and water. There are four main types of Germanic beers: pale lager *(helles Bier)*, dark beer *(dunkles Bier)*, white/wheat beer *(Weissbier* or *Weizenbier)*, and pilsner.

The best place to sample Germanic beer culture is at a *Biergarten*, where long skinny tables stretch beneath shady chestnut trees. This is where Germans meet up with friends and family, relax, and maybe grab a bite to eat. Picnickers can bring their own food or buy it from a self-service stand, then sit at any table without a tablecloth. Covered tables are reserved for people who are being served.

My favorite *Biergarten* (and German beer) is an hour's drive outside Munich at the Andechs Monastery. The stately church stands as it has for centuries, topping a hill at the foot of the Alps. Its Baroque interior—and its beer hall—both stirs the soul and stokes the appetite. The hearty meals come in medieval proportions. Whenever I come here, I get a knuckle of pork, spiral-cut radishes, sauerkraut, a huge pretzel, and a liter of beer (called *eine Mass*, though I'd call it "ein pitcher").

What's more Bavarian than that? Once I asked my German friend if they sell half-liters of beer, to which he replied, "This is a *Biergarten*, not a kindergarten!"

Sausage, Sausage Everywhere

Unless you're a vegetarian, it's hard to leave Germany without sampling sausage *(Wurst)*. Options go far beyond the hometown hot dog. There are literally hundreds of regional variations, including *Nürnberger* (short, spicy, the size of your little finger, and served three in a bun); *Currywurst* (grilled, sliced up, and drenched with a curry-infused tomato sauce); and *Weisswurst* ("white" veal sausage that's boiled, peeled, and eaten with sweet mustard and a fresh soft pretzel).

Most fast-food restaurants (*Schnell Imbiss*) offer sausage on the menu, but I like to go local at a sausage stand (*Würstchenbude*). In Berlin, I look for human hot dog stands. These hot-dog hawkers don an ingenious harness that hangs off the body, allowing them to cook and serve *Wurst* on the fly.

> ## Munich's Oktoberfest
>
> The 1810 marriage reception of King Ludwig I (the grandfather of "Mad" King Ludwig II) was such a success that it turned into an annual bash. These days, Munich's Oktoberfest lasts just over two weeks—from late September into early October. Every night, eight huge beer tents fill with thousands of people eager to show off their stein-hoisting skills. A million gallons of beer later, they roast the last ox. If you plan to come, reserve a room early (Oktoberfest.de).

Christmas Markets

German towns big and small have been lighting up with Christmas markets (*Christkindlesmarkt*) each December for centuries. One of the biggest is Nürnberg's market, with 200 wooden stalls selling handicrafts from local artisans. A traditional center for toy-making in Germany, Nürnberg offers up market ambience that's classier than your average crafts fair, with no canned music, fake greenery, or plastic kitsch. As far back as 1610, a proclamation warned that "indecent joke articles would be confiscated."

Christmas markets are more than a shopping spree; they're places to enjoy a genuinely homey atmosphere. You'll wrap your mittens around a mug of hot-spiced wine while carolers sing in the background. Because a throwaway cup would ruin the experience, you'll pay a deposit for a nicely decorated ceramic mug. You can either return the mug or keep it as a collectible, as each year there's a different model.

Fast, Dependable Trains

At 12:14, I settle into my seat on the luxurious German bullet train, and at 12:16, we glide out of the station. In no time, I'm rocketing toward my next destination. German trains are as slick as can be—clean, modern, comfortable, and on time. ICE trains are the country's fastest, zipping from city to city at up to 200 miles per hour. IC and EC trains are slower, but only relatively—up to 125 miles per hour. Inexpensive

regional trains are substantially
slower, but can help stretch a budget.

Fast trains allow you to maximize
sightseeing. For instance, on an ICE
train, you can get from Munich to
Nürnberg in just one hour or from
Frankfurt to Cologne in less than
90 minutes. German trains are so
quiet and efficient that I almost miss
the old clackity-clackity rhythm
of the rails. It's been replaced by a nearly silent swoosh, as
futuristic trains cut like bullets through the green and tidy
countryside.

Germany Travel Resources from Rick Steves

Guidebooks
Check out Rick's guidebooks covering all of Germany; Berlin; Rothenburg & the
Rhine; and Munich & Salzburg; plus his German phrase book

Audio Europe
Download Rick's free Audio Europe app, with interviews about Germany and self-
guided audio tours, including walks through Berlin, Munich, Rothenburg, and a
best of the Rhine tour

TV Shows
The quintessence of Germany with Rick as your host, viewable on public television and at RickSteves.com. Episodes cover Berlin, Munich and the Alps, Dresden
and Leipzig, Frankfurt and Nürnberg, Hamburg and the Luther Trail, Cologne and
the Black Forest, Rothenburg and the Rhine River, Luther and the Reformation,
and the Story of Fascism in Europe

Organized Tours
Small group tours, with itineraries planned by Rick: Best of Germany in 13 Days;
Germany, Austria & Switzerland in 14 Days; Berlin, Prague & Vienna in 12 Days;
Munich, Salzburg & Vienna in 8 Days; My Way Alpine Europe, Best of Europe (both
include stops in Germany)

*For more on all of these resources, visit RickSteves.com. For Germany trip-planning
tips, see RickSteves.com/europe/germany.*

Switzerland

Mountainous, efficient Switzerland is one of Europe's most appealing destinations. Wedged neatly between Germany, Austria, France, and Italy, Switzerland borrows what's best from its neighbors—and adds a healthy dose of chocolate, cowbells, and cable cars. Fiercely independent and decidedly high-tech, the Swiss stubbornly hold on to their quaint traditions, too.

Despite the country's small size, Switzerland's regions maintain their distinct cultural differences, partly because historically the wild geography has kept people apart. Switzerland has four official languages: German, French, Italian, and Romansh. And yet, regardless of which language is spoken, the entire country is unmistakably Swiss. Everywhere you go, you'll notice a dedication to order and organization, right down to the precision stacking of a woodpile.

Switzerland has more than its share of cosmopolitan cities (Zürich, Luzern, Bern, Lausanne, Lugano), but let's face

it—travelers don't flock to Switzerland for urban adventure. The Alps are the premier destination. Alpine villages (such as Gimmelwald) give you a taste of rural Switzerland, and are the perfect base for riding lifts to dramatic alpine panoramas and taking unforgettably scenic hikes.

FAVORITE SIGHTS AND MEMORABLE EXPERIENCES IN SWITZERLAND

The Swiss Alps in Your Lap

When I say I'm planning to go to Gimmelwald, Swiss people assume I mean Grindelwald, the famous resort in the next valley. When assured that Gimmelwald is my target, they lean forward, widen their eyes, and—with their singsongy Swiss-German accent—ask, "Und how do you know about Gimmelvald?"

This traffic-free village, hanging nonchalantly on the edge of a cliff high above the Lauterbrunnen Valley, has more cow troughs than mailboxes. Here, white-bearded old men smoke hand-carved pipes, and blonde-braided children play "barn" instead of "house." Big stones sit like heavy checkers on old rooftops, awaiting nature's next move. While these stones protect the shingles from violent winter winds, in summer it's so quiet you can hear the cows ripping tufts of grass. There's nothing but air between Gimmelwald and the rock face of the nearby Jungfrau Mountain. Small avalanches across the valley look and sound like distant waterfalls. Kick a soccer ball wrong and it ends up a mile below, on the valley floor.

Gimmelwald was never developed like neighboring towns because its residents made sure it got rated an "avalanche zone," and developers couldn't get building permits. Consequently, while neighboring villages are dominated by

High in the Swiss Alps, farmer Peter cuts hay to feed his cows, gathers it on a tarp *(left)*, and rides his bovine salad down the steep slopes, as if on a barge, to his barn in the humble village of Gimmelwald *(right)*.

condos owned by big-city folks who come by only for vacations, Gimmelwald is still inhabited by locals—about 120 in all—and its traditions survive.

Gimmelwald is a poor town whose traditional economy depends on government subsidies for survival. Each year, its citizens systematically harvest the steep hillside outside their windows. Entire families cut and gather every inch of hay. After harvesting what the scythe can reach, they pull hay from nooks and crannies by hand. Half a day is spent harvesting what a machine could cut in two minutes on a flat field. But this is how the farmers of Gimmelwald have made their living forever—lovingly cutting the hay, to feed the cows, to make the cheese, to feed us people.

From Gimmelwald, a modern gondola goes up the nearly 10,000-foot-high peak of the Schilthorn. For the most memorable breakfast around, I ride the early-morning gondola up to the summit and its solar-powered revolving restaurant. There, I sip my coffee slowly to enjoy an entire panoramic rotation of the Eiger, Mönch, and Jungfrau mountains.

Outside, I watch hang gliders methodically set up and jump into airborne ecstasy. It's possible to hike straight down from the summit, but the first gondola station below the peak, Birg, is the best starting point for high-country hikes. Two minutes from the Birg station and I'm completely alone, surrounded by a harsh and unforgiving alpine world. A black ballet of rocks is accompanied by cowbells and a distant river. Wisps of clouds are exclamation points. After a steep descent, I step out of the forest at the top end of the village I call home. Walking over a pastel carpet of gold clover, bellflowers, and daisies, I'm surrounded by butterflies and cheered on by a vibrant chorus of grasshoppers, bees, and crickets.

Fast Facts

Biggest cities: Zürich (377,000), Geneva (188,000), Basel (165,000), Bern (capital, 126,000)

Size: 16,000 square miles (almost twice the size of New Jersey), population 8 million

Locals call it: Officially it's the Confoederatio Helvetica (Latin for Swiss Confederation); also known as Die Schweiz (German), Suisse (French), Svizzera (Italian), and Svizra (Romansh)

Currency: Swiss franc

Languages: Swiss German (most of Switzerland), French (to the west), Italian (to the south), Romansh (southeastern mountains)

Key date: 1815, Switzerland's borders (and its neutrality) are established at the Congress of Vienna

Biggest festival: Fasnacht pre-Lenten carnival (February/March, countrywide but biggest in Basel, Bern, and Luzern)

Mountain peaks exceeding 10,000 feet: 437

Handy Swiss-German phrases: *Grüezi* (hello; **grit**-see), *Merci* (thank you; **mehr**-see), *Uf Widerluege* (goodbye; oof **vee**-dehr-loo-eh-geh), *Meh schoggi, bitte* (More chocolate, please; meh **shoh**-chih **bit**-teh)

Tourist info: MySwitzerland.com

Switzerland's Top Destinations

Berner Oberland ▲▲▲   allow 2-3 days

High-mountain region popular for its characteristic villages and scenic hikes, lifts, and train rides, in the shadow of the Eiger, Mönch, and Jungfrau peaks

Top Sights

Gimmelwald Time-warp village overlooking Lauterbrunnen Valley
Schilthornbahn Cable car soaring to 9,748-foot Schilthorn peak
Jungfraubahn Train to 11,333-foot Jungfraujoch saddle, with snow activities
Männlichen to Kleine Scheidegg Hike Easy, mostly downhill hike with Eiger views

Bern ▲▲▲   1 day

Cozy Swiss capital, lassoed by a meandering river and embedded with shopping arcades, fine museums, and a Gothic cathedral

Appenzell ▲▲   1 day

Traditional region known for pastoral scenery, appealing folk museums, remarkably fragrant cheese, and the cliffs of Ebenalp

Lake Geneva and French Switzerland ▲▲   1-2 days

Switzerland's best castle, lakeside Château de Chillon; the cute cheese-making village of **Gruyères;** and the steeply situated, urbane, *très* French-speaking city of **Lausanne**

Luzern ▲▲   1 day

Thriving city on a mountain-ringed lake, with historic wooden bridges and well-presented museums; Golden Pass scenic rail journey to Montreux starts here

Zürich ▲▲   1 day

Another tidy city on a pretty lake, bustling with Swiss commerce, upscale shops, and an atmospheric old town

---

The finish line is a bench that sits at the high end of Gimmelwald—one of my "savor Europe" depots. From my perch, I survey the village. Chocolate log cabins are buttressed by a winter's supply of firewood lovingly stacked all the way to the eaves. Grassy fields radiate a vibrant green, as if plugged into the sun. In the Alps, nature and civilization mix it up comfortably, as if man and mountain shared the same crib.

River Swimming in Bern

It's a hot August day, and the waterfront park along the Aare River, in Switzerland's capital city of Bern, is packed with wet and happy people. They're hiking upstream in swimsuits just to float back into town. I join them—marveling at how

Lugano ▲   1 day

Leading city of Italian-speaking Switzerland, with Mediterranean feel; starting point for Bernina Express bus-and-train journey through the Swiss Alps and Italy, passing jaw-dropping mountains, glaciers, and waterfalls

With more time, consider visiting

Murten Walled village, with nearby Roman ruins and museum in **Avenches**
Zermatt Glitzy ski resort with old-fashioned core at the foot of the Matterhorn
Pontresina, Samedan, and St. Moritz Romansh-speaking mountain resort area

this exercise brings out the silly in a people who are generally anything but.

Every hundred yards, concrete steps lead into the swift-flowing river, which looks glacial blue, but is surprisingly warm. Leaping in, I'm immediately caught up in the racing current and propelled toward the grand city center, along with other carefree swimmers and a flotilla of rubber rafts.

Nearing downtown, I stroke over to snare a metal stair railing—I'm nervous that I'll miss the last one and rush toward the city's scary weir and, it seems, oblivion. Hanging onto the railing with me is a tanned and wiry grandmother and several giddy children, clearly enjoying an afternoon going up and down the river.

I crawl out, dry off, and put on the clothes that I'd

stashed here earlier. Setting out for a stroll, I come across more kids beating the heat, splashing in the squirt fountains spurting from the granite plaza in front of the parliament building. There are 26 fountains—one for each canton, or Swiss "state." Kids happily dance with each watery eruption, oblivious to the fact that half of Switzerland's gold stock is buried under the square, in the Swiss version of Fort Knox.

That evening for dinner, I walk downstream, where a trendy restaurant has been built over the river. I'm seated over see-through floorboards that expose the water where my tasty local trout might have been caught. The noisy roar of the rushing river masks the conversations of patrons sipping beer on open-air sofas.

Bern's old town, packed into a tight bend in the river, is a joy to explore on foot. After dinner, I amble through the lanes lined with miles of shopping arcades. This is my kind of shopping town: Prices are so high, there's no danger of buying. The local slang for the corridor under these arcades is *"Rohr"* (German for pipe). To stroll through the town is to go *"rohren"* (piping).

As the city grew over the centuries, its successive walls and moats were torn down, providing vast, people-friendly swaths of land. Today these elongated "squares" are popular for markets and outdoor cafés—the top places to be seen in the evening. I come upon an open-air performance by a jazz band whose lead instrument is a long alphorn, an improbable meeting of tradition and modernity.

Although I've said it's almost criminal to spend a sunny Swiss day anywhere but high in the Alps, the cities of Switzerland can be a delight, and I'd make an exception for urban but easygoing Bern.

Most people come to Switzerland for the mountains, but its cities are worth visiting, too. Located within a tight bend in the Aare River, the capital, Bern, with its fine arcades, is the most charming.

The most I can handle in alpine thrills is a *via ferrata*. Hitched to the cable with carabiners, I worked my way along the cliff high above the Lauterbrunnen Valley floor.

Scared Silly on the *Via Ferrata*

I'm careful not to list activities in my guidebooks that may encourage a traveler to take a risk on something that's dangerous. So when friends in the Lauterbrunnen Valley started talking about a great new outdoor experience called a *via ferrata*—a mountain route with fixed cables—I had to check it out myself.

I enlisted my B&B host, Olle, to join me. We put on helmets and mountaineering harnesses, clipped our carabiners into the first stretch of the 1.5-mile-long cable, and set off with a local guide. My hike on the "iron way" from Mürren to Gimmelwald proved to be the highlight of my entire trip.

The route took us along the very side of the cliff, like tiny window washers on a geologic skyscraper. About half of the route is easily walked, and I was lulled into wondering, what's the big deal? But for several hundred yards, the path literally hangs out over...nothing. The "trail" ahead of me was a series of steel rebar spikes jutting out from the side of the mountain. The cable, carabiner, and harness were there in case I passed out. For me, physically, this was the max. I was almost numb with fear.

At some points, ladders drilled vertically into the cliff made it easier (in my case, possible) to scramble up or down. There were three thrilling canyon crossings—by zipline, on a single high wire (with steadying wires for each hand), and the "iron way," finished with a terrifying hanging bridge.

After one particularly harrowing crossing—gingerly taking one rebar step after another—I said to the guide, "OK, now it gets easier?" And he said, "No. Now comes *die Hammer Ecke* (Hammer Corner)!" For about 500 feet, we crept across a perfectly vertical cliff face—feet gingerly gripping rebar loops, cold and raw hands on the cable, tiny cows and a rushing river 2,000 feet below me, a rock face rocketing directly above me—as my follow-the-cable path bent out of sight.

Three hours after we had clipped in, we finally reached the end. Olle and I beamed, exhilarated that we had survived our little personal test. We hugged our guide like a full-body high-five, knowing this was the thrill of a lifetime. For the next several nights, though, I awoke in the wee hours, clutching my mattress.

More Swiss Experiences

Switzerland's Best Castle: I like to imagine myself as a member of the aristocracy that inhabited Château de Chillon in the Middle Ages. The castle is set wistfully at the edge of Lake Geneva on the outskirts of Montreux. Remarkably well preserved, it has never been damaged or destroyed—it's always been inhabited and maintained. Because it's built on a rocky island, Château de Chillon has a uniquely higgledy-piggledy shape that combines a stout fortress and dank prison (on the land side) with a visually splendid residence (on the lake side). Over the centuries, the romantic castle has inspired a multitude of writers—Lord Byron, Victor Hugo, Charles Dickens, Goethe, Ernest Hemingway. (You can still see where Byron scratched his name into a column.) All the sumptuous detail indoors can't compare with what's outside, though. At the end of my visit, I curl up on a windowsill to enjoy lake views fit for a king.

Riding High: Switzerland's best attraction might just be hiding between the cities and the villages. In this land of rugged mountains and picture-perfect farms—perhaps more

LEFT Château de Chillon

RIGHT Scenic train riding in Switzerland

than anywhere else in Europe—the journey is the destination. Several trains, many with special panoramic cars, run picturesque routes through the country's prettiest places. The Glacier Express, which traverses southern Switzerland, gets my vote for the most scenic of these rides. Designed to maximize sightseeing thrills, the route is a masterpiece of railway engineering, with the train running through 91 tunnels and crossing 291 bridges. A toothed rack between the tracks helps the hardworking train drag itself up steep gradients, and these same teeth help slow the train on downhill sections. Using powerful snowplow engines to keep the track open through the snowy winter, the Glacier Express runs year-round.

CULTURE AND TRADITIONS: EVERYTHING'S SO...SWISS

Cheese Cuisine

The Swiss eat about 150,000 tons of cheese per year. After a few days of cheese plates for breakfast, cheese sandwiches for lunch, and cheese specialties for dinner, even the biggest cheese lovers might find they need a dairy detox.

There are two kinds of Swiss restaurants—with and without cooked cheese. The Swiss eat out at a "cooked cheese" restaurant because they don't want to perfume their houses with the smell. Some cheese dishes are meant for sharing, like raclette and fondue. For raclette, cheese is slowly melted on a special grill; as the cheese softens, diners scrape a chunk off and eat it with potatoes, pickled onions, and gherkins. Fondue is Switzerland's best-known cheese dish, made with Emmentaler or Gruyère melted with white wine, garlic, nutmeg, and cherry schnapps. Eating it is a communal affair, with everyone dipping cubes of bread

From a steamy fondue treat *(left)* to cheering the cows along on the day they head up to the high meadows *(right)*, Switzerland's traditions are alive, well, and accessible for travelers.

into the melted cheese with a long fork. A Swiss friend told me: "When we Swiss plan a cozy party we add '*FIGUGEGL*' to the invitation. It's pronounced like a word: fee-**goo**-geck-ul. This stands for '*Fondu isch guet und git e gueti Luune*' (Fondue is good and gives a good mood). When you read this, you know a good time is planned."

More Cowbells

Swiss dairy farming in the mountains isn't lucrative, but a lifestyle chosen to keep tradition alive. Rather than lose their children to the cities, Swiss farmers have the opposite problem: Kids argue about who gets to take over the family herd.

In summer, farmers strap elaborate ceremonial bells on their cows and take them up to huts at high elevations, where they stay for about 100 days. When the cows arrive at their summer home, the bells are hung under the eaves.

Hired hands get up at dawn to milk the cows, take them to pasture, and then milk the cows again in the evening. It's too difficult to transport the milk down to the village, so it is made into treasured "Alp cheese" right on the mountain. The character of each wheel of cheese is shaped by the herbs and flowers munched by the cows, and locals claim they can tell which valley the cows grazed in by the taste.

Meanwhile, the farmer follows the seasons up into the mountains, making hay while the sun shines and storing it above the huts. In late summer, the cows start down from the high pastures, moving from hut to hut, eating the hay prepared for them. The day the cows return to their home village is an impromptu festival, with the farmers parading their animals through town to their winter barn.

Money, Money, Money

A graffito in Zürich jokes: "Zürich = *zu reich, zu ruhig*" (too rich, too quiet). In a country with a reputation for being one of Europe's most expensive, Zürich is the major hub of international banking and finance. A huge part of the Swiss

Dining on a Budget

Grocery stores and cafeterias are a godsend for thrifty travelers in pricey Switzerland. Larger grocery stores often have a great selection of prepared foods and picnic fixings—perfect for al fresco dining. In most big cities, major department stores have a self-service eatery with lush salad bars, tasty entrées, and fresh-squeezed juices. Swiss hostels usually offer a fine four-course dinner that's often open to nonguests—just call first to reserve a spot.

Quench your thirst at Switzerland's free drinking fountains—with fresh, mountain-chilled water—in squares and other central points around cities and towns. Fill your bottle from the spout of any well-maintained public fountain unless you see a *kein Trinkwasser* ("not drinking water") sign.

economy is based on providing a safe and secret place for wealthy people from around the world to stash their money. (When bank fees are figured in, tax cheats and white-collar crooks actually get negative interest to keep their money anonymously in Switzerland.) Switzerland sticks to its own Swiss franc, partly because adopting the euro currency would require complying with European Union regulations, putting an end to the country's lucrative secrecy.

Switzerland Travel Resources from Rick Steves

Guidebooks
Check out Rick's guidebook covering all of Switzerland; plus his 3-in-1 French, Italian & German phrase book

Audio Europe
Download Rick's free Audio Europe app, with interviews about Swiss culture and sightseeing

TV Shows
The quintessence of Switzerland with Rick as your host, viewable on public television and at RickSteves.com. Episodes cover the Alps, Luzern, Lausanne, Bern, and Zürich

Organized Tours
Small group tours, with itineraries planned by Rick: Best of Switzerland in 12 Days; Germany, Austria & Switzerland in 14 Days; My Way Alpine Europe, Family Europe: London to Florence, Best of Europe (all include a stop in Switzerland)

For more on all of these resources, visit RickSteves.com. For Switzerland trip-planning tips, RickSteves.com/europe/switzerland.

Austria

Austria offers gorgeous alpine scenery, great museums, cobbled quaintness, and decadent pastry. Once the dynastic home of the Habsburg Empire (one of Europe's grandest), Austria is content to bask in good living and its opulent past. The Habsburgs built a vast kingdom of more than 50 million people by making love, not war—having lots of children and strategically marrying them into the other royal houses of Europe.

Today, this small, landlocked country clings to its storied past more than any other nation in Europe. The waltz is still the rage. Music has long been a key part of Austria's heritage. The giants of classical music—Haydn, Mozart, Beethoven—were born here or moved here to write and perform their masterpieces. Music lovers flock to Salzburg every summer to attend its popular festival. Vienna has the much-loved Opera House and Boys' Choir. But traditional

The gardens of Schönbrunn Palace, just outside Vienna, are made for endless wandering.

folk music is also part of the Austrian soul. The world's best-loved Christmas carol, "Silent Night," was written by two Austrians with just a guitar for accompaniment. And don't be surprised if you hear yodeling for someone's birthday.

The country is much more than its famous cities of Vienna and Salzburg. Awash with mountains and waterfalls, Austria is sprinkled with small towns (such as Hallstatt), ruined castles (Ehrenberg), and tucked-away farms (everywhere).

Austrians are relaxed, gregarious people who love hiking in the outdoors as much as enjoying a good cup of coffee in a café. With one of Europe's longest life spans and shortest work weeks, they specialize in *Gemütlichkeit*—meaning a warm, cozy, focus-on-the-moment feeling.

It must be nice to be past your prime—no longer troubled by being powerful, able to kick back and celebrate life, whether engulfed in mountain beauty or bathed in lavish high culture.

> ## Fast Facts
>
> **Biggest cities:** Vienna (capital, 1.8 million), Graz (275,000), Linz (200,000), Salzburg (148,000)
> **Size:** 32,400 square miles (about the size of South Carolina), population 8.2 million
> **Locals call it:** Österreich ("Eastern Realm")
> **Currency:** Euro
> **Key date:** June 28, 1914, Archduke Franz Ferdinand of Austria is assassinated, setting off World War I
> **Language:** German, with many words (especially for food) exclusive to Austria
> **Biggest festival:** Salzburg Festival (late July and August, classical music)
> **Handy German phrases:** *Grüss Gott* (Austrian version of hello, "May God greet you"; grews goht), *Bitte* (please; **bit**-teh), *Danke* (thank you; **dahn**-keh)
> **Tourist info:** Austria.info

FAVORITE SIGHTS AND MEMORABLE EXPERIENCES IN AUSTRIA

Lovely, Lovable Hallstatt

When I think of my favorite towns in Europe, I'll take the offbeat places, where creaky locals walk gingerly on creaky floorboards, and where each balcony sports a one-of-a-kind flowerbox. The tiny town of Hallstatt, positioned picture-perfectly on the shore of Lake Hallstatt, is just such a place.

Hallstatt, a two-hour train ride east of Salzburg, is the pride and joy of the Salzkammergut Lake District. It's a gentle land—idyllic and majestic—where lakes and mountains are shuffled sloppily together...the perfect place to commune with nature, Austrian-style. Even just arriving at Hallstatt is fun—from the train station, people take a shuttle boat across a lake to get to town. It's rare that a place's charm will get

LEFT Hallstatt is the cutest town in Austria.

RIGHT The area around Salzburg is dotted with old salt mines, like the one above Hallstatt. Dressed up like a miner, you'll slide down from one level to the next on wooden chutes.

me out of bed early, but there's something about the glassy waters of Lake Hallstatt viewed from the high end of town. The church spire is mirrored in the tranquil water, and then the shuttle boat slices through the reflection—like a knife putting a swirl in the icing on a big cake.

Bullied onto its lakeside ledge by a selfish mountain, Hallstatt seems tinier than it is. Its pint-size square is surrounded by ivy-covered guesthouses and cobbled lanes. It's a toy town, tourable on foot in about 10 minutes. But the ledge couldn't hold Hallstatt forever, and many of its buildings climb the mountainside. Still, land is limited—so limited that there's not enough room for the dead. Remains evicted from the cemetery are stacked neatly in an eerie chapel of decorated bones. Each skull has been carefully named, dated, and decorated. The men's skulls are painted with ivy, and the women's with roses.

Nearly three thousand years ago, this area was the major salt producer of Europe, when salt—a natural preservative for food—was in great demand. The economic and cultural boom put Hallstatt on the map back in Flintstone times. A humble museum next to the tourist office shows off Hallstatt's salty past. For a better look, I took a guided tour of what's said to be the world's oldest salt mine, located a thrilling funicular ride above downtown Hallstatt. Dressed up in an old miner's outfit, I walked through a tunnel dug in 1719 and into the mountain where the salt was mined, explored several caverns, and screamed down a long wooden chute while praying for no splinters.

These days, it can be a challenge to find vivid cultural traditions that survive in well-discovered places like Hallstatt. But on a recent visit, as the sun rose late over the towering Alps, my friend, who runs a restaurant in town, took me for a spin in his classic boat. It's a *Fuhr*, a centuries-old

Austria's Top Destinations

Vienna ▲▲▲   allow 2-4 days
Genteel and worldly capital city, brimming with a rich
Habsburg heritage (spectacular palaces and top-notch art
museums), grand classical music, a refined café tradition, and
convivial wine gardens

Top Sights
   St. Stephen's Cathedral Enormous, historic Gothic cathedral
   Hofburg Former winter palace of Habsburg emperors, with a treasury of crown jewels
   Schönbrunn Palace Spectacular summer residence, with manicured gardens
   Kunsthistorisches Museum Exhibit of Habsburgs' collection of European masters
   Vienna Opera Internationally renowned opera house

Salzburg ▲▲▲   2 days
Musical mecca huddled under a dramatic castle, with an old town full of winding
lanes, Baroque churches, Mozart landmarks, and *Sound of Music* kitsch

Salzkammergut ▲▲   1-2 days
Scenic land of lakes and forested mountains, starring the dramatically situated,
picturesque village of **Hallstatt**

Danube Valley ▲   1-2 days
Romantic, bikeable valley dotted with ruined castles, offset by the glorious Melk
Abbey and poignant Mauthausen concentration camp memorial

Tirol ▲   1-2 days
Austria's mountain-sports region encompasses view-rich **Innsbruck** and quaint
Hall; farther west, **Reutte** is a good castle home-base

boat design, which was made wide and flat for shipping heavy bushels of locally mined salt across shallow waters. Lunging rhythmically on the single oar, he said, "An hour on the lake is for me like a day of vacation." I asked about the oarlock, which looked like a skinny dog-chew doughnut, and he told me, "It's made from the gut of a bull—not of a cow, but a bull."

Returning to the weathered timber boathouse, we passed a teenage boy with a wooden club systematically grabbing trout from the fishermen's pen and killing them one by one with a stern whack to the noggin. Another man carried them to the tiny fishery to be gutted by a guy who, 40 years ago, did the stern whacking. A cat waited outside the door, confident his breakfast would be a good one. And restaurateurs and homemakers alike—their dining rooms decorated with trophies of big ones that didn't get away—lined up to buy fresh trout to feed the hungry tourists, or a good fish to cook for a special friend.

Traditions are embattled everywhere by the modern world, yet they manage to survive. Despite tourism—and sometimes thanks to tourism—traditional Europe hangs in there. So when I want to cloak myself in *Gemütlichkeit*, flowers, and cobblestones, I visit Hallstatt—where, when friends invite you to visit, they say, "Please come by. I'll cook you a good fish."

Toasting Vienna's Love of Life

If any European capital knows how to enjoy life, it's Vienna. Compared to most modern urban centers, the pace of life here is leisurely. Chatting with friends at a wine garden is not a special event but a frequent occurrence.

For many Viennese, the living room is down the street at the neighborhood coffeehouse, which offers fresh pastries,

From rich chocolate cakes to cozy wine gardens, it's hard not to get caught up in the good life when visiting Austria.

light lunches, a wide selection of newspapers, and a "take all the time you want" ambience (in spite of famously grumpy servers). One of my ritual stops is at Café Hawelka. Draped in its circa-1900 decor, this smoke-and-coffee-stained café seems frozen in time, with paintings by struggling artists (who couldn't pay for coffee), velvet couches, and a phone that rings for regulars. I could be sitting in a chair that had once been occupied by Trotsky, Hitler, Stalin, Freud, or any number of historical figures who rattled around Vienna 100 years ago. Savoring a *Buchtel* (a marmalade-filled doughnut), I ponder how Vienna was a place of intellectual tumult at the end of World War I, as Europe's family-run empires crumbled.

> ## Fast Food, Austrian-Style
>
> In Austria, you're never far from a *Würstelstand* (sausage stand). Most bakeries sell small, cheap sandwiches; look for *Leberkäsesemmel* (roll filled with Austrian meatloaf) as well as *Schnitzelsemmel* (schnitzel sandwich). *Stehcafés* (food counters) usually offer open-face finger sandwiches (*belegte Brote*) with a wide array of toppings. For a quick bite, have a deli make you a *Wurstsemmel*—a basic sausage sandwich.

Another one of my Vienna rituals is to pop into Demel, the ultimate Viennese chocolate shop and bakery. It's filled with Art Nouveau boxes of choco-dreams come true: *Kandierte Veilchen* (candied violet petals), *Katzenzungen* (chocolate shaped like "cats' tongues"), and an impressive cancan of cakes—including the Sacher torte, a local specialty. Apart from its apricot filling, the Sacher-torte recipe seems pretty simple...chocolate on chocolate. Fancy shops like Demel boast "K.u.K." on their signs, meaning good enough for the *"König und Kaiser"*—king and emperor (same guy). Easily the saddest thing I witnessed one summer was when, promptly at closing time, all the unsold cakes and pies on Demel's luxurious shelves were unceremoniously dumped into big plastic garbage bags.

For another royally good experience, I head to Vienna's wine gardens—the *Heurigen*. Clustered in foothills at the city's doorstep, mostly in the legendary Vienna Woods, wine-garden restaurants feature cold-cut buffets paired with fine Austrian wines in an old-village atmosphere with strolling musicians. If I'm in town during fall, I try the *Sturm*, the semifermented new wine made in the fall from the season's first grape harvest. Of the many wine-garden suburbs, I like untouristy Nussdorf.

No matter where I turn in this pleasant city, it's clear that culture is king, and locals are experts at celebrating the art of good living. Here's to Vienna: *Prost!* Cheers!

Alpine Escapes

Even those who know a Rocky Mountain high find something special about the Alps. It's exhilarating to hike on the hilly, wooded trails, passing happy yodelers, sturdy grannies, and dirndled moms with apple-cheeked kids.

In western Austria, the same mountains that put Innsbruck on the vacation map surround nearby Hall. For a lazy look at life in the high Alps around these towns, drive up to 5,000-foot Hinterhornalm and walk to a remote working farm.

Begin your ascent in Gnadenwald, a chalet-filled village sandwiched between Hall and its Alps. Pay at the toll hut, then wind your way upward, marveling at the crazy amount of energy put into this road, to the rustic Hinterhornalm restaurant. This place serves hearty food with a cliff-hanger of a view. Hinterhornalm is a hang-gliding springboard. On sunny days, it's a butterfly nest of thrill seekers ready to fly.

From there, it's a level 20-minute walk to Walderalm, a cluster of three dairy farms with 70 cows that share their meadow with the clouds. The cows ramble along ridgetop lanes surrounded by cut-glass peaks. The ladies of the farms serve soup, sandwiches, and drinks (very fresh milk in the afternoon) on rough plank tables. Below you spreads the Inn River Valley and, in the distance, tourist-filled Innsbruck.

Another alpine escape is Fallerschein, west of Innsbruck. Barely accessible by car, this isolated log-cabin village is smothered with mountain goodness, set in a flower-speckled world of serene slopes, sleepy cows, and musical breezes. Here thunderstorms roll down its valley as if it were God's bowling alley. But the blissfully simple pint-size church on the high ground seems to promise that this huddle of houses will remain standing. The people sitting on benches are Austrian vacationers or clandestine lovers who've rented cabins. Fallerschein is notorious as a hideaway for those having affairs.

More Austrian Experiences

Savoring Salzburg: Salzburg, a musical mecca, is forever smiling to the tunes of Mozart and the *Sound of Music*. The city puts on a huge annual festival as well as constant concerts. With eight million sightseers prowling its cobbled lanes each year, the city can feel pretty touristy. You don't go to Salzburg to avoid the sightseers. You go to experience a town that, in spite of the crowds, is thoroughly entertaining.

After rambling through the old town and past the glorious cathedral, I like to take the funicular up to the towering Hohensalzburg Fortress. One of Europe's mightiest castles, it dominates Salzburg's skyline and offers commanding views of city and countryside.

Another way to take in town and country is on a *Sound of Music* bus tour, sampling Salzburg sights, movie locations, and lovely stretches of the surrounding Salzkammergut Lake District. I took this tour skeptically and actually liked it, even though rolling through the Austrian countryside with 30 Americans singing "Doe, a deer..." is pretty cheesy. But, no matter. With its musical legacies, magnificent scenery, and rich history, Salzburg is a symphony—and you don't have to climb every mountain to enjoy it.

Evocative Castles: Outside the sleepy town of Reutte, not far from the German border, are the ruins of four buildings that once made up the largest fort in Tirol—Ehrenberg. There's the fortified Klause toll booth on the valley floor, which levied duties along the Via Claudia in Roman times; Ehrenberg, the oldest castle on the first hill (from 1296); Fort Claudia, a smaller castle across the valley; and Schlosskopf, the mighty and more modern castle high above. For the best overview of the site, wobble over the 1,200-foot-long pedestrian bridge suspended 300 feet above the valley floor, connecting Ehrenberg with Fort Claudia. (To combine a visit to Ehrenberg with "Mad" Kind Ludwig's castles just across the border, see "Castle Day in Bavaria and Tirol," page 695.)

When I first visited Ehrenberg, one castle crowned its mountain like an ornery barnacle; the others were lost in a thick forest. Inspired, I hiked up into the misty mountain of meaningless chunks of castle wall pinned down by trees, moss, and sword ferns. But now the hungry forest has been

LEFT Salzburg has a main street lined with traditional business signs.

CENTER One of Europe's biggest castles keeps watch over Salzburg.

RIGHT The stark and evocative Ehrenberg ruins above Reutte

cut away to reveal the castle ensemble, and children and adults with medieval fantasies can leap from rampart to rampart...sword ferns swinging.

CULTURE AND TRADITIONS: EVERYTHING'S SO...AUSTRIAN

Musical Notes

Vienna has a long history as Europe's music capital, and music lovers make a pilgrimage of sorts to see the houses of the composers who lived and worked here. The homes of Schubert, Brahms, Haydn, Beethoven, and Mozart all host museums—but they are mostly small and forgettable. For the best music history experience, I like the Haus der Musik, a museum that honors the great Viennese composers with fine artifacts and fun interactive exhibits. You can try your hand at virtually conducting the Vienna Philharmonic—if you mess up, the "musicians" will refuse to play.

Classical music performances are everywhere in town, booking up to 10,000 seats a night. The Vienna State Opera alone belts out 300 glittering shows a year. Fans of toe-tapping waltzes head to the Kursalon, an elegant hall in the main city park, where Johann Strauss directed concerts 100 years ago. The Vienna Boys' Choir performs in the Hofburg's Imperial Music Chapel. Mozart lovers choose the intimate Theater an der Wien, designed in 1801 especially for Wolfie's operas. This gilded high culture can be surprisingly affordable—a standing-room ticket for the opera is about the same price as a cinema ticket. Major events can be sold out for weeks—although there are plenty of live music options available without advance booking.

In Vienna's Haus der Musik, you can virtually conduct the city's famed orchestra.

During the summer, a thriving people scene erupts each evening in the park in front of Vienna's City Hall, where filmed opera and classical music performances are shown for free. Comfy benches with room for about 2,000 viewers face the 60-foot-wide screen. Scores of food stands and picnic tables are set up. There are no plastic cups, thank you, just real plates and glasses—Vienna wants the quality of the dining experience to be as good as the music. And the people-watching? It's *con brio.*

Enjoy some *Germknödel* goodness at high altitude.

Mountains

Much of Austria's character is found in its mountains. Austrians excel in mountain climbing and winter sports such as downhill skiing, which was born in Tirol. When watching ski races, you'll often see fans celebrating with red-and-white flags at the finish line: Austria has won more Olympic medals in alpine skiing than any other country. Innsbruck alone—twice the host of the Winter Olympics—is surrounded by 150 mountain lifts, 1,250 miles of trails, and 250 hikers' and skiers' huts. Ski lifts are busy both winter and summer, taking nature lovers to dizzying heights, where the views are big, and the hiking possibilities are endless.

Taking a break at a cozy, hospitable hut is a traditional part of Austrian mountain fun. High-altitude huts serve fortifying treats such as *Germknödel* (a sweet dumpling topped with poppy seeds and laced with plum jam), *Kaiserschmarrn* (a cut-up and sugared pancake), and *Glühwein* (red wine mulled with cinnamon and oranges).

Coffee

The story of coffee in Austria is steeped in legend. In the late 17th century, the Ottoman Turks were laying siege to Vienna. A spy working for the Austrians infiltrated the Ottoman ranks and got to know the Turkish lifestyle...including their passion for a drug called coffee. After the Austrians persevered, the ecstatic Habsburg emperor offered the spy anything he wanted. The spy asked for the Ottomans' spilled coffee beans, which he gathered up to start the first coffee shop in town. (It's a nice story. But actually, there was already an Armenian in town running a coffeehouse.)

In the 18th century, coffee boomed as an aristocratic

Take your pick of one of Vienna's many elegant and venerable coffeehouses.

drink. In the 19th-century Industrial Age, people were expected to work 12-hour shifts, and coffee became a hit with the working class, too. By the 20th century, the Vienna coffee scene became so refined that old-timers remember when servers brought a sheet with various shades of brown (like paint samples) so customers could make clear exactly how milky they wanted their coffee.

Austria Travel Resources from Rick Steves

Guidebooks
Check out Rick's guidebooks covering Vienna, Salzburg & Tirol; plus his German phrase book

Audio Europe
Download Rick's free Audio Europe app, with interviews about Austria and self-guided audio tours, including a Salzburg town walk, Vienna city walk, and tours of Vienna's St. Stephen's Cathedral and Ringstrasse

TV Shows
The quintessence of Austria with Rick as your host, viewable on public television and RickSteves.com. Episodes cover Vienna and the Danube, the Austrian Alps, and Salzburg

Organized Tours
Small group tours, with itineraries planned by Rick: Germany, Austria & Switzerland in 14 Days; Munich, Salzburg & Vienna in 8 Days; Berlin, Prague & Vienna in 12 Days; My Way Alpine Europe, Best of Europe in 21 Days (both include a stop in Austria)

For more on all of these resources, visit RickSteves.com. For Austria trip-planning tips, see RickSteves.com/europe/austria.

Czech Republic

Despite being wedged between Germany and Austria, and battered by 20th-century wars and communist domination, the Czechs have managed to forge one of the most comfortable and easy-to-explore countries of Eastern Europe. Today, the Czech Republic is enjoying an unprecedented prosperity.

The country is composed of two main regions—Bohemia to the west and Moravia to the east, with a tiny slice of Silesia in the upper-right corner. As the longtime home of the Czechs, Bohemia is circled by a naturally fortifying ring of mountains and cut down the middle by the Vltava River. It's best known for its capital city of Prague and its rollicking beer halls. By contrast, the wine-growing region of Moravia is more Slavic and colorful, and more focused on farming.

Prague's Old Town Square

Ninety percent of the tourists who visit the Czech Republic see only Prague...and for good reason. Prague is one of Europe's best-preserved cities. It's an architectural time warp, filled with sumptuous Art Nouveau facades, high art, grand buildings, and back lanes out of the 18th century. You'll feel like royalty strolling down the "King's Walk" from the cathedral into the old town. And the city offers a wide-ranging menu of classical concerts, and arguably the best beer in Europe.

Outside the capital, you'll enjoy great prices, few tourists, traditional towns, and surprising experiences—whether canoeing through Bohemia, touring the bone chapel in Kutná Hora, or soaking in hot peat soup in Třeboň.

As you travel, talk with Czech people—they bring recent history to life in a way that books can't. And wherever you go, you'll feel the Czech spirit: in the vibrant energy of Prague, the charm of quaint villages like Český Krumlov, and the gentle beauty of the countryside, dotted by wild poppies.

Fast Facts

Biggest cities: Prague (capital, 1.2 million), Brno (380,000), Ostrava (336,000)

Size: 31,000 square miles (similar to South Carolina), population 10.6 million

Locals call it: Česká Republika; Prague is "Praha"

Currency: Czech crown (*koruna*, Kč, officially CZK)

Key date: January 1, 1993, Czechoslovakia peaceably splits into the Czech Republic and Slovakia

Biggest festival: Prague Spring (May-June, international music)

Handy Czech phrases: *Dobrý den* (hello; **doh**-bree dehn), *Prosím* (please; **proh**-zeem), *Děkuji* (thank you; **dyack**-khuyi), *Na zdraví!* (Cheers!; nah zdrah-**vee**)

Tourist info: CzechTourism.com

FAVORITE SIGHTS AND MEMORABLE EXPERIENCES IN THE CZECH REPUBLIC

A Historical Walk Through Prague

Prague is a traveler's dream city: exotic but easy, affordable, and with plenty of great sightseeing. My favorite way to soak up the magic is by connecting Prague's major sights with a stroll through its relatively compact core. You'll get an up-close look at charming cobbled streets and extravagant facades while feeling the sweep of Prague's history, starting at the ninth-century castle from which Czech leaders have ruled for more than 1,000 years, and ending at the square where Czechs gained their freedom from communism several decades ago.

Perched on a hill overlooking the city, Prague Castle is hailed as being the biggest anywhere, with a 1,500-foot-long series of courtyards, churches, and palaces. If exhausting

Czech Republic's Top Destinations

Prague ▲▲▲   allow 2-3 days
One of Europe's most romantic cities, with a remarkably well-preserved old town, a thriving new town packed with Art Nouveau, and fascinating 20th-century history

Top Sights
Old Town Square Beautiful main square with Astronomical Clock
Prague Castle Sprawling hilltop complex of museums, churches, and parks
Charles Bridge Atmospheric, statue-lined bridge enlivened by street music
Jewish Quarter Powerful collection of Jewish sights

Nearby
Kutná Hora Workaday Czech town with offbeat bone church
Terezín Concentration camp memorial
Konopiště, Karlštejn, and Křivoklát Trio of impressive castles

Český Krumlov ▲▲   1 day
Charming Bohemian hill town huddled under a castle and hugging a river bend

Southern Bohemian Towns ▲   1-2 days
Třeboň, home to a famous peat spa; **Telč**, with a spectacular main square; **Třebíč**, with echoes of Jewish history; and sleepy Renaissance gem **Slavonice**

Olomouc ▲   1 day
Moravian cultural capital, vibrant university city, and home of stinky cheese

With more time, consider visiting
Wallachia Time-passed, mountainous region
Mikulov Wine region, highlighted by the cellars of Pavlov

Prague's beloved Charles Bridge, straddling the Vltava River, offers one of the most delightful strolls in Europe.

is a measure of big, I'll buy that claim. Whenever I visit the castle, I feel as if I'm in a pinball machine—rolling downhill, bouncing from sight to sight before funneling out the lower gate. The highlight is St. Vitus Cathedral, where locals go to remember Saint Wenceslas, patron saint of the Czechs. This "good king" of Christmas-carol fame was not a king at all, but a wise, benevolent duke of Bohemia. After being assassinated in 935, Wenceslas became a symbol of Czech nationalism. His tomb sits in an extremely fancy chapel.

From the castle, I follow the "King's Walk" into town. This was the ancient route of coronation processions. After being crowned in St. Vitus Cathedral, the new king would walk through the historic town, cross the Charles Bridge, and finish at the Old Town Square. If he hurried, he'd be done in 20 minutes.

The much-loved Charles Bridge gets my vote for Europe's most pleasant quarter-mile stroll. Built in the 1350s, it now features a chorus line of time-blackened Baroque statues towering above a fun string of street vendors and musicians. I love to be on the bridge when the sun is low for the best light, people-watching, and photo opportunities.

After crossing the bridge, I follow the shop-lined street to the Old

Avoiding Rip-Offs in Prague

Con artists and pickpockets are definitely an issue in Prague. The city's taxis are notorious for hyperactive meters. At restaurants, tourists may be served cheaper meals than what they ordered, given a menu with a "personalized" price list, charged extra for things they didn't get, or shortchanged. Pickpockets—from little children to adults dressed as professionals—target Western tourists. Heed these tips:

- When paying with cash, always count your change.
- In taxis, ask for an estimate up front and insist on using the meter.
- Never let your credit card out of your sight.
- In restaurants, closely examine your bill. Tax is always included in the price, so it shouldn't be tacked on later.

Town Square. One of the city's top sights, the colorful square is bordered by pastel buildings in diverse architectural styles: Gothic, Renaissance, Baroque, Rococo, and Art Nouveau. This has been a market square since the 11th century, though today, many of the old-time market stalls have been replaced by cafés, touristy horse buggies, and souvenir hawkers. The square's centerpiece is a memorial to Jan Hus, a local preacher who complained about church corruption. Tried for heresy and burned in 1415, Hus has long symbolized the fight for Czech freedom.

Memorial to Czech martyr Jan Palach on Prague's Wenceslas Square

Going beyond the "King's Walk," I head to Wenceslas Square, the heart of urban, modern Prague. Whenever I'm here, I'm reminded of the struggles of the Czech people. As my friend Honza explains it, this is where the most dramatic moments in modern Czech history have played out. The Czechoslovak state was proclaimed here in 1918. In 1969, Jan Palach set himself on fire here to protest the puppet Soviet government. And 20 years after his death, massive demonstrations on the square led to the overthrow of the communist government.

"Night after night we assembled here, pulled out our key chains, and jingled them at the president's window, saying, 'It's time to go home now,'" explains Honza. "Then one night we gathered...and he was gone. We had won our freedom." Just being on Wenceslas Square, envisioning the events of November 1989, is compelling. But being here with one of the demonstrators drilled into me the jubilation of a small country winning its freedom from a big one.

Making It Personal with a Local Guide

Prague is one city where, more than just about anywhere else, I recommend hiring a local guide. For about $30 an hour, you get a guide and companion who is expert at giving meaning to your wandering. And if, like me, you are forever fascinated by slice-of-life stories from people who had to live through the Cold War in the Warsaw Pact, it's even more engaging.

On one tour, my guide reminisced about 1989 and how, with the arrival of freedom and the fall of the Iron Curtain,

LEFT With a local guide you can connect with the culture and its history in ways the lone traveler can't.

RIGHT At Kutná Hora's famous bone chapel, the chandelier is just the start of a boney gallery.

Russian-language teachers suddenly had to teach English. There were no textbooks, and Russian teachers took cram courses in English so they could teach their students sentences like "Deez eez my bruder" ("This is my brother"). The fun thing for school kids those first few years was that they knew more English from watching Rambo movies than their teachers did from taking the cram courses.

Another guide talked of how, in her youth, she could only dream of drinking a nice cold Coca-Cola. She said, "We couldn't drink Coke, but we could collect the cans tourists threw away. I had five cans. My friend had ten."

Throughout Eastern Europe, guides artfully weave personal memories like these into their time with you.

Boning Up on Kutná Hora

The refreshingly authentic town of Kutná Hora sits upon what once was Europe's largest silver mine. In its heyday, much of the Continent's coinage was minted right here. If you're not claustrophobic, you can don a miner's helmet and climb down to explore the medieval mining shafts. Centuries of mining in the narrow wet shafts have made the ground beneath town resemble a giant honeycomb.

But I'm more fascinated by the Sedlec Church, just outside town. On the outside, the little church looks normal. But inside, the bones of 40,000 people decorate the walls and ceilings. Plagues and wars in the 14th and 15th centuries provided all the raw material necessary for these creepily creative designs. The display was created 400 years ago by monks. Their mission: to remind you (mid-vacation) that before long, you'll be in the same state—so give some thought to how you might be spending eternity. Later bone stackers at Kutná Hora were more interested in design than theology, as evidenced by an illuminating chandelier that includes every bone in the human body.

Spas and Fishy Cuisine in Třeboň

Třeboň, an inviting medieval town in South Bohemia, sits near a biosphere of artificial lakes that date back to the 14th century. Rather than unprofitable wet fields, the nobles wanted ponds that swarmed with fish. Over the years, what was marshland was transformed into a clever combination of lakes, oak-lined dikes, wild meadows, Baroque villages, peat bogs, and pine woods.

These days, people come from near and far to soak in peat, the dark, smelly sludge that's thought to cure aching joints and spines. So I decided to check it out. Immersed in a *One Flew Over the Cuckoo's Nest* ambience, I was ushered to a changing cubicle. The attendant mimed I should take everything off. I climbed into a stainless-steel tub, she pulled a plug, and I quickly disappeared under a rising sea of dark-brown sawdust broth. When finished, I showered off the sludge, then laid face down in what felt like a nurse's office while my attendant gave me a vigorous massage. I walked out with my shirt stuck to my skin by a mucky massage cream...and without a clue what soaking in that peat soup was supposed to accomplish.

Třeboň is also the fish-raising capital of the country. So if you visit Třeboň, you have to eat fish. Like the Italians do with pasta, the Czechs of Třeboň cook fish with both passion and variety. One time, I went to a local eatery and ordered all the fishy appetizers on the menu. The result was a tapas-style meal of "soused" (pickled) herring, fried loach, "stuffed carp sailor-fashion," cod liver, pike caviar, and something my Czech friends translated as "fried carp sperm." I said, "You can't fry sperm." And everyone at my table insisted that, while female fish have a whole trough full of eggs (caviar), the males have a trough full of the male counterpart—and it's cookable. Fried carp sperm tasted like fried oyster, and it had the same texture, too.

While the Czech town of Třeboň sees few American travelers, it's famous locally for its trout.

As we ate, I noticed that the writing on my beer glass said, "Bohemia Regent anno 1379." It occurred to me that I was drinking and eating the same thing that people here have been consuming for over 600 years: local brew and fish from the reservoir just outside the town gate.

More Czech Experiences

Canoeing in Český Krumlov: With its simple beauty and wonderfully medieval feel, Český Krumlov is the quaint, small-town Europe that many people dream of experiencing. An especially pleasant way to connect with this fairy-tale town is from the waters of the Vltava River. It's easy to rent a canoe or rubber raft from the outfitters in town. Floating down the lazy river, you'll pass through Bohemian forests and other villages, drifting past cafés and pubs happy to welcome you for a break. You'll eventually end up at a 13th-century abbey. From here, hop on the outfitter's shuttle back to town or borrow a bike from them and pedal back along the path.

Prague's Lennon Wall: After John Lennon's death in 1980, Prague's Lennon Wall spontaneously appeared. This was back in Cold War times, when Lennon's visionary ideas inspired many locals. They'd paint "All You Need Is Love," "Imagine," and other graffiti borrowed from Lennon on the wall. Night after night, the police would paint over the graffiti. And day after day, it would reappear. Until independence came in 1989, travelers, freedom lovers, and hippies gathered here. Silly as it might seem, this wall is remembered as a place that gave hope to locals craving freedom. Although the tension and danger associated with this wall are long gone, it remains a colorful, nostalgic, and poignant place to visit.

In the Czech Republic, you can canoe into the wonderfully medieval town of Český Krumlov *(left)* and exercise your freedom of thought at Prague's Lennon Wall *(right)*.

The Stinky Cheese of Olomouc: Try the sour, foul-smelling, yet beloved specialty of the Haná region, Olomouc cheese sticks (*olomoucké tvarůžky*). The milk goes through a process of natural maturation under chunks of meat. Czechs figure there are two types of people in the world: *tvarůžky* lovers and sane people. The *tvarůžky* are so much a part of the Haná and Czech identity that when the European Union tried to forbid the product, the Czech government negotiated for special permission to continue to rot their milk. Zip a few of these stinkers in a baggie, and you can count on getting a train compartment to yourself.

Intrepid travelers can sample the infamous "stinky cheese" of Olomouc.

CULTURE AND TRADITIONS: EVERYTHING'S SO...CZECH

Classical Music

From Antonín Dvořák to Gustav Mahler, the Czech Republic has a rich heritage in classical music. You'll find it everywhere in Prague, which has museums dedicated to the lives and work of Dvořák, Bedřich Smetana (the father of Czech classical music), and Mozart, who hailed from Austria but spent a lot of time here.

Each day, classical concerts designed for tourists fill delightful Old World halls and churches, including the Art Nouveau Municipal House (where the Prague Symphony Orchestra plays), the classical Neo-Renaissance Rudolfinum (home of the Czech Philharmonic), and the National Theater (great for opera and ballet). Or you can simply drop by Castle Square and see Josef and his Prague Castle Orchestra playing for free on the street. A highlight is hearing them play Smetana's masterwork, *Die Moldau* (the unofficial anthem of the Czech Republic). If I were the mayor of Prague, I'd book this trio for the rest of their musical days to bring joy to the city's many tourists at the gateway to its most visited sight and the orchestra's namesake, Prague Castle.

Czech Beer

Czechs are among the world's most enthusiastic beer drinkers—adults drink an average of 80 gallons a year. Whether you're in a restaurant or traditional beer hall, beer (*pívo*) hits your

The Czech Republic is a land where classical music bursts out in the streets and the cuisine sticks to your ribs.

table like a glass of water does in the States. A new serving will automatically appear when the old glass is almost empty. (You must tell the server not to bring more.) On my early trips, I used to have a big beer at lunch and spend the rest of the day wobbly...sightseeing on what I called "Czech knees." Now I resist a momentum-killing beer at lunch and finish each day with a fresh draft beer.

The Czechs invented Pilsner-style lager in Plzeň, and the result, Pilsner Urquell, is on tap in many pubs. Other good beers include Krušovice, Gambrinus, Staropramen, and Kozel. Each establishment serves only one brand of beer on tap (to find out which, look for its sign outside). Unlike many other Europeans, Czechs don't mix beers, and they don't bar-hop. They say, "In one night, you must stay loyal to one lover and to one beer."

Stick-to-Your-Ribs Cuisine

The Czechs have one of Europe's most filling cuisines. Heavy on meat, potatoes, and cabbage, it's hearty and tasty—designed to keep peasants or sightseers fueled through a day of hard work. Expect thick soups, rustic bread, and meaty main dishes such as beef goulash or wild boar. Czech dumplings (*knedlíky*) are a staple. These aren't round, puffy dough balls—they resemble slices of steamed white bread and are meant to be drowned in gravy. There are also sweet dumplings loaded with fresh strawberries, blueberries, apricots, or plums, and garnished with custard and melted butter.

Czech Republic Travel Resources from Rick Steves

Guidebooks
Check out Rick's guidebooks covering Prague & the Czech Republic and Eastern Europe

Audio Europe
Download Rick's free Audio Europe app, with interviews about the Czech Republic and self-guided audio tours, including a walk through Prague

TV Shows
The quintessence of the Czech Republic with Rick as your host, viewable on public television and RickSteves.com. Episodes cover Prague, Olomouc, Třeboň, and Český Krumlov

Organized Tours
Small group tours, with itineraries planned by Rick: Prague & Budapest in 8 Days; Berlin, Prague & Vienna in 12 Days; and Eastern Europe in 15 Days

For more on all of these resources, visit RickSteves.com. For Czech Republic trip-planning tips, see RickSteves.com/europe/czech-republic.

Poland

Poland may not appear at the top of many travelers' wish lists, and that's just one reason you may want to visit. With gorgeous towns, evocative sights, an epic history, and low prices, Poland is a diamond in the rough. While parts of the country are still cleaning up the industrial mess left by the Soviets, visitors today are speechless when they set foot on the country's vibrant main squares, in-love-with-life pedestrian drags, and sophisticated shopping boulevards.

Poland is as big as Italy and nearly as populous as Spain. It's also quite flat, with rolling fields. This lack of natural barriers—and Poland's proximity to powerful neighbors (Germany, Russia, Austria, Sweden)—have left the country with a troubled history that's often meant being part of someone else's empire.

This dynamic past has inspired a powerful patriotism among Poles. They are a kind-hearted people: noble, soft-spoken, and quite shy. Occasionally they strike first-time visitors as brusque. But extroverts quickly learn that all it takes is a smile and a friendly hello (*Dzień dobry!*) to break through the tough exterior that helped these people survive Poland's difficult times.

The 10 million Americans who trace their roots to Poland find something enticingly familiar here, from the comfort food their Busia cooked them to the kindness of distant cousins they encounter. Many return home with a renewed appreciation for their mother country.

Poland's best attractions are its

big cities: the cultural capital and university burg of Kraków; the picture-perfect old merchant town of Gdańsk; and the cosmopolitan business hub of Warsaw. Leaving these population centers, you're immersed in a gently beautiful countryside, where humble farmers work the same plots and live the same uncomplicated, agrarian lifestyle of their great-grandparents.

The resilience of Poland's culture and the warmth of its people inspire me. Thankfully, these are good times in Poland, a nation with a rich past and an exciting future.

FAVORITE SIGHTS AND MEMORABLE EXPERIENCES IN POLAND

Charismatic Kraków

Kraków is easily Poland's best destination: a beautiful, old-fashioned city buzzing with history, enjoyable sights, tourists, and college students. Although the country's capital moved from here to Warsaw 400 years ago, Kraków remains Poland's cultural and intellectual center. Of all the Eastern European cities claiming to be "the next Prague," Kraków is for real.

The old town, within Kraków's medieval walls, converges on one of the most charismatic squares in Europe: the Main Market Square. I choose a café, sink deep into my chair, and absorb the gorgeously intact buildings around me.

Vast as it is, the square has a folksy intimacy. It bustles with street musicians, cotton-candy vendors, gawking tourists, local teens practicing break-dancing moves for tips, and the lusty coos of pigeons. A folk band—swaggering in their colorful peasant costumes—gives me a private little concert. Feeling flush, I tip them royally. (Perhaps too royally. Be warned: A big tip gets you "The Star-Spangled Banner.")

I suddenly hear a bugle call. Glancing around, I eventually pan up to see its source: a trumpet poking out the window of the tallest tower of

Fast Facts

Biggest cities: Warsaw (capital, 1.7 million), Kraków (757,000), Łódź (747,000)

Size: 121,000 square miles (similar to New Mexico), population 38.5 million

Locals call it: Polska

Currency: Polish złoty

Key date: August 14, 1980, Lech Wałęsa leads the first successful workers' strike in Soviet territory

Biggest festivals: Jewish Cultural Festival (late June-early July, Kraków), St. Dominic's Fair (late July-mid-August, Gdańsk, market stalls, musical performances, and general revelry)

Handy Polish phrases: Dzień dobry (hello; jehn **doh**-brih), Proszę (please; **proh**-sheh), Dziękuję (thank you; jehn-**koo**-yeh), Na zdrowie! (Cheers!; nah **zdroh**-vyeh)

Tourist info: Poland.travel

the hulking, red-brick St. Mary's Church. Just as I spot the sun glinting off of the trumpet's bell, the song stops abruptly, causing the crowd below to chuckle and applaud appreciatively. This tune—performed every hour on the hour—comes with a legend: During the 1241 Tatar invasion, a watchman saw the enemy approaching and sounded the alarm. Before he could finish, an arrow pierced his throat—which is why today, the music still stops *subito,* partway through.

Ready to move on from my perch, I toss a few złotys on the table to cover my tab—and head underground into the Rynek Underground Museum. The Main Market Square sits on top of 500 years of history. When it was renovated recently, workers found so many coins, tools, and artifacts of archaeological value that the city opened this excellent museum. Here, at 12 feet below street level, I get an intimate look at medieval Kraków life.

Back on the streets of modern Kraków, I find that this city, more than any other in Europe, is made for aimless strolling. As I linger my way through town, I'm lucky enough to stumble into Staropolskie Trunki ("Old Polish Drinks"), a friendly little place with a long bar and countless local vodkas and liquors—each one open and ready to be sampled. For about $3, I get a complete vodka education with a cheery local bartender who talks me through five different tastes.

Happy after my private vodka tour, I keep walking to clear my head. Eventually I wind up in Kazimierz, the city's historic Jewish Quarter. Once upon a time, the majority of Europe's Jewish people lived in Poland. And Kraków was their social and political base. Few Jews still live in the neighborhood, but the spirit of their traditions survives in a handful of synagogues and cemeteries.

Kazimierz is one of the many places where the big events of World War II intersected with ordinary, everyday lives.

Kraków, with its vast yet people-friendly main square and its countless cafés and pubs, manages to be both trendy and convivial at the same time.

The businessman Oskar Schindler ran his factory here, saving the lives of more than a thousand of his Jewish workers. Now, one of Europe's best museums about the Nazi occupation fills the building where Schindler and his employees worked. While the museum tells the story of Schindler and his workers, it also broadens its perspective to take in the full experience of all of Kraków during the era of Nazi rule.

While tourists come to see Kazimierz's historic sights during the day, this isn't a "preserved" neighborhood. It's lively and fun. Throngs of young clubbers clog the streets after dark. The Kazimierz market square retains the gritty flavor of the town before tourism and gentrification. And countless bohemian-chic restaurants make Kazimierz a destination for dinner. On a balmy summer night, it's the perfect spot to end a day in Poland's "second" city.

Historic, Heroic Gdańsk

A port city on the Baltic Coast of Poland, Gdańsk is truly amazing— and amazingly historic. You may associate it with dreary images of striking shipyard workers from the nightly news in the 1980s—but this is one of northern Europe's most historic and picturesque places.

Milk Bars

All over Poland, you'll find "milk bars" *(bar mleczne)*—cafeterias that combine good, affordable meals with a fun cultural experience. These are leftovers from communist times, when the government subsidized low-cost eateries for its workers. Despite the misleading name, milk bars serve not just milk, but all sorts of traditional Polish dishes.

The idea of a cheap and hearty meal survived communism, and, decades later, you'll still find a wide variety of these budget cafeterias. Some are slick and modern, with excellent food and slightly higher prices. Others are holdovers from the old days (with a certain Soviet *je ne sais quoi*), where you can snare a fast and forgettable meal for about $5. Just head to the counter and point to what you want.

Gdańsk's appealing old town boasts block after block of red-brick churches and narrow, colorful, ornately decorated burghers' mansions. The riverfront embankment, with its trademark medieval crane, oozes salty maritime charm. When the Polish kings came to visit this well-to-do city, they'd gawk along the same route trod by tourists today— which is still called the "Royal Way." Entering through the old town's ornamental gateway, I overheard a fellow traveler gasping, "It's like stepping into a Fabergé egg!"

North of the town center, the charms of the old core fade

Poland's Top Destinations

Kraków ▲▲▲
allow 2-3 days

Poland's cultural, intellectual, and historical capital, with an easy-to-enjoy old town, thought-provoking Jewish quarter, important castle, many churches, and one of Europe's finest town squares

Top Sights
Main Market Square Stunning core of Kraków and a people magnet any time of day
Wawel Castle and Cathedral Poland's historical and spiritual heart
Churches St. Mary's (Gothic altarpiece) and St. Francis Basilica (Art Nouveau)
Kazimierz Jewish quarter with synagogues, cemeteries, and Oskar Schindler's factory

Nearby
Auschwitz-Birkenau Notorious concentration camp, now a compelling memorial
Wieliczka Salt Mine Sprawling underground caverns with sculptures hewn from salt
Nowa Huta Planned workers' suburb, offering an evocative taste of communist times

Warsaw ▲▲
1-3 days

Poland's modern capital, with an appealing urban tempo, stately and sophisticated boulevards, a reconstructed old town, and cutting-edge museums (covering WWII history, Fryderyk Chopin, Jewish culture, Polish art, and more)

Gdańsk ▲▲
2 days

Historic trading city, featuring a showpiece old town lined with marvelous facades, a salty maritime charm, and the shipyard where Lech Wałęsa's Solidarity trade union challenged the communists

as you approach the Gdańsk shipyard. For me, the hike to the shipyard isn't about sightseeing; it's a pilgrimage. This is where the Polish Solidarity union was born, kicking off the beginning of the end of Soviet domination in Eastern Europe. It's remarkable to think that it all came down to the gumption of just a motley collection of workers, led by electrician-turned-labor-organizer Lech Wałęsa.

My guide, Agnus, told the story vividly as we stood at

Gdańsk, a rugged port town on Poland's Baltic coast *(left)*, remembers its shipyard workers who heroically helped bring down the Soviet Union *(right)*.

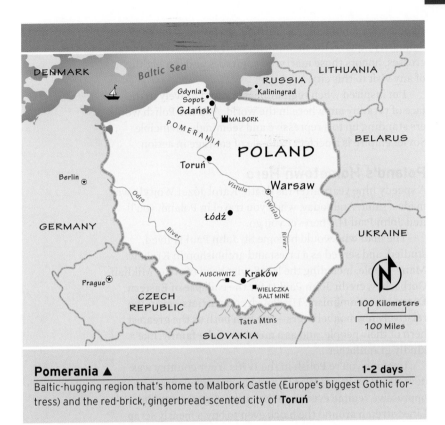

Pomerania ▲   **1-2 days**

Baltic-hugging region that's home to Malbork Castle (Europe's biggest Gothic fortress) and the red-brick, gingerbread-scented city of **Toruń**

the gate under a "Solidarity" banner—draped where a big "LENIN" sign once hung. For 18 days in 1980, protestors huddled behind the shipyard's main gate, refusing to leave until they had won unprecedented concessions from the communists—including the right to strike. A crude yellow board lists the workers' original demands. Their action sparked a wave of strikes and sit-ins that spread along the industrialized north coast of Poland.

When Solidarity negotiated its way to victory in 1980, one of their conditions was that the Soviets let Poland erect a monument to workers killed a decade earlier while demonstrating for the same workers' rights. The government agreed, marking the first time a communist regime ever allowed a monument to be built to honor victims of communist oppression. Lech Wałęsa likened it to a harpoon in the heart of the communists.

The towering monument, with three crucified anchors on top, was designed, engineered, and built by shipyard workers. Just four months after the historic agreement was signed, the monument was finished. Today on Gdańsk's Solidarity Square, the monument, with a trio of 140-foot-tall crosses, honors those martyred comrades and is a highlight of any visit to this city.

I'm inspired when regular people stand bravely in the face of tyranny anywhere in the world. And the Polish workers standing up to a repressive and seemingly invincible Soviet empire is a perfect example of courage in action.

Poland's Hometown Hero

A speedy nine years after his death, Karol Józef Wojtyła was made a saint. And today, when you travel in Poland, you'll find John Paul II wherever you go.

The man who would become St. John Paul II lived, studied, and served as a priest and archbishop in Kraków. Many people, including the last Soviet head of state, Mikhail Gorbachev, credit John Paul II for the collapse of Eastern European communism. His Polish compatriots—even the relatively few nonbelievers—saw him both as the greatest hero of their people, and as a member of the family, like a kindly grandfather.

Imagine you're Polish in the 1970s. Your country was devastated by World War II, and has struggled under an oppressive regime ever since. Food shortages are epidemic. Lines stretch around the block even to buy a measly scrap of bread. Life is bleak, oppressive, and seems hopeless. Then someone who speaks your language—someone you've admired your entire life, and one of the few people to successfully stand up to the regime—becomes one of the world's most influential leaders. A Pole like you is the spiritual guide of a billion Catholics. He makes you believe that the impossible can happen. He says to you again and again: "Have no fear." And you begin to believe it. It's not hard to see why many consider John Paul II to be the greatest Pole in history.

Saint John Paul II is remembered as a favorite son by Poles.

Since his sainthood, the entire country has been ramping up celebrations. At the edge of Kraków, the John Paul II Center is an impressive place to visit. Consecrated in 2013, the church is big and dazzling, with art in the lower sanctuary highlighting the pope's illustrious ministry. A museum displays

his personal effects and gifts given to him from admirers around the world.

About an hour outside Kraków, in the town of Wadowice, the John Paul II Family Home and Museum fills four floors of the tenement building where his family lived through his adolescence. Visitors can see the actual rooms where he grew up and a collection of his belongings.

But for me, one of the best John Paul II experiences is seeing all of the smaller churches throughout Poland, each of which seems to have a chapel dedicated to their saint. Seeing a man of our own time up on the wall, glorified with the apostles and other saints, is powerful. You can almost feel the charismatic presence of this historic figure, who will be honored for ages to come.

More Polish Experiences

Warsaw Reborn: Warsaw is Poland's capital and biggest city. It's huge, famous, and important, but not particularly romantic. (If you're looking for Old World quaintness, head for Kraków.) The fun of Warsaw is to walk through the city's parks, enjoy a little Chopin in the composer's hometown, marvel at its fast-growing skyline, and just connect with big-city people who are as warm and charming as small-town folk.

Warsaw is also an inspiration to visit. To think it was literally bombed flat and rebuilt since 1945 is amazing. When I'm there, I can't help but fixate on the cost of war. I know how lovingly I collect and organize my physical world in my house. But virtually every house in Warsaw was destroyed in 1945...so many cultural and personal treasures simply gone forever.

Warsaw has been rebuilt from the rubble of World War II.

And, now, just two generations later, Germans and Russians stroll through the city on vacation—joking, enjoying ice cream cones, and snapping photos. Of course, we need to forgive and move on. I'm just amazed at how good Poland is at it. Perhaps some other countries—victims of similar horrors—can learn from the Poles.

Look, but Don't Lick: Just outside Kraków is the remarkable Wieliczka Salt Mine, which has been producing salt since at least the 13th century. A tour of the complex, which spreads over nine levels and 100 miles of tunnels, shows how generations of Wieliczka miners

LEFT Outside Kraków, a vast salt mine comes with a cavern carved to be a church.

RIGHT At Auschwitz-Birkenau, death was mass-produced with diabolical efficiency.

spent their days underground, rarely seeing the sun. Some of these miners carved statues from the salt: legendary figures from the days of King Kazimierz, the famous astronomer Copernicus, and even the region's favorite son, Pope John Paul II. Your jaw will drop as you enter the enormous underground chapel, carved in the early 20th century. Everything, from the altar to the grand chandelier, was chiseled from the rock salt. The remarkable relief carving of the Last Supper looks good enough to lick.

Lessons of Auschwitz-Birkenau: A trip to once-upon-a-time Europe can be a fairy tale. It can also help tell the story of Europe's 20th-century fascist nightmare. While few travelers go to Europe to dwell on the horrors of Nazism, most people value visiting the memorials of fascism's reign of terror and honoring the wish of its survivors—"Forgive, but never forget."

No such sight in all of Europe is as powerful as Auschwitz-Birkenau. This Nazi concentration camp—strategically located in the heart of Jewish Europe, in occupied Poland—was the site of the systematic murder of more than a million innocent people.

Today, visitors make the pilgrimage west of Kraków to tour the grounds, with its vast field of chimneys stretching to the horizon. A visit begins by crossing under the notorious gate with the cruelly mocking message *Arbeit Macht Frei* ("Work sets you free"). The broken-down crematoria and the train tracks that delivered their victims are silent remnants of unspeakable horrors.

Why is this somber place worth a bit of our vacations? Because we can learn from it. Auschwitz-Birkenau is committed to making the point that intolerance lives on—genocide is as recent as conflicts in Rwanda, Sudan, and Syria. Even today, Machiavellian politicians can hijack great nations, artfully manipulating fear, patriotism, and mass media to accomplish their destructive agendas.

CULTURE AND TRADITIONS: EVERYTHING'S SO...POLISH

Churchgoing Catholics

Poland is arguably Europe's most devoutly Catholic country. Nearly all Polish children are baptized as Roman Catholics, and almost everyone who gets married has a church wedding. In small Polish towns, there's a strong contemporary tradition of building huge, architecturally daring churches as a sign of civic pride and deep respect for the Catholic faith. The architecture of these modern houses of worship sometimes feels more slapdash and done-on-the-cheap than the great churches of an earlier age (which were often built over centuries). But the spirit that fills them is powerful.

When you travel around Europe, you rarely see new churches. And the old churches you see often feel more dead than alive...kept going more for tourists than for worshippers. But in Poland, churches are alive with the faithful.

Polish Food

Polish food is hearty and tasty, with lots of "cold-weather" ingredients: potatoes, dill, berries, beets, and rye. Polish soups are a highlight, especially *barszcz* (borscht, the savory beet soup) and *żurek* (a hearty sourdough soup with a hard-boiled egg and pieces of *kiełbasa* sausage). Another familiar Polish dish is pierogi, ravioli-like dumplings with various

LEFT During communist times, Poles built bold new churches as a statement.

RIGHT A plate of Polish food fills the stomach and warms the body.

fillings: minced meat, sauerkraut, mushroom, cheese, or even blueberry.

And, of course, there's *wódka* (vodka). The most famous brand, Żubrówka, comes with a blade of grass from the bison reserves in eastern Poland. The bison "flavor" the grass... then the grass flavors the vodka. It's strong—but if you down your vodka quickly, it only hurts once. Poles often mix Żubrówka with apple juice, creating a cocktail called *szarlotka* ("apple cake"). *Na zdrowie!*

Poland Travel Resources from Rick Steves

Guidebooks
Check out Rick's guidebooks covering Kraków, Warsaw & Gdansk, and Eastern Europe

Audio Europe
Download Rick's free Audio Europe app, with interviews about Polish culture and sightseeing

TV Shows
The quintessence of Poland with Rick as your host, viewable on public television and at RickSteves.com. Episodes cover Kraków, Auschwitz, and Warsaw

Organized Tours
Small group tours, with itineraries planned by Rick: Best of Poland in 10 Days; Best of Eastern Europe in 15 Days

For more on all of these resources, visit RickSteves.com. For Poland trip-planning tips, see RickSteves.com/europe/poland.

Hungary

A proud oddball planted firmly in the center of Europe, Hungary mixes a refined elegance (from its days as Vienna's powerful sidecar of the Austro-Hungarian Empire), post-communist rejuvenation, cultural artifacts of a unique Asian heritage, spicy food, exotic thermal baths, endearingly eccentric locals, and Europe's single most underrated capital city. The more you know Hungary, the more you grow to love it.

Throughout history, various cultures from the mysterious East have stampeded to Europe, terrorized the Continent, and eventually retreated home. But only one group stuck around. The original Hungarians—called the Magyars—arrived here in A.D. 896, after a long migration from the steppes of Central Asia. After a few generations of running roughshod over Europe, they decided to convert to Christianity, adopt European ways, and integrate with their neighbors. And even though modern-day Hungarians are fully European, there's still something about the place that's distinctly Magyar.

Budapest—the sprawling Hungarian capital on the banks of the Danube—is a city of nuance and paradox. But those who grapple with it are rewarded with great sights, excellent restaurants, and vivid memories.

While one in five Hungarians lives in Budapest, the countryside plays an important role in Hungary's economy—this has always been a heavily agricultural region. The country's large towns and small cities—including

The grand spas of Hungary recall the glory days of the Austro-Hungarian Empire.

my favorites, Eger and Pécs—offer the visitor a refreshing contrast to the congested metropolis at the country's heart.

FAVORITE SIGHTS AND MEMORABLE EXPERIENCES IN HUNGARY

Budapest Remembers the Cold War

Traveling in Europe in the 1980s, I got in touch with my Czech friend, Lída, and told her I was coming to Prague for a visit. "If you don't mind," she said, "maybe we can meet in Budapest instead? I have been dying to try a Big Mac!"

If communism was a religion during the Cold War, Budapest was sin city. Offering tourists from communist countries a taste of the decadent West, Budapest had a famously progressive economic system dubbed "goulash communism." Meeting up with Lída in Budapest, we strolled down the shopping street called Váci utca. An excited mob gathered in front of a shop that was selling Adidas shoes. Lída explained that this was the only place in all of Eastern Europe where wannabe capitalists could drool over window displays featuring fancy sportswear that cost two months' wages. Up ahead, Ronald McDonald stood on the street corner like a heretic prophet cheering on the downtrodden proletariat. I'll never forget waiting an hour—in a line that stretched around the block—for American "fast" food. But as Lída finally bit into that long-awaited Big Mac, a deeply satisfied smile spread across her face. That evening, we went to hear Bruce Springsteen at the local stadium. With 50,000 rock fans, you could feel freedom ready to combust all around.

Today, that time feels like ancient history, and Hungarians under age 30 have no living memory of communism. But Budapest still has one of Eastern Europe's best sights for those fascinated by the Red old days: Memento Park.

When regimes come crashing to

Fast Facts

Biggest cities: Budapest (capital, nearly 2 million), Debrecen (205,000), Miskolc (165,000)

Size: 36,000 square miles (similar to Maine), population 10 million

Locals call it: Magyarország

Currency: Hungarian forints (Ft or HUF)

Key date: A.D. 896, seven original Magyar tribes arrive in the Carpathian Basin after a long migration from Central Asia, creating what would become Hungary

Biggest festivals: Formula 1 races (July, Budapest), Sziget Festival (August, Budapest, one of Europe's biggest rock and pop music events)

Handy Hungarian phrases: *Jó napot kívánok* (hello; yoh **nah**-pot kee-vah-nohk), *Kérem* (please; **kay**-rehm), *Köszönöm* (thank you; **kur**-sur-nurm), *Egészségedre* (cheers; **eh**-gehs-shay-geh-dreh)

Tourist info: GotoHungary.com

In Budapest's Memento Park, the sculpted figures that once glorified the communist goals of the state are now gathered together in a nostalgic game of statue maker.

the ground, so do their monuments. And, while most Eastern Europeans quickly disposed of any statues of Stalin, Lenin, and their local counterparts, some clever entrepreneur collected Budapest's into an open-air museum. The result is Memento Park, located in the countryside several miles outside the city center, boasting an entertaining jumble of once fearsome, now almost comical statues, gesturing frantically in an otherwise empty field, as if preaching their ideologies to each other for eternity.

A visit to Memento Park is a lesson in Socialist Realism, the art of communist Europe. They took censorship to new extremes: Under the communists, art was acceptable *only* if it furthered the goals of the state. Aside from a few important figureheads, individuals didn't matter. Everyone was a cog in the machine, a strong and stoic automaton, an unquestioning servant of the nation.

The gift shop hawks a fun parade of communist kitsch. On one visit, I picked up a CD featuring 20 patriotic songs— *The Greatest Hits of Communism*—and a Stalin vodka flask. Observing the capitalist bustle of today's Budapest, it occurs to me that Stalin, whose estate gets no royalties for all the postcards and tacky souvenirs featuring his mug, must be spinning in his communist grave.

Heat Wave in a Budapest Ruin Pub

Budapest's trendiest clubs are called "ruin pubs." Inhabiting ramshackle old buildings in the city center, they feel like a gang of squatters made a trip to the dump yesterday and grabbed whatever was usable, moved in today, and are open for business tonight.

This fast-combusting nightlife scene fills the city's long-derelict, now-gentrifying Jewish Quarter. On hot nights, the pubs spill out into shoddy courtyards, creating the feeling

Hungary's Top Destinations

Budapest ▲▲▲   allow 2-3 days
Grand, Danube-spanning cityscape peppered with opulent
buildings, fine restaurants and cafés, rejuvenated streets and
squares, and avant-garde "ruin pub" nightlife

Top Sights
Thermal Baths Fun Széchenyi, genteel Gellért, and classic Rudas
Hungarian Parliament Riverside behemoth with over-the-top interior
Hungarian State Opera House Neo-Renaissance splendor and affordable opera
House of Terror Remembrance of Nazi and Soviet crimes
Buda Castle Historic hilltop ensemble of palaces, churches, and museums

Nearby
Memento Park Open-air museum of communist statues
Szentendre Colorful, Balkan-feeling riverside artist colony
Esztergom Unassuming town with Hungary's biggest and most important church
Gödöllő Palace Summer palace of Habsburg monarchs

Eger ▲▲   1 day
Strollable town with inviting main square, gorgeous Baroque buildings,
invigorating thermal baths, and fine wines

Pécs ▲▲   1 day
City featuring a unique mosque-turned-church, good museums, and colorfully
tiled facades

With more time, consider visiting
Sopron Charmingly well-preserved old town
Hollókő Intriguing open-air folk museum, still inhabited by villagers

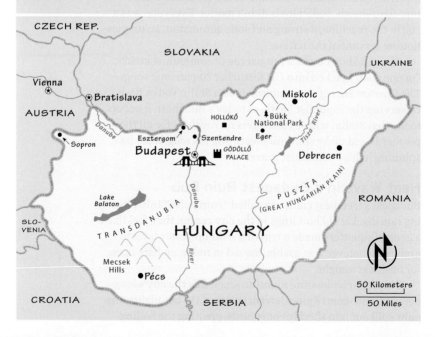

of a cozy living room missing its roof...under the stars.
Enjoying a drink here, I'm
reminded of creatures that
inhabit discarded shells in a
tide pool. The formula really
works. With the come-as-you-
are atmosphere, these clubs
attract people who make a
point not to be fashion slaves.
And, for adventurous travelers

of any age, it's easy to meet people.

Budapest's ruin pubs provide a great chance for travelers to connect with locals (and the local hard liquor).

I end up sitting with Peter (who designs ruin pubs), Laura
(who works at a hotel), and Sandra (whose father's company
introduced pornography to Hungary after freedom in the
1990s). I say how much I like the shabby lounge atmosphere
of a ruin pub, and Laura declares that this one, Szimpla Kert
(which means "Simple Garden"), is the mecca of ruin pubs.

Ruin pubs come with a bit of communist kitsch. Many
of the regulars who love these lounges were toddlers during
the last years of communism. Never having experienced its
downside, they have fond memories of those "good old days,"
when the pace of life was slower and families were tighter-
knit. Ruin pubs sell nostalgic commie soft drinks along with
cocktails.

Peter buys everyone a round of spritzes (rosé with soda
water). He's excited about the new ruin pub he just designed
across town, and wants us to go there. I comment on how
well the design works. He explains how these clubs are the
soul of underground culture here. It's the anti-club: flea market furniture, no matching chairs, a mishmash of colors. It's
eclectic—"designed to be undesigned."

More Hungarian Experiences

Enchanting Eger: The small city of Eger, in northern
Hungary, remains refreshingly off the tourist trail. Egerites
socialize in their inviting main square, watched over by one
of Hungary's most important castles, and go about their daily
routines in a people-friendly, traffic-free core amidst lovely
Baroque buildings.

The town is also at the heart of one of Hungary's best-
known wine regions. A good place to sample local wines is
Sirens' Valley, a series of atmospheric wine caves burrowed
into the hillsides just outside of town. A wine-tasting must
is Eger's famous Bull's Blood blend of reds. When asked to

Eger, with striking architecture *(left)*, and Pécs, with decorative tilework *(right)*, are the two most interesting towns in Hungary outside of Budapest.

explain the name, one vintner told me: "In 1552, when the Ottomans laid siege to Eger, they were astonished by the ferocity of the town defenders. Local wine sellers knew that the Muslim invaders wouldn't drink alcohol, so they told them it was bull's blood." Of course, since locals only started making this wine in the 1850s, the story is bunk. But as the vintner says, "If it convinces visitors to buy a bottle, where's the harm?"

Colorful Pécs: It takes a lot to get me excited about decorative tiles. But the small Hungarian city of Pécs—at the southern tip of the country—somehow manages. This is the hometown of the Zsolnay family, who innovated the "pyrogranite" method for creating architectural tiles that are as delicate-looking and vibrantly colorful as a fine vase, but frost-proof and as hard as stone. During Hungary's late-19th-century heyday, buildings all over the country were slathered with vibrant ornamentation. Today, Pécs retains the highest concentration of this distinctively Hungarian form of art, the old tile factory has been turned into a crisp and colorful cultural center, and local museums and shops explain the story of the Zsolnay clan and their finest creations. My favorite tiles are glazed with eosin, another Zsolnay invention that shimmers with a

The Tricky Hungarian Tongue

The Hungarian language is of Asian origin—unrelated to any other tongue in Europe (except distant cousins Finnish and Estonian). The language befuddles their neighbors and tourists alike. For example, the letter *s* by itself sounds like "sh," while the combination *sz* is "s." That's why the capital is called "boo-daw-pesht," while "Liszt" sounds like "list." Like other Eastern cultures, Hungarians list a person's family name first, and the given name last. So the composer Franz Liszt is called "Liszt Ferenc" in his homeland.

Hungarians tend to be traditional and formal in the way they speak—a waiter greets diners with *Tessék parancsolni* (Please command, sir) while a polite young man greeting an older woman might say, *Kezét csóko-lom* (I kiss your hand). On the other hand, Hungarians use two different words as a *ciao*-like informal "hi" and "bye": the local word *szia* (which sounds like "see ya") and the English word "hello." So you may hear a Hungarian begin a conversation with "See ya!" and end it with "Hello!"

unique range of subtly shifting colors—like the gossamer wing of a butterfly.

CULTURE AND TRADITIONS: EVERYTHING'S SO...HUNGARIAN

Taking the Plunge

I don't feel like I'm *really* in Hungary until I take a dip in one of the country's many thermal baths. While it may sound intimidating, enjoying a hot-water soak is very accessible, even to tourists. Thermal baths are basically like your hometown swimming pool...except the water is superheated, there are plenty of jets to massage away your stress, and you're surrounded by Speedo- and bikini-clad Hungarians. It's sightseeing, a cultural experience, and relaxation, all rolled into one.

Locals brag that if you poke a hole in the ground anywhere in Hungary, you'll find a hot-water spring. Budapest alone has 123 natural springs and some two-dozen thermal baths (which are actually part of the health-care system—doctors might prescribe a soak and a massage instead of medicine). At most baths, men and women are usually together, and you can keep your swimsuit on the entire time. But there are also a few gender-segregated, clothing-optional areas.

A typical bath complex has multiple pools: Big pools with warm water are for serious swimming, while the smaller, hotter thermal baths are for relaxing and soaking. You'll also usually find a dry sauna, a wet steam room, a cold plunge pool, and sunbathing areas. Many baths have fun flourishes: bubbles, whirlpools, massage jets, wave pools, and so on.

One of my favorites is Budapest's Széchenyi Baths—a big, yellow, copper-domed complex in the middle of City Park. Stepping into the lobby, I survey the long price list. I then try to explain what I want to the cashier: a bath ticket with a private changing cabin (for just a few dollars more). Once inside, I'm immediately lost in a labyrinth of hallways, until a white-smocked attendant directs me to my cabin. After I rent a towel and slip into my swimsuit, I'm finally ready for some hot-water fun.

Immersed in 100-degree water under glorious Baroque

ceilings, I enjoy some of Europe's most memorable people-watching. Hungarians of all shapes and sizes stuff themselves into tiny swimsuits and strut their stuff. Young people float blissfully in warm water. Pot-bellied elders stand in chest-high water around chessboards and ponder their next moves. Easing my way into the steaming water, I submerge myself nostril-deep—and feel the accumulated impact of a day of busy sightseeing ebb away.

Budapest's Cafés

In the late 19th century, a vibrant café culture boomed in Budapest, just as it did in Vienna and Paris. The *kávéház* (coffeehouse) was a local institution, allowing workers to get a jolt of caffeine to power them through a 12-hour workday and giving city dwellers a place to escape their tiny flats (and avoid having to pay for heat at home). For the price of a cup of coffee, they could come to a café to enjoy warmth, companionship, and loaner newspapers.

Realizing that these neighborhood living rooms were breeding grounds for dissidents, the communists closed the cafés or converted them into *eszpresszós* (with uncomfortable stools instead of easy chairs) or *bisztrós* (stand-up fast-food joints with no chairs at all). Today, nostalgia is bringing back the *kávéház* culture. A favorite activity is whiling away the afternoon at a genteel coffeehouse, sipping a drink or nibbling a delicate layer cake. Budapest has many impressive cafés, but the undisputed champ is the palatial New York Café—which makes other fancy coffeehouses feel like a strip-mall Starbucks.

Hungarian Cuisine

Hungarian cuisine features meat, tomatoes, and peppers (*paprika*) of every shape, size, color, and flavor. Peppers can be stewed, stuffed, sautéed, baked, grilled, or pickled. For seasoning, red shakers of dried paprika join the salt on tables. There are two main types of paprika spice: sweet (*édes*), used for cooking, and hot (*csípős* or *erős*), used to adjust your own plate to your preferred amount of heat.

On menus, chicken or veal *paprikás* comes smothered in a spicy, creamy red stew, and is served with dumpling-like boiled egg noodles. Hungarian *gulyás leves* (shepherd's soup) is a clear, spicy broth with chunks of meat, potatoes, and other vegetables—not the thick "goulash" stew you may be expecting. Cold fruit soup *(hideg gyümölcs leves)* is a sweet, cream-based treat—generally eaten before a meal, even though it tastes more like a dessert.

Wine and Spirits

Hungary boasts 22 designated wine-growing regions, scattered across the country. In addition to the standard international grapes (such as Riesling and Chardonnay), Hungary corks up some interesting alternatives. Tokaji—which French King Louis XV called "the wine of kings, and the king of wines"—is a sweet, late-harvest, honey-colored dessert wine made from noble-rot grapes, which burst and wither on the vine before being harvested.

Hungary is also proud of its fruit-flavored firewater *(pálinka)* and—most of all—Unicum, a bitter liquor made of 40 different herbs and aged in oak casks. Featured in a series of whimsical, vintage, Guinness-like ads, Unicum is a point of national pride and has a history as complicated as its flavor. To sample this local answer to Jägermeister, look for the round bottle with the red-and-white cross.

Hungary Travel Resources from Rick Steves

Guidebooks

Check out Rick's guidebooks covering Budapest and Eastern Europe

Audio Europe

Download Rick's free Audio Europe app, with interviews about Hungarian culture and sightseeing

TV Shows

The quintessence of Hungary with Rick as your host, viewable on public television and at RickSteves.com. Episodes cover Budapest

Organized Tours

Small group tours, with itineraries planned by Rick: Best of Eastern Europe in 15 Days; Prague & Budapest in 8 Days

For more on all these resources, visit RickSteves.com. For Hungary trip-planning tips, see RickSteves.com/europe/hungary.

Slovenia

Tiny Slovenia is one of Europe's most unexpectedly rewarding destinations. At the intersection of the Slavic, German, and Italian worlds, Slovenia blends the best of each culture. And though it's just a quick trip away from the tourist throngs in Venice, Munich, Salzburg, and Vienna, Slovenia has stayed off the tourist track—making it a more authentic Back Door destination.

Though only half as big as Switzerland, Slovenia will surprise you with all it has to offer. You can hike on alpine trails in the Julian Alps, go spelunking in some of the world's best caves in the Karst, get your urban fix in the vibrant capital of Ljubljana, and ride a romantic *pletna* boat across beautiful Lake Bled. And be sure to make time to relax with a glass of local wine and a seafood dinner while watching the sun dip into the Adriatic.

Today, it seems strange to think that Slovenia was ever part of Yugoslavia. In fact, Slovenia feels more like Austria, both in its landscape and in the personality of its people. Slovenes are more industrious, organized, and punctual than their fellow former Yugoslavs...yet still friendly, relaxed, and Mediterranean. They won't win any big wars (they're too well-adjusted to even try), but they're exactly the type of people you'd love to chat with over a cup of coffee. And the Slovenian language is as mellow as the people. The worst they can say in their native tongue is, "May you be kicked by a horse." Rather than say "Damn it!" they'll exclaim, "Three hundred hairy bears!"

Slovenia is an endearing, undiscovered gem. Just make sure when planning a trip to Slovenia that you allow enough time to explore this delightful land.

FAVORITE SIGHTS AND MEMORABLE EXPERIENCES IN SLOVENIA

Bells and Bridegrooms in Lake Bled

With its sweeping mountain panoramas and Romantic Age aura, Lake Bled is Slovenia's top alpine resort. Since the Habsburg days, this is where Slovenes have taken their guests—from kings to cousins—to show off the country's natural wonders.

The focal point of any Lake Bled visit is to ride a *pletna* boat to the fairy-tale island in the middle of the lake. Boarding my *pletna*, I strike up a conversation with the oarsman, Robert. With close-cropped blonde hair and piercing blue eyes, he's younger than I'd expect for such a traditional profession. He explains that he built his boat by hand, following a design passed down from father to son for centuries. There's no keel, so Robert must work hard to steer the flat-bottomed boat with each stroke. Leaning back, I appreciate his rhythmic rowing, which sends us gliding smoothly across the lake's mirrored surface—neatly bisecting a perfect reflection of the cliff-capping castle overhead.

From the boat dock where Robert drops me off, I look up a long, stony staircase. Lake Bled is a popular wedding location, and after the ceremony, it's traditional for grooms to carry—or *try* to carry—their brides up all 99 of these steps to prove themselves "fit for marriage." On summer Saturdays, you'll see a steady procession of brides and grooms here. Trudging up the stairs carrying only my camera—and getting winded near the top—I'm glad not to be hauling a spouse.

Summiting the island, I'm face-to-face with the pretty Baroque Church of the Assumption. Inside, a long rope hangs down in front of the altar. Visitors take turns grabbing hold, pulling hard, and being lifted momentarily off their feet to the sound of a clanging bell in the adjacent campanile. Supposedly, ringing the bell three times with one pull will make your fondest wish come true. I can't resist giving the rope a tug.

Fast Facts

Biggest cities: Ljubljana (capital, 270,000), Maribor (158,000)

Size: 7,800 square miles (size of New Jersey), population 2 million

Locals call it: Slovenija

Currency: Euro

Key date: June 25, 1991, Slovenia declares independence from Yugoslavia

Language: Slovene

Biggest festivals: Ljubljana Festival (summer-long music fest), Kurentovanje (spring Mardi Gras celebration, town of Ptuj)

Handy Slovene phrases: *Dobar dan* (hello; **doh**-behr dahn), *Prosim* (please; **proh**-seem), *Hvala* (thank you; **hvah**-lah), *šnopc* (schnapps; "schnapps")

Tourist info: Slovenia.info

The Slovenian mountain resort of Lake Bled has an enchanting church on its island and hardworking boatmen to get you there.

After Robert gives me a lift back to shore, I stroll the promenade around Lake Bled. Handsome villas line the lake, including what was once the vacation getaway of the Yugoslav president-for-life Tito, who huddled here with foreign dignitaries like Indira Gandhi and Nikita Khrushchev. After Tito died in 1980, his villa was converted into a classy hotel with a James Bond ambience. In one suite, you can actually sleep in the dictator's bed.

Completing my circle around the lake, I settle in at a waterfront café and dig into a Lake Bled specialty: a delicate layer cake of vanilla custard, whipped cream, and crispy wafers. Slovenes are proud of their local pastries—and the beauty of their land. Eating my delicious cream cake, surrounded by the majesty and serenity of Lake Bled, it's easy to see why.

Laid-Back Ljubljana

As a tour guide, I enjoy introducing my American travelers to Slovenia's capital, Ljubljana. Although Slovenia is known as the most industrious of the Balkan countries, this vest-pocket capital's mellow ambience and lively riverfront café scene are revelations. The leafy riverside promenade crawls with stylishly dressed students sipping *kava* and polishing their near-perfect English. Surveying this scene, invariably one of my tour members wonders aloud, "Doesn't anybody here have a job?"

Ljubljana's residents work hard. But, with the country's main university campus right downtown, the city also knows how to play hard. Socializing and people-watching seem to be the national pastimes.

While Ljubljana has slick new museums opening each year, ultimately this town is all about ambience. The cobbled core of

Slovenia's Top Destinations

Ljubljana ▲▲   allow 1-2 days
Vibrant capital oozing with cobbled ambience, trendy
boutiques and eateries, unique architecture by Jože Plečnik,
and inviting riverside promenade

Lake Bled ▲▲▲   1-2 days
Alpine lake resort with a church-topped island, cliff-hanging castle, famous
desserts, and proximity to mountain thrills

Julian Alps ▲▲   1 day
Cut-glass peaks, tranquil Soča River Valley, adventure-sports capital Bovec, and
fine WWI museum in Kobarid, all connected by a twisty mountain road

Karst Region ▲   1 day
Arid plateau with world-class caves (Škocjan and Postojna), Lipizzaner stallion
stud farm at Lipica, scenically situated Predjama Castle, great wines, and "slow
food"

With more time, consider visiting
Logarska Dolina Remote mountain valley with traditional lifestyles
Piran Atmospheric seaside resort town
Ptuj Charming-if-sleepy historic town topped by a castle

Ljubljana is an idyllic place that sometimes feels too good to be true. The spunky mayor is on an eternal crusade to pedestrianize the entire city, block by block. Fashion boutiques and al fresco cafés jockey for control of the old town, and people enjoy a Sunday stroll any day of the week. Easygoing Ljubljana is the kind of place where graffiti and crumbling buildings seem elegantly atmospheric instead of shoddy.

Ljubljana, the trickiest capital in Europe to pronounce, is shaped by the artistic genius of Jože Plečnik, the greatest Slovenian architect of the 20th century.

The Ljubljanica River, lined with cafés, restaurants, and a buzzing market hall, bisects the city. The outdoor farmers market is a hive of activity, where big-city Slovenes buy directly from the producers. Some farmers still use wooden carts to hand-truck veggies in from their garden patches in the suburbs.

After being damaged by an earthquake in 1895, Ljubljana was rebuilt in the Art Nouveau and Art Deco styles that were so popular at the time. A generation later, the homegrown architect Jože Plečnik bathed the city in his distinctive classical-meets-modern style: sleek and eye-pleasing, artfully ornamented with columns and geometrical flourishes.

Like Gaudí shaped Barcelona and Bernini shaped Rome, Plečnik made Ljubljana what it is today. Because he walked to work each day and had to live with what he designed, Plečnik was particularly thoughtful about incorporating aesthetics, nature, and human needs into his projects. The result is like feng shui on an urban scale. Enjoy his picturesque market colonnade, Triple Bridge, and Cobbler's Bridge.

For a more personal look at the architect, I enjoy visiting his home, decorated exactly as it was the day Plečnik died in 1957. On my first visit, this nondescript house underwhelmed me. But as the docent, Ana, proudly walked me from room to room—revealing the quirky but beautiful furniture and artful bric-a-brac Plečnik designed, as well as souvenirs from around the world that inspired him—I found myself seduced by his genius.

Standing in Plečnik's bedroom, Ana explained with emotion how important this great man was to her tiny nation. Inspecting a table strewn with his drawings, equipment, and personal items (including his glasses and the hat he was famous for wearing), I began to feel as though Plečnik himself had invited me over for dinner.

That's a feeling I get again and again throughout Slovenia. This cozy land and its welcoming people just have a way of making visitors fall in love with them.

High in the Slovenian Alps

The Julian Alps, crowning the northwestern corner of Slovenia, are laced with hiking paths, blanketed with deep forests, and speckled with ski resorts and vacation chalets. Beyond every ridge is a peaceful alpine village nestled around a quaint Baroque steeple.

The single best day in the Julian Alps is spent driving up and over the breathtaking Vršič Pass and back down via the Soča River Valley. Navigating the pass takes 50 hairpin turns—24 on the way up, 26 on the way back down—each one numbered and labeled with the altitude in meters. Curling on twisty roads between the peaks, I am treated to stunning high-mountain scenery and charming hamlets.

But as beautiful as this area is, it has a dark side. During World War I, 10,000 Russian prisoners of war labored here, building the pass road. At switchback #8, I leave my car by a rushing mini waterfall and hike up through the woods to a humble little Orthodox chapel. In 1916, an avalanche thundered down here, killing more than a hundred workers. The surviving prisoners erected the rustic chapel where the final victim was found.

Just after switchback #24, I reach the summit at just over 5,000 feet, where a mountain hut offers amazing alpine views. Twisting back down the other side of the mountains—and getting dizzy on the serpentine roads—I get my first view of the Soča River Valley. The Soča—with water somehow both crystal clear and spectacularly turquoise—is a mecca for kayakers and other whitewater adventurers, who call it "Adrenaline Valley."

Though peaceful now, this area saw some of the fiercest fighting of World War I. Known as the Soča Front—or

Don't Skip the Sticker

Slovenia's sleek network of expressways is one of Europe's best—but these aren't "free"-ways. Drivers on expressways must display a toll sticker, called a *vinjeta*. If renting a car in Slovenia, it probably comes with a sticker (ask just to be sure). If you're driving in from elsewhere, buy one at a gas station near the border. Be warned: This rule is taken very seriously. Police check frequently, and drivers without stickers are given a large fine on the spot.

Slovenia's beautiful Julian Alps *(left)* were the scene of fierce and bloody fighting during World War I, as the mausoleum at Kobarid *(right)* attests.

the Isonzo Front in Italian—the million casualties here gave it the nickname "Valley of the Cemeteries." The fighting between the Italian and Austro-Hungarian armies was waged not in the valleys, but at the tops of the mountains.

Finally, I reach the humble village of Kobarid, with the valley's best collection of World War I sights. The town was immortalized by Ernest Hemingway, who drove a Red Cross ambulance nearby (and later wrote about Kobarid in *A Farewell to Arms*).

I stop at Kobarid's excellent museum, which tells the story of the Soča Front and humanizes the suffering of this horrific but almost forgotten corner of World War I. The exhibits focus not on guns and heroes, but on the stories of the common people who fought and died here. I gaze into the eyes of a generation of young men—imported from the farthest reaches of the Habsburg Empire to fight a hopeless battle on a frigid mountaintop. Graphic images of war injuries are juxtaposed with a display of medals earned—suggesting the question, was it worth it?

Next, I head up to the hilltop mausoleum just above town. The octagonal pyramid holds the remains of 7,014 Italian soldiers—victims of just one battle. Standing on the broad terrace at the top of the gigantic monument, I'm surrounded by a 360-degree panorama of cut-glass peaks. Visually tracing the twinkling Soča River back the way I've come, I think: Only Slovenia combines epic scenery and poignant history, all in one dizzying corkscrew drive.

More Slovenian Experiences

Spectacular Spelunking: About an hour south of Ljubljana, Slovenia's Karst region is honeycombed with a vast network of caves and underground rivers. Spelunkers agree that this region has some of the most remarkable caves on the planet, including my favorite, the Škocjan Caves. Visitors begin by

LEFT The Škocjan Caves

RIGHT The Lipica Stud Farm

seeing a multitude of formations in a series of large caverns. Guides tell the story as, drip by drip, stalactites grow from spaghetti-thin strands to mighty sequoia-like stone pillars. The experience builds and builds as you go into ever-more-impressive grottoes, and you think you've seen the best. But then you reach the truly colossal final cavern, where the sound of a mighty river crashes through the mist. It's a world where a thousand evil Wizard of Oz monkeys could comfortably fly in formation. Crossing a breathtaking footbridge 150 feet above the torrent gives you faith in Slovenian engineering. Finally, the cave widens, sunlight pours in, and you emerge—like lost creatures seeking daylight—into a lush canyon.

World-Class Horses: Lipizzaner stallions—known for their noble gait and Baroque shape—were made famous by Vienna's Spanish Riding School. The Lipica Stud Farm, near the Škocjan Caves, was founded in 1580 to provide Lipizzaners for the Habsburg court in Vienna. While the stuffy Viennese cousins of Slovenia's Lipizzaners still perform under chandeliers, at Lipica visitors can get nose to nose with the stallions. You'll learn how they're raised and trained, and—on most days—get to watch them train or perform. The Lipizzaners' clever routine—stutter-stepping sideways to the classical beat and hopping in the air on their hind legs—thrills horse lovers and casual viewers alike.

CULTURE AND TRADITIONS: EVERYTHING'S SO...SLOVENIAN

Hayracks and Beehives

Coming from such a small country, locals are proud of the few things that are distinctly Slovenian. Two such icons of Slovenian culture are roofed hayracks and beehive panels.

Because of the frequent rainfall in Slovenia, hayracks are protected by a roof that allows the hay to dry. You'll see these distinctive roofed hayracks scattered across the hillsides, especially in the northwest. Souvenir shops sell postcards and miniature wooden models of this unlikely national symbol.

Slovenia also has a strong beekeeping tradition. Slovenian beekeepers believe that painting the fronts of the hives makes it easier for bees to find their way home, so for centuries, they have illustrated their hives with vivid, whimsical scenes of folk life, bible stories, historical events, and so on. A lovable beekeeping museum in the village of Radovljica (near Lake Bled) explains the history of beekeeping. But if you can't make it there, replica beehive panels—a favorite form of folk art—are sold everywhere as souvenirs.

Slovenian Food

Traditional Slovenian food has a distinctly Germanic vibe—including the "four S's": sausage, schnitzel, strudel, and sauerkraut. One local dish to look for is *štruklji*, a dumpling-like savory layer cake, which can be stuffed with cheese, meat, or vegetables. But cosmopolitan Slovenia—at an intersection of cultures—isn't too hung up on traditional grub. Locals favor a wide range of cuisines: Mediterranean, French, Asian, Mexican, and so on. Ljubljana has some of the best—and most varied—restaurants in the former Yugoslavia.

Drinking in Slovenia

Slovenia is proud of its good wines, its many varieties of flavored brandies, and the local lager with a warm-and-fuzzy name that suits the culture: Smile. But its most unusual beverage is Cockta, a cola with an unusual flavor (which supposedly is made from berry, lemon, orange, and 11 herbs).

Slovenia's charms are subtle—like its trademark hayracks and its passion for the berry-flavored cola, Cockta.

Originally called Cockta-Cockta, the drink was introduced during the communist period as an alternative to the difficult-to-get Coca-Cola. These days, even though Coke is widely available, nostalgic Slovenes still have a taste for the Cockta they grew up on. Be adventurous, buy a bottle to drink, and ponder the power of an acquired taste.

Slovenia Travel Resources from Rick Steves

Guidebooks
Check out Rick's guidebooks covering Croatia & Slovenia and Eastern Europe

Audio Europe
Download Rick's free Audio Europe app, with interviews about Slovenian culture and sightseeing

TV Shows
The quintessence of Slovenia with Rick as your host, viewable on public television and at RickSteves.com. Episodes cover Ljubljana, Lake Bled, Soča Pass, Škocjan Caves, Predjama Castle, and Lipica Stud Farm

Organized Tours
Small group tours, with itineraries planned by Rick: Best of Eastern Europe in 15 Days; Best of the Adriatic in 14 Days

For more on all these resources, visit RickSteves.com. For Slovenia trip-planning tips, see RickSteves.com/europe/slovenia.

Croatia

Sunny beaches, succulent seafood, and a taste of
la dolce vita...in Eastern Europe?

Croatia, with thousands of miles of coastline,
is Eastern Europe's Riviera. Holiday makers love
its pebbly beaches, predictably balmy summer
weather, and dramatic mountains. Croatia is also
historic. With ruined Roman palaces, Byzantine
mosaics, Venetian bell towers, medieval walls,
Habsburg villas, and even communist concrete,
past rulers have left their mark.

One tragic exception to Croatia's mellow history came
in the early 1990s, when the country declared independence
from Yugoslavia, sparking an ugly war. Today the bloodshed
is in the past. While a trip to Croatia offers thoughtful travelers the opportunity to understand a complicated chapter
of recent history, most visitors focus instead on the appealing towns and natural wonders the country has long been
known for.

Dubrovnik is still the "Pearl of the Adriatic," with its
old town encircled by a medieval wall. The town of Split is—
astonishingly—built in, on, and around a Roman palace. The
stunning Plitvice Lakes National Park, sparkling with waterfalls, attracts hikers and pho-
tographers. And, for a coastal
getaway, it's easy to fall in love
with the village of Rovinj, on
the Istrian Peninsula.

Dubrovnik,
with its mighty
walls and
inviting beach

Over the last several years,
Croatia has reclaimed its
status as a tourist hotspot. In
the summer, its long coastline
is crawling with a Babel of
international guests. And yet,

despite the tourists, this place remains distinctly and stubbornly Croatian.

FAVORITE SIGHTS AND MEMORABLE EXPERIENCES IN CROATIA

Romantic Rovinj

Idyllic Istria, a wedge-shaped peninsula at Croatia's northwest corner, is an engaging mix of Croatia and Italy. While most of the Croatian coast was Italian-dominated for centuries, Istria remained part of Italy for even longer. Today, bilingual street signs remind visitors that both languages are still official.

My favorite little town on the Istrian coast is Rovinj. Surrounded by the Adriatic on three sides, this town is like a little hunk of Venice draped over a hill. A visit here produces a collage of vivid travel memories: Boats laden with kitschy shells for sale bob giddily in the harbor, while the bell tower's rickety staircase tests climbers' faith. From the top, on a clear day, you can see Venice. And capping the tower, a patron-saint weathervane valiantly faces each menacing cloud front that blows in from the sea. She swivels with the breeze to provide locals with a primitive, but eerily accurate, weather report.

Walking through the market puts me in a good mood. I feel like Marilyn Monroe singing to a bunch of sex-starved GIs. Babushkas push grappa and homemade fruit brandies on me. Istria is one of Europe's top truffle regions, and small, pricey bottles of pungently flavored oils invite me to bring that taste home with me. The merchants' sample walnuts are curiously flavorful. I'll buy a bag on my way out of town.

Strolling the cobbled back lanes, I wander into a time-warp bar that takes "untouristy" to almost scary extremes. The town fishermen and alcoholics (generally, it seems, one and the same) are smoking, bantering loudly, and getting too

LEFT Rovinj, on the tip of the Istrian Peninsula, is my favorite stop between Venice and Dubrovnik.

RIGHT Croatians are clever at turning their rocky shores into romantic cocktail bars.

drunk on cheap homemade beer to notice the nude pinups plastering the walls. Suddenly, all eyes are on me... and I feel like a rabbit at the nocturnal house at the zoo. But they quickly go back to their chattering, laughing, and drinking. My friend explains that they're speaking the local Istrian vernacular—a Croatian-Italian hybrid.

That evening, walking along "restaurant row"—the seafront promenade where interchangeable fish joints desperately vie for diners' attention—I stumble on Valentino Cocktail Bar, where travelers nurse drinks on the rocks...literally. Patricia, the elegantly coiffed and exactingly made-up owner, hands out pillows and invites you to plunk down in your own seaside niche. Fish, attracted by the bar's underwater lights, swim by from all over the bay. The sun sets on a gorgeous Istrian evening, classy candelabras twinkle in the twilight, and couples cozy up to each other and the view. Sipping my white Croatian wine, I keep thinking, simply, "romantic."

> ## Fast Facts
>
> **Biggest cities:** Zagreb (capital, 790,000), Split (178,000), Rijeka (129,000)
> **Size:** 22,000 square miles (similar to West Virginia), population 4.5 million
> **Locals call it:** Hrvatska
> **Currency:** Croatian kunas (kn)
> **Key date:** October 8, 1991, Croatia declares its independence from Yugoslavia
> **Biggest festivals:** Dubrovnik Summer Festival (July-August, music), Moreška sword dance (twice a week in summer, on the island of Korčula)
> **Handy Croatian phrases:** *Dobar dan* (hello; **doh**-bar dahn), *Molim* (please; **moh**-leem), *Hvala* (thank you; **hvah**-lah), *plaža* (beach; **plah**-zhah)
> **Tourist info:** Croatia.hr

Wandering Dubrovnik's City Walls

Jockeying my way between cruise-excursion groups, I climb the steep steps to the top of the still-stout medieval walls that surround Dubrovnik. As I begin a slow, circular, hour-and-a-half walk around the fortified perimeter of one of Europe's best-preserved medieval towns, I snap photos like crazy of the ever-changing views. On one side is a sea of red rooftops; on the other side, the actual sea.

My B&B host holds a mortar shell—a souvenir of the 1991 shelling of Dubrovnik *(left)*. Houses that were hit are the ones with newer, brighter red tiles *(right)*.

Near the Pile Gate, I pause to enjoy a full frontal view of the Stradun, the 300-yard-long promenade that runs through the heart of Dubrovnik's old town. In the Middle Ages, merchants lined this drag; before that, it was a canal. Today this is the main artery of the city: an Old World shopping mall by day and sprawling cocktail party after dark.

Farther along, I look down and see a peaceful stone terrace perched above the sea, clinging to the outside of the city walls. Generously shaded by white umbrellas, this is my favorite Dubrovnik escape, a rustic outdoor tavern called Buža. The name means "hole in the wall"—and that's exactly what you'll have to climb through to get there. Filled with mellow tourists and bartenders pouring wine into plastic cups from tiny screw-top bottles, Buža comes with castaway views and Frank Sinatra ambience.

Looking inland from my ramparts perch, my eyes fall on a random arrangement of bright- and dark-toned red roof tiles. In this complex and often-troubled corner of Europe, even a tranquil stroll around the walls comes with a poignant history lesson. After Croatia declared independence in 1991, the Yugoslav National Army laid siege to this town and lobbed mortars over the hill. Today, the new, brighter-colored tiles mark houses that were hit and have been rebuilt. At a glance, it's clear that more than two-thirds of the old town's buildings suffered bomb damage.

Surveying the rooftops, my thoughts turn to Pero, my B&B host, who spent years after the war turning the bombed-out remains of his old-town home into a fine guesthouse. Upon my arrival last night, Pero uncorked a bottle of *orahovica* (the local grappa-like firewater). Hoping to write that evening with a clear head, I tried to refuse the drink. But this is a Slavic land. Remembering times when I was force-fed vodka in Russia by new friends, I knew it was hopeless. Pero made this hooch himself, with green walnuts. As he slugged down a shot, he handed me a glass, wheezing, "Walnut grappa—it recovers your energy."

Pero reached under the counter and held up the mangled tail of a mortar shell, describing how the

Croatian Beaches

Croatia is known for its glimmering beaches. However, most are pebbly or rocky rather than sandy—and spiny sea urchins are not uncommon. In addition to a swimsuit, pack a pair of water shoes for wading, as well as a beach towel and sunscreen. You might also want to bring a hat, bug spray, and sturdy shoes (for hiking to more secluded beaches).

Many of Croatia's beaches are nude. If you want to work on an all-around tan, seek out a beach marked *FKK* (from the German *Freikörper Kultur*, or "free body culture").

Croatia's Top Destinations

Dubrovnik ▲▲▲   allow 1-3 days
The "Pearl of the Adriatic," highlighted by walkable medieval walls; great beaches; and Mount Srđ, a Napoleonic fortress with spectacular views

Nearby
Mljet National Park Undeveloped island retreat
Cavtat Art-packed resort village
Pelješac Peninsula Dramatic coastal scenery and Croatia's best vineyards
Ston Small town with giant fortifications

Dalmatian Islands ▲▲   1-2 days
Low-key **Korčula**, with walled old town and fjord-like backdrop, and ritzy **Hvar**, with seductive beaches

Split ▲▲   1 day
Bustling city with extensive Roman palace ruins and busy seaside promenade

Istria ▲▲   2-3 days
Italian-feeling region with Croatia's prettiest town **(Rovinj)**, Roman ruins **(Pula)**, and picturesque wine-and-truffles hill towns **(Motovun)**

Plitvice Lakes National Park ▲▲▲   1 day
Forested canyon filled with crystal-clear lakes, stunning waterfalls, and easy trails

Zagreb ▲▲   1-2 days
Capital city boasting quirky museums, lush parks, and a colorful urban bustle

---

gorgeous stone and knotty-wood building he grew up in suffered a direct hit in the siege. He put the mortar in my hands. Just as I don't enjoy holding a gun, I didn't enjoy touching the twisted remains of that mortar. Pero explained that he gets a monthly retirement check for being wounded in the war, but he got bored and didn't want to live on the tiny government stipend—so he went to work rebuilding his guesthouse.

I took Pero's photograph. He held up the mortar and smiled. I didn't want him to hold up the mortar and smile, but that's what he did. He seemed determined to smile—as if it signified a personal victory over the destruction the mortar had wrought.

It's impressive how people can weather tragedy, rebuild, and move on. Despite the terrors of war just a couple of decades ago, life here is once again very good, and, from my perch here atop the city walls, filled with promise.

Magical Motovun

Croatia is more than the sea, and diverse Istria offers some of the country's most compelling reasons to head inland. In the Istrian interior, between humble concrete towns crying out for a paint job, you'll find vintners painstakingly reviving a delicate winemaking tradition, farmers pressing that last drop of oil out of their olives, trained dogs sniffing out truffles in primeval forests, and a smattering of fortified medieval hill towns offering sweeping views over the surrounding terrain. The best of these hill towns is Motovun, featuring a colorful old church and a rampart walk with the best spine-tingling vistas in the Istrian interior.

On my first visit to this region, I drove halfway across Croatia and arrived late at night. Through a driving rainstorm, I wound and wound up through the dark to Motovun's summit. The road got narrower and narrower. When I ran out of road, I parked, got out, and walked to my hotel, with no sense of what the town even looked like. The next

Croatia's Istrian Peninsula is famed for its hill towns like Motovun *(left)* and its a cappella singing groups *(right)*.

morning, I awoke before my alarm rang and pushed open my lumbering shutters. The heavy rainstorm had cleaned the air, and an early-morning light invigorated the colors of the glistening red-tile roofs, the rustic stone rampart, and a lush landscape of rolling hills and simple farms.

The next year, I returned to Motovun with my film crew. During a break, while strolling the town's cobbles and marveling at how dead it was, I heard a men's a cappella group practicing. I snooped around to find out where they were. Around the corner, I went up a short flight of stairs and stared at a closed door separating me from their heavenly singing. I gently pushed the door open just a crack to see the singers. It was a traditional *klapa* group of a dozen men, sitting in a half-circle with their backs to me. Standing before them was the group's director, a woman with springy hair who looked like a mad, young, female Beethoven. She saw me, ran to the door, and invited me in. I pulled out a chair and savored the chorus.

A short time later, I ran to get my film crew. We unanimously agreed it was a magic moment, and we filmed it. The group ended up kicking off our Croatia episode with a wonderful bit of serendipity. Not only did it make for good television, but it was also a reminder to me of an important travel lesson: When out wandering, be bold. Remember, it's worth running the risk of having a door shut in your face—in order to risk being welcomed in.

More Croatian Experiences

Quirky Zagreb: In addition to its cosmopolitan bustle, generous parks, and in-love-with-life café-and-restaurant scene, Croatia's capital is home to some of Europe's most delightfully offbeat museums. The Museum of Naive Art showcases a uniquely Croatian art form: paintings by untrained peasant artists. (In the early 20th century, art-world highbrows embraced this sort of unschooled art as

evidence that artistic ability is inborn rather than taught.)
The movement's founder, Ivan Generalić, typically painted
wintry scenes on glass (in winter, he wasn't busy working
the fields, and glass was the cheapest material available).

Just across the street is the equally endearing Museum of
Broken Relationships, featuring true stories of failed couples
from around the world, told in their own words. Displayed
alongside their story is an actual item that embodies the
relationship (from angry gnomes to sex toys to discarded
wedding albums), in addition to the predictable "he cheated
on me so I broke his favorite fill-in-the-blank" items. The collection has struck such a chord, they've taken it on the road,
garnering fans in cities worldwide.

Hiking in a Waterfall Wonderland: Plitvice Lakes National
Park, two hours south of Zagreb, is one of Europe's most
spectacular natural wonders. Imagine Niagara Falls diced
and sprinkled over a heavily forested Grand Canyon. There's
nothing like this lush valley of 16 terraced lakes, laced
together by waterfalls, boat rides, and miles of pleasant plank
walks. Countless cascades and water that's both strangely
clear and full of vibrant colors make this park a misty natural
wonderland. Before I came here, I thought I really knew
Europe. Then I discovered Plitvice and realized you can
never exhaust Europe's surprises.

Layers of History in Split: Croatia's "second city," Split, has
an atmospheric old town core that's built amid the foundations of a fourth-century Roman palace. When the Emperor
Diocletian retired, he built a vast residence for his golden
years here in his native Dalmatia. After Rome fell and the
palace was abandoned, a medieval town sprouted from its
shell. The hallways of the palace became streets, the rooms
morphed into squares, and to this day, residents are actually living inside the walls of Diocletian's palace. Squeezed

Croatia's
charms range
from the
Museum of
Naive Art in
Zagreb *(left)*,
to Plitvice, a
dramatic natural
wonderland
(center), to
the town of
Split, whose
nucleus was the
fourth-century
palace of
Roman emperor
Diocletian
(right).

between the old town and the harborfront is a nicely landscaped pedestrian promenade called the Riva, where the sea of Croatian humanity laps at the walls of the palace. Strolling locals finish their days in good style here—just enjoying life's simple pleasures in a city that so seamlessly weaves its past and present into one.

CULTURE AND TRADITIONS: EVERYTHING'S SO...CROATIAN

Staying with Locals

Private accommodations throughout Croatia (and especially along the coast) offer travelers a characteristic alternative to big, overpriced resort hotels. There are *sobe*—individual rooms for rent—or *apartmani*, which are a bit larger and have a kitchen. The simplest *sobe* allow you to experience Croatia on the cheap, at nearly youth-hostel prices, while giving you a great opportunity to connect with a local family. The fanciest *sobe* are still affordable and can be downright swanky, with hotelesque amenities (private bathroom, air-conditioning, satellite TV, and so on) and as much or as little contact with your host family as you like.

Succulent Seafood

While Italian-style pastas and pizzas are common throughout Croatia, it's more memorable to splurge on a seafood dish, especially when vacationing on the coast. Croatians say that a fish should swim three times: first in the sea, then in olive oil (as you cook it), and finally in wine (when you eat it). But be careful when ordering: Most fish dishes are priced by

weight rather than by the portion (a one-kilogram portion feeds two hungry people).

Be open and adventurous. Seafood items that may sound unappetizing can be a delicious surprise. For instance, a good, fresh anchovy, done right, has a pleasant flavor and a melt-in-your-mouth texture. The menu item called "small fried fish" is generally a plate of deep-fried minnows. Another specialty is octopus salad, a flavorful mix of octopus, tomatoes, onions, capers, and spices.

Harmonious Croatian Voices

Traditionally found in Dalmatia, *klapa* music features the hauntingly beautiful sound of men's voices harmonizing a cappella, like a barbershop quartet with a soothing Adriatic flavor. Typically the leader begins the song, and the rest of the group follows behind him with a slight delay. Mariachi-style *klapa* groups perform in touristy areas, including what was once the entry vestibule of the Emperor Diocletian's palace in Split. Just listening to a few glorious tunes in this grand space with grand acoustics provides an unforgettable soundtrack for your trip.

Croatia Travel Resources from Rick Steves

Guidebooks
Check out Rick's guidebooks covering Croatia & Slovenia; Dubrovnik; and Eastern Europe

Audio Europe
Download Rick's free Audio Europe app, with interviews about Croatian culture and sightseeing

TV Shows
The quintessence of Croatia with Rick as your host, viewable on public television and at RickSteves.com. Episodes cover Split, Plitvice Lakes National Park, Zagreb, Rovinj, Dubrovnik, and the Dalmatian Coast

Organized Tours
Small group tours, with itineraries planned by Rick: Best of Eastern Europe in 15 Days; Best of the Adriatic in 14 Days

For more on all of these resources, visit RickSteves.com. For Croatia trip-planning tips, see RickSteves.com/europe/croatia.

Greece

With its classical past and hang-loose present, Greece offers something for every traveler. As the cradle of Western civilization, Greece boasts some of the world's greatest ancient monuments. But it also has plenty more to offer, including succulent seafood, inviting islands, whitewashed houses with bright-blue shutters, and an easy, mellow ambience.

Most tourists come here for a quick visit to Athens to bask in the greatness of the Acropolis and then head to an island to bask in the sun. But for more of a true Back Door experience, consider some of my favorite destinations on the mainland, such as the home of the ancient oracle at Delphi, the birthplace of the Olympics in Olympia, the Gibraltar-style fortress at Monemvasia, the stark Mani Peninsula, or the elegant-but-cozy port town of Nafplio, near two of Greece's greatest ancient sites—Mycenae and Epidavros.

Greece is easy on travelers. The people are welcoming and accommodating. Greeks pride themselves on a concept

called *filotimo*—literally "love of honor," but roughly translated as openness, friendliness, and hospitality. Social faux pas by unwary foreigners are easily overlooked by Greeks.

The country has gone through some tough economic times, but the pace of life remains relaxed. People work in the mornings, then take a midafternoon siesta, when they gather with their families to eat the main meal of the day. On warm summer nights, they stay up very late, even kids. Families spill into the streets to greet their neighbors on the evening stroll. For entertainment, they go out to eat, ordering large amounts and sharing it family-style.

It's a joy to surrender to the Greek way of living. All the things you're looking for—deep-blue water, mouthwatering food, striking scenery, and the thrill of connecting with ancient history—are here waiting for you. With its long history and simple lifestyle, Greece has a timeless appeal.

> ## Fast Facts
>
> **Biggest cities:** Athens (capital, 800,000), Thessaloniki (375,000), Piraeus (172,000)
> **Size:** 51,485 square miles (roughly the size of Alabama), population 10.8 million
> **Locals call it:** Hellas
> **Currency:** Euro
> **Key date:** 776 B.C., the first Olympic Games are held
> **Biggest festivals:** Athens & Epidavros Festival (June and July in Athens and Epidavros on the Peloponnese), Carnival Season, a.k.a. Apokreo (weeks prior to Orthodox Lent)
> **Annual per-capita cheese consumption:** 55 pounds (mostly feta, highest in the world)
> **Handy Greek phrases:** *Gia sas* (hello; yah sahs), *Parakalo* (please; pah-rah-kah-**loh**), *Efharisto* (thank you; ehf-hah-ree-**stoh**), *Ne* (yes; neh), *Ohi* (no; **oh**-hee)
> **Tourist info:** VisitGreece.gr

FAVORITE SIGHTS AND MEMORABLE EXPERIENCES IN GREECE

Cockcrow on Hydra

Hydra—less than two hours south of Athens by ferry—offers the ideal Greek island experience, without a long journey across the Aegean.

Hydra has one real town, no real roads, no cars, and not even any bikes. Zippy water taxis whisk you from the quaint little harbor to isolated beaches and tavernas. Donkeys are the main way to transport things here. These surefooted beasts of burden, laden with everything from sandbags and bathtubs to bottled water, climb stepped lanes. Behind each mule-train toils a human pooper-scooper; I imagine picking up after your beast is required. On Hydra, a traffic jam is three donkeys and a fisherman.

On Greece's idyllic isle of Hydra, the only traffic is donkeys.

While the island is generally quiet, dawn here taught me the exact meaning of "cockcrow." On Hydra, the end of night is marked with much more than a distant cock-a-doodle-doo: It's a dissonant chorus of cat fights, burro honks, and what sounds like roll call at an asylum for crazed roosters. After the animal population gets that out of its system, it's like one of the old gods hits "snooze" and the island slumbers a little longer.

Tourists wash ashore with the many private and public boats that come and go, but few venture beyond the harborfront. Today, after my barnyard awakening, I decided to head uphill, and my small detour became a delightful little odyssey. While I had no intention of anything more than a lazy stroll, one inviting lane after another drew me up, up, up to the top of the town. Here, shabby homes enjoyed grand views, tired burros ambled along untethered, and island life trudged on, oblivious to tourism.

Over the crest, I followed a paved riverbed down to the remote harbor hamlet of Kaminia, where 20 tough little fishing boats jostled within a tiny breakwater. Children jumped fearlessly from rock to rock to the end of the jetty, ignoring an old man rhythmically casting his line.

As I trudged into town, a rickety woven-straw chair and a tipsy little table at Kodylenia's Taverna were positioned just right, overlooking the harbor. The heavy, reddening sun commanded, "Sit." I did, sipping ouzo and observing a sea busy with taxi boats, ferries connecting this oasis with Athens, freighters—like castles of rust—lumbering slowly along the horizon, and a silhouetted cruise ship anchored like it hadn't moved in weeks. Ouzo, my anise-flavored drink of choice on this trip, and my plastic baggie of pistachios purchased back in town were the perfect complements to the setting sun. Blue and white fishing boats jived with the chop. I'd swear the cats—small, numerous as the human residents of this island, and oh so feminine—were watching the setting sun with me. An old man flipped his worry beads, backlit by the golden glitter on the harbor. Three men walked by, each reminding me of Spiro Agnew.

As darkness settled, my waiter—who returned here to his family's homeland after spending 20 years in New Jersey, where he "never took a nap"—brought a candle for my table. My second glass of ouzo came with a smudge of someone's big fat Greek lipstick. Wiping it off before sipping seemed to connect me with the scene even more. The soft Greek lounge music tumbling out of the kitchen mixed everything like an audio swizzle stick. I glanced over my shoulder to the coastal lane home. Thankfully, it was lamplit.

Walking home, under a ridge lined with derelict windmills, I tried to envision Hydra before electricity, when spring water flowed and the community was powered by both wind and burros. At the edge of town I passed a bar filled with noisy cruise-ship tourists, and was thankful I'd taken the uphill lane when I left my hotel that morning. Locals, proud of the extravagant yachts moored for the night, like to tell of movie stars who make regular visits. But the island is so quiet that, by midnight, all the high rollers seem to be back on board watching movies. Sitting on a ferry cleat the size of a stool, I scanned the harbor—big flat-screen TVs flickered from every other yacht.

Back in Hydra town, I observed the pleasant evening routine of strolling and socializing. Dice clattered on dozens of backgammon boards, entrepreneurial cats seemed busy, children chased soccer balls, and a tethered goat chewed on something inedible in its low-profile corner. From the other end of town came the happy music of a christening party. Dancing women filled the building, while their children mimicked them in the street. Farther down, two elderly, black-clad women sat like tired dogs on the curb.

Succumbing to the lure of a pastry shop, I sat down for some honey-soaked baklava. I told the baker I was American. "Oh," he said, shaking his head with sadness and pity, "you work too hard."

I answered, "Right. But not today."

Communing with Athens' Ancients

For decades, I recommended that travelers to Athens—long infamous for its sprawl, noise, and pollution—see the big sights, then get out. But visiting it recently, I saw a dramatic change. New driving laws, along with a marvelous subway system, have made the city less congested. While it used

Greece's Top Destinations

Athens ▲▲▲   allow 2-3 days

Greece's sprawling, congested capital, featuring first-class ancient ruins, atmospheric old Plaka quarter, and thriving ramshackle nightlife

Top Sights
Acropolis Hilltop capped by architectural jewel, the Parthenon
Acropolis Museum Glassy modern temple for ancient art
Ancient Agora Marketplace and meeting point of ancient Athens
National Archaeological Museum World's best collection of ancient Greek sculpture

Nafplio ▲▲▲   1-2 days

Tidy midsized town with a cozy port, elegant old town, hilltop fortress, and easy day trips to two amazing ancient sites

Nearby
Mycenae Ancient fortress city with iconic Lion Gate and beehive tomb
Epidavros Best-preserved theater of the ancient world, with astonishing acoustics

Hydra ▲▲▲   1-2 days

Idyllic car-free island with picturesque harbor, casual beaches, and enticing coastal hikes

Santorini ▲▲   1-2 days

Black-sand beaches and postcard-perfect towns clinging to the rim of a caldera (flooded volcano crater)

Mykonos ▲▲   1-2 days

Quintessential Greek isle with whitewashed village and pulsating nightlife

---

to turn my hanky black in a day, the air now seems much cleaner. And the city is much more people-friendly, with welcoming pedestrian boulevards and squares filled with benches, shade-giving trees, and inviting cafés rather than parked cars. But the big draw still remains its ancient sites. Nowhere else in the world will you feel like you've journeyed back in time to the birthplace of Western civilization itself.

Crowned by the mighty Parthenon, the Acropolis rises ethereally above the sprawl of modern Athens. I consider the Parthenon the finest temple from the ancient world: Simple, balanced, and orderly, it sums up the Greek Golden Age. Unlike most ancient sites, the Acropolis we see today was started and finished within two generations—a snapshot of the Golden Age set in stone. I visit late in the day, as the sun goes down, when the white Parthenon stone gleams a

Kardamyli and the Mani Peninsula ▲   1-2 days

Unspoiled beach town of Kardamyli and jumping-off point for the Mani Peninsula's dramatic hill towns and jagged coastlines

With more time, consider visiting

Olympia Stunning temple and stadium ruins at birthplace of the ancient games
Monemvasia Gibraltar-like rock peninsula with million-dollar views
Delphi Where ancients came to consult the oracle

creamy golden brown, and what had been a tourist war zone is suddwenly peaceful.

While the Acropolis was the city's ceremonial showpiece, the ancient Agora, at its foot, was the real heart of classical Athens. For some 800 years, this marketplace was the hub of all commercial, political, and social life, as well as home to many of the city's religious rites.

Little remains of the Agora, other than one very well-pre-served temple and a rebuilt portico. But wandering this field of humble ruins with an Athenian guide reminds me of the value of connecting with great local guides. Fay ("like Faye Dunaway," she explained) was a wealth of insights mixed with attitude: "We Greeks smoke, hate breakfast, and just can't get along with each other. But give us a common enemy and we become tight as a fist."

Still stately after all these centuries, the Parthenon tops Athens' majestic Acropolis. And at the base of the hill is the state-of-the-art Acropolis Museum.

She also explained that Greeks designed on a human scale—appropriate for their democracy. When the Romans came, they added gigantism. As Romans didn't have democracy, their leaders had a taste for grandeur—putting an "un-Greek" veneer of power on the Agora with pompous staircases, fancy pavement, and oversized temples and statues. You can tell Roman statues from Greek ones because Roman ones are larger than life, not freestanding (always propped on something), with "too much robe" and interchangeable heads. Masters of both imperial ego and efficiency, they reused stone bodies, economically replacing just the head with each new emperor. That's why lots of Roman statues are headless, with scooped-out necks.

From the Agora, it's on to Athens' best modern attraction, the Acropolis Museum. Housed in a striking, glassy building that gives a postmodern jolt to the otherwise staid, concrete cityscape, the museum houses various artifacts from the Acropolis. It's well worth a visit, although for me, the main attraction will always be the Parthenon itself.

At the end of the day, a ritual for me is to wander the old town under the floodlit Parthenon, munching a souvlaki rolled in greasy pita bread and pretending that Athens is the same small, charming village at the foot of the Acropolis that it was many centuries ago.

Greece Goes Wild

The Mani Peninsula—the southern tip of mainland Greece—feels like the end of the road. It's stark and sparse. If Greece had an O.K. Corral, this is where it would be. And the town of Kardamyli would be the saloon where everyone goes for a drink.

Today the Mani is a peaceful region of rustic villages and untrampled beaches. Only goats thrive here. While mountains edged with abandoned terraces hint that farming was

once more extensive, olives have been the sole major Mani export for the last two centuries. Many Mani towns feature sumptuous, old, fresco-slathered churches—pockets of brightness in this otherwise parched land.

Greece's rugged Mani Peninsula is dotted with ghost towns, souvenirs of a tough environment and a hard-fought past.

Sealed off from the rest of the country by a ridge of mountains, the peninsula has—over the centuries—harbored refugees, fleeing whatever crises were gripping the rest of Greece. People would hide out in the mountains, far from the coast and marauding pirate ships. And when they weren't fighting foreign invaders, they would fight each other.

Clambering up ridges are empty, ghostly villages fortified with towers. The most characteristic is Vathia. Built on a rocky spur, Vathia was an extreme example of what can happen when neighbors don't get along. In this vendetta-ville, 80-some houses were split north/south into two rival camps, which existed in a state of near-permanent hostility.

After spending a day driving around the Mani, exploring its rugged landscape and contentious history, I enjoy unwinding in Kardamyli, a humble beach town with a "Bali in a dust storm" charm. This handy base for exploring the Mani Peninsula works like a stun gun on my momentum. On my last trip, I felt as if I could have stayed for days, just eating well and hanging out. It's the kind of place where travelers plan their day around the sunset.

Having dinner at my favorite beach taverna under a leafy canopy brings back memories of my first meal here 20-some years ago: I had settled my chair into the sand under a bare and dangling lamp, and felt a faint but refreshing spritzing. Looking around for the source of the mist, I saw a tough Greek teenager in a swimsuit the size of a rat's hammock tenderizing a poor octopus to death by whipping it like a wet rag, over and over, on a big flat rock. The octopus would be featured that night on someone's dinner plate—but not mine.

These days, light bulbs still swing in the breeze—but, no longer naked, they're dressed in gourd lampshades. I sit under an eave enjoying the view. I love gazing into the misty Mediterranean, knowing the next land is Africa. The inky waves churn as the red sun sets.

More Greek Experiences

The Allure of Nafplio: My vote for the most charming town in Greece is Nafplio, on the Peloponnesian Peninsula. Nestled under cliffs at the apex of a vast bay, Nafplio has a unique pride. Its role as the first capital of independent Greece once made it a prestigious port town. And although its glory days have faded, the town retains a certain genteel panache, with palm-tree waterfronts, and narrow and atmospheric back streets that are lined with stately Venetian houses and inviting shops. Owing to its prestigious past, Nafplio's harbor is guarded by three castles (all wonderfully floodlit at night): one on a small island, another just above the old town, and a third capping a tall cliff above the city. With its harborfront setting and pleasant present-day vibe, Nafplio doesn't even need tourists—and doesn't disappoint them.

Nafplio also serves as a handy home base for touring the historic ruins of Mycenae and Epidavros. Mycenae, as ancient to Golden Age Greeks as Socrates and Plato are to us, has an archaeological mystique to it. And Epidavros entices visitors to actually try out the famed acoustics of the best-preserved theater in the ancient world.

Olympic Original: For more than a thousand years, the Olympic Games were held in their birthplace—Olympia, a sacred village in the Peloponnese. Besides the stadium, Olympia's Temple of Zeus was one of the great tourist destinations of the ancient world, boasting a then-world-famous 40-foot statue of Zeus by the great sculptor Pheidias. Today, Olympia is one of the best opportunities for a hands-on antiquity experience. Despite the crowds that pour through here, Olympia is a magical place, with ruins nestled among lush, shady groves of pine trees. Its once-majestic temple columns—toppled like a tower of checkers by an earthquake—are as evocative (with the help of the excellent museum) as anything from ancient times. And you just have to play "On your mark, get set...go!" on that original starting block from the first Olympic Games. As you line up, crank up your

imagination, light a torch, and refill the stadium with 40,000 fans. Olympia can still knock you on your discus.

Magnificent Monemvasia: This gigantic rock juts up improbably from the blue-green deep, just a few hundred yards offshore from the Peloponnese peninsula. Often referred to as the "Gibraltar of Greece," it is a fascinating showcase of Byzantine, Turkish, and Venetian history dating back to the 13th century. Its remarkably romantic walled Lower Town hides on the sheltered side of the burly rock, tethered to the mainland by only a skinny spit of land (Monemvasia means "single entry"). A steep, zigzag path leads up to the even bigger Upper Town, whose fortress, in its day, was considered the mightiest in Byzantine Greece. Today its scant ruins sprawl evocatively across the broad summit. Climbing Monemvasia takes only about half an hour, but on top, spend as long as you want, getting lost in the Middle Ages.

LEFT Nafplio is a delightful home base for exploring the wonders of the Peloponnesian Peninsula.

RIGHT Visitors to Olympia, home of the ancient Olympic Games, can't resist the chance to line up at the original starting block.

CULTURE AND TRADITIONS: EVERYTHING'S SO...GREEK

Greek Cuisine

The food in Greece is simple...and simply delicious. The Greeks have an easy formula, and they stick with it. The four Greek food groups are olives (and olive oil), salty feta cheese, ripe tomatoes, and crispy phyllo dough. Virtually every dish you'll have here is built on a foundation of these tasty building blocks.

My favorite way to eat in Greece is to order a main dish and a medley of *mezedes* (appetizers) to share with my companions. The selection, while predictable and routine after 10 dinners, never gets old for me: *tzatziki* dip, garlic dip,

fava bean dip, or a mix of all three on a single serving platter; fried eggplant or zucchini; Greek salad; and big grilled
peppers—red or green—stuffed with feta cheese. Usually
there's also something from the sea, such as grilled calamari,
sardines, or a plate of fried small fish (three inch), very small
fish (two inch), or very, very small fish (one inch). With
three-inch fish, leave the head and tail on the plate (and try
not to wonder about the once inky, now dry black guts). With
the smaller fish, you'll leave nothing but a line of greasy fin-
gerprints on the fringe of your paper tablecloth.

My go-to fast-food meal in Greece is souvlaki—meat
grilled on a skewer and served on a plate or wrapped in
pita bread to make a sandwich. When you get it "to go," the
meat (often pork or lamb) is tucked into a wonderful greasy
pita pocket with lettuce, tomato, onions, and *tzatziki*. It's
often bulked up with doughy French fries and wrapped in
wax paper that you peel back as you eat. As international
fast-food places move in, the traditional souvlaki stand is
harder to find...but more worthwhile than ever to seek out
and enjoy.

Religion

The Greek Orthodox Church remains a strong part of everyday
life here. Ninety-five percent of all Greeks consider themselves
Orthodox, even if they rarely go to church. Their faith was
a rallying point during centuries of foreign occupation, and
today the Greek constitution recognizes Orthodox Christianity
as the prevailing religion of Greece. Greek lives are marked by
the age-old rituals of baptism, marriage, and funeral.

Orthodox elements appear everywhere. Icon shrines dot
the highways. Orthodox priests—with their Old Testament
beards, black robes, necklaces, cake-shaped hats, and families in tow—mingle with parishioners on street corners. During the course of the day, Greeks routinely pop into churches

to light a candle, asking for favors. Greek lotharios in track suits reverently bend at the waist to kiss an icon, which is already slathered with lipstick from a steady stream of devout visitors. Even local teens who seem far from religious make the sign of the cross when passing a church.

Orthodox Easter, which is often later than the Catholic/Protestant Easter, is celebrated with gusto and tradition. For instance, on Good Friday in Kardamyli, a processional passes through town and the priest blesses each house. At midnight on Holy Saturday, townspeople turn off their lights and come to the main square. The priest emerges from the church with a candle and spreads light through the candle-carrying crowd, who then take the light home with them. Gradually the entire town is illuminated...and the fireworks begin.

Drinking in Greece

Greece is a rough land with simple wines. A local vintner told me there's no such thing as a $50 bottle of fine Greek wine. I asked him, "What if I want to spend $30?" He said, "You can buy three $10 bottles." With dinner, I like to order *retsina* wine, a post-WWII rotgut with a notorious resin flavor that's long been famous as the working man's Greek wine. It makes you want to sling a patch over one eye and say, "Arghh." The first glass is like drinking wood. The third glass is dangerous: It starts to taste good. If you drink any more, you'll smell like it the entire next day.

With a new generation of winemakers (many of them trained abroad), Greece is receiving more recognition for its wines. More than 300 native varietals are now grown in Greece's wine regions. But like many locals, I often skip the wine and go for a cold beer, or the cloudy, anise-flavored ouzo, supposedly invented by monks on Mount Athos.

Greek Dance

In Greece, dancing is a part of everyday life. If you go to a special occasion such as a wedding or baptism, you can see all ages dancing together. With arms outstretched or thrown across one another's shoulders, Greeks form a circle to perform their traditional dances. (In the old days, mixed couples were linked by handkerchiefs instead.) Often they dance to folk songs accompanied by a *bouzouki*, a long-necked mandolin. These days the music is usually amplified, fleshed out with a synthesizer, and tinged with pop influences.

Some of the dances you might see are the graceful *kalamatianos* circle dance, the *syrtaki* (famously immortalized

by Anthony Quinn in *Zorba the Greek*), and the dramatic solo *zimbetikos*. A few dancers might get carried away, "applaud" by throwing plates or flowers, and then dance on the tables into the wee hours. Wherever you are in Greece, ask locals where you might enjoy some live music and dancing with dinner or after. It can be a smashing time.

Greece Travel Resources from Rick Steves

Guidebooks
Choose from Rick's regional and city guides on Greece and Athens

Audio Europe
Download Rick's free Audio Europe app, with interviews about Greece and self-guided audio tours, including a walk through Athens and tours of the Acropolis, Ancient Agora, and National Archaeological Museum

TV Shows
The quintessence of Greece with Rick as your host, viewable on public television and at RickSteves.com. Episodes cover Athens, the Peloponnese Peninsula, and the islands of Hydra, Santorini, Mykonos, Rhodes, Samos, and Lipsi

Organized Tours
Small group tours, with itineraries planned by Rick: Athens & the Heart of Greece in 14 Days

For more on all these resources, visit RickSteves.com. For Greece trip-planning tips, see RickSteves.com/europe/greece.

Index

Start your trip at

Our website enhances this book and turns

Explore Europe

At ricksteves.com you can browse through thousands of articles, videos, photos and radio interviews, plus find a wealth of money-saving travel tips for planning your dream trip. And with our mobile-friendly website, you can easily access all this great travel information anywhere you go.

TV Shows

Preview the places you'll visit by watching entire half-hour episodes of *Rick Steves' Europe* (choose from all 100 shows) on-demand, for free.

ricksteves.com

your travel dreams into affordable reality

Radio Interviews

Enjoy ready access to Rick's vast library of radio interviews covering travel tips and cultural insights that relate specifically to your Europe travel plans.

Travel Forums

Learn, ask, share! Our online community of savvy travelers is a great resource for first-time travelers to Europe, as well as seasoned pros.

Travel News

Subscribe to our free Travel News e-newsletter, and get monthly updates from Rick on what's happening in Europe.

Classroom Europe®

Check out our free resource for educators with 500+ short video clips from the *Rick Steves' Europe* TV show.

Audio Europe™

Rick's Free Travel App

Get your FREE Rick Steves Audio Europe™ app to enjoy...

- Dozens of self-guided tours of Europe's top museums, sights and historic walks
- Hundreds of tracks filled with cultural insights and sightseeing tips from Rick's radio interviews
- All organized into handy geographic playlists
- For Apple and Android

With Rick whispering in your ear, Europe gets even better.

Find out more at ricksteves.com

Pack Light and Right

Gear up for your next adventure at ricksteves.com

Light Luggage

Pack light and right with Rick Steves' affordable, custom-designed rolling carry-on bags, backpacks, day packs and shoulder bags.

Accessories

From packing cubes to moneybelts and beyond, Rick has personally selected the travel goodies that will help your trip go smoother.

Shop at ricksteves.com

Rick Steves has

Save time and energy

My guidebooks are toolkits for independent travelers. But for all they deliver, it's still up to you to devote the time and energy it takes to manage the preparation and logistics that are essential for a happy trip. If that's a hassle, there's a solution.

Rick Steves Tours

A Rick Steves tour takes you to Europe's most interesting places with great guides and small

great tours, too!

with minimum stress

groups. We follow Rick's favorite itineraries, ride in comfy buses, stay in family-run hotels, and bring you intimately close to the Europe you've traveled so far to see. Most importantly, we take away the logistical headaches so you can focus on the fun.

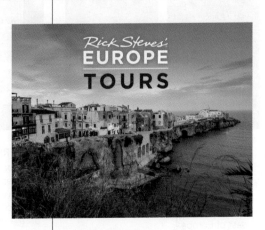

Join the fun

This year we'll take thousands of free-spirited travelers—nearly half of them repeat customers—along with us on 50 different itineraries, from Athens to Istanbul. Is a Rick Steves tour the right fit for your travel dreams?

Find out at ricksteves.com, check seat availability and sign up. Europe is best experienced with happy travel partners. We hope you can join us.

See our itineraries at ricksteves.com

A Guide for Every Trip

BEST OF GUIDES

Full-color easy-to-scan format, focusing on Europe's most popular destinations and sights

Best of England
Best of Europe
Best of France
Best of Germany
Best of Ireland
Best of Italy
Best of Scotland
Best of Spain

COMPREHENSIVE GUIDES

City, country, and regional guides with detailed coverage for a multi-week trip exploring the most iconic sights and venturing off the beaten track

Amsterdam & the Netherlands
Barcelona
Belgium: Bruges, Brussels,
   Antwerp & Ghent
Berlin
Budapest
Croatia & Slovenia
Eastern Europe
England
Florence & Tuscany
France
Germany
Great Britain
Greece: Athens & the Peloponnese
Iceland
Ireland
Istanbul
Italy
London
Paris
Portugal
Prague & the Czech Republic
Provence & the French Riviera
Rome
Scandinavia
Scotland
Sicily
Spain
Switzerland
Venice
Vienna, Salzburg & Tirol

THE BEST OF ROME

Rome, Italy's capital, is studded with Roman remnants and floodlit-fountain squares. From the Vatican to the Colosseum, with crazy traffic in between, Rome is wonderful, huge, and exhausting. The crowds, the heat, and the weighty history of the Eternal City where Caesars walked can make tourists wilt. Recharge by taking siestas, gelato breaks, and after-dark walks, strolling from one atmospheric square to another in the refreshing evening air.

...dmired **Pantheon**—which ...e largest dome until the ...e nearly 2,000 years old ...k a day over 1,500).

...hool of Athens in the **Vat-** ...embodies the humanistic ...aissance.

...**eum**, gladiators fought ...one another, entertaining ...,000.

...t this Rome *ristorante.* ...guards at St. Peter's ...work seriously.

Rick Steves books are available from your favorite bookseller.
Many guides are available as ebooks.

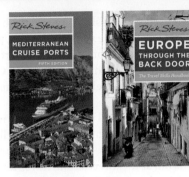

POCKET GUIDES

*Compact, full-color city guides with
the essentials for shorter trips*

Amsterdam
Athens
Barcelona
Florence
Italy's Cinque Terre
London
Munich & Salzburg
Paris
Prague
Rome
Venice
Vienna

SNAPSHOT GUIDES

Focused single-destination coverage

Basque Country: Spain & France
Copenhagen & the Best of Denmark
Dublin
Dubrovnik
Edinburgh
Hill Towns of Central Italy
Krakow, Warsaw & Gdansk
Lisbon
Loire Valley
Madrid & Toledo
Milan & the Italian Lakes District
Naples & the Amalfi Coast
Nice & the French Riviera
Normandy
Northern Ireland
Norway
Reykjavík
Sevilla, Granada & Southern Spain
St. Petersburg, Helsinki & Tallinn
Stockholm

CRUISE PORTS GUIDES

Reference for cruise ports of call.

Mediterranean Cruise Ports
Scandinavian & Northern European
  Cruise Ports

Complete your library with...

TRAVEL SKILLS & CULTURE

Europe 101
Europe Through the Back Door
Europe's Top 100 Masterpieces
European Christmas
European Easter
European Festivals
For the Love of Europe
Postcards from Europe
Travel as a Political Act

PHRASE BOOKS & DICTIONARIES

French
French, Italian & German
German
Italian
Portuguese
Spanish

PLANNING MAPS

Britain, Ireland & London
Europe
France & Paris
Germany, Austria & Switzerland
Iceland
Ireland
Italy
Spain & Portugal

Be creative! You can combine the
"Two, please," or "No, thank y
"Please, where can I buy a ticke
any language, especially in French. If y
want, such as the bill, simply say *La*
please).

HELLOS AND GOO

Pleasantries	Bonjour
Hello.	Parlez-
Do you speak	par-lay
English?	Oui. /
Yes. / No.	Je ne
I don't speak	zhui
French.	Dés
I'm sorry.	S'il
Please.	Me
Thank you (very	m
much).	E
Excuse me. (to get	
attention)	
Excuse me. (to pass)	
OK?	
OK. (two ways to	
say it)	
Good.	
Very good.	

HOW WAS YOUR TRIP?

If you enjoyed a successful trip with the help of my books and would like to share your discoveries, please fill out the survey at RickSteves.com/feedback. We're all in the same traveler's school of hard knocks...and it's OK to compare notes. Your feedback helps us improve this book for future travelers!

For our latest travel tips, tap into our information-packed website: RickSteves.com. To check out fellow readers' hotel and restaurant reviews—or leave one yourself—visit my travel forum at RickSteves.com/travel-forum. For updates to my guidebooks, check RickSteves.com/update.

Rick Steves' Europe is more than Rick Steves. All 100 of us are pooling our travel experience and working hard to help you enjoy the trip of a lifetime!

ACKNOWLEDGMENTS

Dank u wel to the entire Book Department at Rick Steves' Europe for their travel expertise, original writing, fact-checking, editing, photo selection, map-making, and many other contributions to this book. *Merci* for support from my entire well-traveled staff at Rick Steves' Europe.

Grazie to the following for sharing their knowledge: Risa Laib and Cameron Hewitt (travel savvy and original writing); Tim Tattan (radio); Joan Robinson and Margaret Cassady (women's packing tips); Elizabeth Holmes (travel agents, overseas flights); Laura Terrenzio (train travel); Gretchen Strauch (train travel and accommodations); our colleagues at Auto Europe/Kemwel (car rental and leasing); Chris Rae (driving and navigating); Stefanie Bielekova (gluten-free eating); Ruth Arista (wine transport); Alan Spira, M.D., and Craig Karpilow, M.D. (health for travelers); Lisa Friend (travel apps, family travel, and health); Amy Lysen (Couchsurfing); Marcy Lay (home swaps and cultural exchange); France Freeman (home exchange); Kevin Williams and Cory Mead (technology for travelers); Tara Swenson (health advice); Arlan Blodgett, Stewart Hopkins, Chris Luczyk, and Sabine Schrader (photography); Gabe Gunnink (LGBTQ and student travelers); and Audrey Edwards and Leiane Cooke (travelers of color); John Sage, Susan Sygall, Carole Zoom, and Carmen Papalia (travelers with disabilities); Heidi Van Sewell and Michelle Kono (bus tours); Yumiko Sato (bus tours and cruises); and Todd and Carla Hoover (cruising). *Muchas gracias* to Simon Griffith for directing and producing our *Rick Steves' Europe* television series with such passion and artistry.

Finally, *tusen takk* to my parents for dragging me to Europe when I didn't want to go.

Photo Credits

Front Cover: Dolomites, Italy © Maurizio Rellini, Sime, eStock Photo

Additional Credits: 322, 641 (right), 727 Public Domain via Wikimedia Commons; 376 (right) © iStock; 493 © Jordan Reznick

Additional Photography: John Adkins, Dominic Arizona Bonuccelli, Ben Cameron, Jennifer Davis, Trish Feaster, Barb Geisler, Gabe Gunnink, Jennifer Hauseman, Cameron Hewitt, David C. Hoerlein, Sandra Hundacker, Anne Jenkins, Michaelanne Jerome, Jane Klausen, Suzanne Kotz, Rosie Leutzinger, Cathy Lu, Lauren Mills, Pat O'Connor, Gene Openshaw, Rhonda Pelikan, Carol Ries, Sabine Schrader, Steve Smith, Robyn Stencil, Andy Steves, Rick Steves, Gretchen Strauch, Susan Sygall, Ashley Sytsma, Laura Van Deventer, Ragen Van Sewell, Honza Vihan, Ian Watson, Kevin Williams, Rachel Worthman, Robert Wright. Photos are used by permission and are the property of the original copyright owners.

Avalon Travel
Hachette Book Group
1700 Fourth Street
Berkeley, CA 94710

Printed in Malaysia for Imago.
First printing January 2022.

ISBN 978-1-64171-409-9
39th Edition

For the latest on Rick's talks, guidebooks, tours, public television series, and public radio show, contact Rick Steves' Europe, 130 Fourth Avenue North, Edmonds, WA 98020, 425/771-8303, www.ricksteves.com, rick@ricksteves.com.

Rick Steves' Europe

Managing Editor: Jennifer Madison Davis
Assistant Managing Editor: Cathy Lu
Editors and Researchers: Glenn Eriksen, Suzanne Kotz, Rosie Leutzinger, Jessica Shaw, Carrie Shepherd
Editorial & Production Assistant: Megan Simms
Graphic Content Director: Sandra Hundacker
Maps & Graphics: David C. Hoerlein, Lauren Mills, Mary Rostad
Digital Asset Coordinator: Orin Dubrow

Avalon Travel

Senior Editor and Series Manager: Madhu Prasher
Associate Managing Editors: Jamie Andrade, Sierra Machado
Indexer: Stephen Callahan
Interior Design: McGuire Barber Design
Production: Lisi Baldwin, Jane Musser
Maps & Graphics: Kat Bennett
Cover Design: Kimberly Glyder Design

More for your trip!
Maximize the experience with Rick Steves as your guide

Guidebooks
Make every trip smooth and affordable with dozens of European city and country guides

Phrase Books
Rely on Rick's French, Italian, German, Spanish, and Portuguese phrase books

Rick's TV Shows
Preview your destinations with more than 100 episodes of *Rick Steves' Europe*

Rick's Audio Europe™ App
Get free audio tours of Europe's top museums, sights and historic walks

Small Group Tours
Take a lively, low-stress Rick Steves tour through Europe

For all the details, visit ricksteves.com